AUSTRALIAN INDUSTRIAL RELATIONS

in a South East Asian Context

AUSTRALIAN INDUSTRIAL RELATIONS

in a South East Asian Context

S. Petzall

Deakin University, Geelong

N. Timo

Griffith University, Gold Coast

K. Abbott

Deakin University, Geelong

Melbourne, Australia

Published by
ERUDITIONS® PUBLISHING
P.O. Box 555
Emerald Victoria Australia 3782
Telephone: 03 5968 4532
Facsimile: 03 5968 5823
International Phone: 61 3 5968 4532
International Fax: 61 3 5968 5823
email: publisher@eruditions.com
internet: www.eruditions.com

© S.Petzall, N.Timo, K.Abbott 2000

This book is copyright. All rights are reserved. Apart from any fair dealing for the purpose of private study, research, criticism or review, as permitted under the Copyright Act, no part of this publication may be reproduced, stored in a retrieval system, or transmitted, in any form or by any means, electronic, mechanical, photocopying, recording or otherwise without the prior written permission of the publisher.

National Library of Australia
Cataloguing-in-Publication entry:

Petzall, Stanley B.

Australian industrial relations: in a South East Asian context.

Bibliography.
Includes index.
ISBN 1 86491 007 0.

1. Industrial relations - Australia. 2. Personnel management - Australia. 3. Labour unions - Australia. 4. Comparative industrial relations. 5. Industrial relations - Asia, Southeastern. 6. Industrial relations - East Asia. 7. Industrial relations - China - Hong Kong. I. Abbott, Keith, 1956- . II. Timo, Nils. III. Title.

331.0994

Printed by Corporate Printers, South Melbourne, Australia.

CONTENTS

Authorship and Acknowledgments vi

On-line teaching assistance vi

Preface vii

Case Study: The Australian Waterfront Dispute, 1998 1

1. Conceptual and Analytical Tools 15
2. Industrial Conflict 37
3. Management and Industrial Relations 65
4. Employer Organisations 85
5. Trade Unions: Structures, Functions and Future 109
6. The State and Industrial Relations 163
7. The Law and Industrial Relations 181
8. Wage Fixation in Australia 203
9. Enterprise Bargaining and Workplace Change in Australia since 1996 237

Case Study: CRA Individual Contracts and Strategic HRM Practices 283

10. Negotiation Skills 293
11. Equity in Industrial Relations 311
12. Multinational Corporations 333
13. Five Selected South East Asian Countries 357

Appendix: Sample Certified Agreement 389

References 401

Index to References by Author 433

Index 441

AUTHORSHIP AND ACKNOWLEDGMENTS

Stanley Petzall wrote chapters 10 (Negotiation), 12 (Multinational Corporations) and 13 (South East Asian countries), the latter with some early contributions by Bernard O'Meara and Cec Pedersen. Stanley was also responsible for the South East Asian material throughout the book, with the exception of Chapter 4.

Nils Timo wrote wrote chapters 5 (Trade Unions), (together with Stanley Petzall), 8 (Wage Fixing) and 9 (Enterprise Bargaining), as well as the MUA and CRA Case Studies.

Keith Abbott wrote chapters 1 (Conceptual and Analytical Tools) and 7 (The Law) (with a contribution by Laura Bennett), and worked together with Stanley on Chapters 2 (Industrial Conflict), 3 (Management) and 6 (The State).

Bernard O'Meara wrote Chapter 4 (Employers Associations). Laura Bennett wrote Chapter 11 (Equity) (together with Stanley Petzall).

The authors would also like to thank the many colleagues and anonymous referees for their helpful comments during the drafting of this book over a number of years. Thanks too, to Sandy Powrie for her assistance in typing the manuscript. Particular thanks must go to Diana Guillemin, without whom this book may not have been published, and also to the editorial staff at Eruditions Publishing. Last, but not least, the authors would like to thank their respective families for their patience, tolerance and support during a long and arduous undertaking.

ON-LINE TEACHING ASSISTANCE

For lecturers adopting this book, an on-line website is available.

The site contains additional material to keep you up to date and add interest to your course. It also contains valuable teaching resources, examination questions and additional content, such as material on industrial democracy and wage fixing in the five selected South East Asian countries. Lecturers should contact the publisher for further details.

PREFACE

The workplace is an important part of most people's lives. It is also undergoing enormous change in Australia today. Much of what we take for granted about employment is changing. Union membership has never been so low. Industrial laws have never been so tough. The centralised wage fixing system that most adult Australians grew up with has been severely restricted. Standard working conditions, which once enjoyed the virtual status of law under the Award system, are no longer certain. New laws and practices founded on economic rationalism are changing the face of Australian industrial relations. New terms like employee relations, labour flexibility, individual contracts, and enterprise bargaining are the language of the future. Rarely before has the study of industrial relations involved such a significant and practical relevance as it does today.

It is important, therefore, for future employees and managers to have some understanding of industrial relations in the current climate of change. Rapid globalisation of national economies and the growth of multinational corporations throughout the world is forcing new approaches to the management of labour in the push for greater competitiveness. In Australia, the Federal Government has responded to calls by business leaders to speed up the decentralisation of traditional bargaining frameworks. With reduced union power and more pro-active labour management strategies, employees need to have some understanding of how the workplace changes affect them. Employees need to understand how to protect their existing rights and get the best deal in bargaining with their employers. For employers, the climate of change is creating new challenges and opportunities in the management of labour. It is equally important, therefore, that managers and employers have an understanding of the current changes if their organisations are to function harmoniously and profitably.

About This Book

The present book is a general introduction to Australian industrial relations. In complexity, the book is written as an introductory text for students of industrial relations at Australian universities and other post-secondary institutions. It is suitable for second or third level undergraduate programs as well as post-graduate course-work programs. The book is fully up to date and thoroughly referenced. Each chapter has learning objectives, useful review questions and a list of key additional readings for the better student.

The contents are structured in line with the traditional approach of many courses, moving from broad theoretical concepts, to the major actors, to processes and procedures, and finally to outcomes. However, this book also differs from traditional approaches. First, the book endeavours to communicate the very real and exciting changes occurring in the workplace. For example, the book commences with the high profile case study on the MUA v Patrick waterfront dispute. Whilst it may be necessary for students to revisit this case later, it is intended to provide a motivating example for the more conceptual material that follows. Second, there is a more than the usual exploration of the various theories of industrial relations together with a stronger focus on the international context of industrial relations. These features are intended to provide students with the conceptual tools for making sense of industrial relations outside western industrial settings.

An additional feature of the book is the detailed coverage it provides on the 'practice' of industrial relations. There are several case studies and a sample Certified Agreement. There is an important chapter on Enterprise Bargaining, which includes a substantial analysis of the actual content and consequences of enterprise agreements in Australia today. It also includes a practical guide on how to engage in the enterprise bargaining process. There is also a brief chapter on negotiation to give some exposure to the majority of students who will not go on to study a full negotiation unit.

The South East Asian Context

We are mindful of the fact that many South East Asian students undertake management courses in Australian universities, and in so doing undertake labour management units as part of their degrees. We are also mindful that many Australian managers are looking to establish firms in South East Asia or are having increasing contact with managers within this region. For both these reasons this book also covers industrial relations practices and issues in five selected, economically significant South East Asian countries: Japan, South Korea, Malaysia, Singapore and Hong Kong. These countries have been chosen because they are significant trading partners of Australia, and the prospect of contact between Australian managers and managers in these regional countries is probably high. They have also been chosen because South East Asian student enrolments at Australian universities are highest from three of these five countries: Malaysia, Hong Kong and Singapore. It is hoped therefore that this material will make the course more relevant to students from these countries.

Whilst the book sets out to look at the industrial relations systems of six countries in all, the student should be mindful that this is not a comparative study. Such a study is beyond the scope of an introductory industrial relations text. The authors have tried to ensure the book covers all major relevant Australian material, as well as English-written sources dealing with the industrial relations issues pertinent to the five selected South East Asian countries.

Stanley Petzall
Nils Timo
Keith Abbott

June 2000

CASE STUDY

The Australian Waterfront Dispute, 1998
(MUA v Patrick Stevedores)

BACKGROUND

For students of HRM and industrial relations, this MUA Case Study provides great insight into the complex processes that shape management and labour relations. The waterfront dispute highlights the differences between capital and labour and illustrates how the workplace can become a site of significant conflict and change. The dispute also offers an unusually clear view of the interaction between several recurring themes in the study of industrial relations: managerial approaches to labour; the impact of competition on business strategies; the place of unions in shaping workplace regulation; the role of government; and the political influences that shape our perception of labour relations. Whilst it is not essential to begin this book with this case study, it has been placed at the beginning to help students grasp the practical relevance of the material that follows. On first reading, students should not expect to fully understand all the issues raised or all the terminology used in the case study. Rather it is recommended that they refer back to this case again later in their course and see just how much deeper their understanding of various issues has become.

The Australian waterfront dispute of 1997-1998 has been described as a battle that changed the nation (Trinca and Davies 2000). It is an example of an attempt to the use direct state intervention to deregulate waterfront labour by removing union monopolies over wage setting and conditions of labour. Other examples include the 1996 Liverpool Dockers strike, and the breaking of New Zealand waterfront unions during the late 1980s by the use of contract labour. This case study must be seen within this broader context and was conducted at the time of a wide-ranging debate about the role of Australian unions, the effectiveness of the industrial relations system, and the efficiency of the Australian waterfront. At times, the debate turned into a series of arguments concerning workplace change, the role of unions, managerial power and what constitutes 'the public' interest. On the one hand, Australia's economic progress was seen as being held hostage by 'lazy' and 'overpaid' warfies. On the other hand, the dispute raised serious questions about the role of government, the legality of contrived corporate restructuring, the adherence to the rule of law, and whether the end justifies the means.

However, before embarking on this case study, we need to explain the term 'waterfront' a little more fully. The waterfront forms part of the transport industry associated with the loading, unloading and movement of cargo between ports around the world. 'Stevedoring' refers to the loading and unloading of ships' cargoes (often in the form of containers, measured as '20-foot equivalent units' or TEUs). A 'stevedore' is a company or terminal operator that is engaged in stevedoring. A 'wharfie' or 'docker' or 'waterside worker' is an operational employee employed by a stevedore (Productivity Commission 1998b, xiii).

The Australian waterfront has a long and bloody history of militant unionism. The waterfront has always been a conflict-ridden industry, known for its hard, dangerous work and its bitter disputation. The Maritime Union of Australia (MUA) grew from the amalgamation of the Waterside Workers Federation (WWF) and the Seaman's Union of Australia in 1993. Historically, the MUA's militant tradition was based on a strong collective reaction to the low pay, poor conditions and dangerous work that were commonplace on the wharves. It was a system based on casual labour, involving daily 'auctions' of workers. Militant unionism became the only effective tool for achieving a more equal bargaining position for workers (Beasley 1996). However, the result of these hard beginnings was a union dominated by the Communist Party of Australia (especially at ports such as Sydney), which enshrined a rigid union delegate structure that was resistant to change. The union was always tough and tenacious, fully prepared to take both industrial and political action (such as banning the berthing of U.S. warships during the Vietnam War). However, it was also adept at holding on to out-dated work practices, and inept at understanding and negotiating workplace change (McIntyre 1998).

The waterfront dispute must be located in the context of broader political manoeuvring (Wiseman 1998). By the 1980s, significant numbers of Australian employers had come to the conclusion that centralised wage fixing should be abandoned. They began to canvas strategies to break the power of unions and reintroduce individual contracts between employers and workers. Much of the initial strategic planning was driven by members of the 'H.R. Nicholls Society', a right wing industrial relations think-tank named after an early twentieth century opponent of central wage fixing. The National Farmers Federation (NFF) is a key employer group representing graziers and rural commodity producers. Their fighting fund (reputedly of around A$7 million dollars) had financed strikebreakers from New Zealand during the 1984-shearing dispute. The NFF had also funded common law action against striking meat workers over live sheep exports in 1978 and striking abattoir unionists in 1986. Officials from the NFF played a central role in the 1998 waterside dispute. The incoming conservative Howard Government in 1996 came to office with a clear intent to follow Margaret Thatcher's model of union busting, targeting the MUA monopoly on the docks (Sheridan 1998, 144). The 1998 dispute is inseparable from this political context.

GLOBALISATION AND RESTRUCTURING WORK PRACTICES ON THE AUSTRALIAN WATERFRONT

Ports play an important role in the Australian economy as a primary handler of goods and agricultural produce for international trade. In 1995-1996, the total value of cargo moved through Australian ports was A$120 billion, representing 70 per cent of the value of all imports and 78 per cent of exports (Meyrick and Associates and Tasman Asia Pacific 1998). Historically, the debates about economic reform on the waterfront focused on the role of the MUA. It was seen as impeding competition with its entrenched monopoly on waterfront labour, which fostered outdated and inefficient work practices. During the 1990s, the Business Council of Australia (BCA) called for the total restructuring of the waterfront. The aim was to provide a waterfront that operated with world-class efficiency, delivering minimum costs to the shipment owners (BCA Bulletin, October 1992, 8).

The election of the Federal Labor Government in 1983 ushered in a number of changes to industry policy including planned changes to the waterfront. In 1989, the Government received the Australian Inter-State Commission report on the waterfront reform that recommended the introduction of redundancies, a greater focus on workplace employment arrangements, job redesign, multi-skilling and the use of casual/contract labour (Inter-State Commission 1989). Arising from this Report, the Labor Government set up in 1989 the Waterfront Industry Reform Authority (WIRA), a tripartite forum charged with gaining improvements on the waterfront. Under the WIRA, the stevedoring workforce was reduced by 4,900 employees (57 per cent of the workforce) through government funded redundancies. One outcome of the process was to change the age profile of the stevedoring workforce from an average of 55 to 45 years of age. Another outcome of workforce reductions was a productivity increase of 64 per cent in container handling through the port of Sydney. The WIRA also introduced a degree of multiskilling by encouraging employers to adopt new technologies. The outcome, according to WIRA documents, was an overall lift in waterfront productivity by about 75 per cent (WIRA 1991). However, according to some, long term productivity improvements on the Australian waterfront continue to remain elusive (Sloan 1998).

Whilst the industry's quarterly benchmarking survey *Waterline* (published by the Bureau of Transport Economics) suggested that productivity had improved considerably since the WIRA reforms, the various methodologies used by subsequent inquiries resulted in substantially different conclusions about ship and freight movements, port charges and labour costs. For example, in 1995 the Bureau of Industry Economics (BIE) measured the timeliness and reliability of Australian container ports. The BIE concluded that it generally took between 50-100 per cent longer to load and unload a container ship in Australia than it did in comparable overseas ports. There were also higher than average time delays for ships in port (BIE 1995). In 1998, the Productivity Commission reviewed waterfront efficiency and productivity. In its first Report on *International Benchmarking of the Australian Waterfront* (1998a) the Productivity Commission concluded that Australian ports had improved productivity over the previous decade, although port users still experienced higher overall port and handling charges than was the case for our major international competitors. Poor stevedoring practices and lower net crane productivity (the productivity of an individual crane while it is working) were found to be related to over-manning levels, greater down time due to work stoppages or go slows, and equipment malfunction which reduced the number of container movements or lifts per employee. The Report also concluded that the lack of an integrated terminal-transport system dealing with the reception and delivery of containers resulted in longer truck queues than at overseas ports (1998a).

In its second Report on *Work Arrangements in Container Stevedoring* (1998b), the Productivity Commission concluded that stevedoring work was characterised by complex, inflexible and highly prescriptive work practices that constrained workplace productivity. The most significant of these practices related to:

- the 'order of engagement' (i.e. the order in which different types of employees are engaged per shift and what job they perform) which was dominated by strict union rules relating to rostering
- allocation of pre-planned overtime according to a union roster
- high shift premiums and penalty rates
- excessive and overgenerous redundancy arrangements.

The Report identified a number of factors that impeded change on the waterfront including:
- an adversarial work culture
- a strong union monopoly encouraging poor labour practices on the waterfront
- lack of competition in the industry, with the result that costs could easily be passed on to consumers.

The Drewry Report (1998) adopted a different view. It argued that Australian ports compared favorably with overseas ports and benchmarks. For example, when taking into account quay length, cargo congestion, crane cycle times, size of container, the pattern of ship arrivals, size of vessels, and the number of containers moved as a proportion of the capacity of the vessel, Australian ports were close to or exceeded international benchmarks. Measuring waterfront productivity is clearly complex and depends on what is measured. During the Australian waterfront dispute of 1997-1998, each of the protagonists relied upon a raft of alternative statistics to prove their cause was just.

PATRICK STEVEDORES: THE COMPANY, PRODUCT MARKETS AND TRADE UNIONS

While there are other unions on the waterfront such as the Transport Workers Union (TWU) and various trade unions covering maintenance workers, the MUA is the dominant union on the waterfront. A small union with some 10,000 members, the industrial militancy of the MUA is founded largely on its monopoly bargaining power and absence of strong competitive pressures on the waterfront. Patrick Stevedores is a stevedoring company operating across all the main Australian ports. Prior to the dispute with the MUA, it employed approximately 1,400 stevedores. It is a wholly owned subsidiary of a larger conglomerate named Lang Corporation. Patrick moves about 1,500 containers per day across Australian ports and is one of two stevedoring companies, the other is P&O Ports Container Terminals of Australia Ltd (Lang Corporation 1997 *Annual Report*). The only assets of stevedoring companies (apart from equipment, plant etc.) are:
- their commercial contracts to handle containers on behalf of port users
- their lease over the docks that control the access to stevedoring cargo.

Stevedoring is capital intensive and the two largest stevedoring companies have been able to protect their investments by shutting out competitors. Competitors are denied access to docks because Patrick and P&O have long-term leases over docks with port authorities. These leases provide the stevedoring companies with a right of first refusal on the renewal of the leases, thereby making it impossible for new competitors to start operating. The U.S. based shipping company, International Purveyors, which services the large Freeport copper mine in Indonesia, was squeezed out of the Australian stevedoring industry after its access to the Melbourne docks was restricted. (This company also lost a skirmish with the MUA earlier in 1997 over an attempt to use non-union labour to load their ships in Cairns.) Newcomers are also reputedly 'warned off' as part of an alleged long and secretive collusion between the major operators (Tull 1997). These arrangements have enabled the larger stevedoring companies to control the product market through exclusive contracts with port users. The stevedores could also rely upon the MUA to vigorously impose established waterfront wages and working conditions on any new entrant into the industry.

The relationship between the stevedores and the MUA is therefore more appropriately described as a powerful duopoly: the stevedores control the product market and the MUA exercises a tight control over all wages and working practices. As a result, the two stevedoring companies have an entrenched, financially rewarding dominance of the waterfront, between them controlling over 95 per cent of cargo movement on Australian wharves, while the MUA is entrenched as the sole representative of labour. This duopoly has four major effects. First, with new entrants facing major set-up costs and entry barriers, the two major stevedoring companies have generally operated with little accountability. Second, in the absence of competitive pressures, Patrick in particular failed to develop effective HRM and industrial relations practices at workplace level. Instead it surrendered the day to day control of work to the MUA. Third, the militancy of the MUA effectively scared off any potential new entrants and discouraged improvements in work organisation and efficiency. Finally, lack of competition led to entrenched poor management practices (such as the use of older machinery, poor maintenance that leads to machinery break downs) and poor labour practices. In effect the MUA controlled the conditions under which labour was used on the docks (leading to such problems as over-manning, excessive overtime, poor rostering, and an unfavourable adversarial work culture). In the absence of competition and fresh ideas, port consumers simply paid up.

A 'GRAND PLAN' PLAN FOR DE-UNIONISING THE DOCKS

The subsequent dispute between Patrick and the MUA can be traced to strategies being developed at the highest level of the Australian Government. In April 1997, a government consultant began work on a strategy to eject the MUA from the waterfront. The Federal Cabinet subsequently received this document (described as a 'Cabinet briefing paper' according to subsequent press leaks) on the 7 July 1997. Entitled 'Waterfront Strategy' (1), the document advocated a strategy of creating a dispute with the MUA to take advantage of various legal remedies dealing with strikes and secondary boycotts. It was hoped that this would ultimately lead to the destruction of the MUA. (The Howard Coalition Government has denied that the document represented a 'strategy' for the waterfront.) The objectives of this strategy (as later tabled in Federal Parliament, see end note) were listed as:

> Increased economic growth and employment opportunities, through the establishment of a reliable and cost efficient waterfront; removal of MUA/ACTU control over the waterfront and therefore its use as a political/industrial weapon; to demonstrate the effectiveness of the Government's industrial relations and transport reforms, which will have a flow-on effect into other sectors of industry (Australia. Cabinet Briefing Paper 1997, 1).

The Cabinet briefing paper went on to argue that:

> Stevedores would need to activate well-prepared strategies to dismiss their workforce, and replace them with another, quickly, in a way that limited the prospect of, for example, the [Australian Industrial Relations] Commission ordering reinstatement of the current workforce (Australia. Cabinet Briefing Paper 1997, 3).

The briefing paper argued that the key to the success of the strategy was 'to get the main ports going as soon as possible and then to establish a national pattern of growing movement on a daily basis until the strike collapses or becomes irrelevant' (1997, 4). In order to achieve this, it argued that the government would need to be prepared to actively assist stevedores (such as Patrick) with a wide range of supportive actions, including:

- the provision of strategic advice
- legal assistance and physical security services
- managing public and business opinion
- chartering overseas tugs
- the employment of foreign skilled labour including the arrangement of visas and accommodation
- substantial public expenditure including (in a later decision) up to $250 million to fund redundancies (1997, 3-5).

The Cabinet briefing paper recommended that the option of an 'evolutionary' approach to waterfront reform be rejected in favour of an 'activist' approach involving the provocation of industrial action which 'would provide stevedores with the option of dismissing their employees and rehiring new (or selected current) employees under different arrangements'. This document did not publicly surface until June 14th, 1998 (when it was leaked to the *Australian Financial Review*, 25th June, 1998) where it effectively destroyed the Howard Government's credibility concerning the extent of its involvement (and frequent denials) in orchestrating the waterfront dispute.

Of the two major existing stevedoring companies operating on the Australian waterfront (P&O and Patrick), Patrick was chosen because of its greater enthusiasm for an immediate confrontation with the MUA. Indeed, under the leadership of Managing Director Chris Corrigan, Patrick had already developed its own plans for de-unionising its operations, using currently serving and former military personnel. Patrick was communicating with a Hong Kong registered company called Container Management Services, established as part of the front for the recruitment and training operation. Patrick also contracted a former army special services (SAS) officer, Mike Wells, to recruit and train the non-union stevedoring workforce. Wells established another new company, Fynwest, and advertised in *Army* magazine in late October 1997 for 'trade specialists'. The advertisement suggested it was looking for soldiers who were considering leaving the army although, in the end, currently serving military personnel on leave were also recruited. In order to secretly train the new workforce, Patrick had hired a section of docks in Dubai in the United Arab Emirates (UAE) for $800,000. It was calculated that about 260 workers would be hired, with a core group of about 70 being trained in Dubai. The plan was for them to leave Australia secretly in early December and be ready to commence Australian operations by late March 1998.

According to Wells, the operation was conducted with the assistance of the Government (e.g. the issuing of passports to servicemen). The secrecy of the operation was lost when the MUA was tipped off about the Dubai operation and the media quizzed the 'tourists' as they were boarding a flight to Dubai. Ten days later, with threats of international union action, the operation was abandoned. Patrick shortly after abandoned Wells and his men with monies outstanding. Subsequently, these ex-service men have launched unfair dismissal actions against Patrick seeking $120 million in damages, using similar legal arguments that the MUA successfully used against Patrick Stevedores (Wells affidavit, dated 6 May 1998). After denying his involvement at the time of the Dubai mission, Mr Corrigan later admitted he knew of the mission, had financed it and claimed it was the act of a desperate man (interview on the '7:30 Report', ABC TV, February 3, 1998).

Patrick did not give up here, but continued its efforts to rid itself of an unwanted unionised labour force. A new plan was devised whereby Patrick and the National Farmers Federation (NFF) would break the MUA union monopoly by establishing a new and completely non-unionised workforce. At this time, both the Howard Government and Patrick continued a media campaign about 'lazy and over-paid warfies' holding Australia to ransom. The NFF plan was to set up a new stevedoring company known as Producers and Consumers Ltd (P&C) to train stevedores and run stevedoring operations on docks leased from Patrick. This plan was soon implemented.

CREATIVE ACCOUNTING, COMPANY RESTRUCTURING AND UNION EXCLUSION

By the beginning of 1998, the NFF had leased part of Patrick operations at Melbourne's Webb Dock. On 28 January 1998, armed security guards overran a small union picket, changed all the locks and took over 5 Webb Dock. On 23 February, non-union workers began training at 5 Webb Dock with the clear intent of being available to work on other docks if required. P&C Stevedores was now in business.

In February, the MUA commenced a series of hearings before the Australian Industrial Relations Commission (AIRC) in an attempt to prevent what the MUA saw as a real likelihood of MUA members being sacked in the near future. The AIRC was unable to conclude that Patrick intended to provoke a dispute to justify replacing its current unionised workforce with a non-union one. Patrick agreed during the hearings to give undertakings that all existing employees would continue in employment, despite the sub-lease to P&C Stevedores at 5 Webb Dock, and to maintain staffing levels based on current levels of business (Australian Financial Review, 14th February, 1998). At this time, the MUA had also commenced proceedings in the Federal Court regarding alleged breaches of the Stevedoring Industry Award - 1991 relating to the company's failure to consult with the union on issues such as job security, redundancy requirements and proposed changes on the docks. The MUA argued that the actions of the company breached the Patrick Melbourne Enterprise Agreement 1996.

The AIRC found the conduct of Patrick to be in breach of its agreement with the MUA (the company had failed to abide by the dispute and grievance handling procedures and consultation requirements under the award regarding workplace change) but found that the MUA strike action was an inappropriate response. MUA members immediately went out on strike protesting the decision of the AIRC. Both Patrick and the MUA continued to argue matters before the AIRC, especially an application for orders under Section 127(1) of the Workplace Relations Act 1996 that empowered the

AIRC to make orders to stop industrial action. Patrick was afraid that the MUA would use the Section 127 hearings as an opportunity to supoena officers of Patrick and NFF for cross-examination and so sought an injunction against the MUA from proceeding with strike action. The application before the Victorian Supreme Court was heard before Justice Beech, who issued the broadest of strike action injunctions against 'anyone, anywhere' and 'at anytime'. Justice Beech justified this order on the basis that the then current Patrick Melbourne Enterprise Agreement 1996 was in force and thus prohibited strike action (Supreme Court of Victoria, Patrick Stevedores Operations Pty Ltd and ors v Maritime Union of Australia and ors, (1998) 79 *Industrial Reports*, 268 and (1998) 79 *Industrial Reports* 276). These broad orders were subsequently overturned on appeal (Supreme Court of Victoria, Court of Appeal, Maritime Union of Australia and ors v Patrick Stevedores Operations Pty Ltd and ors, (1998) 79 *Industrial Reports* 317).

At 11 p.m. on 7 April 1998, armed guards, some in black balaclavas and with dogs, moved in on Patrick dockside operations by boat and mini bus, securing gates and changing locks. Each one of Patrick's 1,460 MUA workers was informed that they had been sacked because the labour hire companies they worked for had become insolvent and had no assets to pay wages. In effect, the employees were now locked out. Prime Minister John Howard was quoted as saying the sackings were a 'defining moment' in the history of Australian industrial relations. The Patrick/NFF strategy followed essentially the blue print detailed in the earlier 7 July 1997 Federal Cabinet briefing paper. The strategy was based on a swift and surgical strike to lock out the MUA and replace a unionised workforce with a non-union one. In order to rid itself of the unwanted unionised workforce, a series of company arrangements (corporate restructuring) was put in place enabling financial assets to be quietly transferred out of the Patrick companies employing labour. These assets were presumably transferred to Patrick's parent company Lang Corporation where they vanished. This reduced these now cashed strapped companies to mere shells, with very tenuous contracts as their only assets.

The Patrick group of companies is part of and controlled by Lang Corporation. Prior to 23 September 1997, four Patrick companies, Patrick Stevedores No. 1, Patrick Stevedores No. 2, Patrick Stevedores No. 3 and National Stevedores Tasmania were in the business of providing stevedoring services in ports around Australia. These companies owned plant and equipment and employed labour in stevedoring industry. They obtained contracts from customers and provided labour to service these contracts. These four Patrick employer companies owned not only the assets and business of the stevedoring operation at a number of ports, but also employed the labour for this operation. However, on 23 September 1997 the companies (National Stevedores - Tasmania was finalised in March 1998) sold their assets and business to Patrick for approximately $315 million under a Business Purchase Agreement (BPA). At the same time the employer companies entered into Labour Supply Agreements (LSAs) with Patrick.

According to Patrick's ultimate holding company, this restructuring was put in place to avoid customer confusion as to which corporate entity owned which assets. They also argued that it allowed for better performance monitoring and better rates for bank borrowing. However, as a result of the September 1997 restructuring, somewhere between $60 million and $70 million from the employer companies, which would otherwise have been available to finance their business operations, was returned to shareholders. The shareholders' funds in the employer companies were reduced to about $2.5 million by the restructure and those funds were exhausted by April 1998. (Whilst the employer companies were said to be owed about $16 million by other companies in the Patrick Group, these funds were unavailable to the employer companies.) In effect, MUA members became the major unpaid creditors of the Patrick employer (labour hire) companies, which now had no assets to pay the (former?) Patrick workforce. If the MUA members were dismissed, either because there was no work for them, or because there were no funds to pay them, it would result in the loss of accrued leave entitlements and severance pay in the order of A$125 million outstanding (and with no capacity to pay) by the now defunct labour hire companies.

Following the restructure, one Patrick company was left as the owner of the plant and equipment as well as being in control of the stevedoring services provided under the Labour Supply Agreements. In effect Patrick was attempting to outsource labour to itself, and strip the labour supply companies of any tangible assets. The labour supply contracts included tight productivity targets and the capacity to hire non-union labour. They also had a 'no disruption' to supply clause, prohibiting any delaying, interference or interruption with the supply of their labour services. Neither the MUA nor the Patrick's workforce had been informed of the restructuring or its implications. It was all done with much secrecy. A strike by the MUA (arguably provoked by Patrick) created the opportunity to terminate the labour supply contracts with the effect that the labour supply companies were then placed in receivership, under an administrator, as required under Part 5.3A of the *Corporations Law*. This requires administrators to be appointed when a company is no longer able to meet its debts so that the administrators can maximise (if possible) a better return to creditors.

The employer strategy was twofold. First, to use the situation at no. 5 Webb Dock to goad the MUA into taking industrial action, thereby opening themselves up to actions for damages in tort law and under the secondary boycott Sections 45D and 45E of the Trade Practices Act 1974 (Commonwealth). Second, the strategy relied upon negative opinion of the MUA by the public who would accept 'creative' corporate restructuring for the 'good' of all.

The Australian Council of Trade Unions (ACTU) decided to pursue a more thoughtful response than simply union pickets lines. Instead, they used 'people power' in the form of 'peaceful community assemblies' at the picket lines at wharves around the country. Despite provocation on both sides, police generally refused to act as strike breakers. Consequently, the action moved to the courts. The union response was cautious, legally sound and disciplined.

THE UNION RESPONSE

The success of the MUA action against Patrick Stevedores needs to be seen in the context of the provisions of the *Workplace Relations Act 1996*. The introduction of the Workplace Relations Act 1996 ushered in a number of provisions to curtail the collective organising capacity of trade unions. Under various guises, the Act used freedom of association to prevent unions from adopting traditional union security arrangements (e.g. union membership arrangements, deductions of union dues etc.). For example, Section 298K(1) of the Act makes it an offence (a 'prohibited reason') for an employer to dismiss, refuse to employ or injure an employee based on whether (or not) they are in a union. The Federal Court decides whether any of the above 'prohibited' actions have occurred. The Court has power under Section 298U to make a number of orders (including consequential orders) in order to enforce its findings (including granting injunctions to prevent sackings and/or imposing fines). Sections

298K and 298U were originally intended as a 'union buster' by prohibiting unions from either compelling employer's to give them 'closed shops' or forcing an employee to join a union. The purpose was to bring union recruitment methods within the tort of conspiracy making certain types of union activity unlawful and the onus of proof was reversed and placed on the defendant (e.g. a union) to show that they are not in contravention of these clauses. However, these clauses ultimately became the undoing of Patrick's case. The MUA and the ACTU relied upon these Sections in the reverse by arguing that Section 298K(1) (applying to employers) and 298K(2) (applying to any person) must equally apply to employers or other persons who conspire to 'dismiss' or 'injure' or 'alter an employee's position to the employee's prejudice' solely because of their union membership. The tort of conspiracy could therefore equally apply to employers engaged in prohibited conduct. Ironically, the union case was helped along by the Prime Minister John Howard who had already said on national television (Channel 9 '*A Current Affair*' on 12 April 1998) that these employees were sacked because of union membership of the MUA. Whilst the MUA maintained industrial discipline and pursued this logical legal argument, Patrick was trusting that the Courts would accept 'commercial' reality (being unable to unscramble the omelette) and allow their contrived corporate restructuring to prevail.

Alarmed at the imminent threat of mass sackings, the MUA tried unsuccessfully to restrain Patrick in the AIRC. Undeterred, the MUA moved to the Federal Court on 6 April 1998, seeking an interim injunction against Patrick or the administrators (now the employer of Patrick's 'former' workforce) from sacking its workforce, pending trial. (Mass sackings took place at 12 midnight on the 7th of April.) This time, however, the MUA was successful before Justice North in the Federal Court. Here the Court took seriously a charge that Patrick had contrived to unlawfully sack its entire workforce of some 1,600 workers and in the process was involved in a tort of conspiracy against its own workforce. He drew attention to the July 1998 Howard Cabinet briefing paper (as well as other documents) setting out a detailed plan for dismissing an entire workforce. Particular attention was given to details of a meeting dated the 12 March 1997 that canvassed options for:

- manufacturing a dispute on the waterfront with the MUA
- reducing the MUA's ability to organise
- limiting the capacity of AIRC to deal with the re-instatements that would follow, such as by dressing them up as 'bona fide' redundancies (Federal Court of Australia, Maritime Union of Australia and ors v Patrick Stevedores No. 1 Pty Ltd and ors, (1998) 79 *Industrial Reports* 281 at 288).

His Honour went on to find that there was evidence to suggest that Patrick 'had a role in facilitating the training of a new waterfront workforce in Dubai'. Justice North concluded that Patrick's corporate restructuring was designed to facilitate the sacking of MUA members and 'the evidence raises a serious question to be tried'. Justice North went on to say:

> Patrick contended that the (MUA) could not succeed in (their) claim under Section 298K(1) because the real cause of harm to employees was (not from the restructuring) but rather the threatened termination of their employment. The termination could only be achieved by a decision of the administrators and that decision would not be made for a prohibited reason (under the Workplace Relations Act 1996) but for the reason that the employers were insolvent.

> I do not accept this approach for the purposes of this interim application. It is arguable that the conduct alleged to be in breach of Section 298K(1) was undertaken so that the administrators would have no option but to dismiss the workforce. The conduct was arguably designed so that the termination would be the probable outcome. The threatened termination was the effect of the conduct in breach of Section 298K(1). It does not matter that the final act was to be the act of the administrators, if that act was intended and likely to occur as a result of the prior conduct of the employers. The Court has powers to make orders to remedy the 'effects' of conduct in breach of Sections 298K(1) and 298U(e) (relating to 'prohibited reasons') ((1998) 79 Industrial Reports 281 at 288-290).

The issue was whether the actions by Patrick Stevedores to use company restructuring in order to rid itself of an unwanted unionised workforce brought the commercial actions of the company within the purview of industrial law. On this question, Justice North was emphatic:

> It is an objective of the (Workplace Relations) Act to ensure freedom of association, including the right of employees to join (a union) of their choice It (the Act) prohibits victimisation on the ground of union membership The Court should take into account as favouring the (union claim) that the context of the (union) claims is not a commercial dispute about money but an attempt to vindicate the rights of employees to earn a living free of victimisation ((1998) 79 Industrial Reports 281 at 291).

In deciding to favour the MUA, Justice North gave a clear signal that in particular circumstances (such as in this case), Courts will undue 'sharp' business and commercial practices the principal purpose of which is to victimise or prejudice employees in their employment. The decision of the Court was to order Patrick Stevedores to reinstate all sacked MUA members (pending a trial of all the issues) and to restrain the company from terminating the labour supply agreements with the labour hire companies. The Court issued orders to that effect. In justifying the need for making the orders, Justice North recognised the precarious position of employees in the face of a determined and secretive company campaign to injure them in their employment. He said:

> At a final hearing the Court may determine that the employees should be reinstated. If orders are not made now, it will be practically impossible for the Court to make such orders later because there will be so many irreversible changes flowing from the employees' absence from the workplace. In a practical sense, the failure to grant orders now will deny the employees the possibility of the remedy which they seek and as to which they have raised a serious question to be tried. The passage of time and events would defeat this remedy ((1998) 79 Industrial Reports 281 at 291).

The Courts' decision was influenced by undertakings furnished by the MUA that it would not continue its industrial action, and its members would sacrifice salaries to enable the administrators of the now cash strapped labour hire companies to trade out of insolvency. The orders of the Court effectively restored the status quo prior to the sackings of 7 April 1998. Patrick appealed the decision of Mr Justice North. A Full Bench of the Federal Court found the decision by Mr Justice North 'free from any appealable error' and rejected Patrick's appeal (Federal Court of Australia, Appeal to Full Court, Patrick Stevedores Operations No. 2 Pty Ltd and ors v Maritime Union of Australia and ors, (1998) 79 *Industrial Reports* 305).

Patrick then appealed to the High Court of Australia. The decision of the High Court was split according to three separate decisions. However, essentially, the High Court rejected Patrick's appeal. While upholding the general thrust of Mr Justice North's orders, the High Court varied the orders to allow the administrators greater flexibility in trading. However, the orders on Patrick to continue to employ sacked MUA members remained intact (High Court of Australia, Patrick Stevedores Operations No. 2 Pty Ltd and ors v Maritime Union of Australia, (1998) 79 *Industrial Reports*, 339). This, however, was not the end.

REFORM ON THE DOCKS?

Subsequent to the decision of the High Court, Patrick and the MUA finalised agreements, after considerable public posturing. The Minister for Workplace Relations and Small Business, Peter Reith, had in April prior to the High Court decision issued a document entitled *Waterfront Reform: Seven Benchmark Objectives*. This document set out a series of objectives (rather than benchmarks) that included improvements in training, crane rates, better use of technology, etc. that was meant to guide the negotiations between Patrick and the MUA. The agreements recognised the continued representational role of the MUA. In return, the MUA agreed to a number of changes. These included:

- approximately 600 redundancies
- introduction of casuals
- allocation of crews on shifts to be made by management
- introduction of aggregate hourly rates
- less manning
- introduction of productivity measures
- contracting out (Patrick Terminals Enterprise Agreement 1998; Patrick General Stevedoring Enterprise Agreement 1998).

Patrick also agreed to meet the MUA's legal costs ($A1.5M), as well as to settle action against the MUA by the Australian Consumer and Competition Commission (ACCC) for businesses hurt by the MUA strikes and stoppages during the dispute. A fund of A$7.5M was set up by Patrick to compensate businesses damaged during the dispute. Finally, the 600 redundancies were financed by the establishment of a $10 levy on containers under the Stevedoring Levy (Imposition) Act 1998. The MUA, at the conclusion of the dispute, remained on the docks, albeit reduced in number of members. For employees, the new Company regime involved closer time and work surveillance, tighter supervision, introduction of casual labour and low base rates to be topped up with individualised bonus and productivity payments. For Patrick, the result netted a slashed workforce from 1427 to 601, new agreements, a slight increase in productivity. Lang Corporation's share price nearly tripled in the months after the dispute closing in December around $7.50 up from a low of $1.16 during the dispute. Lang Corporation reported a profit of A$36 million for the year ending 30 September 1999 as compared to a loss of $A63 million in 1998 following the dispute (Trinca and Davies, 2000, 284). The major cost outcome of the dispute, namely the funding of the redundancies under the Government's redundancy program was paid for by a levy on port users based on the number of containers moved. Patrick Stevedores emerged relatively unscathed (Trinca and Davies 2000). Despite the dispute, all parties (including the Government) conceded that the restructuring would not decrease waterfront user fees or charges (*The Age*, 27 February 1999).

This case demonstrates the need for trade unions to be more disciplined. It also shows that they need to develop coherent and effective legal strategies to counteract employer de-unionisation strategies. The case is a good example of the increasing tendency of specialist industrial law courts such as the Federal Court (at least in cases dealing with 'prohibited reasons') to read into employment relations a charter of employee rights when interpreting employer conduct.

NOTES

The document entitled 'Waterfront Strategy' was reported to have been written during April 1997. Cabinet subsequently received it on the 7 July 1997. It was leaked to the *Australian Financial Review* and published on the 25 June 1998. This document along with others were formally made public when tabled by the ALP Opposition in the Senate in July 1998. The Howard Coalition Federal Government has denied that the document represented a 'strategy' for the waterfront.

REVIEW QUESTIONS

1. Why did the employer in this dispute resort to the tactics of trying to use corporate law to override industrial law? Is this strategy typical of employers in other disputes?
2. What role did the Government play in the dispute? Should Governments intervene in this manner?
3. How was the MUA able to resist the threat to de-unionise the waterfront? Could other unions act as effectively as the MUA did in this case? Explain.
4. In what ways might Patrick (and the Government) have better planned, or acted differently, so that they might have succeeded in their endeavour to break the MUA stevedoring monopoly on the waterfront?
5. What light does this dispute cast on the role of the law, and the Courts in industrial relations?

FURTHER READING

Trinca, H. and Davies, A. (2000) *Waterfront: The Battle that Changed Australia*, Doubleday, Random House, Milsons Point, NSW.

Wiseman, J. (1998) 'Here to Stay? The 1997-1998 Australian Waterfront Dispute and its Implications', *Labour and Industry*, 9(1), 1-16.

CHAPTER 1

Conceptual and Analytical Tools

'There is nothing so practical as a good theory.'

Kurt Lewin

LEARNING OBJECTIVES

After reading this chapter, you should:

- understand the major debates surrounding the definition of industrial relations
- be familiar with the scope of the subject matter of industrial relations and the disciplines which contribute to its scholarship
- be familiar with the different conceptual 'frames of reference' embodied in the unitarist, pluralist, and Marxist approaches to industrial relations
- be able to describe the role of theory in explaining and predicting industrial relations
- provide an outline of the main industrial relations theories, and explain their strengths and weaknesses.

INTRODUCTION

From personal experience we know that differences of opinion are commonplace, whether between family members, friends, social interests, ethnic groups, political parties or nations. This is no less true amongst individuals and groups in the workplace. Because modern industrial organisations rely on hierarchies of authority and control to produce economic output, it is inevitable that employees and managers will at times have different expectations about the distribution of tasks and the allocation of rewards. How these differences are reconciled is an important part of the day-to-day work of managers. Yet there is little agreement in our society on how this reconciliation should be achieved for the benefit of all. Wide differences of opinion exist over how to best regulate workplace relations, what level of interaction is necessary or appropriate between managers and employees, and how breakdowns in relations should be avoided or resolved. It is in the very nature of the subject matter of industrial relations that such differences are often clouded by strongly held ideological convictions or simplistic assumptions about human nature and the nature of work itself. At the same time, the management of industrial relations is rarely straightforward, made more complex by an array of uncertain economic, sociological and political factors. To assist practitioners to manage industrial relations, a variety of theories and models have been developed.

This chapter outlines the various approaches, models and conceptual tools commonly used to analyse industrial relations. While some concepts may require careful reading, they all contribute to a good general understanding of industrial relations.

DEFINING INDUSTRIAL RELATIONS

The definition of industrial relations has long been a source of considerable debate, particularly over what is included in the field of inquiry. Some scholars have taken a narrow view, defining industrial relations in terms of the institutions that regulate relations in the workplace. Using this definition the objects of study have typically included:

- employers (or managers) and their representatives (i.e. employer associations)
- employees and their representatives (i.e. trade unions)
- various government agencies with an interest in industrial relations (i.e. labour courts and public departments)
- institutionalised processes that regulate work and resolve workplace conflict (e.g. labour laws, contracts of employment, collective bargaining mechanisms, informal, and formal rules and practices that govern the workplace) (see, Dunlop 1958; Flanders 1965; Clegg 1979).

Other scholars have looked beyond institutions and defined industrial relations in terms of the social psychology and interaction of individuals in the workplace (see, Marginson 1969; Somers 1969; Laffer 1974). Still others have taken an even broader view, defining industrial relations in a way that embraces wider social and economic influences outside the workplace. These scholars link industrial relations to the wider distribution of economic power and the class divisions of contemporary capitalism (see, Hyman 1989).

Whether narrowly or broadly defined, the major debate in recent years has centred on how the rapidly changing patterns of work and changing institutional processes can be best accommodated within existing definitions of industrial relations. The major changes prompting this debate include:

- the increasing adoption of new Human Resource Management (HRM) practices
- the recent decline in trade union membership
- the decreasing coverage of the collective bargaining process
- the retreat of government intervention in workplace relations.

All these developments have raised significant new questions about the definition of what has traditionally been covered by 'industrial relations' (see, Kelly 1994; Kaufman 1993). If industrial relations is only about the institutions of job regulation and processes of conflict avoidance, how, for example, is the declining influence of both trade unions and the role of collective bargaining to be treated? Or if industrial relations is more about the study of macro-level economic and social influences on workplace behaviour, how are the new micro-level HRM practices to be incorporated? Questions such as these are forcing scholars to redefine industrial relations in a clearer and more relevant manner.

One attempt to redefine the subject, mainly from academics outside traditional industrial relations, has involved integrating its subject matter in the functions of HRM (see, Stone 1998, chapter 15; Mabey, Salaman and Storey 1998, chapter 9). The key to this approach is said to be HRM's strategic approach to the management of people. Put briefly this means that human resource policies are integrated with overall business strategy. Emphasis is placed on the importance of people and the promotion of organisational commitment. A common value system is promoted between management and employees. Industrial relations in this treatment is seen as merely one of many functions of a fully operational HRM program. Such functions can include the recruitment and selection of staff, training and development, on-the-job health and safety, the placement of staff by strategic job analysis and design, and the management of employee performance and remuneration. In other words, industrial relations is defined as a sub-set of HRM, applied to the specific management function of dealing with the settlement of disputes and contracts of employment, involving trade unions, labour courts, worker collectives, and the like. Such a view has not been without criticism. It has been noted for instance that there is little agreement in the literature over a precise meaning of HRM (Kaufman 1993), with one study in particular finding the term had been variously used as a concept, a theory, a metaphor, a research topic and an ideology (Kelly 1994, 7). The key assumptions of HRM have also been questioned. Some, for instance, have argued that its definition is either too prescriptive (Legge 1989), is contradictory (Noon 1992), or simply fails to recognise that conflict is an inevitable part of the workplace (Hyman 1989). A practical problem that arises from including industrial relations in HRM, is that few organisations operate fully-fledged HRM programs.

Another attempt to redefine industrial relations in more contemporary terms, including the practices of HRM, has involved the advancement of a new catch-all term know as 'employment relations' (see, Bamber and Lansbury 1998; Keenoy and Kelly 1998). However, such attempts also have their problems. For example, much of the American literature uses the term for describing HRM functions and associated interactions between individual employers and employees at the level of the firm. Applied in this way, 'employment relations' means something quite different to the older terms 'personnel management' and 'industrial relations'. The British literature, on the other hand, applies a far wider meaning to employment relations that goes beyond the workplace, to cover the interactions between the state, employer associations and organised labour. This version of employment relations embraces the micro-level relations between individual managers and employees, as is the case in the American usage, and also the macro-level relations between the institutions that govern the workplace (Legge 1995, Chapter 2).

The important point about the wider institutional references in the British use of the term 'employment relations' is that these have always been a part of traditional 'industrial relations' scholarship. What most British literature in fact does is use the term 'employment relations' in two senses. First, it uses it generally to describe the functions and activities of HRM. In other words it reflects the orthodox American usage, in which the employment relationship is simply the sum of the collaborative interactions between managers and employees. These include responsibility for: the flexibility, skill and loyalty of employees; the absence of workplace conflict and trade unions; and the achievement of the high performance outcomes of the firm. Second, the literature uses the term to describe the institutional and regulatory environment in which the functions, activities and interactions of HRM take place. This second usage is a simple recognition that trade unions and state intervention in the form of substantive labour laws and industrial tribunals are an inescapable part of the British workscape - a situation not so true in the United States (and also in the American literature). Applied in this second way the employment relationship takes on a different meaning that acknowledges the diversity (or plurality) of workplace interests and the potential for conflict. This can be seen where the employment relationship is described as governed by formal regulations and informal practices determined by dispute settlement and negotiation procedures.

This dual use of the term 'employment relationship' is also becoming more prevalent in the Australian HRM and industrial relations literature. Those articles or chapters, for example, which deal with the functions of HRM, invariably do so by portraying the employment relationship in terms of its collaborative, common purpose characteristics (or unitarist attributes, see below). Articles or chapters dealing with trade unions, industrial courts and legal matters, on the other hand, invariably portray the employment relationship in terms of its diversity and conflicting interests (or pluralist attributes, see below) (see, Kramar, McGraw and Schuler 1997; Stone 1998; Mabey, Salaman and Storey 1998). This duality is hardly surprising. Australia, like Britain, has a vibrant and legally protected trade union movement that cannot be easily ignored or suppressed. What is surprising is that this duality is rarely acknowledged, although this may have something to do with the contradictions that such an acknowledgment would immediately present. How, for example, can an employee be committed to the objectives of an organisation (a core functional outcome expected of HRM practices), and at the same time be a member of a trade union? Or, how can the functional flexibility of a firm (another expected outcome) be squared with multi-unionism and associated demarcation lines that often exist between jobs and union territories? (Legge 1995, 247). The answer to such questions has so far involved little more than changing the definition of employment relations to suit the particular subject matter being discussed.

Whilst this is wholly unsatisfactory, this book is not the place to resolve the problem. For present purposes, we will be happy to accept the view that the functions, activities and interactions of HRM may constitute the 'employment relationship', but only when they occur in workplaces without dual loyalties and internal conflicts, and only where there is little or no outside interference in the way a firm decides to manage its employees. In workplaces where the contrary characteristics are in evidence, HRM practices must be held to operate within a broader diversity of interests or pluralist frame of reference (see below). In summary, because the terms and conditions of employment for the vast majority of workers are still regulated through the agency of such things as trade unions, industrial tribunals, labour laws, and the like, the bulk of this book will draw upon this broader pluralist frame of reference.

Thus the approach taken in this book is consistent with traditional 'industrial relations' scholarship. Two definitional levels are applied to the term 'industrial relations': one intellectual and one practical. At an intellectual level industrial relations is defined as 'an interdisciplinary field that encompasses the study of all aspects of people at work. The field includes the study of individuals, groups of workers who may or may not organise into a union or an association, the behaviour of employer and union organisations, the public policy or legal framework governing employment conditions, the economics of employment problems and the comparative analysis of industrial relations systems in different countries' (Kochan 1980, 1). At a practical level industrial relations is defined as the processes of regulation and control over workplace relations, the organisation of tasks, and the relations between employers and their representatives, and employees and their representatives, and is the sum of economic, social and political interactions in workplaces where employees provide manual and mental labour in exchange for rewards allotted by employers, as well as the institutions established for the purpose of governing workplace relations (Gospel and Palmer 1993, 2). The term 'industrial' not only includes the interactions that take place within organisations involved manufacturing, but also those that take place within service sector organisations and public sector enterprises. Similarly, the term 'relations' not only includes interactions that take place between managers and blue-collar manual workers, but also those that occur between managers and white-collar employees. In this chapter on the conceptual basis of industrial relations, it is the intellectual definition of IR that is largely used.

FRAMES OF REFERENCE

Debates over the scope of industrial relations are largely moulded by the perceptions held by individuals. Because such individuals are social beings and industrial relations itself is a social phenomenon, individuals rarely come to the practice or study of industrial relations value-free. Scholars, apart from coming from different disciplinary backgrounds, quite often bring different values and assumptions to their analysis, whether they acknowledge them or not. Practitioners also often hold different values, which in turn may be accentuated by the vested interests they represent. A starting point in the study of industrial relations is, therefore, to identify the major perspectives, or frames of reference (Fox 1966, 1-2), which are normally adopted in studies in this area. Although there is a vast array of conceptual approaches, most can be broadly categorised within three frames of reference, which differ in their perception of the nature of work and workplace conflict. These can be identified as unitarist, pluralist and Marxist.

Unitarism

It is difficult to pin down the beginnings of the unitarist view of industrial relations, but it probably stems from a set of philosophical ideas that hold the world is generally one of harmonious order, despite the appearance of occasional conflict, muddle and formless happenchance. If this is the case then its intellectual beginnings can be traced to social philosophers who have long held society to be a kind of super-oganism, in which the constituent parts of civil society display a certain interdependence which is not unlike the way organisms combine to give life to the human body (see, Ely 1890; Carlye 1911; Hobson 1920; Hayek 1960; Tawney 1961). This idea views the actions of individuals and social groups in terms of their contribution to the survival and well-being of the society, in which all have a common interest. It argues that this harmony of interests compels individuals and social groups to prefer the common interest over their own interest in the event of a clash.

Present-day unitarist thinking about industrial relations starts from the broad assumption that there is a mutual interdependence of interests between the constituent parts of modern-day business organisations. Accordingly, conflict between employers and employees is not seen as inevitable. Subscribers to this view do not deny that conflict between the two groups may sometimes occur, but they believe such occurrences are mere aberrations in an otherwise cooperative relationship. In a manner not unlike organisms, employers and employees are held to have a shared interest in the survival of their organisation, such that workplace conflict, when it does occur, is unlikely to get to the point of making a firm insolvent. The divisions that do exist are, according to unitarists, the product of personality disorders, inappropriate recruitment and promotion practices, the deviance of dissidents, the work of agitators, or poor internal communications. To ensure such divisions do not thwart the natural harmony of things, it is often argued that the rational management team must pay careful attention to removing the sources of potential conflict. To this end, it must ensure that recruitment and promotion processes are fair and equitable. It must also ensure that communication systems are in place to alert employees of where their true interests lie, and that individuals who are 'difficult' or prone to personality conflicts are either counselled, suppressed or dismissed. Lastly management must ensure that the organisation is promoted amongst the work-force as the single source of authority, and that alternative sources of authority, such as shop stewards or trade unions, are eliminated from the workplace (see, Fox 1966; Fidler 1981, 148-67; Kochan and Barocci 1985; Storey 1989; Stone, 1998).

A number of criticisms have been directed at the unitarist perspective. Some have argued that the approach fails to understand the nature of conflict and ignores the distribution of power within modern-day organisations (Hyman 1975). Others have argued that the political processes within such organisations are not adequately taken into account, and that it over-emphasises consensus and mutuality of interests within business organisations, whilst ignoring the complex historical, economic, social, industrial and technological factors that cause workplace dissension and conflict (see, Osborne 1992). Still others have asserted that the approach is little more than a type of management ideology, one which serves to legitimise management authority, blame conflict on employees, threaten the existence of trade unions and is both manipulative and exploitative (see, Guille, Sappey and Winter 1989).

Pluralism

Pluralism is a term drawn from the field of political science. It emerged as a critique of the concept of sovereignty and the idea that the stability of political systems is dependent upon the existence of a final source of authority. Setting aside underdeveloped countries, pluralists argue that in highly developed countries there are sufficient resources to satisfy the competing demands of the different social interest groups. In such societies, it is asserted by pluralists, political stability is not maintained through any recourse to a single source of sovereign authority, but instead by continuous mediation processes (e.g. elections, independent judiciary) and by institutions (e.g. parliamentary democracy, impartial public service) put in place to resolve the competing demands made by multiple sources of authority (e.g. landowners, farmers, financiers, industrialists, workers, army, and the like) (see, Truman 1951; Dahl 1961; Lindblom 1977; Richardson and Jordan 1979).

Industrial relations pluralists draw an analogy between the governance of western democratic states and the running of industrial enterprises. Managers of enterprises are admittedly selected in a very different manner to the government of a democratic state, but in common with governments they often claim 'special authority' and responsibilities within their domain. Accordingly, pluralists assert that there is a similarity between the questionable doctrine of political sovereignty and the notion of managerial power or 'prerogative'. They also see similarities between the behaviour of trade unions in the workplace and the behaviour of organised social interest groups operating in the political arena, and between the processes and institutions of collective bargaining and the processes and institutions of mediation used in wider civil society (Clegg 1975).

It is this broad analogy with civil society with its endless potential for conflict that distinguishes the pluralist perspective of industrial relations from the unitarist. Typical of this view is that business organisations are inherently complex social organisations made up of different interest groups, and that workplace conflict within them is inevitable. Management and employees are viewed as two such interest groups, who, by of the very nature of the factory system, will always pursue different values and objectives. From the pluralist frame of reference, therefore, there will always be both different sources of authority within an organisation, and potential for conflict between them over the organisation of work and the allocation of rewards. By recognising the inevitability of conflict, those holding this perspective tend to regard it as necessary for the health of an enterprise. First, it serves to bring workers' grievances to the surface. Second, the ever-present potential for conflict is said to provide a spur for managers to find innovative ways to handle it to produce the best results. Third, recognising competing sources of authority, particularly shop stewards and trade unions, allows industrial relations issues to be dealt with on a collective basis. This, it is argued, not only gives management the most efficient way to implement employment rules, but also creates fairer outcomes by allowing employees to counter the power of management when negotiating workplace contracts. Fourth and finally, on a more general level, a certain amount of visible conflict is said to show that the workers' aspirations have not been totally undermined by hopelessness or suppressed by power. It may also show that prevailing work rules are inadequate, are in need of change, or that management is failing to find workable compromises (see, Fox 1966; Fox 1971; Fox 1974; Clegg 1975).

The industrial relations implications of pluralism are that management should accept the reality of competing interests and that workplace conflict is a normal part of the social dynamics of modern industrial organisations. It is the task of management to keep workplace conflict to manageable proportions and, if possible, turn it into a positive influence within the organisation. This can only be achieved, it is argued, by managers recognising the legitimacy of trade unions and accepting their right to participate in company decision-making processes. In order to do this, managers must accept the need to relinquish certain rights and recognise that trade unions are not the cause of conflict but are instead the organised expression of diverse workplace interests which exist anyway. They must also recognise that conflict is rooted in the very nature of social relations and so try to manage workgroup structures, relations and policies to minimise conflict.

Like unitarism, the pluralist approach also has its critics. Some have suggested that it assumes the existence of articulate and organised interests without explaining how they are generated in the first place. In other words the approach assumes the existence of different social groups in the workplace without considering the conditions that cause them to develop (Hyman 1975). Others have argued that the approach neglects the role of individuals in industrial relations, as well as the different contexts in which workplace struggles take place. In this regard the approach is said to be methodologically flawed because it assumes some groups have more power than others without inquiring sufficiently into the way each group acquires power and authority. It also fails to inquire into the constraints that can prevent any group from fully exercising that power (Hyman and Fryer 1977). Still others have asserted that the approach is lacking because it fails to accommodate the influence of politics on the conduct of industrial relations and the role of the state in setting its boundaries (e.g. Dabschek 1989). Finally, it has been suggested that the approach merely focuses on how conflict is expressed organisationally but fails to explain why the inherent potential for conflict should exist in the first place (Edwards 1986).

Marxism

A Marxian perspective may seem no longer relevant given the break-up of the Soviet Union, the collapse of communism in Eastern Europe and the decline of 'radical' thinking in the West over the past decade. There are, however, a number of studies from this school of thought which remain influential. This is because, first, they are based on vastly different assumptions about the nature and cause of workplace conflict; and second, because they act as valid critiques of the previous two perspectives. Those arguing from a radical perspective draw principally on the work of Karl Marx, a nineteenth century German philosopher, sociologist and economist. Although Marx said very little directly about the institutions and processes of industrial relations, his theories are very relevant to these areas.

Marx argued that capitalist societies were characterised by perpetual class struggle. This struggle is caused by inequalities in the distribution of wealth and the skewed ownership of the means of production. Wealth and property ownership, he observed, were highly concentrated in the hands of a small number of bourgeoisie (or capitalists), whilst the vast mass of the proletariat (or workers) lived in poverty and had nothing to sell but their labour. The dominant capitalist class controlled the levers of political and economic power, and were forced to exploit the working class by extorting 'surplus value' from their labour. Capitalism generated this exploitation because, by its very nature, it required capitalists to engage in ruthless competition with each other. Each round of new investment placed increasing competitive pressures on profits and created the need to cut costs and rationalise productive operations.

This dynamic was seen by Marx as forcing capitalists to perpetually drive down the wages of workers and reduce their numbers. As the latter constituted by far the larger number of those consuming the output of their own productive labours, each new round of investment thus produced its own inherent contradiction. Marx argued that societies organised along these lines developed political systems and class-based values that legitimise the dominant position of the capitalist class and coerce the working class into a 'false consciousness' that accepts the status quo. At the same time, however, he argued that capitalist political systems and class-based values are incapable of indefinitely controlling the internal inconsistencies of capitalism. Consequently, the deepening impoverishment of workers eventually moves them to recognise their common class interests and spurs them to organise against their exploitation (Marx [1857][1891]; for contemporary commentaries see, Hyman 1971; Edwards 1979).

Applying this Marxist frame of reference to industrial relations, social conflict is viewed as a natural outcome of capitalism, with the result being a struggle between two social classes. The expectation is that the working class will eventually rise up to overthrow the capitalist class and redistribute wealth in a new social order without private property. Consequently, those who later followed Marxist beliefs came to view industrial relations as merely another example of the class struggle already being played out in wider society. Vladamir Lenin, for example, used Marx's analysis to write extensively about the role trade unions should take in society. This role, he argued, required them to raise workers' revolutionary consciousness as a means of leading them to overthrow the system. Unions limiting their actions to merely improving the material lot of workers were held to be misguided, because the capitalist class would always be in a position to claw back any gains it was temporarily forced to concede. Lenin argued that the leaders of such trade unions needed to be replaced by revolutionary intellectuals who understood the true political and educative purpose of unionism. The leading modern-day industrial relations scholar using a Marxist frame of reference is Richard Hyman (1971; 1975, 1977; 1978; 1980; 1989), who identifies two consistent themes from this approach: first, that capitalism produces a structured antagonism between capital and labour; and second, that such antagonism encourages workers to organise collectively and creates among them the urge to challenge the priorities of capitalist method of production (1980, 42). According to Hyman, employers are naturally moved under capitalism to contain costs, whilst workers are constantly moved to maximise wages as this is their only source of livelihood. This inevitably leads to conflict as employers resist the cost increases associated with the wage demands of workers (1975, 19). Industrial relations is thus conceived as being inherently prone to conflict, with collective bargaining merely representing temporary accommodations and unstable compromises which invariably break down because of the contradictions inherent within capitalist society. The source of industrial conflict, on this understanding, is a product of the class struggle occurring within wider society. The remedy for such conflict thus requires nothing less than a complete change in the way wealth and property ownership are distributed.

As a critique of pluralism, Marxism calls for fundamental changes that extend beyond the workplace. Pluralism, it argues, merely acts to gloss over the inequalities of wealth, power and class domination in capitalist societies, when the real need is to change the whole structure of such societies. In the same vein, it claims that pluralist talk about checks and balances hides the fact that power is highly concentrated in the hands of a small 'ruling stratum' which makes a genuine balance of power between the propertied and the propertyless impossible. Thus, it is argued, the pluralist analogy between the constitution of a democratic state and the procedural rules of industrial relations is false. Democratic constitutions, it suggests, provide equal opportunities for major political parties to win power in government, but in industrial relations the parties do not compete for power. Power is instead permanently vested in one party, namely, the owners of the means of production and their representatives, the management. Unions may occasionally provide a check on this power, but their main role is really one of a permanent opposition (Frenkel 1977). On another tangent, it has been claimed by Marxists that union officials representing the interests of members are socialised to accept most aspects of the inequality of work, so that when negotiating with managers they are still serving the purposes of the true power holders in society. In fact, it is precisely because of this that the true power of owners and managers is rarely displayed or used in public. Employees and their unions are simply bought off through marginal concessions which protect the really important managerial rights (Hyman 1971).

The Marxist frame of reference has also been criticised. At a general level, for instance, it has been suggested that it is difficult to demonstrate the existence of a coherent, dominant, capitalist class and an exploited working class in advanced industrial societies. Furthermore, capitalists do not appear to be an homogenous social group. There are vast differences in the values and interests between such groups as small shop owners, farmers, shareholders, and the like. On the other hand, the increasing misery and exploitation of the working class in advanced industrial societies, as predicted by Marx, has not in fact occurred. As a consequence, it is hardly surprising that the revolutionary conflict predicted between these two competing classes has not occurred either. Indeed, most of the available evidence indicates that it is possible for social conflict to be regulated and controlled, resulting in slower and more evolutionary forms of change (Dahrendorf 1959). Others have noted that despite Lenin's advocacy, trade unions have continued to concentrate on securing economic benefits for members, and in so doing have been responding to what their members actually want. Indeed, they have not sought to foster revolutionary consciousness, and charges of 'false consciousness' levelled at union leaders and workers are little more than a form of 'social mysticism', coming largely from intellectuals unfamiliar with the facts of economic life (Perlman 1949). Still others have asserted that the state is not simply a tool of the capitalist class, and can often be seen to act in the interests of labour and other organised social groups (Dabscheck 1983). Similarly, the state is often seen to act in the interest one group of capitalists to the disadvantage of others (Jessop 1982).

Most people, either in part or in full, subscribe to one or other of the above three perspectives. Much, of course, depends how people view the world and what assumptions they hold about the nature of work and workplace conflict. As a general rule, however, those believing in social and economic individualism tend to be unitarist, and are typically found among the ranks of employers, managers and conservative politicians. Those who believe collectivism produces better social and economic outcomes are more inclined to be pluralists, and tend to be found among the ranks of trade union officials, employees and labour politicians. As for those who believe capitalism is economically exploitative and socially divisive, they are probably a small but influential minority on the left-wing of the labour movement. However, within Australia, even amongst this grouping, they tend to take a Marxist view without going so far as to advocate Marxist revolutionary change. It is also worth noting that these three perspectives largely apply only to western industrial societies governed by mature democratic systems - a point we will expand further later in this chapter.

The important point to take from this section is that in understanding the foundations of our own perspective, and that of others, we can make much better sense of industrial relations. Nowhere will this become more apparent than if we find ourselves engaged in workplace bargaining processes, unable to fathom the logic of the person we are negotiating with.

THEORIES OF INDUSTRIAL RELATIONS

What we have considered so far are three broad frames of reference with their underlying ideologies and assumptions about workplace relations. However, none of these amounts to an empirical, scientific theory on industrial relations, designed to interpret and predict industrial relations phenomena. According to Dabscheck and Niland (1981), theories serve two essential functions. First, they provide a means of explaining what is happening, and second, by virtue of this explanation they provide a means by which to predict the future. Of course, many industrial relations practitioners deny the value of theories, claiming to be pragmatists who operate successfully on the basis of experience and intuition. However, we do need integrating ideas or theories to help create order in disconnected data from different sources and disciplines.

The development of theories typically follows several stages. The first is a rudimentary stage, in which empirical data is ordered and classified in a relatively simple manner. The second is a more rigorous system of classification, in which the relationship between the variables is specified. The third stage involves the development of a simple theory that links causes and effects and allows simple generalisations to be made. The fourth and final stage sees a full-blown theory emerge, which can be tested to explain experience and used to make empirical predictions (Parsons 1951, 50). This scheme is a useful yardstick for measuring how far a theory has developed, and what functions it is capable of performing.

Scientific Management

Scientific Management is generally regarded as the first modern management theory, and was developed in the early years of the 20th Century. Although not specifically developed to explain or predict industrial relations, it nevertheless has elements that have been used in this way. Frederick Taylor [1911], a self-trained engineer developed the theory based on what he saw as scientific principles, mainly for the purpose of raising the efficiency of industrial enterprises. As a system of management, the theory was intended to maximise output through time and motion studies which would identify the most efficient methods of performing work. To this end, the theory identified the need to select a staff of 'first class men', to train them in the best work methods and to use incentive payment schemes to motivate them. It also stressed the need for rationality, clear objectives and the maintenance of managerial authority. It furthermore emphasised the need to reduce tasks to their basic elements elements, so that they might be performed by low-skilled, low-paid employees in assembly line production. Managers were expected to treat workers impersonally and collectively, and their relationship with them was calculative, focussed on extrinsic rewards and incentives. The theory argued that firms using these techniques in a systematic and scientific manner would maximise output, whilst enabling workers to maximise their pay.

Scientific management techniques clearly demonstrated their unitarist assumptions by the fact that both managers and workers were seen as beneficiaries, with a common interest in the success of the enterprise. Given the right selection techniques, work-force training and incentive payment schemes, the expectations of both managers (i.e. profits) and workers (i.e. pay) could be realised. Consistent with this unitarist interpretation, the theory had no role for trade unions. Indeed, trade unions were held to interfere with the close relationship that would otherwise naturally exist between managers and workers. In fact Taylor saw the practice of 'soldiering' (i.e. the deliberate restriction of output to levels below what workers could actually attain) and the prevalence of poor selection techniques as directly caused by the influence of trade unions. Collective bargaining also had no role, and was viewed as standing in the way of suitable payment schemes to motivate workers individually. Over the early part of the 20th Century, scientific management provided employers and management with a rational for excluding unions and for implementing systems of work supposedly capable of delivering superior output and pay on the basis scientific and objective rules. Taylor's theory was widely applied over the early part of the 20th Century and became the cause of considerable industrial unrest in the United States (Tillett et al. 1970). It retained considerable appeal in a vastly modified form in many organisations up until the late 1960s and early 1970s, and the general idea of 'objective rules' is still evident in some recent human resource management techniques (1970, 86).

Human Relations Theory

Human relations theory emerged in the late 1920s and early 1930s and was influenced by the new discipline of industrial psychology. It also was not primarily developed for the purpose of explaining or predicting industrial relations, but like scientific management was also used for this purpose. The theory itself grows out of studies conducted by a team of researchers at the Western Electric Company in the United States, who carried out a series of experiments and observations of work group behaviour (Mayo 1933). These studies concluded that group activities and their related social satisfactions were crucial factors in worker motivation. The role of pay incentives as theorised earlier by Taylor, was therefore down-played. Instead, managers with leadership skills were needed to create and maintain work group cohesion, which was fundamentally important in maximising worker satisfaction, motivation and productivity. Managers were urged to recognise that people are different to other resources used in production. Attention had to be given to the nature of supervision and of the working of groups and teams. It was important to find ways of involving employees through job design and inclusive managerial techniques. However, despite these clear differences with scientific management, the key elements of this theory remained consistent with the unitary frame of reference. This is evident in the theoretical focus on the social satisfaction of work groups, and in the assumption of common interests between the work groups and management. Indeed, the theory goes so far as to hold workplace conflict to be pathological, dysfunctional for all concerned, and the result of either poor internal communications or the failure of management to understand the social needs of workers.

Interestingly, in the Mayo studies both the contested internal power relations within the organisation and the role of trade unions, were all but ignored (Bramel and Friend 1981). This is surprising given the organisation at the time had invested thousands of dollars to pay spies for the purpose of reporting on and subverting pro-union tendencies among employees. Human Relations theory fell into disrepute over the early post-war period as result of on-going theoretical inconsistencies and mixed results in practice. It nevertheless paved the way for more sophisticated approaches represented later in *neo-human relations* or *behavioural theories*. These theories are best seen in the works of Maslow (1943), McGregor (1957), Herzberg (1966) and Roethlishberger (1965), all of whom, in various ways, focussed on individual satisfaction and motivation, including the need for 'self actualisation' through a 'hierarchy of needs'. Applied in industrial settings, theories of this type suggested different sources of job satisfaction and dissatisfaction. Their key element was that high job satisfaction led to high worker motivation, which in turn led to high job output. This has led to techniques of 'job enrichment'. Despite the more sophisticated approach of neo-human relations and behavioural theories, they share many of the same unitary assumptions of earlier theories. In other words, they fail to account for the role of trade unions and the nature of workplace conflict. Nevertheless, their contribution to industrial relations theories remains important for identifying the link between employees' work effort and the type of psychological contract they have with managers (for more detailed contemporary discussion of both human relations and neo-human relations theories see, Huczynski 1993). The dominance of this type of thinking among practicing managers spanned a brief but notable period between the mid-1960s and late 1970s, but may still be detected in the new human resource management practices.

Systems Theory

Systems theory was developed by an American academic, John Dunlop (1958), who argued that industrial relations was a sub-system of the wider social system. A system, he pointed out, is an abstraction. It is designed to highlight relationships, focus attention on critical variables and assist in historical inquiry and statistical testing. Work, Dunlop observed, is a system governed by rules and regulations covering everything from recruitment, wages, and performance, to hours, holidays and a myriad of other employment details. These rules range from the formal, such as legislation and written collective agreements, to the informal, such as the unwritten customs known to everyone in the workplace. Dunlop argued that industrial actors try to establish this body of formal and informal rules and regulations, and that their establishment is influenced by wider environmental circumstances. He also argued that all actors share an interest (a binding ideology) in maintaining the process of negotiation and conflict resolution. This model of workplace relations is made up of the following four key features.

First, the *Actors* are made up of employers and their representatives, employees and their representatives, and external agencies. 'Employers' include the owners of enterprises and/or the managers acting on their behalf, as well as those public administrators who control public sector employees. The 'representatives of employers' are those associations that act on behalf of employers and/or managers from the same industrial sector. 'Employees' are those who undertake work at the direction of owners and managers of enterprises. The 'representatives of employees' include both formal organisations, such as trade unions, and informal organisations such as groups of non-union employees who have worked together for sufficient time to develop common values and beliefs. 'External agencies' are taken to be government departments and institutions, including courts with industrial relations responsibilities.

Second, the *Environmental Contexts* mean the prevailing market and budgetary circumstances, the technological conditions, and the distribution of power in the wider society, all of which influence and/or constrain the actors engaged in industrial relations. 'Market and budgetary contexts' means the prevailing product market and the internal budgetary conditions under which an enterprise operates. These contexts influence both an enterprise's employment levels and its ability to pay wages, undertake training, meet worker demands for improved conditions, and so on. 'The technological context' means the nature, scale and degree of change in the technology being used by an enterprise, all of which have a bearing on the size and skill of the work force, training levels, employee supervision, accident rates, and so on. 'The distribution of power context' refers to the power relations between the actors and society. Societies governed under a military dictatorship, a despotic family elite, the church or a colonial administration, for example, will produce quite different industrial relations outcomes to societies governed under the rule of democracy.

Third, the *Body of Rules* governs the employment relationship and is the outcome of the interaction of the actors. The degree of influence of each actor in establishing the rules is said to depend on the balance of power between the actors. In some systems, employers will have almost a completely free hand. In others, they will be constrained by the power of unions or the actions of government. The body of rules includes procedural rules, such as those for making rules (e.g. collective bargaining and compulsory arbitration) and those that apply to particular situations (e.g. disputes settlement procedures and disciplinary procedures). They also include substantive rules, such as those pertaining to the establishment of pay rates and conditions of employment. Such rules can take many forms, ranging from government legislation and enterprise regulations, to workplace custom and practice.

Fourth, a *Binding Ideology* is the set of beliefs held by each actor that encourages compromises for the sake of maintaining the system. The role of the ideology is to bind the system together and provide stability by a common set of beliefs and values. The ideology of each actor may not be identical, but there must be enough in common to prevent the system disintegrating. The actors may not even be fully conscious of their ideology. Sometimes intellectuals and publicists may be used to express the ideology of the actors.

An important aspect of Dunlop's Systems Theory model is that the industrial relations are always seen to be self-adjusting towards an equilibrium. As soon as change in one part has repercussions on any other part, it is said to set in motion a series of processes that must ultimately re-impose a sense of order on the system. By way of example, the introduction of new technology could normally be expected to require changes in existing work practices. These changes may require the retrenchment of some workers and the retraining of others. This in turn would lead to trade unions responding to protect those workers being retrenched and to seek better wages for those being trained for new equipment. Any dispute that arises out of such actions may be resolved between the parties (or actors) at the level of the workplace. If not, then the government may be called upon, though its labour courts, to adjudicate on an appropriate retrenchment package for the dismissed workers and a new wage rate for the re-skilled operators. No matter how the dispute is resolved, adjustments to the pre-existing employment relationship will need to occur if work with the new technology is to proceed without further incident. The introduction of new equipment can thus be expected to set in motion a range of negotiations which will unfold until a new equilibrium is reached. An interesting aspect of this scenario is that all the parties are assumed to have little or no interest in resisting the introduction of the new technology, if it is deemed necessary for the future survival of the firm. In this way each actor is said to share a common acceptance of the ultimate outcome of the conflict resolution procedures. It is this common acceptance (or binding ideology) which, it is argued, stabilises and sustains the industrial relations system.

Dunlop's Systems Theory model was the first attempt to develop a general theory of industrial relations that could be applied at the enterprise, industry and national levels. It could also be used for making comparisons between the entities at each of these levels. It is still a widely accepted framework used for describing the key elements of industrial relations and for identifying and analysing their interrelationships. However, it has not been without its critics. Some, for instance, have argued that the model misconceives the nature of social conflict by over-emphasising the stabilising influences of a shared ideology (Wood 1978). From a Marxist perspective, the evidence of social stability, for instance, might merely be a sign of oppressed workers being unable to break the domination of their employers. A more pluralist view suggests that in specifying three types of actor and assuming each has a mutual interest in the survival of business organisations, the model discounts the possibility that one or other of the actors may seek to eliminate rivals in certain circumstances (see, Frenkel 1977). For example, there is ample evidence in recent years of organisations trying to omit trade unions from workplace negotiations over wages and conditions. Other critics have noted how some workplace conflicts have been so severe that, far from demonstrating Dunlop's 'binding ideology', they have resulted in managers and employees actually rallying around opposing ideals. In such instances, it is argued, ideology has *reinforced* the conflict rather than promoted cooperation between the parties (see, Kochan, Katz and McKersie 1986). Other critics have argued that with its focus on rules and the fixed roles of actors, the theory ignores individual attributes such as personality, motivation and free will, important variables that can have an influence on some industrial relations outcomes (see, Schienstock 1981).

Strategic Choice Theory

Strategic choice theory was developed by Kochan, Katz and McKersie (1986) in an attempt to update Dunlop's systems theory by including a number of recent changes in the practice of industrial relations. Four trends in particular were identified as changing the way business managers deal with industrial relations:

1. the recent decline in union membership and the rise of new service industries not covered by unions
2. the way collective bargaining structures and outcomes involving trade unions have altered
3. the emergence of new managerial values and strategies which reject older pluralistic assumptions about the need to recognise trade unions (managers preferring instead to have greater information sharing, workplace cooperation, performance incentive schemes and autonomous work teams)
4. the decline of active government involvement in making regulations about the terms and conditions of employment.

It is argued by the authors that these changes have made industrial relations far more complex than has traditionally been the case. In the first place, the decline of trade unionism, decentralised bargaining processes and the advance of human resource management practices, have all caused a re-distribution of decision making authority. Orthodox industrial relations specialists have lost much power to human resource and line managers. Second, the growing popularity of unitarist (or consensus) ideas among human resource managers is said to have led organisations to take a more pro-active approach to the management of employees. This can be seen in the way senior executives are integrating the development of both human resource and business strategies. Third, as a consequence of this, managers are no longer simply passive reactors to the demands and initiatives of organised labour. Indeed, according to Kochan and his colleagues, the integration of human resource and business strategies has meant that day-to-day workplace industrial relations are being increasingly influenced by decisions about marketing, production, finance, investment, and so on. Finally, the retreat of government from the role of neutral umpire and regulator of employment conditions has further hastened these changes by creating a shift in the balance of power in favour of management over unions.

Table 1.1 Three levels of industrial relations activity

LEVEL	EMPLOYERS	UNIONS	GOVERNMENT
Long-term strategy and policy-making	Business strategies Investment strategies Human resource strategies	Political strategies Representation strategies Organising strategies	Macroeconomic and social policies
Collective bargaining and Personnel policy	Personnel policies Negotiation strategies	Collective bargaining strategies	Labour law and administration
Workplace and individual/organisation relationships	Supervisory style Worker participation Job design and work organisation	Contract administration Worker participation Job design and work organisation	Labour standards Worker participation Individual rights Individual rights

Reprinted with permission from *The Transformation of American Industrial Relations* by Thomas A.Kochan, Harry Katz and Robert B. McKersie. Copyright 1986 by Basic Books Inc.1986, 17.

The dispersion of power and authority identified in this analysis is shown by the authors in Table 1.1. The table shows three levels of activity and decision making for each of the three major actors of Dunlop's systems theory. The first row is the strategic decision making level. This refers to the organisational level where long term strategy and policy are decided within businesses, trade unions and government. The participants at this level are typically senior managers, union executives and government leaders (or the heads of government departments and agencies). They not only decide broad strategies but do so being mindful of the strategies and policies of others. In Australia, an example of an exchange at this level is the national wage case heard before the federal industrial relations tribunal, where trade unions, employers and government come together to plead their points of view. The second row or tier is called the collective bargaining or personnel policy level. This refers to exchanges between personnel managers, union officials and public department administrators. It is at this level that industrial relations have traditionally taken place. This can be easily seen in the way business organisations have traditionally engaged personnel specialists to negotiate with trade unions and to satisfy labour laws. The third tier is the workplace level, and this refers to day-to-day relations that are not directly controlled by players from either the second or first levels. It is at this level that line managers and workers interact, giving effect to formal collective bargaining outcomes, human resource management policies and workplace regulations. It is also at this level that many informal customs and practices directly impact the conduct of workplace relations.

An important element of the Strategic Choice theory is that it recognises relationships between decisions at different levels of a business organisation, and between that organisation and its wider industrial relations environment. Thus, to return to our earlier example, a decision taken at the strategic level to introduce new technology will almost certainly effect the conduct of collective bargaining (e.g. over future training and manning levels). This in turn will have an effect on the conduct of day-to-day workplace relations (e.g. when manning levels are altered or jobs re-organised). The framework also recognises the effects of strategic decisions on different actors in the system. Strategic changes made by government to macroeconomic policy settings, for instance, may influence a company's long-term investment strategy because of bank interest rates. If it is believed bank rates will rise, diminishing the need for existing manning levels, then this will almost certainly affect the organisation's future employment strategies, personnel policies, collective bargaining position, and ultimately, the relations between line managers and employees in the workplace.

Whilst Strategic Choice theory has many advantages over Dunlop's original systems theory, especially by focusing on the inner workings of management, it nonetheless has its critics. Much of the criticism harks back to earlier arguments directed at Dunlop's theory. However, one additional criticism has centred on the view that the theory fails to provide a clear definition of strategy in an industrial relations context. The criticism is that almost any form of managerial behaviour could be labelled strategic. For example, industrial relations initiatives taken by management might be little more than ad hoc adjustments caused by external competition, rather than a carefully thought out strategic plan (Hilibrand 1988). Other critics have suggested that the case studies and data in the research are inadequate to truly test the key hypotheses (Lewin 1987). Still others have argued that the Strategic Choice model is even weaker than Dunlop's in analysing the role of government institutions, not to mention the role of groups and organisations other than management and trade unions (Dabscheck 1994).

Labour Process Theory

Labour Process is another industrial relations theory which attempts to deal with contemporary issues. The foremost proponent of this theory is Harry Braverman (1974) He draws on classical Marxist analysis of the labour process to explain the nature and causes of modern industrial conflict, the inequality of ownership and the exploitation of workers. The argument begins with three Marxist assumptions:

1. the primary role of management is to convert raw materials into products through the use of labour and machinery
2. the only way management is able to do this is through structures of power and control that convert the capacity of employees to perform work (labour power) into actual work effort (labour)
3. only through this conversion can profitable production and capital accumulation take place.

On the basis of these three assumptions, Braverman asserts that since the beginning of the 20th Century managers have increasingly controlled the activities of workers through the advancement of technology and the spread of scientific management techniques. These developments, he suggests, have changed the labour process by de-skilling work and fragmenting tasks until they are devoid of any meaningful content. This has occurred because managers and owners are perpetually compelled by competition to introduce ever-more systematic control over the labour process. They have achieved this in two ways. First, by gradually centralising the knowledge of production with managers so that the autonomy of employees to control the pace and conduct of work has been diminished. Second, by breaking up the elaborate work tasks previously performed by skilled workers into smaller constituent tasks which has allowed work to be performed by less skilled workers at lower rates of pay. Moreover, these changes have enabled management to increasingly divide and rule the work force, and thereby reduce opposition to managerial direction. These developments, it is argued, are a result of the logic of modern capitalist production, and are the outcome of the constant need for businesses to find new ways to employ labour more efficiently and cheaply. The other side of this logic, however, is that the workers increasingly resist their deepening alienation and exploitation, either openly or covertly. This in turn makes them unreliable contributors to the labour process, prone to act in ways against the interests of the very organisations that employ them. Viewed under Labour Process theory, workplace conflict is not simply the result of inappropriate management selection and promotion practices, or the recalcitrant behaviour of individuals (as unitarists assert). Nor is it simply the product of competing group interests in the workplace (as pluralists assert). Instead, it is inherent in the very nature of capitalist industrial development.

While Braverman's (1974) labour process theory has been influential, it has also been criticised. The main areas of concern are the generalisations, particularly the concepts of de-skilling and control, which are seen as too crude and mechanistic. It has also been argued that the effects of technological innovation, which Braverman (1974) views as an integral part of competition between employers under capitalism, never operate in one direction alone. Not all workers are always disadvantaged. Certainly, in some industries some workers may be de-skilled, but demand may also be simultaneously created for new skills in new industries (Littler and Salaman 1984). In relation to control, it has been argued that employers do not always pursue total control strategies as ruthlessly as Braverman (1974) suggests. There is ample evidence of employers accepting more limited control, as evidenced by the many organisations that presently give workers considerable job autonomy as a means of encouraging loyalty. In the same vein, there is also significant evidence to suggest worker resistance to de-skilling and job specialisation has been more successful than Braverman's (1974) analysis allows (Knights et al. 1985).

Other Theories

The above theories cover the main schools of thought in the field of industrial relations. There are several lesser schools, which are perhaps worthy of brief comment. The first, *transaction cost theory*, is limited to theorising about the costs of workplace governance in labour contracts. Theories of this type are based on the premise that all economic transactions incur some cost. The most productive organisations are those that minimise the costs of production and economic transactions. The relevance to industrial relations of this view is in relation to the formulation, negotiation, administration and enforcement of employment contracts. All these aspects are seen as economic transactions involving costs. These costs can be financial and non-financial, both as set out formally in the contracts and as occur informally in coordinating, monitoring and motivating employees. The theory stresses the efficiency gains that can be made when managers structure employment relations and contracts to obtain employees' 'consummate', as opposed to 'perfunctory' cooperation. The theory asserts that open-ended labour contracts that enable employers to allocate workers flexibly avoid many costly negotiations. This is held to be better workplace governance because the more detailed employment contracts are, in relation to tasks and responsibilities, the more complex and costly they are. Furthermore, because managers who attempt to create detailed contracts often have difficulty anticipating and detailing all the tasks employees may be expected to perform (a limitation referred to as 'bounded rationality'), employment contracts often remain ambiguous or unclear about specific tasks. This leads to still further costly negotiations (for an elaboration of theories of this type see, Williamson 1985; Milgrom and Roberts 1990).

A second minor school of thought, known as *regulation theories*, focuses on the relationship between economic agents (or interests) and various state entities set up to regulate their activities. There are several models in this school, for example so-called 'capture theory' and 'bargaining theory'. Capture theory argues that regulatory agencies charged with governing relations between economic agents are invariably 'captured' by those they seek to regulate. Accordingly, they are prone to serve the interests of both labour and capital (or the dominant one), rather than the interests of society as a whole (see, Stigler and Friedland 1970). Bargaining theory takes an alternative view, arguing that regulatory agencies, whilst remaining independent of economic agents, enter bargaining relationships as a way of guiding them to the benefit of the society as a whole (Joskow 1974). Both these theories have been useful for examining governmental agencies set up to regulate such things as occupational health and safety, anti-discrimination laws, equal employment opportunity laws, and the determination of wages and conditions of employment. They have also been useful in providing insights into the interaction between various parts of the state and other institutions involved in industrial relations. Other regulation theories that similarly look at the role of the state in industrial relations are 'life cycle theory' (see, Bernstein 1955), public interest theory (see, Owen and Braeutign 1978), and (neo)corporatist theory (see, Schmitter and Lehmbruch 1979). (For an elaboration of theories of this type see, Barbash and Barbash 1989; Dabscheck 1993.)

A third minor school of thought, called *labour market theories*, is based upon neo-classical economic theories. Theories of this type are generally built around two economic assumptions. The first is that resources are scarce in relation to the wants of individuals, so that they must make choices about how to allocate them. In making these choices, individuals act as 'rational economic maximisers'. That is to say, individuals are forced to make choices to maximise the economic satisfaction (or 'utility') that they obtain from limited resources. The second assumption holds labour markets to be 'perfectly competitive'. This idea assumes that there are a large number of small, independent employers competing for labour, and a large number of independent workers competing for jobs. It assumes all jobs undertaken within the same labour market require the same level of skills and that all workers are equally productive (i.e. possess the same level of skills and ability). It assumes workers can enter and leave the labour market freely and can move between jobs freely. It assumes that the only cost to employers of hiring labour is the wage, and that there is perfect information in the sense that all workers and employers know the state of the labour market at any given time.

Whilst labour market theories use these heroic simplifications of the real world, what they are arguing is that it is the market, and not employers and workers that actually set wage levels. Therefore, they predict in general terms, in any given labour market there will be a uniform wage, and wage differences between organisations cannot exist. Thus, if workers are being underpaid they know about it and move to organisations paying higher wages. If a low paying organisation wishes to remain in business it must raise wages in order to retain workers. The same logic also applies to a high paying organisation, which will reduce wages when faced with queues of workers competing for jobs. Consequently, the only decision organisations have to take is how many workers to employ at any given point in time. This in turn is said to be controlled by the 'law of diminishing returns', which holds that when successive units of labour are added to fixed factors of production, the amount each successive labour unit adds to total output diminishes. Thus employers will hire successive hours of labour only up to that point at which the addition to revenue equals the hourly wage. In summary, these broadly based labour market theories are typically seeking to explain how wage rates and employment levels are determined. They may also be seeking to show how such things as union activity and government regulation divert the expected outcomes of an otherwise competitive labour market (see, Friedman and Friedman 1963; Olsen 1971; Freeman and Medoff 1984; Kaufman 1989; Kaufman and Hotchkiss 1999).

The last minor 'school of thought' considered here is called *institutionalist theories*. Theories of this type generally focus on the history, origins and development of industrial relations 'institutions'. Such institutions can take the form of trade unions, employer associations and government agencies with industrial relations responsibilities (e.g. industrial tribunals, public departments). They may also include formal and informal processes which serve to govern workplace relations (e.g. dispute settlement procedures, collective bargaining, legal frameworks). A wide range of theories is often held to fall within this school of thought. Both systems theory and strategic choice theory are good examples. Indeed, the Marxist, labour process and regulation theories might also be said to be institutionalist. As a general rule, institutionalist theories have pluralist assumptions and focus their attentions on institutions that they argue govern the pattern of workplace relations. To name but a few: some have looked at the history of trade unionism (see, Webb and Webb 1894; Commons, 1913); others the purposes of trade unions (see, Perlman 1928; Tannenbaum 1951); still others the role of collective bargaining (see, Clegg 1976; Kochan 1980); and still others a combination these institutions and others (see, Dabschek 1994).

CONCLUSION

In this chapter we have surveyed the various frames of reference people use to make sense of industrial relations. The advantage of being familiar with these is that they enable researchers, students and practitioners to identify the values that underlie industrial relations theories. Such values may often be unstated or even unconscious. Whilst there is no dominant framework in the study of industrial relations, pluralism is probably dominant among theories developed in western industrial democracies. This is hardly surprising given that most theoretical frameworks used to explain social and political developments in these societies are based on a reality of social tolerance and democratically negotiated political settlements. Theories of industrial relations relevant to conditions in South East Asia have not been examined in this chapter. This is partly because the literature is sparse (Kurunila and Venkalaratnam 1996; Verma et al. 1995). What can be said is that there appears to be a strong tendency to repeat the theories already mentioned, but perhaps with a particular emphasis being placed on those theories with Marxist and unitarist assumptions. Among those theories with Marxist assumptions, they tend to view industrial relations as shaped by the region's colonial history, or as the product of contemporary economic imperialism. Among the unitarist theories, the tendency is to view industrial relations as shaped by national cultures of social collectivity which distinguish societies in South East Asia (Kuwahara 1996).

We have also looked at specific industrial relations theories, some of which attempt to encapsulate the entire subject matter, and some of which have a more limited focus. Whilst all of the theories discussed have the potential to increase our understanding, we should remember that none of them alone is capable of providing a total understanding of the complexities and nuances of industrial relations. The astute practitioner should nevertheless be aware of them, cautiously using each where it provides the best explanation of a particular situation. In this book, we have used Dunlop's systems theory as a useful model upon which to organise the remainder to the contents. The model gives us a simple structure of actors, processes and outputs of industrial relations. This is also a valuable structure to help us compare and understand the five different national industrial relations systems in South-East Asia covered by this book.

REVIEW QUESTIONS

1. What are the key elements in a definition of industrial relations?
2. How do the unitarist and pluralist 'frames of reference' differ in their assumptions about the nature of workplace relations?
3. In what ways does a Marxist approach to industrial relations differ from the pluralist approach?
4. How do the assumptions contained in the various 'frames of reference' determine the construction of industrial relations theories?
5. What does the role of theory play in analysing industrial relations?
6. How do theories of scientific management and human relations theory treat trade unions and industrial conflict?
7. What are the main features of Dunlop's systems theory, and what are the main criticisms of this theory?
8. How is Marxist theory different from systems theory, and what are the main criticisms of this theory?
9. How does strategic choice theory advance upon systems theory?

FURTHER READING

Adams, R. and Meltz, N. (eds.), (1993) *Industrial Relations Theory: Its Nature, Scope and Pedagogy*. Scarecrow Press, London.

Bamber, G. and Lansbury, R. (eds.), (1998) *International and Comparative Employment Relations*. 3rd Edn. Allen and Unwin, Sydney, Chapter One.

Barbash, J. and Barbash, K. (eds.), (1989) *Theories and Concepts in Comparative Industrial Relations*. University of Carolina Press, Columbia, SC.

Dabscheck, B. (1994), 'A General Theory of (Australian) Industrial Relations', *Journal of Industrial Relations.* vol.36, no.1, 3-17.

Hyman, R. (ed.), (1989) *The Political Economy of Industrial Relations: Theory and Practice in a Cold Climate.* Macmillan, London.

Kochan, T., Katz, H. and McKersie, R. (1986) *The Transformation of American Industrial Relations.* Basic Books, New York.

CHAPTER 2

Industrial Conflict

'Those who make peaceful revolution impossible will make violent revolution inevitable'

John Fitzgerald Kennedy

LEARNING OBJECTIVES

Upon reading this chapter, you should:
- be able to define industrial conflict
- have an understanding of the various forms of industrial conflict
- be able to evaluate the different general theories explaining the causes of industrial conflict
- be able discuss the incidence and pattern of strikes in Australia, and five Asian countries.

INTRODUCTION

Conflict and cooperation are two sides of the same human condition. As social beings, we are inclined to cooperate with one another to achieve goals we could not achieve as individuals. However, when we look at the way people interact, we also discover that some social interactions are marked by conflict. It is clear, for example, that individuals may at times actually work against social systems and the achievement of common objectives. Similarly, the social systems themselves can be found wanting, making it difficult or even impossible for people to cooperate effectively. For example, crime (an individual behaviour) and unemployment (a social system) are two social interactions that can operate against the common good. So, although most social relations tend to be cooperative, there is an ever-present potential for conflict. This is so, whether it is within a family, a social group, a business organisation, or even between nations. Our concern in this chapter is with the potential for conflict in industry, and in particular the industrial conflict that periodically occurs between managers and workers. It is important that we understand this conflict if we are to make sense of its impact on industrial relations and the wider society. It is also important if we are to understand the different interests involved in the workplace, and the strategies used to minimise conflict between them.

DEFINING INDUSTRIAL CONFLICT

The classic definition of industrial conflict still widely used in the literature (see, Keenoy and Kelly 1998, 304-5) and first proposed by Kornhauser et al. in 1954, is 'the total range of behaviours and attitudes that express opposition and divergent orientations between industrial owners and managers, on the one hand, and working people and their organisations on the other hand' (1954, 13). As a general definition this has served well, but the main elements it contains have been the subject of considerable discussion. Two elements in particular are worth considering more carefully.

The first relates to the parties identified, namely, the 'industrial owners and managers, on the one hand, and working people and their organisations on the other hand'. In this regard Dabscheck and Niland (1981, 35) have claimed that the definition is too narrow because it excludes other groups that may also be involved. In particular, it excludes those government departments and instrumentalities that intervene to resolve industrial conflicts, and may at times even be directly involved in disputes. They also pointed out that other groups, academics, churches, media, community bodies, and even members of the public, can all affect public and political opinion, and these in turn may influence the course of industrial conflict. Accordingly, Kornhauser's definition should also include the 'total range of behaviours and attitudes' of these 'outside' groups, and any part they may play mediating or otherwise affecting the behaviour and attitudes of the two sides in any given industrial dispute.

The second element of Kornhauser's definition to consider is the 'total range of behaviours and attitudes that express opposition and divergent orientations'. Speculation has centred on the question: what types of 'behaviours and attitudes' are included in this definition of industrial conflict? One way of answering this question involves categorising oppositional behaviours and attitudes as organised and unorganised. Thus, organised conflict is said to be behaviours and attitudes that are collective, that is, two or more individuals combining in the workplace to engage in some form of industrial action. Conflict of this type includes such things as strikes, overtime bans, work-to-rule bans, lockouts, political demonstrations, and so on. All of these involve some form of organised collective action by those involved. Unorganised conflict, on the other hand, is said to be behaviours and attitudes that are individually based, such as absenteeism, labour turnover, low productivity, low morale, sabotage, indiscipline, and the like. Both organised and unorganised conflict is said to occur in response to discontent and dissatisfaction in the workplace. Whilst organised conflict is a conscious strategy to remedy a source of discontent, unorganised conflict represents individual withdrawal from the source of discontent. Unorganised conflict may not even be recognised by individuals as being a form of conflict (Hyman 1989, 56). An additional distinction between these two categories is whether the conflict is overt (open) or covert (hidden). Thus, overt and organised forms of conflict typically coincide. Covert conflict, on the other hand, is said to coincide with unorganised conflict. That is to say, because organised conflict is collective in nature and based on a conscious strategy, it is difficult to hide. Indeed, it is usually the intention of organised conflict to gain publicity as part of the strategy for change. Unorganised conflict, however, is typically much less visible because of its scale and lack of a conscious purpose to change a situation. Often the intent is to withdraw from the source of discontent in a way that does not publicise the action for fear of reprisal (Kornhauser et al. 1954, 8).

COMMENTS ON OVERT AND COVERT FORMS OF INDUSTRIAL CONFLICT

The distinction between overt, organised forms of conflict (e.g. strikes, lockouts, etc.), and covert, unorganised forms of conflict (e.g. absenteeism, labour turnover, etc.) is important to ensure that all forms of industrial conflict are identified. It is also important in understanding the rate of change in contemporary industrial conflict. Some analysts, for example, have argued that overt industrial conflict serves the interests of wider society on several fronts. First, it makes clear the grounds separating the opposing groups, and brings issues into the open where they can be subjected to public opinion, political regulation and social control. Second, it forces the prospect of a rapid resolution, and in the process, clarifies which groups hold power at key points in society (Kornhauser et al. 1954, 16-8). Others have suggested that overt, organised conflict helps foster loyalty and internal cohesion within groups, and may also promote innovation, change and progress in the search for competitive advantage. Thus, the wages and working conditions enjoyed by workers might not exist but for past industrial struggles, including strikes and lockouts. At the same time, the productivity improvements gained by employers from new technology might not have occurred without the periodic spur of open, organised conflict with unions and workers. Overall, based on this argument, overt industrial conflict has served to improve rather than undermine the operation of industrial society (Lan 1997, 30).

From this (pluralist) viewpoint, covert industrial conflict serves no socially useful purpose, apart from acting as a safety valve for pent-up individual discontent (Ford and Hearn 1987, 8). Indeed, there is ample evidence to suggest that attempts to suppress overt industrial conflict merely diverts it into other, less visible forms. Put another way, these two forms of conflict appear to be interchangeable (see, Scott et al. 1963; Turner et al. 1967; Edwards et al. 1995). Hyman (1989) has observed that in any industrial situation where workers experience sufficiently acute deprivations, conflict will occur in one form or another. If no effort is made to remedy the underlying discontent, the effect of any measures of suppression will merely divert the conflict from one form to the other (1989, 57-8). Where, for example, there are strong and effective legal sanctions against strikes and other forms of open and organised conflict, the likely effect is the diversion of the discontent into more covert and unorganised forms of conflict. Good examples of this phenomenon are provided by the industrial relations systems of the former Soviet Union and Nazi Germany. In both instances, independent trade unions were abolished, strikes and other forms of open and organised conflict were banned, and draconian penalties of imprisonment (and in some cases even execution) were applied (Galenson 1954; Neumann 1968). The effect of these measures was that collective overt and organised industrial conflict was abolished, but was replaced by high levels of individual covert industrial conflict in the form of 'passive resistance', such as absenteeism, shoddy workmanship and low productivity.

More recently, Edwards et al. (1995) noted a similar rise in covert forms of industrial conflict in Europe. This, they suggest, was the result of persistently high levels of unemployment since the late 1970s, and the growing incidence of job insecurity since the late 1980s. Both of these trends have reduced the will and ability of workers and unions to organise traditional forms of overt industrial action. At the same time, changed job structures and the spread of less secure forms of employment have increased both the work effort of many workers and also the level of managerial power. The result, according to the authors, is rising levels of worker dissatisfaction, along with a growing tendency to 'resist' these developments in hidden ways by:

- exerting minimum effort on the job
- engaging in petty theft
- restricting the flow of information to management
- 'whistle blowing'
- 'foot dragging' and similar behaviours.

The same can be said in Australia. Laws are making it increasingly difficult to take legal industrial action, while award and trade union coverage of the workforce is shrinking at unprecedented rates. Consequently, there are strong indications that covert forms of industrial conflict are replacing overt forms. Wooden and Baker (1994), for instance, provide evidence that the rate of labour turnover is greater in Australian workplaces without unions or union delegates. This finding supports the view that Australian workers express dissatisfaction by 'voice' (i.e. collective industrial action) where suitable channels are available (i.e. trade unions), and by 'exit' (i.e. covert behaviour culminating in leaving the organisation) where no such channels are available. Statistics on covert conflict, such as absenteeism, labour turnover, restrictions on output, and low productivity, are difficult to come by, often unreliable, and subject to problems of interpretation. The evidence from qualitative studies, however, is significant (see, Taylor and Walton 1971; Dubois 1979; Edwards 1986; Wooden 1995). Taken together, the findings of these studies suggest that lost time and productivity through covert forms of conflict are far in excess of losses as a result of strikes. This has interesting implications for employers holding a unitary perspective of industrial relations (see Chapter 1), and also for conservative governments planning to remove unions from the workplace. For while the belief may be that non-union workplaces are more productive, the reality may be that older forms of organised conflict are simply diverted into newer forms of unorganised conflict such as increased labour turnover, which, on a large scale, is widely recognised as being very costly to employers. (Unitarists and HRM practitioners, of course, might argue that employers would be forced to reduce such costs by addressing the underlying causes of discontent.)

It is therefore clear that the 'total range of behaviours and attitudes that express opposition and divergent orientations' in industrial conflict occur in two ways: one overt and organised on a collective basis, the other covert and unorganised on an individual basis. Why then has research and media attention focused primarily on the overt and organised forms of conflict, and particularly on strikes. The 'strike' has been defined as any temporary work stoppage by a group of employees for the purpose of expressing a grievance or enforcing a demand (Hyman 1989, 17). Several reasons have been put forward to account for the inordinate interest shown in this type of industrial conflict. Ford and Hearn (1987), for example, have argued that the interest comes from the obvious newsworthiness of strikes, while researchers find strike statistics fairly easy to gather compared to figures relating to other forms of conflict (1987, 9-10). Waters (1982) has further suggested that the interest in strikes stems from the fact that they normally affect people other than the strikers themselves, and impose costs on groups beyond those directly involved. He also notes that because strikes disrupt economic activity, they tend to evoke the opposition of business interests, whose views are influential in the media. It is finally suggested that the interest is inspired by the way strikes, and particularly their resolution, are immensely important for the political stability of governments of all political persuasions (1987, 1-2).

The strike, then, is clearly a noteworthy form of industrial conflict, though it is not the only one, and often these days, not even the most significant one. Later (see Chapter 3) we will examine the underlying causes of industrial conflict, looking closely at how conflict may be the inevitable result of the internal tensions built into a modern-day business. Briefly stated the argument is that the achievement of organisational goals within a business depends upon managers and owners having more power than employees. This power gives managers the right to give orders and control most aspects of the daily working lives of employees. This right is invariably contested, if not by the employees themselves, then by trade unions, interest groups and governments acting on their behalf. In other words, because of the unequal distribution of power between competing workplace interests, potential conflict exists at the very core of the modern business organisation. In its most extreme form, this conflict emerges as strike action, and it is to the causes of strikes that we now turn.

THEORIES OF INDUSTRIAL CONFLICT

There are numerous theories that attempt to explain industrial conflict and strikes. All the evidence assembled by sociologists, political scientists, industrial psychologists, economists, historians, industrial relations specialists, and the like, suggests that strikes are very complex social phenomena. We should therefore be wary of single-cause explanations of strike action. The following, whilst not a complete listing, provides a brief summary of the main theories that have been put forward to explain the causes and patterns of industrial strikes.

Strikes as a Product of Industrialisation

Industrial conflict has often been linked to the very nature of industrialism itself. One of the more important explanations along these lines was by Ross and Hartman (1960), who asserted that the pattern of strikes in any given country was influenced by its industrial relations system. Four different 'patterns' were identified as being broadly representative of the various systems found in industrial (and industrialising) societies.

The first was called the North European (type 1) pattern. Countries in this category were said to have following common features:

- well established labour movements
- influential left-wing political parties
- effective trade unions with high coverage rates, stable memberships and few internal leadership struggles
- industries which accepted trade unions as legitimate representatives of workers
- centralised collective bargaining frameworks
- governments that confined their industrial relations role to regulating and enforcing collective bargaining.

It was found in countries having this type of industrial relations system that the propensity to strike was low and the duration of strikes was short.

The second was called the North European (type 2) pattern. These countries have many of the same industrial relations features as the previous pattern, but they had far less government intervention. In such countries industrial conflict was found to be less frequent, but the stoppages were longer than in the previous pattern.

The third was called the Mediterranean/Asian pattern. In this case the countries had the following features in common:

- labour movements that were relatively new
- left-wing political parties were almost ineffective
- trade unions were poorly patronised, had unstable memberships and significant internal leadership conflicts
- industries generally ignored trade unions as industrial relations actors
- governments were highly interventionist in determining the terms and conditions of employment.

In countries where this type of system prevailed, it was found that the propensity to strike was high and the duration of strikes was short.

The final system was called the North American pattern. Countries in this category had the following common features:

- labour movements were older than those found in the Mediterranean/Asian pattern, but younger than those found in the North European patterns
- trade unions were only partially effective, with moderate coverage and relatively few internal leadership struggles
- left-wing political parties were inactive or non-existent
- collective bargaining was highly decentralised
- government involvement in industrial relations was negligible.

Countries with this type of system tended to have fewer strikes of longer duration.

The explanation Ross and Hartman (1960) gave for these differences was that as industrialisation advances, labour movements are forced to turn away from strikes in favour of broader political objectives. Therefore, as industrialisation increases industrial systems typically progress from the Mediterranean/Asian pattern towards the North European (type 1) pattern. Simultaneously, governments become more and more involved in national economic life, as increasingly important employers of labour, providers of welfare, and participants in the industrial relations system. It was argued that all these developments reflect an on-going integration of a nation's political economy. Hence, the process of industrialisation not only accounts for why different countries have different patterns of industrial conflict, but also why strike activity in most countries has undergone a long-term decline, a 'withering away' (Ross and Hartman 1960). Kerr et al. (1962) used this thesis to predict that, as the 'logic of industrialisation' proceeded, trade unions would become more and more 'accommodated within the system' as a way of managing labour problems. Moreover, all countries would ultimately move in the same direction, their industrial relations systems adopting similar methods and looking ever more like one another. Hence, it was concluded that regardless of different social, cultural and political settings, the global rate of industrial conflict would decrease as industrialisation advanced throughout the world.

Another explanation for industrial conflict also draws on the processes of industrialisation, but looks more closely at the structure of industry and how it shapes the roles of individuals and groups in the workplace. Theories along these lines generally start from two assumptions. First, that individual and group behaviour is controlled by the roles each play. Second, that the workplace and the roles it produces, generates predictable behaviour. One important study by Ingham (1974) analysed how the organisation of industries and production systems affected the likelihood of conflict. Ingham found that the smaller the number of parties in a workplace and the less divergent their interests, the less likely conflict between them was. This occurred most clearly under conditions of 'high industrial concentration', or situations where a small number of large firms had similar structures, technologies and product specialisations. Ingham argued that, first, a small number of large firms reduced the number of employers and unions. Second, firms with similar organisational structures and technology reduced divergent interests in the wider workplace. Third, high levels of product specialisation empowered workers reducing divergent interests within firms. These conditions, he suggested, tended to centralise decision making with employer associations and trade unions, making it easier for both sides to develop a shared understanding, reach agreements, and impose the terms of those agreements on individual firms and unions (1974, 40-4).

Still related, though not altogether consistent with industrialisation theories, are the arguments relating to technology and technological change as determinants of industrial conflict. Woodward (1958) for example suggested that forms of production can be grouped along a spectrum, with labour intensive, small-scale, batch production processes standing at one end, and capital intensive, large-scale, continuous production processes at the other. Woodward (1958) found that pressures on workers and management resulting from assembly line technology in large-scale, continuous production processes, normally led to poorer relations between management and workers, and to more industrial conflict as a consequence. In another important study by Kuhn (1961), the links between technology and conflict were explored more directly. Kuhn's argument was that 'fractional bargaining' (i.e. the way workers press demands not authorised either by their unions or by means of sanctioned action) tended to occur in direct response to the changing state of workplace technology. Changes in the following areas were involved:

- work methods, standards or materials
- the opportunity for social interaction between workers
- the grouping of workers
- sequential materials processing for single-end products.

Kuhn's (1961) study found that the first and second changes made workgroups more willing to engage in fractional bargaining; the third weakened the political authority of the union over workgroups; and the fourth allowed workgroups to disrupt production at high cost to employers and low cost to themselves.

Taking a broader view of industrialisation beyond a single industrial sector or an individual workplace, are those studies which draw on the work of Karl Marx (1857). One of the leading contemporary proponents of this school of thought is Hyman (1975, 1989) (see Chapter 1). In the manner of Marx, he argues that the cause of industrial conflict lies in the unequal division of economic resources and the existence of a capitalist class. The capitalist system, it is argued, inevitably produces opposing class interests. On the one hand is a proletariat class, composed of workers who have nothing to sell but their labour, and who are compelled to sell their labour to survive. On the other hand, there is the bourgeois(capitalist) class, composed of the owners of the means of production, who are compelled to buy labour in order to maintain the profitability of the enterprises, which supports their position in society. This type of economic organisation, it is argued, requires workers to generate 'surplus value' on the goods they manufacture - that is to say, they are required to produce goods which attract a higher price than the cost of labour used in the production of the goods. This surplus value is retained by the buyers of labour (i.e. the owner of the means of production) in the form of profit. In Marxist analysis, the size of the profit is the measure of workers' exploitation. In other words, the un-remunerated labour used to produce surplus value on goods manufactured by workers, is held by Marxists to be a form of theft - a theft perpetrated by the few who own and run industry on the many who have nothing to sell but their labour.

From a Marxist viewpoint, industrial conflict is the inevitable result of the exploitation of workers by the owners and managers of the means of production. It occurs when workers become 'conscious' of their common class interest and decide to organise against their exploitation. This resistance may take the form of sabotage, disobedience, strikes, or even political campaigns leading to revolution. Whatever the form of industrial conflict, it is held to be an extension of the class conflict of wider society, which is in turn a direct result of the unequal division of wealth and ownership of private property (product producing private property in particular). The inference from this type of analysis is that the processes of (capitalist) industrialisation will see the incidence of industrial conflict become more and more severe, leading eventually to the overthrow of the existing economic and social order and the emergence of a new order based on communitarian ideals.

It is interesting to note that among the numerous theories of industrial conflict based on industrialisation, there is no consistency in their predictions of the future incidence of industrial conflict.

Strikes as a Product of Institutionalisation

The institutionalisation of industrial relations and the influence this has on industrial conflict has already been mentioned. However, there are a number of studies that deal with this issue more directly. One, by Wright Mills (1948), looked at the institutionalisation of trade unions over time, and how this relates to patterns of strike activity. Four stages were identified. In the first stage, trade unions come into existence to counter the bargaining power of businesses. Industrial conflict at this stage is confined to individual enterprises, is aimed at protecting and advancing members economic interests, and is typically irregular, uncoordinated and often violent. In the second stage, businesses form associations to counter the growing power of trade unions. This in turn drives trade unions to organise and take industrial action on an increasingly industry and national basis. Bargaining frameworks consequently become more national and industry based, with conflict becoming more regular and systematic, but less violent. This leads to a third stage, in which the state is moved to become more active in resolving disputes between the two sides of industry. This in turn leads to the fourth stage, where political questions come to dominate trade union thinking and action. In this final stage, trade unions are faced with political issues and the need to defend the gains already made. Trade union leaders adopt strategies that lead their unions to evolve into institutions, effectively integrating the industrial worker into the national political economy. This evolution sees industrial conflict diminish, as trade unions adopt institutionalised routines for the management of discontent. This can be seen in their participation in labour contracts and dispute resolution processes that regulate what would otherwise be disruptive (1948, 9, 234).

Another important group of studies has looked at institutionalised collective bargaining and its relationship to industrial conflict. Collective bargaining is when employers and unions jointly negotiate the terms and conditions of employment. This is in direct contrast to 'unilateral regulation', where one side alone determines conditions of employment, and 'statutory regulation', where the government determines workers' employment conditions. The argument is that formalised collective bargaining is associated with a low incidence of industrial conflict. Dubin (1954) has argued that collective bargaining provides a system which regulates industrial conflict and keeps it within acceptable bounds (1954, 46). In other words, collective bargaining provides a mechanism for systematic change in the rules governing management-worker relations. It does this, Dubin argues, by allowing those in dispute to look at the situation more dispassionately, and to reflect on the possible consequences of their actions over an extended period of negotiation. At the same time workers have an opportunity to express their dissatisfaction and put their claims to management in an orderly fashion. It also provides a forum in which communication lines and relations between management and workers can be improved. Based on this theory, industrial conflict is likely to be higher where formalised collective bargaining processes are not observed or are non-existent.

A similar study identified a link between the incidence of strikes in various countries and the structure of their collective bargaining. The study looked at the number of stoppages, the size of the workforce involved, the duration of the stoppages and the number of working days lost. These factors were compared with the following aspects of collective bargaining:

- the extent of bargaining (i.e. the proportion of employees included in the process)
- the level of bargaining (i.e. whether at plant level, industry level, or national level)
- the depth of bargaining (i.e. the degree of involvement by local officials)
- the degree of control (i.e. the extent to which negotiated agreements are obligatory and enforceable)
- the scope of agreements (i.e. the extent of the coverage of terms and conditions of employment).

The conclusions were that plant-level bargaining tended to involve small numbers of workers in long strikes, whereas industry-level and national-level bargaining tended to involve larger numbers of workers in short strikes. Plant-level bargaining also showed a higher incidence of strikes than industry and national bargaining. Comprehensive and efficient dispute procedures were also associated with a low number of unofficial strikes. On the other hand, where dispute procedures were absent or defective, or where the distinction between unofficial and official strikes was blurred or non-existent, the number of strikes was likely to be higher. In summary, industrial conflict was more prevalent where formalised processes and procedures for collective bargaining were absent or ignored (Clegg 1976).

Strikes as a Product of Political Factors

Another explanation for strikes centres on the distribution of political power, or more specifically, the extent to which the labour movement is able to exert influence at government level. Shorter and Tilly (1974) analysed developments in France during the 1920s and 1930s, and then again after World War II. The authors put forward the theory that 'strike waves' were linked to a combination of two factors: the organisational ability of trade unions and periodic crises in a nation's political history. Trade union organisational ability was considered essential for successful strike activity, but was equally important for the success of union political campaigns. The theory implies that all strikes at their base level have political aims and implications. Trade unions are held to be more than just organised economic interests seeking material gain for those they represent. They are all this, but they are also political organisations, which if unable to exert political power, will invariably use strike action to put pressure on those who can. As such, strikes occur not only because wages are low or living costs are high. They occur not simply as a result of workers feeling alienated, frustrated or aggressive. Instead, strikes occur when workers believe a situation is of critical importance both for their own interests and for the politics of the nation (1974, 344-5). From this political perspective, the authors plotted various 'strike waves' in France, which coincided with periodic crises in the nation's political history. From this they concluded that differences in strike rates in other countries might be explained by the extent to which their labour movements were able or unable to exert power in government politics.

Similarly, the political dominance of the Social Democratic Party in Sweden has been used to suggest that in countries where labour movements have acquired political power then strike activity would be low. In Sweden, it was observed, both the political and industrial wings of the labour movement had renounced the strike weapon because working class objectives could be pursued more effectively in the political arena. But in order for this to happen, the authors argued, the political power of the labour movement needed to be secure and enduring. In other words, labour had to have held office for significant periods of time. The organisation of the labour movement also needed to be secure and enduring, with a high degree of centralised leadership. So, in countries where the internal authority structures of the labour movement were not so centralised, or where its industrial and political wings were fragmented, or where it lacked the ability to gain and hold political power for significant periods of time, then, the authors asserted, the incidence of industrial conflict was likely to be higher (Korpi and Shalev 1979).

A further study described two different kinds of political situation. The first involved a labour movement that was politically effective, where trade unions were relatively strong and where the institutions of collective bargaining were well established. Under such circumstances, it was argued strikes would be more likely caused by economic (rather than political) factors. This was because political access legitimised trade union participation in collective bargaining on economic issues at industry level. The second situation was where a labour movement was politically ineffective, trade unions were relatively weak, and institutions of collective bargaining were not well established. In these circumstances, economic factors would play a lesser role in strikes. This was because without a role legitimatised by the state, trade unions would not be strong enough to pursue economic objectives. Strikes therefore would be caused by the political need of the trade unions to achieve legitimacy within a collective bargaining environment. Thus, whether a labour movement had access to political channels, whether trade unions were organisationally effective, and whether collective bargaining was institutionalised, were all factors controlling whether industrial conflicts were primarily aimed at economic rather than political ends (Snyder 1975).

Another key study suggested industrial conflict was a product of political factors. It argued that the type of government policy being pursued was the critical factor in long-term trends in industrial conflict. High levels of public sector expenditure, particularly on welfare provision, tended to shift disputes over the allocation of scarce economic resources to the level of politics. Conversely, low levels of public expenditure on social welfare tended to shift disputes to the private sector (i.e. to industry). In situations where left-wing parties dominated government, welfare provisions were usually high, and industrial conflict was typically low, because public resources were allocated more favourably towards labour. This had a tendency to short-circuit the need for trade unions to pursue demands through action taken at the level of industry. In situations where right-wing parties dominated, and where public expenditure on welfare provision was low, the opposite outcome was observed. Trade unions pressed demands more fiercely at the level of industry and strike activity was consequently higher. Thus, the crucial issue in explaining patterns of strike activity was not the assumption of political power by left-wing parties as such, but instead the changes in the distribution of national income under welfare policies pursued by left-wing governments (Hibbs 1976).

Strikes as a Product of the Business Cycle and Economic Factors

A number of writers have related the level of industrial conflict to the business cycle. One of the earliest noted how periods of falling prices were often accompanied by trade unions adopting defensive strategies to protect workers against reductions in wages, lengthening work hours and the worsening conditions of employment. It was argued that during periods of economic recession, pressures were placed on businesses to reduce wages and working conditions. Consequently, conflict between labour and capital would be more severe and strikes more numerous than in times of stable prices. Conversely, in periods when long-term prices were rising, the theory suggested, trade unions would go on the offensive and conflict would once again rise. This would occur because living costs for workers would rise and trade unions would take action to protect real wages. In addition, larger business profits would give rise to conflict over their distribution. Thus, it concluded that incidence of strikes was inversely related to the long term business cycle during periods of falling prices, and directly related to the long term business-cycle in periods of rising prices. In other words, the incidence of industrial conflict is likely to be lowest when prices are neither rising nor falling (Hansen 1921, 620).

A later study introduced another dimension to business cycle explanations of strikes by suggesting that the peak in strike activity consistently preceded the peak in the business cycle. This argument centred on the view that employers and trade union leaders hold different economic expectations. Unions, it was suggested, paid attention to rates of employment, which generally lagged behind peaks in the business cycle. They also paid attention to other economic variables such as wage increases gained by other unions and rises in the cost-of-living. Employers, on the other hand, tended to pay attention to other trends, such as rates of investment, business failures and orders, which all generally change in advance of peaks in the business cycle. Employers were consequently prone to resist demands on issues for which trade unions were still willing to fight. It is thus in the period leading up to the business cycle peak that industrial conflict will be at its highest. Once the cyclical peak has been reached, however, the theory suggests the more pessimistic expectations of business leaders come to be shared by trade union leaders, and the incidence of industrial conflict falls off as a consequence (Res 1952).

Another business-cycle explanation argued that the overall level of strike activity is related to changes in unemployment and real wages. Thus, in periods of economic growth, when the demand for labour is high and business profit margins are healthy, the expectations of workers in pursuing a wage demands are said to exceed those of trade union leaders. In such cases, the leaders can seek to lower the expectations of members as a means of reaching an agreement with employers. But if they are unable to do so, they are forced to either conclude agreements that are unacceptable to members or organise industrial action. It is conjectured that union leaders are more likely to use strike action as a means of lowering the aspirations of rank-and-file members so that they might reach an agreement with employers. Seen in this way, industrial conflict is linked to the business cycle when rank and file expectations exceed the willingness and capacity of businesses to meet them. The incidence of strikes therefore rises when these differences are highest during periods of economic growth (Ashenfelter and Johnson 1969).

Other economic explanations do not specifically refer to the business cycle, but instead look at changes in leading economic indicators. Some of the more influential studies along these lines have dealt with changes in wage structure and inflation. One study asserted that wage changes are the dominating force behind changing patterns of industrial conflict. Their theory suggested that industrial conflict is generated by tensions experienced by individuals over their actual and desired positions in the wage structure. The argument was supported by the increasing incidence of industrial conflict when the wage structure changed, altering the relative position of different groups of workers. Particularly when the average wage increased, the wage structure narrowed and a rise in industrial conflict followed as trade unions tried to re-establish lost relativities (Paldam and Pederson 1982). A further study went on to argue that industrial conflicts and wage rises were mutually reinforcing phenomena. An initial round of wage inflation induced industrial conflict over lost wage relativities, which in turn produced new rounds of wage inflation, more industrial conflict, and so on (Paldam 1983).

Another study, in a decade of high inflation, concluded that strike activity depended on the extent that unions and employers differed over actual and expected rates of inflation (Davis 1979). Thus, during periods when inflation was fairly constant, the actual inflation rate and the inflation rate expected by employers and trade unions were likely to be similar, making it easier to be accounted for in wage settlements. However, during periods of high or changing rates of inflation, the actual and expected inflation rates were likely to be different, making it more difficult for the parties to reach agreement and raising the probability of strike action to enforce wage demands.

Still focussing on the issue of wages, it has been argued that industrial conflict over wages is inevitable in capitalist societies, where a tension always exists over the distribution of scarce economic resources between wages and profits. Furthermore, because wages are the only source of livelihood for most workers, problems of job security and the effects of progressive income tax compound this conflict. In other words, workers may suffer a variety of deprivations, absolute and comparative, which lead to industrial conflict. Those workers who are forced to subsist 'below the breadline', or the minimum wage necessary to survive, suffer 'absolute deprivation'. But a more potent cause of industrial conflict is 'relative deprivation'. This form of deprivation, according to the theory, involves comparisons which individuals and groups make about their living standards in relation to the community as a whole and other groups with which they historically compared themselves. As those who live in a state of relative deprivation generally have more power to make their dissatisfaction felt than those living in a state of absolute deprivation, it is the former who are held to be the more potent source of industrial conflict (Runciman 1966).

Still looking at economic factors, there may be a relationship between unemployment levels and industrial conflict. The argument is that during periods of low economic growth and high unemployment, employers are less willing to give in to trade union demands than when economic growth is high and unemployment is low. Under growth conditions employers are likely to take whatever actions are necessary to avoid disruptions caused by strikes. Consequently, strikes are held to be more likely during periods of low economic growth. Furthermore, when low growth is accompanied by high unemployment, strikes are likely to last longer than if they occurred during periods of high economic growth and low unemployment (Creigh and Makeham 1982). This thesis is in direct contrast to one which suggested that high levels of unemployment can be expected to coincide with low levels of industrial conflict. It argued that workers generally lack the willingness to go on strike during periods of high unemployment for fear of being put out of work at a time when the labour market is weak. In addition, when low unemployment returns after a period of high unemployment, trade unions frequently go on the offensive, taking advantage of the buoyant labour market to make up the ground lost during the preceding period (Hibbs 1976).

One study brings together a number of diverse labour market indicators to explain industrial conflict. Produced in the United Kingdom by the Department of Employment, the study analysed industry variations in strike activity and identified four explanatory factors.

1. Earning levels. Industries paying high wages tended to be more strike prone than industries paying low wages. Workers in high paying industries were more likely to engage in industrial action because of previous histories of success, and because they had the financial wherewithal to endure stoppages for periods necessary to achieve success. Furthermore, workers in these industries had a greater interest in developing the earnings of their jobs because they were unlikely to find better paying jobs in other industries.

2. Labour intensity. Industries where labour costs constituted a high proportion of the total production costs appeared to be more strike-prone than industries were labour costs accounted for a low proportion of the total production costs. It was thought that this was because high labour cost industries were more likely to resist the wage demands of workers because of the costs involved, thereby increasing the likelihood of industrial conflict.

3. **Establishment size.** Here it was found that industries above the average size were more likely to be strike-prone than industries below average size. One explanation for this was that larger establishments tended to experience more problems in communication and control than smaller establishments, giving rise to greater levels of conflict.
4. **Prevalence of women workers.** Industries which had a high proportion of female employees were less likely to be strike-prone than industries employing high numbers of males. This may be because the psychological and cultural inclination of women towards industrial action was less well developed than in men (see, Smith, et al. 1978).

Strikes as a Product of Social Factors

Although social factors have been mentioned in preceding sections, there are nonetheless a number of studies dealing directly with them as a cause of industrial conflict. Social interaction theory is based on the fact that some industries are more strike-prone than others. The authors argue that industry differences can be attributed to the social location of workers and the type of jobs they perform. In brief, industries are likely to be more strike-prone when workers form homogenous groups, and when these groups are spatially or culturally isolated from the wider community. Conversely, industries are less likely to be strike-prone when workers are individually deployed on the job, are unorganised in terms of trade union membership, and are drawn from across the wider community. For example, the strike proneness of miners and maritime workers is explained by the self-contained communities they live in, largely isolated from the rest of society. They typically have their own codes of conduct, myths, heroes, and social standards. They also share common industrial hazards, periodic unemployment, poor living conditions, low wages and intermittent work. Moreover they are often unable to escape these communities because of a lack of skills and a lack of alternative job opportunities. These conditions are said to explain why workers in these industries combine to think and act collectively. They also explain why such isolated communities and their industries attract tough-minded individuals who are more combative and more inclined to strike action as a means of advancing their interests. By contrast, workers who live in multi-industry towns, who have skills and an abundance of alternative jobs, who mix with a wide variety of occupations and social groups, and who belong to associations with diverse memberships, are less likely to experience the same isolating hardships. Social interaction theory uses two polar opposites to demonstrate the strike-proneness of some industries relative to others. On one side are isolated communities of hardened workers doing unpleasant work, who think and act collectively and hold combative attitudes. On the other are socially integrated workers in more attractive work, less tough-minded and less inclined to take industrial action to achieve their objectives (Kerr and Siegal 1954).

Human relations and neo-human relation theories also look at social factors as a means of explaining industrial conflict. However, these theories are more directly concerned with workplace social relations. The general theme contained in the early human relations theories is best exemplified in Mayo's so-called 'Hawthorne Studies', (1933) (see Chapter 1) which emphasised that workers have social as well as economic needs. These theories argued that focusing on satisfying the economic needs of employees to the neglect of their social expectations of work ran the risk of lowering workplace morale and raising the potential for industrial conflict. To avoid these dangers, managers should encourage workgroup cohesion, recognise that people are different to other productive resources, and find ways of involving employees in decision making about work. In short, industrial conflict was associated with poor internal communications between managers and employees. Later theories from the neo-human relations movement argued that economic and social factors were important in explaining the incidence of industrial conflict, but added that it was also important to acknowledge that employees required social rewards as well.

Most people are aware of Maslow's 'self actualising' hierarchy of human needs, and these were proposed as important in the workplace for ensuring employees were both contented and motivated (Maslow 1954). Consistent with Maslow was the important neo-human relations thesis called 'theory X and theory Y'. This argued that managers were prone to view employees as solely concerned with the financial rewards of their work (theory X). But industrial confrontation would only be avoided and employees would only be truly motivated if managers paid attention to workers' broader demands (theory Y). The implication of this theory was that organisational frameworks which legitimised only 'theory X' in the workplace would always maintain the potential for conflict. Hence these frameworks needed to be eliminated to minimise this potential. Of course, trade unions, shop stewards and collective bargaining processes were seen as falling into this undesirable category (McGregor's 1966). Another study identified a combination of so-called 'hygiene factors' (e.g. good wages and working conditions) and 'satisfier factors' (e.g. responsibility and recognition) as being critical to work-force morale (Herzerg 1968). The assumption behind all these studies was that industrial conflict occurred because managers failed to tap the real potential of workers. It was best avoided by providing structures for workers to make full use of their personal abilities.

Summary of Industrial Conflict Theories

In this section we have set out some of the major theories used to explain the causes of strikes and industrial conflict. The list is far from exhaustive, and none of the interpretations can claim universal acceptance or applicability. Indeed all theories are subject to major criticisms (for a useful survey of the literature in this regard, see, Jackson 1987), and none alone is capable of explaining all the complexities of industrial conflict.

INDUSTRIAL CONFLICT THEORIES APPLIED TO AUSTRALIA AND THE SOUTH EAST ASIAN REGION

We will now look at some of the problems that arise when we apply the major theories on industrial conflict to Australia and other South East Asian nations.

The Marxist analysis appears to offer a viable general explanation of why industrial conflict occurs. This is because it is relatively easy to show disparities of wealth and power as one of the causes of industrial conflict in most capitalist societies. However, the Marxist analysis does not explain why some countries are more strike-prone than others. To overcome this problem Marxist theorists explain the differences in terms of residual feudal elements persisting long after capitalism has been introduced. This is particularly directed at places like Japan and other South East Asian countries, where cultural attachments to older ways of life are said to reinforce a 'false consciousness' among workers. It has also been suggested that differences in the maturity of a country's capitalist economic development are the cause of differences in the incidence of industrial conflict. However both these explanations have problems. For example, it would be reasonable to expect Japan, the most advanced capitalist society in the South East Asian region, to be the country least subject to residual feudal influences and therefore the most conflict-prone. However, both assumptions are clearly not the case.

Interpretations based on economic factors also have problems. This can be demonstrated in two Australian studies. The first drew on strike statistics between 1913 and 1963 and found that high levels of strike activity were associated with periods of strong economic growth. Conversely, low levels of strike activity coincided with periods of economic recession and depression (Oxnam 1971). The explanation given was similar to the one by Hibbs (1976) (discussed earlier). Restated briefly, conditions of economic prosperity enhance the bargaining power of organised labour and create conditions requiring change in workplace rules. There are thus major issues to bargain over, generating industrial conflict at a time when the bargaining power of organised labour is strongest. The converse is the case during periods of economic decline. There are fewer major issues and organised labour is at its weakest. The second Australian study looked at business cycles between 1952 and 1970. This study agreed with Oxnam's (1971) conclusion that periods of prosperity coincided with increased strike activity, but only in relation to disputes about changed working conditions and managerial policy. No relationship was found to exist between the state of the economy and the frequency of strikes over wages and conditions. The study concluded, in agreement with Ashenfelter and Johnstone (1969)(see above), that the main cause of cyclical movements in strikes was the perception held by workers of the likely effectiveness of strike protests, which was related to up-swings in the business cycle (Bentley and Hughes 1971).

These different findings suggest some caution should be exercised when relying on theories that involve correlations between business cycles and industrial action. One could add the general observation that the 1960s were years of great prosperity, with low unemployment, low inflation, moderately rising real wages and strong economic growth. They were also years of historically high levels of industrial conflict compared to the 1970s, when unemployment and inflation were far higher and economic growth was far more uncertain. This outcome stands in contrast to the business cycle explanations offered by Creigh and Markem (1982) and Paldam (1983). One should also use caution when seeking to apply economic explanations to different nations. The wave of strike actions recorded in South Korea between 1987 and 1989, for example, had little to do with economic causes and more to do with dramatic changes in the country's domestic political climate (see, Leggett 1997, 64-76; Park and Leggett 1998). In this case, Shorter and Tilly's (1974) political crises theory, or the distribution of political power theories of Snyder (1975) and Korpi and Shalev (1979), seem more appropriate for the purpose of explaining the pattern of industrial conflict.

Political explanations of strike activity also have their problems. Whilst they appear to offer plausible explanations of industrial conflict in many European countries, with the exception of South Korea, they appear to have difficulty explaining the low level of strike activity in South East Asia. In contrast to Korpi and Shalev's (1979) theory, for example, very few left-wing political parties have enjoyed consistent political power throughout the region. The only left-wing political party of any significance is in Japan, and it has only very recently been accepted as a partner in a governing coalition. Yet strikes in Japan have remained consistently low, both before and after the left-wing Social Democratic Party came to power (Matsuda, 1993). Singapore is the only other South East Asian country that can claim to have left wing political parties, but they have never held office. Indeed the country's ruling Peoples' Action Party has suppressed independent trade unionism to the interests of creating a favourable climate for international investment (Anantaraman 1990), and this has kept the incidence of industrial conflict low. Hong Kong and Malaysia have no left-wing parties, and yet both these countries have similar low levels of strike activity. The strike experience of these countries is thus contrary to Korpi and Shalev's (1979) expectations that the unequal distribution of political power in favour of capital will result in high levels of strike activity. Indeed, one could offer the counter example of the Australian Labor Party, which has held office for significant periods of time, yet Australia has historically had high levels of industrial conflict by international standards.

This is not to say all political explanations cannot be applied to South East Asia. Indeed, there is state intervention in industrial relations throughout the region. In Singapore and Malaysia, for example, severe legal restrictions are imposed on trade unions and particularly strike action, which is undoubtedly the main reason for the low levels of industrial action experienced in these countries. The few strikes that have occurred have tended to be spontaneous political protests rather than strikes aimed at material gains. In Australia the outcome of state intervention has been very different. For example, at the beginning of the 20th century the Australian government established a system of compulsory arbitration, a third party to act in the prevention and settlement of industrial disputes. It is interesting to note that it has had far less impact on dampening the level of strike activity than might be expected. Indeed, it has been argued that the system has only served to reduce the commitment by employers and trade unions to labour contracts (i.e. industrial awards) (Waters 1982, 27-8). Furthermore, genuine collective bargaining, including grievance procedures at the workplace level, have failed to develop under the influence of compulsory arbitration (Niland 1978). Thus, despite the relatively high level of state intervention represented by the conciliation and arbitration system, the consequent reduction in strike activity has been less than that achieved by other South East Asian countries. Moreover, in contrast to other regional countries, the type of strike activity in Australia has historically been in the form of short-term demonstration stoppages aimed at economic objectives. In other words, Dubin's (1954) institutionalised collective bargaining thesis seems supported by the Australian experience but contradicted by several Asian countries, while Snyder's (1975) Swedish-based political power argument seems contradicted by Australia and most other examples in our region.

Other problems with industrialisation, institutional and technological change interpretations of strike activity can be demonstrated by contrasting the economic experiences of Japan and Hong Kong. In Japan, the concentration of a few large corporations using mass production techniques and sophisticated forms of technology has not been accompanied by the development of a unified trade union movement using sophisticated strategies, which was outcome predicted by Ross and Hartman (1960), Kerr et al. (1962) and Wright Mills (1948). Nor have collective bargaining frameworks become more centralised and institutionalised, as envisaged by Dubin (1954) and Clegg (1976). Yet the incidence of industrial conflict in Japan has remained low by international standards, an outcome that differs markedly from the predictions of these various theories. In Hong Kong, industrialisation has created a highly decentralised and fragmented industrial structure. Trade union membership has remained low, and union organisation has remained highly decentralised. The existence of collective bargaining is notionally recognised in certain economic sectors. Nevertheless, this country also has a low level of industrial action despite the apparent contrast with the Japanese model. This outcome stands in direct contrast to Ingham's (1974) technology and organisational structure theory. In summary, in both Hong Kong and Japan the causes of industrial conflict, or lack of it, are better understood by considering cultural factors rather than industrialisation, institutional and technological factors.

Finally, human relations theories have been criticised for their unrealistic assumption that conflict is pathological in nature. They have also been criticised because they are prone to exaggerate the significance of interpersonal actions, and ignore the possibility that the causes of conflict may be structural rather than personal in nature. Indeed, some have argued that improved communication, one of the key measures seen by Mayo (1933) as resolving potential conflict, can actually increase rather than reduce the incidence of conflict. For example, communicating information about job changes or planned redundancies is likely to provoke conflict and strike action. Other aspects of the neo-humanist stable have also been criticised, particularly where they suggest trade unions, shop stewards and collective bargaining are causes of industrial conflict. In this regard the clearest criticisms are in a Royal Commission Report (1968) conducted in Britain, which suggested that shop stewards and trade unions generally had a calming effect on workplace conflict. Their presence, it reported, through organised collective bargaining frameworks, lowered the incidence of unregulated strike action.

It should be clear by now that theories purporting to explain industrial conflict should be applied with caution. Indeed, if there is a single lesson in this section, it is that one theoretical interpretation should never be relied on to the exclusion of others. To do so runs the risk of over-simplifying something that is complex in both its causes and characteristics. Different parties in any dispute invariably interpret, rightly or wrongly, the same situation in different ways. Thus, a full explanation of any industrial conflict should explore the different points of view and interactions of all involved. It should also explore the interaction between the various structures and processes that may encourage or diminish industrial conflict. In short, the causes of each strike (and other forms of industrial conflict) are unique. Understanding these causes can only improve the prospect of minimising or resolving future conflict. Understanding a variety of theories on industrial conflict can help guide our thinking by providing the analytical tools necessary to make sense of the unique causes in each different situation.

MEASURING INDUSTRIAL CONFLICT

Measuring industrial conflict is an imprecise activity at best. Gauging employee dissatisfaction from covert expressions, such as labour turnover, sick leave, sabotage, and so on, immediately runs up against problems. Employees, for example, may not be expressing dissatisfaction when they move to another job, or when they take sick leave, or when they happen to break something. They may very well be genuinely sick, or inclined to relocate for personal reasons, or simply accident-prone. The difficulty is discovering the real cause in any particular case. This is the reason overt forms of conflict, and in particular strikes, are used as the key measure of employee dissatisfaction. In short, whilst recognising that strikes are a very inadequate measure of the totality of industrial conflict, the fact is quantitative indicators are almost exclusively confined to this form of conflict.

Various statistical measures have been used to record strikes. They have included:
- the number of strikes
- the numbers of workers involved in strikes (which may include workers involved both directly and indirectly)
- the number of working days lost through strikes
- the money lost in production and wages as a result of strikes.

In Australia, the ABS (Australian Bureau of Statistics) is responsible for recording the level of strike activity and uses each of these measures as a means of undertaking this task. It also makes records the major causes of strikes. We will return to Australian strike statistics shortly, but before doing so it is worth noting that the different methods are used to collect strike statistics in different countries. In Table 2.1, for example, we compare the information sources and methods used to collect strike data in Australia and the five South East Asian countries which we examine in this book (Hong Kong, Japan, Malaysia Singapore, and South Korea).

Table 2.1 Information sources and methods of collecting strike data in selected countries

Country	Minimum criteria for inclusion in statistics	Are political stoppages included?	Are workers indirectly affected included?	Sources and notes
Australia	Ten or more days lost	Yes	Yes	Information gathered from arbitrators, employers and unions
Hong Kong	At least ten workers with at least one days duration involved	No	No	Information gathered from Conciliation Service, media reports, employers and employees
Japan	None. However, official disputes are excluded	Yes	No	Legal obligation on employers and unions to Labour Relations Commission or prefecture governor
Republic of Korea	None. However, sympathy strikes are excluded	No	No	Employers and employees are legally required to report to Labour Relations Commission, regional government and Ministry of Labour
Malaysia	Duration of at least one day	Yes	Yes	Legal obligation on employers and trade unions to report strikes to Industrial Relations Dept and Dept of Trade Union Affairs
Singapore	No statistics available from ILO, owing to virtual non-occurrence of strikes			

Source: International Labour Office, 1993

As Table 2.1 shows, there are significant differences exist between the countries listed. These differences include:
- the minimum criteria used for the inclusion of strikes
- the treatment of political, unofficial and sympathy strikes
- the counting of workers directly and indirectly involved in strikes
- the sources used to gather strike statistics.

(For a discussion of the problems associated with comparing national strike statistics, see, Jackson 1987, Chapter 2; Bamber and Lansbury 1998, 6-7).

Added to these differences, there are also problems with actual methods used to gather the information on strikes. The official ABS statistics collected in Australia offer a case in point. In this regard Waters (1982, 7-8) made the following observations:

1. There may be reporting problems, resulting in under-estimation of the number of strikes. This is because data collection is voluntary, with none of the participating firms being legally obliged to provide information. Also, for some stoppages, the data is only an estimate, particularly for strikes involving two or more establishments.
2. The ABS excludes stoppages of less than ten man-days lost. This compounds the problem of under-estimation of short strikes. The data is also ambiguous about when strikes begin and end. It is not clear for instance whether 'rolling strikes' should be counted as one strike or a series of strikes.
3. While the ABS makes an estimate of the numbers of workers involved directly and indirectly in strikes, this refers only to workers in establishments where some workers are on strike. There is no attempt to measure the impact on other establishments.

Despite these problems, however, the methods used to collect strike data in Australia are relatively comprehensive by international standards. So much so that it has been suggested that they tend to over-exaggerate Australia's strike record by comparison to other countries (Beggs and Chapman 1987, 139). In summary, therefore, we can say that considerable differences exist in the methods and problems associated with the collection of strike data, which make international comparisons extremely difficult.

INTERNATIONAL COMPARISONS

Despite the problems just mentioned, it is still worthwhile reviewing the strike statistics of a number of different countries. This will allow us to obtain a broad idea of their relative strike-proneness, and also give some understanding of international trends in industrial conflict. To this end, Table 2.2 sets out International Labour Organisation (ILO) strike and lockout data for the years 1980 to 1998. The countries include Australia, our five selected South-East Asian countries, and five other industrialised countries.

Although it must be stressed that direct comparisons are imprecise at best, from Table 2.2 it is clear that Australia is more strike prone than the South East Asian countries, but it is only a middle ranking country when compared to other industrial economies outside the region. Compared to the South East Asian countries, Australia's relative strike proneness may be attributed to its liberal democratic political and cultural traditions. Australian society has long acknowledged the right of workers to freely organise and bargain collectively under the protection of national laws. These circumstances are notably lacking among the other countries in the region. The other major conclusion to be drawn from the figures is that the trend in industrial disputes has been a general decline over the period covered by Table 2.2. This trend, however, has been more marked in countries outside the South East Asian region.

HISTORY: AUSTRALIAN STRIKE STATISTICS

Having looked at Australia's strike-proneness regionally and globally, we will now turn to Australia's strike history. Strike statistics in Australia have been collected by the Federal Bureau of Statistics since 1913. As Table 2.3 indicates, there have been wide fluctuations in the numbers of industrial disputes, workers involved, working days lost, and average days lost per worker.

Table 2.2 ILO international strikes and lockouts, selected years, 1980-1998

Australia (1997 working population = 9,220,500)										
	1980	1982	1984	1986	1988	1990	1992	1994	1996	1997
D/C	2,429	2,060	1,965	1,687	1,508	1,193	728	560	543	447
W/T	n.a.	n.a.	n.a	n.a	893.4	729.9	871.5	265.1	577.7	315.4

SOUTH-EAST ASIA

Hong Kong (1997 working population = 3,216,000)										
	1980	1982	1984	1986	1988	1990	1992	1994	1996	1997
D/C	37	34	11	9	8	15	11	3	17	7
W/T	5.0	7.0	2.3	2.1	0.9	1.5	1.8	0.1	1.7	0.4

Japan (1996 working population = 67,870,000)										
	1980	1982	1984	1986	1988	1990	1992	1994	1996	1997
D/C	1133	944	596	620	498	284	263	230	193	n.a
W/T	562.9	215.7	155.0	118.0	74.8	84.3	109.2	49.0	23.2	n.a

Malaysia (1997 working population = 8,569,200)										
	1980	1982	1984	1986	1988	1990	1992	1994	1996	1997
D/C	28	26	19	27	9	17	17	15	9	4
W/T	3.4	3.3	2.8	5.1	2.2	98.5	6.1	2.3	1.0	0.7

South Korea (1997 working population = 21,604,000)										
	1980	1982	1984	1986	1988	1990	1992	1994	1996	1997
D/C	206	88	114	276	1873	322	235	121	85	78
W/T	48.0	8.0	16.4	46.9	293.6	133.9	105.0	104.3	79.0	43.9

Singapore (1997 working population = 1,516,000)
No statistics are available from ILO, owing to virtual non-occurrence of strikes.

OTHER INDUSTRIALISED COUNTRIES

United Kingdom (1997 working population = 28,715,869)										
	1980	1982	1984	1986	1988	1990	1992	1994	1996	1997
D/C	1,330	1,528	1,206	1,074	781	630	253	205	244	216
W/T	833.7	2,102.9	1,464.3	720.2	790.3	298.2	148.0	107.0	364.3	130.0

United States (1997 working population = 125,182,378)										
	1980	1982	1984	1986	1988	1990	1992	1994	1996	1997
D/C	187	96	62	69	40	44	35	45	37	29
W/T	795.3	655.8	376.0	533.2	118.3	184.9	363.8	322.0	272.7	338.6

Italy (1996 working population = 22,849,000)										
	1980	1982	1984	1986	1988	1990	1992	1994	1996	1997
D/C	2,238	1,747	1,186	1,469	1,769	1,094	903.0	861.0	791.0	n.a.
W/T										

France (1997 working population = 26,403,900)										
	1980	1982	1984	1986	1988	1990	1992	1994	1996	1997
D/C	2,118	3,113	2,537	1,391	1,852	1,529	1,330	1,671	n.a	n.a
W/T	500.8	397.7	42.1	21.8	46.3	29.3	15.2	n.a	n.a	n.a

Canada (1997 working population = 15,354,000)										
	1980	1982	1984	1986	1988	1990	1992	1994	1996	1997
D/C	1,028	677	717	735	548	579	404	374	328	279
W/T	441.0	444.3	186.7	483.6	206.8	270.5	149.9	80.8	281.7	253.9

D/C = Number of strikes and lockouts   W/T = Workers involved (thousands)

Source: International Labour Organisation, *Yearbook of Labour of Labour Statistics*, ILO Office, Geneva, various annual issues

Table 2.3 Industrial disputes in Australia, selected years, 1913-1998

Year	Number of disputes	Number of workers involved	Number of working days lost ('000)	Average per worker involved
1913	208	50.3	622.6	12.38
1918	298	56.4	539.6	9.56
1923	274	76.3	1146.0	15.02
1928	287	96.4	777.3	8.06
1933	90	30.1	112.0	3.72
1938	376	144.0	1338.0	9.29
1943	785	296.1	990.2	3.34
1948	1141	317.1	1662.7	5.24
1953	1459	496.0	1050.8	2.12
1958	987	282.8	439.9	1.56
1963	1250	412.7	581.6	1.41
1968	1713	720.3	1079.5	1.50
1970	2738	1367.4	2393.7	1.75
1972	2298	1113.8	2010.3	1.80
1974	2809	2004.8	6232.5	3.10
1976	2055	2189.9	3399.2	1.70
1978	2277	1075.6	2130.8	2.00
1980	2429	1172.8	3320.2	2.83
1982	2060	722.9	2158.0	2.99
1984	1965	560.3	1253.5	2.20
1986	1754	691.7	1380.7	2.00
1988	1508	894.4	1713.8	1.90
1990	1193	729.9	1376.5	1.90
1991	1058	1181.5	1610.5	1.40
1992	728	871.5	941.2	1.10
1993	610	489.6	635.8	1.30
1994	560	265.1	501.6	1.90
1995	642	344.0	546.8	1.60
1996	524	576.5	924.5	1.30
1997	444	310.5	534.2	0.75
1998	514	347.0	524.9	0.72

Source: ABS, *Industrial Disputes*, Cat. Nos. 6321.0 and 6322.0, *various*

The pattern of strikes over the interwar period was essentially one marked by a small number of long strikes. The highest levels over the period were recorded during World War I (1914-1918) and on the eve of the Great Depression (1929-33). Unrest during World War I had several causes: opposition to the Hughes Government's policy of conscription which sent Australian troops to fight abroad; inflation caused by the war; and, the activities of the syndicalists, a group of violent revolutionaries in the labour movement (Turner 1976, 63-70). The peak in the late 1920s occurred after a sustained period of post-war prosperity, in which workers had made substantial material gains. Then, after the onset of the Great Depression, economic conditions became more difficult for both employers and workers. This inspired employers to resist the wage demands of workers and trade unions, and when strikes occurred, they involved some major trials of strength, particularly in the coal and timber industries (Turner 1976, 80-4).

During the years between the Great Depression and World War II, the position of organised labour was weak. Record high levels of unemployment during the Great Depression were followed by patchy economic recovery in the late 1930s. Both of these circumstances reduced the leverage trade unions could exert on employers by strike activity. Full employment was restored and economic growth picked up during World War II, but the threat of Japanese invasion and national mobilisation as part of the war effort kept a lid on strikes (Turner 1976, 86-97). Following World War II the country experienced a sustained economic boom and full employment. The incidence of industrial conflict increased dramatically as trade unions flexed their muscles on the back of pent-up wage demands. Conflicts within the labour movement, between Communists and anti-Communists seeking to wrest leadership in key industrial sectors, aggravated the conflict well into the 1950s (Turner 1976, 98-109).

Politically, the defeat of the Chifley Labor Government in 1951 saw the beginning of a long era of conservative Liberal-Country Party dominance, which was to last until 1972. During this time the economy underwent a series of major structural changes, full employment was maintained and real wages rose. At the same time rapid technological changes saw the character of the trade union movement change. By the early 1960s the number of blue-collar workers, traditionally the 'bedrock' of the labour movement, began to be challenged by a growing number of white-collar workers. This change gave rise to a period of relative industrial stability. In the late 1960s the number of strikes increased both in quantity and in number of working days lost. This increase was in large measure closely tied to the social and political movements of dissension at this time. Some strikes were associated with the Labor movement's opposition to Australia's participation in the Vietnam War. Others were associated with conservation-minded unions imposing so-called 'green bans' on historic buildings in Sydney and Melbourne, as a means of saving them from destruction by developers (Turner 1976, 126). Still others were associated with unions sympathetic to issues being raised by the womens' movement.

Strikes rose to a post-war peak in 1974, mainly due to unprecedented high inflation and the trade union efforts to protect the living standards of members. However, the increase at this time was also aggravated by policies of the Whitlam Labor Government. These encouraged wage claims in the public sector, which ultimately had 'flow-on' effects in the private sector (Turner 1976, 127-9). There were some minor rises in the incidence of strikes in 1978 and 1981, largely due to the policies of the Fraser Coalition Government (1975-83) and a wages campaign by metal worker unions. Since the early 1980s there has been a general downward trend on all indices in Australia.

RECENT HISTORY: AUSTRALIAN STRIKE STATISTICS

Looking at the detail of Australian strike statistics over the more recent past, Table 2.4 sets out ABS data on working days lost per employee on an industry basis, between 1984 and 1998. There are a number of conclusions that can be drawn from this table. The first is that the mining industry is the most strike-prone industry in Australia, and coal mining in particular. As most mining occurs in isolated or country areas, Kerr and Siegal's (1954) social isolation theory (see above) would seem to go some way towards explaining the high incidence of strikes in this industry. Second, manufacturing, transportation, storage, communication and construction appear to be significantly more strike prone compared to other industries. On detailed analysis the reason for this prominence may, of course, differ from industry to industry. But, what can be said is that:

- individual firms in these industries tend to be on average larger than most other firms
- these industries are a prominent source of employment for full-time, blue collar male employees
- as a consequence, these industries are particularly conducive to trade union coverage and activism.

Australian Industrial Relations

These factors are consistent with industrialisation explanation by Woodward (1958) and the Department of Employment labour market study (see: Smith, et al. 1978) mentioned above.

The final conclusion to be taken from the Table 2.4 is that the incidence of strikes has generally declined across all the listed categories, although the trend in this direction is at times patchy.

Table 2.4 Working days lost per thousand employees by industry in Australia, 1984-1998

Year	Mining		Manufacturing		Transport, Storage and Communication	Construction	Other Industries (a)	All Industries
	Coal	Other	Metal products, machinery, equipment	Other				
1984	3,913	3,745	343	416	372	503	91	248
1985	6,898	1,931	255	312	432	666	71	228
1986	10,773	3,328	445	328	135	458	72	242
1987	8,902	1,069	479	305	217	773	69	223
1988	15,543	1,777	750	183	177	725	85	269
1989	5,505	642	473	283	160	374	97	190
1990	4,879	1,631	1,293	212	299	204	62	217
1991	4,507	735	1,820	296	237	428	63	265
1992	2,970	997	352	275	214	151	60	158
1993	3,288	322	474	141	42	51	44	108
1994	5,964	323	117	123	137	59	16	76
1995	4,660	1,359	142	160	84	115	12	79
1996	7,171	73	146	70	43	892	17	131
1997	4,206	19	189	107	101	290	11	75
1998	2,732	23	71	106	114	524	7	72

(a) Excludes community services from 1991

Source: ABS, *Industrial Disputes*, Cat. Nos. 6321.0 and 6322.0

The ABS also gathers statistics that provide a breakdown of the causes of strikes. These must of course be treated with some caution, particularly given what has already been said about the complexity of industrial disputes and the danger of looking for single cause explanations. Nevertheless, the statistics in this regard give some idea about the main issues, at least as they were perceived by those involved. A compilation of these data covering the period between 1984 to 1998 is given in Table 2.5. What the table shows is that managerial policy is the main cause of industrial disputes in Australia, followed by physical working conditions, wages, trade unionism, and so on. One notable feature of the data is the relatively low proportion of disputes over wages. This can probably be accounted for by the centralised wage fixing system which operated for all but two of the years covered by the data. This system was supported by the various Prices and Incomes Accords concluded between the two wings of the Labor movement, the Australian Council of Trade Unions (ACTU) and the Australian Labor Party (ALP), during the Hawke (1983-1991) and Keating (1991-6) Labor Governments. These Accords saw wage issues settled mainly through the federal conciliation and arbitration system (see Chapter 8). Another interesting feature is the high proportion of disputes caused by managerial policy, which increased significantly around 1987.

There are probably a number of overlapping factors involved here:
- the introduction of new human resource management practices which became more widespread around this time
- the introduction of new technologies and associated re-organisation of work
- the aftermath of tariff reforms and financial deregulation
- stock-market uncertainties
- the introduction of productivity and enterprise bargaining principles into the country's centralised wage fixing processes.

One year, 1992, is also worth noting. That year saw a large amount of politically inspired strikes against the industrial relations policies of the Kennett government in Victoria. This accounts for the high proportion of strikes falling in the 'other' causes category in that year.

Table 2.5 Industrial disputes by cited cause in Australia, 1984-1998 (per cent)[1]

Year	Wages	Hours of Work	Leave, Pensions Compensation	Managerial Policy	Physical Working	Trade Unionism	Other
1984	24.6	5.9	8.4.	32.5	16.3	8.7	3.6
1985	23.1	3.8	3.2	24.8	14.9	16.5	13.7
1986	40.0	1.0	10.8	35.6	6.9	3.3	2.4
1987	43.6	1.7	16.	27.4	7.3	3.0	1.5
1988	29.6	1.8	2.9	52.4	9.2	2.0	2.0
1989	13.9	0.5	12.	52.4	5.1	6.0	10.2
1990	10.9	0.3	1.4	74.7	7.0	3.7	2.0
1991	2.3	0.2	1.4	53.6	3.7	1.9	36.8
1992	2.5	-	1.6	23.7	2.9	5.0	64.3
1993	23.	0.6	2.1	46.2	3.2	1.8	22.8
1994	27.3	1.0	3.7	30.9	3.4	1.5	32.2
1995	28.0	0.5	3.0	37.3	4.5	4.1	22.2
1996	26.5	0.9	-	45.8	2.1	5.0	19.7
1997	24.4	0.9	1.0	52.6	3.4	1.6	16.1
1998	6.1	-	0.6	61.7	6.8	2.2	22.6

[1] figures based on thousands of working days lost.

Source: ABS, *Industrial Disputes*, Cat. No. 6322.0

The ABS also gathers data on the length of industrial disputes and how they are settled, which are presented in Tables 2.6 and 2.7. From the figures in these two tables it should be clear that the majority of strikes are over in a day, with workers returning to work without the issue in dispute being settled. This pattern of industrial action is a product of Australian conciliation and arbitration processes. Issues in dispute will typically continue for longer periods of time and be the subject of on-going negotiations whilst work continues. It is only when negotiations stall that actual stoppages occur. Demonstration strikes are used by trade unions as a way of getting the matter heard by industrial tribunals. In some instances, however, they are the product of ineffective shop floor organisation, inexperienced managerial actions or the non-observance of local dispute handling procedures (Dabscheck 1992, 77-9). Longer strikes lasting two or more days have historically been rarer, but have shown signs of increasing in recent years as collective bargaining frameworks have moved closer to the shop-floor.

Table 2.6 Industrial disputes in Australia by duration, 1984-1998 (per cent)[1]

Year	Up to and including 1 day	Over 1 and up to 2 days	Over 2 and less than 5 days	Over 5 and less than 10 days	Over 10 and less than 20 days	20 days and over
1984	14.9	15.5	17.1	16.2	14.6	21.7
1985	26.1	10.5	21.2	16.6	19.8	5.9
1986	32.3	4.8	7.2	16.1	29.2	10.5
1987	28.9	15.0	13.2	21.6	9.6	11.6
1988	30.1	16.5	11.2	31.9	7.7	2.5
1989	19.4	29.7	15.7	11.3	15.0	9.0
1990	11.3	22.3	46.1	6.6	5.1	8.0
1991	11.2	51.4	28.5	3.3	4.0	1.4
1992	71.5	10.9	7.8	3.3	1.8	4.8
1993	24.3	44.7	18.1	6.8	5.5	0.5
1994	14.2	24.0	20.3	28.6	11.4	1.5
1995	23.9	18.8	27.9	17.6	5.1	6.7
1996	21.7	15.6	50.1	5.7	1.9	5.0
1997	27.1	23.1	10.4	17.6	8.8	13.0
1998	18.6	50.5	6.7	9.0	6.1	9.1

[1] Figures based on thousands of working days lost.

Source: ABS, *Industrial Relations*, Cat. No.6322.0

Table 2.7 Method of settling industrial disputes in Australia, 1984-1998 (per cent)[1]

Year	Negotiation	State Legislation	Federal and joint Federal and State Legislation	Resumption without Negotiation	Other Methods
1984	25.1	20.8	6.5	46.7	1.0
1985	14.8	10.5	15.1	56.1	3.5
1986	12.1	8.1	42.2	34.2	3.4
1987	17.5	14.2	24.6	42.1	1.6
1988	10.3	6.0	46.0	34.9	2.8
1989	15.2	10.0	20.5	53.5	0.8
1990	15.0	11.8	26.4	46.5	0.3
1991	9.9	5.0	33.8	50.9	0.4
1992	11.4	2.0	3.0	83.1	0.6
1993	17.0	2.4	18.7	61.3	0.5
1994	15.2	3.6	32.2	46.9	2.1
1995	16.2	3.9	11.6	68.1	0.1
1996	16.7	3.1	4.6	74.4	1.1
1997	16.4	5.8	8.1	68.4	1.3
1998	33.9	1.4	12.0	52.3	0.3

[1] Figures based on thousands of working days lost.

Source: ABS, *Industrial Disputes*, Cat. No. 6322.0

WHY HAS STRIKE ACTIVITY DECLINED IN AUSTRALIA?

The major question arising out of the above statistics is why there has been a relatively dramatic decline in the time lost through industrial disputes in Australia in recent years. There are a number of reasons that could account for this, many of which could also account for the same trend in other mature industrial economies with settled liberal democratic political systems.

1. Historically high levels of unemployment since the late 1970s, together with a long-term decline in inflation and general maintenance of real wages, have tempered the ability and willingness of workers to take industrial action.
2. The introduction of new management techniques has promoted more cooperative forms of employee relations, reducing the propensity of many workers to use strike action to address their grievances.
3. The passing of new legislation has assisted a general shift from centralised forms of collective bargaining to enterprise and individual forms of bargaining. This has encouraged employers to adopt more sophisticated pay systems and personnel practices, generating greater harmony between workers and managers.
4. There has been the development of more flexible labour markets, represented in the growing number of part-time, casual, temporary, contract and self-employed workers. This has reduced the ability of a growing segment of the work-force to undertake collective action in the form of strikes.
5. The ability of the trade union movement in Australia to organise industrial action has been reduced by a number of factors:
    - persistent mass unemployment
    - declining coverage of the total work-force
    - overall failure of trade unions to recruit new members in the high-tech service industries
    - waning influence of unions in their traditional strongholds of coal mining, manufacturing, stevedoring and construction
    - a gradual reduction in wage differentials between union and non-union workers due to lower long-term rates of inflation
    - some state governments have endeavoured to set an anti-union example by attacking public sector conditions of employment.
6. Perhaps the most important, the earlier mentioned Prices and Incomes Accord, negotiated between the ACTU and ALP between 1983 and 1996, has removed a sizeable portion of industrial conflict from the workplace. It has been moved into the political and legal arenas where it is resolved through reasoned argument rather than recourse to industrial muscle (Lewis and Spiers 1990; Dabscheck 1992).

All these developments will be expanded upon in subsequent chapters. For the present, it is enough to say that Australia has, for much of its industrial relations history, had the unenviable reputation of being a 'land of strikes'. However, the experience of the past fifteen years would suggest that this reputation is no longer warranted.

REVIEW QUESTIONS

1. How important is the strike as a form of conflict?
2. What is the relative significance of other forms of conflict, such as labour turnover, absenteeism, poor workmanship, low productivity and even sabotage?
3. 'General theories of industrial conflict are too broad-brush to be of any value to students of industrial relations.' Do you agree? Discuss.
4. What social factors have been attributed to the causes of industrial conflict?
5. Which theories of industrial conflict start from a pluralist 'frame of reference', and which start from a unitarist 'frame of reference'?
6. What are the various economic explanations of industrial conflict?
7. What problems are there in the measurement of strikes?
8. Of what value are comparative strike statistics for different countries?
9. Why have strikes declined in Australia since the early 1980s? Will this trend continue in the future?
10. 'Asian countries are different from Australia - they are much less strike-prone.' Discuss.

FURTHER READING

Edwards, P. (1986), *Conflict at Work. A Materialist Analysis of Workplace Relations*, Blackwell, Oxford.

Hyman, R. (1989), *Strikes* (fourth edition), Fontana, London.

Ingham, G. (1974), *Strikes and Industrial Conflict*, Macmillan, London.

Jackson, M. (1987), *Strikes: Industrial Conflict in Britain, U.S.A. and Australia,* Wheatsheaf Books, Brighton.

Kornhauser, A. Dubin, R. and Ross, A. (eds.), *Industrial Conflict*, McGraw-Hill, New York.

CHAPTER 3

Management and Industrial Relations

'The only two professions for which no qualifications are required are motherhood and management'

Anonymous

LEARNING OBJECTIVES

Upon completing this chapter you should be able to:
- outline the key features of different business organisations
- outline the main causes of internal organisational conflict within business organisations
- understand the role of management in resolving internal organisational conflict
- describe how managerial ideology and style impacts the way business organisations approach industrial relations issues
- outline some of the broader economic influences that have increased the importance of management in workplace relations in recent years
- detail one of the more important contemporary methods used for analysing the role management in industrial relations
- have some understanding of the management approaches to industrial relations in the five selected South East Asian countries.

INTRODUCTION

The role of management in industrial relations has received little coverage in the literature. This is in part because management has traditionally been seen as a passive player in industrial relations, and so has not attracted the same attention as trade unions. Recently, however, there has been an upsurge of research interest, particularly in the way management deals with labour relations at both strategic and workplace levels (see, Kochan, Katz & McKersie 1986; Purcell 1987, 533-48; Ahlstrand 1990, chapter two). This interest has been inspired by companies being forced to radically alter their traditional methods of work and job design because of declining productivity rates and increased levels of global competition. This has had a significant impact on the way managers and workers relate. In particular, it has generated new and complex problems in the way companies utilise their employees. It has also seen managers become increasingly important players in workplace industrial relations. The policies and practices adopted by the modern business organisation to deal with industrial relations are no longer passive, or simply managerial responses to the demands of workers and their representatives. Instead, they have become far more strategically central and pro-active than in the past. It is these new management policies and practices as well as the influences that guide them that are the subject of this chapter.

BUSINESS ORGANISATIONS, STAKE-HOLDERS AND INHERENT CONFLICT

An organisation can be described as a collection of people working together in a coordinated and structured way to achieve one or more common goals. Normally an organisation has a continuous, autonomous existence supported by a structure of authority, formal division of responsibility, and established rules and procedures. These attributes enable an organisation to plan strategies, undertake actions, and achieve objectives that individuals alone would be incapable of doing (Ippolito and Walker 1980, 270; Pross 1992, 3-4). In so doing, members of organisations undertake a range of tasks, which are normally horizontally sub-divided according to the skills of the individuals doing them, the complexity of the task, and the state of technology. In most cases, there is also a vertical sub-division governing the way the tasks are performed. This vertical sub-division in business organisations is normally expressed in hierarchical structures that divide the owners, those they employ to manage the tasks, and those they employ to complete the tasks.

These structures and relationships are important to any understanding of management's role in industrial relations, as they inevitably involve issues of power and control. Indeed it is intrinsic to the way companies operate that the achievement of organisational objectives depends upon managers and owners having far more authority than their employees. Not only does this give managers and owners the right to give orders, to hire and to fire, it also gives them substantial control over most aspects of the day-to-day working lives of those they employ. In this sense business organisations are not just places of employment, or places where goods and services are produced for everyday consumption. They are all of this, but they are also social entities that serve to legitimise the power of the few (owners and managers) over the many (employees). Furthermore, the hierarchical structures that are a part of business organisations often provide owners and managers with powers that go well beyond the simple direction of work. For example, many are able to impose on employees their own personal definition of what is the right and proper in the ethics of work. To put it another way, the power of owners and managers not only includes the right to provide or deny employment and to decide the goals to which the resources of their organisations are directed. It also includes the control of the cultural context in which work takes place (Perrow 1986, 12).

While the power and control of organisations is exercised through hierarchical structures, it is the accumulation of power in the hands of managers and owners that has always been problematic. This is because the unequal distribution of power is invariably contested, first, by employees (and their representatives) eager to protect themselves from the arbitrary decisions of managers and owners; and second, by governments fearful of the social and political problems large companies can cause if their activities go unchecked. Arguably, it is this conflict over power and control that is at the root of most industrial relations problems between management and labour.

An important part of the literature that examines this conflict focuses on the role of management. The most prominent contemporary theorist looking at this role is Braverman (1971). This scholar's work has already been discussed in some detail (see Chapter 1). To briefly restate his main argument, managers, pursuing competitive production, have a constant need to find new ways to employ labour more efficiently and more cheaply. Consequently, there is an ever-present need for workers to resist work practices that are alienating and exploitative. From the employer's perspective, this means that workers are prone to act in ways not always in the employers' best interests. It is thus a part of modern capitalism that management must constantly build structures of power and control to ensure that the workers contribute in a positive and sustained way.

Braverman's (1974) thesis provides a valuable insight into why strong differences exist between management and employees. These differences are frequently expressed as conflict over how work should be allocated, organised and regulated; what wages and conditions should be applied; and what distribution of workplace rights, obligations and responsibilities are appropriate (Edwards 1979, 13). This propensity for conflict quite naturally complicates the task of management. It is further complicated by the fact that, in comparison to other production resources, employees are qualitatively different, requiring ongoing, careful management to achieve organisational goals. Unlike land, capital, raw materials and equipment, employees interact personally with managers. They have emotions, expectations and ambitions, as well as social, political, religious, ethnic and family loyalties, which may compete with loyalty for their employer. Workers also differ individually in their potential and ability, and may have different creative or physical needs that need to be addressed. In short, the very nature of people makes their management far more difficult than the management of the other resources of production.

It is the complexity of people, the intrinsic tensions within companies and the need to maintain power and control to resolve those tensions, that pushes management into directing and organising work to achieve a minimum of disruption. While managers deal with many other issues, such as planning, finance, production, marketing, compliance, reporting and other business-related matters, they will inevitably also be called upon to make industrial relations decisions to reconcile the competing interests within their organisations. In other words, management is what keeps an organisation from breaking apart from internal tensions, it makes it work, secures its survival and, depending on the type of organisation, maintains its profitability and effectiveness (Beardwell and Holden 1994, 36).

MANAGEMENT AND THE RESOLUTION OF ORGANISATIONAL TENSIONS
Introduction
What, then, are the choices that confront management when dealing with a conflict within a business organisation? Tensions can exist between the stakeholders at any level of an organisation, but as already suggested in Braverman's (1974) thesis, they are most visible between workers and managers. Organisations have historically used a variety of strategies and techniques to resolve such conflict (see, Wren 1987). Most have consisted of the establishment of managerial structures to either control the actions of employees or to solicit their cooperation. In both cases, the techniques have tended to blend

the formal or legal requirements of employment, with the informal psychological expectations about how the work should be performed. The theories that interpret management strategies for dealing with industrial conflict can be said to fall into one of three general categories:

1. scientific management
2. human relations
3. human resource management.

Before examining these theories a few points need to be made. First, it should be noted that the general features of these theories have already been discussed in Chapter 1. So here we simply highlight the managerial approach to resolving conflict that each theory takes. Second, it is important to recognise that the strategies chosen by managers are rarely guided solely or even primarily by the detailed arguments of management theories. Such theories do not give the whole picture of how any business organisation manages its employees. Nevertheless, it is clear that management decisions about industrial relations strategy are rarely made without some reference to the general concepts and language of these theories. This may be so, of course, even when the manager adopting a management strategy is unaware of any underlying theory.

The last point concerns the concept of 'power'. Since it recurs in each of the following theories, it needs additional comment. At the risk of oversimplifying, it is generally agreed that, in industrial relations, power means the ability to apply coercive sanctions or positive inducements. The application of power, whether by way positive inducement or negative sanction, is commonly said to have occurred if one party brings about a change in the behaviour of another party that would not otherwise take place. A further agreed characteristic of applied power is that its consequences in any given relationship must be intended (Bacharach and Lawler 1980, 16-7). In any business organisation, the application of power invariably involves a number of these factors. One important study observed that the exercise of power in organisations normally takes one of five forms:

1. 'coercive power', which relies on fear and is most evident in the way managers use the right to hire and fire labour as a means of disciplining workers
2. 'reward power', which is based on the ability of management to distribute things of value to workers, such as overtime and promotion
3. 'legitimate power', which is based on the position managers hold within the formal hierarchy of an organisation
4. 'expert power', which is based on the specialist knowledge of managers and the way workers rely on this knowledge to resolve work-related problems or complete assigned tasks
5. 'referent power', which is derived from the personal traits of managers, such as charisma and leadership (French and Raven 1959).

All these forms of power are utilised by management to control the workplace and deal with employees, although coercive and legitimate power are the forms most widely used in modern business organisations. Recently reward power has also become more popular as managers have sought to use bonus schemes, profit-share plans and other incentives to encourage employees to comply with their directions (O'Neill 1995, 23). Now let us turn to the theories which underlie management strategies in industrial conflict.

Theories of Management Strategy for Industrial Conflict

The first theory comes from the scientific management school of thought and deals with structures of power and control (see, Taylor 1911). Following this approach managers seek to reduce internal tensions by direct and highly rigid control of employee workplace activities. Workers, in this theory, are assumed to be immature, prone to avoid work whenever possible and have limited, self-centred aspirations and time horizons. It is therefore necessary for management to show rational leadership in recruiting and directing workers, to have a clear understanding of the tasks employees are expected to perform, and to have an unrestricted right to control the pace and processes of work tasks. Companies subscribing to this form of management practice normally reduce work tasks to their basic elements. The skills required of workers are thereby kept to a minimum. Employees are also treated impersonally and collectively, with any industrial relations issues being referred to negotiation with trade unions. Under these conditions, internal tensions are tempered by the superior knowledge of management, and by the vested authority (legitimate power) to direct workers. Strategies based on these ideas have been the traditional approach to industrial relations by business organisations for most of this century, particularly in Australia.

The second theory comes from the so-called human relations school (see, Maslow 1954; Mayo [1933]; Child 1967). The key assumption of this theory is that the resolution of organisational conflict comes from the ability of individuals to achieve self-fulfilment in the workplace. Achieving this goal starts by recognising that self-fulfilment is a fundamental right of workers, and that workers are qualitatively different to other resources used in the production. It is then argued that if workers are denied autonomy on the job, if they are reduced to acting as mere extensions of the machinery they operate, or if they are given work that limits their capacity to create and think, then they will invariably find ways to subvert methods of control that enforce these conditions. (Arguably, this is an individualistic, psychological interpretation of what Marx described collectively as class resistance to alienation and exploitation.) From this theory, the role of management principally involves managing the social relations and personal satisfactions of the workplace. Companies operating on this basis take an industrial relations approach that recognises the right of employees to have a say in how they are governed at work. Managers confer this right by establishing an agreement of formal or informal rules about the organisation of work. Employees are consulted by management to strengthen the psychological contract based on cooperation. This type of strategic approach has gained popularity in Australia over the past decade, and can be seen in the increased level of investment in training, the spread of multi-skilling, and the introduction of new job designs to encourage employees to work across traditional boundaries.

The most recent management theory is known as human resource management (see, Guest 1987; Blyton and Turnbull 1992; Stone 1998). This approach differs from the previous two. It argues that internal conflict can be resolved by establishing workplace conditions that encourage autonomous individuals, whether employees or management, to work collaboratively for the common good. Companies adopting this type of industrial relations strategy apply a humanistic approach that regards employment relations as a whole. Collaboration between employees and management is encouraged through the development of a unifying culture, strong leadership and a clear vision of organisational goals. The aim of these strategies is to replace destructive workplace interest groups with communication between different stakeholders and a collective understanding that the interests of all are better served by minimising internal conflict. Participatory management practices in the form of workplace teams, performance appraisals, performance related pay and individual contracts of employment, are typical activities of these types of strategies.

MANAGEMENT IDEOLOGY

Management theories have long played an important part in shaping the assumptions and beliefs that managers have about the nature of people and how to manage them. They have been important in supporting or justifying managerial ideologies about the appropriate distribution of power and the determination of goals within the organisation. For example, many managers, following traditional scientific management ideas, see their organisation as altogether separate or independent from their employees, or more to the point, they see the operation and survival of their organisation as highly dependent upon their own individual actions. These managers, who may be given the task of achieving organisational goals over which they have had little say, nevertheless identify personally with these same organisational goals. As a result they tend to see that they have a sacrosanct right (and duty) to manage work in whatever way they see fit, and view any challenge to this right as a threat to their personal goals. But their scientific management assumptions are rarely stated openly, and, if they are, they are rarely challenged. Indeed, it could be argued that many employees are prone to accept the basic assumptions of management, even when they serve to justify actions on the part of management that all but disempower or disenfranchise employees. (Such acceptance may even be carefully cultivated in organisations whose managerial ideology, based on HRM assumptions, includes creating a unifying organisational culture.) The situation was described by Jaynes (1996), who suggested that managerial ideologies foster an organisational consciousness that ignores power and structural inequalities in favour of a shared way of thinking. The willingness of an organisation's members to act cooperatively is the measure of the effectiveness of the managerial ideology. This occurs, Jaynes argued, because organisation members internalise the ideology, including its full set of delusions and distorted reasoning (1996, 88).

There are a number of models about the relationship between management ideology and industrial relations. Two of the more important, the pluralist and unitarist frames of reference, have already been discussed in Chapter 1. To briefly recap, the pluralist perspective holds that:

- different sectional groups exist within organisations and that the interests of each rarely coincide
- workplace conflict between these groups is both inevitable and legitimate - 'inevitable' because there is a natural propensity for inter-group rivalry over organisational strategies and objectives; and 'legitimate' because this rivalry can be utilised to promote a constructive equilibrium between competing group interests
- the best way to achieve this equilibrium is to put in place negotiation mechanisms that recognise the right of organised labour to participate in decision making processes about the structure and nature of work
- such mechanisms serve management objectives by making the resolution of workplace conflict predictable.

The key point this ideological perspective holds for management's role in industrial relations is that managers tend to accept the inevitability that workers will hold loyalties to trade unions which are greater than any loyalty they may hold towards their companies. As such, they are prone to accept trade unions as legitimate bargaining agents on behalf of workers (see, Fox 1971).

The ideological position of most Australian managers for much of the 20th Century would seem to be along this pluralistic line of thinking. However, the general acceptance of trade unions has not been so much a matter of choice as a response to the practical necessity of dealing with Australia's unique system of state-sponsored industrial relations regulations (see, Plowman 1989). Given the chance, most managers have historically tried to resist any restrictions placed on their workplace rights. The actions of trade unions and government regulations in the area of industrial relations have long constituted two such restrictions. They can be seen in practice in the State and Federal industrial relations tribunals, where organised labour has certain rights to represent workers in bargaining processes over wages and conditions. What these legally imposed rights has meant for managers is that it has long been impossible for them to oppose trade unionism outright. They have instead been forced to utilise the existing regulatory frameworks to contain trade union influence and to limit the scope of bargaining to matters that do not overly impinge on their right to manage their companies as they see fit. This has been particular true in industries such as manufacturing, mining, transport, public utilities, communication, construction and ports, where unions have traditionally attracted strong support and been prone to undertake militant action to achieve their objectives. Thus, if not willingly embraced, it has nonetheless been pluralism which has dominated management thinking in its approach to industrial relations for much of the 20th Century.

This dominance, however, has been significantly eroded in recent times. There has been a growth of management strategies based upon a unitarist perspective. To recap, the unitarist perspective holds that:

- employees and managers have interlocking responsibilities and an overriding common interest in cooperating to secure the survival of the organisation they both work for
- workplace relations do not naturally tend towards conflict but towards harmony and trust
- organisations can be likened to teams, where one source of authority should exist and there should be only one focus of loyalty
- industrial conflicts are aberrations caused by malcontents, outside agitators, poor communications or abrasive styles of supervision
- trade unions actually create internal conflict because they provide unnecessary competition with management for the loyalty and commitment of employees (Fox 1971).

It is difficult to know how prolific this perspective is in the thinking of Australian management. If pluralist notions have long dominated for reasons of necessity, it is no less the case that elements of the unitarist perspective have long been held just below the surface. Trade unions may have historically been accepted as a legitimate part of the industrial relations scene. But it is also clear that many managers have long held the views that workers should work judiciously and cooperate with management for the good of the firm; that they should strive for the same objectives as management; and that workplace conflict is the result of trade union interference. These views could be argued as having come more to the fore in recent years. Certainly this interpretation is supported by the rise of new right groups such as the H.R.Nicholl's Society, the aggressive anti-union strategies adopted by some of Australia's larger companies (e.g. CRA) and employer associations (e.g. Business Council of Australia), and the growing appeal of human resources management practices. Whatever the case, one thing is certain. High levels of unemployment, declining trade union memberships and the growing popularity of enterprise bargaining have all diminished the former influence and legitimacy of organised labour in the eyes of a growing number of Australian managers. Accordingly, the legacy of pluralism may linger in many sectors of the economy, but unitarist ideals are gaining popularity. Consequently more and more managers are applying anti-union strategies and devoting time and resources to persuading employees that loyalty and commitment towards the company they work for is in their best interests.

MANAGERIAL STYLE

Just as managerial theories serve to support managerial ideologies, so also managerial ideologies have an important influence on the style of management in industrial relations. In business organisations, management style essentially refers to the way owners and managers chose to coordinate and control those in their charge. It includes a set of principles that define the limits and provide the guidelines for appropriate management practice in dealing with employees. Whilst it is difficult to categorise with any degree of precision different styles of management, two important studies have gone some way towards identifying the key elements of various approaches.

The first study is by Purcell (1987, 523-46), who draws a distinction between two managerial styles. The first refers to styles that treat employees as individuals. Seen in terms of a continuum, at one end, this particular style of management regards individual workers as commodities, a necessary cost to the organisation to be employed, utilised and retrenched as business conditions require. The development of an individual's capacity to work is of little concern. Industrial relations policies are therefore confined to controlling, disciplining and coordinating the workplace activities of individual workers. At the other end of the continuum, policies and practices are again directed at individual workers, but in this case workers are regarded as a resource to be nurtured and developed as a means of improving their contribution to the operation and output of the firm. Further, whilst management functions are again directed towards controlling, disciplining and coordinating workers, they also involve the implementation and administration of programmes designed to encourage commitment and develop the skills of employees. Typical of industrial relations programmes to achieve this end are performance pay systems, career development schemes and participatory decision making mechanisms. Between these two extremes, a third style is identified as management that takes a paternal approach to its employees. Here industrial relations policies and practices are essentially benevolent. They are principally directed towards maintaining the welfare of individual workers as a means of building up their sense of obligation and loyalty to management.

The second management style identified by Purcell (1987) treats employees as collectives. That is to say, it refers to management policies and practices that are formulated and planned with a view to being applied to groups of employees, not individuals. The continuum again ranges across three possibilities. At one end a high degree of collectivism is held to exist and the style of management recognises the legitimacy of trade unions to bargain on behalf of workers. Alternatively, worker representatives are granted substantial rights of participation in company decision making processes. Here the control sought by management is built on the establishment of forums and mechanisms which are intended to bring about the cooperation of employees and their representatives. The assumption is that such frameworks will encourage them to support organisational objectives and temper their propensity to cause disruption. At the other end of the continuum a low level of collectivism is identified in styles of management that deal with groups of workers, but actively denies the legitimacy of trade unions. The aim of industrial relations policies in this case is to neutralise the influence of trade unions by dealing directly with workers collectively at the level of the firm. Furthermore, this collectivist style of management views employees as part of a wider whole that includes all members of the organisation (it is worth noting that this managerial style is consistent with the unitarist ideology mentioned earlier).

Between these two extremes a third variation is identified by Purcell (1987) in styles that reluctantly accept the legitimacy of trade unions, as well as the collective participation of employees in decision making processes. Forums and mechanisms established to facilitate these processes are not, however, benevolently aimed at facilitating worker cooperation. They are instead aimed at minimising the disruption caused by conflicts between management and organised labour. The industrial relations policies and practices applied are accordingly adversarial in their approach, used primarily by management to limit the scope of bargaining to issues that do not encroach too heavily on their power. (This particular style replicates the elements of the pluralist approach noted above).

A second study that looks at categorises of managerial styles is by Poole (1986). In this study four styles are identified - authoritarian, paternal, constitutional and participatory. Poole (1986) divides these styles in accordance with their unitarist and pluralist characteristics. Authoritarian and paternal managerial styles are equated with a unitary ideology. Organisations operating under these managerial styles are viewed as having a unified authority structure where industrial relations policies and practices are either directive or welfare-orientated. This means that control and coordination is essentially an uncontested managerial right, exercised for the exclusive interests of the firm and/or in the paternal interests of workers. Constitutional and participatory management practices, on the other hand, are equated with a pluralist ideology. Companies employing these managerial practices are regarded by Poole (1986) as being composed of coalitions of individuals and groups that have objectives and values that differ from those of management. Management's approach to industrial relations is thus essentially about reconciling these differences by reaching agreements with organised labour or allowing employees to participate directly in company decision making processes. Poole's (1986) categorisation of management styles is set out in Figure 3.1.

Although the empirical evidence is somewhat thin, the preferred managerial style in Australia appears to be closest to the constitutional and participatory approaches noted by Poole (1986), and some way between the adversarial and cooperative approaches noted in Purcell's (1987) collectivism continuum. We should be careful to recognise that management styles are nonetheless far from universal or static. Much depends on the type of business and economic environment in which an organisation operates, the type of legal and trade union constraints its management confronts, and its size, complexity and location. Thus, a small company operating under highly competitive conditions, making simple products and employing a non-unionised, largely unskilled workforce is likely to have few incentives to use cooperative forms of management.

Figure 3.1 Strategy, 'style' and frame of reference: the industrial relations of managers

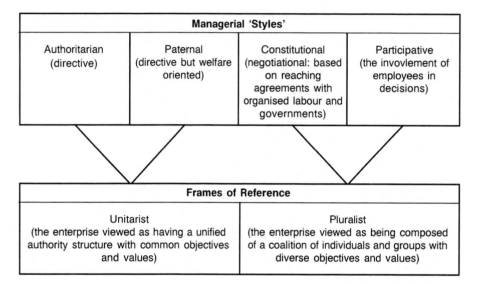

Source: M. Poole 1986, 44

The opposite might be expected where a large company operates in a monopolistic product market, employing a highly a unionised, militant workforce to produce complex items. Having said this, however, if any general trend exists, it is likely that managerial styles in the near future will drift more towards the authoritarian-paternal axis described by Poole (1986), and the labour control-unitary axis noted by Purcell (1987). This seems inevitable given the present trend towards decentralised forms of industrial bargaining, the expansion of enterprise bargaining, the persistent decline in trade union membership and the growing popularity of human resource management techniques.

ECONOMIC INFLUENCES

While managerial ideologies and styles have a substantial influence on workplace industrial relations, developments in the wider environment are also influential. Over the past two decades there have been several major changes which have forced companies to re-evaluate how they manage their workforces. Foremost among these changes has been the increasing globalisation of manufacturing, marketing, trading and finance. Throughout much of the western world, national tariff barriers have been gradually reduced and replaced by regional trading blocs of transnational proportions. National financial services have become more open to overseas participants and the fixing of exchange rates has become more subject to the ebbs and flows of international currency movements. Communication and transport technologies have improved, as have business information flows. Trading and marketing possibilities have also become more global. All these developments have placed increasing competitive pressures on national and multinational companies and made the business environments in which they operate far more unpredictable. To meet these challenges many companies have been forced to alter their organisational structures and to consider new industrial relations practices to utilise their workforces in a far more productive and efficient manner. Because Australia relies heavily on international trade it has been particularly vulnerable to these changing global influences. For example, the reduction of tariff protection for manufacturing industry has resulted in increased price competition and with less opportunity to pass costs onto consumers. This has forced employers to change existing policies in an effort to reduce costs, improve quality and increase efficiency.

These changes have been reflected in recent years by the flurry of political and business activity aimed at encouraging managers to take a more pro-active, strategically grounded approach to workplace industrial relations. Business forums have been established to discuss the problems of altering management practices, which was most clearly seen in the Hilmer Report (1995). This high profile report recommended that trade union structures be rationalised and the prevailing system of centralised wage fixing be dismantled. The argument from business more generally has been that changes along these lines will improve the productive output of workers and thereby improve the international competitiveness of Australian companies. The trade union movement has similarly identified the need for new trade union structures and a new industrial relations system. Less centralised wage fixing mechanisms and less rigid award provisions have been advocated as the best way to improve the productivity of labour, as well as improving the career and training opportunities for workers (Abbott 1993, 151). The Federal Government and various state governments have accepted many of these arguments and have passed a range of legislation designed to decentralise employer-employee bargaining processes.

All these developments have served to move management-employee bargaining down to the level of the firm. In so doing they generated a growing level of interest in the conduct of workplace relations, not just at the level of specialist managers who have traditionally had the sole responsibility for dealing with industrial conflict, but across management as a whole. In short, companies are being forced to respond more quickly to volatile business conditions. As a result they are also being compelled to find a management style that places greater emphasis on collaboration and less emphasis on conflict between commercial goals and industrial relations practices and outcomes.

MANAGEMENT AND STRATEGIC CHOICE THEORY

One of the more important contemporary studies dealing with management's role in industrial relations has been the strategic choice theory (Kochan, Katz and McKersie 1986). This theory has also been outlined in Chapter 1 (the reader is urged to re-read that section for a more comprehensive account). This theory argues that it is the changes to business and economic conditions that generate new managerial values and labour management strategies. Hence, the decline of trade unionism, the decentralisation of workplace bargaining, and the growing acceptance of human resource management practices, are all identified as influential external changes. They all act to re-direct managerial responsibility for industrial issues away from industrial relations specialists to human resource managers and line mangers. They also encourage management to take a more pro-active role in managing employees, and a more integrated approach to human resource functions in broader business strategy. As such, the theory suggests that contemporary managers are now more active players in seeking industrial relations change than in the past. It also suggests that the authority to deal with industrial relations has now spread throughout the managerial hierarchy.

Indeed, the participation in industrial relations is said to increasingly involve chief executive officers, senior and middle managers, and line managers, with each adopting new responsibilities for the management of employees. Those at the highest management level are involved with formulating the broad strategies related to human resource planning. They also liaise with trade union executives, government ministers and senior public servants to advocate those strategies both for their organisation and often for the industrial sector as a whole. Those in senior and middle management positions, and particularly personnel and human resource managers, continue to be responsible for implementing human resource plans, as well as negotiating with trade union officials, shop stewards and individual employees for labour contracts consistent with those plans. They also continue their responsibility for liaising with public departments to ensure that organisational policies conform to government labour laws. Lastly, line managers are being increasingly held accountable for ensuring that the formal workplace rules and regulations, which arise from human resource policies, labour contracts and government laws, are being properly adhered to by the organisation's workforce. They are also being increasingly held responsible for ensuring that informal customs and practices assist in maintaining harmonious relations between the organisation's personnel.

Industrial relations decisions and activities can thus be seen to increasingly involve all levels of the managerial hierarchy, and not just personnel managers, as has been the case in the past. Critics of strategic choice theory have suggested that it exaggerates the importance of corporate strategies in the conduct of industrial relations; that it overstates the widespread practice human resources management techniques; and that its methodology and supporting data are deficient (see, Hilderbrand 1988; Strauss 1988; and Lewin 1988). In response to these criticisms Purcell and Ahlstrand (1989) set about trying to cast light on the links between strategic decisions made at the corporate level and those made at the middle and line management levels. They did this by making a distinction between 'first', 'second' and 'third' order strategies in diversified multi-divisional firms. First-order strategies were held to be the province of executive management, who determine the long-term objectives of the firm and the broad mix of activities required for their achievement. Strategic items at this level covered issues such as divisional liquidations, takeovers, acquisitions, and major capital investments. Second-order strategies involved middle management and were principally concerned with maintaining, or restructuring, or realigning systems of control in accordance with the objectives of first-order strategic items. 'Third-order' strategies were said to be undertaken by line managers and involved decisions about production, marketing and the management of employees. The choices about industrial relations strategy at this line management level are listed in Figure 3.2.

Drawing on case studies, the authors provided two examples of linkages between corporate strategy and strategy formulated at the levels of middle and line management. The first concerned the influence of line and middle managements on corporate strategy, with the evidence suggesting that influence in this direction is generally limited. Executive managers, it seemed, rarely consider industrial relations issues when formulating long-term corporate strategies. The exception to this general rule was when corporate plans have the most obvious industrial relations implications, the most notable example being decisions to close plants or retrench workers.

Figure 3.2 'Third Order' (or line management) strategy choices

---
1. Management style - should a single style or approach be cultivated across the entire corporation?
2. The way resources should be deployed and where decision making should occur within personnel and industrial relations.
3. The workforce structure and employment policies, especially job-grading, evaluation systems and worker mobility
4. The selection of bargaining and consultative groups and agendas
---

The second example, however, showed that the opposite does occur. Strategic decisions taken at the corporate level have a substantial impact on the management of industrial relations at lower levels. In their example, Purcell and Ahlstrand (1989) found among the companies they investigated, traditional bargaining levels were changed when separate companies were formed out of former divisional units. These reforms were considered more the result of second order strategy than the product of any strategic intent to deal with industrial relations issues (1989, 409).

MANAGEMENT AND INDUSTRIAL RELATIONS IN SOUTH EAST ASIA

While managers in Australia may have been compelled in the past to adopt a more pluralistic outlook by trade union power and tribunal regulation of industrial relations, the same has not been true of the five South East Asian countries examined in this book. For most of the histories of these countries, trade unions have been relatively weak, or have been forced to submit to the will of the political regime in power. Indeed, managements in these countries are deeply imbued with unitary frames of reference for cultural reasons and because they have never had to confront strong trade unions unlike managements in Australia. We will conclude this chapter therefore by examining management and industrial relations practices in these five South East Asian countries. We will begin by looking specifically at management practices in Japan and South Korea, and then more generally at the management style used by ethnic Chinese in the other three countries (i.e. Hong Kong, Malaysia and Singapore). This latter selection is based on our limited space and the fact that the Chinese communities in each of these countries are the dominant business elite, especially in the case of Hong Kong. In any case, the three descriptions that follow should be considered broadly representative of the different managerial styles of the region. (It is worth noting that the subject matter of this section is elaborated in more detail in Chapter 13.)

Japan

Japanese management practices and strategies have always been based on the need to maintain close relations between employer and worker, and the need to ensure that there is a sharing of interests between both. In this regard one of the most fundamental characteristics of Japanese management is the strong emphasis placed on 'groupism'. This style of management can be traced far back into Japan's history. Clark (1983), for example, has argued that, despite its advanced state of industrialisation, the Japanese have long had a village mentality which has fostered a strong collectivist culture. This is best observed in the strong sense of family and kinship that many Japanese feel in their social relations, and by extension, in their workplace relations. Many Japanese employees, whether holding managerial positions or simple labouring positions, see the firms they work for as extended families. Indeed, in many senses large companies have come to replace feudal overlords, which were held in the highest esteem in earlier Japanese society both because of the protection and the largesse they gave local communities. Although undergoing some challenge from economic downturn, many Japanese workers still look to their companies as a source of lifetime employment, a privilege which at present is only extended to about one-third of the workforce.

Keys and Miller (1984) have identified three common factors which underlie Japanese management practices. The first is a long-term planning horizon, which involves business strategies that have long time-lines and a commitment to both the extended time and necessary resources to implement them. The second is a commitment to lifetime employment, which leads to practices such as careful selection and recruitment processes, extensive socialisation, comprehensive welfare provisions, detailed employee training, and programs to facilitate a climate of trust between management and workers. The third factor is the emphasis placed on collective responsibility, which involves managerial efforts to encourage consensus decision making, teamwork and cooperation. As Dollinger (1988) goes on to point out, each of these managerial characteristics has strong links to Confucian ideals. The commitment to lifetime employment, for example, is an extension of the reverence accorded to community and family in Confucian thought. The same reverence is also accorded to values such as loyalty, diligence and individual deference to the needs of the community. All of these values, it is argued, translate readily into the modern business corporation, encouraging consensus in managerial approaches to industrial relations issues.

Confucian philosophy, however, cannot alone account for Japanese management practices. There are of course more pragmatic reasons why Japanese companies act as they do when dealing with industrial relations issues. The commitment to lifetime employment, for example, has also been explained by the desire of Japan's business and political leaders to secure a stable workforce, prevent labour shortages, and minimise employee turnover for the purpose of advancing the country's industrial development. Much of the international competitive advantage of Japanese companies has been accredited to those human resource management practices which support the concept of lifetime employment. The effect of lifetime employment on the conduct of industrial relations is that it has tended to tie workers closely to their enterprises, which in turn has inhibited any tendency to undertake industrial action to satisfy their workplace needs (Koike 1988, 260; Chen 1995, 184).

The system of lifetime employment essentially consists of three practices. First, recruitment is not from the open job market. Most employees come directly from school or university. Second, the company expects these employees to spend their entire working life in its employ, in return for which the company guarantees job security. Third, recruitment is not based on technical skills but rather on general characteristics and abilities of candidates, and on their perceived ability to fit into the group. The application of these practices has extensive consequences. Great care, for example, is taken in employee selection, as mistakes can be costly and difficult to rectify. On the other hand, the potential recruit also has to be very careful in selecting the right company, with good long-term prospects. It is really an exchange of commitments, so to speak, with each side pledging loyalty to the agreed exchange. There is also a down side. A Japanese lifetime employee fired by a company in mid-career, for instance, will usually find it much harder to obtain alternative employment than his or her western counterpart. It is in the sense of this difficulty that the company assumes some of the obligations of a family when it hires permanent workers. It must be prepared to make sacrifices for its employees in economic downturns, but in return they are expected to give their absolute loyalty to the company, even to the extent of making considerable sacrifices in their personal lives. To the extent that the company becomes an extension of an employee's family, nothing is feared more by the employee than exclusion from the company 'group'. After a new recruit has been hired extensive socialisation begins. The employee is rotated between departments, to learn how each functions, its history and culture, and how each fits into the whole. New recruits typically live in a company dormitory and socialise outside of work with fellow employees. In this way, the company assumes the characteristics of a real family-type of organisation. New recruits are also expected to develop close relationships with their superiors, who are expected to act as mentors and role models, providing on-the-job training and forming close personal bonds with those in their charge (Chen 1995, 188-9).

Closely related to lifetime employment is the system of promotion by seniority. Since most employees are recruited directly from school or university, the age and length of service of members of a particular cohort are closely parallel. Seniority therefore becomes a logical basis for promotion once recruits have 'learned the ropes' by working in all major company areas. It used to be the case that most recruits had a good chance of becoming a section or department head if they stayed with the company throughout their working lives. However, in more recent times the promotion prospects of lifetime employees have declined as a consequence of the general slowdown of the Japanese economy. Even in the faster growing companies, the chance of promotion remains consistent with traditional patterns, because faster growing companies tend to have lower average labour costs than slower growing companies, and therefore have a proportionally lower need for managers of labour.

Related to the system of seniority is the compensation system used by many Japanese companies. The level of remuneration paid in Japanese companies tends to be more egalitarian than that paid in their western counterparts. The differential between senior executives and base level employees is narrower, with the latter being able to share equally with the former in gaining access to cash benefits when the company is successful. Indeed, part of the competitive advantage of Japanese companies rests in the fact that approximately one-third of total annual remuneration is paid to employees in the form of annual or semi-annual bonuses. This component of workers' pay is flexible, and can be readily reduced when companies confront periodic downturns (though it is interesting to note that it is common practice for companies to first discharge part-time and temporary workers before cutting bonuses). Another important component of this pay system is the way retirement benefits are calculated on base rates of pay, such that the payment of bonuses to workers during times of strong economic performance will not increase a company's financial obligation to employees at their time of retirement. In addition, most Japanese companies provide other forms of payment, such as family allowances, housing assistance and separation pay, all of which contribute to employees' sense of shared destiny with the companies they work for, both in good times and in bad (Chen 1995, 192-3).

It is in the context of these managerial efforts to develop a good rapport with employees, and the more general Japanese cultural attribute of placing 'group' interests over individual interests, that we can gain some understanding of the way Japanese managers deal with industrial relations. The combination of these factors tends to ensure that Japanese workers are deeply concerned about the fortunes of the company they work for. The growth of Japanese trade unions with an independent existence outside the firm has been negligible, in large part because unions of this type have not been able to persuade Japanese workers that their interests would be better served by this form of representation. Enterprise-based unions are thus the norm, and in most cases have been set up and financed by the companies themselves. This system of trade union organisation was originally established by labour laws passed by the occupying forces after World War II. It has never been challenged because of the managerial practices applied by Japanese firms in their treatment of their workers. All permanent employees, both blue and white collar, and without regard for rank and status, are eligible for membership of company enterprise unions. Indeed, it has been estimated that as many as one in six senior Japanese executives have had experience as union officials (Whitehill 1991, 245-6). The company and the union thus have a uniquely inter-dependent relationship, which has meant that union members have been very hesitant about undertaking industrial action that may damage the company's reputation or prospects. It has also meant that managers have tended to regard union membership as a valuable training ground for gaining managerial expertise, a view that contrasts markedly to the way managers view trade union membership in the west. When Japanese strikes do occur, they are typically of a symbolic nature, with stoppages confined to lunch-hours and rarely taking a form likely to damage a company's economic interests.

In closing, it is a fact that the entire Japanese industrial relations system is coming under increasing pressure to change, and so also, presumably, is the traditional approach of Japanese management to industrial relations issues. First, there are the on-going problems with the Japanese economy since the mid-1990s, which have seen an increasing number of large companies abandon the principles of lifetime employment and seniority promotion as they search for new ways to improve their declining economic fortunes. Second, many younger Japanese, in any case, are showing a declining interest in committing themselves to lifetime employment in one organisation and the prospect of slow promotion by seniority (Chen 1995, 188-92). Third, there are signs that the post-war system of enterprise unionism is breaking down as newly formed independent trade unions covering entire industries gather increasing interest among employees. This has been particularly so among the casual and temporary workers that service major companies, but is also the case among the permanent workers of these companies. It is too early to say how widespread or how quickly these changes will become, but it will almost certainly have an impact on the way Japanese managers approach industrial relations in the future.

South Korea

The characteristic that distinguishes South Korean management practices has been described as akin to 'clan management'. This loosely describes the way managers identify closely with each others interests in the manner of family. This clannishness draws significantly on the same Confusion thinking as that in Japan, but unlike Japan it rarely extends to include the workers within the organisations. Thus, Confucian ideals about work ethics and company loyalty only profoundly permeate the level of management. Such ideals also support management labour practices that are formalised, bureaucratic and paternalistic (Lee and Yoo 1987; Chen 1995, 220-2). Other significant differences also exist. The Japanese practice of lifetime employment, for example, is uncommon in South Korea. Consequently there is far more labour mobility than in Japan. Credentialism is also more important in the hiring employees in South Korea, whereas personality is more important in Japanese recruitment. For this reason South Koreans place a great emphasis on gaining a sound education, and particularly in gaining the type training and professional qualifications demanded by South Korean industry. As a result, the country enjoys one of the highest literacy rates in the South East Asian region, with 98 per cent of the population able to read and write. Over 80 per cent of high school leavers go on to some form of post-secondary vocational or professional training. (Chen 1995, 220).

Nevertheless, South Korean management practices have some ambiguity in style. While there are those bureaucratic and autocratic practices which reflect Confucian thinking, there is also a certain flexibility similar to that commonly found in American management systems (Lee and Yoo 1987, 76). This second aspect is partly due to the large numbers of American troops in South Korea, a dominant feature of the country's social and political life since the end of the Korean War. The support organisations set up to service these troops, with their American managerial practices, have no doubt had a major influence on South Korean management ideas. It is also partly the result of many South Korean business executives studying management in American universities. There has thus been a grafting of United States flexibility and Confucian hierarchical traditions in South Korean management systems, which are thereby rigid and formal in some areas, and flexible and adaptable in others. In the area of industrial relations this can be seen in a managerial approach that is flexible on workers' wages and conditions of employment, but rigid when dealing with the demands of trade unions and workers acting collectively. In consequence, South Korean companies have much less community of interest between mangers and workers than is commonly found in Japanese corporations.

At the same time, the level of trade union membership in South Korea is much lower than in Japan. In South Korea unions are industry-based rather than enterprise-based. Part of the reason for this is that trade unions in South Korea are largely controlled by the state, which has strong links with the country's largest corporations. The government also has a positive interest in curtailing labour unrest in pursuit of its economic development strategies. This has served to limit the value of trade union membership for large numbers of South Korean workers. The hostility displayed by government and business towards independent forms of trade unionism has also diminished the interest of workers in joining these types of organisation. Consequently, collective bargaining is also much less institutionalised in South Korea than it is in Japan. Managers have less interest and need to engage in industrial relations issues. Indeed, when South Korean workers are moved to undertake industrial action, which they are more inclined to do than in Japan, it is normally in pursuit of political change from government rather than industrial objectives from managers (Lie 1990).

Overseas Chinese Management

Japanese management systems have long been the main focus of interest among scholars with an interest in South East Asian business practices. However, the dramatic growth of so-called 'Tiger Economies' in the region has seen this focus shift to management systems in companies run by ethnic Chinese nationals in Hong Kong, Malaysia and Singapore. While the Chinese communities in these countries share a Confucian heritage with the Japanese and South Koreans, there are sharp differences in the way they see their place in society. Fukuda (1988), for example, has noted that in Chinese Confucian thinking the family is placed above the individual and the community, while in Japanese thinking the community is placed above the individual and the family. Thus, while both societies are collectivist rather than individualistic in nature, the 'group' is differently defined, with the Chinese conceiving it more in terms of the sociological clan, meaning those united by common ancestry, name, property and marriage.

What this means is that the Chinese business managers in places like Hong Kong, Malaysia and Singapore rarely trust anyone beyond the family and the clan, and are profoundly suspicious of wider social and community institutions such as the nation, the government and the public sector. This unwillingness to trust anybody beyond the familial 'group' has created a particular kind of business organisation and a particular style of management. So, for example, nearly all Hong Kong businesses owned by ethnic Chinese employ 200 people or less, a pattern that is similar to businesses in other countries where ethnic Chinese dominate the private sector (see, Redding 1990, 146-7; Chew 1988). This dominance of small-scale businesses has much to do with the inability of Chinese owners and managers to trust the necessary number of people in senior positions necessary to make larger-scale businesses work. The generally small size of Chinese-run businesses, in turn, means that managerial systems are marked by a relatively low degree of structure and formality. That is to say, the extent of labour specialisation is typically low, there are few standardised rules and operating procedures, very few written records are kept, and decision making tends to be highly centralised and very secretive (Redding 1990, 154-63).

It is for these reasons that the management style of many Chinese managers towards industrial relations issues has been described as 'didactic'. This means that managers typically seek to control and centralise organisational information within their ranks. They maintain a significant organisational distance between themselves and those in their charge, and they are intolerant of challenges by workers to their managerial power (Chen 1995, 88). Indeed, most Chinese managers (who, incidentally, are often owners at the same time) are highly suspicious of workers, and although they demand their loyalty it is rarely taken for granted. This is particularly so in the case of companies which have grown beyond the immediate control of the family. There is perhaps some basis for the concern given a cultural tendency among Chinese non-family employees to strike out on their own once they have learned the ropes of a business. Tam (1990) summed up the relationship between managers and workers in Hong Kong as one of widespread disloyalty and absence of commitment by employees to companies, systematic neglect of human resource development by companies, severely limited trust between employers and employees, and a constant breakdown of companies into smaller units (1990, 153). This description, it could be said, is equally applicable to small companies run by ethnic Chinese in Singapore and Malaysia.

Another notable feature of this type of management is the disdain it holds for workers and worker collectives. For example, it is not uncommon for Chinese managers to actively employ 'divide-and-rule' type tactics as a means of frustrating support for trade unions. As for the idea of managers working alongside employees in a manner commonly found in Japan, it is almost unheard of (Redding 1990, 155-67). It is for these reasons that trade unionism is generally low in countries where this type of managerial practice dominates. Workers in these countries tend to respond to poor working conditions by voting with their feet (exiting) rather than taking coordinated industrial action (voice). This partly explains the tendency of non-family Chinese workers to move on to start their own business when they feel dissatisfied. Of course, Chinese workers with family ties to their employer are obviously disinclined to take industrial action, preferring to resolve differences as any family would. For all these reasons, those working for Chinese-run firms, whether family or non-family, tend to make poor trade unionists.

CONCLUSION

It is clear that there are considerable differences in the management of industrial relations both between South East Asian countries and in comparison with Australia. Confucian cultural ideals figure prominently in any explanation of both the similarities and differences between management strategies in South East Asian countries. In the case of Japan, the management approach to industrial relations appears to be strongly influenced by unitarist ideals, which are supported by the Confusion belief that the community should be placed before the individual.

The management style in South Korea is more mixed, with Confucian elements combining with elements of American origin. The frame of reference is consequently more pluralistic, with a greater divergence of interests existing between management and labour. The management approach among ethnic Chinese nationals in Hong Kong, Malaysia and Singapore is different again. Here the Confucian belief that family (or sociological clan) should be placed above all else, explains the distrust that tends to exist between managers and workers. Its approach consequently tends to be adversarial (or at best paternalistic).

The management approach in Australia tends to be unitarist by preference but pluralist in practice, another variation that can be traced to this country's cultural and political values. These values are largely based on liberal democratic traditions and a pluralistic division of social interests. This has translated into a managerial tendency to support the merits of individualism (over and above community and family), and labour tendency to support the merits of class-based collectivism (aside from community and family). As a mature democratic industrialised society, the tussle between these two competing visions in Australia has led managers to accept the existence of institutions and processes established to mediate workplace conflict, which is effectively a pluralistic approach in both style and practice.

REVIEW QUESTIONS

1. Why has it been argued that tensions between stake-holders is an inherent part of a modern business organisations?
2. Why is the exercise of power through hierarchical structures an essential part of business organisations, and why can the possession of this power by managers become problematic?
3. Explain the key aspects of the three most common theories used for interpreting management industrial relations strategies.
4. 'Management ideology has a significant influence on the way business organisations approach the management of employees'. Discuss.
5. Compare and contrast the central features of the models put forward by Purcell (1987) and Poole (1986) in relation to management style and its influence on industrial relations policy.

6. What are the major recent economic and political developments which have heightened the importance of management's role in industrial relations?
7. What are the major changes which have inspired senior Australian management to take a more active interest in industrial relations?
8. How does management ideology in South East Asian countries differ from that in Australia?
9. What role does Confusian thinking play in the way managements in South East Asian countries approach industrial relations issues? In what ways are they similar, and how do they differ?
10. Why have the management styles and practices of companies run by ethnic Chinese nationals in South East Asian countries not led to more industrial unrest?

FURTHER READING

Ahlstrand, B. (1990), *The Quest for Productivity: A Case Study of Frawley After Flanders*, Cambridge University Press, Cambridge.

Edwards, R. (1979), *Contested Terrain*, Basic Books, New York.

Kochan, T., Katz H. and McKersie, R. (1986), *The Transformation of American Industrial Relations*, Basic Books, New York.

Legge, K. (1995), *Human Resource Management: Rhetorics and Realities*, Macmillan Business, Houndsmill.

Perrow, C. (1986), *Complex Organisations*, Random House, New York.

Poole, M. (1986), 'Management Strategies and 'Styles' in Industrial Relations: A Comparative Analysis', *Journal of General Management*, vol.12, no.1.

Purcell, P. and Ahlstrand B. (1989), 'Corporate Strategy and the Management of Employee Relation in the Multi-Divisional Company', *British Journal of Industrial Relations*, vol. 27, November.

CHAPTER 4

Employer Organisations

'The stronger man's argument is always the best.'

Jean De La Fontaine

LEARNING OBJECTIVES
After reading this chapter you should be able to:
- understand the role of employer organisations in industrial relations
- look at the relationship between employer organisations and other players in the industrial relations framework
- briefly review the history of these associations
- review the theories attempting to explain the emergence and development of employer associations
- discuss bargaining structures and provide examples of how these arise
- briefly provide an Asian perspective on employer associations.

INTRODUCTION
Employer associations are the natural counterpart of trade unions in a capitalist economy. While trade unions developed in response to the needs of workers, employers have also recognised the value of joining together for support and protection. This chapter examines these organisations. First, we look at the history of Australian employer associations. We then review contemporary developments: the structure, strategies and objectives of business organisations in Australia, and their role in the conduct of industrial relations. However, it needs to be said from the outset that information and literature on these organisations are sparse. This is partly because employer associations have not traditionally been very prominent players in industrial relations. But it is also because their activities are rarely viewed in the same way that trade union activities are seen, as a direct challenge to society's economic and power status quo. This chapter concludes by reviewing employer associations in the selected five South East Asian countries.

DEFINITION OF EMPLOYER ASSOCIATIONS

The term 'employer association' is applied to business organisations that have a specific interest in industrial relations (see Plowman 1989; Bell 1994). It is this specific industrial relations interest which distinguishes these 'associations' from other organisations that represent employers across a range of other interests. This distinction can be set out in the following way:

1. 'Employer organisations' undertake a variety of functions when seeking to serve their membership. These functions can include informing and educating members on issues pertinent to the industry they operate in, gathering statistical information, monitoring industry developments, running trade conferences, publishing trade journals, lobbying politicians, conducting publicity campaigns or some combinations of these.

2. 'Employer associations' also engage in these essentially political and commercial activities, but in addition are actively involved on behalf of members in processes that determine employee conditions (Plowman 1982). This may involve:
   - giving employer support to government policies on labour and social issues in return for policies that protect or advance business interests in particular industries
   - providing employer representation at industrial tribunals on wages and working conditions
   - facilitating collective action amongst members as a means of resisting trade union demands
   - some other action conducive to employers in the balance of power between labour and capital.

It is this involvement in employee relations by employer associations that we are essentially concerned with here. Unfortunately, this distinction sometimes becomes blurred, as some employer organisations occasionally engage in industrial relations activities, for example during times of crisis. In addition, some organisations indirectly influence industrial relations when, for instance, they lobby governments for changes in business practices which have profound ramifications for working conditions of employees. An example was the push for extended shopping hours in Victoria by some employer groups. This led to the need to formulate appropriate pay rates and conditions for workers expected to work outside the normal hours.

HISTORY OF EMPLOYER ASSOCIATIONS

In the last half of the 19th Century, the growth of trade union influence and the threat of compulsory unionism were of great concern to employers. By 1885, the Trades and Labour Councils had become very effective at focussing the combined strength of unions against less organised employers. This focus and coordination allowed unions to exert more pressure on employers to implement compulsory unionism in their establishments. These conditions encouraged adversarial workplace relations and eventually led employers to seek a similar focussed and coordinated approach to the industrial environment.

A dispute between employers and unions over an eight-hour workday led to the formation by employers of the Iron Trades Employers Association in 1873 (Dabscheck and Niland 1982, 172). This body has been more commonly known as the Metal Trades Industry Association (MTIA) until it merged with the Australian Chamber of Manufacturers (ACM) in 1998 to form the Australian Industry Group (AIG). It is now an extremely powerful national lobbyist for employers.

In Victoria, in November 1884, the Operative Bootmakers' Union members were in dispute with employers over an industry wide log of claims. This resulted in a thirteen-week stoppage and a high degree of animosity between employers and the union. As a consequence of this action, in 1885 employers formed the Victorian Employers Union, the precursor of the Victorian Employers Federation (VEF), (Thomas 1985, 1-2).

As these adversarial conditions continued and worsened in the 1890s depression, other employer unions were established. With compulsory arbitration and the establishment of wages boards and tribunals, unions acquired legal status and the employers' dominance of the employment relationship was challenged. For employers, these developments served to reinforce the collective benefits of employer unions (Wright 1995, 29-30).

While many employer unions have survived as can be seen from the examples above, many more disappeared either through merger or by disbandment. The disbandment of employer unions occurred predominantly in situations where such associations were formed in response to a specific strike or threat. Once these issues were resolved, the need for the association disappeared and the association was disbanded.

The role and purpose of early employer associations were quite specific. They provided a united retaliatory mechanism against union initiatives. Wright (1995, 29) also points out that while employer coordination was a response to the growth of unionism in many industries, it was also greatly concerned with trade issues and tariff protection. Employer associations were also subject to a great deal of disunity, as members vied to have their individual needs satisified at the expense of the collective.

The period between 1901 to 1913 saw the second highest growth rate of population that Australia has experienced (Coppell 1994, 90). This in turn stimulated strong growth in industry, employment and the economy. This growth intensified the density and penetration of trade unions, and led to the development of permanent employer associations closely resembling those we have today.

As the influence of employer associations grew throughout the 20th Century, so the dependence that employers placed on them also grew. By the end of the century, with the increasing complexity of the business environment and the industrial relations system, their role and function were expanding. A wider range of employer associations was established. These included:

- 'umbrella associations' such as the VEF and the former ACM, whose members come from a variety of industries.
- 'industry associations' such as the former MTIA and the Oil Industry Industrial Committee, whose members come from a specific industry. Some of these organisations are sufficiently large to be autonomous, providing member services with no support from other associations. Others are part-time operations, depending on other associations for assistance.
- 'peak employer associations' such as the Australian Chamber of Commerce and Industry (ACCI) and the Business Council of Australia. The emergence and development of these peak associations has to some degree mirrored the evolution of the ACTU and the Trades and Labour Councils.

All of these associations have provided employers with greater coordination, unity and dissemination of information. They have also allowed more effective lobbying of governments on policy issues.

THE DEVELOPMENT OF PEAK ASSOCIATIONS

There is a variety of definitions available for employer associations. In London in 1968, Lord Donovan (Donovan 1971 Report, 7-8) stated that employer associations undertake a number of activities such as the negotiation (directly or indirectly) of wages and working conditions. However, he went on to distinguish other associations that engage in such things as the standardisation of products and trading contracts. This introduces a differentiation based on industrial relations and other functions.

In Australia too, employers associations can be grouped into those with a main focus on industrial relations, and those whose main purpose is to act as industry associations, formed to protect common trade interests. The latter type of organisation has little or no industrial relations function, but typically acts as a pressure group, for example lobbying governments on issues such as protection or free trade. There is also the 'hybrid' association that may engage in both types of activities.

It is useful to understand the origin of employer associations because as Dufty and Fells (1989, 82) contend, these associations went through a learning experience when they were formed. Responding to the prevailing conditions of their time, they were originally concerned more with trade and tariff protection and specific industrial conflicts rather than longer term industrial relations issues (Wright 1995, 29).

Plowman (1992, 225-226) contends that employer associations are essentially reactive in nature and that they engage in 'Reactive activity' in order to maintain power and bargaining structures. He argues that the role and purpose of associations have changed very little from their inception. Although this view has been challenged by Barry (1995, 543-545), it is still a major theme within industrial relations literature.

Despite Plowman's argument, the original employer associations that were formed around regional, state, trade and occupational demands have evolved. During the 1920s the first Peak associations started to appear. As Carney (1988, 76-77) discusses, these were committees with member drawn from umbrella organisations such as the Australian Council of Employers Federation (ACEF), a part-time organisation, the Associated Chambers of Manufacturers of Australia and others. These committees met mainly to decide a united approach to national wage claims and then disbanded later.

It was not until 1977 that one major 'Peak' association emerged, the Confederation of Australian Industry (CAI). The CAI was formed through the amalgamation of ACEF and the Associated Chambers of Manufacturers of Australia. This association was designed to unite all other umbrella organisations and their member employers. However, the CAI itself amalgamated with the Australian Chamber of Commerce in 1992 to become the Australian Chamber of Commerce and Industry (ACCI) an even stronger peak employer association (Alexander and Lewer 1998, 98).

The other main peak employer association is the Business Council of Australia (BCA). This association was formed in 1983 when the Business Round Table joined the Australian Industries Development Association. It brings together over 80 chief executives from the nation's leading organisations and promotes discussion and research on major issues affecting the business community (BCA 1994, 4).

THEORIES CONCERNING EMPLOYER ASSOCIATIONS

A number of theories have been formed to explain the emergence and development of employer associations. Whilst we will examine the most recent ideas, including Plowman's Reactivity theory mentioned above, several of the early explanations also deserve scrutiny.

John Commons

Commons (1909) undertook research in the US and produced a work entitled, 'American Shoemakers, 1648-1895'. Commons argued that as improved transportation and communication services became available, employer and employee functions became separated. This allowed expansion of the marketplace and nurtured the formation of both unions and employer associations for mutual protection and greater penetration of the market. The Commons thesis saw market growth and the increasing inequality between employers and employees as instrumental in the development unions and associations to protect respective collective interests.

Hoxie

In the 1920s in the US, R.F Hoxie put forward an opposing power thesis to explain why unions and employer associations form and develop. Hoxie argued that employers and employees use a number of m7echanisms to ensure that each has either a comparable or superior organisation to the other. While Hoxie saw both these parties as critical players in industrial relations, he emphasised that each has opposing interests to the other. Both parties then engage in activities to offset the power developed by the other. Each strives to develop more sophisticated structures and coordination than the other. The objective is to maximise the interests of one group over the other.

In Australia, the spread and threat of unionism together with the role played by the Trades and Labour Councils were central reasons for the emergence of employer associations. In support of Hoxie's view, the ACTU emerged as the peak union body in 1927 following attempts by employers to establish peak associations of their own earlier that decade. This competitive copying of organisation follows Hoxie's model well, although it does not address the issue raised by Wright (1995, 29), that employers formed organisations to deal with issues of trade and tariff protection as well the industrial relations issues.

McCaffree

Again in the US, early in the 1960s, *K.M McCaffree* developed the thesis that employer associations were created in response to the dynamic environment in which they operate. McCaffree argued that employer needs, such as a means to achieving greater dominance in the employment relationship, played a less important role in the development of employer associations than was previously believed. Instead, he argued, the need to establish such associations was imposed upon employers by their environment. McCaffree argued that the establishment and development of employer associations could be explained by looking at the growth in complexity and sophistication of the political, economic and market conditions. He conceded that the growth of unionism was also an environmental influence that could pressure employers into a state of consolidation. However, he emphasised the external environment of organisations and argued that it was here that the major factors influencing employers occurred.

In the early Australian context, the gold rush brought an influx of migrants to the established cities. These people brought with them professions, skills and trades that encouraged the growth of new industries. We can apply McCaffree's thesis to this early Australian period by showing how the growth of population and new industries encouraged the division of labour and lead to the spread of unionism.

As a more complex market developed, unions consolidated into the Trade Councils and employment legislation was enacted. With the nature of work and the employment contract changed, employers were pressured to establish associations to gain protection from environmental influences and to provide a means to deal more effectively with them.

Jackson and Sisson

In the mid 1970s, Jackson and Sisson produced three models which they believed explained the emergence and development of employer associations (Plowman 1986). These models, built upon earlier research, attempted to both explain a wider range of issues and integrate them into one cohesive thesis. Jackson and Sisson also argued that if their three models did not largely explain the origin and development of employer associations, then variants of the models certainly would.

The first model was the defensive model. They contended that employer associations originated as a defense mechanism that would protect them from the threat that united and coordinated unions posed. In this instance they argued that the development of union structures was an aggressive action and that employers formed similar structures in order to offset the power and coordination achieved by the union movement.

In the Australian context this could explain the emergence of employer associations, however once established there would be little need to develop further. If the model is varied to the extent that one party is aggressive (unions) while the other is defensive then we can assume a continuing spiral where every new aggressive action is met by an opposing defensive counter-action. This would certainly support the view that employers and their associations are reactive but it would not necessarily explain employer initiatives or joint consultative processes.

An example of employer initiatives through their associations can be seen in the establishment of the Employee Relations Study Commission by the Business Council of Australia in 1987. The purpose of this commission was to seek methods of improving the ways in which people work together by changes to the existing industrial relations system (BCA 1994, 28). Other examples are the BCA's *Australia 2010* document or the *Joint Statement on Participative Practices* that was made by the CAI and the ACTU in 1988. This sub title of this document was 'A Cooperative Approach to Improving Efficiency and Productivity in Australian Industry'.

The second model proposed by Jackson and Sisson was the procedural (political) model. This model builds on the defensive model. Once employers and unions have constructed their respective representative bodies they are able to formally recognise each other. The employer associations acknowledge the role and purpose of the union movement while the latter recognises the employers' role and purpose, and their right to manage within their organisations. This mutual recognition then allows for the construction of an agreed framework within which bargaining and negotiation can take place.

In the Australian context, this second model may help to explain the continuing role of both union and employer associations. The emergence of the chambers of commerce and employer federations as well as trade councils allowed a framework to be constructed that allowed the two key parties, employers and employees, to air and settle their grievances. This is in keeping with Dunlop's model and an extension to his web of rules (Dunlop 1977) (see Chapter 1). Also, as Kerr, Dunlop, Harbison and Myers (1964) argued, conflict is necessarily associated with employment as both employers and employees seek security through opposing means and often at the expense of each other. The second model of Jackson and Sisson could explain how these continually arising differences are settled so that they do not totally disrupt industry to the detriment of both parties.

The third model is the market (economic) model and this also builds upon the previous model. This model argues that employers organise along product lines, frequently colluding to reduce market wages. However, although this model may apply to highly competitive industries, it does not apply to less competitive and more labour intensive industries.

The three models put forward by Jackson and Sisson are probably better described as a single three-part model than three independent models. However, they do provide a useful background for explaining how employer associations form and why they continue to evolve and develop. It is yet to be seen if these models will remain applicable to Australia as we further develop Workplace Agreements and enterprise bargaining. They may also be challenged by the Howard Governments' the second wave of industrial reforms which will see further changes to the roles of both trade unions and employer associations.

Streeck

In West Germany in the early 1980s, W.Streeck's research on employer associations also found that the environment played an important role in determining their role and nature. However, Streeck found that role of the 'State' or government was an important influence in determining the issues dealt with by employer associations. Streeck argued that even though associations may have begun as private, state-free organisations, they are used by the state for collective discipline and responsibility.

Dunlop

John Dunlop (1977, 119-128) also noted that the role of governments in the industrial relations system has increased. In Australia the three levels of government (federal, state and local) are significant employers in their own right. Therefore they not only create the political and legal framework in which industrial actors operate, but they also decide industrial relations policies as employers. This 'leading by example' approach can encourage both unions and employers to adopt similar policies. The Federal Government in particular has created mechanisms that not only allow involvement by various parties, but actively encouraged participation.

The National Wage Cases, the various Accords, and the Workplace Relations Act 1996 have all created the need for involvement and research by all parties affected. Similarly, in 1996 when the Victorian Government handed back responsibility for Industrial Relations to the Federal Government, this necessitated greater involvement by all the parties affected.

To a large extent in these and other examples, government has set the agenda for all parties, not just employer associations. Carney (1988, 77-78) discusses the role of employer associations as lobby groups trying to influence government policy and this supports Streeck's thesis that the 'State' can alter the role and nature of such associations. However, this does not mean that the role of employees and their unions, or employers and their associations, are completely responsive to and directed by government policy. On the contrary, it is more often the initiatives of these parties that influence government policy. Nevertheless, Streeck rightly identified the role of government as an active player in an industrial relations system.

Windmuller

In the early 1980s, Windmuller argued that there were five objectives that create the need for employers to band together for the benefit of their collective interests. He believed that one or more of these objectives could influence employers to seek such communal support. He also argued that while the need to achieve these objectives continues, there is a continuing need for the employer association. Windmuller's objectives can therefore be seen not only as reasons for the establishment of employer associations, but also grounds for their continued existence.

The five objectives identified by Windmuller (1984) are set out in Table 4.1. In identifying these objectives Windmuller noted that it is sometimes difficult to separate the trade and industrial relations functions of employer associations, because they are often so interlinked that they are inseparable. It is the last three objectives that are of interest here as they relate specifically to the industrial relations system.

Table 4.1 Windmuller's five objectives of employers forming employer organisations

Objectives of employers forming collective associations to represent their interests
• To regulate mutually agreed issues of trade and competition
• To obtain legislative protection in trade, especially regarding imported goods
• To present a united front against trade unions
• To provide services in labour and personnel management
• To lobby for relevant social and labour legislation

Source: Based on material from Windmuller, J. 'Employers Associations in Comparative Perspective: Organisation, Structure, Administration.' In *Employers Associations and Industrial Relations: A Comparative Study.* Edited by J.P. Windmuller and A. Gladstone. Clarendon Press, Oxford, 1984

The third objective is quite specific, a practical approach for employers to deal with trade unions. Without an employer association, unions can effectively divide and defeat employers. In trying to obtain the best wages and conditions for their members, unions generally can only push toward the industry benchmarks with larger well-informed employers. However, smaller employers can be coerced by industrial action to engage in over award payments, setting a useful precedent. If one employer pays certain wages and provides certain conditions (e.g. a 36 hour week), then unions can use this as the basis for disputes with other employers to gain similar benefits.

However, if employers form an employer association, they not only negotiate centrally, but can ensure that all members are aware of the negotiated benefits. It then becomes much more difficult for individual employers to be served with a log of claims in these areas. The contribution of relevant information to the association, and the dissemination of information to members, provide employers with a powerful communication tool. It allows a uniform flow of information about existing and potential industrial issues, and permits a united front.

Windmuller's fourth objective seeks to establish an association that can provide accurate information and advice. While many large organisations employ specialist staff to deal with human resource and industrial relations issues, the overwhelming number of smaller organisations in Australia do not.

In addition, because the industrial relations system in Australia is rapidly and continually changing, even large organisations with specialist staff still need advice. The employer association is able to provide a range of services that meet the needs of its members. These services generally include expertise in the interpretation of award clauses and support in the construction and wording of workplace agreements. When, for example, the Victorian State Government handed over its responsibility for industrial relations to the Federal Government, many Victorian employers, who were still party to state awards, experienced a great deal of concern and confusion. Many sought advice from their employer association. It is clear, therefore, that the provision of such services is critical to employer associations.

The fifth objective is concerned with employers having input into the construction of legislation that will impact upon them. Such legislation could involve direct changes to industrial relations legislation or it could also concern legislation that could indirectly result in industrial strife. For example, the Labor Government's Button plan, which was designed to improve efficiency within the vehicle industry, included the gradual reduction of industry protection through government import tariffs. This eventually saw Nissan close its major operations and other vehicle manufacturers were forced into retrenchments and redundancies.

Yet while issues such as tariff protection are a common interest among employers and employer associations, these same issues can often cause friction when they bring out diverging opinions and interests. This friction can occur within employer associations or between them. However, the result is often a fragmented approach that inhibits these organisations from presenting an effective united stance. This internal conflict can therefore weaken the influence of employer associations significantly.

In Australia there has also been a growing awareness of the broader role that trade unions and employers can have within the community. There is also a greater awareness of the inter-relatedness of industrial issues with social, economic, political and legal issues. As a result both trade unions and the larger peak employer associations are now concerning themselves with a wider range of issues and acting as lobbyists to the governments on behalf of their members. The governments have responded to this approach by adopting a more consultative approach themselves and gaining views on important issues from a much wider section of the community. This has allowed employer associations to argue that they, like their union counterparts, do indeed represent a large section of the community and therefore should be consulted.

Plowman's Reactivity Thesis

David Plowman who has completed a great deal of research on employer associations in Australia, developed his 'reactivity' thesis to explain the origin and development of employer associations. Plowman believes that the introduction of compulsory arbitration to our nation brought forward the response from employers to band together in associations. Within this framework, employer associations have continued to be predominantly reactive to their environment, as disunity amongst these associations has stifled any proactive initiatives. Plowman argues that several causes are to blame for this reactivity. The multiple award situation that has dominated much of Australia's industrial history has meant that employers have in many instances had to deal with a multitude of unions. Plowman (1992) notes that one company was respondent to over 120 awards at both state and federal level. This, he argues, is one reason why trade unions are proactive and employer associations are reactive.

Another reason he gives is that of the nature of the award-ambit. While employers have moved to contain costs, unions have moved to increase the benefits available to their members. Ambit and the establishment of minimum standards have allowed trade unions the initiative in negotiating for such benefits, while employer associations have waited upon the union movement to utilise this initiative and then respond to it.

The membership of employer associations also limits their ability to respond proactively. Plowman notes that membership of associations consists of small, medium and large organisations with varying degrees of capacity to pay and provide working conditions. In order to overcome this, associations use the lowest common denominator principle, which in turn severely limits the responsiveness of the associations. He also notes that formulating proactive industry-based policies becomes even more difficult for larger and peak associations.

Thornthwaite and Sheldon (1996) and Barry (1995) have recently put forward a number of alternatives to those embraced by Plowman. The former suggest alternative definitions of the terms 'reactivity' and 'proactivity'. They used the former MTIA as an example to develop their view. This association, they argued, rapidly changed in the 1990s as society moved away from traditional industrial relations to non-union collective bargaining, enterprise bargaining and workplace agreements.

Barry (1995, 545-549) attacks the Reactivity thesis on the grounds that the way in which employer associations have emerged and developed in Australia is not unique to this nation. He also does not believe that the thesis explains the development of permanent pre-arbitral associations such as the VEF.

It is an interesting co-incidence that the theories put forward to explain the emergence and development of employer associations also resemble theories put forward to explain the emergence and development of trade unions (see, Tannenbaum 1951; Beatrice and Sidney Webb 1896; Commons 1909).

While the theories reviewed in this section provide an historical perspective of the emergence and early development of employer associations, the late 1990s will offer new challenges for researchers. Employer associations have been given new opportunities without some of the restraints they were previously under. The necessity for a change in their role, function, structure and the services that they provide is clearly shown by the merger of the MTIA and the ACM to form the Australian Industry Group (AIG) (discussed below).

STRUCTURE

The structure of employer associations varies and is dependent upon the number of employer members, the range of services they provide and the type of association they are. Employer associations also provide managers of member organisations with two opportunities. First, they represent the individual and collective interests of member organisations at various levels such as regional, state and federal. This caters to the specific needs of managers of member organisations. Second, the input of members allows managers of member organisations to influence the development of association policies to reflect management philosophy. A predominance of either an individualist or collectivist style management amongst members will therefore show itself through association policies with a tendency towards a unitarist or pluralist stance respectively. Such differences can also lead to internal and inter-association dissension.

Industry Associations

Industry Associations refer to those employer associations that represent a single industry. This would include the AIG, the Oil Industry Industrial Committee, the Australian Paint Manufacturers' Federation Inc, the Retailers Council of Australia, the Housing Industry Association and many others. These associations are national and draw upon members in several or all states. They have a specific focus on one or more specific industries and membership comes from that sector, although in 1995, the MTIA described itself as 'Australia's Manufacturing, Engineering and Construction Industry Association'.

The MTIA and AIG

The MTIA in 1995 had a membership, including affiliates of 6622. These organisations were engaged in those areas listed above. The National Office was located in Canberra while it had Branch Offices in New South Wales, Victoria, Queensland and affiliate offices in Adelaide and Perth. It also had an office in Jakarta. The MTIA was an autonomous association, meaning that it was big, independent and not reliant on support from other associations to provide its member services. Instead, the MTIA provided management services to a number of smaller associations including the Australian Constructors Association (ACA), the Association of Australian Aerospace Industries (AAAI) and the Office Equipment Industry Association (OEIA).

A group of elected members formed the National Executive of the MTIA. The office bearers included a National President, a Deputy National President, National Vice Presidents, the National Secretary-Treasurer and, the Immediate Past National President. Assisting the office bearers were 14 elected members, a small number of alternate members and representatives from the Affiliated Member associations and the National Construction Council (MTIA Annual Report 1995). Elections were held annually. The National Executive members were elected by the state branches and affiliates while the branches elected their own office bearers from representatives of their member organisations. Regular elections were held for the branch office bearers and national committee representatives. This structure ensured that the three state branches, the National Construction Council and affiliates had representation on the National Executive. It also ensured that there was full input into the special groups and task forces at the national level.

A full time Chief Executive oversaw the permanent staff of the association and there was a Director for each of the three main state offices. Other full time staff were responsible for the internal running of the association and the provision of services. These roles included the following areas of responsibility: Finance and Administration, Trade and Commercial Services, Public Affairs and, Industrial Relations.

While Industrial Relations was a major area of interest for the MTIA it also undertook research and reports into a number of other areas, including its role as a shareholder in the Superannuation Trust of Australia. Other areas included International Trade Initiatives, Environmental Issues, Training and Development, Occupational Health and Safety as well as the development of policies into these and other areas affecting members. At the national level there were also specialist groups such as the National Personnel and Industrial Relations Group and the MTIA National Business Strategy Group. The MTIA not only addressed issues of concern to members but it also lobbied the government of their behalf and attempted to influence policies accordingly. The scope of activities varied on different issues due to make up, size and needs of its member organisations.

On 1 July 1998, the MTIA and the Australian Chamber of Manufacturers (ACM) formally merged to form a single industry association known as the Australian Industry Group (AIG). This new Industry Association boasts a membership of over 11,500 companies producing more than $100 billion in output. These member companies employ over 1 million people and produce exports worth more than $25 billion. Specific segments such as the Defence Industry take a high profile within the AIG. Nevertheless, an interesting feature of its activities centres on its recognition of the need for Australian industry to participate and be represented fully in the global economy.

The AIG represents employers from a range of industries but predominantly from the 'Industrial' sector. The structure has remained similar to that of the MTIA in that there are national, state, regional and branch Councils comprised of elected members (mostly Chief Executive Officers of member organisations) under the guidance of a National Executive. The combined resources of both the MTIA and the ACM now provide members with a wider range of services. AIG member services include:

- representation in public policy issues; lobbying; surveys and research; communications; and publications
- trade and international services
- industrial/employee relations issues; enterprise bargaining; contracts of employment; unfair dismissals; equal opportunity; discrimination; disputes avoidance and resolution
- environment, energy and safety including workers compensation and compliance
- training technical skills; group training; management training; training policy and programs
- workforce strategies; human resource consulting/outsourcing
- telephone advice network
- regional services; association management; and industry sector programs.

Services provided by the membership subscription include information, assistance and advice on:
- contract of employment issues
- awards (wage rates and employment conditions)
- tribunal representation
- employee/management negotiations
- award simplification
- dispute resolution
- termination of employment, including redundancy
- workplace agreements (negotiation, drafting, representation)
- recruitment, selection, induction
- contracting out.

Source for the AIG membership information: Herbert 1999, AIG web page

The AIG also provides a range of chargeable services to members and non-members.

The merger of the ACM and the MTIA is consistent with survey findings reported by Mortimer and Still (1999). In this 1998 survey, it was reported that there were a number of employer association mergers and that there was a trend towards fee for service activities. The survey also showed that associations were necessarily drawing on expertise and contacts beyond their state boundaries so that they could provide members with a wider range of services and expertise. However, the most interesting findings were that employer associations were adopting a range of strategies to cope with decentralisation. These included the fee for service activities, providing a wider range of services, better marketing and sensitivity to client needs and drawing on broader levels of expertise.

Thus the merger of the ACM and the MTIA, the array of chargeable services, the broader business and global emphasis are all roughly consistent with those results reported by Mortimer and Still. The AIG has therefore resulted from a recognition of changing Industrial Relations practices in Australia and the need to realign structure, services and activities with a decentralised market.

PEAK ASSOCIATIONS

The Business Council of Australia (BCA) and the Australian Chamber of Commerce and Industry (ACCI) are examples of two peak associations in Australia however their respective memberships and structures are quite different. Both associations are reasonably new in comparison to the ACTU. Both are considered by industry and the Trade Union movement to be peak bodies and both have been highly influential in industrial relations.

ACCI

ACCI came into being in 1992 following the merger of two other employer associations and by 1994 its Annual Report stated that it was representative of over 300,000 organisations. It also stated that its membership included all state and territory-based chambers, employer and national industry associations. (ACCI, Annual Report, 1994). The membership is composed of other smaller associations across a range of industries, rather than individual corporate members, and so it represents these associations on a wide scope of issues at the national level.

Hamilton (1993, 88-90) notes that there were a number of mergers between employer associations at the state level that made the merger to form ACCI go smoothly. These mergers occurred in Western Australia where the Confederation and State Chamber of Commerce merged to form the Chamber of Commerce and Industry of Western Australia. Similar mergers had already occurred in Victoria in 1991 and in South Australia in 1972.

MacIntosh (1993, 60) states that ACCI was a lot more critical of government reform that its predecessors and that a subtle shift in policy occurred after its formation. ACCI supported the replacement of arbitration with individual and collective bargaining at the enterprise level. The previous CAI had wanted to retain the arbitration system as well as introduce a greater emphasis on enterprise bargaining. MacIntosh argued that the change in policy was a reflection of the different membership make up, with a greater emphasis on the needs of small business.

In discussing the formation of ACCI, Hamilton (1993, 90) also points out that the association represents the peak associations at the regional and state levels and most of the national industry associations. This makes it the only national peak council of employer associations in Australia.

BCA

The Business Council of Australia was formed in 1983 but unlike ACCI, it does not have smaller associations as the base of its membership. The BCA has some 80 large Australian Organisations as its members and the Chief Executives of these organisations form the Council and its Board. The Board consists of a President and three Vice Presidents. There are three standing Panels of CEO's forming the following:

- the Economic and Financial Panel
- the Human Resources Panel
- the Business Law and Regulation Panel.

These panels then have a number of committees that investigate and report on specific areas of interest. These include the Employee Relations Committee, the Australia 2010 Action Committee, the International Relations and Trade Committee, the Innovation Task Force and the Greenhouse Reference Group. Executives, other than the CEO's, from the companies represented on the council also staff these committees.

Both ACCI and BCA are supported by full time staff. The BCA is supported by a Secretariat that is headed by an Executive Director. Other positions within the secretariat include an Economic Adviser, a Director for Policy Analysis and Research, and a number of Assistant Directors, Executive Assistants and support staff.

In discussing national employer coordination and structure, Plowman (1991, 146) identified a number of structural models including the following:

1. the mutual defence model
2. the federation model
3. the alliance model
4. the secretariat model
5. the confederation model.

These were models of national employer coordination and each could be located at different stages of history within the development of associations in Australia. The earliest model, the mutual defence model emerged in New South Wales in 1890 during the Maritime Strike when 700 employers decided that it was in their interests to form the Employers Defence Association of Australasia. It was explicitly stated in the organisation's objectives that it was for mutual defence and protection (Plowman 1991, 147).

The federation model saw the joining together of associations to form an employer federation at each state. These state federations then joined to become a confederation at the national level. This allowed member associations to concentrate on their respective areas of interest while joining together at a state level to determine policies and action plans on industrial relations issues that affected them all. However, the diverse range of interests represented, created difficulties of coordination while still allowing for member autonomy.

The alliance model was an attempt to improve on the federation model. Plowman (1991, 152-156) identified the alliance model period from 1917 to 1958 and noted that among the many alliances formed, there were a number of similarities. The similarities were that the alliances were loose-knit and voluntary; employed no full time staff; were restricted to specific roles such as test cases; and that they brought together a large range of state and national employer associations. However once the specific issues were resolved these alliances disbanded.

The secretariat model was describes efforts to achieve coordination on a more permanent basis and first emerged in the 1950s following concerns about the alliance model. The National Employers Association structure followed this model. However, factional disunity lead to its demise and the consequent formation of the confederation model.

The confederation model was an attempt to overcome the difficulties experienced in the formation of previous structures. Plowman (1991, 161) notes that there were at least three variants of this model. They tried to bring into being a confederation that confined its activities to industrial relations and trade related activities.

Plowman does note that these five models were practical given the circumstances of the time and were only superseded as the conditions and needs of employers altered. ACCI can be described as a confederation structure as it brings together the major state associations and provides a permanent form of national representation on issues affecting its members.

The Business Council on the other hand is an authoritative body that relies on the power of its member organisations, which are some of the largest organisations in Australia. It can also become embroiled in industrial relations by initiating research such as that undertaken by its Employee Relations Study Commission. The third report of this committee was released in 1993, was based around McKinsey's new management model and was supported by Fred Hilmer (O'Brien 1994, 468-469).

BARGAINING STRUCTURES

Employer associations undertake a range of functions and provide a number of services to their member organisations. These functions may be stated in the association's charter, constitution or its regulations. These functions may also grow out of the needs of the members or because there is an expectation that such activities will be undertaken (Gladstone 1984, 24-43). The type and range of member services will vary greatly and is dependent upon the size of the association, the resources available to it, the range of employer interests covered and the needs of its members. The provision of services with regard to industrial relations can include:

- research on topics effecting their members
- lobbying governments and influencing policy decisions
- advocacy support and the representation of individual members in settlements
- specialist advice on the interpretation of award clauses, the construction of enterprise agreements etc.
- advice on human resource and occupational health and safety issues
- the provision of training and seminars for members to up-date them on important issues such as legislative changes
- collective bargaining with the trade union movement.

The associations carry out the majority of these functions regularly. They are in constant contact with a range of employers they become aware very quickly of the concerns of their members and any trends that may be emerging. The larger associations also have regular contact with government departments and union officials. They monitor closely issues raised at the AIRC. The associations have regular contact with the majority of players comprising Dunlop's system. They, like their union counterparts, are representative organisations. While they have contact with the management of organisations, they have little if any contact with non-management employees of their member organisations.

Following the move toward greater collective bargaining, this has become a major role of employer associations at the regional, state and national levels. However, given the confrontational approach they have taken towards the unions until the 1980s, mechanisms such as bargaining structures have needed to be put in place to allow effective collective bargaining to occur. The role the associations play as a representative has meant that they have necessarily been involved in the construction of these bargaining structures and procedures, which are used to discuss, investigate, negotiate, collaborate and resolve disputation.

Where a dispute can be settled between an employer and employee or union delegate, employer associations have tended to encourage the settlement of the dispute at this level. Association officers simply provide advice on how best to handle the situation. However, if a dispute escalates to a stage where it involves the majority of the workforce of one or more organisations, or an industry, then the involvement of the association would increase accordingly. Bean (1985, 73) observed that the level of bargaining is more centralised at the national and industry-wide levels than at the enterprise and plant levels. The more widespread the impact, the greater the involvement of employer associations as the dispute impacts on more member organisations.

The change from conciliation and arbitration to enterprise bargaining represents a change in bargaining structure, as well as a change from a centralised level of bargaining to a decentralised level (Thornthwaite and Sheldon 1996, 174). It also allows for less involvement by governments and unions and is a shift towards returning the responsibility for resolving industrial conflict to the parties engaged in the employment relationship: the employer and employees. This also alters the role of the employer association as well. Nevertheless, in contradiction of Plowman's reactivity theory, a number of employer associations have shown strong initiative in seeking change.

Both the BCA and ACCI, key peak employer associations, have taken the initiative as proponents of change to these different bargaining structures. Prior to the late 1980s there was more evidence of Plowman's reactivity theory among employer associations. They were disorganised and there was widespread disagreement as to how the bargaining structures should be shaped. The period prior to the Accord was characterised by decentralised militancy (Thornthwaite and Sheldon 1996, 175). However, the emergence of the CAI and later the BCA, saw not only national coordination of employer associations but also a more coherent approach to the bargaining process. The recent role of ACCI and BCA has shown how important effective national employer associations can be in influencing bargaining structures.

Another key employer association, the MTIA, was also proactive during this period. In 1986 the association undertook a survey of its members and the outcome of this survey was a shift in policy with regard to reforming the industry bargaining structure and a focus on bargaining at the enterprise level. A range of initiatives to achieve these objectives was put to the metal industry unions in that year. As the MTIA pursued its objectives for structural change, other employer associations and the Federal Coalition in Opposition also began to push for decentralisation. However, the MTIA considered that its members wished to retain the federal award-based framework while moving towards enterprise bargaining. So it was in open conflict with other associations pushing for deregulation and even greater decentralisation. In 1988 the MTIA obtained its goal, when the introduction of the Structural Efficiency Principle allowed enterprise bargaining to be explored within the existing confines of the Arbitration Commission.

In the 1980s, there was also a push by new right employers and their associations for change to industrial bargaining levels and structures. A number of aggressive individual employers, supported and encouraged by their equally determined employer associations, actively challenged the role and rights of the Trade Union movement. These cases included Mudginberri (1985), Robe River (1986) and the Dollar Sweets case in 1988.

Another change to the structure and levels of bargaining occurred when the Kennett Government in Victoria, a significant employer in itself, decided to abandon state responsibility for industrial relations in favour of Federal Government control. If other states were to follow, the Australian system of industrial relations would certainly be streamlined and potentially more effective. (However, following the power dispute in Victoria in February 2000, the Victorian Bracks Labor Government may try to revive a state industrial relations system. If Victoria recovers the powers it ceded to the Federal Government, this would check the trend described above.)

In summary, it is clear that at the national level there has been a substantial change in policy by employer associations, which are now more effectively organised and more willing to take the initiative in seeking industrial change. In fact, the combined efforts of these associations, together with overall union agreement and political pressure, have brought about change in the structure and level of collective bargaining. The ongoing move towards workplace agreements and enterprise bargaining also reduces the need for state intervention, although it does lend itself to central coordination by federal legislation. These changes mean a change to the role and services provided by employer associations, the trade union movement, and the state and federal governments.

THE WORKPLACE RELATIONS ACT 1996

The Workplace Relations Act 1996 introduced sweeping changes to the Australian industrial relations system and its participants. As trade unions began to react to these changes, so too did the employer associations. The changes that were introduced included an emphasis on enterprise bargaining and a reduction in the centralised functions of the Australian Industrial Relations Commission. Employer associations adapted in some or all of the following ways:

- attempting to achieve economies of scale through mergers
- the provision of fee for service arrangements
- the provision of services for those members affected by globalisation
- increased competition
- increased work based flexibility
- more accessible and 'user friendly' structures.

These changes in the structure and activities of employer associations cannot be seen as simply a reaction to a threat to their relevance or existence under the new Act. Indeed, the Workplace Relations Act 1996 provides recognition of employer associations and their ongoing role within the industrial relations system. The Objects of the Act refer directly to employer associations: Object (f) ensures the freedom of employers and employees to join or not join the association of their choice; Object (g) ensures that employer and employee associations properly represent their membership and are accountable to them. (See also Chapter 9 for a discussion of the Workplace Relations Act 1996.)

THE ASIAN PERSPECTIVE

Compared to our Asian neighbours, Australia has a rather unique form of industrial relations. However, it is not unique within the western world. Much of our system was established in the 1800s and was heavily influenced by the British heritage of the first European settlers. The first settlers brought with them the foundations of our culture, which while it clashed with the indigenous culture, was to become the dominant culture of the nation. Our industrial relations system, like our legal and political structures, therefore closely resembles the British system. This is not the case in most Asian countries. With regard to employer associations, Barry (1995, 543) noted that just as Australian associations have received little attention from researchers compared to trade unions, much the same can be said about our Asian neighbours.

Japan

Japan has a history and culture that is ancient in comparison to that of Australia. However, the devastation of World War 11 saw the American military occupation government attempt to eradicate political groups, including trade unions. In order to suppress these possibly communist organisations, the occupation government encouraged the growth and development of enterprise-based unions which are now a feature of modern Japan (Deery and Mitchell 1993, 6). As a result, enterprise unions negotiate with the management of individual enterprises, rather than seeking wider forms of collective bargaining such as industry or national bargaining. The level and structure of bargaining is therefore somewhat different to Australia and the role of employer associations is correspondingly different.

There is nevertheless a bargaining role for employer associations in Japan. This is because the enterprise unions are linked together and do join up for the annual 'Spring Offensive' (or 'Shunto') in which the Japanese Trade Union Confederation ('Rengo') negotiates an annual percentage increase in the wages of members. The counterpart of the Rengo is the 'Nikkeiren' or the Japanese Federation of Employer Associations. While negotiations take place between these bodies first, they are both severely restricted by enterprise bargaining. They tend to negotiate only the procedures and policies. It is the enterprise unions that negotiate directly with their individual enterprises for the minimum wage and conditions, so the impact of the national campaign is minimal. Similarly, the close working relationship between management and union members at the enterprise level in effect means that most negotiation on wider issues also takes place here. It is interesting to note that it is common for the unions to be the active pacesetters for such negotiations and for the employer associations to undertake a more reactive role.

Singapore

The tripartite relationship between the government, employers and unions in Singapore is very close. The Secretary General of the union peak body the National Trade Union Congress (NTUC) is a senior minister in the ruling government. The focus of the government is on continual economic improvement, with industrial relations as a high priority. The government therefore takes an active and controlling role. With government control and a strong tripartite industrial system, bargaining structures and levels are set. While employer associations still represent the interests of their members, the government consults publicly and regularly with both the employer associations and the NTUC.

The most important of Singapore's tripartite bodies is the National Wages Council (NWC), which comprises the NTUC, the government and employer associations. Among the largest associations are the Singapore National Employers Federation (SNEF), which represents over 900 local and international employers, and the Singapore Manufacturers Association. There are only five registered employer associations in Singapore representing over 1000 organisations (Leggett 1994, 100).

Collective bargaining is not restricted to the NWC. Employer associations and unions are free to negotiate outside this and other government advisory bodies. However, legislation restricts the issues that can be discussed. The role of employer associations, therefore, is to provide research and member services, while representing members' interests within the tightly controlled government framework. These limitations also apply equally to the unions and peak bodies such as the NTUC. Where disputes arise, employer associations may provide representation and advocacy. However, the dispute will generally be resolved by conciliation arranged through the appropriate government department.

With the role and function of employer associations and unions so openly controlled and directed by the government, Streeck's theory could perhaps be said to apply. (Streeck argued that the agendas of employer associations are strongly moulded by government policy and that governments may even draw free associations into the legal and enforcement structure.) While Streeck's study was in West Germany, the governments of both of these countries aim to achieve economic superiority for their respective nations. However, the reason for the adoption of this controlled system and the methods used to achieve it are predictably different.

Malaysia

In 1990, less than 10 per cent of the workforce in Malaysia was unionised and, due to controlling legislation, most of these unions were small. Only the public service sector was dominated by larger unions. Legislation provided that membership of unions, including employer associations, must be from Malaya, Sabah or Sarawak, and that members must belong to similar occupations, trades or industries. Ayadurai (1994, 71) points out that even union federations must conform to the second requirement, that is to have members from specific or related occupations. Malaysian bargaining structures and levels of bargaining are controlled by legislation. While employer associations can provide advice, advocacy and representation, over 80 per cent of disputes are resolved through conciliation.

The peak employer association is the Malaysian Employers' Federation (MEF), which advises its members on collective bargaining issues as well as representing their interests on tripartite national bodies. The MEF was formed in 1978 with a membership comprising over 1000 individual corporations and seven employer associations. This diversity means that it is required to provide a wide range of membership services. After breaking away from the MEF, the Malaysian Council of Employers' Organisations (MCEO) was formed in 1982, comprising two employer associations.

The MEF's union counterpart is the Malaysian Trades Union Congress (MTUC), the peak union body, which represents over half the country's union members. However, as its membership does not in conform to industrial legislation, it is registered as a society. The MTUC's power is therefore somewhat limited and there would appear to be an imbalance of power between the two peak bodies. However, both peak organisations may be represented in industrial forums and both are consulted by government on relevant industrial issues. Similarly, both form part of fact-finding bodies and are able to make submissions to the government.

The Malaysian Government has actively striven for industrial peace to further its aim of greater economic performance, as outlined in its Industrial Master Plan and its Vision 2020. It has used its interventionist policies and legislation to ensure compliance by both industrial parties to the national objectives. Through tripartite bodies, voluntary collective bargaining, the maintenance of small and fragmented unions, and its push for greater efficiency and productivity, the government has ensured that the peak bodies have focussed on the intended agenda and are working closely together.

Hong Kong

The Hong Kong industrial relations system has been heavily influenced by the British, who have controlled the country, and by the culture of the Chinese. Because union involvement at the workplace is poorly developed, union intervention has been limited. There is also no legislation requiring an employer to recognise or bargain with a trade union, and so collective bargaining is considered to be underdeveloped.(Levin and Ng Sek Kong 1994, 28-42).

There are several kinds of employer associations in Hong Kong, with many registered as societies. There are the industry specific associations, chambers of commerce and manufacturers' associations and merchant associations. The industry-based associations and the umbrella associations are more reminiscent of the Australian types of associations. This is not surprising as both were heavily influenced by British models.

The Employers' Federation of Hong Kong is one association that was specifically created to deal with industrial relations issues. However, with less than 4 per cent of labour being covered by collective agreements, the role of the employer association is quite different. Levin and Ng Sek Hong (1994, 41) noted that the craft unions and the respective employer associations produce documented agreements annually, which focus on minimum wages and overtime. In the more modern manufacturing sectors such as printing, open-ended agreements have been reached between the unions and the relevant employer association. Similarly in the cotton textile sector, collective agreements have been reached between the employer association and the unions.

However, in many other parts of industry, union membership is low and therefore collective agreements do not exist. This low level of collective bargaining limits the role of the employer associations to providing advocacy and representation. They also provide advice, research, feedback on important issues, representation on national tripartite bodies, and lobbying on trade issues. While these services may be vast in themselves, the industrial relations component is significantly less than in their Australian counterparts.

Equally, however, the FTU, the peak union federation, does not see itself as having a role in collective bargaining on behalf of its members. Evidence suggests that member unions deliberately avoid confrontation with employers and the government. Suggestions have been made that an older and ineffectual leadership is the problem (Levin and Ng Sek Kong 1994, 42). In any case, such circumstances suggest that while the structure of employer associations in Hong Kong is similar to that of Australia, its role and functions are differ.

The hand-over of Hong Kong to China has seen intense pressure put on the Hong Kong economy and business community to continue to perform well rather than deteriorate. Therefore, it is expected that it will take some years for the formal industrial relations framework to alter to conform to any changes in work practices that the new government may introduce. The role and status of the unions and of the employer associations could therefore also be expected to remain unchanged for some time.

South Korea

As in the cases of Malaysia and Singapore, the South Korean Government has pursued an active interventionist policy in industrial relations, although this policy may have softened in recent years. Unlike neighbouring nations, legislation exists that guarantees collective bargaining to those employed in the private sector, with more limited rights for those in the public domain (Young - Ki 1994, 142-143). A low level of unionism is characteristic of South Korea. The only union body registered with and recognised by the South Korean Government is the Federation of Korean Trade Unions (FKTU). While there are other national bodies in existence, these do not have official recognition.

There are two types of employer association in South Korea. The first deals exclusively with labour issues. For example, the Korean Federation of Employers' Associations (KFEA) was formed in 1970 and draws members from the manufacturing sector (organisations employing 300 or more employees) as well as from the banking and insurance sectors. The second type concerns itself with overall management problems including labour related issues. For example, the Korean Chamber of Commerce and Industry (KCCI) was founded in 1884 and membership is mandatory to all businesses founded as a legal person. It deals with all business issues and is the official representative of all business sectors in South Korea. Another example is the Federation of Korean Industries (FKI), which was founded in 1961. FKI membership is dependent upon sales or budget and is open to organisations with annual sales of 50 billion won or more (and trade associations with a budget of 1 billion won or more). Both the KCCI and the FKI undertake research, collect data and provide members with advice on labour related issues. Another major association is the Korean Foreign Trade Association (KFTA) which was formed in 1946. Membership is mandatory for all organisations involved in import and export. It promotes and protects the interests of its members.

The Labour Union Law (LUL) has an important bearing on the role and activities of employer associations. This law requires employers to bargain collectively with a unionised workforce. Collective bargaining takes place at three levels; the national level, the multi-employer or regional level, and local enterprise level. Employer associations may be involved at any level to provide advice, but are normally involved at the regional and national levels. As unions are organised along industry lines, this is also where employer associations are usually most active. An interesting point is that the LUL requires only the chief executive of a union or an empowered worker representative to bargain. However, penalties on employers engaged in a prohibited practice are quite severe.

Industrial conflict can cause a great deal of disruption and in South Korea the interests of the public are paramount. Under South Korean legislation, disputes are dealt with by the Labour Relations Commission (LRC), which also operates at the national, local and at special levels levels. The Commission operates on a tripartite system, which requires representation at the national level by employers, unionists and public interest representatives. The employers and union officials nominate their representatives for a period of three years. In effect, the South Korean Government's tight control of the industrial relations system through legislation, and its restrictions on unions and workers, have also forced employer associations to accept their part in this government-dominated tripartite system.

CONCLUSION

The Australian industrial relations system has a number of key players. This chapter has attempted to present an overview of one of these players, the representative body of employer collectives, the employer associations. These associations started to appear informally from the 1850s onward, although they were transient and were generally formed to cope with a specific industrial crises, or to promote and discuss trade and tariff related issues. Once these issues were adequately dealt with, the associations were disbanded.

These early associations were based around regions, states, trades and occupations, with the result that a number of diverse associations emerged. However, the introduction of compulsory arbitration was a strong signal to employers that they needed to work toward greater unity and coordination. The early establishment of the Trades and Labour Councils and the ACTU, as well as the political movement of the Labor Party, were also spurs to employers to seek greater coordination.

Three types of employer associations emerged, although their functions and activities varied. Only those with an industrial relations focus have been discussed in this chapter. The first of these is the 'umbrella association' that draws its membership from a range of industries such as employer federations, chambers of commerce and industry, and chambers of manufacturers. These associations are generally formed on a regional and state basis. The second type is the 'industry association'. These associations draw their membership from specific or related industries. The third employer association discussed is the 'peak association'. These are formed at a national level.

Several theories have been examined in an attempt to explain the emergence and continued development of employer associations. These theories, where possible, have been reviewed in chronological order to illustrate how the theories evolved over time. An attempt was also made to apply these theories to the Australian system.

- Commons argued that improved communication and transportation were factors contributing to market expansion and hence to the need for mutual protection.
- Hoxie argued that the opposing interests of each party saw employers and unions engage in activities that promoted their individual cause.
- McCaffree's argued that growth in political and economic conditions, more sophisticated markets and the growth of unionism were all environmental influences that necessitated improved employer coordination and national structures.

- Jackson and Sisson put forward three interlinked models to explain the employer association phenomenon: the 'defensive model' offsetting union initiative and aggression; the 'procedural (legal) model' where union and employer associations were necessary for the parties to bargain; and the 'economic model' which suggested collusion for mutual benefit.
- Streeck argued that in West Germany, the state played a part in the function of associations.
- Windmuller suggested that there were five main objectives that could explain employer associations. These were listed in Table 4.1.
- Plowman's Reactivity Thesis in which employers through their disunity, poor coordination and diverseness were basically reactive parties while the unions took the initiative. Alternatives by Barry, Thornthwaite and Sheldon were put forward to counter or explain Plowman thesis.

The MTIA (AIG), ACCI and the BCA were examined to give an indication of the similarities and variations in structure, role and function. The MTIA/AIG and BCA were the primary examples used to highlight the structures of these associations although it was noted that other structures were common.

The bargaining structures, in which employer associations and their counterparts operate, were also examined. Recent examples were used to show how these structures operate and how they have changed.

The role of employer associations was examined in the five selected Asian countries: Japan, Singapore, Malaysia, Hong Kong and South Korea. The differences and similarities between employer associations in Australia and these nations were examined. In particular we have looked at their structure; the factors that have influenced their development; the type of bargaining structures and their role in them; and their relationship with government.

REVIEW QUESTIONS

1. Discuss the emergence and early development of employer associations in Australia.
2. Discuss the nature and role of the three major types of employer associations.
3. Identify the means of interaction between the three major types of employer associations and each of the following:
    - trade unions
    - employers
    - employees of organisations
    - state and federal governments
    - other employer associations
    - the AIRC

4. Discuss the theories presented. Identify those that you feel adequately explain the emergence and development of employer associations in Australia. Are there any other possible explanations?
5. Have association's structures continued to change?

6. Given the nature of bargaining structures, can you identify the potential future role of employer associations?

7. Discuss the different structures and roles of the BCA, AIG and ACCI.

8. Are Australian employer associations significantly different compared to those of our Asian neighbours? Why? If not, why not?

9. Given the impact of the Workplace Relations Act 1996, what role will employer associations play in the future?

FURTHER READING

Plowman, D. (1989) *Holding the Line: Compulsory Arbitration and National Employer Coordination in Australia.* Cambridge University Press, Sydney.

Plowman, D. (1992) 'Employer Associations and Industrial Reactivity' in Dabscheck, B., and Griffin, G. (eds.) *Contemporary Australian Industrial Relations*, Longman Cheshire, Melbourne, 225-242.

Michael, B. (1995) 'Employer Associations: Assessing Plowman's Reactivity Thesis.' *Journal of Industrial Relations*, vol. 37, no. 4, 543-561.

Plowman, D. (1989) 'Countervailing power, organisational parallelism and Australian employer associations.' *Australian Journal of Management*, vol.13, no 3.

Deery, S. and Mitchell, R. (eds.) (1993) *Labour Law and Industrial Relations in Asia.* Longman Cheshire, Melbourne.

CHAPTER 5

Trade Unions: Structures, Functions and Future

'Adversity has the effect of eliciting talents, which in prosperous circumstances would have lain dormant.'

Horace (Roman Poet, 65-8 B.C.)

LEARNING OBJECTIVES

This chapter deals with the role of trade unions in contemporary society. It also attempts to identify contemporary issues of relevance to trade unions. Towards the end of this chapter trade unionism in our five selected South East Asian countries is also reviewed. At the end of this chapter you should be able to:

- understand the role of trade unions
- identify the different types of trade unions
- highlight the changing role of trade unions
- understand the reasons for the decline in trade union membership in Australia in the 1990s
- briefly identify trends in trade union structure, functions and activities in five selected South East Asian countries.

INTRODUCTION

Why study trade unions? Trade unions have historically played an important role in regulating wages and conditions. Trade unions also have other functions. As labour market institutions, trade unions influence the way in which labour is bought and sold in the labour market. In this sense, unions seek to remove labour from the forces of competition. As political and social agents of change, unions are complex organisations and they influence government social, economic and political decisions. How do trade unions come to exercise such influence? To answer this, we need to know what trade unions are?

The classic definition is that a trade union is an ongoing association of wage-earners with the purpose of maintaining or improving their working conditions (see, Webb and Webb 1894, 1). As Martin points out, the single constant defining feature of trade unions is that they organise workers collectively (1989, 97). However, the goals unions pursue and the way they organise varies considerably according to the characteristics of the union, industry location and history.

Trade unions have existed in Australia since soon after European settlement. They have grown from a small collection of mutual benefit associations (for the purpose of supporting members in social and employment issues) to large sophisticated organisations influencing a range of political, social and economic issues. These issues sometimes take shape in what the media often refers to as the 'union agenda'. Modern trade unions were borne out of the sometimes-bitter struggle and upheavals between employers and employees during the late eighteenth and early nineteenth centuries over the right of working men and women to collectively negotiate their wages and conditions. Union activity has always been fraught with danger. During medieval times, those who sought to organise workers to gain improvements in working conditions may have been jailed, put to death or worse, conscripted into the army! Indeed, even in the 20th Century, union organisers and striking workers have been jailed and shot by police. Despite the dangers, the notion of mutual benefit societies set up to control the supply of labour is not a new one. The craft guilds and artisan collectives during the Middle Ages were essentially performing a trade union function of protecting the welfare of their members.

While the media made much about the role of the Maritime Union of Australia (MUA) during the 1998 waterfront dispute (see MUA Case Study), professional associations are also powerful 'guilds' set up to protect the economic or political interests of their members. The Australian Medical Association (AMA) and the specialist medical colleges exert considerable influence in the labour market by setting fees and limiting the numbers of persons who are licensed to practice medicine. This ensures that the medical profession remains one of the most influential professions in Australia.

Trade unions are important labour market regulators because they act to control the supply and conditions under which skill or labour is employed. Unions also ration labour in order to ensure work for their members. Some researchers see the role of trade unions as a counteracting force in the workplace, overcoming what is often seen as an unequal or a–symetrical bargaining relationship between employers and workers. At its simplest, this tension between unions and employers can be described as the conflict between a collectivist (institutional) and an individualist (human resource management) approach to workplace regulation.

Trade unions in Australia during the late 19th Century took a significant step in actively influencing the political agenda by forming a political 'wing' which subsequently became known as the Australian Labor Party (ALP). The purpose was to encourage Parliament to pass labour laws more favourable to working men and women. The study of trade unions therefore is also the study of social and political institutions. Trade unions are complex and diverse organisations. They differ in size, structure, membership composition, organisational strength and militancy. This leads to a number of questions such as, what do trade unions do? Why do people join unions? Why do we have the types of unions that we do? Finally, how is the role of unions changing? This chapter examines the role of trade unions and looks at the debate about the role of trade unions in the workplace.

THEORIES OF TRADE UNIONISM

Why have trade unions developed? A number of theories have been advanced to explain the origins, purpose, functions and strategies of trade unions. Here we provide a brief overview of some of these theories, and examine their relevance to Australia and the five Asian countries discussed in this book.

Sydney and Beatrice Webb Labour Theories

The pioneers in the study of trade union history in the UK were Sydney and Beatrice Webb, referred to above. As Fabian Socialists, they were committed to a philosophy of gradual change, by working within the institutions of liberal democratic capitalism to bring about socialism by evolution. They carried out a exhaustive examination of trade union records to write the first comprehensive history of trade unionism in the UK. In the process, they developed theories about the origins, functions and strategies employed by the British labour movement. As Australia began as a British colony, and the early Australian trade unions were branches of their British parent bodies, as we point out below, it might be expected that the Webbs' ideas would have considerable relevance to Australian unions.

In their analysis of the British labour movement, the Webbs (1894) argued that its *modus operandi* could be reduced to the use of two devices, three methods and three doctrines. The devices were named 'restriction of numbers' and the 'common rule'. The restriction of numbers was a method used by craft unions to restrict entry to their trades. It involved imposition of rules involving lengthy and demanding apprenticeship requirements, as well as relatively high entrance fees. This was an obvious attempt to protect job rights, and establish favourable conditions of employment for those who became fully qualified in their respective trades. The Webbs condemned these tactics, on the grounds that they were both unfair, in excluding large numbers of aspiring workers from certain occupations, and that they retarded economic progress. They initially believed that pressure of public opinion would compel unions to drop these tactics, but later conceded that this was unrealistic thinking. The Webbs, also identified the union device known as the 'common rule' concerned with establishing and enforcing a 'going rate'. The purpose of this was to prevent employers from pushing down wages and working conditions to subsistence levels, and thus forcing workers into the position of an exploited under class competing with one another for jobs.

The Webbs distinguished three methods used in the creation of unionism. The first involves the method of mutual insurance. This encompassed activities such as the collection of funds to assist workers who lost their jobs or fell on hard times despite the efforts of unions to protect them. Insurance benefits covered contingencies such as accidents, funeral benefits, unemployment, pensions, and payments to widows. Historically, together with job protection, provision of these mutual and self-help benefits were among the oldest objectives of British trade unions. Such benefits might enable workers to survive when they encountered hard times and provided incentives to individuals to join trade unions. The benefits also gave trade unions muscle in bargaining with employers, as the funds built up could be used to support workers on strike. They could also serve to ensure that members did not seek work at starvation wages, and thereby helped to keep up the general level of wages to at least a minimum level.

The second method, collective bargaining, was a tactic to try to ensure that workers negotiated collectively with employers to achieve the common rule. Workers united in a group enjoyed greater strength dealing with employers than if they were compelled to negotiate individually. The Webbs observed that collective bargaining could be employed at a local level in the workplace, at a regional level or at a national level. The ultimate objective was the establishment of machinery at each of these levels, with a view to spreading the benefits of collective bargaining as broadly and as evenly as possible. Interestingly, the Webbs viewed conciliation and arbitration as part of the process of collective bargaining (that is, using an external third party in the negotiation process). They actually visited the Australian colonies in 1898, and were interested observers of the early experiments in Australia with compulsory conciliation and arbitration. In the Webbs' view, conciliation and arbitration could add professionalism to the rather random, haphazard and amateurish practice of collective bargaining that existed in Britain. They argued that trained conciliators and arbitrators allowed employers and trade unions to reach swifter, better and more mutually acceptable agreements.

The third method was to seek legal enactment. This effectively involved trade unions acting as pressure groups, to secure benefits for organised labour and encouraging parliament to pass legislation favourable to working people. The Webbs saw considerable advantages in this method. Once an Act had been passed, it represented the most enduring protection for workers, and was much more recession-proof than collectively bargained agreements, which could always be altered or abandoned if economic conditions worsened. However, ironically, the Webbs warned trade unions of the dangers of becoming involved in party politics, for fear of creating divisions in the ranks of workers. But while British workers enthusiastically embraced pressure group lobbying in the 19th Century, they ignored the Webbs' warnings about involvement with party politics. The British Labour Party was established in 1899 with strong trade union backing, and trade unions became an integral part of its internal structure.

Finally, the Webbs referred to three different doctrines which trade unions use to justify their activities. First, the doctrine of vested interests or protection of job rights was seen as analogous to property rights and the right of business to trade. Workers were justified in resisting attempts to undermine their established employment conditions and their 'job rights' just as much as property owners and business owners in protecting their interests. Second, the doctrine of supply and demand conceded that trade unions operate in a competitive capitalist environment. Trade unions should use their collective strength in good times when their bargaining power is strong to improve the lot of their members, though in bad times they might be forced to give ground. The Webbs' deplored the fact that economic power determined outcomes in this way. As they pointed out, it was particularly unfortunate that such matters as hours of work and safety could be determined in this manner, rather than through the needs of different trades and occupations. Finally, there was the doctrine of state power as a public good. They hoped that the establishment of a national minimum wage might help to reduce the impact of economic recessions on workers.

Much of what the Webbs' wrote about British trade unions is readily applicable to Australia. Australian unions have employed all the methods outlined by the Webbs', including political lobbying, active use of the conciliation and arbitration tribunals, and in more recent times, collective bargaining. They have also used essentially the same doctrines as those outlined by the Webbs to justify their actions. On the other hand, the Webbs' concept of conciliation and arbitration was very different from the way a system of compulsory conciliation and arbitration developed in Australia. Arguably, Australian unions could almost be seen as creatures of the system using it for the benefit of their members. However, the most enduring aspect of the work of the Webbs may be their methodology. As empiricists, the Webbs were responsible for examining the ways in which trade unions actually went about their business. They thereby highlighted the need to understand key institutions in the labour market and the ways in which they interact.

The Webbs' theory seems less applicable to the development of trade unions in the Asian countries. Essentially, the theory was based on the assumption that trade unions are a legitimate institution in a developing liberal democracy. In both Britain and Australia, these conditions were met. In the Asian countries, this was not necessarily the case. For example, until relatively recently, Malaysia, Singapore, and Hong Kong were colonies, with at best very limited forms of representative government. Trade unions were not encouraged by the British colonial regime, which sought to maximise employer power and market forces to create an important centre of trade and commerce. Neither Singapore nor Malaysia could be considered a liberal democracy following independence, and both placed considerable restrictions on trade unions. In Japan, unions were subject to tough restrictions during the early period of industrialisation. Japanese Governments were never really democratic, and a military dictatorship with fascist overtones seized power in Japan in the early 1930s. Independent trade unions were effectively suppressed or were used by the military regime to support the war. Only following World War II, did Japan develop into a genuine democracy with the American occupation authorities using unions to help break up the large Japanese pre-war military/industrial conglomerates. The occupation government also promoted democratic unions in the face of the communist victory in China in 1949. But even after World War II, significant cultural differences in Japan make the Webbs' analysis of trade unions of limited value in understanding the Japanese industrial relations system. Korea, on the other hand, was a colony of Japan from 1910-1945, with brutal suppression of any institutions that might oppose the Japanese colonial government. Following liberation from Japanese rule, South Korea became a military dictatorship until the late 1980s, with continuing restrictions on the labour movement.

Marxist Theory of Class Conflict

In Chapter 1, we examined the Marxist frame of reference. As we saw there, Marxist theory is based on the idea of class conflict, or exploitation by the ruling class of the underclass of workers or proletariat. Lenin, the leader of the Bolshevik Revolution in Russia, spelt out the role of trade unions in the struggle to replace capitalism and exploitation with socialism and the classless society. According to Lenin (1928), the role of trade unions was to raise revolutionary consciousness among workers. He noted that trade unions originally arose under capitalism to improve the economic lot of workers. However, according to most Marxists, it is futile for workers to attempt to redistribute wealth through methods such as collective bargaining and political lobbying within a democratic framework. This is because of the inevitable tendencies of capitalism, with its fierce competition between enterprises, forcing wages down to subsistence levels. Thus any gains won by means such as collective bargaining or political lobbying are purely temporary, and will be taken back by employers in the long run.

Therefore, the true objective of trade unions, according to Lenin, was political rather than economic - to raise revolutionary consciousness among workers to ultimately overthrow the whole capitalist system. Strikes, whatever their outcome in economic terms, were seen as a useful means of raising this consciousness. Lenin noted that many trade union leaders, who rose from within the working class, were only concerned with the narrow objective of improving the wages and conditions of their members. He called this approach 'reformism', and considered that they were misled, or were suffering from 'false consciousness', and had to be replaced by revolutionary intellectuals, who understood the true purpose of trade unions. Lenin was aware of the role and activities of Australian trade unions before World War I, and was very scornful of their reformist character. In Chapter One, we examined some criticisms of Marxist theory, including its view of unions and the assumption that intellectuals are the true union leaders. According to contemporary writers such as Hyman, (1975) the Marxist perspective shows the real nature of the capitalist system and its inherent class conflict between the owners of capital and workers. However, the Marxist approach has declined in popularity since communist system in Eastern Europe and the Soviet Union collapsed and China adopted State sponsored capitalism.

In Australia, particularly during the period from the Great Depression until the early 1950s, communists who accepted Lenin's ideas held office in some important unions (see below). However, while the communist leaders of trade unions were believers in the Marxist political ideology, most of those who supported them were not. Their support was for the communists' industrial policy, which secured economic gains for the members. Once the communists overplayed their hand, as they did in the coal strike of 1949 (see below), their support in the unions rapidly declined. According to Howard (1977, 257), the communists in Australian trade unions generated no real revolutionary impetus, and thus failed in the ultimate objective of trade unions in Marxist theory. Similar observations could be made about the role of communists in trade unions in Japan and Singapore. In those countries, there was considerable turbulence in the 1940s and 1950s, as communists exploited the industrial grievances of workers in the post-war era. However, once these societies began to experience rapid economic growth, and workers achieved genuine gains in their standard of living, communist influence declined rapidly. In Singapore, of course, the former government of Lee Kuan Yew also assisted this decline by measures to suppress the Communist Party in all political and social spheres.

Perlman's Theory

Perlman was an American writer of Russian origin, who was more or less a contemporary of the Webbs. Perlman (1949) developed a theory from his examination of the development of trade unions in Britain, Germany, Russia and the United States. Originally a follower of Karl Marx, Perlman later abandoned Marxist ideas, and adopted instead the ideas of the American writer John Commons (1913) as his guiding philosophy. Commons had developed the thesis that trade unions and collective bargaining were essential parts of the democratic fabric of American society, and a bulwark against totalitarianism. Perlman argued that the character and form of the labour movement in any society was governed by the interplay between three groups in that society: capitalists or the business class, manual workers and intellectuals. The business classes were the risk-takers in society. They were opportunity conscious, and prepared to seize economic opportunities for profit, even though their ventures might fail. Perlman viewed this class as essential to the progress of society, as their willingness to take risks was necessary to found business enterprises that would provide employment for workers and taxes for governments.

The manual workers, on the other hand, were security or scarcity conscious. As the demand for jobs tended to exceed the supply, workers were anxious to hold onto the jobs they had succeeded in getting. Perlman argued that workers formed and joined unions for the purpose of controlling and administering scarce job opportunities. The role of unions was to establish job rights, and ensure that employers adhered to those rights as far as possible. This, of course, involved placing limits on employers' rights to hire and fire. The character of unions was thus essentially non-ideological. In the US, it became known as business unionism. Unions accepted the legitimacy of capitalism, and sought benefits from it, but wished to place limits on its excesses in the interests of their members. Perlman believed that craft unions were the most cohesive form of union and created, through craft consciousness, the strongest bonds between workers. However, scarcity consciousness could also create other forms of union structure. Perlman also argued that unionists could employ any method of industrial action in pursuit of their goal of job preservation, including collective bargaining, strikes and political lobbying.

The third group, intellectuals, come from outside the trade union movement. They were typically of middle-class origin. Intellectuals sought to influence and re-direct the activities of trade unions towards their own vision of a better society. Trade unions were the vehicles chosen by intellectuals to realise their vision. There were three kinds of intellectuals, according to Perlman. Revolutionary intellectuals who were interested in replacing capitalism with some form of socialism, and using any means to achieve their ends. Marxist intellectuals were a typical example. Ethical intellectuals were interested in inspiring workers to throw off the chains of authority in industry, but not to the extent of smashing the whole social system. Their thrust was towards industrial democracy, with elected managers, and workers' rights to participate at the highest levels of industry. Examples of this type of intellectual were the Christian Socialists, who advocated self-governing workshops, and the anarchists, who argued for labour communes. The final group of intellectuals was described as efficiency intellectuals, attracted to the idea of a planned economic order. Their vision of society was one in which disorganisation was replaced with order, and waste and social deprivation were progressively eliminated. An example of this type of intellectual approach was the English Fabian Socialists, including the Webbs, who viewed organised labour as having a strong economic and moral function.

Perlman was critical of intellectuals, and warned trade unions to be wary of outsiders who might attempt to interfere by framing policies and programs not in the best interests of workers. He also differed from the Webbs, in opposing their notion that workers should abandon the device of restriction of numbers and leave it to the employer to decide who should work at the level of pay set by the common rule. Based on his comparative study of trade unions in four different countries, Perlman concluded that three factors shaped the direction of trade union movements:

- capitalism's power to resist the demands of organised labour
- the extent of the influence of intellectuals (who were seen as often naive, in underestimating the resilience of capitalism and overestimating labour's commitment to radical change)
- the degree of maturity in the outlook of the trade union movement.

Perlman's theory has some application to Australia. The basic notion of scarcity consciousness helps explain the way in which Australian unions have gone about pursuing benefits for their members. The concept of tensions between trade union leaders who spring from the working class and intellectuals who compete with them for leadership, was also illustrated in the years between the Great Depression of the 1930s and the 1950s. During that period Communists and the Movement struggled for ascendancy in many unions as discussed below. However, there are also significant differences. Perlman's theory best explains the American style of non-ideological business unionism. It does not account so well for Australian unionism, with its strand of socialism and its close association with the Australian Labor Party (ALP).

The concept of scarcity consciousness also has considerable relevance to Asian societies. At the time when trade unions first became a significant force in the five Asian countries, unemployment was high and jobs were scarce. Undoubtedly, this situation shaped the original objectives and strategies which unions adopted. Also, in the case of Japan and Singapore, as in Australia, Communist intellectuals played an important part in trade unions during the 1940s and 1950s. It could be said, too, that Perlman's notion of the forces shaping trade union direction has some explanatory value in relation to these Asian societies. In each case, the power of capitalism to resist attacks has proved immense, when the post-war boom set in. The influence of intellectuals in the trade union movement has proved very limited (apart from the Communists, referred to above). With the exception of Korea, the trade union movements in these Asian societies have learnt to live within the capitalist system. In the case of Singapore, the National Trade Union Council (NTUC) has developed a 'symbiotic relationship' with the governing PAP, and a philosophy of tripartism characterises the industrial relations system (see Chapter 13). In Japan, trade unions are mainly enterprise unions, whose fate is closely interwoven with their enterprises. This demonstrates a business unionism ideology, and a philosophy of pragmatism. Many managers have also previously served as union officials (see Chapter 13 and Chapter 6). Capitalism has also proved triumphant in Malaysia. Malaysian unions are relatively weak and divided, with their power circumscribed by government (see Chapter 13). Only in South Korea does it appear that unions have reached less of an accommodation with capitalism, but in that case the struggle for workers' rights has become intertwined with the more general struggle for democracy (see Chapter 13).

The above discussion broadly covers the role of trade unions in developed and emerging industrial economies. Unions also have a role in newly industrialising economies, often playing a key-democratising role. But they may also go the other way and develop close ties to political parties (as they do in industrialised economies). In these cases unions may fulfil political functions, such as public relations (demonstrating that labour's organised voice); control of the labour supply (for the benefit of the government); and acting as an outlet for otherwise revolutionary pressures (that could threaten the government). Thus, unions established in newly industrialising economies may function either as agents of the government or, alternatively, act to promote democratic structures (either with the support of the ruling political party or alternatively, suffering at the hands of the regime). Once a more or less democratic or non-colonial regime emerges, committed to economic development, unions tend to be seen as a continuing necessity. However, new regimes tend to be anxious to ensure that unions do not have any real say in wage determination. Government priorities tend to be to encourage savings and exports, rather than the immediate consumption (which most rank and file workers prefer).

Thus, such new regimes often encourage unions to assume a political rather than an economic role. This assists politicians in widening their support bases, and it may be acceptable to many union officials, who have aspirations to use unions as vehicles for moving into political careers. Such theories offer some insights into the origins of trade unions under colonialism, and their continuing role in some instances, for example in Malaysia and Singapore. In Singapore, in particular, this seems a reasonably accurate description of the role unions have assumed after independence from Britain. As we have already seen the Singaporean NTUC has virtually become a part of the PAP Government (see also Chapter 13).

Relevance of Trade Union Theories

Each of the theories examined above throws some light on the origins, functions and strategies of trade unions in Australia and the five Asian countries. However, none could be considered a full explanation of the development and role of unions in any of the countries examined. Howard (1977) argued that, in general terms, the Australian labour movement does not fit well within any accepted theory of unionism. The main reason for this is the role of Australia's centralised industrial relations system. This system, generally referred to as the 'centralised or compulsory arbitration' system, is a complex process of voluntary conciliation and compulsory arbitration enforceable by law. The Australian system has two 'tiers' that complement each other, operating under federal and state legislation. The two levels vary in form, composition, jurisdiction, power and procedures. Trade unions play an integral role in this framework, which in turn has become essential to trade union strategies. Howard (1977) suggested it was the introduction of compulsory centralised conciliation and arbitration, particularly at the federal level, which was responsible for the creation and subsequent growth of many trade unions. The system encouraged union registration and award making throughout the early part of the 20th Century (see Chapter 8). Labour organisations were essential for the efficient operation of the new system, which was required to prevent, and particularly to settle industrial disputes. According to Plowman (1989) the creation of the centralised arbitration system had the effect of forcing employers to recognise the newly established legal rights of unions to represent their members. Prior to this, employers were had used a range of common law rights (e.g. tort, law of trespass, contract law) and other means, such as employing strike breakers, as a way of refusing to deal with unions.

The relationship between the centralised tribunal system and the growth in trade unions had several practical effects. It was impractical for arbitrators to deal directly with individual employees who were not organised into groups, as their numbers would have flooded the tribunals. Consequently, for greater efficiency, the tribunals rapidly moved to the position of wanting to make awards that would have industry-wide application. The first step in the process of securing wider coverage for awards was for employees to organise to be represented by one body, which was then made party to an award. Formation of unions, therefore, helped to make the number of parties to disputes manageable and allowed awards that settled disputes the maximum coverage. The second step came with legislation based on Section 51(xxxv) of the Australian Constitution, which provided the Commonwealth Parliament with power to make laws on 'conciliation and arbitration for the prevention and settlement of industrial disputes extending beyond the limits of any one state.' The jurisdiction of the Court established by Parliament therefore needed unions that both included substantial numbers of workers, and were organised geographically on an interstate basis.

Howard's (1977) research suggests that the early Registrars, who granted registration to trade unions, were particularly willing to register applicant bodies to help collective organisation and so enable the system to operate effectively. Having once become registered, a trade union was virtually assured of perpetual legal existence, protected from competition from rival bodies, unless its membership fell so low that it became defunct. Its members were also assured of the benefits of industrial awards. An impartial Court looked after the welfare of the members, thus leaving union officials with minimal need to develop grass roots organisation or service members' needs. However, the result was that trade unions were very much creatures of the compulsory arbitration system, and, in many cases, lacked the industrial muscle to function effectively without its protection. As Howard argued, all these considerations seem to have contributed to the dramatic growth of trade unionism in the early twentieth century. The union numbers increased by 275 per cent during the years 1901-11, which coincided with the establishment of the various arbitration systems (Howard 1977, 266). He concluded that the twentieth century labour movement in Australia should be seen as a labour movement in form and intent, rather than by tactic and achievement (1977, 163).

However, the history of trade unions in Australia is not quite as simple and untroubled as this account would suggest. Australian trade unions pre-dated arbitration and were very active in political lobbying very early in their history (see below). Indeed, it was partly their pressure that created the institution of compulsory arbitration, and helped shape its later development. Whilst the introduction of arbitration certainly influenced the behaviour and characteristics of Australian unions, it is less certain that it lead them to be 'dependent' upon the arbitration system for their existence. Writers such as Gahan (1996) have rejected this 'dependency theory' arguing that unions are more influenced by other non-arbitration factors, such as political orientation, membership characteristics, industry location, and a range of social and economic factors. Nevertheless, Howard's view that compulsory arbitration played a key role in trade union growth and development after the great strikes of the 1890s remains valid. It is clear that under the Conciliation and Arbitration Act of 1904 (a predecessor of the Workplace relations Act 1996) unions traded-off independent action in favour of registration.

In the five selected South East Asian countries considered in this book, there are similar arguments about the role of historical events and institutions in the growth and development of unions. However, as in the case of the conflict theories discussed in Chapter 2, these trade union theories also have their limitations.

We turn now to an examination of the history of Australian trade unions, as background to their current functions, structure and objectives. Some brief comments about the history of trade unions in Japan, Singapore, Malaysia, Hong Kong and Korea are to be found in Chapter 13.

THE HISTORY OF AUSTRALIAN TRADE UNIONISM

By Australian standards (measured from European settlement) trade unions have a long history. Their origins and history go back to the gold rush of the 1850s. Temporary combinations of workers for common industrial action can be traced back even further. However, in this section, we will simply outline some of the significant factors that have shaped unions, and evaluate some of their early achievements to provide a brief background to the modern trade union movement.

The first recorded combination of workers to raise the price of labour in Australia occurred in 1795, during the convict era, but the action was rapidly suppressed (Turner 1976, 10). In the United Kingdom, legislation, the Combinations Act, was passed in 1791, following the French Revolution, outlawing the formation and membership of trade unions. They were seen as potential sources of unrest and as importing the ideals of the French revolution. Those who breached the Act could be, and were, transported to Australia by way of punishment. When the colony of New South Wales acquired its first legislature, the Masters and Servants Act was passed in 1828. This restrictive legislation, which purported to legally regulate the rights of employers and employees, soon fell into disuse (Turner 1976, 13). This is clear from the fact that the first important, successful strike in Australian history, by printers, was recorded in 1829. As early as 1831, there were attempts to form permanent trade unions or societies, in the Webbs' sense, though these were mostly short-lived. Nevertheless, in 1850, there were 20 such societies in existence in Sydney, and 12 in Melbourne, the capital of the newly proclaimed colony of Victoria (Turner 1976, 14).

On the political front, it is also clear that organised labour was active at an early stage in Australian history. In the early 1840s, a successful 'working class' political action compelled the New South Wales Legislative Council to abandon attempts to enact restrictive labour legislation, to make it easier for employers to prosecute their employees for breach of contract (Turner 1976, 16-17). But it was really the discovery of gold in 1851 that marked the beginning of the era of successful trade union organisation. Between 1851 and 1861, the population of Australia nearly trebled to 1.2 million people. Transportation to the colonies was abolished in all colonies except Western Australia, and free settlers flocked in. Permanent trade unions were established, including engineers, carpenters and printers. Other workers who successfully organised themselves during the period 1855-79 included tanners, leather dressers, tailors, agricultural implement makers, ironworkers, painters and bookmakers. Predominantly these were skilled tradesmen, and the early unions were normally branches of English parent organisations.

Unskilled and semi-skilled workers were not far behind in establishing and joining trade unions. Some examples include: the first union of coal miners, formed in 1860; a gold miners union set up initially in Bendigo in 1872, and later extended to include other geographic regions; and seamen's unions formed in 1874 in Sydney and Melbourne. Waterside workers organised themselves into unions in 1882 in Sydney and 1885 in Melbourne. In 1886, the first shearers unions appeared in New South Wales, Victoria and Queensland, and later became the backbone of the Australian Workers Union. Between 1880 and 1900, the first white collar unions of post office workers and teachers were formed, though they did not become industrially significant until well into the 20th Century.

Most of the period between 1850 and 1890 was an era of relative economic prosperity in the Australian colonies, and there was a strong demand for labour, both skilled and unskilled. It was this factor which outweighed the unfavourable legal environment for trade unions. During this time also, inter-union forms of cooperative organisation appeared. Between 1857 and 1884, trades and labour councils were established in the eastern states. Their original purpose was to provide common meeting places for trade union members. However, they soon began to acquire other functions, such as intervening to conciliate in industrial disputes involving more than one affiliated union and acting as pressure groups agitating for favourable legislation from colonial governments. There was also a movement towards more cooperation between unions in different colonies. In 1879, the first Inter-colonial Trade Union Congress was held, followed by similar conferences at intervals of between 3 and 5 years.

During this era, the evidence suggests that trade unions were remarkably successful in improving the terms and conditions of their members. An early example was the achievement of the 8-hour day or 48 hour week in the Sydney and Melbourne building trades as early as 1856, (Turner 1976, 24-25). This occurred at a time when a 60-hour working week was much more common in most industries and occupations. By 1890, many unionists throughout the colonies enjoyed the benefits of the 8-hour day, perhaps the great single benefit yet achieved by workingmen (Turner 1976, 26).

This era of early success ended abruptly with the great strikes of the early 1890s (1890-4). These strikes were a watershed in the development of trade unions. They affected Australia's two key burgeoning industries - shearing and maritime transport. They paralysed the eastern colonies, and extended as far away as New Zealand. The main issue in these strikes involved attempts by employers to break union working conditions in favour of the right to contract. The timing was ill chosen, as Australia suffered its worst economic depression to that time, beginning in 1891 and extending through the rest of the century. The employers espoused a platform of 'freedom of contract', or the right, in effect, to hire non-union labour. With assistance from colonial governments, they emerged completely victorious. Scab labour was escorted onto the wharves, into the mines and into the shearing sheds, under the protection of colonial troops. Many unionists lost their jobs, and many unions went out of existence. Unemployment rose as high as an estimated 30 per cent. (Turner 1976, 47; Hagan 1983, 32-33). Historians tend to view these strikes as a watershed because of their dramatic long-term consequences for the labour movement (Turner 1976, 52-3).

One direct result of the great strikes was the decision of unions to turn to political action. The Australian trade union movement divided into two wings, one industrial and the other political, later to become the Australian Labor Party. Previously they had used only the weapons of collective bargaining and industrial action to secure their ends. Now Labor Parties were formed in all the colonies, through the agency of the trades and labour councils, to provide separate working class representation. In the elections of 1894, the New South Wales Labor Party won a quarter of the seats in the colonial legislature. It thereby established itself as the first organised political party, and forced the anti-labour interests to draw together into similarly organised groupings. The Labor Parties in New South Wales, South Australia and Queensland were able to hold the balance of power in their respective legislatures, and extract concessions from the governments of the day (Turner 1976, 50). In 1899, the first Labor Government in the world was formed in Queensland. Though short-lived, it pre-dated the first Labour Government in the United Kingdom by 25 years. Labor would soon be strong enough in New South Wales, Queensland and federally, to hold power in its own right.

Another significant effect of the great strikes was the decision to experiment with compulsory arbitration as a means of preventing and settling industrial disputes. The colonial governments were shaken by the economic dislocations caused by the great strikes. They sought new methods of dealing with industrial disputes that would not involve such widespread and disruptive trials of strength between employers and organised labour. Trade unions threw their support behind compulsory arbitration, based on the principle of impartial judicial tribunals, as a means of redressing the balance of their industrial weakness, but employers opposed the new institution.

Based on Section 51 of the new Commonwealth Constitution of 1900 (discussed earlier in this chapter), the Federal Parliament passed the Conciliation and Arbitration Act in 1904, and established the new Commonwealth Arbitration Court in 1905. At state level, between 1900 and 1912, the governments of New South Wales, Queensland, South Australia and Western Australia all set up their own arbitration courts, to deal with industrial disputes confined within the boundaries of their states. The significance of this development was considerable, as a union could force an employer to have pay and conditions for his workers set by a tribunal. However weak it might be industrially, therefore, a union could have recourse to arbitration to discharge its primary function in representing its members' interests. This, in turn, enabled it to attract recruits. Thus, arbitration directly promoted union growth

(Martin 1980, 5-6). The Harvester Judgement in 1907 showed unions just how powerful the new tribunal could be. In that case Justice Higgins (the second President of the Arbitration Court) declared for the first time, the concept of a minimum or basic wage, to enable unskilled workers and their families to subsist in conditions of 'frugal comfort' (Turner 1976, 59). The basic wage was followed by judgments, awarding margins for skill to those in occupations above the level of labourer. The Commonwealth Court was popular with trade unions, as its awards appear to have been generous by the standards of the time.

The extent to which arbitration seems to have promoted trade union growth in the period 1900-1914, (see the discussion earlier in this chapter) is illustrated by the growth in the number of unionists. From an estimated 100,000 in 1900, it grew to 500,000 at the beginning of World War I, when trade union statistics began to be formally recorded (Martin 1980, 2). The growth of unions continued unabated until 1927, when a level of 50 per cent unionisation of the workforce, very high by the international standards of the time, was achieved. As the trade union movement consolidated during these years, pressure increased for a national trade union centre. This resulted in part from the influence of the revolutionary International Workers of the World, emanating from the United States. It was also partly from the influence of the powerful Australian Workers Union, which was spearheading a push to become the 'One Big Union'. The push for a national trade union body was to some extent an expression of distrust of Labor politicians in the industrial movement. It was also about building influence in ALP branches and the desire to rely more on industrial action to achieve industrial objectives (Martin 1980, 8-9).

The ultimate outcome was the formation of the Australian (originally Australasian) Council of Trade Unions (ACTU) in 1927. Its role was to act at a national level as the trades and labour councils did at the state level. It would control and direct interstate disputes involving more than one affiliated union, and it would lobby federal governments on behalf of the national trade union movement. The ACTU was relatively weak in its early years, because it was structured to be under the control of the trades and labour councils collectively. Some large unions such as the Australian Workers Union (AWU) stood aloof from it until as late as 1967. But once other large unions joined the ACTU, the organisation became the first stable national trade union organisation in Australia (Turner 1976, 78-9). In the years following World War I, the white-collar sector of the workforce became more unionised. Bank officers, insurance staff, local government officers, surveyors, professional engineers and draughtsmen, all established their own trade unions. A coordinating body for trade unions in the federal public service, the High Council of Commonwealth Public Service Organisations, was also set up in 1919.

Trade union growth came to an abrupt halt, however, in the late 1920s with the onset of the Great Depression, the worst in Australia's history. Three major militant unions, the waterside workers, timber workers and coal miners, all suffered severe defeats in big strikes between 1928 and 1930, as employers sought to cut their costs, including wages. Unemployment escalated rapidly, reaching a peak of 27 per cent of the workforce in 1932. For the first time, wages were cut by the Arbitration Court in 1931. At the political level, Labor Governments, both state and federal, were swept away, and replaced by conservative governments, intent on dealing with the depression by austerity measures. The number of workdays lost through strikes plummeted, as the effects of the Great Depression became more widespread. In 1930, 1.5 million working days were lost. By 1931, this number had fallen to 110,000.

Between 1929 and 1935, union numbers declined to 42 per cent of the workforce. Another result of the Depression was the growth of Communist Party influence in trade unions. The party had been founded in Australia in 1920, but had little influence until this time. In 1934, the Communists captured control of the Coal Miners Federation, in 1936 the Ironworkers and in 1937 the Seamen and Waterside Workers. Recovery from the Depression was very slow. 1937 restored the 1929 wage level, but unemployment remained very high, between 10 and 12 per cent, until 1941, after the outbreak of World War II. The importance of the 1930s was the legacy of bitterness caused by mass unemployment. There was a sense of disillusionment among workers and unions both with the arbitration system, which had for the first time cut living standards, and to some extent with Labor politicians. During this decade, too, Communists emerged as significant trade union leaders (Turner 1976, 91). In 1941, the Menzies-Fadden Conservative Government was replaced by a Labor Government headed by John Curtin. This Government mobilised Australia for a total war effort against the looming threat of invasion by Japan, following Japanese entry into the war of 1941. Trade unions of all political complexions joined in cooperation in the war effort. After the Nazi invasion of Soviet Russia in 1941, Communist support also swung behind the war. Both wages and prices were pegged for the duration of the war.

In 1945, following the Allied victory over the Axis forces, the Australian economy was still beset by shortages and rationing. While full employment had been achieved for the first time during World War II, 1945-9, the period of post-war reconstruction, was turbulent in terms of strike activity. The Communists sought to exploit industrial grievances in a push to destroy capitalism from within the unions they controlled. The anti-Communist Movement, originating with Catholic elements within the Labor Party, took up the cudgels with the Communists in the unions through pro-ALP Industrial Groups. There were fierce battles for control of key trade unions especially in mining and iron working (such as over the control of the Federated Iron Workers Union). Unions such as the AWU maintained a special clause in their constitution to 'destroy the communist party in all its guises'. In 1949, the coal miners called a national coal strike, which imperilled the main national source of fuel. This finally led the Labor Government, now under Prime Minister Chifley, to intervene, by ordering troops into the coalmines. The coal strike was broken, but the Labor Government was crippled and lost the election of 1949. Between 1949 and 1951, the Communists were defeated in most trade unions. However, the divisions between Communists and anti-Communists ultimately split the Labor Party. A new anti-Communist political party, the Democratic Labor Party, was formed in 1955, and disputes with the left wing of the ALP was instrumental in helping to keep Labor out of office at the federal level until 1972.

By 1956, trade unions reached a peak of strength in Australia, with 61 per cent of the workforce unionised (Turner 1976, 116). Although full employment in the Australian economy was largely maintained until 1974, trade union membership began to decline from the mid 1970s. This was largely a consequence of structural changes in the economy, with the number of workers in the key blue-collar, manufacturing sector, which had always enjoyed the highest level of unionisation, no longer growing. The shift to service industries produced growth in the number of white-collar workers. During the period 1949-1972, the blue-collar workforce increased by 50 per cent, but the white-collar workforce jumped by 250 per cent (Hagan 1983, 45). Unfortunately for unionism, white-collar workers were less likely to join trade unions. However, a white-collar peak organisation, a counterpart of the

ACTU, the Australian Council of Salaried and Professional Associations (ACSPA), was formed in 1956. Despite the reluctance of many white-collar workers to unionise, during the 1960s there was an increasing tendency for white-collar workers in the more unionised industries (such as teaching and the public service) to imitate blue-collar union tactics. They increasingly adopted rolling strikes in order to improve their position. Whereas white-collar workers had previously stood apart from manual workers, there was now increasing cooperation between their unions and their peak organisations (Martin 1980, 15). White-collar workers also began to show themselves more willing to affiliate with the Labor Party, whereas they had previously largely remained aloof from such links. By 1977, the barriers had broken down, and an agreement was reached for ACSPA to merge with the ACTU. Two years later the Council of Australian Government Employee Organisations (CAGEO), the successor of the High Council of Commonwealth Public Service Associations, also merged with the ACTU.

The year 1974 marked the end of the long post-war boom. In that year, over 6 million working days were lost in strikes, an all-time record. From that time, however, unemployment again became a dominant economic problem, with which successive governments, Labor and Coalition, had to wrestle. At the federal level, a Labor Government under Gough Whitlam was elected from 1972-5. In the early years of the Whitlam Government, there was a wages explosion, partly encouraged by the Government's initial use of the public service as a wage pacesetter. However, rapidly rising unemployment and inflation forced the Whitlam Government to adopt more conservative economic policies and to call for wage restraint after 1974. Problems of unemployment and inflation continued to dog the economy after the defeat of the Whitlam Government and the election of the Fraser Liberal-National Federal Government, from 1975-83.

The Fraser Government initially continued with its Labor predecessor's policy of supporting wage indexation. This policy allowed no wage claims outside those approved by the Commonwealth Conciliation and Arbitration Commission (as it was then known, now the AIRC). It compelled unions to abide by national wage fixing principles (Hagan 1983, 53) as an anti-inflationary measure. However, the Government gradually withdrew supporting mechanisms, such as attempts at price restraint, until the policy finally collapsed in 1981. It also passed a number of anti-union measures. These included giving employers rights to sue trade unions for their conduct in industrial disputes under Trade Practices legislation. They also included re-enacting fines to be imposed on unions within the arbitration system for breaches of industrial awards occurring through industrial action (Martin 1980, 25-6). However, in practice, these measures had little impact. After a post-war low of 49 per cent unionisation of the workforce in 1970, trade union membership picked up to 56 per cent, levelling out at 55 per cent by the end of the decade. There were a number of reasons for this. In the federal public service, the Whitlam Labor Government had implemented measures to encourage the growth of unionism (Hagan 1983, 51). In the private sector, the growth in unionism was partly the result of the insertion of preference clauses into key industrial awards. These clauses gave preference to unionists over non-unionists in employment and at the point of retrenchment. It was also partly the result of 'closed shop' agreements between employers and unions in some industries.

The growing participation of women in the workforce also provided unions with a new source of recruits. For example, the number of women joining the workforce between 1947 and 1971 increased by 138 per cent as compared with only 47 per cent for men. By 1971, they comprised about one-third of the total labour force, but two thirds of employed women were in white-collar occupations, the most rapidly growing sector of the workforce. In 1969, a test case run by the ACTU in the Conciliation and Arbitration Commission resulted in a decision for equal pay for equal work, which saw female wages increase to that of their male counterparts. This provided a powerful recruiting tool for white-collar unions with strong female memberships in the 1970s (Hagan 1983, 51).

In 1981, there was another serious recession, following a wages blowout in the metal trades industry. Technological change, which had already appeared in the 1970s as a threat to overall employment numbers, also began to gather pace. The Fraser Government was defeated in the election of 1983 ushering in 13 years of federal Labor government. The Hawke and Keating Governments' labour policies were dominated by the Accord (an agreement on wages and prices) between the government and the ACTU (discussed in chapter 8). Then, in 1996 the Federal Government changed again with the election of the Howard Coalition government. Both periods of government ushered in major economic, social and political reforms that were to impact on the role and influence of Australian trade unions.

Thus, as this brief overview illustrates, trade unions in Australia are an institution with a relatively long history. To a considerable extent, the attitudes of unions were shaped by their historical experience, and the long struggle to win acceptance for their legitimacy as representatives of the working class. Over time, enormous improvements in wages and working conditions have been won, sometimes at considerable cost. Labor created a political wing, and trade unions alternated between industrial action and political pressure group activities to achieve their objectives. Relations between the two wings of the Labor movement have not always been cordial, and the benefits won from Labor Governments were often below the expectations of the industrial wing. Nevertheless, trade unions had won their place as one of the significant and enduring institutions in Australian society by the early twentieth century.

LEGISLATIVE CONTROL AND TRADE UNION DEMOCRACY

Historically, Australian Governments have always sought to regulate the affairs of trade unions. For example, Section 31 of the old Trade Union Act of New South Wales, passed in 1881, defined a trade union as:

> ...any combination whether temporary or permanent for regulating the relations between workmen and employers or between workmen and workmen or between employers and employers or for imposing restrictive conditions on the conduct of any trade or business ... (see, Brookes 1988, 3).

The capacity of trade unions to collectively organise and their ability to influence the activities of employers and employees by direct action has led to their regulation by the State. This arises because the objectives of unions whilst primarily those of a labour market institution, also include political objectives. These political objectives may be industrial, defensive or related to economic conditions. A feature of trade union growth, has been the growing role of the state in the statutory regulation of trade unions. Often the state has actively sought to promote internal union democracy and membership participation through statutory regulation. Both at state and federal levels, governments in Australia have sought to control the activities of unions. Among the more important matters covered by legislation include: the registration and de-registration of unions; defining union members; voting procedures, union governance; prohibiting strikes; regulating the financial management of unions; and penal provisions relating to participating in banned strikes or failure to enforce their rules (such as refusing to admit a person who is eligible to be a union member. As Creighton observed the state has a significant array of weapons to ensure labour does not win too many battles or especially the war. One of the most important of these weapons is the law (Creighton 1982, 121).

Unions, without the legal status and protection granted by industrial legislation, are vulnerable organisations. Unions are in effect alien intruders in the common law contract of employment. The protection offered by industrial legislation allows unions to gain a legal persona through registration and 'incorporation', without facing the prospect of being pursued under common law for a range of matters including trespass and tort of conspiracy. The process of registration and incorporation also grants the rights to acquire and hold property, and to exclusively represent members with employers and before industrial tribunals. Exclusive representation rights come with registration because a union is made a bargaining agent for workers under the so-called 'conveniently belong' provision. This provision restricts a union to a particular coverage (to avoid multiplicity of unions covering the same work) and then protects and encourages its legally enforceable monopoly. In summary, therefore, registration is important because the activities of unions at times conflict with an employee's contract of employment (such as in the case of strikes) and it gives unions legally enforceable representational rights. However, despite these rights, unions have often had to defend themselves against tendencies to control them through the law, both statutory and common (tort) law.

The position of trade unions to influence the supply of labour has implications for union 'government' and democracy. Union government is a term that refers to the processes for representing membership, for communicating the ideas and demands of membership to leadership, and for translating union policies into action. Child et al. (1973) has described this as the cycle of union activity, in which membership views are communicated to union leadership, and these are then interpreted and implemented. Child et al. (1973) argue that a number of factors influence the union's activities and, in particular, the effectiveness of the representative system, such as the size of the union, membership diversity and industry coverage. A significant question therefore in the regulation of trade unions is how to keep them democratic. The publication of Michels' classic work *Political Parties* in English in 1915 illustrated the problem of maintaining democratic control over unions. In his opinion, trade unions would inevitably find a need to develop bureaucratic structures in order to become more effective in achieving their objectives. As a result, unions tended to concentrate power at the top of the organisational hierarchy and lessen the influence of the rank and file. An oligarchy was therefore the inevitable result, where trade union leaders could be expected to pursue policies designed to enhance and entrench their own power and status in the organisation and prevent others from gaining control of the trade union. In Michels' view, the objectives of trade unions inevitably take on the personal objectives of its leaders rather than those of the membership (rank and file) in general and this is maintained by the development of an elite oligarchy (see Michels 1959).

The extent to which Michels 'iron' law of oligarchy (as he referred to this process) prevails in today's trade unions is debatable. As union members become more educated and articulate, they are more likely to ensure that their unions are running effectively and democratically, or they may leave the union movement, resulting in a decline in trade union membership. On the other hand, participation in union affairs has become increasingly complex, time consuming and requires increasing amounts of resources to be effective. There are also other reasons why members may not be active. Some may be apathetic (most union elections are decided by a small proportion of eligible voters); many members lack skills and resources to run against incumbent union officials; and others may be satisfied with union activities and policies. Nicholson (1978, 33) lists a number of criteria that can be used to assess union democracy. These include:

- constitutional arrangements that encourage electoral contests
- systems of checks and balances to guard against the entrenchment of factional power
- accessible channels for the upward transmission of information and grievances
- mechanisms for the maintenance of a credible relationship between membership goals and union policies
- systems of accountability
- procedures and practices that encourage membership participation in decision-making
- union journals and reporting procedures (financial and union governance matters).

Governments have also attempted to legislate for union democracy. For example, the current Workplace Relations Act 1996 has adopted many of the earlier legislative provisions relating to promoting union democracy. One of the chief objects of the Act is to 'encourage the organisation of representative bodies of employers and employees and their registration under this Act' (Section 3(e)). To achieve this, a wide range of regulations exists to deal with membership enrolment, union registration, elections, industrial action and financial reporting of unions. Before the Industrial Registrar will permit the registration of a union, the Registrar must ensure that its constitution and rules are not undemocratic, harsh, oppressive, or unreasonable in terms of its dealings with members. Section 196(c) requires that the rules of an organisation 'shall not impose upon applicants for membership, or members, of the organisation, conditions, obligations or restrictions which ... are oppressive, unreasonable or unjust'. Section 261 protects the rights of individuals to join and not be unjustifiably refused. This right is subject to the qualification that a union may refuse admission to persons of 'general bad character'. Once an employee is admitted to membership, that person is entitled to remain a member so long as he or she complies with the rules of the union. This aims to ensure that unions provide each member with the ability to participate in the affairs of the union. Nevertheless, legislative regulation cannot ensure the democratic control of unions. It cannot guarantee membership participation, nor can it compel unwilling members to take more active roles in their union.

Government intervention can also have ulterior motives, such as 'democratising' unions in order to weaken them. For example, the Workplace Relations Act 1996 (WRA, see also Chapter 9) continues a legacy established under the Conciliation and Arbitration Act 1904 of legislating for union democracy. However, the Howard Coalition Federal Government has gone further in using this Act to achieve the broader political objective of reducing the role and power of unions. The objects of the Act include the encouragement of workplace or enterprise agreements (Section 3(d)); removing union representational monopoly by introducing freedom of association (enabling an employee to join or not to join a union, or to set up their own union (Sections 3(f) and Part XA); and ensuring that trade unions remain accountable to their members (Section 3(g)). The Act encourages direct employer – employee arrangements through the use of non-union workplace agreements (either Australian Workplace Agreements (AWAs) or Certified Agreements (Parts VIB and VID)).

The Act also prohibits the closed shop. It removes the power to grant preference clauses to unionists under awards, and frees up the requirements for registering a trade union or association including contractors (Section 188(1)). The Act reduces the requirements for registration of a trade union from 1,000 to 50 employees (Section 189(1)(c)). The Act also removes the restraints on a new trade union being registered in an industry where there is an already existing union registered, if the new union would be more effective in representing union members (Section 189(1)(j)(ii)). The Act also provides a mechanism for 'disamalgamation', so that the large amalgamations persuaded by the ACTU during the mid 1980s can be broken up. Former amalgamated unions can be reconstituted and re-registered as if the amalgamation had not occurred (Section 253ZH). However, the application of this Section is in doubt, because it appears to apply only to amalgamated unions. In fact, most trade union 'amalgamations' did not involve the creation of a new union. One union normally acted as host and the other (usually the smaller union) de-registered. (At the time of writing there was only one application for disamalgamation before the Federal Court. The Victorian Bakers were attempting to break away from the Australian Liquor, Hospitality and Miscellaneous Workers' Union (ALHMWU)).

A further feature of the Act is the ability to form enterprise or company unions where workers are performing work in the same enterprise (Section 188(1)(c)). The aim here is to reduce the influence of established unions in favor of creating company-based unions. One of the first attempts to register an enterprise union under the Act involved the SMQ Enterprise Union (Suncorp/Metway QIDC Staff Pty Ltd the former Metway Staff Association) in 1999. After extensive hearings, the Commission refused to register the company union finding that it was not independent from the company and could not properly function as an independent union (Vice President McIntyre, Application for Registration by SMQ Enterprise Union, 27th October 1999, December 1269/99 S Print S0298). Overall, the ostensible aim of the Act is to promote freedom of choice. In practice, however, it is a serious attempt to reduce the bargaining power of the large national and industry unions in favour of smaller unions, and to bring enterprise unions more closely under the scrutiny of company management. The Act also reduces the importance of union registration by recognising 'industrial associations' whether registered or unregistered in an attempt to break the monopoly of established unions. However, the impact of such union competition is questionable. In countries like Japan, despite having some 85,000 mostly enterprise unions, the trade union movement has continued to organise around the logic of collective action (such as the annual spring wages offensive).

The extent to which legislation can limit the influence of trade unions is uncertain. In Australia, unions and centralised arbitration have grown in tandem, each reinforcing the other. The Australian industrial relations system is founded on collective regulation and processes of dispute resolution. Trade unions play a primary role in providing terms and conditions of employment at the workplace. Whilst under the Workplace Relations Act 1996, the role of unions is diminished, their role as labour market institutions continues and unions have adopted a broader 'safety net' role in maintaining minimum award conditions (see Chapter 8).

TYPES OF TRADE UNIONS

The structure of the union movement in Australia can be said to reflect the way trade unions have been regulated and controlled by legislation. Initially this encouraged the growth of craft and occupational unions. This unique framework has developed under a stable legal environment (union registration and legally enforceable bargaining rights) to include the following five basic forms of union: craft unions, occupational unions, industrial unions, general industry unions, and enterprise unions. Although that division is overly simple, it does provide a means of distinguishing the broad organisational features of unions.

Craft unions organise workers on the basis of a particular craft or trade, whatever industry they may be employed in. The term 'craft' is commonly used to describe a skilled occupation that recruits and trains workers by means of an apprenticeship system. Many early craft unions adopted the same structure as their UK parent union (e.g. coal miners).

Occupational unions cover workers who belong to a particular occupational classification or to a related group of occupations. Occupational unions are termed 'horizontal' (meaning a broad selection of workplaces with workers of broadly similar occupations and skills). The membership may cut across industry boundaries, such as clerical unions, or public service unions. Here a worker's union coverage is acquired because of an employer (e.g. government), or the job (e.g. teaching), or a specific range of occupations performed (e.g. clerical).

Industry unions are often organised according to industry coverage as opposed to being organised along skill or occupational boundaries. Industry unions seek to cover all workers in a particular industry, irrespective of the job they perform (e.g. automotive industry unions). Membership is based purely on the industry rather than on the skill, trade or occupation of the workers. Both manual and non-manual employees are included. They represent a 'vertical' form of organisation, and are often referred to as industry 'chain' unions borrowing notions from the natural sciences (i.e. covering extraction, manufacture, production and distribution).

A fourth category of trade union is the general union. This is often very large and organises workers regardless of skill, occupation or industry. There are very few unions of this type in Australia, although the Australian Workers' Union (AWU), one of this country's oldest and largest labour organisations, and the Australian Liquor Hospitality and Miscellaneous Workers Union (ALHMWU) can be described as general unions.

A final category of trade unions is company or enterprise unions. These unions are limited to representing workers (or sections of workers) within a company. These can either be registered or recognised under industrial relations legislation (such as the Commonwealth Bank Officers Association) or operate unregistered. While enterprise unions are commonplace in Japan for example, and despite favourable federal legislation, these unions are rare in Australia at the end of the 20th Century. Most that did exist were among the many smaller unions amalgamated with larger general and industry unions under the ACTU's union amalgamation policy during the 1980s and early 1990s.

THE PURPOSE, AND GOALS OF TRADE UNIONS

Unions have both objectives and goals. For example, Deery (1989) argues that unions have four principal objectives namely:

1. the provision of direct services to members, e.g. legal aid and insurance benefits
2. improved conditions of employment, because employees wish to retain and increase their share of the product of their labour
3. organisational security, such as protection of the union membership through arrangements with employers and protection against 'poaching' by rival unions
4. political objectives (Deery 1989, 76, 78).

According to Byrt (1985, 129-136) the goals of trade unionism can be viewed in terms of three broad activities: economic, political and. The economic role of trade unions is principally to seek higher wages. There are two main means through which unions seek higher wages. The first is through arbitration. An important feature of Australian industrial relations is the existence of an extensive and complex network of legally constituted industrial tribunals established for the purpose of dealing with labour disputes, wage fixation and industrial matters. This compulsory system was dominant in wage fixation up until the 1990s (see Chapter 8). The second, following on from the 1990s is collective bargaining and a shift towards workplace agreements (collective bargaining has always been a feature of the Australian system in terms of negotiating workplace outcomes) (see Chapter 9). Trade unions also have a political role. In Australia, the political role of trade unions is played out through their affiliation with the Australian Labor Party.

Byrt's the third goal of unions is job control and protection. In fact, the most important source of union power derives from a union's capacity to restrict or control the supply and price of labour. Clarke and Clements referred to this as a form of 'defensive job control' (1977, 290). Job control has two elements. The first element is controlling the supply of labour. Unions restrict the supply of labour through monopolising the supply of particular skill (as in the case of craft unions and the apprenticeship system). Similarly, they may use their membership rules to recruit and dominate a particular occupation or industry. This kind of territorial control is expressed in the formal rules of a union (for example, the eligibility rules, where the occupations or industries from which a union is allowed to recruit are decided and recorded by the Industrial Registrar). Vast arrays of rules and practices have also been formed between unions, detailing each union's territory, membership and political affiliations. Demarcation disputes occur when these rules and membership territorial boundaries clash.

The second element of job control is controlling the way work is carried out. Unions control the conduct of work through the imposition of on-the-job rules, which may be in writing or may simply be custom and practice. But whether formal or informal these rules govern the conditions under which a job is performed. Both the elements of job control involve controlling the supply and the cost of labour, and protecting the job entitlements of members through rationing. (For example, a union may require that only union members are employed, and then, that jobs are distributed according to seniority, that is, the number of years in the union). According to Byrt (1985), job control can be exercised in many ways such as:

- prescribing conditions of entry into an occupation or skill area
- enforcing the 'closed shop' (requiring union membership to obtain or retain employment)
- enforcing health and safety regulations

- prescription of work methods
- setting output targets, quotas or piecework (contract rates)
- regulating the hours and intensity of work (e.g. allocating overtime)
- controlling methods of payment
- regulating technological change
- providing welfare services and legal advice to members.

THE METHODS AND STRATEGIES OF UNIONS

Gardner (1989, 58) has suggested four ways or methods used by unions to achieve their goals. These are:

1. autonomous or unilateral job regulation
2. collective bargaining or joint negotiation
3. arbitral or third party regulation
4. political action.

The first method used in the 19th Century, is little used today. In the Webbs' description (see above), unilateral regulation is associated with a craft union's control the labour supply through apprenticeship regulation, enforcement of the closed shop and collection of relatively high membership dues. While the notion of craft is still important today, the introduction of multi-skilling, competency-based training and team working has tended to reduce the importance of craft.

The second method is collective bargaining or joint negotiation between employer and union. Typically this negotiation involves the use of various forms of industrial action to demonstrate strength, enforce agreements and make further gains. Compulsory unionism through the enforcement of the 'closed' shop is a mechanism for increasing numerical strength and reinforcing solidarity during direct action (i.e. strikes) and collective bargaining. A common tactic used in collective bargaining is the 'common rule' - generalising gains from one group across total union membership, or from members to non-members. This is achieved by setting so-called industry standards that both restricts the supply of labour and prevents undercutting of wages and conditions. Collective bargaining tactics often focus on setting and enforcing these 'common rule' standards. (This differs from the first method, unilateral regulation, which restricts supply but allows market forces to determine a rates of pay (Gardner 1989, 59).) This approach has also been termed 'pattern bargaining' (e.g. using a standard negotiating strategy and common outcomes across a particular industry, such as in the metal industry).

The third method for achieving union goals is arbitral or third party regulation. This is about using an independent arbitration system. In the Australian context, the establishment of various federal and state arbitral industrial tribunals has seen the growth of a system of legally binding awards regulating wages and conditions (see Chapter 6). Such a system is connected to collective bargaining because trade unions are given legal recognition to bargain on behalf of members (and non-members) through the award system. This gives the concept of the 'common rule' a legally enforceable status. Unions have expended considerable effort in building expertise in presenting cases in arbitration.

The final method of trade union activity, political action, involves pressure for legislation or other state action through lobbying and influencing political parties, particularly those representing labour. In Australia, close links have been forged between trade unions and the ALP. However, as Gardner (1989) goes on to observe, distinguishing between the three union methods of collective bargaining, arbitration and the political action in Australian is difficult. This is because of the close interrelationship between trade unions, politics and government policy (1989, 60). Despite the move in the early 1990s towards a system of enterprise bargaining, it has been argued that collective bargaining occurs in the shadow of arbitration in Australia (Howard 1977). Furthermore, it has been pointed out, arbitration is itself rarely a process of third party decision making. Rather it relies to a large degree on agreement and negotiation between the major parties to a dispute (Rawson 1986).

Unions adopt a variety of strategies when implementing the objectives, goals and methods discussed above. Broadly, these strategies fall into two categories, bargaining strategies and membership strategies (see Table 5.1). These strategies both operate at the national political level, at the workplace level, and at the representational level.

Table 5.1 Two types of trade union strategy

Bargaining Strategy	**National/Political Level** the Accord, occupational superannuation, taxes, social wage etc.
	Workplace Level wage negotiations, negotiating physical/working conditions etc.
Membership Strategy	**Representational Level** membership recruitment, legal services, union issues, representation etc. at the workplace.

Trade union bargaining strategy refers to the tactics and approaches used by trade unions to achieve political as well as industrial aims in their dealings with governments and employers. Trade union bargaining strategy broadly parallels trade union membership strategy in that it operates at a national/political level as well as workplace level. There may be considerable overlapping between the two strategies. For example, political strategies might be aimed at reducing the legal constraints on recruiting members through closed shops, preference clauses etc. (referred to as 'union security arrangements'). Political bargaining strategy may also seek welfare benefits to help membership recruitment.

In practice, few unions pursue a purely ideological bargaining strategy. Rather union bargaining positions vary between militancy (hostility to capital) to cooperation (pragmatism) through to incorporation, where the trade union offers little or no resistance to managerial authority. Union bargaining strategies may also be the outcome of a range of variables including:
- political/ideological outlook of the union
- attitudes of union officials, members and management to workplace issues
- level of union workplace activism and strength of delegate structure

- degree of state regulation
- history of the employer-employee relationship
- award coverage and custom and practice
- strategic location (or bargaining strength) of union (and members) in the production process
- market position (impact of competition) of the company.

These factors may influence both union strategy and the degree of cooperation in the workplace. For example, BHP has traditionally had close union cooperation. During the 1980s the company and steel unions cooperated on a wide range of productivity issues. As a result the company benefited from substantial government assistance under the ALP Government's steel industry plan. However, this cooperation has not lasted. The BHP/Union dispute occurred at BHP's iron ore mines in the Pilbara over the company's attempt to introduce non-union contracts. The Company justified the dispute by the need to achieve greater productivity due to increased competition (especially from Rio Tinto) despite widespread support for maintaining collective union agreements by workers (*Australian Financial Review*, 25 January 2000. See CRA Rio Tinto Case Study.)

TRADE UNION ORGANISATION

Trade unions are typically structured on the basis of four tiers of activity:

1. **Workplace, plant or shop:** The workplace is theoretically where union members get to know the union. A member's first contact with the union is usually through the job representative (also referred to as 'shop steward' or 'job delegate'). As a consequence, the role of the job representative becomes important in establishing a union presence at the workplace. Some larger workplaces may have collectives of shop stewards drawn from various work sections known as shop committees, or combined union committees, which coordinate recruitment, union issues, activities and negotiations.

2. **District or regional:** Sub-branches based on localities comprise the district or regional level of the union. These convene general meetings of members, usually at monthly intervals.

3. **State or Branch:** At the state level there are branch offices in the relevant state capital that are directed by an annual conference. There is a state council or committee of management that meets monthly. These bodies are made up of paid and elected officials. There is also a state secretary and state organisers, who may be either elected or appointed by the committee of management (depending on the union's internal rules). They are responsible for the day-to-day operation of the union, provide advice to members, coordinate negotiations with employers and control the operation of the union office.

4. **Federal:** Most unions operate with some form of a federal level council, or national office responsible for coordinating union strategies, determining union policies (through a national executive or conference), conduct negotiations with employees and conduct federal industrial tribunal cases. The extent and power of a federal or national office vary according to unions, and their branch strength (often according to the size of membership in each state). An example of a strong federal office is the Australian Liquor and Hospitality and Miscellaneous Workers Union (ALHMWU). The Australian Workers Union (AWU) is predominantly organised along a state branch structure.

TRADE UNIONS AT THE WORKPLACE

The Australian Workplace Industrial Relations Survey 1995 (AWIRS) provides a snapshot of the role of trade unions at the workplace. Unions operate a wide range of workplace representational and delegate structures that can involve establishing union site committees or site delegate committees. The AWIRS Survey (AWIRS, Morehead et al. 1997) illustrates the range of tasks undertaken by union workplace delegates. For example, 79% of delegates spent time on resolving individual grievances, 67% spent time recruiting new members, 64% spent time negotiating over work practices and 57% spent time on joint consultative committees. Preparation of newsletters occupied only 41% of delegates and negotiating pay increases was only undertaken by 32% of delegates. Of time spent on the tasks performed by union delegates, the most time consuming were handling individual grievances (37% of delegates spent a lot of time on this task), followed by participating on joint consultative committees. Less than 17% of time was spent negotiating pay increases (AWIRS, Morehead et al. 1977, Table 8.2, 168).

The AWIRS 1995 survey also illustrates the increasing precarious nature of trade union presence in the workplace. For example, 48% of workplaces with 20 or more employees had no union delegate. However, this first group of workplaces included the smaller ones, employing only 30% of the workforce. This first group was made up of 26% of workplaces (or 14% of employees) with no union members what so ever (confirming that most employees work in workplaces with at least one union member). The other part of the first group, 22% of workplaces (or 16% of employees) had union members but no delegate. The second group, 52% of all workplaces (employing 70% of employees) had both union members and delegates. According to AWIRS, larger workplaces were more likely to have union members and delegates than smaller workplaces (Morehead et al. 1997, 140-141). The AWIRS survey also found that the proportion of workplaces with at least one union member declined from 80% in 1990 to 74% in 1995. The decline was greatest amongst workplaces employing between 20 to 49 employees, where the proportion of workplaces with at least one union member fell from 73% to 64% by 1995 (Morehead 1997, 139). Where union delegates are present, they were more likely to be involved in workplace bargaining. 43% of all delegates said that they had negotiated enterprise agreements, two-thirds having spent a lot of time on this activity in the year preceding the survey. Delegates also reported spending more time communicating between the union head office and members (51%), handling queries about award conditions (31%), or mediating between management and members (33%) (Morehead, et al. 1997, 168).

Table 5.2 The role of a union delegate

ROLE OF A UNION DELEGATE OR SHOP STEWARD
• Carry out union policy
• Consultation and advice to union and membership
• Recruiting campaigns for new membership
• Representing members with management (often with the assistance of a union organiser)
• Participating in a local union committee
• Ensuring that the award or workplace agreement conditions are enforced
• Grievance and dispute handling
• Health and safety

The role of a union delegate is an important component of the collectivist approach adopted by unions. Typical job duties of a delegate are illustrated in Table 5.2.

A MODEL OF UNION BEHAVIOUR

In the previous section, we examined the work of trade unions. However, trade unions can also be viewed as organisations. Freeman and Medoff (1984) proposed a model of union behaviour that defines union activity according to two broad dimensions, 'monopoly' and 'collective voice'. This implies that trade unions are labour market institutions and actively seek to influence and shape labour markets and workplace relationships. These two dimensions provide an analytical framework within which most of the outcomes of trade union activity can be considered. This model is shown in Table 5.3.

Table 5.3 Monopoly and collective roles of trade unions

	Union Effects On Productivity Of The Firm	Union Effects On Income Distribution	Unions As Social Organisations
Labour Monopoly Characteristics (Labour Market)	Unions raise wages above competitive levels, acting as a disincentive to employ labour due to increased labour cost. Firms attempt to reduce costs by introducing labour replacing technology. Union work rules decrease productivity.	By increasing the income of their members, unions contribute to income inequality between union and non-union labour. Unions create horizontal inequities by creating differentials among comparable workers.	As political organisations, unions attempt to advance their own political agendas. Unions (individually or collectively) fight for their own interests in the political arena. Union leaders attempt to monopolise their influence by holding on to union power contributing to non-democratic union practices.
Collective Action (Institutional Characteristics)	Unions have some positive effects on the productivity of the firm. They act as a vehicle for resolving grievances (thereby reducing employee quit rates or turnover). They induce management to alter methods of production and adopt more efficient policies, based on productivity enhancement rather than simply cost cutting. They can also help as an agent of change by improving consultative processes, improving morale and cooperation among workers. Unions harness the views of employees and are better able to negotiate with management improvements in wages and conditions and adoption of better HRM practices.	Unions reduce inequality amongst workers by establishing an industry or common rule approach to wages and conditions. Unions interfere with managerial power by ensuring that workers are treated fairly and limit the scope for arbitrary managerial practices in employee relations (such as promotions, retrenchments, performance appraisals etc). Unions may alter wage relativities by reducing differences between workers, supervisors and managers leading to the adoption of different HRM practices and policies in relation to wages and conditions between union and non-union firms.	Unions as political organisations, represent the views of their membership especially those in lower income groups and workers in weaker bargaining positions.

Modified from Freeman, R. and Medoff, J. (1984), What Do Unions Do? Basic Book Inc., New York, 8

The monopoly face of unionism refers to the ability of unions to raise their members' wages above their competitive levels by use of collective (monopolistic) market power and control over the supply of their members' skills. The monopoly face of unionism may also be manifest in relation to variables other than wages. Unions may use their power to impose non-wage constraints on employers such as work rules and manning levels.

Collective voice face is the second component of the model and refers to the purpose which trade unions represent through collective (membership) action. The benefits of collective voice (and therefore unionism) are seen as opening up communication channels between workers and their managers through collective bargaining, grievance and disputes procedures and reductions in absenteeism which provide for orderly industrial relations and for information flows which may modify the behaviour of all parties. As Miller and Mulvey (1992) observe, such communication channels are unlikely to be found in non-union settings, even where management positively tries to create them through such devices as 'open door' policies, because non-union workers (unlike union members) will always be inhibited by their vulnerability to managerial retaliation. Freeman and Medoff argue that management can use the information flowing through the channels of voice to understand and improve the operation of the work environment and the production process, with the result that unionism can be a significant advantage to enterprise efficiency. The exit/voice model involves the union in a regulatory way at the workplace. Unions for example, create rules that govern such matters as benefits resulting from seniority and work rules. These rules reduce rivalry among workers, encourage cooperation and assist in the process of passing on skills through on-the-job training (Freeman and Medoff 1984, 12).

However, there are problems with the Freeman and Medoff model. The benefits of collective voice depend very much on a positive management attitude to unionism rather than the assertion of managerial power. In addition, the beneficial effects that are held to flow from the presence of unionism are dependent on a positive industrial relations climate at the workplace level. In addition, some employers have adopted a much more interventionist approach (often referred to as the 'individualistic' or 'new' HRM') whereby collective bargaining structures are replaced by individual performance and payment systems, such as individualised contracts with no union involvement. In the case of CRA, the process involved deliberate de-unionisation. Despite this, the Freeman and Medoff model attempts to give us a glimpse of how unions work.

WHY DO WORKERS JOIN UNIONS?

Having examined what unions do, it is relevant to ask why do people join unions? The role of unions in representing the working class has historically preoccupied labour historians for a long time (for example, the Webb's, as discussed earlier). More recently, with the decline in the numbers of union members the reasons for joining unions have preoccupied researchers. Why do workers join unions? There is no straight answer here because trade unions perform a variety of roles and attract a range of human sentiments from commitment through apathy to outright hostility. Unions also tend to attract similar sentiments from governments. The activities of unions often produce two outcomes or commodities: public and private 'goods'. Public goods are associated with the political, economic and social representation that unions provide on behalf of its members (e.g. campaigning for increased unemployment benefits, better training and improved social or educational policies). Private goods are often associated with those functions that directly affect individuals such as wage increases, grievance handling or representational matters with their employer.

The demand for union services is complex. The circumstances whereby workers choose to join a union are almost or varied as human behaviour itself. The decision to join a union can be affected by a number of variables such as:

- level of satisfaction/dissatisfaction with the worker's economic circumstances
- the extent to which the worker chooses to influence their work situation
- the extent to which they see the union as representing their views with management
- peer or coercive pressure
- the costs of unionism (cost of union membership includes both financial cost and things such as the likelihood of employer antagonism, etc.).

There are a number of explanations for why employees join unions. These are discussed in turn below.

Instrumental/Utilitarian Reasons

First, there are instrumental reasons for joining a union. This view suggests that the decision to join a union is related to the desire by workers to gain improvements in unsatisfying working conditions, or alternatively as insurance to prevent exploitation. Second, there is the utilitarian view which sees union membership as a commodity exchange, that is the value of the decision to join is one of a number of choices that workers make under particular circumstances (Crouch 1982). In this sense, workers are seen as economic 'rational' beings and join unions solely because the benefits outweigh the costs. Third, there is a view that union membership is something deeper and philosophical, where the decision to join or not to join is based on political and ideological reasons (following the Marxist view of unions as class institutions) rather than for rational or utilitarian reasons.

Ideological Reasons

Ideological or political motivations to join unions are complex and tend to be related to social and economic class. Bain and Price (1983) in a study of trade unionism in the United Kingdom found that male manual workers employed in traditional manufacturing industries were more likely to join trade unions for ideological reasons than women or white-collar workers. This propensity to join was related to political beliefs as well as the extent to which these industries had a craft tradition. As Jackson (1982) notes, the growth in trade union membership has traditionally been related to the growth in factory production and industrialisation, which contributes to the growth of a union consciousness. The emergence of union services has challenged traditional notions of craft and a 'worker' consciousness. Price and Bain (1983) suggest that trade unions play an important labour market function in rationing and allocating jobs according to union membership (e.g. ensuring that the more long serving union members have access to promotion through seniority, overtime, etc).

Deery and De Cieri (1991) show that demographic factors such as age, gender, education and marital status are not significant in predicting the probability of workers joining unions. They found that workers who were ideologically committed to the labour movement, join unions not for the practical benefits of union membership, but from a sense of duty or a commitment to the principle of unionism (1991, 62). They also emphasised nature of unionism varies in particular industries. Industry characteristics and the ability of the union to maintain services affects members' opportunities to improve in working conditions and promotion (e.g. the study of the ideological orientations of the building and metal unions in Australia by Frenkel and Coalican (1984)).

Involuntary Conscripts

A final reason for joining a union may be due to the requirements of the job (i.e. compulsory unionism such as working in a 'closed shop'). Rawson (1978) argues that trade union membership can be distinguished between 'volunteers' and 'conscripts' (required to belong to a trade union as a requirement under their contract of employment). Compulsory membership was found to affect men more than women. 44 per cent of men in the private sector (predominantly manufacturing, transport and retail/warehousing) indicated this as a reason for joining, compared to 26 per cent of women (1978, 4). However, since the early 1990s, the union closed shop has declined in significance as a reason for joining a union, as most industrial tribunals and courts were reluctant to enforce compulsory union membership. Since 1996, the closed shop has been outlawed under the Workplace Relations Act 1996.

What Do We Know?

Much of the literature supports the idea that the majority of workers join unions for instrumental and utilitarian reasons and at times the two are indistinguishable. Some studies also analyse the decision in terms of collective versus individual benefits. Collective benefits are those that relate and depend on collective bargaining power of the union to improve pay and conditions. For example, according to Rawson (1986), trade unions are made up of people who individually are in a weak position and unions exist in order to maximise individual gains through collective means in order to advance improvements on their pay and conditions (1986, 12-13). In this vein, workers join unions in order to maximise their collective bargaining power. Individual benefits include training and education and personal enhancement in terms of pay and conditions.

Phelps Brown (1990) has argued that as society has become more consumerist and individualistic, workers increasingly join unions for individual or personal reasons. Kerr (1992) found that hospital workers in the UK joined for instrumental and collective reasons in both negotiating pay and conditions or representing members in grievance and disciplinary matters rather than merely accessing union financial services or union shopping discounts etc. Waddington and Whitston (1997) in a study of UK workers found that most workers predominantly joined for collective reasons such as improving pay and conditions or representational matters. They found that whilst many workers first made contact with the union themselves, the regularity of union contact was a significant factor in the decision by workers to remain union members. In a study of New Zealand workers, Tolich and Harcourt (1999) found strong support for the collective role of unions, but found a small proportion of workers joined because management recommended they should (1999, 70). Peetz (1997a 1997b 1997c and 1998) found that the principal utility of unions is their capacity to provide representational benefits (such as job protection, advice, improvements in wages and conditions etc.) and these collective functions remain important motivating factors behind the decision to join.

The propensity to join and remain a member of a union appears conditional upon whether the union is adequate in supporting its members through effective workplace representation (Peetz 1998). Activism, especially under collective bargaining and regularity of contact, are also factors (Wooden and Hawke 1999). Shop floor delegates also report that the regularity of personal contact between the union and members and is a key determinant of why people not only join but stay as members (AWU Official). The notion of union membership as 'industrial insurance' is also borne out by other surveys particularly amongst female workers. However, workers with greater work experience are less likely to join unions (Pocock 1994, 22-23). In this vein, some unions have attempted to attract members by providing a range of financial services, such as the union shopper, financial benefits (cheaper insurance, credit cards etc) in addition to traditional collectivist and representational roles.

THE STATISTICS ON THE STRUCTURE OF AUSTRALIAN TRADE UNIONISM

The pattern of trade union membership in Australia can be divided between industry/occupation and gender. The information from the Australian Bureau of Statistics (ABS) shows the distribution and pattern of Australian union membership in Table 5.4.

Table 5.4 Trade union industry penetration, August 1999

INDUSTRY	PERCENTAGE OF ALL EMPLOYEES UNIONISED IN EACH INDUSTRY		
	Males	Females	Persons
Agriculture, forestry, fishing and hunting	3.5	7.4	4.6
Mining	38.8	---	35.5
Manufacturing	36.4	22.2	32.8
Electricity, gas and water	55.1	25.9	50.1
Construction	28.5	3.0	25.7
Wholesale trade	11.7	5.0	9.6
Retail trade	14.7	19.8	17.4
Accommodation, cafes and restaurants	8.3	11.6	10.1
Transport and storage	45.0	20.6	38.7
Communication services	55.8	33.3	48.3
Finance and insurance	24.0	30.0	27.5
Property and business services	10.5	8.8	9.7
Education	49.9	43.9	45.8
Government, administration and defence	45.8	35.6	41.2
Health and community services	30.7	30.7	30.7
Cultural and recreation services	17.6	13.6	15.7
Personal and other services	40.4	18.8	30.5
TOTAL	**27.7**	**23.4**	**25.7**

Source ABS, Employee Earnings, Benefits and Trade Union Membership, Australia, August 1999, Cat. No. 6310.0, Tables 21, 22, 23

According to the ABS data as set out in Table 5.4, the highest rates of trade union membership were in electrical, gas and water supply (50.1%) followed by communication services (48.3%) and education (45.8%). The lowest rates of trade union membership was found in agriculture, forestry, fishing and hunting (4.6%), followed by wholesale trade (9.6%) and property and business services (9.7%). The distribution of union membership shows the dominance of trades and blue-collar occupations which have a much stronger trade union culture (or 'craft culture') then clerical services that showed much lower levels of union membership.

Union membership appears linked to occupational status. For example, the 1996 ABS survey of trade union membership found that the highest level of union membership was found in intermediate production and transport occupations (such as plant and machine operators and drivers) where 48.8% of employees were union members (or 50% of males and 41% of females). Low levels of union membership was recorded in advanced clerical and service workers occupations, where only 13% of employees were union members (31% of males and 11% of females) whereas intermediate clerical workers was 26.5%. Professional occupations recorded 35.0%. Managers were less likely to join, with only 16.3% found to be union members (ABS, Trade Union Members, Australia, August 1996, Cat No. 6325.0, 6). The ABS survey also found that union membership has traditionally been higher in public sector employment for both male and female employees. However, even here there has been a gradual decline from 46.9% in August 1996 to 41.2% by August 1999 (ABS, Employee Earnings, Benefits and Trade Union Membership, Australia, August 1999, Cat. No. 6310.0, Tables 21, 22, 23; Trade Union Members, Australia, August 1996, Cat No. 6325.0, 6).

Returning to the 1999 ABS survey (Table 5.4), in relation to gender, a higher proportion of male employees were trade union members (27.7%) than females (23.4%). This was most marked in mining (38.8% were males as compared to 0.0% females or too small for the ABS to record), construction, 28.5% were males as compared to 3.0% for females, transport and storage 45.0% for males as compared to 20.6% females. Women were more likely to be found in retail trade 19.8% as compared to 14.7% males, and accommodation, cafes and restaurants 11.6% as compared to 8.3% for males. The majority of female union membership was found in education 43.9%, government administration and defence 35.6%, communication services 33.3%, health and community services 30.7%, finance and insurance 30.0%, electricity, gas and water supply, 25.9%, manufacturing, 22.2% and transport and storage 20.6% (ABS, Employee Earnings, Benefits and Trade Union Membership, Australia, August 1999, Cat. No. 6310.0, Tables 21, 22, 23).

There are a number of differences between male and female union membership and job status (whether full-time or part-time or casual). Males generally recorded a higher rate of trade union membership than females in all occupations. 31.2% of all full-time employees and 30.8% of all part-time employees were trade union members. Male full-time employees have higher rates of trade union membership (32.5%) than female employees (28.7%). However, this pattern was reversed for part-time employees (30.8% for females, 25.5% for males). 10.3% of casual employees are likely to be members of a trade union (ABS, Trade Union Members, Australia, August 1996, Cat No. 6325.0). However, the relationship between employment status and union membership is a complex one. During the period 1992-1999, the number of part-time employees have increased by 37% and casuals employees have increased 37%, whereas the increase in overall employee numbers has gone up by 15%. According to Cully (2000, 13-14) during this period, the number of union members fell by 35.1%. In terms of employment status, for casual employees, union membership fell by 38.6% for men and 38.2% for women. The drop was also proportionately greater amongst male part-time employees. However, according to Cully, when viewed as a proportion of employment, part-timers have improved their relative position to full-timers accounting for 19.6% of union members (up from 15.7% in 1992), in particular, casual male employment has grown at a faster rate than permanent male employment. However, Cully observed that union membership does not necessarily mean higher wages, rather the picture is more complicated and dependant upon skill levels and industry (Cully 2000, 14-15).

Cully goes on to suggest that, despite taking into account the changes in the composition of the labour force, there appears to be three fundamental shifts in the location of union membership. First, the decline in union membership amongst casual and part-time employees is not as great as that of permanent employees suggesting a gradual shift in union membership from permanent to part-time. Second, unions have been successful in increasing membership amongst female part-time employees. Third, casual male employment has grown faster than permanent male employment, however, the rate of unionisation for both continues to decline. Such a shift in unionisation has implications for union recruitment strategies particularly with new jobs increasingly involving part-time and casual male workers.

THE DEBATE OVER UNION STRUCTURE

Historically, the main structural features of trade unionism in Australia have been the dominance of small craft unions. Consequently, there are a large number of trade unions, 295 according to the ABS in 1996 (ABS, Trade Union Statistics, June 1996, Cat. No. 6323). In 1990, union membership was concentrated in a relatively small number of very large unions. Only 15 per cent of trade unions (45) had membership in excess of 20,000 persons, but these unions accounted for over 80 per cent of total union membership in Australia (ABS Trade Union Statistics, June 1990, Cat No. 6323.0). In addition, 45 per cent of all trade unions have less than 1,000 members and together, account for only 1.3 per cent of total union membership.

Small trade unions have proven resistant to change. For example, in 1981, the majority of organisations had less than 2000 members. Moreover the structure and distribution of unions has remained relatively stable, indicating that small unions have shown remarkable durability. According to Deery (1983), the growth in small trade unions can be traced back to the reluctance of Governments (particularly conservative governments supported by employer groups) to allow the aggregation of union resources and the extension of union power through the creation of amalgamated or general unions. Changes made to the Conciliation and Arbitration Act in 1972 effectively prevented unions from merging until the mid 1980s. They also tended to reinforce the built-in inertia of Australian trade unions. In addition, the laws controlling trade union registration have been complex and the requirements for amalgamation have been onerous. Both of these factors have acted as a disincentive to union rationalisation. Lastly, the cost of amalgamations was high, almost unaffordable for smaller unions unless subsidised by a larger host union. (This factor has been offset since the Australian Electoral Commission became involved in conducting union elections free of cost).

The structure and status of Australian Unions has become a matter of debate in Australia to the point, according to some, of being overdone (Gill and Griffin 1981). There are a number of strands to this debate. First, there is a view that there are simply too many unions in Australia. Too many unions are incompatible with a productive and efficient workplace (Blandy et al. 1989). Former ACTU Secretary, Bill Kelty, endorsed this view in a speech in September 1989 in which he argued that the number of unions in Australia was ludicrous and inefficient for both unions and management. (September 1989, *Business Review Weekly*, 92-97). Second, there is the view that union structures are remote and dominated by a small number of large unions that have lost touch with ordinary members (Crosby and Easson 1992). Finally, there is the view that unions are loosing relevance and need to embark on new types of recruiting campaigns (ACTU 1999).

According to some researchers, Australian trade union structures have developed haphazardly through a combination of statutory encouragement, union conservatism, and occupational, trade or craft loyalties. Instead of developing a national, or industry basis, unions as a result have:

- developed in a piecemeal fashion, according to trade and skill and without any central guiding authority
- been encouraged to multiply by compulsory arbitration, which has also protected small and weak organisations
- lost the incentive to combine into larger unions because the wage fixing system has led to the terms of awards flowing from one union to another, irrespective of bargaining power
- developed internal vested interests and political conservatism that are strongly resistant to amalgamation
- historically rationalised only during periods of membership decline or phases of extended collective bargaining (Rimmer 1981).

The BCA Critique of Australian Trade Unions

The Business Council of Australia's (BCA) attack on trade union structure is part of a broader debate about Australia's centralised industrial relations system (the AIRC) and the role of trade unions as third parties in the employment relationship (see Chapter 4). Whilst the debate initially commenced as a review of union structures (Laughlan 1989, 64), it soon involved broader questions about the role and function of unions (Sloan and Wooden 1991). At its core, the debate is essentially about two competing models of regulating the workplace. On one hand, there is the collectivist or pluralist system of industrial relations with a strong centralised independent industrial tribunal and a body of industrial laws that regulate the rights of employers, employees and trade unions. On the other hand, there are those such as the BCA that promote a more individualist or unitarist system based on a strong HRM function, where the employment relationship is dominated by common law contracts with no role for trade unions.

The BCA has been very influential in directing the debate over industrial relations and trade union reform. During the mid 1980s, the BCA published a range of reports (often through the National Institute of Labour Studies, or NILS) in order to promote an industrial relations debate. A number of reports were commissioned such as *Enterprise Bargaining Units: A Better Way of Working* (1989), *Avoiding Industrial Action: A Better Way of Working* (1991), *Working Relations: A Fresh Start for Australian Business* (1993) and a series of lead articles in the BCA Bulletin (e.g. BCA Bulletin, May 1990). Broadly, the BCA approach argued that the structure of trade unions impeded efficiency by:

- centralising bargaining processes away from the workplace
- perpetuating multi-union representation at any one workplace
- creating 'pattern' bargaining (e.g. standardised union wage claims across an industry) which inhibits the development and spread of enterprise bargaining
- limiting the scope of labour flexibility (such as multi-skilling)
- promoting adversarial labour relations (Sloan and Wooden 1990).

The BCA argued that the current trade union workplace coverage was inefficient and adversely affected the bargaining processes at workplace level. For the BCA, the large number of unions at the bargaining table meant that unions were unable or unwilling to take into account individual business situations. The result was wages and conditions not being related to productivity. In addition, the BCA argued that unions were ineffective in representing the 'best' interests of their members (Drago et al. 1992). According to the BCA what was needed was either more 'contestable' or 'competitive' unionism, or no unions at all. The most appropriate form of bargaining according to the BCA would be that which occurs directly between the employer and employees. The BCA has promoted an 'employee relations' model that involves a direct contractual relationship between employer-employee through individual contracts; a stronger HRM focus; greater labour flexibility; and the use of performance pay (see CRA case study).

The BCA model has been subject to criticism on academic grounds for taking a managerialist approach, whilst ignoring the class basis of industrial conflict (Sheldon and Thornthwaite 1993; 1996). It has also been criticised for promoting a unitarist model of industrial relations and failing to recognise the broader safety net role played by of the collectivist centralised industrial relations system (Jamieson 1990; see reply, Hilmer 1990). However, the BCA has had a significant influence on the reform agenda.

Stemming the Decline in Union Membership: the ACTU Response

A longstanding objective of the Australian trade unions has been to restructure unions along industry lines. The first congress of the ACTU in 1927 declared its policy as the better organisation of the workers by the transformation of the trade union movement from the craft to an industrial basis by the establishment of one union in each industry (Hagan 1977, 18). Support for industry based unionism was also helped the establishment of the larger, general industry unions. For example, the AWU still has an objective, first listed at registration in 1916, of establishing (through amalgamation) 'one big union' (OBU). At the core of the debates concerning 'bigger is better' in union structures, was the idea that greater size meant better resources to stem a gradual decline in union membership (Davis 1996).

According to Briggs (1999), ACTU and member union strategies during the 1980s and 1990s fall into two categories. The first, referred to as 'economic mobilisation', covers the period of the Accord when the ACTU was an active partner with the Labor Government in seeking widespread economic and social changes (see Chapter 8). The second category is referred to as 'political mobilisation' and refers to a shift of focus in union strategy from macro-economic and social issues, to the adequacy of union structures and membership services given the ongoing decline in union membership. This second stage which began in the mid 1980s, can be seen in the publication of two reports, which strongly influenced the direction of union strategy, *Australia Reconstructed* (a joint effort by the ACTU and the Trade Development Council 1987) and *Future Strategies for the Trade Union Movement* (ACTU 1987). These documents served to highlight the fragile state of Australian unionism by demonstrating the inadequacies of current union thinking in terms of economic and industry structure, education and training, and the necessity to rationalise structure of unions themselves. Both reports were an attempt by the ACTU to focus on services and coordination of union recruitment strategies as the 'core business' of the union movement. The reports became important components in the total strategy for the renewal of the trade union movement.

Australia Reconstructed called for the adoption by Australian unions of 'strategic unionism' derived from an analysis of the trade union policies of a number of European countries, particularly the Scandinavian countries. Trade union policies in these countries were comprehensive, integrated and designed to achieve long-term objectives, rather than simply being short-term responses (1987, 169). The European trade union policies extend beyond the narrow traditional focus of Australian trade unions on wages and working conditions (i.e. income distribution) and focus on wealth creation through economic growth and productivity enhancement. Income policies were also to be linked to wealth creation. Strategic unionism meant the adoption of centrally coordinated goals; integrated strategies; tripartism; strong local and workplace union organisations; comprehensive education, training and research services; and, the active pursuit of all of these goals both within and outside the traditional forums of industrial relations (1987, 169-170). The report also recommended restructuring Australian unions into larger and more effective organisations through a policy of union amalgamation (1987, 190).

Whilst *Australia Reconstructed* promoted the strategies adopted by various European unions, *Future Strategies* (ACTU 1987), focused on the mounting pressures facing Australian unions and the need to develop survival strategies to promote membership growth. The report identified a number of threats to the trade union movement including:

- poor or indifferent community attitudes to unions
- the policies and practices of the New Right (including the use of common law, legal sanctions and the Trade Practices Act)
- the declining proportion of union coverage
- the disinterest and/or disenchantment of union members
- the inadequate level of services provided to union members
- the inability of the trade union movement to respond to rapid change
- the changing structure of the workforce
- increasing technological change
- the internationalisation of the economy
- the growing importance of anti-union employment practices.

Future Strategies sought to link union re-organisation with improving communication with members by establishing 20 so-called 'super' unions. Whilst the policy was never achieved in full, the ACTU campaign of union amalgamations between 1989 and 1994, fundamentally altered the structure of Australian trade unions as illustrated in Table 5.5.

Table 5.5   Results of ACTU union amalgamation policy 1989-1994

Success of ACTU Amalgamation Policy: 1989-1994
Australian trade unions have undergone substantial changes over the last decade:
• between 1986 and 1996, the number of unions fell from 506 to 312 (194 fewer)
• amalgamations have been the major source of change. In 1995 - 1996, 7 unions amalgamated to form 3 larger unions
• at June 1996, 132 trade unions had a total of 2.4 million financial members (and 350,000 members who were unfinancial)
• trade union membership between June 1995 and June 1996 increased by 10,700
• between 1992 and 1996 the number of unions with membership of 100,000 and over increased from 9 to 12. The number of unions with less than 1,000 members has declined from 26 in 1993 to 11 in 1996. But the proportion of unions with less than 1,000 members remained approximately the same at around 46 per cent of all unions.

Source ABS, Trade Union Statistics, Australia, June 1996, Cat no. 6323.0

Future Strategies also justified a radical policy of union amalgamation and membership exchanges in the name of greater union efficiency and membership servicing. This involved the ACTU becoming active in determining union coverage. The Industrial Relations Act 1988 and subsequent amendments (brought in by the then ALP Government with the support of the ACTU) contained Section 118 (and later s.118A) that allowed AIRC to decide union coverage at workplace or industry level. The legislative purpose was to further trade unionism through exclusive union coverage. This was to be achieved by allowing a successful union to legally recruit all workers at a particular workplace or within an industry (Kallmargen and Naughton 1991). Examples of single-site agreements include Flagstaff Industries, Olex Cables, Warner Bros. Movie World, Sea World, and Dream World. This aspect of ACTU policy comes close to a U.S. labour law concept of 'union recognition rights', which means that once a union has established an initial right to cover a particular workplace, it is then able to recruit all workers at the site. At the time, the ACTU union rationalisation policy was very controversial and many ACTU affiliated unions objected to the idea of the ACTU picking 'winners' and 'losers'. In addition, many arbitrated cases under Section 118A involved transfers of existing union members between competing unions rather than generating new membership.

EXPLAINING THE DECLINE IN UNION MEMBERSHIP

Despite ACTU attempts to restructure trade unions, union membership in Australia has continued to decline. According to the ACTU during the period 1982 to 1996, union membership fell from a high of 49.5% to a low of 24%. The problem facing Australian unions was both the recruitment and the retention of union members. Not only had these two factors not kept pace with employment growth, they had in fact declined. Between 1982 and 1994, when the labour force increased by 1,337,900 employees [25.8%], union membership declined by 284,200 [11.1%]. In the first half of this period 1982 to 1988, union membership increased by almost 5%, with unions recruiting 26 of every 100 new employees. However, in the second half 1990 to 1994, union membership declined by 376,200 [14%]. The ACTU has concluded that without an infusion of new members, union membership will continue to decline in absolute terms (ACTU, *The Future of Unions in Australia*, Background Paper, ACTU Congress May 1995a, 5).

Why has Australian trade union membership declined so dramatically? There are a number of complex reasons. First, there has been a significant decline in manufacturing industries, which has traditionally had a high level of union membership. For example, during the period 1966 to 1988, the number of employees in manufacturing fell by 34%, and union membership fell by 20% (Shaw et al. 1990, 93). Second, whereas manufacturing has declined, employment in the service sectors particularly retail, financial services and tourism has increased substantially. Union membership in service sectors is, however, low. For example, union membership in retailing is 17.4%, accommodation, hotels and cafes 10.1%, finance and insurance 27.5%, health and community services 30.7% and personal and other services 30.5% (ABS, Employee Earnings, Benefits and Trade Union Membership, Australia, August 1999, Cat. No. 6310.0, Table 20). The explanation for low union membership in the services sector appears to be that workplaces tend to be smaller and more decentralised than in manufacturing and the public service. In addition, services are more likely to employ casuals and part-time workers. They may also have higher turnover and job mobility rates, which makes worker recruitment into unions more difficult.

A third reason for the decline in union membership is about gender. Historically, unions have opposed the participation of women in the workforce, seeing them as a threat to full-time male employment. Women were often seen as poor union members for their alleged lack of militancy. In addition, as many women are employed casual or part-time, they are often employed in areas of work that lack affinity with unions, because of the absence of a labour consciousness (or craft) tradition in their areas of work. There are also other explanations for low rates of female membership. For example, women may be less favourably disposed towards unions because they feel that their specific needs are not being addressed. Consequently they see few advantages in joining a union (Pocock 1994; Pocock 1995). It may also be that the poor record of trade unions in attracting more women members may be due in part to the under absence of women officials in trade unions. According to a survey of women officials in trade unions in South Australia, women are less than proportionally represented among union officials in three-quarters of the unions surveyed. Women officials were found to hold only 25% of all union positions, being concentrated in a relatively small number of larger unions, mostly covering white-collar workers in the public and private sectors, and in unions with a large proportion of women members (Pocock 1995, 14).

In addition, women often lacked the necessary representational skill. Women were often found to have taken a back seat in workplace negotiations. According to Pocock (1994; 1995) women's share of all types of workplace representation (including workplace delegates, health and safety, equal employment opportunity, training and consultative representatives and their deputies) was only 31 percent. Women made up only 12 percent of deputy shop stewards (only six of the fifty-six respondent unions could supply this data); 37 percent of health and safety representatives (in twenty-nine unions); 22 percent of consultative committees (in eighteen unions); and a mere 11 percent on training committees in a small number of unions (Pocock 1995, 11).

A fourth reason for union membership decline concerns societal and attitudinal changes at work. A 1995 survey by the Labour Council of New South Wales found that unions were failing to maintain membership loyalty amongst blue-collar workers. The survey of 1200 workers found that one in five union members would quit their union membership if closed shops were abolished, and there was major dissatisfaction among blue-collar workers with the performance of unions. The survey found that while 67% of workers believed Australia was better off with unions, only 48% would join a union if they were given a free choice. The survey also found that dissatisfaction with unions was almost 10 per cent higher with blue-collar workers than among professional or white-collar workers. In addition, the survey also found low levels interest amongst young people in joining unions (Survey 'Attitudes to Work and Unions' - Focus Group Research Study, Labour Council of New South Wales 1995).

A fifth reason for the decline of unionism relates to the role management plays in union success in the workplace. Kochan, Katz and McKersie (1986) and Kochan and Tamir (1989) argue that the decline in union organisation in the USA has been a function of increased globalisation and deep-seated unitarist managerial attitudes towards unions. They also suggest that technological change and shifting product markets have placed greater cost pressures on management to pursue anti-union strategies. Decentralisation and globalisation are associated with a weakening of the institutions of labour regulation (such as arbitral labour courts and trade unions) (Macken 1997). This has allowed employers greater choice in deciding the type of workplace relations' practices enabling management to pursue more individualist employee relations' policies that freeze out unions. Employers are increasingly hostile towards trade unions and adopting HRM practices that aim to exclude or weaken unions at the workplace (Peetz 1998). The move towards individualising the contract of employment is often justified on by the need to make labour relations as flexible as possible in response to product market conditions. In response to more competitive product markets, employers want to be able to link the pay and conditions of the workforce more tangibly to 'the needs of the business'.

A sixth reason for the decline of unionism concerns the role of the State. The State can play a significant part in encouraging or discouraging unionism and influence the ability of unions to recruit new members. The state can, as lawmaker, decide the legal environment in which trade unions operate. For example, the election of conservative governments in Victoria and Western Australia have reduced the role of their industrial tribunals in the award making and dispute settling, and reduced the extent of collective bargaining by introducing individual contracts between employers and employees. Such agreements are enforceable at common law. Unions are locked out as parties to such agreements and have no representational rights. In the case of Victoria, the introduction of a system of contracts was also accompanied by the removal of the award system. (This caused a widespread shift of Victorian workers to the federal jurisdiction, aided by the then Federal Labor Government. The conservative Kennett Government then ceded all its industrial relations powers to the Commonwealth, following the election of the conservative Coalition Federal Government in 1997.) The current Victorian Labor State Government is grappling with the problem of 're-acquiring' is former industrial relations power back from the Coalition Federal Government.

The impact of government on unionism can also be seen across the Tasman Ocean. New Zealand has adopted far-reaching labour market reforms that have influenced the Coalition Federal Government's changes to trade union regulation in Australia. The New Zealand industrial relations system was, from 1894 until 1984, essentially a system of compulsory conciliation and arbitration similar to Australia's system. This system generated awards, primarily national and occupational in coverage, establishing terms and conditions of employment. The Labor Government elected in 1984 passed several pieces of legislation intended to persuade the industrial parties to restructure industrial relations along industry lines and to decentralise industrial relations to the enterprise level. The New Zealand Labour Government also removed the power of compulsory arbitration in 'interest disputes' (i.e. bargaining matters at workplace level, but excluding interpretations of agreements and awards) from the Arbitration Court. The Court retained a role in voluntary arbitration, but was required to settle disputes having regard to market-based criteria, such as industry efficiency, workplace productivity, and labour costs. The emphasis was on greater voluntarism in workplace issues, including union membership.

The election in 1990 of the Nationals to Government in New Zealand saw the introduction of the Employment Contracts Act, which took effect in May of 1991. The philosophical basis to the Employment Contracts Act 1991 was maximisation of individuals' choice, through a regime of completely free contracting consistent with ideas found in the common law. The Employment Contracts Act disbanded the arbitral model. Conciliation and arbitration became a private (and voluntary) matter. The Labour Court was abolished, with contract enforcement left to the civil courts. As awards expired their terms were to be imputed into individual contracts of employment, unless varied by subsequent agreement between the individual worker and employer. In essence, the Act made it possible to bargain on almost any condition of employment. Unions lost their exclusive representational and coverage rights over employees and employees were given the choice to either represent themselves or nominate a bargaining agent (that could be any union). Whilst the Act required the employers to recognise employee bargaining agents, there was no requirement on employers to bargain in good faith (i.e. to meet, provide information and negotiate honestly) with employee bargaining agents. According to Douglas (1993), and Harbridge and Moulder (1993) the impact of these reforms on trade unions in New Zealand was dramatic. Union membership declined fastest in services such as clerical, retail, cafe/restaurant, and tourism sectors. Union membership in manufacturing and engineering was more resilient due to stronger union delegate structures. With a dramatic reduction in the collective role of trade unions, it is argued that many employees lost out in wage bargaining under the new employment contracts.

A final explanation concerns the Accord. Some researchers see a link between the decline in Australian union membership during the 1980s and 1990s and the Labor Federal Government's Accord (see Chapter 8 for a discussion of the Accord). For example, Kenyon and Lewis (1996) have argued that under the Accord many workers saw little reason to remain union members. The majority of workers received pay adjustments under the centralised national wage case, so union membership made little difference to their rates of pay. In fact the support of the union leadership for the Accord may have been seen by many unionists as against their interests especially amongst skilled workers who believed that they could have negotiated better pay outcomes directly with their employer than that allowed under the Accord (1996, 4).

Other researchers argue that the corporatist nature of the Accord and its link to broader government policy contributed to membership decline. Ordinary workers questioned the benefits of union membership especially as the benefits of the Accord were distributed equally to members and non-union members alike (Bray and Walsh 1995; Hampson 1996). In addition, ACTU union rationalisation policies were seen as having a negative effect. Potential members were not being attracted and existing members were leaving the new amalgamated unions, which were seen as large and remote (Costa and Duffy 1991 and Davies 1996). As one union report *Can Unions Survive?* (Berry and Kitchener 1989) argued, under the Accord, unions were focused on a relationship with the then Labor Government rather than the day to day problems of working Australians (1989, 6). A similar conclusion was reached by the Evatt Foundation, in their report *Unions 2000 (1995)*. This report observed that the big union issues of the 1980s, such as the role of the Accord, union amalgamations, restructuring and industry superannuation, were essentially top-down unionism, frequently delivered with little membership understanding or involvement in either ideas or their implementation. The effect was to create a distance between members and their own unions, increasing passivity and leading members to doubt their union's loyalties and priorities (1995, 57).

In analysing the decline in union membership in Australia, Hawke and Wooden (1998), argue that changes to industrial relations and a move towards workplace bargaining have both benefited and hurt unions. They observe that union membership has fallen from a high of 50% in the 1970s to 28% by 1998. Moreover, the decline in union density appears to have accelerated since the late 1980s with the move towards workplace bargaining. According to Wooden and Hawke (1999) there is a strong association between union presence and bargaining structure, with collective bargaining being overwhelmingly dominated by unions and individual bargainers (individual agreements) predominantly non-union. They argue that unions are more successful in maintaining a strong presence where they are involved in workplace bargaining, but a strong presence does not always generate increased union membership (1999, 44-45).

When we move away from analysing raw union membership numbers and focus attention on the decline in union density (i.e. proportion of workers covered by unions), according to Griffin and Svensen (1996), the decline is far more complex matter than. Their comprehensive review and analysis of the literature dealing with the decline in Australian union density found a number of shortcomings in our approach and knowledge of the issue:

- current approaches place too much emphasis on union membership, rather than on union density
- more sophisticated models of change are needed to examine the precise nature of long-term trends in unionisation
- studies which assess the impact of occupational changes and industry shifts often rely on different methods of data gathering which do not allow for realistic comparisons of findings of change in trade union membership
- because trade unionisation varies according to number of employees (i.e. the smaller the size of the business, the more likely there will be lower level of unionisation) the tendency towards mergers and company takeovers is may have a diluting affect on density measures

- trade union amalgamations and the employment of more union officials with tertiary qualifications are seen as discouraging union democracy and alienating membership, yet there is little evidence to support this view
- attitudinal studies and the personal characteristics of workers are seen as important variables in relation to a worker's propensity to join a union. However, such studies over emphasise the relationship between intention and behaviour. Such research is often based on questionnaires and the tenuous relationship between attitude and intention, as attitudes do not necessarily relate to any given behaviour on the part of workers
- studies of declining trade union density need more sophisticated and multi-casual models that include the social context of unionisation, trade union bargaining strategy and worker motivations (Griffin and Svensen 1996, 6-26).

WHAT SHOULD UNIONS DO?

Australian unions are not alone in facing membership decline. The impact of economic, social, political and attitudinal changes are relevant to understanding why union membership is declining. Buchanan (1996) argues that unions need to adopt four principles in trade union bargaining strategy that he sees as essential for rejuvenating trade unions with their members (and potential members) at the workplace. He suggests unions should:

- maintain organisational and ideological autonomy by remaining independent of employers and the State (e.g. no more Accords)
- give greater resources to establishing regional and workplace level organisations more attuned to members needs
- adopt bargaining strategies which do not involve conflict between unions and members (e.g. no negotiation of agendas which contain disadvantages for members)
- increase inter-union cooperative networks tailored to achieve specific trade union objectives, such as labour market objectives, reorganisation of working time, and more appropriate approaches to enterprise bargaining (Buchanan 1996).

Kenyon and Lewis (1996) argue that unions need to re-connect with the workplace and accordingly need to develop more effective workplace representational structures (1996, 11-12).

Stemming the Tide: The ACTU's 'Organising Works' Campaign

In order to improve the membership recruitment and retention, the 1993 ACTU Congress, Executive and Council meetings in March and May 1995 formulated a new strategy aimed at a major expansion in the number of recruiting officers and the diversification of the services offered by unions (ACTU 1995a; 1995b 1995c). Consequently, the ACTU and its affiliates introduced a new scheme called 'Organising Works'. Originally funded by the ACTU for the employment of 60 trainee organisers, the role of Organising Works was to recruit new union members using a servicing model of trade unionism. By 1995, Organising Works organisers had, according to the ACTU, recruited some 9,000 new union members and boosted trade union revenue by $2M. This income was approximately double the costs associated with the program. The program also sought to expand the number of workplace delegates by an additional 20,000 and to achieve a target of 200,000 new union recruits by the end of the program. The May 1996 meeting of the ACTU Council approved the employment of additional 300 recruiters into the Organising Works scheme. It also encouraged unions to consider services such as the provision of holiday homes at discounted rates and discounted insurance and health cover schemes (Davies 1996, 169).

An Organising Model of Unionism

Key planks in trade union strategy since the introduction of the Organising Works program have been to move towards a member services-oriented recruitment approach and the creation of a 'recruitment' culture. This approach was based on the experiences of U.S. unions. This member services or 'organising' model of union recruitment attempts to move unions closer to their membership and workplace level. It differs from the old model of unionism (or 'servicing' model) built around 'core' functions of advocacy and legal representation. The new ('organising') model of unionism increases the members' role in determining union priorities and improves marketing of union services at workplace level. Following an overseas mission by ACTU officers in 1999, the ACTU released a report called *Unions @t Work* (1999). The report contained a number of initiatives for improving union services and membership recruitment campaigns and adopted a 'sink or swim' approach including:

- increasing the effectiveness of union bargaining claims
- organising more effective union recruitment campaigns
- making better use of the media to push the union point of view
- maintaining an equitable safety net of wages and conditions below enterprise bargaining
- campaign for greater job security and a better balance between family and working life
- developing and fostering greater workplace activism (*Unions @ Work*, ACTU 1999).

The release of *Unions @ Work* was also accompanied by an internal restructure of the ACTU. ACTU staffing and operations were rationalised and the role of workplace union services and representational structures increased. The numbers of industrial officers were increased to improve workplace support and the ACTU Council was expanded to enable representatives from every union, and all state and provincial branches of the ACTU to be represented.

UNIONS UNDER THE COALITION FEDERAL GOVERNMENT

With the election of a Federal Coalition Government in 1996, Australian trade unions are undergoing a period of reflection and consolidation. Union amalgamations, whilst once a key platform of ACTU policy, is no longer a key priority. Unions are no longer involved in macro economic policy planning as they once were under the Labor Government/ACTU Accord. The introduction of the Workplace Relations Act (WRA 1996) by the Coalition Government has important implications for union membership recruitment strategies. According to Peetz (1999), whilst the Act encourages greater workplace cooperation, the strategy behind the Act involves a number of anti-union elements (see Chapter 9). These include:

- undermining union membership by removing union preference clauses from awards and agreements
- removing obstacles from employers wishing to resist unionism and remove collective bargaining from employment relations
- diverting union time and resources in defending 'freedom of association' actions
- encouraging fragmentation by disamalgamation and the growth of enterprise unions
- diverting union resources to the defence of long standing award conditions
- threatening unions financially by creating large areas where employers can seek damages after union action (1999, 2899).

TRADE UNIONS IN THE FIVE SELECTED SOUTH EAST ASIAN COUNTRIES

A brief outline of the role of trade unions in our five selected South East Asian countries is provided in Chapter 13. Here we examine in more detail the structure and functions of trade unions, and comment on recent trends affecting them.

Japan

As will be discussed in Chapter 13, trade unions in Japan originated in the period of industrialisation following the Meiji Restoration in 1868. The development of an independent trade union movement was never encouraged by the state, but by the 1920s, such a movement could be said to have come into existence. However, the militaristic regime of the 1930s destroyed independent trade unions, and reorganised them as state-controlled bodies.

It was not until the imposition of the post-war constitution on Japan that trade unions re-emerged as independent entities. In the new democratic era, unions quickly re-attained their pre-war strength, and reached a peak density level of 56%, comprising 6.6 million members in 1949. However, with the end of the struggle between Communists and anti-Communists in the union movement in the 1950s, union density again declined. By 1970, it was down to 35%, and thereafter there was a period of stagnation and further decline. In 1996, Japanese union membership totalled 12,451,000, or a density of only 23%.

There are a number of reasons for the decline in union membership. A principal cause has been the change in the industrial structure of the Japanese economy. Like other advanced industrialised economies, Japan experienced a shift towards the service sector, and a decline in manufacturing. This has undermined the base blue-collar membership, as the proportion of white-collar workers has grown. An associated trend has been that in the service sector, the size of firms tends to be small, making it more difficult for unions to organise.

The rise in living standards has been advanced as another reason for the decline in unionism, with many workers less enthusiastic about joining. In the period following the oil crisis of 1973, many employers also took a tougher line towards unions. Further, as discussed in chapter 13, Japanese workers have a strong commitment to their enterprises, and the system of lifetime employment has discouraged job-hopping at least among the one-third of employees who are counted as permanent. As in other advanced industrial societies, the level of unionisation is higher among male workers than female workers. The permanent workforce consists mainly of males, while females are more likely to be consigned to temporary positions. They are therefore less interested in joining trade unions.

However, Taira (1993, 229) points out that the statistics on union density ignore one important fact. Many firms that officially have no labour unions have 'employee associations' that behave very much like unions. These associations are not unions only because they have failed to register with the labour administration under the labour law. If these associations were counted, then the level of union density would rise considerably.

The main form of contemporary trade unionism in Japan is enterprise unionism. See Chapter 13 for the reasons for the evolution of this form of unionism in Japan. A specific cultural factor is what Dore (1973) calls 'enterprise consciousness', in which workers see the firm not merely as a place to make a living, but as a community with which they identify. Workers leaving the company automatically lose union membership, as do those promoted to management positions. However, despite their name, enterprise unions do not exist for the benefit of the enterprise. They enjoy legal protection against employer interference in their affairs, and other unfair labour practices. There was an estimated 70,839 unions in 1996, with density greatest among regular employees in large firms. Around 97% of enterprise union members work in firms with over 100 employees. There are other types of union, including craft, industrial and general unions, but these are a much rarer form of organisation in Japan.

Most of the enterprise unions are affiliated with industrial federations, of which there are over 100 in Japan. The functions of these federations include coordination of the activities of enterprise unions to improve wages and conditions, dealing with common industry problems, assisting member unions in particular disputes, and political lobbying in members' interests. These federations in turn belong to national centres. The main centre is called Rengo (Japan Trade Union Confederation - JTUC). Rengo was formed in 1989, with the adherence of 78 industrial federations and nearly 8 million members. Originally public sector unionism was more strongly represented in its members, but over time union membership has declined and the balance has shifted towards the private sector.

Rengo has followed a general policy of promoting cooperative labour-management relations. It has links with the Japan Socialist Party, which formed Government in a coalition in 1994, but the Government was short-lived. Rengo has mainly concentrated on political campaigns, and has found it hard to represent the interests of grass-roots workers. Rengo's structure has been challenged by a number of problems: an unfavourable economic climate; high unemployment in the long recession of the 1990s; job shortages for university graduates; and industry and enterprise re-structuring. (Kuwahara 1998, 252-257).

The influence of the trade union movement on overall economic policy in Japan is also very limited. On two of the most powerful Advisory councils, the Economic Council, which deliberates on economic planning, and the Industrial Structure Council, which shapes industrial policy, labour union leaders are hopelessly outnumbered by representatives of business interests. This has led to a phenomenon which has been called 'corporatism without labour', but this probably underestimates the power of organised Japanese labour, with its constitutional rights to take collective action (Taira 1993, 226).

Because of the strong association between workers and their enterprises, the relatively low level of industrial disputes, and the often symbolic nature of those disputes, Japanese unions have typically been portrayed as 'tame cat' in nature. However, Koike (1988, 251-257) disputes this assessment. He argues that Japanese unions play a very active role in many important issues in their enterprises, including transfers, promotions, redundancies and wage rates. There is also real participation by unions in managerial decision-making through joint-consultation over important issues (separate from collective bargaining), such as labour conditions, the shopfloor environment, safety and fringe benefits. And Japanese workers show considerable enthusiasm to participate in the affairs of their enterprises.

Internally, unions are very democratic. Officials are typically elected by members for one or two year terms. This applies at all levels of organised labour, from enterprise unions to Rengo. Power is centred at the bottom, and gingerly delegated upwards by the enterprise unions. There is also a turnover of unions in enterprises. Where members feel that an existing union is not serving their interests sufficiently well, they will often replace it with a new one. Sometimes more than one union exists per enterprise. The possibility of competition helps to keep unions ' adversarial' enough to prove that they are fighting for the members' benefit. (Taira 1993, 229). This supports Koike's assertion above that Japanese unions are not totally 'tame-cat'.

Elected union officials do not lose their employee status in their companies, they are treated as being on leave. They may even earn promotions in absentia, and return to higher positions than those they left. (Taira 1993, 227). This, of course, helps to cement the relationship between the enterprise and its union.

Thus, to sum up, Japanese unions are typically structured around enterprises, with the greatest density among permanent male workers. They have a generally cooperative attitude towards labour relations, based on enterprise consciousness. Their numbers have also been declining for reasons similar to those in other advanced industrial societies, but the statistics probably overstate this trend because of the existence of numerous 'employee associations'.

Singapore

The history of trade unions in Singapore is briefly outlined in Chapter 13. Trade union activity was always regulated by colonial ordinances, but for the decade following independence from Britain, Singapore did experience independent trade unions, with a struggle for control between Communists and anti-Communists, and a turbulent era of strikes and conflict. However, since the late 1960s, trade unions have been so much subordinated to the Government and its economic objectives, that the relationship is typically described as 'symbiotic', with a senior Government minister always holding the post of the National Trades Union Congress (NTUC). The commitment of the NTUC to cooperative labour relations from the late 1960s initially caused a decline in union membership. However, there was a subsequent membership recovery because of the association with the National Wages Council (NWC), the expansion of the labour force, and the organising zeal of some trade union leaders (Leggett 1993, 101-102). However, as Chew and Chew (1995, 65) have pointed out, seeking full employment as a strategy creates a problem for the NTUC. There is no incentive for workers to join trade unions and pay dues when they can receive the benefits without joining.

Trade union density had declined to 14.6% of the workforce by 1998 (Yearbook of Statistics, Singapore 1998). In the early 1980s, the Government decided that, in the interests of labour-management cooperation, its favoured form of union organisation was enterprise unionism along Japanese lines. The NTUC unions were therefore re-structured in 1984, after which there were 20 enterprise, 18 industry, 20 craft and 4 general unions. In 1989, 3 more house unions affiliated with the NTUC were registered (Leggett 1993, 100). By 1993, the total number of trade unions had grown to 74 (Ariff 1993, 352).

Strikes in Singapore are virtually impossible without tacit government approval, and none has been recorded since 1986. However, industrial disputes (as opposed to strikes) are still at about half the level of earlier years. Ariff (1993, 359) explains this apparent contradiction. Apart from the legislative prohibition on strikes, he points out some economic reasons for the scarcity of strikes. First, Singapore workers are able to draw on their Central Provident Fund contributions to buy their own homes. 92% of Singaporeans own their own homes, compared with only 20% in 1960. This has given workers a substantial stake in the economy. Second, substantial wage increases have occurred as a result of National Wages Council recommendations (with unions being represented on the council). For example, wages doubled in the 1970s', and then again in the 1980s. A third reason has been the general labour shortage, which has made employers willing to pay higher wages. Thus, a general consensus seems to have emerged that it is better to settle disputes collaboratively within a nationally determined wages policy than to engage in industrial confrontations.

The role of trade unions in Singapore is probably best explained within a framework of state corporatism. Corporatism, as outlined in Chapter 6, involves economic and political subordination of particular social groups, such as organised labour, to the interests of the state. In corporatist state-union relations, unions are seen as auxiliaries of ruling parties, or a means for implementing economic development policies. As such, they may be required to play a 'productionist' role instead of pursuing the goals of increased consumption in terms of wages and benefits for their members. Unions may be asked to educate, train or discipline members, to raise productivity, discourage industrial conflict, restrain wage demands and make whatever sacrifices may be necessary in the interests of national development.

Under a corporatist model, conciliation and arbitration typically replace the right to autonomous bargaining, with outcomes determined by what is seen as the national interest. Other typical union resources, such as the right to strike, legality of involvement in politics and legitimacy of collective bargaining, may be limited. The state may also replace unions in playing a social welfare role. Thus the attractiveness of union membership to individuals is typically reduced, as unions are seen as increasingly irrelevant in improving wages and working conditions. The overall outcome is a decline or stagnation in trade union membership and increasing apathy among members (Anantaraman 1991, 116-7). This corporatist model provides a good explanation of the main trends in trade unionism in Singapore during the last three decades.

Notwithstanding the above, the standard of living for most workers in Singapore has risen dramatically during the past 3 decades, with per capita GNP rising to over $US 27,000 in 1998, and making Singapore one of the five richest nations in the world by this measure.

Malaysia

Malaysia has had ambitious national development plans since the 1960s. Trade unions have had only a very limited role in these plans. From the mid 1970s until the mid 1990s, the Malaysian economy was one of the fastest-growing in the world, registering a 5.7% per capita growth rate of GNP from 1985-1995, making it the eighth fastest-growing economy in the world. . However, the Asian financial crisis hit Malaysia hard, with real GDP declining 6.7% in 1998, and the official unemployment rate increasing from 2.5% in 1996 to 3.9% in 1998. 84,000 workers were retrenched in 1998, compared with only 19,000 in the previous year. By 1999, a small economic recovery had begun, but it was clear that it would take some time for Malaysia to resume its previous growth path (Edwards 2000, 670).

As in the case of Singapore, trade unions are subject to stringent legal controls in Malaysia. A more detailed account of these controls is provided in Chapter 13. Trade unions can only achieve legal legitimacy if they are registered. They have to conform to strict rules at the point of registration. The Director General for Trade Unions has the power to register unions, and may refuse to do so if he believes that any of the unions' objectives are unlawful. The Act states bluntly that the objectives of unions may only be economic, not political. If unions have any political objectives, they are outside the scope of the law. If the Director General refuses to register a union, there is an appeal to the Minister of Human Resources, whose decision is final.

Unions are required to submit to detailed rules concerning their objectives; the purposes for which funds may be used; the way in which branches can be established; matters that have to be decided by secret ballots; methods of election of officers; and all matters relating to strikes or lockouts. There are also restrictions on the types of persons who can join unions. Only workers over the age of 18 years are eligible to join, and membership is confined to the trade or occupation for which the union was established. Employees of the federal or state governments are prohibited from joining unions, unless specifically exempted by the King from this prohibition. Those employed in managerial or professional capacities are also prohibited from being union members, unless similarly exempted (Ayadurai 1993, 72-3).

As in Singapore, strike activity by trade unions is very strictly controlled, though there have been more strikes in Malaysia than in Singapore. After a major dispute in 1979, the Malaysian Airlines System dispute, the Industrial Relations Act was amended to give the Minister wide-ranging powers beyond those already in the Act, in particular to prohibit strikes in 'essential services'. This concept is broadly defined, and could include airlines, food processing, electrical, road transport or any other industry deemed to be in the national interest (Kuruvilla and Arudsothy 1995, 170).

A further problem for trade unions is that they can only effectively engage in collective bargaining with employers if they are recognised by those employers. Formal recognition depends on whether the union is registered; has appropriate coverage of a trade or occupation; has approved members; and is representative (Ayadurai 1993, 73-4). In practice, few employers voluntarily recognise trade unions. In the case of a dispute with a recognised union, the Director General of Industrial Relations has the right, in the first instance, to determine the matter. However, the Minister of Labour can make a final and binding decision. At least half of the claims with union recognition have been in the low-cost, labour intensive manufacturing areas of textiles and light electrical. This is also where the greatest number of recognised claims has been rejected by the Minister (Kuruvilla and Arudsothy 1995, 171.)

In 1985, trade union density was only about 10% of the employed workforce. In 1989, there were 370 trade unions, 210 in the public sector and 160 in the private sector. The Malaysian Government has followed a deliberate policy of fragmenting trade unions, and limiting their growth (Kuruvilla and Arudsothy 1995, 172). Those unions that do exist are small in membership and have limited resources. The Director General of Trade Unions has also used his discretion to register unions on the basis of particular trades, occupations and industries to thwart new membership drives, particularly in the foreign owned and economically vital electronics industry (Ayadurai 1993, 80-81). The Malaysian

Government, like the Singapore Government, has sought to foster enterprise unionism as the main form of unionism, so as to foster more cooperative labour relations. In 1988, 54.5% of unions were enterprise unions (Kuruvilla and Arudsothy 1995, 173).

Trade union federations do not fall within the definition of trade unions, but may be registered as societies. The Malaysian peak union organisation is the Malaysian Trades Union Congress (MTUC). It is registered as a society, but is effectively prevented by the law from functioning as a true union federation. An attempt to unify the two main labour federations in 1985 was frustrated by the Government (Kuruvilla and Arudosthy 1995, 174). About 50% of the unionised workforce is affiliated with the MTUC through their unions. The federation exercises little control over its affiliates and has limited involvement in industrial matters. Its main function is to liaise with government, undertake research and conduct educational programs for members (Ayadurai 1993, 82).

Thus, Malaysian trade unions, while not quite as fettered as in Singapore, have been kept relatively weak as part of the Government's national development policy. In particular, unions have effectively been excluded from the key electronics industry, which is largely foreign-owned. The corporatist model described above in relation to Singapore also applies to a lesser degree to Malaysia. However, apart from Government controls, another factor limiting the growth of trade unions is the very high proportion of foreign workers in the labour force. According to an authoritative estimate, in 1995 there were 1.7 million foreign workers in Malaysia, accounting for just under 20% of total employment. Foreign labour has been particularly important in plantation agriculture, construction, services, textiles and clothing. In addition, many of these foreign workers are working illegally in Malaysia (Edwards, 2000, 671). However, it is surprising that, given the severe straits in which the economy found itself in the late 1990s, that there was no record of increases in trade union militancy.

Hong Kong

As described in Chapter 13, the overall role of the British colonial government in the Hong Kong economy could be described as laissez faire. Within the framework established by the British colonial administration, trade unions were allowed relatively free reign. Under Hong Kong law, trade unions may seek registration, the effect of which is to grant them corporate status, immunity from action in some civil cases, protection of those pursuing trades disputes, and freedom from liability for criminal prosecution for conspiracy (Levin and Ng 1993, 32). The Registrar of Trade Unions' discretion to refuse registration is limited (Ng and Fung 1989, 62-3).

As in the UK, collective bargaining between employers and trade unions is a purely voluntary matter, and any agreements entered into are not enforceable in the courts. A law to compel employers to bargain collectively if unions which wished to do so, was repealed following the hand-over of Hong Kong by Britain to China (Slater 1999). There are no prohibitions on strikes as such, as is the case in Singapore and Malaysia. However, the relevant legislation appears to permit only strikes whose causes are primarily economic, that is, trade disputes, with objectives relating to employment (Levin and Ng 1993, 34). There is provision for voluntary conciliation where such strikes do occur.

The number of trade unions increased steadily since the late 1960s, but union density has declined. After a peak of 23.9% in 1975, it declined to 15.8% in 1987. The main area of growth for trade unions has been in the community, social and personal services sector. In practice it is in the civil service that unions have flourished and been most active. However, membership in manufacturing has been declining, but this is largely a reflection of the fact that the manufacturing sector in Hong Kong has shrunk in recent years, or rather that it has moved offshore to mainland China. In 1987, there were 415 unions in Hong Kong, covering a total of 381,685 employees (Levin and Ng 1993, 37).

These unions were also organised into federations. There are two organisations - the Confederation of Trade Unions (which is pro-democracy in its political line) and the Federation of Trade Unions (which is pro-government). Their main functions are coordination of industrial campaigns (such as they are in Hong Kong) and political lobbying of governments in relation to labour matters.

Levin and Chiu (1995) suggest the following reasons for the decline in trade unionism in Hong Kong:

- structural change in the economy
- the decline of some traditionally unionised trades e.g. seafaring and spinning and weaving
- the rising standard of living of the population
- internal movement of people and jobs to new towns
- expansion of government provision for housing, education and welfare benefits
- provision of new channels for dispute resolution such as the Labour Tribunal.

Another significant factor in the decline appears to be ignorance about trade unions and hostility towards them, which is demonstrated by survey data. Partly, this may be the result of poor marketing by trade unions. But another factor that certainly plays a part is the attitude of employers. The reason why unions are better established in the civil service has been the willingness of governments to deal with them, as compared with their private sector employer counterparts (Levin and Ng 1993, 40).

Generally, the Hong Kong trade union movement has been portrayed as docile and weak. Outside the civil service, strike activity has been very limited, and few collective agreements have been negotiated. Some reasons that have been advanced for the relative weakness of trade unions in Hong Kong include:

- the politicisation and division of the Hong Kong union movement between left and right wing unions
- the history of a refugee labour force with materialistic values and little taste for collective organisation
- the Chinese dislike for confrontation situations
- a preference for dealing with conflict by indirect methods.

Another explanation is that the labour movement has deliberately adopted a low profile, following a distinctive Chinese strategy not based on western models of trade union objectives, models and policies. As in Singapore, it has also been suggested that the buoyant nature of the labour market until 1997 enabled workers to improve their position by individual job-hopping, thus obviating the need for trade union representation (Ng and Fung 1989, 78; Levin and Ng 1993, 46; Levin and Chiu 1995, 191-6).

However, the picture of an industrial relations system with low union density, limited collective bargaining, little overt conflict and worker apathy towards unions altered dramatically when the Asian financial crisis hit Hong Kong after 1997. There were numerous collapses and corporate shutdowns. The most spectacular failure was that of Peregrine Securities, a company with offices in 16 countries, which collapsed owing $1 billion. There was a string of smaller brokerage failures, and 3 major

Japanese chain department stores, Yaohan, Matsuzakaya and Daimaru, also closed their doors (*Asia 1999 Yearbook*, 17). Other employers responded to the crisis by attempting to cut costs. There were widespread pay freezes and pay cuts, dismissals, and the highest unemployment rate on record. In the 3 months to the end of April 1999, the official rate of unemployment reached an estimated 6.3%, the highest ever recorded. Trade unions and labour representatives, however, insisted that the true rate was 10-12% (Lewis, 2000, 303). In 1998, statistics told a story of increasing friction between employers and employees. The number of labour disputes involving 20 or more employees seeking government intervention jumped 110% over the previous year to 337. The number of individual party to such claims climbed 205% to 34,000. At the same time, 20 new unions were registered in 1998, compared to only 3 in 1997 (Slater 1999).

In May and June 1999, the national airline, Cathay Pacific, experienced a 12 day pilots' strike over proposed pay cuts. This followed a labour-shedding exercise in which 470 jobs were cut (*Asia 1999 Yearbook*, 17). The cuts were imposed, but the airline paid in disrupted business, and the pilots won a quid pro quo for their lost pay in the form of stock options.

According to Eden Woon, Director of the Hong Kong General Chamber of Commerce, the recession in Hong Kong has made unions more vocal and has led people to have greater sympathy for them than in the past (Slater 1999, 56). Unions have become more active in seeking to recruit new members and to compel employers to bargain collectively with them. The Federation of Trade unions, one of the two umbrella organisations, set a target of increasing union membership by 10% in 1999-2000. Unions have also moved to build popular support among the public because they have few other means of influencing employers.

Cathay Pacific was unusual being one of the few major private employers which recognises unions and bargains collectively with them. But other employers have been finding that they have to take unions seriously for the first time. For instance, about 400 workers employed by the American shipping giant Sea-Land recently formed a union after the company dropped a discretionary bonus, and introduced a plan to increase hours, which it later withdrew. The regional human resources director acknowledged that the formation of the union had forced the company to pay closer attention to labour relations.

Workers employed by Citybus, one of the Hong Kong's major bus companies, also formed a union. Though the employer refused to recognise it, the union took successful industrial action to slow down the bus service to protest at forced transfer of drivers and threatened pay cuts. The action at least compelled the company to stop the forced transfers.

In an unusual move, the two labour federations, separated by a political divide, also cooperated in building up a public outcry against Hong Kong Telecom's plan to cut the pay of its 10,000 employees, and the company eventually abandoned the plan. There were also signs of unrest in the civil service, over a plan to privatise some government departments after the Government had retreated from its stated intention of reducing civil service salaries (Slater 1999). The trade union movement also played an active role in lobbying against plans to increase the flow of workers from mainland China into Hong Kong (Lewis 2000, 303).

Structural changes in the Hong Kong economy probably indicate that the Territory will experience higher rates of unemployment than previously, as the loss of manufacturing jobs has not been compensated for by the creation of new jobs in the services sector. This may also create more fertile ground for unions than in the past, when Hong Kong experienced virtually full employment.

Thus, overall levels of unionisation in Hong Kong have remained low, and union activity has traditionally been largely confined to the civil service. The reasons, however, have been different from those in Singapore and Malaysia, as the Hong Kong Government has traditionally played a very non-interventionist role. Mainly it appears that Hong Kong workers have had a distaste for union membership and methods. This has been partly due to Chinese cultural values, and partly due to the nature of the labour market, which has enabled workers to better their position without joining trade unions. However, the experience of the recent recession suggests that things may be changing. Faced with job losses, pay cuts and deteriorating working conditions, many workers have become more militant, and have shown themselves more willing to turn to trade unions. Even employers, though refusing officially to recognise unions, have been compelled to adjust their labour relations policies, and in some cases abandon pay cuts because of union pressure. Structural problems in the Hong Kong economy also suggest that unions may have more opportunities to strengthen their position than was true in the past.

South Korea

A relatively full account of trade unions in South Korea is offered in Chapter 13. The development of the trade union movement has been closely bound up with the democracy movement, and as the country has moved towards fuller democracy, trade unions have been accorded a more legitimate role in industrial relations.

South Korean unions are organised at three levels. The grass roots level of organisation is at the plant or enterprise. All union members at a particular plant, regardless of occupation, join the same local union. Elected local union leaders then bargain collectively with employers over enterprise-specific issues on behalf of the members. Local unions affiliate with occupational federations and regional councils. In turn, these form national centres. However, the power to negotiate terms and conditions of employment is vested firmly in the local unions.

There are a few unions, such as the Korean Federation of Communication Trade Unions and the Federation of Korean Taxi Transport Workers Union, which are occupationally structured, and bargain collectively at regional and national levels.

Since 1987, there have been many attempts to form a rival national centre to the KFTU. The problems of this organisation, effectively a Government front, are detailed in Chapter 13. In 1991, the main rival organisation, the Korean Trade Union Congress (KTUC) was formed, and soon had more than 300,000 members. In 1995, the KTUC amalgamated with other non-recognised bodies to form a new federation, the Korean Confederation of Trade Unions (KCTU). Despite official non-recognition, a representative of this organisation was invited to join the Industrial Relations Reform Commission, advising the Government on changes to industrial relations. The KCTU claims a membership of 400,000, including unions representing workers in three major chaebol, Hyundai, Daewoo and Kia. It also covers unions from other key sectors in the Korean economy. As might be expected, KCTU has been more aggressive and assertive than the officially recognised FKTU.

Amendments to labour laws made in 1987 have made it easier for trade unions to use the official conciliation machinery. This has resulted in a jump in the number of unions, but not by a proportionate increase in membership. In 1995, there were 6,606 trade unions, with a density of 12.7%, compared with 3,500 unions with a density of 12.6% in 1970 (Park and Leggett 1998, 278-9).

A number of trends can be identified in union membership in South Korea (Kim 1993). First, as heavy industry has grown, men have displaced women in union activity. Second, there has been an increase in the unionisation of white-collar workers as their numbers have grown. Third, structures have developed within unions that promote 'solidarity' and 'cleavage'. Examples have been joint councils based on region, occupation and industry, as well as enterprises. The establishment of enterprise councils to promote solidarity has been a tactic to counter divisive tactics of the chaebol. Hyundai in particular has taken an aggressive stance towards the new unionism. Other chaebol, however, such as Samsung, adopted softer and more progressive human resource management policies that helped to reduce union militancy. The labour militancy of the 1980s and early 1990s seemed to have subsided until the changes in the law in 1996, revived it again (see Chapter 13). The decline in trade unionism in Korea during the 1990s, despite favourable legislative changes, is probably explained by industrial re-structuring, particularly with the decline of mining and manufacturing. However, trade unionism remains strong in organisations with over 250 workers (Park and Leggett 1998, 280).

Thus, while trade union density in South Korea remains low, even less than in Singapore, the trade union movement has played a major role in the democratisation of the country. It has also made an increasing impact in industrial relations in the big business sector in particular. Militancy, which flared in the past mainly over political issues, has flared again as the country has sought to take harsh economic measures to recover from the Asian financial crisis. But overall, it appears that the industrial relations system, and trade unions that form a part of it, are moving towards a more mature phase.

CONCLUSION

This chapter has outlined a number of key roles that unions play. The most important of these is the role that unions play in the employment relationship by acting as a collective 'voice' on behalf of members. Those researchers who study the a-symmetrical power relationship at work consider this role to be paramount in protecting the rights of workers. We also have another group of researchers who argue that employers and employees have much more in common and the role of unions as third parties in the employment relationship is unwarranted. (See also Chapter 1.) A number of theories have been detailed concerning the origins and functions of trade unions. Trade unions play an important role in collectively producing public and private goods. The way these are produced highlights a second function of trade unions, that is, as labour market structures that attempt to influence the demand and supply for labour. The collective aim is to remove or insulate wages from the forces of competition. This illustrates a key role played by unions in providing 'industrial insurance' on behalf of their members.

Discussion on the legal regulation of trade unions and union democracy illustrates the complex nature of trade unions. They are at once service organisations that aim to provide workplace representation, improve wages and conditions and deal with employee grievances, and political organisations designed to represent the class (political) interests of members. Australian unions have generally fared well under registration. However, in return for subjecting themselves to regulation, they have traded-off freedom of action in order to gain the benefits associated with registration. These benefits have included such things as bargaining rights, legal status, and the ability to intervene in the employment relationship in their own right.

This chapter has also examined the reasons why workers join unions, mostly for better pay, job security, and improvements in working conditions. The state has been shown to directly interfere with the ability of unions to operate freely by legislating controls on union government and membership in order to encouraging democratic participation in union affairs. As the world of business has been transformed over the past decade, so too has the role and structure of Australian trade unions. This chapter has examined union structure and the work of unions. A key factor during the 1980s and 1990s has been an on-going concern about declining union membership. Union amalgamation was promoted by the ACTU as a mechanism to form large well-resourced and efficient unions. The Coalition Federal Government's industrial relations reforms have reduced the role of unions by promoting individualism. The reduction poses major challenges not only for existing trade unions but also employers in terms of how to best regulate the workplace whilst maintaining a committed and productive workforce.

A brief examination of trade unions in our five selected South East Asian nations indicates that trade unions in these countries have always been less powerful and prominent than their Australian counterparts for a variety of economic, political and social reasons. However, as in Australia, trade union density has also been in decline over the last two or three decades, with South Korea perhaps being the only example of a country where independent trade unions have increased their influence without significantly increasing their membership.

THE ROLE OF THE ACTU

The Australian Council of Trade Unions (ACTU) is the peak national union council and national centre representing the Australian workforce. The ACTU is made up of 65 affiliated unions representing nearly 3 million workers. There is a branch of the ACTU in each state. These are generally called State Labor Councils. The ACTU was formed in 1927 following increasing recognition by the State Labor Councils and federal unions that there was a need for an organisation to represent the national interest of the Australian trade union movement. The ACTU has been located in Melbourne since its inception. The ACTU speaks on behalf of all workers including those in manufacturing, finance, government and the service sector generally. It includes trades, sales, clerical, technical and professional workers amongst its affiliated union membership.

ACTU policies and its most important operational decisions are established through democratic processes that involve:

- An Executive made up of representatives of ACTU officers, union and industry areas and women's' representative that numbers 40 in total. The Executive meets every quarter
- A Council of around 100 representatives of unions which meets yearly
- A Congress of around 1,000 delegates representing all affiliates held every three years, which sets policy.

The ACTU often conducts research and advocacy on behalf of affiliates and plays a lead role in conducting national wage cases before the Australian Industrial relations Commission (AIRC).

REVIEW QUESTIONS

1. Henry Ford once said that 'history is bunk'. Comment in respect of trade unions.
2. How helpful are trade union theories in explaining the structure and functioning of contemporary trade unions?
3. What are the most important reasons for joining a trade union?
4. What criteria would you use to determine the effectiveness of unions?
5. What role (if any) do you believe that unions should play today?
6. 'Amalgamate' or 'perish': what's best for the unions, for the employees?
7. What factors have contributed to the relatively low trade union density in the five selected South East Asian countries?
8. Explain the differences in trade union militancy in the five selected South East Asian countries.

FURTHER READING

Australian Council of Trade Unions (1999) *Unions @t Work: The Challenge for Unions in Creating a Just and Fair Society*, ACTU, Melbourne.

Bamber, G. and Lansbury, R. (eds) (1998) *International and Comparative Employment Relations*, 3rd Edn, Allen and Unwin, Sydney.

Freeman, R. and Medoff, J. (1984) *What Do Unions Do?* Basic Books, New York.

Frenkel, S.(ed) (1995) *Organised Labor in the Asia-Pacific Region. A Comparative Study of Trade Unionism in Nine Countries*, ILR Press, Ithaca, New York.

Peetz, D. (1998) *Unions in A Contrary World: The Future of the Australian Trade Union Movement*, Cambridge University Press, Melbourne.

Rothman, M., Briscoe, D. and Nacamulli, R. (eds) (1993) *Industrial Relations Around the World*, De Gruyter, Berlin and New York.

ACKNOWLEDGEMENTS

The assistance of staff of the ACTU (Melbourne) and the AWU (Queensland) is greatly appreciated in the preparation of this chapter.

CHAPTER 6

The State and Industrial Relations

'A State which dwarfs its men, in order that they may be more docile instruments in its hands, even for beneficial purposes - will find that with small men no great thing can really be accomplished.'

John Stuart Mill (On Liberty, 1859)

LEARNING OBJECTIVES

After reading this chapter you should:
- have an understanding of what institutions might broadly be said to constitute 'the state'
- have an understanding of the various theories used to explain which social interests are served by state intervention
- be able to apply these theories to assess whose interests are served by state intervention in industrial relations
- be able to provide an overview of how the state intervenes in industrial relations
- be able to assess the roles of government in industrial relation systems in the Asia-Pacific region.

INTRODUCTION

Governments of all political persuasions in all industrial (and industrialising) countries have a deep interest in industrial relations. An industrial relations system marked by perennial conflict can greatly damage a country's prospects of attracting overseas investment and stifle the ability of its exporting industries to deliver on time. A general disruption of services, employment and production, as well as the loss of taxation revenue, are all outcomes of a poor industrial relations system that few governments can ignore. Indeed, more than a few have lost office and even entire states have been challenged for their seeming inability to maintain peace between the two sides of industry. For all these reasons state involvement in the conduct of industrial relations is more the norm than the exception. This is no less so in Australia and the five Asian countries studied in this text, each of which has been highly active in establishing institutions and enacting legislation designed to promote industrial peace. This chapter looks at the role played by the state in industrial relations.

DEFINITION OF THE STATE

Defining what 'the state' is has long been the subject of considerable debate. The term has been used to identify an historical entity (see, Dyson 1980), a philosophical idea (see, Bosanquet [1899]), a form of human community (see, D'Entreves 1967) and a specifically modern phenomenon (see, Poggi 1978). As a modern phenomenon, it has been defined narrowly as constituting those organisations that have a monopoly on the legitimate use of force (Weber, [1919]). Used in this way it has typically referred to the government, the courts, the police, the armed forces, and organisations capable of compelling certain behaviours among individuals that make up society. Others have defined the state more broadly, seeing it as including the complete apparatus of formal public rules, roles and institutions that exercise political authority over the people in a defined territory (Bell and Head 1994, 3). This type of definition refers to almost any authority or organisation that is not part of the private sector. These definitions may be useful in specific contexts, or when applied for different analytical purposes. However, one major problem is that they do not separate political and industrial authority. For example, Australian trade unions are registered under government legislation, so when they set about exercising power or authority over members it could be argued under some definitions that they are in fact part of the state. Of course such a construction quickly becomes unworkable when we distinguish the state, responsible for making and administering industrial laws, from the employers and employees. Nevertheless it is useful to distinguish the state from other industrial relations actors, if only because the various institutions and processes of the state do not operate with the same degree of coherence and autonomy as trade unions, employer associations, and the like. One definition that fulfils this requirement and has a clear industrial relations focus was provided in a British study by Gosper and Palmer (1992). Those authors suggested that the state might be defined as the institutions and processes of political government, which have monopolies over taxation and the legitimate use of force. They argued that state institutions are composed of the legislature (parliament) and the executive (cabinet); the judiciary (courts) and central administration (the public service); the police and armed forces, which occasionally play a significant role in industrial relations, especially during industrial conflict; local government and special agencies including industrial tribunals, conciliation and arbitration services, equal opportunity commissions and occupational health and safety authorities (1992, 154).

THEORIES OF STATE INTERVENTION

The distribution of political power can have an important impact on the way the state interacts with its industrial relations system. One way to understand this interaction is through the various theories of state intervention. In general terms, four theories can be used to summarise the literature in this area. They can be distinguished by how they answer the question: in whose interests does the state act when it intervenes in people's lives? The answer each theory gives to this broad question helps to explain whose interests are served when the state intervenes in industrial relations.

PLURALIST THEORIES

The first theory comes from the pluralist school of thought (see also Chapter One). It starts from the observation that the state is the provider of rules, regulations and policies, which organised social interests (or 'pressure groups') attempt to influence. In the struggle to exert political influence, pressure groups such as trade unions and organised business interests, amongst others, are said to invariably come into competition with one another, but do so on unequal terms. Some pressure groups will have greater access to money, organisation, size and status (Dahl 1961, 228). Others will be part of self-enclosed policy communities or hold institutionalised or semi-institutionalised relations with government (Richardson and Jordon 1979, 13). Still others will be conferred with particular advantages because of their pivotal role in the national economy (Lindblom 1977, 172-5). However, regardless of their political resources, avenues of access or economic role, pluralism holds that none will be consistently relevant in all political circumstances. In other words, political power can never accrue exclusively to any single organised social interest. All will have some capacity to influence the policy outcomes of government. Indeed, when any one group grows too dominant in its relations with government, it is argued by pluralists that processes are set in motion which cause other social interests threatened by this domination to organise and allocate resources as a means of counteracting such dominance (Galbraith 1963, 123-5). State intervention under this interpretation is essentially about resolving the conflicting interests of groups with the greatest concerns about issues of the day. Industrial relations issues are just one of many contested by numerous social groups. Policy outcomes are merely the result of shifts in the balance of competing social and political forces throughout society (Schattsneider 1960, 141), although the state too can have independent interests and be a major participant in the struggle to determine policy (Smith 1990, 305).

ELITIST THEORIES

Elite theories of state intervention challenge the view that power is distributed in the manner described by pluralists. Classical elite theorists (see, Mosca [1896]; Pareto [1916]) argue that societies are always dominated by a minority (or 'elite') who take the major political and economic decisions within society and concentrate power in their own hands. This is so whether the society in question is governed under a monarchy, an aristocracy or a democracy. Such elites gain their position as a result of possessing resources or attributes valued by the societies over whom they rule. In some societies the elite's domination may be based on their ownership of material or economic resources. In others it may be based on religious dogma or doctrine, with power concentrated in the hands of religious officials. In still others, it may be based on military power, with power concentrated (either overtly or covertly) in the hands of army officers. Contemporary elite theorists (see, Bottomore 1966; Nordlinger 1981) argue that the position of elites in the modern state is sustained by the large-scale organisations covering most areas of social and economic life. From this perspective, large firms, trade unions, and political parties, for example, embody organisational forms in which effective power is vested in an oligarchic leadership. The significance of this is that bureaucratic control and institutional position are said to be primary sources of political power. In short, the leadership of large organisations confers elite status on those holding such positions. Contemporary elite theorists also argue that there are different kinds of elites apart from those holding formal political power. Bottomore (1966), for example, draws a distinction between political elites and a political class. Political elites are said to include people who actually exercise formal power, such as government ministers, senior public officials, military leaders, important business leaders, and influential members of aristocratic and royal families. The political class, however, is said to be a broader group including people capable of wielding political power under certain conditions, such as the leaders of opposition political parties, senior trade union officials, business leaders and politically active intellectuals (14-5). On the basis of this classification elite power is based on a variety of sources, ranging from the occupation of formal office, the ownership of wealth, technical expertise, knowledge, and so on. State intervention, and thus state intervention into industrial relations, is undertaken to serve the interests of ruling elites, whether these be the leaders of large firms, senior trade union officials, politicians, intellectuals, and the like.

MARXIST THEORIES

Marxist theories start from the assumption that it is not the political process itself that determines the type of intervention undertaken by the state but the form of economic organisation of production. In advanced industrialised societies the capitalist system is said to dominate the political and social affairs of people, and to divide them into two competing social classes: the bourgeoisie and the proletariat. Contemporary Marxists (see, Miliband 1969; O'Connor 1973; Poulantzas 1973) point to the concentration of income and wealth in a small section of the property owning population, who, because of their economically dominant position in society are able to exercise decisive political power. Taking the cue from the work of Karl Marx [1856], a common theme in these theories is that the state is not neutral when it intervenes in national life. Instead it is used as an instrument by the bourgeoisie for class domination - or as Marx famously expressed it: 'the executive of the modern state is but a committee for managing the common affairs of the whole bourgeoisie' ([1848], 35). Miliband (1969), for example, has argued that under contemporary circumstances this still occurs because the bourgeoisie come from the same social background as members of the state apparatus (i.e., government ministers and senior civil service officials, military leaders, members of the judiciary and other state institutions). It is also occurs because the bourgeoisie is able to exercise power through personal contacts and though associations representing business and industrial interests at the level of politics. Lastly it occurs because state officials are limited in their freedom of action by their dependence on a successful economic base for their continued survival in office. The state thus acts in the long-term interests of the bourgeoisie because of common class associations and the need to create conditions conducive to the processes of capital accumulation. It does this most notably by maintaining order and control within society and industry. From the Marxist point of view, the establishment of publicly funded physical resources (e.g. roads, ports, railways), the administration of regulatory measures (e.g. police, courts, industrial tribunals), the operation of educative agencies (e.g. schools, colleges, universities), and the provision of public services (e.g. housing, health, welfare), are all state actions designed to reduce the cost of labour to capital.

CORPORATIST THEORIES

The final theory is the product of corporatist thinking (see, Schmitter 1974; Lehmbruch 1977; Cawson 1978; Williamson 1989). As applied to liberal democracies, this theoretical approach starts in a similar fashion as pluralism, viewing the state as the main provider of rules, regulations and policies. It parts company with pluralism by regarding decisions taken by the state as primarily the outcome of negotiations with major producer groups. This bias toward producer groups stems from the state's power to grant rights of 'incorporation' (the recognition or legitimisation of a representative body). This means that the state has the power to license or recognise the exclusive right of certain groups to represent particular interests, and on the basis of this right, to grant them power to influence the development and administration of public policies. The most important reason for incorporating a particular producer group is its ability to frustrate the administration of national policies. In this regard the key producer groups are considered to be those representing the interests of 'labour' (i.e. trade unions) and 'capital' (i.e. large business corporations and employer associations). These particular groups are seen as having political resources that are significantly more important than those representing other areas of social life. The most important political resource of these groups is of course the capacity to decide income, employment and investment outcomes. Uncontrolled, this capacity is potentially disruptive to the state's effective conduct of economic policies. It reflects a balance of influence that is biased against the state (Williamson 1989, 204-5). The legitimising or granting of rights of incorporation to such groups is thus seen as a measure to control their behaviour, and thereby reduce their potentially disruptive influence. Another feature of corporatism is the assumption that the incorporated producer groups are capable of delivering on commitments. For the state (and in particular the government) to be assured that obligations extracted from incorporated groups will ultimately benefit the conduct of policy, they require negotiating partners that have monopolies over the interests they represent. Hence, a necessary precondition for state intervention along corporatist lines is that 'chosen' trade unions and business groups have the ability to control the behaviour of members, either through rewards or the threat of exclusion (Schmitter 1979, 13-4, 21-2).

In summary, the key aspects of the four theories could be said to apply to industrial relations as follows. Pluralist interpretations see the state intervening in industrial relations for the purpose of reconciling competing social interests represented in the workplace. As such, the interests served can favour employees, employers, the state itself, or all three, with none being dominant. Much will depend on the issue provoking the intervention and the type of political resources each player brings to bear on the process. Elite theories see the state intervening for the purpose of accommodating the interests of a ruling elite. In this case the interests served can favour employees, employers, the state itself, or all three. Again no elite group is dominant and much rests on what will serve the interests of those in control of the relevant organisations and resources. Marxist interpretations see state intervention as serving the class interests of the bourgeoisie. In industrial relations, this can only favour employers, as the proletariat has few connections with those holding political power and few economic resources to draw upon as a means of influencing the political process. And finally, corporatist theories see the state intervening in industrial relations for the purpose of maintaining control over national policies. The interests served can favour employers, trade unions, the state, but is typically all three, with much depending on the ability of producer groups to deliver on their commitments in agreements with the state.

KEY ROLES PLAYED BY THE STATE IN INDUSTRIAL RELATIONS

The theories just outlined provide a broad understanding of the ways we might identify *who* benefits from state intervention. In this section we will look at *how* the state intervenes and especially how the state can influence a country's industrial relations system.

State Influence through Procedural and Substantive Rules

The state exercises influence over the industrial relations system by the way it regulates relations between parties (Dabscheck 1992, 341). 'Rules' in the form of laws are central to this form of regulation. In Australia, for example, the Federal Government is involved in establishing both substantive and procedural rules. Substantive rules directly regulate the terms and conditions of employment (e.g. annual leave, sick leave, equal employment opportunity, occupational health and safety, working hours, termination of employment, and the form in which wages are paid). It is worth noting that the ability of the Federal Government to create substantive rules is restricted by the Constitution (see Chapter Seven, The Law and Industrial Relations). When seeking to make substantive rules for the private sector, for instance, it must argue its case before the relevant industrial tribunal (i.e. the Australian Industrial Relations Commission), along with other interested parties. In relation to the federal public sector, however, its can simply create new substantive rules without restriction. In so doing it may often acts as 'pacesetter', resulting in the same rules eventually adopted by the private sector. Procedural rules regulate the behaviour of parties participating in bargaining. For example, they establish industrial relations tribunals with legal powers to decide bargaining issues and industrial disputes. They give these tribunals legal power to formalise and enforce negotiated agreements, and power to create the bargaining procedures between employers and employees. They also provide legal recognition for the participating parties, and set out the procedures for dispute resolution (see Chapter Seven). Procedural rules provide the mechanism for establishing substantive rules. In other words, they are rules used in the process of making rules.

State Influence through Manipulation of the General Social and Economic Environment

The state is also influential in the way it manipulates the general economic environment. Government policies that deal with economic matters such industrial development, taxation, unemployment, inflation, incomes, tariffs, and so on, all have a direct impact on labour market and industrial relations outcomes. High inflation, for example, can trigger wage campaigns by unions seeking to offset rising costs of living for members. High unemployment can reduce labour mobility and the spread of workplace grievances as people move between jobs. How the government deals with these and other economic problems will have a decided impact on workplace relations. In addition, the government is also influential through its ownership and management of public services and utilities. Not only does it provide infrastructure for businesses in the form of ports, roads, railways and bridges, it also provides essential services such as health and education. It furthermore owns or regulates the provision of water, electricity, gas and public transport, and may compete with the private sector in areas such as insurance and civil aviation. In all these activities the state is responsible for investment and manning decisions, both of which have significant implications for the conduct of industrial relations in these areas.

State Influence as a Major Employer

The state is furthermore influential as a major employer. Almost one-third of the Australian workforce, for example, is employed by the various levels of government, with public sector employees engaged in such things as the provision of immigration, pension and unemployment services. They also operate prisons, provide law enforcement, preside over the judiciary, operate ports, drive trains and collect garbage. They furthermore work in the electricity, gas, water, sewerage, sanitation, transport, banking, insurance and communications industries, and are employed in a wide array of occupational categories. As the wages and conditions of public sector employees are set by the government responsible for their activities, whether federal, state or local, the state has a major direct role in the conduct of industrial relations for a sizeable section of the Australian work-force.

To this it can be added that governments throughout Australia have frequently tried to use their position as major employers to set the pattern of wages and conditions in the private sector. They have done this most clearly in the past by setting better conditions in the public sector and then leaving it to unions to argue the case of comparable worth before industrial tribunals hearing private sector disputes. This practice has become less prevalent in recent years, with governments seeking to set an example of restraint and to down-grade public sector conditions.

State Influence as a Signatory to International Conventions

The state is also influential because of its obligation to fulfil international commitments. Australia, for instance, is a member of various international organisations, the most important in terms of labour issues being the International Labour Organisation (ILO) and the Organisation for Economic Cooperation and Development (OECD). As a signatory to the charter of these international organisations, Australia is obliged to implement laws and practices that comply with their standards and conventions. The most obvious application to industrial relations of these obligations has been the enactment of laws dealing with the forty-hour working week, equal pay for work of equal value, and anti-discrimination in employment and occupation. It is worth noting that whilst the Federal Government is constitutionally limited in its power to directly legislate on wages and employment conditions in the private sector, it can do so on matters that fulfil Australia's international treaty obligations and through use of the corporations power. (See also Chapter 7, the Law and Industrial Relations.)

State Influence through the Attitudes and Policies of Political Parties

In countries with mature liberal democratic systems, political parties are a key institutional feature of the state. In Australia, they have had a significant influence on the conduct of industrial relations. Throughout Australia's brief history, different parties have formed governments with significantly different industrial relations agendas. Of the two major parties, the Labor Party has tended to pursue policies which have been sympathetic towards trade unions, whilst the Liberal and National parties have tended to be more sympathetic towards business interests. Changes in government have usually been accompanied by changes in industrial relations policy. This has been particularly true in recent years, when these changes have significantly changed the pattern of centralised bargaining and the level of trade union involvement in public policy. The contrast between the Labor Government between 1983 and 1996, and its successor, the Liberal-National Coalition Government, is particularly instructive.

The former Labor Government, for example, was strongly wedded to corporatist notions of state involvement. Through its Prices and Incomes Accords, a series of agreements made with the trade union movement (see Chapter 8), the government used negotiated social wage trade-offs as a means of managing economic and social policies. Central to these trade-offs was government support for centralised collective bargaining. In return the trade union movement made a commitment to wage restraint. A secondary aspect was that trade unions gained significant influence over the formulation of public polices dealing with the employment conditions of Australian workers. This type of policy approach stands in sharp contrast to that taken by the Liberal-National Coalition Federal Government. Its *Workplace Relations Act 1996,* for instance, was enacted primarily to undermine the centralised bargaining system (see Chapter 9). This was achieved by first, broadening the scope by which individual and enterprise bargaining agreements could be concluded without trade union involvement; and second, by diminishing the powers of industrial tribunals that supported a centralised bargaining system. At the same time, the trade union movement has been ostracised from the political process of the government in the belief that public policies are better served by resisting influence from unions (see, Keenoy and Kelly 1998, 118-123).

RECENT TRENDS IN STATE INVOLVEMENT

These different policy approaches are part of a larger debate which developed in recent years over the most appropriate role governments should play in industrial relations. This debate has been fuelled by periodic recessions, flagging productivity, historically high unemployment, advancing globalisation, declining fiscal resources, and the ascendancy of neo-liberal, neo-economic ideals in the thinking of policy-makers and business leaders. The details of the different public policy outcomes arising from this debate are given in Chapter 8, Wage Fixation in Australia. In this section we will look at the current trends in state involvement in industrial relations.

The Australian debate is typical of other industrial societies. The debate essentially involves two competing visions, both of which have centred on the view that traditional labour practices are too rigid in contemporary business circumstances. This view has gained great strength from theories of competitive labour markets supported by neo-classical economists. These theories have already been touched upon in Chapter 1. To briefly restate their main argument (see, Friedman and Friedman 1963; Olsen 1965; Freeman and Medoff 1984; Kaufman 1989; Kaufman and Hotchkiss 1999), labour markets are said to be made up of individuals, who, when left to their own devices, will make choices about how best to allocate their time and energy to satisfy their day-to-day wants and needs. In perfectly competitive labour markets, it is argued, these choices will invariable see the allocation of individual workers to forms of employment where they are most wanted and most able to perform. At the same time employers will invariably pay wages at the most efficient margin consistent with the profitable employment of labour. Supporters of this type of analysis typically regard any external agency that interferes with the way individuals make choices about occupation, employment, pay, working conditions, and the like, as inconsistent with the efficient labour market outcomes.

The issue under debate is how much state interference is necessary or desirable to ensure that changes in traditional labour practices occur in both a productive and equitable manner. Business leaders and conservative politicians have viewed the problem as a product of excessively powerful trade unions and the country's centralised bargaining system. The modern workforce, they argue, must become more flexible if it is to secure its future employment prospects. It must be more fully exposed to the rigour of market forces if it is to function more productively and more efficiently for the interests of all. This will require a radical reduction in the degree of state intervention into industrial relations (see, Blandy and Sloan 1986; Costello 1989). To this end, they advocate that the power of industrial tribunals to decide wages and conditions be limited, that bargaining frameworks be decentralised down to the level of the firm, and that the role of trade unions in the settlement of workers' wages and conditions be curtailed. At the same time, they recommend that companies embrace more strident anti-union policies; pursue individual rather then collective contracts with employees; and implement human resource management practices. These proposals are typically rationalised by arguing that any outside interference in agreements between individual employers and individual employees is contrary to the efficient and productive allocation of labour.

The alternative vision comes from trade union leaders and Labor politicians, who have similarly recognised the need for changed trade union structures and decentralised bargaining practices (see, Evatt Foundation 1995). Unlike business and conservative leaders, they argue that labour market failure is more about a failure of opportunity than one of institutional interference. The remedy they advocate, therefore, has sought the restructuring of trade unions along industry lines to open the way for the multi-skilling of workers. They have also supported a 'managed' system of decentralised wage bargaining and award provisions to improve productivity and employment prospects though greater career and training opportunities. These recommendations are based on the belief that, if left to their own devices, many individuals entering the labour market will confront insurmountable obstacles to obtaining appropriate employment and fair rates of pay. Particular social groups, such as women and those from non-English speaking backgrounds, are seen as particularly disadvantaged in unregulated labour markets. A certain degree of state intervention in industrial relations is thus necessary to ensure that disadvantaged workers have the opportunity to gain the skills and knowledge most desired by business.

Prior to the election of the Liberal-National Coalition Government in 1996, the 'failure of opportunity' argument clearly held the ascendancy. The Labor Government, working with the trade union movement, introduced a series of legislative measures that facilitated enterprise bargaining. Bargaining outcomes had to meet certain minimum conditions and had to be ratified by the Australian Industrial Relations Commission before they had the force of law. The trade union movement, under the guidance of the Australian Council of Trade Unions (ACTU), rationalised its organisational structure along industry lines, and awards contained provisions for productivity-based wage increases, training, career development and multi-skilling. With the election of the Coalition Government the ascendancy moved in favour of the business and conservative position. The Coalition's *Workplace Relations Act 1996*, although far from fully satisfying the labour market model, went a significant way towards reducing both the influence of trade unions and centralised bargaining as a means of settling wages and conditions. These moves, at the very least, signalled the general intention of a retreat of state intervention from the industrial relations scene, a shift which has been broadly repeated in other industrialised countries (see, Abbott 1999).

THE STATE AND INDUSTRIAL RELATIONS IN SOUTH EAST ASIA

In this final section we look at the role of the state in the five selected Asian countries. A more complete description of the industrial relations histories and systems of each of these countries is provided in Chapter 13. Our aim here is to provide a brief overview that makes specific reference to the way the state regulates the conduct of industrial relations in each of the selected countries. In reading this section it should be noted how each state plays a vastly different role to the one played in Australia. What this role is depends on each country's unique historical experience, cultural traditions, relations with business, and overall economic policy objectives.

Japan

Japan is famous for the close relationship that has long existed between business and the state - which is perhaps nowhere better symbolised than in the oft-quoted slogan 'Japan Incorporated'. The nature of Japanese state involvement in industrial relations can be traced back to the turn of the century when Japanese governments formed a strong alliance with employers in a conscious effort to advance the country's industrialisation. During these early years, both the government and employers regarded themselves as a single body with little to differentiate their core aims and interests. As part of this identity of interest, numerous attempts were made to suppress Japanese trade unionism. These efforts largely failed and over the first two decades of the twentieth century independent trade unions were able to achieve some measure of recognition. However, by the 1930s, militaristic elements within the Japanese government renewed their efforts to suppress the trade unions, partly to temper opposition to the government's imperialist plans, and partly to minimise disruptions to its war preparations. Initially the government tried to apply measures similar to those of Nazi Germany and Fascist Italy, organising workers into a patriotic labour front, the SANPO. This, however, only proved partially successful, which prompted the government to introduce a new policy in 1940 which banned trade unions altogether. After World War II, a democratic constitution was imposed on Japan by the occupying forces. Its provisions guaranteed, for the first time, the right of labour to organise and bargain collectively. It provided a legal framework establishing an industrial tribunal (i.e. Labour Relations Commission) to deal with industrial disputes and collective bargaining issues. Most post-war Japanese governments have since delegated the regulation of industrial relations to this tribunal (and other similar agencies set up on a regional or industry basis), whilst retaining the right to determine the wages and conditions of workers in the public sector (Komatsu 1994, 118-22). For the most part, it has seen the state take a relatively benign role towards industrial relations, with interventions occurring only during periods of severe economic crisis.

Having said this, it is nonetheless the case that state remains particularly close to business. Three reasons account for this closeness. The first relates to the nature of Japanese economic development. Industrialisation in Japan occurred much later than in western industrialised nations, and was then all but destroyed during the Second World War. Consequently, there is a long legacy of state involvement in nurturing and later re-establishing industry. In other words, there is a long and sustained history of active government involvement in developing the country's economic capacity, which has seen a political culture grow up that largely accepts the merits of close cooperation between the state and business. Second, most post-war governments have been led by conservative political parties that have had close ties with business. Indeed, except for a short period between 1947 and 1948, the conservative

Liberal Democratic Party has either held office in its own right (Matsuda 1993, 173), or been the dominant force in ruling coalition governments. Third, many large companies owe their present success to generous state assistance provided in the past. One early example of this can be seen in the role played by the Ministry of Trade and Industry (MITI), which provided early post-war guidance and incentives in the form of tax concessions and capital aid to companies with the potential to compete abroad (Petzall and Selvarajah 1991, 201). This type of assistance has long been a prominent part of Japanese business life, and has given rise to a phenomenon known as 'Amakudari'. This refers to the tendency of senior public service officials and government ministers to retire to key positions in the private sector. While there is some debate about the impact of this movement, there can be little doubt that it creates significant networks of influence between powerful government departments and big businesses (see, Colingnon et al. 1997, 171-7).

In summary, the post-war role of the Japanese state in industrial relations could be described as generally neutral in a formal institutional sense, but pervasive in an informal non-institutional sense. In other words, while Japanese governments have maintained their long held informal associations with business, they have not acted overtly against trade unionism in any political or policy sense. Although they have established independent institutions in which collective bargaining and industrial disputes can be settled, they have generally refrained from directly intervening into the conduct of the country's industrial relations.

Singapore

By comparison to the Japanese post-war experience, the industrial relations role of the state in Singapore is far more interventionist. This stems largely from the country's colonial past and its long history of dependency on international trade for economic survival. As a colony Singapore was a major South East Asian trading port used by various European powers for the exchange of oriental spices and wares. However, since gaining its independence in the early 1960s, Singapore has moved into manufacturing electronic components and optical instruments, as well as petroleum refining, shipping and the provision of financial services. The country's long dependence on external markets has pushed it in the direction of economic openness, free trade and free markets. It accordingly has no currency controls, few tariffs and no controls on foreign investment. These economic freedoms on the international front, however, are not matched by the same freedoms on the domestic political front. The state has long been highly interventionist, seeking to control most aspects of Singaporean life. The Government maintains that this is necessary if the country is to have the capacity to adjust quickly to economic changes beyond its borders. General statistical data from the early 1990s show the extent of this control. The state owns around three-quarters of the country's small landmass and takes responsibility for housing around four-fifths of the population. The state is also the largest single employer, exerting strict control over wage movements in both the public and private sectors. It also compels Singaporean workers to contribute around a quarter of their salaries to a government-controlled superannuation fund (Sullivan 1991, 121-3).

Although economic reasons account for the high level of Singaporean state involvement in the country's domestic affairs, political reasons are also involved. These can be traced to a number of interrelated factors in Singapore's early political history. First, there was political turmoil surrounding the country's independence in the early 1960s, when it was expelled from the Malaysian Federation during the latter's confrontation with Indonesia. Second, the British naval bases subsequently withdrew from the country between 1968 and 1971. Both of these events 'created a sense of siege and encouraged a crisis mentality' (Low 1990, 292), which prompted governments of the day to oversee the development of a form of state corporatism to ensure the country's future survival. This political form has continued with the on-going re-election of the same government under the administration of the People's Action Party (PAP). Singapore's state system now incorporates a limited number of organised interests in the form of associations, societies and even trade unions. All, however, are linked to the corporate state, in that their leaderships are chosen by government and are charged with the responsibility of developing the 'spirit of national solidarity' among their memberships (Anantaraman 1991, 77-9). The National Trades Union Congress (NTUC), for example, was formed under the stewardship of the national government, and is effectively part of the machinery of state. It has little power to act independently in the manner of the trade unions found in western industrialised countries, and its primary function is to promote industrial harmony among workers for the purpose of advancing the country's industrial growth strategies. Political opposition, whether it occurs within the party system or within the trade union movement, has only ever been symbolically tolerated. Indeed, many unbending leaders of opposition parties and trade unions have been driven out of office and, in some cases, out of Singapore itself by libel suits brought by leaders of the PAP. In addition, the industrial tribunals set up to decide workers wages and conditions are also part of the machinery of state. The National Wages Council (NWC), for example, is also policy arm of government, set up for the specific purpose of ensuring wages growth does not exceed the country's productivity growth.

The Singapore state system is therefore one where there are very high levels of government intervention in industrial relations. It is a system that has proved highly successful at providing a cheap and compliant labour force to attract foreign investment and multinational companies to the country. These in turn have generated Singapore's near-meteoric rate of economic growth. There is emerging evidence that the government is beginning to soften its approach towards trade unions and political dissension generally. This has occurred in the wake of political and social upheavals in Indonesia and the Philippines, and the recent South East Asian financial crisis, all of which have inspired the government to adopt a more conciliatory approach to industrial relations and social policy.

South Korea

Like Singapore, for much of its modern industrial development the role of the state in South Korea's system of industrial relations has been highly interventionist. Unlike Singapore, however, the policy objectives of state intervention have been driven by a desire to develop local heavy industries capable of exporting elaborately produced goods for international sale. From the close of the Korean War in 1953 until the early 1980s, various governments have provided significant political and financial support to domestic business conglomerates known as 'chaebol'. This support included the active suppression of organised labour, and the legal enforcement of harsh employment regimes in the form of long working hours and low pay. It also involved major public financial assistance and subsidies to industry. Although these types of assistance were largely welcomed by big business, privately owned companies have always had some reticence about the degree of control they give government over business objectives and activities. Companies nevertheless accepted the government's overall economic strategy, which served to cement close ties between them and state officials.

This general long-term situation came under pressure during the early 1980s, when the military dominated government of the time introduced a series economic policy measures aimed at liberalising the domestic economy. These measures sought to promote greater competition by de-concentrating key industrial sectors monopolised by the chaebol. Attempts were made to force the chaebol to divest themselves of subsidiaries and to identify and concentrate only on core business interests. These efforts largely failed, and served to sour relations between the state and big business. The next decisive turn occurred in 1987, when the country's first directly elected president, began a renewed push to break up the chaebol, in an effort to court the growing middle class and distance himself from a previous military regime. Despite widespread popular appeal, this attempt also meet with limited success, largely because of the onset of a serious economic slump. More significantly, the attempt inspired chaebol leaders to criticise the government publicly for the very first time. The government nevertheless continued to press for de-concentration and ordered the largest chaebol to sell off their idle land and buildings. They were also once again ordered to nominate core businesses and to sell off others. New anti-monopoly and fair trading laws were passed, curtailing cross-subsidisation, transfer-payment guarantees and other anti-competitive activities. The chaebol leaders responded with open hostility, so much so that the then chairman of Hyundai was moved to found a new political party to contest the 1992 presidential election. Although a compromise was ultimately reached, the incident marked a new low in relations between big business and the state. There was a growing intolerance of government intervention in the way companies were managed and operated (Chung-in-Moon 1994, 154-60).

Relations between the trade unions and the state tell a mixed story. On one hand, South Korean governments have actively resisted independent trade unionism. The history of organised labour and the state is littered with periods of intense hostility. On the other hand, trade unions sympathetic to government economic policies have been encouraged by the state, and relations between the two have been sound. This is a legacy from the era prior to the democratic reforms of 1987, from when many laws are still operable. Until this time, trade unions were largely organised by the state under a legal framework established by successive military governments. Its laws limited the number trade unions to one per enterprise, and each trade union had to be affiliated with the only officially recognised trade union centre: the Korean Federation of Trade Unions (KFTU). The leaders of this organisation were normally associated with government. It was not uncommon for many of them to move to government or senior public sector posts when a career move was in order. For many union members and potential members, these machinations reeked of political corruption and favouritism and, for long a time, this diminished interest and support for the country's trade unions. The laws also provided for free collective bargaining. But this was rarely practiced because any supporting industrial action was invariably held illegal due to the complex procedures involved (Park 1993, 158).

In 1987, as part of the democratic movement of the times, major changes were made to the country's legal framework, which in turn led to changes in the way trade unions operated. These changes followed a great wave of strikes in support of a wider community push for democratic reform in the country's political institutions. The end result saw the abolition of compulsory arbitration of industrial disputes, and the Ministry of Labour became more sympathetic to registering trade unions other than those covering production workers. This latter development saw trade union coverage extended to various clerical and professional occupations that were previously excluded from representation. It was also extended to Chaebol workers, who had also previously been excluded. At the same time new trade union federations were formed which challenged the dominance of the KFTU. Popular democratic sentiments flowed over to trade unions and saw their leaderships elected by secret ballots rather than appointed by government officials. As a consequence, many pro-government trade union officials were swept from office. The response to these developments among employers was hostile. Many chaebols employed private union-busting militias, but failed to prevent the spread of unionism within their industries. By the early 1990s, the trade union movement was significantly revitalised, its tarnished image among workers somewhat repaired, and union officials acted more in the interests of members than the state.

Since this time the South Korean economy has been opened further to international competition, which has greatly reduced the former dependence of big business on state assistance. At the same time there has been a significant improvement in business-state relations, despite the fact that the government still possesses considerable leverage to coerce the corporate sector. The government is now committed to playing a much less restrictive role in industrial relations. It presently confines most of its activities to supporting a legal framework set up to decide minimum employment conditions. However it is not averse to engaging in activities designed to frustrate the formation and operation of independent trade unions. Employers also are still prone to engage in unfair labour practices, and industrial disputes still tend to be marked by high levels of violence and political confrontation. Nevertheless, the general trend is towards an emerging trade union movement that is more independent and democratic. Free collective bargaining between employers and trade unions is more widespread, and the fear of communist North Korea is used less frequently by the state to justify authoritarian rule and repression of organised labour.

Malaysia

State intervention into Malaysian life has been high for much of the country's brief history. Unlike the previous countries mentioned, where state intervention was based very early on a desire to secure national economic prosperity, the driving force behind state intervention in Malyasia during the early post-independence years was the ethnic diversity of the country's population. This diversity was (and still is) made up of around 60 per cent native Malays, who were mainly poor, worked as agricultural or factory labourers. The remainder of the population was made up of ethnic Chinese and Indians, who were generally wealthier than their Malay counterparts, and owned and operated most of the country's major businesses. The leadership of the Malay-dominated coalition government, which ruled Malaysia from the time of independence (and still does), developed very early a policy of extensive private sector regulation as a means of improving the lives of Malays. The New Economic Policy (NEP), as it was referred to, did this by acquiring holdings in key sectors of the Malaysian economy. The government consequently developed stakes in the country's rubber plantations, tin mines and financial sector, and later in the petroleum industry. The principal purpose of these holdings was to facilitate a re-distribution of national wealth and economic opportunities from Chinese and Indian minorities to native Malays. Public sector organisations were also used to increase the labour market participation by the Malay workforce. Government subsidises and tax concessions were furthermore provided to Malay businesses as a means of nurturing them to a point where they could viably compete with non-Malay businesses. Great policy emphasis was also placed on educating Malays in business management. Laws were established to compel non-Malay businesses to take on Malay partners and employ Malay workers.

For many years national economic considerations played a secondary role in government policy to these socio-economic ethnic policies. The first decisive steps to address economic considerations were taken during the 1970s, when the NEP was turned to developing heavy industry and the country's export capacity. Progress on both the heavy industry and export fronts, however, was slow. Non-Malay businesses continued to resist attempts to have them take on Malay partners and hire Malay employees, and local (mainly Chinese) investment in manufacturing remained low. The government responded by establishing free trade zones and industrial estates, which housed cheap and compliant labour and where trade unions were excluded. Such sites were specifically aimed at encouraging foreign investment and manufacturing for export production, but were only moderately successful.

The next decisive steps took place in 1980, when Prime Minister Mahatir introduced his new 'Look East' policy. This policy continued measures aimed at stimulating industrial development but, in addition, sought to reduce the country's dependence on foreign machinery. It was a policy that drew substantially on the export-promotion, import-substitution model which at the time had been successfully employed by South Korea. The main difference, however, was that state enterprises would be used to develop heavy industry rather than private sector conglomerates. This model was chosen because it originated from a non-Chinese society, and state enterprises were targeted because Malays controlled them. It was a policy that was almost immediately bedevilled with problems, not least because it coincided with an emerging world recession that had a significant impact on Malaysia's traditional export commodities. By the end of the 1980s, the government was forced to accept it had been made a mistake expecting Malay pubic servants to successfully run heavy industry. Malay managers were consequently replaced by Japanese expatriates and even local Chinese, an outcome that would have been unthinkable during the early years of the NEP (Bowie 1994, 172-9).

As far as industrial relations were concerned, the 'Look East' policy sought to promote industrial peace and increase productivity. The approach, in addition to drawing on the Korean model of industrial development, also drew on the Japanese experience of enterprise unions. Laws were passed to encourage the re-organisation of trade unions along these lines. The government introduced legislation to constrain free collective bargaining and secure industrial order through the establishment of conciliation and arbitration machinery. It also tried to promote an approach to industrial relations reminiscent of Singapore. To this end, a blueprint for cooperative industrial relations practices was agreed between the state, employer associations and trade unions under a Code of Conduct for Industrial Harmony. This Code encouraged employers and trade unions to refrain from victimisation, intimidation and strikes, and to cooperate at all levels of industry for the sake of the national economic good. It also covered joint responsibility of the parties for industrial relations in enterprises, as well as employment, collective bargaining, communication and consultation issues. A committee chaired by the Minister of Human Resources was established to enforce the Code, and the Industrial Court was required to take the Code into account when making awards. Neither of these institutions, however, was capable of reaching decisions without deferring to government wishes, and although employer associations and trade unions largely abided by the Code, there were threats of breaches from time to time (Ayadurai 1993, 87-90).

Overall, Malaysian state intervention in industrial relations involves the exercise of considerable powers by the Minister of Human Resources and the Director-General of Industrial Relations. These powers give the government substantial influence over industrial relations in the private sector. In addition, they are augmented by active government curtailment, both formally and informally, of independent trade unionism. In the public sector, the power of the government to influence industrial relations is even more dominant, and organisations are entirely bound by government machinery designed to control workers' wages and conditions. Under the present political regime there is little sign that government intervention will diminish in the foreseeable future.

Hong Kong

By comparison to the other countries described, Hong Kong's state intervention in industrial relations is negligible. This approach is largely a legacy of British colonial policy, which from the very beginning sought to develop the country's economy in accordance with the principles of laissez faire capitalism. To this end, British colonial governments consistently refrained from intervening in the affairs of the private sector, and taxes and public expenditure came to be among the lowest in the industrialised world. This approach has a long history of support among the population, the more so since Hong Kong was returned to Chinese rule in 1997. The same approach has extended to industrial relations. Collective bargaining has long been a voluntary process, and in a manner similar to Britain has been entirely dependent upon the willingness of employers to recognise and negotiate with trade unions. Indeed, formal collective bargaining has rarely been practised outside the public service. Also in line with British traditions, collectively bargained agreements have never been legally enforceable, and institutional provisions for conciliating industrial disputes have never been compulsory. On the other hand, Hong Kong trade unions are registered as corporate entities for the purposes of freeing members and officers from criminal prosecution when engaging in industrial action. Finally, both trade union coverage of the Hong Kong workforce, and the level of industrial disputes have remained consistently low. Whatever the reason for this situation, unlike many of the other countries discussed in this section, it has had little to do with government intervention since it has been neither supportive nor suppressive of trade unions and industrial action (Ng and Fung-Shuen 1989).

With the return of Hong Kong to Chinese rule, however, it appears that there may be a change in policy direction as the new government has indicated its intention to operate a more interventionist policy. The chief executive of the government, for example, has lamented the lack of a high-tech manufacturing sector in the province, and indicated that the government should promote one. It has been reported that the government is in favour of financing a 'science park' to attract high-tech multinational companies. Behind these developments is a growing popular fear that Hong Kong will become less competitive in international markets. The present low wages paid to workers in Guangdong province, where most of Hong Kong's manufacturing is now done, are rising rapidly, and there is widespread fear that Beijing may support the development of Shanghai at the expense of Hong Kong (*The Economist* 1997, 25). If as a consequence government policies become more interventionist, it is highly likely that they will affect the country's existing system of industrial relations. Attempts may be made, for example, to re-structure the system along the lines of other South East Asian countries who have introduced such measures to attract foreign investment. It is also possible that there may be a clampdown on independent trade unions for political and ideological reasons. Any form of worker dissension may be regarded by China's communist leadership as amounting to treachery in the workers' state. However, these matters remain in the realm of speculation, and only time will tell whether the level of state intervention in Hong Kong remains minimalist or follows a more interventionist path.

CONCLUSION

This chapter has outlined the role of the state in industrial relations. As Keenoy and Kelly (1996) observe, the state's main role is one of a 'manager of discontent', which, as the above discussion suggests, can vary greatly from county to country. While this chapter has focussed mainly on the role of the state in Australian industrial relations, it has also looked at five selected South East Asian countries. In these countries, the extent of state intervention in industrial relations tends to follow the pattern in other policy areas. This in turn tends to follow each country's geo-political history, and its cultural, ethnic, economic, and political circumstances. State policies and institutions that have been highly interventionist in the economy and social life as a whole, have typically also been interventionist in the area of industrial relations (e.g. Malaysia, Singapore and South Korea). In these countries, the governments have sought to promote industrial development partly to catch up with the industrialised west, and partly to secure their political position from challenges both internal and external. This has usually been led to high levels of state involvement in supporting business and controlling the availability, price and management of labour. This has tended to create industrial relations systems marked by active state suppression of independent trade unionism and significant legal constraints placed on the practice of collective bargaining and industrial action. In countries where state intervention has been less pervasive over the economic and social life of the country, there has been a tendency for the state to be less intrusive in industrial relations (e.g. Hong Kong and, to a lesser extent, Japan). In these cases, the legacy of western imperialism or occupational powers is clear. The industrial relations institutions and processes are essentially a South East Asian version of the domestic circumstances of Britain and the United States. Nevertheless, no clear trend is emerging in the pattern of state intervention among the five countries discussed. Some states are becoming less interventionist as a result of economic liberalisation and political democratisation (e.g. South Korea). Others seem to be on the verge of becoming more interventionist (e.g. Hong Kong), whilst other are experiencing little or no change at all (e.g. Japan, Malaysia, Singapore).

In Australia, the pattern of state intervention in industrial relations is both a product of its colonial legacy and of its long democratic traditions. State intervention in Australia at times of industrial conflict, in the organisation and activities of trade unions, and in the conduct of collective bargaining, is less direct than in most of the South East Asian countries reviewed (except of course, Hong Kong). It has long been conducted through industrial tribunals that are legally or constitutionally independent of the government. In other words, the Australian state has played a moderately interventionist role in determining the pattern of industrial relations. But it has done so with a more liberal view of control than most South East Asian countries when seeking to 'manage discontent' between the two sides of industry. This is partly due to the influence of Britain's industrial tradition, where independent trade unionism, the right to strike, and free collective bargaining, have long been accepted as a matter of course. It is also a product of the more pluralistic nature of Australian politics, and particularly of government periodically alternating between political parties with very different ideologies. Democratic political systems favour moderate forms of policy, which try to accommodate the broadest range of social interests, including both business and organised labour. In Japan, Malaysia and Singapore this democratic influence is not so clear, largely because the same political regimes have been in power for decades. In South Korea and Hong Kong the existence of democratic institutions is a relatively recent phenomenon. It should also be noted that the moderate pattern of Australian intervention is partly attributable to the fact that Australian governments are constitutionally limited in their power to intervene directly in industrial relations. Governments in the selected South East Asian countries do not operate under the same constraints.

REVIEW QUESTIONS

1. What institutions and processes are said to constitute the state?
2. Why do states invariably see the need to intervene in industrial relations?
3. In whose interests does the state act when it chooses to intervene in industrial relations?
4. How do pluralist and corporatist theories of state intervention differ in their treatment of government involvement in industrial relations?
5. In what ways can the state influence the pattern of a country's industrial relations?
6. In your opinion, should the state be involved in industrial relations? Give reasons for your answer
7. What are the limitations of government intervention in industrial relations?
8. 'A country whose politics is dominated by a one-party authoritarian government, and which is seeking the rapid industrialisation of the economy, will invariably employ policies that suppress the organisation and activities of independent trade unions.' Discuss.
9. The role of the state in industrial relations in South East Asian countries differs from the role played in Australia. Discuss.

FURTHER READING

Ball, A. and Millard, F. (1986), *Pressure Politics in Industrial Society*, Macmillan, London

Bell, S. and Head, B. (eds.) (1994), *State, Economy and Public Policy in Australia*, Oxford University Press, Melbourne.

Dabscheck, B. (1992), 'Industrial Tribunals and Theories of Regulation', in B. Dabscheck, G. Griffin and J. Teicher (eds) *Contemporary Australian Industrial Regulations: Readings*, Longman Cheshire, Melbourne, 340-59.

Galbraith, J. (1963), *American Capitalism: The Concept of Countervailing Power*, Pelican, London.

Jessop, B. (1990), *Putting the Capitalist State in its Place*, Polity Press, Cambridge.

Miliband, R. (1969), *The State in Capitalist Society*, Weidenfeld and Nicolson, London.

CHAPTER 7

The Law and Industrial Relations

'Laws grind the poor and rich men rule the law'

Oliver Goldsmith, 1728-74

LEARNING OBJECTIVES

At the end of this Chapter, you should be able to:
- understand the different sources of law relevant to industrial relations
- recognise the important contribution of case law in clarifying the obligations and responsibilities of employers and employees under a contract of employment
- outline the Constitutional provisions which enable the Australian Federal Government to intervene in industrial relations.

INTRODUCTION

As the last Chapter showed, governments have a strong interest in regulating the conduct of industrial relations. Not only do they do this for political reasons, they do it to prevent industrial conflict causing significant social and economic damage. One of the main ways they achieved this is through the law. The law (and the political values that underlie it) plays a crucial role in any country's industrial relations. This role may be highly visible and difficult to ignore. Alternatively, it may also be subtle and far-reaching. For workers, the law is important for enforcing employment conditions and for defining acceptable behaviour when negotiating with employers. For example, industrial law may require workers to bargain one-to-one with their employer, or it may require them to join national unions, which bargain on their behalf. For employers on the other hand, the law may define how they should act when directing workers, or that they guarantee health and safety standards. It is important therefore to recognise that the law plays a major role in both the conduct of industrial relations and in the interaction of conflicting parties. Consequently, this chapter focuses on Australian industrial law. Whilst it is beyond the scope of this book to give a detailed account of the industrial law of our five selected South East Asian countries, some coverage can be found in Chapter 13.

SOURCES OF INDUSTRIAL LAW

We can begin by saying that the law is not monolithic. It does not consist of a clear, consistent and logical body of rules that apply to all workplaces at all times. Instead, there are conflicting and often competing bodies of law. In Australia, both the courts and the state and federal governments have played important roles in establishing industrial relations law (often simple called 'industrial law'). In addition, those courts, parliaments and industrial tribunals that create industrial laws often have very different views on trade unions and employment relations. Such differences can have profound effects on industrial relations. Conflicts about the values underlying industrial law occur both within and between our major law-making institutions. We will now examine the principle law-making institutions in Australia, the laws they have created, and the values that underlie those laws.

The Courts and Common Law

The courts play an important role in industrial relations. To describe their function, they have both independent law-making power (often referred to as 'common law'), and power which flows from their interpretation of Acts of parliament (legislative law). The common law they have developed over the years clearly reveals the values they bring to the field of industrial relations. These laws develop through the case law or precedent system, in which judges generate legal principles in their decisions on particular cases. They do this, in part, by looking at the reasoning given in the decisions of previous cases (precedent). The doctrine of precedent operates through an understanding of the existing legal rules, identification of the underlying principles and, in some cases, at an even deeper level, of the values on which the principles are based. The common law's stress on past values is highly conservative. Many of the values it maintains about employment are taken from the nineteenth century, which in turn are derived from even older, almost feudal views about the relationship of masters and servants. Inevitably, such views involve a commitment to managerial rights. That is, the values that underpin the common law tend to view employers as possessing inalienable rights to run their business without interference from outside parties. Workers are seen as not only subordinate to the direction of employers, but obliged to avoid engaging in collective action. Areas of the common law that are particularly important in industrial relations are the contract of employment and the regulation of industrial action.

The Courts and the Contract of Employment

The values behind the common law are most clearly revealed in the 'contract of service', which is the contract most employees work under. The essence of the contract of service is that work is exchanged for payment. In the Australian context, Awards, Enterprise Agreements, Australian Workplace Agreements (see below), and individual contracts of labour, are all examples of formalised contracts of service. Such contracts normally set out the wages to be paid, the hours to be worked, holidays and sick benefits, performance expectations, and so on. Contracts are normally formal, in writing and signed by both parties or their representatives. But there is no need for the contract, or all of its provisions, to be established in writing, though if the contract is wholly oral or partly written and partly oral, it may be more difficult to prove the oral terms. (For a summary of the relevant cases, see Creighton and Stewart 2000, 221.) In more casual workplaces, for example, the contract of service may be purely oral or quite brief. The parties may have only talked about wages, the work to be done, and how long the job will last. Also, a contract need not include all the terms the parties have agreed to, whether written or oral. The common law imposes a series of duties on the parties to the contract whether or not they have been discussed. It does this by 'implying' a series of terms into a contract. Thus, even though either party may not know of these implied terms, and even though, had they known, they might not have agreed, nevertheless they are regarded by the courts as having agreed (see, Macken et al. 1997, 140-52).

This doctrine of implied terms allows the courts to construct the employment contract according to their idea of what the employment relationship is, or should be. Brooks (1993) has suggested that the courts see 'servitude' as the underlying feature of the employment relationship. (In feudal England, where the common law began, 'servitude' was in fact the appropriate term for employment.) Brooks argues that the courts have used the doctrine of implied terms to construct a contract where the employer essentially 'purchases the employee' for a period of time. In addition, based on the obligations then imposed on an employee, the employer gains further 'added value' (or additional benefits) from the relationship. These additional obligations imposed by the law on employees include: acting in the employer's best interests; obeying all lawful orders, in a manner both reasonable and in the employer's best interests; not taking any pecuniary reward for work done for the employer from any third party; granting all rights in any inventions made by the employee to the employer; and performing all required work with reasonable care and skill (Brooks 1993, 19).

The duties imposed on the employer are less far-reaching. For instance, the employer is not required to act in the employees' interests or, indeed, to take their interests into account when making business decisions. Brooks suggests that the rights given by common law to the employee do not involve 'added value' (additional benefits) for the employee. An employee's rights under the implied contract are simply about compensation for losses caused by the employment. An employee can be compensated for losses caused by: not receiving payment for work done; damage to the employee's bodily health; expenses incurred by the employee on the employer's behalf; and premature termination of the employment contract (Brooks 1993, 19).

At the same time, the common law assumes that the contract of service is based on a bargain between equals. In practice, however, individual workers are often in a weaker bargaining position when negotiating contracts of employment with employers. Without representation, workers are frequently offered conditions on a 'take it or leave it' basis. Negotiations, where they do occur, often centre on a standard contract and are normally limited to a small number of issues. However this may depend on the scarcity of the skills being employed. If, for example, the labour (or skill) being employed is scarce, then the bargaining power of potential employees is higher, and workers may be able to insist upon certain conditions before a contract of employment is concluded. In such cases the equality of the bargaining relationship more closely matches the equality assumed at common law. However, great inequality occurs when labour is abundant and this is clearly the normal situation for the vast majority seeking work.

The Courts and the Tort of Conspiracy

The courts have also played a major role in the area of industrial sanctions and strikes. Courts have actively established laws allowing employers to obtain court orders that prohibit industrial action by trade unions and workers. In contrast to many areas of the law where it may take years to obtain an order, court orders against trade unions can often be obtained within twenty-four hours. This has become a major area of common law. The courts have become increasingly active in attempting to curtail industrial action under legal principles that deal with economic and industrial 'torts'. (Tort law, or the law of civil wrongs, as opposed to criminal wrongdoing, offers remedies of damages and orders, and includes a variety of actions from negligence to defamation.) The industrial torts, at the present time, include the torts of intimidation, conspiracy and contractual interference (for an elaboration of these types of torts, see: Creighton and Stewart 1994, 267-78; McEvoy and Owens 1990, 104-29). To illustrate how trade unions, union officials and individual workers can be held liable at common law for industrial action, we will look at an example, the tort of conspiracy by unlawful means.

Three key elements are required to establish conspiracy by unlawful means. The first, 'the conspiracy element', occurs when two or more individuals act together. The second, 'the damage element', occurs when the individuals acting together deliberately inflict loss on a third party. And the third, 'the unlawful element', occurs when the losses inflicted are the result of an unlawful act. To illustrate how easily these elements can be established in an industrial conflict, we will take the example of a employee badly injured at work as a result of faulty machinery. In such a situation, if fellow workers walk off the job in protest at the employer's negligence (whether or not their trade union becomes involved in the strike action), the three elements are satisfied. The conspiracy element is satisfied by the fact that two or more workers walked off the job (and more so, if they also call on their trade union to become involved). The damage element is satisfied by the employer (the third party) suffering economic loss due to the cessation of work. Finally, the unlawful element is satisfied by the collective breach of employment contracts. Under common law, the workers and their trade union have done enough to establish a conspiracy by unlawful means, and can thereby be held individually liable for their actions. The reasons for the walkout are irrelevant. The fact that the workers were motivated by a concern for the safety of their fellow workers does not provide a defence. The fact that the walkout could have been caused by the employer's breach of occupational health and safety regulations is also irrelevant. Even if the employer's beach of the law is far more serious than that committed by the workers, the employer cannot also be held liable for conspiracy since there was no joint action (conspiracy) and no deliberately inflicted loss (Creighton and Stewart 1994, 270-72).

It could be argued, of course, that this is simply doubling the penalty for the same wrongdoing. For if a worker walks off the job to protest at the behaviour of the employer, that worker is in breach of his or her employment contract, but that is the extent of his or her common law liability. However, where two or more workers walk off the job in exactly the same circumstances, they are each liable for both breach of contract and conspiracy. This demonstrates the common law's historical attempts to suppress collective action taken by workers (Bennett 1994, 92-3).

What this means is that all industrial action in Australia constitutes a conspiracy by unlawful means and all those involved in such action are liable at common law. This includes workers, union officials and trade unions. An employer may seek a number of remedies when this wrong has been committed. In fact, not all of these remedies even require the employer to establish a case. An employer may, for instance, obtain a temporary court order (i.e. an interim injunction) against striking workers and their trade unions. (An injunction is an order for a specific action, such as an order to cease picketing and return to work.) The employer will be granted an order provided it can show that its claim involves a 'serious question' which the court will hear at a later date. (The court's theoretical purpose in granting the injunction is to return the parties to the status quo prior to the conflict pending the hearing of the dispute.) So long as the 'balance of convenience' favours the granting of an injunction (and it nearly always does), the interim injunction may be heard *ex parte*: that is, in the absence of workers, their trade unions and their legal representatives. It may also be heard very quickly, within 24 to 48 hours (subject to a 72-hour cooling-off period imposed by current federal legislation). The effect of such an injunction is to break a strike, because workers who defy such an order can be held in contempt of court and may, at the court's discretion, be fined or imprisoned. Employers may also choose to proceed to a full trial and obtain damages and/or a permanent injunction. The 1989 air pilots' dispute resulted in the Australian Federation of Air Pilots being ordered to pay the airlines $6.48 million in damages (Creighton and Steward 1994, 272-74). But this is rare. Generally, an interim injunction, combined with the threat to pursue the action, is sufficient to end a strike.

Interestingly, the principles of tort law do not apply to employers who lock workers out or who bar trade unions from a workplace. The common law provides no similar laws to the torts applied to trade unions and workers who take industrial action against employers. Thus, the claim that the courts are a neutral forum for resolving industrial disputes must be questioned.

The Courts and Interpretative Power

In addition to their common law powers, the courts also have interpretative powers when there is disagreement over the meaning of the words in an Act of parliament. In theory, laws made by parliament (i.e. statutes) prevail over those made by the courts. In practice, however, it is the courts that interpret legislation and declare the correct meaning of its provisions. Hence, the law created by an Act of parliament depends on the interpretation of the wording by the courts. The courts can play a crucial role in determining how legislation, including industrial relations legislation, operates in practice. Generally speaking, the courts have not been overly sympathetic to legislation that protects workers and their trade unions. Instead, they have tended to adopt interpretations that rely on common law values (e.g. enforcing managerial rights), even when these values are inconsistent with the values expressed by the legislation.

Court decisions about whether a worker is an 'employee' and therefore entitled to the full benefits of protective legislation provide an example of this tendency. This question has usually been decided in terms of whether the person concerned is employed under a 'contract of service' or 'a contract for services'. In order to decide the question, the courts have typically focused on the employer's right to control the activities of the employee, which is a key common law value as mentioned earlier. Where there has been sufficient control, the courts have normally found that a contract of service exists, and that the worker concerned is entitled to the benefits of legislation. Where no such control is found, the worker is said to be engaged under a contract for services. The person concerned is consequently designated a contractor, for whom no legislative benefits are applicable. To ascertain the extent of control, the courts have typically looked at contracts to see whether their provisions permit the worker to work for other employers. They have also looked at the value of equipment a worker is expected to bring to the job and whether a worker is entitled to organise the work to be performed by someone else. Consequently, it has proven relatively easy for employers to alter the terms of employment contracts, so that workers are categorised as contractors rather than employees, thus absolving the employer from various legislative responsibilities (Creighton and Stewart 1994, 132-35; Macken et al.

1997, 8-20). The point being made here is that the interpretations of the courts are often at odds with the intent or spirit of legislation. Hence, by concentrating on the question of control rather than protection, the courts have shifted the focus onto how employers manage the activities of workers (a key common law value) rather than whether workers should attract the benefits of protective legislation.

The Constitution

The courts also have a further interpretive role that stems from the federal nature of the Australian political system. In Australia, legislative power is divided between state and federal parliaments by the Australian Constitution. The words of the Constitution, however, are extremely general and it is the High Court that interprets them and allocates legislative power between the states and the commonwealth. The Constitution is another source of law that plays an important part in the country's industrial relations by defining the Federal Parliament's powers to intervene. These powers are conferred on the Federal Parliament (and thereby on any industrial tribunal it may establish) by the following Constitutional articles:

Section 51 (xxxv): The 'conciliation and arbitration power' enables the Federal Parliament to make laws with respect to 'conciliation and arbitration for the prevention and settlement of industrial disputes extending beyond the limits of one state'. This section empowers Federal Parliament to establish a federal industrial tribunal with powers to conciliate and arbitrate on disputed issues arising between employers and workers.

Section 51 (xxxix): The 'incidental power' is a Constitutional article that allows the Federal Parliament to legislate on 'matters incidental to the execution of any power vested by the Constitution'. It is this particular provision that allows compulsory arbitration, which is an incidental matter relating to the establishment and regulation of conciliation and arbitration tribunals. This provision also allows the Federal Parliament to make legislation to regulate the activities and organisation of trade unions.

Section 51 (xxix): The 'external affairs power' is a provision that confers responsibility on the Federal Parliament for the external affairs of the nation. This allows it to pass legislative measures with respect to industrial relations in fulfilment of the country's obligations as a signatory to international treaties.

Other articles in Section 51 identify 'constitutional corporations', and allow the Federal Parliament to make specific industrial relations laws for businesses operating in the following areas: interstate and international trade and commerce (*Section 51(i)*); navigation, shipping and railways (*Section 51(v)* and *Section 98*); communications (*Section 51(vi)*); banking (other than state banking)(*Section 51 (viii)*); insurance (other than state insurance) (*Section 51 (xiv)*); fisheries in Australian waters (*Section 51 (x)*); and foreign corporations (*Section 51 (xi)*). A constitutional corporation is also considered to be any organisation incorporated in a Territory and any Commonwealth Authority (*Section 4 (i)*).

Section 52 (iii): The 'exclusive power' allows the Federal Parliament to make laws on 'matters relating to any department of the public service'. It is this provision which allows it to regulate directly the terms and conditions of employment for workers in its administration.

Section 52 (vi): The 'defence power' allows the Federal Parliament to regulate directly the employment conditions of members of the armed forces, as well as those specifically employed in military research and military service during peace time.

The Federal Government, via its majority in the parliament, uses these provisions to enact legislation for the purpose of regulating industrial relations in organisations that fall within its province. For the most part, it has relied on *Section 51 (xxxv)*, 'the conciliation and arbitration power', to achieve this purpose. It is this provision that has been used to pass industrial relations laws, including establishing an independent industrial tribunal charged with the responsibility of maintaining industrial peace. We will return to look at these laws in some detail, but first we will examine how recent governments have turned to other constitutional powers in an effort to influence industrial relations in organisations historically outside federal jurisdiction.

In recent years, for example, the Federal Government has made more extensive use of the external affairs power, the trade and commerce power, and the corporations power to exert more control over industrial relations. As set out above, the external affairs power enables the Federal Parliament to enact legislation to comply with international treaties to which Australia is a signatory. The government is a signatory to International Labour Organisation (ILO) conventions and has used these to extend its industrial relations reach. The Keating Labor Federal Government, for instance, in its 1993 amendments to the Industrial Relations Act, used its external affairs powers to extend existing legislation by complying with ILO conventions on minimum wage fixing, equal remuneration for equal work, termination of employment, parental leave and 'freedom of association' (Creighton 1995, 111). One of the key advantages of the use of such conventions has been that they enable legislation to be passed that covers the entire workforce. This is not possible in the case of the other constitutional powers, which all have some limits to their coverage of workers. The Howard Coalition government has also made use of Constitutional provisions other than those involving conciliation and arbitration matters. For example, it has used its corporations power and its trade and commerce power to remove obstacles supposedly standing in the way of free labour markets. In so doing it has enacted legislation which restricts third party involvement in industrial conflict within trading and overseas companies, as well as in companies registered in a territory. Such legislation is of course limited because it does not cover workers employed by unincorporated businesses (e.g. small local businesses, small construction firms, cafes, shops, and the like). To reach some of these workers, the government has used its trade and commerce power to include any organisation engaged in overseas or interstate trade and commerce, whether incorporated or not (Wallace-Bruce 1998, 15-23).

Industrial Relations Legislation

Legislation passed by parliament is another source of law. There are industrial tribunals in every Australian state and territory, and each operates in accordance with statute-based law. The most important tribunal, in terms of coverage and leadership, is the federal Australian Industrial Relations Commission (AIRC). This body is established by power vested in the Federal Parliament under *Section 51 (xxxv)* of the Constitution. Its role is put into practice the principle objectives of government industrial relations legislation. The relevant legislation at present is the *Workplace Relations and Other Legislation Reform Act 1996* (WRA), which, in accordance with *section 51 (xxxv)* of the Constitution, seeks to 'provide a framework for cooperative workplace relations that promotes the economic prosperity and welfare of the people of Australia'. This goal is to be achieved by the following objectives:

1. encouraging high employment, improved living standards, low inflation and international competitiveness through higher productivity and a flexible and fair labour market

2. giving primary responsibility for determining matters affecting the employment relationship to those operating in the workplace
3. enabling employers and employees to choose the most appropriate form of agreement for their particular circumstances
4. allowing wages and conditions to be determined as far as possible by agreement at the workplace and upon a foundation of minimum standards
5. maintaining an effective awards safety net and enforceable minimum wages and conditions
6. conferring rights and responsibilities which support fair and effective agreement making and ensuring that all abide by awards and agreements applying to them
7. providing for freedom of association, including the right of employees and employers to join or not join an organisation or association of their choice
8. ensuring that representative organisations are representative of and accountable to their members and are able to operate effectively
9. enabling the Commission (i.e. the AIRC) to prevent and settle industrial disputes as far as possible by conciliation and, where appropriate and within specified limits, by arbitration
10. assisting employees to balance work and family responsibilities
11. helping to prevent and eliminate discrimination
12. assisting in giving effect to Australia's international obligations in relation to labour standards (*Workplace Relation Act*, Section Three). (See also Chapter 9 for a discussion of the content and impact of WRA 1996.)

The Australian Industrial Relations Commission

These objectives guide the Australian Industrial Relations Commission (AIRC) in its decisions and actions. The key officials of this body are the (1) president, (2) vice-presidents, (6) senior deputy-presidents, (15) junior deputy-presidents and (48) commissioners, all of who are appointed by the Governor-General. There are also (13) members of state tribunals appointed by the Commission (AIRC 1996). The president is in charge of the day-to-day operation of the Commission and assigns members to work on particular industry panels or disputes. Senior and junior deputy-presidents are in charge of industry panels and have special duties in relation to Full Bench cases (see below). Commissioners carry out most of the conciliation and arbitration work, and are normally drawn from the ranks of unions, employer associations and public departments that deal with industrial relations issues.

As a source of law the major purpose of the Commission is to prevent and settle industrial disputes. To this end the commissioners usually work alone in trying to assist parties resolve their differences. It should be noted that the Commission settles only 12 per cent of strikes. This is because most Australian work stoppages are undertaken as demonstrations of resolve, lasting little more than 24 hours (see Chapter 2). The work of commissioners normally deals with trying to resolve differences during the period leading up to the settlement of an award or agreement (see below), and in which no strike (or lock-out) is at the time being undertaken. It is one of the quirks of the arbitral system, as it is known, that there need not be a strike for the Commission to become involved. All that is required is a dispute and that only needs one party to reject the demands of another. If the dispute is deemed to fall within the jurisdiction of the Commission under its constitutional mandate, then it has the right to intervene to settle the matter. An important aspect of the process is that in practice the Commission has an almost perpetual right to intervene in most cases. This is because of what are referred to as 'paper disputes'. These disputes are based on unrealistic ambit claims and counter-claims made by unions and employers, and may date back a decade or more. Claims of this type are on-going. They are served on employers by unions to avoid the administrative cost of approaching each employer with every new round of demands. At the same time, these claims are in turn rejected by employers on an on-going basis. This broad unresolved dispute creates the necessary legal context for the Commission to intervene in more immediate disputes (often over more realistic, substantive matters). This process thereby defuses developing industrial unrest more quickly. This also means that annual or bi-annual awards and agreements determined by the Commission are often in fact part settlement of an on-going 'paper dispute' (Wallace-Bruce 1998, 26-32).

Some of the more important work of the Commission is undertaken by a full bench, which consists of three members (two of whom must be presidential members). Full benches are convened to hear:

- national wage cases
- cases involving major changes to wage setting principles
- cases seeking to change the guidelines on key issues such as standard hours of work, paid leave, parental leave, superannuation, and so on.

The Commission is assisted in its work by:

- the Australian Industrial Registrar, whose office is responsible for the Commission's administration and the publication of its records
- the Employment Advocate, who, whilst not formally part of the AIRC, provides assistance to employees and employers about their rights and obligations concerning Australian Workplace Agreements (see below)
- the Federal Court, which is responsible for enforcing provisions of the *Workplace Relations Act 1996*, awards, certified agreements, and for hearing termination of employment cases.

One important point should be noted. Under the *Workplace Relations Act 1996*, the Commission is required to encourage individual enterprise level agreements (see Chapter 9). To ensure this occurs, new legal restrictions limit the award-making power of the Commission to twenty 'allowable matters'. These matters include:

1. classifications of employees and skill-based career paths
2. ordinary hours of work and the times within which they occur, rest breaks, notice periods and variations to working hour
3. rates of pay, such as hourly rates and annual salaries, rates of pay for juniors, trainees or apprentices, and rates of pay for employees under the supported wage system
4. piece rates, tallies and bonuses
5. annual leave and leave loadings
6. long service leave

7. personal and carer's leave, including sick leave, family leave, bereavement leave, compassionate leave, cultural and other like forms of leave
8. parental leave, including maternity and adoption leave
9. public holidays
10. allowances
11. loadings for overtime or for casual or shift work
12. penalty rates
13. redundancy pay
14. notice of termination
15. stand down provisions
16. dispute settlement procedures
17. jury duty
18. types of employment, such as full-time, casual, or regular part-time employment, and shift work
19. superannuation
20. pay and conditions for outworkers, but only to the extent necessary to ensure that overall outworker pay and conditions are fair and reasonable compared to a relevant award for workers performing the same kind of work at an employer's business or commercial premises (*Workplace Relations Act 1996*, Section 89A(2)).

In practice, however, the Act extends these limited 'matters' by allowing the Commission to make decisions on 'incidental' matters. For example, enterprise flexibility clauses have been widely applied in awards. (Such clauses arise from Enterprise Flexibility Agreements (EFA), under the Industrial Relations Act 1988, as amended in 1994. EFAs were enterprise level agreements between employers and employees which varied an award, but were subject to the no disadvantage test and approval by the AIRC. A union affected by an EFA was entitled to be heard at the approval hearing. See Chapter 9, case 3.) The Commission can also, in certain situations, make an award to settle an on-going dispute, even if the issue in dispute is not an 'allowable matter'. Nevertheless, the overall principle of limiting the scope of awards, is designed to encourage employers and employees to reach workplace agreements that expand upon the limited matters covered in awards. The *Workplace Relations Act 1996* allows for direct workplace negotiations between employers and employees, with no intervention by trade unions or employer associations. The resulting detailed agreements are then expected to be formally registered as Certified Agreements and Australian Workplace Agreements (see below). Two other elements in the Act are also designed to encourage enterprise bargaining. First, the Commission is required to avoid deliberating on issues more appropriately dealt with at the enterprise level. Second, the Commission must allow agreement at the local workplace level on how award provisions should best be applied.

Awards

Awards are made by the Commission under the 'conciliation and arbitration powers' of the Constitution. There are single and multi-employer awards, industry and occupational awards, and primary and secondary awards. The procedure of award making can be summarised as follows. Within the context of an ongoing 'paper dispute' (see AIRC above), when an industrial dispute occurs over the settlement of substantive matters contained in an award, the employer(s) and trade union(s) (or government minister with an interest in the dispute) notify the Commission Registrar. The Registrar then notifies the presidential member heading the panel covering the industry concerned, who decides whether or not the dispute falls within the jurisdiction of the Commission. If it does, the presidential member either presides over the conciliation process or delegates this responsibility to a more junior member of the panel. Initially, the Commission calls a compulsory conference of the parties to encourage them to resolve their differences. If conciliation fails, then the case will go to arbitration, in which case the commissioner responsible will make a decision on the outstanding matters and file it with the Registrar. If one of the parties objects to the decision, an appeal can be lodged on the ground that the matter is of such public importance that it warrants review by a full bench. The Full Bench will decide if this is the case and, if so, will convene to either confirm, modify or overturn the decision. Once an award is made, it is then the role of the Industrial Court to enforce its provisions (Wallace-Bruce 1998, chapter 4).

Certified Agreements and Australian Workplace Agreements

The *Workplace Relations Act 1996* also provides for parties in the workplace to make their own agreements. Negotiations at the level of individual businesses are expected to lead to agreements containing provisions that either supplement or displace the minimum terms and conditions set out in awards. Agreements of this type were once called 'over-award' agreements, but are now recognised by the Commission as Certified Agreements and Australian Workplace Agreements.

a) **Certified Agreements** (See sample Certified Agreement in Appendix at the end of this book).

A Certified Agreement has the force of law once the following requirements are fulfilled:

1. the agreement must pass a no-disadvantage test, i.e. its passing will not result in an overall reduction in the terms and conditions of employees under relevant federal and state awards and laws (*Workplace Relations Act 1996*, Part VIE)
2. a valid majority of persons employed at the time and whose employment would be subject to the agreement must have genuinely made the agreement
3. the explanation of the terms and conditions set out in the agreement must take account of the particular circumstances and needs of those employed (for example the needs of people from non-English speaking backgrounds)
4. the agreement must include procedures for preventing and settling any disputes relating to the agreement
5. the employer must not use coercion to prevent employees seeking representation by a union
6. the agreement must specify a nominal expiry date which cannot be more than three years after the day on which the agreement comes into operation
7. the agreement must satisfy the minimum entitlement provisions with respect to equal pay, parental leave and termination of employment as prescribed by the Act
8. the employer must not contravene the freedom of association provisions of the Act
9. the agreement must not discriminate against an employee because of sex, colour, disability, pregnancy, religion, political opinion, age, marital status, sexual preference and national extraction
10. the agreement must apply to all 'comparable employees' in the business unless there are reasons for not doing so (*Workplace Relations Act 1996*, Part VIB). (see also, Wallace-Bruce 1998, Chapter 6).

Certified Agreements are recognised and given the force of law by the Commission under the *Workplace Relations Act 1996,* based upon the 'corporations power' and the 'conciliation and arbitration powers' of the Constitution. They may be concluded between workers and employers in unionised and non-unionised businesses, so long as the businesses concerned are 'constitutional corporations'. This includes those organisations identified under the corporations articles in *Section 51* of the Constitution; 'arbitration companies' which are organisations that fall specifically within the jurisdiction of *Section 51(xxxv)* of the Constitution; and 'greenfield' businesses which are newly established organisations. All agreements concluded must be lodged in writing with the Registrar of the Commission, and they are open to public scrutiny.

Trade unions can act as bargaining agents during periods of negotiation, but must be invited to do so by existing or potential members. The trade unions that can be involved in Certified Agreements are of two types: (1) those which have been traditionally registered under the legislation; and (2) the new category of 'enterprise associations'. The latter may be very small and, indeed, may cover only a small part of a particular business. The requirement for registration of an enterprise association is that it must cover persons employed at a business carried on by a single employer or one or more operationally distinct parts of such a business.

Certified agreements may be made between employers and unions or between employers and employees.

b)   Australian Workplace Agreements

Australian Workplace Agreements can only be made in constitutional corporations. There is thus no requirement that a 'paper dispute' exist between the parties. Nor is there any requirement that the issues under negotiation be limited by the ambit of a dispute. These type of agreements are the same as individual contracts. The main requirements for an agreement of this type are as follows:

1. it must contain provisions relating to discrimination
2. it must not contain provisions preventing a party disclosing details of the agreement to any person
3. it will normally operate for three years and can be extended for another three years
4. an employer must not refuse to deal with an employee's bargaining agent, if the agent is authorised in writing
5. an agreement can be varied by written agreement if it meets all the conditions for an Australian Workplace Agreement
6. the Employment Advocate (see above) must issue a receipt and certified copy of the agreement if signed and authorised by the employer and employee
7. existing employees must receive a copy of the agreement at least 14 days before signing and new employees at least five days before signing
8. the employer must explain the effect of the agreement to the employee between receiving and signing it
9. the employee must have genuinely consented to making the agreement
10. if an agreement in the same terms was not offered to all comparable employees, it must state that this was not unfair or unreasonable
11. if an agreement is referred to the Commission by the Employment Advocate for breach of agreement, the Commission must also apply the no disadvantage test as required for the certified agreement (*Workplace Relations Act 1996*, Part VID).

The Employment Advocate (see *Workplace Relations Act 1996*, Part IVA) is required to approve an Australian Workplace Agreement if it meets these requirements and passes the no disadvantage test. Once in operation, an agreement of this type excludes any federal and state award that would otherwise apply (other than a 'bargaining termination award'). It also operates to the exclusion of state laws, except those relating to the termination of employment, occupational health and safety, workers' compensation and apprenticeships. It further operates to the exclusion of federal employment laws.

Australian Workplace Agreements (AWA) must be agreed between an individual employee and employer (whether the employer is an individual or an organisation). It must be individually signed and employees may appoint bargaining agents such as trade unions, labour consultants or consultative committees to act on their behalf. The employer, however, is not required to negotiate with such representatives, although they must be 'recognised'. Before an AWA can be filed and have legal effect, it must be approved by an Employment Advocate. The Employment Advocate is not part of the AIRC, but is a position held within the Department of Industrial Relations. If the Employment Advocate has doubts about whether the agreement meets the required conditions, it may advise the parties to amend the AWA or accept an 'undertaking' from one of them that the agreement will not disadvantage the employee(s) in its operations. If the Employment Advocate's concerns are not met, the matter may be referred to the AIRC (see, Wallace-Bruce 1998, Chapter 6).

In summary, it appears that both these types of agreement have been introduced as part of the Howard Coalition Government's desire to make enterprise bargaining an intermediate stage on the path to direct (presumably non-unionised) employer-employee negotiations. Under the existing legislation, enterprise bargaining can proceed through either Certified Agreement or an Australian Workplace Agreement, whilst the number of matters which can be covered by awards registered with the AIRC has been drastically reduced (see above), with all non-award matters being negotiated between the parties.

Non-Industrial Legislation

In addition to legislation that deals directly with the establishment of industrial tribunals and the way contracts of employment are negotiated and settled, there is also legislation that regulates specific aspects of industrial relations. There are, for example, major statutes at the state level covering occupational health and safety (OHS). The principal OHS Act of each state and territory imposes a series of general duties on employers, manufacturers, designers, suppliers and employees. A primary duty of care is placed on employers to provide a safe system of work. Failure to comply with this duty can result in a variety of sanctions, including prohibition or improvement notices by inspectors, or the prosecution of firms and individuals. The legislation of most states also creates mechanisms (e.g. joint committees, and employee health and safety representatives) for workers to participate in OHS. In recent years, a closer link has been drawn between workers' compensation and the prevention of injury or disease in most jurisdictions. There is also anti-discrimination legislation, which renders certain forms of workplace discrimination unlawful. The forms of discrimination covered by such legislation include marital status, disability, sex, race, ethnic origin and others. Most states and the Federal Government have such legislation. Australian anti-discrimination legislation is not general, but instead is targeted at specific situations. In other words, it does not create a general human right or make discrimination illegal as such. Rather it makes discrimination illegal in the context of particular employment decisions, such as hiring, firing or promotion (for an elaboration of the technical aspects of how discrimination is determined, see, Hunter 1992; Macken, et al. 1997, chapter 16).

The *Trade Practices Act 1974* is legislation covering anti-competitive behaviour and consumer protection. In 1977, the Fraser Coalition government introduced provisions against secondary boycotts (Bennett 1994, 84-96). These provisions were aimed at industrial action where trade unions sought to put pressure on a target employer by taking action against someone with whom that employer had dealings. In *Ascot Cartage Contractors Pty. Ltd v. Transport Workers Union of Australia* (1978, 148), for example, the Transport Workers Union (TWU) and oil company drivers placed black-bans on a company which contracted out drivers to oil companies and undercut employee drivers. Pressure was put on the oil companies not to deal with the contracting company. In other words, the contracting company was the target and it was subject to a secondary boycott because of pressure placed on its customers. Since this case, trade unions that breach the secondary boycott provisions of the Act can be subject to very powerful sanctions. In the Mudginberri dispute, for instance, the Australasian Meat Industry Employees' Union (AMIEU) was found to be in contempt of an injunction granted by the court, and was fined $100,000. To pay these fines, union property was confiscated, and it was later ordered to pay the Mudginberri meat works a total of $1,458,810 in damages (Pittard 1988, 29-30).

ISSUES AND PRACTICES

We have already discussed how political values underlie industrial relations legislation. To help understand the way these values influence the type of industrial laws we get, we will examine three major issues often dealt with in industrial relations legislation. In so doing, we will look at the different legislative approaches taken by the Australian Labor Party and the Liberal-National Coalition parties (or what we will hereafter refer to as the 'Coalition'). The issues to be examined are: (1) how workers organise and bargain; (2) how social justice and equity issues are maintained; and (3) how industrial action and sanctions are viewed.

Organisation and Bargaining

In Australia, a most employment occurs within organisations. The form organisations take and the opportunities available to them depend heavily on the legal system under which they operate. Influential legal constraints on organisations include the types of organisation recognised by law, the powers granted to them and the responsibilities or duties imposed upon them. In Australia, the powers, responsibilities and freedoms given to employer organisations are decided by a mixture of corporate and industrial relations laws. Similarly, a mix of other laws, including trade practices and tax law, regulate their activities in areas important for industrial relations, such as their market size and position. So too, for trade unions, there are features of their operation that are regulated by laws. For example, what industries unions are entitled to cover, what minimum size of membership is allowable, what right of access to firms is granted, what types of industrial action are possible, and so on.

Until the early 1980s, it would be fair to say that there was a bipartisan (agreed by both parties) political approach supporting the concept of nationally organised trade unions as an integral part of the system of conciliation and arbitration. The Labor Party viewed the national organisation of trade unions as assisting their operation within the system, and providing a necessary counter-balance to the power of capital. The Coalition parties similarly viewed the national organisation of trade unions favourably, although their reasoning was that this was the most effective means of controlling the activities of organised labour (Hagan 1981). As a result of this bipartisanship, both sides of politics generally accepted the value of arbitral law and changes in its provisions were relatively few. However, this bipartisan approach began to breakdown during the 1980s. In 1984, the Australian Council of Trade Unions (ACTU) sought to strengthen the weakening position of unions by creating 'super unions' (Evatt Foundation 1995). The Federal Labor Government of the time passed amendments to the *Industrial Relations Act*, raising the legal minimum size of union membership. This effectively forced the amalgamation of many small and medium-sized trade unions. At the same time, the growing weakness of many unions encouraged the Coalition parties to denounce national unionism altogether. They began to openly support the alternatives of enterprise unionism and non-unionism. It was over a decade before the Coalition had the opportunity implement their initiative, but it was eventually realised with the introduction of the *Workplace Relations Act*. This act, for the first time, legally endorsed the concept of enterprise associations and contained provisions that allowed the de-amalgamation of trade unions.

This legislation places greater emphasis on the rights of individual workers to organise, gather information and bargain with employers. It contrasts sharply with the Labor Party view that the arbitration system should support effective worker organisations and temper the inevitable inequalities in bargaining power between employers and employees. The Labor view is, of course, that the balance of power between the two depends on how, and whether, workers are organised. It argues that an enterprise association, covering only a small number of workers working for a multinational firm, will be in a different bargaining position to that of a nationally organised trade union. The resources available to the association will also be far less, and it will be unable to undertake multi-workplace industrial action to support its bargaining position. It is also less likely to be able to exert political pressure to advance its claims than nationally organised trade unions. And even if an enterprise association covers workers occupying very powerful positions within the labour process, the advantage this confers in bargaining may not be enough, as the airline pilots discovered in 1989. Even irreplaceable workers, it seems can be replaced.

Social Justice and Equity

As we said earlier the common law treats the parties to a contract of employment as equals. It thus makes no distinction between an employee who happens to be the managing director of Shell Oil, and a Vietnamese outworker who earns subsistence wages for an eighty-hour week. The unwillingness of the common law to make this distinction has long had social justice and equity implications for workers, and is one of the key reasons for why governments on both sides of politics have long supported various forms of legislative protection. This support, however, has been applied differently by different governments. Coalition governments, for instance, have normally taken the view that widespread exploitation of workers is a strictly nineteenth century phenomenon, with such employment circumstances having long ago disappeared with the emergence of a more educated work-force and more enlightened management attitudes. Where exploitation does exist, it is seen as an aberration, confined to relatively few work sites with unsavoury managers. For these reasons the Coalition's approach to issues of social justice and equity in the workplace has been essentially 'abstentionist'. That is to say, their approach is based on 'small state' liberalism and economic rationalism (small government and free market forces). This is apparent in its current legislative approach, which has been aimed at preventing workplace inequalities by encouraging individuals to pursue problems through their common law and statutory rights, rather than relying on legislative protection, as has traditionally been the case.

The Labor Party has long taken a different approach to issues of social justice and equality. It identifies exploitation as a property of certain markets and often beyond the control of individual employers or employees. On this view, social injustices and inequalities are not about wrongdoing on the part of managers, or the degree of work-force education. Instead they occur where workers are easily replaced, where firms are marginal, and where both these conditions combine in a highly competitive business environment. In these circumstances, it is argued, there are overwhelming pressures to cut labour costs, such that without the protection of legislation, even good employers find it difficult to pay a living wage because more marginal competitors undercut them. From this view, businesses may get caught in a 'vicious circle', where wages and conditions are driven perpetually lower and lower. This idea of 'ruinous competition' was the major issue concerning those who originally conceived the idea of arbitration. They believed that only third party intervention and effective enforcement could prevent workplace injustices and inequalities as a result of over-competition. Arbitration, the award system, and a variety of protective legislation were seen as necessary to counter 'ruinous competition'.

The current *Workplace Relations Act 1996* reflects a mixture of both political approaches. It is reasonable to believe that, given free rein, the Coalition would have enacted legislation based on the view that social injustice and inequality were random and relatively infrequent occurrences. The position of industrially weak groups, however, was a key election issue and the Australian Democrats used their balance of power in the Senate to maintain a degree of protection in the Act for such workers. They ensured that third parties (such as the AIRC) retained a role in maintaining a degree of equity in industrial relations through the application of the 'no disadvantage test'. They also ensured that provisions limited competition between trade unions and strengthened trade union representation of workers. Prior to these Democrat amendments, the Bill had stripped the AIRC of its powers to decide whether awards and agreements were equitable; removed trade union rights of entry to a workplace without a written invitation from a member; and denied award coverage to outworkers.

The fact that these protections still exist in the Act indicates the limitations governments confront in their desire to change industrial laws. In this case, it was the influence of organisations outside the trade union movement that were successful. Organised interest groups representing women, migrants, aboriginals, the disabled, the economically disadvantage, and other groups in weak bargaining positions in organisations and the labour market generally, lobbied fiercely for the maintenance of legislative protection of the interests of workers.

Industrial Actions and Sanctions

Industrial law has long been seen as a way for governments to achieve their economic objectives. However, the degree of emphasis governments place on this and the connection they see between industrial action and economic conditions has varied. Coalition governments have typically seen trade union 'militancy' and excessive wage demands as the principal reasons for poor economic performance, both nationally and at the level of firms. They have therefore tended to introduce laws that limit industrial action and make it more difficult for trade unions to obtain wage increases. In line with this approach, they have also long supported the courts' approach to collective action. Labor governments, on the other hand, have been keen to limit employers' use of 'labour injunctions', and have sought to channel disputes through industrial tribunals rather than the courts. The Labor emphasis has been on dispute resolution rather than confrontation. This is made clear in the Labor government's *Industrial Relations Reform Act 1993*, which denied employers access to common law actions until they had a certificate from the AIRC (Naughton 1994, 7). The same Act also introduced the concept of 'protected' industrial action, which limited the right to strike and lockout while parties were negotiating an agreement. It was also subject to notice requirements, intervention by the AIRC, and the protection of property and personal safety (Naughton 1994, 6-7). The *Workplace Relations Act 1996* continues the concept of protected action and maintains the notice and protection provisions.

THE IMPACT OF INDUSTRIAL LAW: A COMMENT

It would be wrong to assume that the law, as set out in legislation and common law cases, operates the same way in practice. There is often a gap between the 'law on the books' and the 'law in action'. The effect of a particular law can only be understood over a period of time by observation or some other form of empirical analysis. This is particularly true if we consider that a law may have different effects in different workplaces, or even different effects on the same workplace over time. A good illustration of this point is minimum standards legislation. This particular law is expressed in terms that apply to all employees equally. Whether employees are actually granted minimum standards, however, depends on where they work (Costello 1996, 6-15). A large corporation, with a significant public profile and large market share, a strong union presence and well-established mechanisms for ensuring regulatory compliance, will normally have the interest and financial wherewithal to maintain minimum entitlements for its employees. A small, financially strapped restaurant employing non-union labour in the highly competitive hospitality industry, however, may find it impossible to abide by legal minimum standards. This will be particularly so when these are breached as a matter of course among competitors. Compliance, therefore, is often dependent on factors beyond the scope of law. In the example we are using, the market position of firms, their ability to comply, the level of government enforcement, the extent of trade union scrutiny, and the degree of social disgrace for non-compliance, are all factors which can affect the impact a law has on firms. The law-abidingness of a particular workplace may also change over time. The factors affecting this include such things as the vigour with which a law is enforced; the views of management; whether the firm is operating in a recession or an expansionary environment; and the nature of public opinion. The level of compliance with occupational health and safety laws, for example, is often dependent upon whether the work is performed by permanent employees or contract labour, with more strict adherence normal in the case of employees (Quinlan and Bohle 1991, 18).

Technical or legal aspects of legislation may also alter the impact of a law. For example, it not uncommon for a gap to emerge between written and practised law because legislation is based on a misunderstandings of a particular issue. The same thing can occur because the world changes in ways that leave the legislation ineffective. Or, it may occur because the legislation was never intended to work. The policies of political parties, for example, are often based on long standing beliefs. If those beliefs are not kept up to date, they can produce some unintended consequences if they become the basis for legislation. The Howard Coalition government, for instance, described small business as the 'victim of over-regulation'. It argued that the removal of certain restrictions imposed by industrial law was essential if this sector was to prosper. AWAs were particularly designed with their interests in mind, and on the assumption that freeing small business from the rigidity of awards would improve their performance and profitability. But for years it has been standard practice for small business to simply ignore awards. This has been especially true since state and federal governments downgraded or cutback the resources of enforcement agencies. Consequently, it seems likely that AWAs will hold little attraction, if small businesses are already offering less pay and conditions than is provided under the minimum standards legislation.

Adherence to laws such as 'freedom of association' offers another example of legislation having an unintended consequence. For example, the *Workplace Relations Act 1996* gives workers the right to appoint a bargaining agent. The stated aim of this provision is to increase workers' choice by providing the freedom to choose to either represent themselves, or to have representation from a trade union or some other third party. Its effect, however, depends very much on the economics of representation, because workers requiring the representation will have to pay for it. Under the previous arbitral legislation, negotiations around industry awards provided trade unions covering small workplaces with crucial economies of scale. Poorly paid workers and non-union workers were offered a degree of representation because negotiations were centralised. This was particularly important for women workers in areas such as retail and hospitality, where there are many small workplaces, and where workers are poorly paid and the number of casual positions is high. In the new climate of enterprise and sub-enterprise bargaining, representation is more expensive, particularly in industries made up of thousands of small workplaces. Poorly paid workers, particularly casuals will also find it difficult to afford the services of a bargaining agent, and trade unions covering such industries will not have the necessary resources to commit officials to separate negotiations across a large numbers of work sites. The most likely result will be to deprive the most disadvantaged workers of any representation at all. The impact of this on such workers will depend on the effectiveness of the other protections offered by legislation. If this protection is insufficient, the price of the so-called legal right to 'freedom of association' is likely to be a very real loss of wages and conditions.

It is also easy to fall into the trap of seeing law as a set of rules imposed on individuals or organisations. But the role of law, particularly in industrial relations, is far more complex. Many laws only function if triggered by an individual or an organisation. In order to obtain an injunction, for example, an employer must apply to a court. The law can be understood not just as a set of rules, but as a resource to be utilised, a means by which individuals or organisations may achieve their objectives. In the Australian industrial relations scene there is a long history of various groups using the law against other groups. It is not, however, simply a matter of unions using the law against employers and vice versa. Groups, which are often seen as sharing common interests, have at different times been in conflict and have not hesitated to use industrial law to strengthen their positions. Trade unions have invoked the law against other unions, employers against other employers. The law has also played an important role in intra-union struggles. Indeed, because the Australian legal system contains different institutions that are often at odds in their approach to industrial relations, it is possible for employers and unions to play one legal institution off against another. Employers, for example, have used the common law to undercut arbitral protections, and unions have sought legislative changes to reduce the opportunities given to employers by the courts.

Therefore, a key question in industrial relations is: who has access to the law? The answer is often decided by what are called procedural provisions. These provisions decide how the law is utilised by deciding who has access to legal remedies; under what the conditions such access occurs; and who has standing to make submissions to courts and tribunals. Take, for example, the 'no disadvantage' test in the *Workplace Relations Act 1996*. This test, as mentioned earlier, provides workers with certain rights to minimum conditions, by insisting that workplace agreements do not disadvantage employees in relation to terms and conditions of employment. In most cases, departures from the award involve a work-wages trade-off. These trade-offs often involve changes to provisions relating to hours (e.g. extending normal working hours, abolishing restrictions on weekend work, doing away with penalty rates) (ACIRRT 1996, 10). They also raise complex issues, many of which involve considerations of health and gender. What, for instance, are the health implications of changes to work hours? Does the deregulation of shift work, particularly in certain industries, raise the probability of increased rates of occupational injuries and illness? Would such changes have family or gender implications? Will the parents of young children have access to adequate childcare outside of the traditional nine to five working day? Will the cost of such out of hours child care exceed the amount they receive as a trade-off for such extensions to standard hours? Do such changes involve work intensification and, if so, how will they impact on women who already carry heavy domestic loads?

It is up to the Employment Advocate to identify whether the new conditions involve a 'disadvantage', but clearly the concept of 'disadvantage' is more complex than first appears. Whether the workers are disadvantaged depends, in part, on the nature of the work process, and the characteristics of the worker (e.g. gender, age, health, and marital status). Thus, the procedural provisions that control what information is available to the Employment Advocate when it comes to deciding whether the new terms and conditions would disadvantage employees are crucial. In the past a wide range of industry, union, community and special interest groups made submissions to tribunals adjudicating on industry and occupational awards. This allowed the tribunals to identify a large range of community views on key issues and gave them information on complex issues. Special interest groups, such as the ACTU, industry groups or women's groups, such as Women's Electoral Lobby, have the resources and the interest to research such issues. Unfortunately, the present legislation excludes such groups from providing information to the Employment Advocate.

The onus is instead placed on the parties to AWAs. The information supplied must either come from the Employment Advocate, the employer, or the workers concerned with an AWA, or their bargaining agents. *The Workplace Relations Act 1996* provides that other parties may not make submissions or be heard with respect to an AWA and that if the matter is forwarded to the Commission from the Employment Advocate, Commission hearings must be in private. Yet individual employers and employees, particularly in small business, do not have the resources or expertise to deal with the complex issues raised by the no disadvantage test. Nor can informed public criticism of the outcome of AWAs influence future outcomes. The present legislation minimises comment. It provides that Commission hearings must be in private and that where the Commission chooses to publish its decisions, it must not identify the parties. In the past, because hearings were open, a decision of the Commission was subject to public scrutiny and media comment. Several decisions were heavily criticised in the media and were subsequently reversed (including one which allowed workers to 'cash in' sick leave). It seems inevitable therefore that, under the present restrictive provisions on workplace agreements, serious issues arising from changes to conditions will be obscured, including not least gender and health implications.

The shortcomings in the procedure also have implications for employers. Short-term changes may offer advantages that become swallowed up by longer-term costs. Over the medium to long-term, for instance, changes to hours provisions may be associated with a rise in labour turnover, absenteeism and health problems. Where this occurs the disruption and costs may exceed the advantages of any changes. Indeed, a study by ACIRRT (1995) found that there was inadequate recognition of the occupational health and safety implications of changes to work processes under enterprise bargaining (134-49). Changes to labour conditions may also affect the competitive position of small employers in way they have not foreseen. It is difficult to avoid the conclusion that many of these changes are driven by big business and easily sold to small business because of its historical hostility to government regulation. This is despite the fact that such changes may weaken the long-term position of small business. In the retail sector, for instance, changes to working hours which allow extension of trading hours may allow large retailers to take market share away from small businesses. Employers are not the same. The impact of labour laws will depend on the nature of their business.

CONCLUSION

Understanding the various sources of law is important for understanding the legal responsibilities and constraints on those who participate in the procedures and processes of industrial relations. Court-made law has long been characterised by a set of uniform values which are largely conservative and supportive of the right of employers to manage their firms as they see fit. This has not, however, been true of law made by various parliaments, which has historically been made to resolve problems arising from unfettered managerial control. The nature of legislative law in Australia has, in turn, depended very much on whether the Labor Party or the Coalition parties has held office. Normally Labor seeks to counter-balance the power of capital, and the Coalition seeks to control the activities of organised labour. Since federation, both state and federal governments have maintained an active role in formulating, administering and enforcing industrial law. Each successive government has sought to reshape industrial law in ways that best suited their particular policy and electoral interests, as well as their favoured interest groups. For the most part, this has been done within the general legislative framework of arbitration, which was long accepted by both sides of politics. Trade unions were assigned certain rights and duties consistent with the representation of their members and workers generally. Conditions of employment were uniformly secured through a system of awards. Arbitration was a core element in the Australian political economy, even if there were disagreements about what form it should take. The AIRC played a key role in preventing and settling industrial disputes through conciliation and arbitration.

In recent years this system has come under increasing attack from large business interests, conservative political leaders and right-wing think-tanks. This reflects a determination on the part of the business community to eliminate what it sees as rigid workplace structures and employment conditions. This attitude is coupled with the changing economic conditions of a rapidly globalising economy; declining trade union influence; uncertain productivity growth; and historically high levels of unemployment. As a result, a series of changes in industrial law have occurred which largely reflect the employers' agenda. The most significant have seen the introduction of a non-union bargaining stream into the arbitration system; a weakening of the powers of the AIRC; and a downgrading of the role of awards. Supported by 'free market' economic assumptions, the current *Workplace Relations Act 1996* has sought to decentralise employer-employee bargaining down to the level of the firm. Its implementation has been based on the view that arbitral processes and trade unions produce distortions in the labour market, which in turn result in the inefficient allocation of labour and the inappropriate payment of wages. The ideal relationship in the workplace is now held to be a 'one-to-one' relationship between employer and employee, with agreements being tailored to accommodate the specific needs of those directly involved. Such a view rejects older ideas about the need to redress the imbalance of power between labour and capital. Instead it argues that a concerted effort is required to restructure industrial relations down to the level of the firm, and that this can be greatly facilitated by changes to industrial law. These changes amount to a significant movement down a path towards a de-collectivised and decentralised system of industrial relations. Further legal developments will depend on the how the balance of power in the political and industrial systems unfolds in the future.

REVIEW QUESTIONS

1. What values underpin common law judgements towards industrial relations issues?
2. What powers do courts wield with respect to industrial relations Acts passed by parliament?
3. What role does the Australian Constitution play in industrial relations?
4. What are the various powers used by the Federal Parliament to enact industrial law?
5. What are 'paper disputes', and what is their role in allowing the Australian Industrial Relations Commission to conciliate and arbitrate industrial relations matters?
6. What are the main differences between Awards, Certified Agreements and Australian Workplace Agreements?
7. The political values that underlie industrial relations legislation can have a significant influence on the type of industrial laws we get. Discuss.
8. What social justice and equity issues are at stake under the new deregulated legal framework for industrial relations?
9. There is often a gap between the 'law on the books' and the 'law in action'. Discuss.
10. What reasons have been offered to justify the need for change to the arbitral system of industrial relations?

SAMPLE CERTIFIED AGREEMENT

A genuine sample of a Certified Agreement can be found in the Appendix at the end of the book.

FURTHER READING

Creighton, B. and Stewart, A. (2000), *Labour Law: An Introduction*, 3rd Edn, Federation Press, Sydney.

Macken, J., O'Grady, P. and Sappideen, C. (1997), *Macken, McCarry and Sappideen's The Law of Employment*, 4th Edn, LBC Information Services, Sydney.

Wallace-Bruce, N. (1998), *Employee Relations Law*, LBC Information Services, Sydney.

Wallace-Bruce, N. (1994), *Outline of Employment Law*, Butterworths, Sydney.

CHAPTER 8

Wage Fixation in Australia

'We will now discuss in a little more detail the Struggle for Existence'

Charles Darwin (The Origin of Species)

LEARNING OBJECTIVES

When you complete this chapter you should:

- have an understanding of the Australian wages policy
- be able to outline the role that government, employers and trade unions play in wage fixation processes
- be able to elaborate the structural changes that are currently affecting the processes of wage fixation
- have an understanding of the link between wages policy and macro-economic objectives.

INTRODUCTION

The Australian wage fixation system has undergone numerous changes since the early 1980s. It has shifted from a highly centralised system to one that is more workplace focused. The issues confronting the Australian system during this period have been shared by wage fixation systems in many other countries, issues such as equity, productivity, efficiency, flexibility, and conflict minimisation. These themes have been deeply entwined in the evolution of Australia's wages system over the last two decades. A key factor in the direction of wage setting has been the agreement on prices and incomes between the Australian Labor Party (initially while still in opposition, but later as the Federal Government) and the Australian Council of Trade Unions (ACTU). Known as the Accord, it provided the consultative framework for setting wages between 1983 and 1996. The election of a Federal Coalition Government saw the demise of the Accord era. This chapter examines wages policy from the Accord period through to enterprise bargaining under the Howard Coalition Federal Government, illustrating how Australia's wages system gradually shifted from award to enterprise level. It is important to understand these trends in wage fixation as they play an important part in the Australian workplace reform debate. Because of space constraints, wages policy in the five selected South East Asian countries is not discussed.

DEFINITION

With the exception of one slight qualification, defining the term 'wage fixation' is relatively easy. It simply refers to the fixing of the price for labour. The only qualification is that in most cases it is not the *wage* that is fixed, but rather the *wage rate*. That is to say, it is the remuneration one receives for a period of time worked instead of the total weekly or annual income. For salary earners, wage and wage rates are the same, because their weekly or annual income is fixed, regardless of the time they work. This type of payment system is normal among professional employees, although it is becoming more common in other occupations. For wage earners, wage and wage rates can differ, depending on the quantity and quality of the work performed. For example, wages can exceed wage rates whenever overtime is worked or whenever production bonuses are paid. This is often the case among employees paid on an hourly basis, such as trades people, production personnel, and clerical workers. So when we hear the term wage fixation, it is actually the wage rate that is fixed, the rate of payment, not the total income received for a given quantity and quality of labour.

There are three ways in which wage rates are fixed. The first involves individual bargaining between an employer and an employee, in which a wage rate is agreed. The average rate across all bargaining agreements is the average wage rate for a given occupational group. The second way involves informal bargaining, both individual and collective, between an employer and an employee, or a group of employees. The wage rate is fixed across occupational categories in accordance with customs and practices. Limitations on this approach include the inability of employees to move between occupations and work-sites, and the ignorance of employees (and even employers) of prevailing labour market conditions. The third way wage rates can be fixed is through formal, institutionalised processes. This can include both collective and individual bargaining, in which employers and individual employees or groups of employees act within prescribed processes to fix the rate of wages. These processes may include direct negotiations between recognised representatives of employers and employees, the mediation of independent industrial tribunals, the adherence to statutory regulations, or a combination of all three.

In this chapter we are principally concerned with the fixation of wages for groups of employees through formal, institutional processes. This is, of course, the main way wages are decided for the vast bulk of Australian workers.

BACKGROUND

Australia has long had a centralised system of industrial relations. Arbitration and conciliation tribunals, industrial peace boards, industry wages boards, industrial magistrates and industrial law courts, have all been a normal part of the industrial relations landscape for the better part of a century. The origins of the system date back to the late 1890s and early 1900s. At this time industrial disputes between capital and labour were particularly bitter. Underlying the conflict was a debate over what contractual model of labour relations was the most appropriate. Employers wanted their right to manage their firms as they saw fit enshrined in legally binding individual contracts. Trade unions wanted the legal right to challenge these powers on a collective basis whenever they saw them as unfair, dangerous or exploitative. The battle over these issues was at its fiercest in the mining, maritime and pastoral industries. It was the failure of trade unions to reduce managerial power through industrial conflict during the 1890s that ultimately led to establishment of the Australian Labor Party (ALP). The trade unions had come to believe that the lot of working men and women could only be advanced through political activity. The influence of the ALP at the Constitutional Conventions of the late 1890s, in turn, resulted in the adoption of Constitutional provisions which specifically allowed the Federal Parliament to establish institutions for the purpose of resolving conflict between the two sides of industry. The wording of the key provision (i.e. Section 51 xxxv) was as follows:

> The Parliament shall, subject to this Constitution, have the power to make laws for the peace, order and good government of the Commonwealth with respect to Conciliation and Arbitration for the prevention and settlement of industrial disputes extending beyond the limits of any one State

This particular provision of the Australian Constitution is the main source of the Federal Government's industrial relations powers, and it is through it that a comprehensive industrial relations legislative framework was introduced. This first took form in the *Conciliation and Arbitration Act 1904*, which sought to set up a system of labour regulation that aimed at preventing strikes and lockouts through a system of tribunals whose primary function was to maintain industrial peace. The flagship of this system was the Australian Conciliation and Arbitration Commission (ACAC), the forerunner of the present day Australian Industrial Relations Commission (AIRC). The Commission was charged with the responsibility of:

1. encouraging the settlement of disputes by mediation or arbitration
2. establishing and maintaining an effective framework for settling and protecting wages and conditions of employment through awards
3. having regard for national economic and social conditions when making determinations
4. setting wages and conditions by application
5. regulating the rights and responsibilities of employers and employees
6. setting up and regulating a system of union registration and encouraging the democratic control of unions
7. eliminating industrial disputation.

Its chief industrial judge of the period, Justice Higgins (1922), was to later describe it as embodying 'the process of conciliation, where arbitration is in the background to substitute for the rude and barbarous processes of strike and lock-out. Reason is to displace force; the might of the State is to enforce peace between industrial combatants as well as between other combatants; and all in the interest of the public' (1922, 2).

Essential to this new 'province of law and order' (Higgins 1922, 2) was an attempt to control and regulate employers and trade unions. This was done by giving the Commission power to arbitrate and conciliate disputes between them, while having regard for the interests of the wider community. In effect, this meant defining the rights and duties between capital and labour according to the Commission's standard of 'fair dealing', or as it said at the time, between the 'average good employer and a competent and honest employee'. To this end, the Commission established a system of 'awards', which were legally enforceable labour contracts binding employers and employees (or collections of employees) to certain agreed wages and conditions. The system itself related each award to others, for as Higgins (1922) noted, to do otherwise would only 'breed unnecessary restlessness, discontent [and] industrial trouble' (1922, 41).

During these early years the Commission established the first of an important series of wage fixing principles. This occurred in the Harvester judgement of 1907, when Justice Higgins established the 'basic wage'. The fixation of this wage was based on a rate, which would provide 'frugal comfort' for an unskilled worker, his wife and three dependent children. A margin for skill was also set down, and both rates were subsequently varied from time to time as a means of providing automatic cost-of-living adjustments. While the original Harvester decision was overturned on appeal, the decision provided an important benchmark for fixing Australian wage rates in the following years. Its most important legacy was that, from a very early stage, a high degree of centralisation and uniformity was imposed on the way wage rates were fixed. It also gave priority to workers' needs over employers' capacity-to-pay in determining what level of wages should be paid to workers (Drago et al. 1992, 12). Higgins justified his decision by arguing that workers' wages were not to be gambled away in the same way that share speculators might gamble on the stock market, and that if an enterprise could not compete without cutting workers' wages, then the enterprise should be abandoned (1922). On the one hand, critics such as Evans have argued that what Higgins laid down was a doctrine of bankruptcy, that is, he would rather see firms go broke instead of adjusting wages downwards as a response to falling market prices (1985, 38). Nevertheless, Higgins decision established the principle that ensured that workers' wages were not to be treated as speculative capital, but rather that wages were to be protected as a contractual commitment to workers in return for their labour.

The Federal Government (or 'the Commonwealth', as it was then known), already facing disputes between states over tariff policy, was confronted with employer opposition to the new system of conciliation and arbitration. To resolve both issues, it linked the introduction of award wages to levels of industry protection (i.e. tariffs and import quotas). In return, employers were expected to accept Commission rulings to pay 'fair and reasonable wages' to their workers. This expectation was frequently expressed in legislation that had little to do with settlement of workers' wages. For example, the *Excise Tariff (Agricultural Machinery) Act 1906* provided for an exemption on the duty of Australian produced equipment if the president of the Court of Conciliation and Arbitration deemed that wages paid by the industry were 'fair and reasonable'.

Thus, the system of compulsory conciliation and arbitration in Australia was introduced in order to bring conflicting parties together before an independent third party mediator. The system was largely designed to give unions the ability to gain improvements in wages and conditions without the need to resort to damaging strikes. A major reason for compulsory rather than voluntary arbitration was the government's concern for the public interest. The needs of the community were to be given equal importance when the Commission was resolving disputes between employers and trade unions.

THE EMERGENCE OF THE AWARD SYSTEM

The development of a centralised system of conciliation and arbitration had a number of effects. First, it gave rise to some important procedures. These grew out of a number of High Court decisions about the power, jurisdiction and processes of the Australian Conciliation and Arbitration Commission. For example, in order to give the Commission jurisdiction, unions (or employers) needed to create a 'paper' interstate dispute. Unions achieved this by serving a log of claims in excess of anything that any employer could be expected to accept. This established the concept of an 'ambit claim'. An award of the Commission (i.e. a contract of employment covering an occupational group, or group of employees in an industry or firm) could only be made within the range of demands claimed by the parties, as set out in the original dispute finding. As long as subsequent claims were made within this same ambit, then the lengthy and costly procedure of serving a log of claims on all the employers who were party to the award became unnecessary. This allowed unions to seek a series of award variations within established ambits, without having to first obtain a dispute finding from the Commission. The effect of this was to encourage the growth of the award system. These arrangements also had other ramifications. Unions, for example, could serve a log of claims on an employer who was not a respondent (a party) to an award, and following a finding of a dispute, the employer would be made a respondent. This process became known as 'roping-in'. Unions could also serve a log of claims on an employer association and thereby bind individual members of that association to an award. These and similar developments became the principle focus of the tribunal system. The tribunals, concerned to maintain a rational system among the developing awards, turned to the issue of 'comparative wage justice', or distributing wages uniformity across trades and industries.

In 1956, the High Court found that the federal tribunal could not exercise both judicial and arbitral powers (i.e. it could not both make awards as an arbitral function, and enforce those awards, a judicial function). This decision grew from the constitutional principle of the separation of powers, that is, the separation of legislative and judicial functions. Following this decision, the tribunal system was split between industrial tribunals responsible for arbitral functions (creating new rights, agreements and awards between the parties) and the Industrial Courts (such as the Federal Court) responsible for judicial functions (defining and interpreting the agreements between parties).

The award system was complex both in the way it covered workers and in the conditions of employment it often specified. Some awards (such as the metal and engineering awards) became the pacesetters for workers' wages and conditions. Awards became a key factor in how labour was used and remunerated in Australia. They set wage rates and specified job conditions including job definitions and classifications, hours of work, leave entitlements etc. Many awards also contained very narrow job definitions. For example, the Federal Metals Award, (a key award for wage relativities) contained several hundred different, narrowly defined jobs. Unions covering individual vocations or occupations encouraged the growth of awards.

Because awards still have a quasi-legal status, they have tended to become entrenched and subject to change only with further disputation and arbitration. Whilst it could be argued that Australia's management practices are often a factor behind this high level of disputation (see Chapter 3), the centralised industrial relations system has been widely criticised by employers. Some of the key criticisms are:

- the coverage of so many different awards has institutionalised restrictive work practices, encouraged demarcation disputes relating to union coverage, and reduced the capacity of enterprises to respond flexibly to changing market pressures
- the award system generated a multiplicity of trade unions representing different employees in every organisation which increased the costs of negotiation and discouraged agreement
- relative wages were rigid and compressed, making it difficult to link pay to performance (BIE 1996, 52).

UNIONS AND AWARDS

In an endeavour to secure industrial peace and encourage compliance with its orders, the early arbitration courts recognised trade unions through a process of registration. Registration, or incorporation allowed unions to legally represent employees (whether members or not) in industries covered by each union in the dispute settlement and award process. The broader impact of registration was to recognise trade unions as the near exclusive voice of workers (whether members or not) and, together with employer associations, as the major clients of the tribunal system. Registration also protected the membership territory and skill domain of a union from competition from other unions. This led to the development of a form of 'tribal' unionism based on union custom and practice, award coverage and exclusive work practices across tribal (industry or vocationally based) boundaries. Unions became the major parties to awards and 'preference to unionist' clauses (e.g. a union member is entitled to first preference of work on engagement or at retrenchment) linked awards to union membership. Under state tribunal systems, this process was given further impetus by the creation of 'common rule awards', or awards applying to all employees and their employers performing particular callings or vocations. In comparison, federal awards were limited to those parties respondent to the dispute finding which created the award.

Unions developed a system of work rules and defensive forms of job control. This usually involved:

- controlling and prescribing the terms and conditions of entry into an occupation, vocation or trade
- establishing a craft tradition and ethos that controlled the way that work was conducted
- the rigorous enforcement of union membership at the point of entry into employment by use of the closed shop (e.g. union labour only) and protecting union members' job rights
- enforcing occupational health and safety as a means of controlling the work process
- prescribing what work can be performed by members through established custom and practice (informal work rules) and demarcation
- protecting members from the impact of technological change through resisting change, or negotiating manning levels (Clarke and Clements 1977, 290).

CRITICISM OF THE AWARD SYSTEM

Critics have argued that the net effect of Australia's system of centralised tribunals and awards was to:

- encourage the resolution of issues away from their source - generally at levels outside the enterprise, with longer time frames and often with outcomes showing little concern for the real interests of the parties directly operating at the enterprise level
- encourage the proliferation of representative bodies, both unions and employer groups
- establish wages and conditions appropriate to a 'national norm' or a comparative wage justice concept, often with little regard for, or flexibility to accommodate the employee relations environment or business circumstances of the individual enterprise (Bongarzoni and Compton 1986, 133).

This system of determining wages and conditions has been further criticised in recent times. Growing debate over the economic direction of Australia and the impact of globalisation has focused increasing attention on the role of the centralised system of arbitration. The system is particularly criticised for its constraining effects on enterprise performance and productivity (Sloan 1995). According to the Business Council of Australia (BCA) a major critic of the arbitration system, the interventionist and institutional features of Australia's industrial relations system placed constraints on the ability of business to effectively compete in a global economy. The BCA advocated a new industrial relations system that:

- made it much more practicable for enterprises and employees to leave the award system and agree on the terms of their employment at the enterprise level, including the content of agreements, how they are adjusted, renewed or terminated and whether they are individually based or collective
- allowed employee representation arrangements to be based on decisions by employees individually or collectively about who can best represent their interests in their dealings with employers and how those interests can be best represented; the role of unions in bargaining would be dependent on the authority given to them by their members
- changed the legislative framework to better encourage employers and employees to stick to their agreements by enabling them to decide how their agreements would be adjusted and enforced
- contained arrangements to safeguard and enhance the welfare of individuals in their employment relationships by establishing statutory minimum conditions of employment and means for redressing unfair treatment (BCA *Working Relations* 1993, 12).

THE ECONOMIC DEBATE
Tariffs - the 1950s to 1980s

Much of the debate during the 1980s and early 90s has concerned microeconomic reform and labour market deregulation. Underlying this debate was a concern about the impact of Australia's institutional arrangements that dominated the labour market. Throughout the 1950s and 1960s tariff protection acted as a buffer against foreign competition for domestic employment. However, some saw the role of tariffs as restraining the capacity of industry to become more productive.

To take the manufacturing sector as an example, tariffs continued to increase until the 1980s, but domestic employment continued to decline. In 1965 manufacturing employed 25 per cent of the total Australian workforce, but by 1991 the figure was only 14 per cent. Writing in the early 90s, Gregory (1992) saw this as a two-fold dilemma. First, high tariff levels cannot protect employment levels. If manufacturing employment is to grow the sector must look outwards and export. Furthermore, if manufacturing is to sell on world markets it must be efficient and flexible. Second, because the Australian manufacturing sector remained undeveloped throughout the 1970s, unless microeconomic reform in manufacturing was substantial, it was now simply too small to make a large contribution to rising living standards (Gregory 1992, 308). However, according to Rimmer and Zappala (1988, 564) manufacturing faced a number of challenges. These included: increasing rates of product obsolescence; rapid technological change; the saturation of some product markets; decreasing levels of real productivity; a change from traditional mass production methods to small-scale batch production; and intensified pressure to respond more quickly to changes in demand.

Ignoring Reform in the 1970s and early 80s

In the 1970s, after years of indifference and inward looking economic and industry policies, Australia was unprepared to take the necessary economic decisions to prepare for the emerging global markets and free trade (Pappas et al. 1990).

To understand the background of the reforms of the 1980s and 90s, it is important that we have some knowledge of the developments in the previous decade. In 1973 Australia experienced a boom driven by high growth rates in government expenditure following a recession of 1971-72. . However this economic boom slowed following a unilateral 25% across the board tariff cut in July 1973 by the Whitlam government. Australia's growing economic difficulties were then compounded in December 1973 when sharp increases in oil prices by the Oil Producing and Exporting Countries (OPEC) gave rise to a worldwide recession. As prices of almost everything began to rise, there was a domestic wage explosion in the first half of 1974 as unions sought to protect members' wages. This inevitably further fuelled inflation. Unemployment rose sharply, and business confidence and investment were weakened. The result was that the policies of future Australian governments became focussed for a lengthy period on correcting 'imbalances' in the share of national income going to wages rather than to profits and reducing the size of the budget deficit (Sheehan, et al. 1994, 77). Real unit labour costs as measured by the Economic Planning Advisory Council (EPAC) had risen by 23% between the final quarters of 1972 and 1974, and were not to return to the 1972 level until 1980 through tighter monetary policies (Argy 1992, 216).

In the Australian manufacturing sector, the 1970s were seriously detrimental. Manufacturing, which had risen by some 70% over the decade to 1973-74, increased only marginally in the decade to 1983-84. The share of total private investment devoted to manufacturing fell sharply from an average of 50% during the 1960s to a low of 24% by 1983-84. The net trade deficit on manufactured goods increased rapidly as a proportion of Gross Domestic Product (GDP). Management generally remained inward looking, struggling with problems of cost competitiveness, technology and economies of scale. Manufacturing looked to have a bleak future (Sheehan, et al. 1995, 77-78). This was compounded by a decline in the demand for domestic manufactured goods leading to a rise in imports, especially from Asia and Japan. As a result, between 1979 and 1993, the ratio of imports to GDP (expressed in 1989-1990 prices) rose from 13.7% in 1979 to 18.5% by 1993 (Sheehan, et al. 1995, 50).

For a brief period during the 1970s Australia experimented with automatic cost-of-living adjustments to wages. It began in 1974 at a time of both rapidly rising prices and unemployment. The Whitlam Federal Labor Government and the ACTU asked the AIRC to introduce automatic cost-of-living adjustments to wages to offset increasing prices (i.e. full wage indexation) as part of a national incomes policy. The AIRC issued guidelines on the principles and procedures of the new wage-fixing system. Under these guidelines, wage increases could only be granted in accordance with the criteria set down by the AIRC (Davis and Lansbury 1993, 111). In December 1975, however, the newly elected Conservative Fraser government opposed full wage indexation, mainly on the grounds of the depressed state of the economy. It also argued that unions had failed to comply with the AIRC indexation guidelines by seeking wage increases outside the ceiling imposed by the AIRC. Between 1975 and 1981, wage increases determined by the AIRC were regularly below increases in the cost of living and many wage increases were obtained outside AIRC guidelines through industrial action. The system of wage indexation was abandoned by the AIRC in 1981 in favour of direct industry level negotiations.

By the early 1980s Australia returned to rapidly rising wages. Some very large pay increases were won in key industries, such as transport, warehousing, oil, maritime and waterfront, and these began to flow-on to other sectors, causing a general wages explosion. Real unit labour costs rose 15% between the final quarters of 1980 and 1982. At the same time, there was a sharp fall in demand for goods and services and a rise in unemployment. The Federal Fraser Government initiated a 'wage pause' first within the Commonwealth public service and then successfully sought its general implementation by the AIRC during 1982 to early 1983 in an attempt to control rising inflation. However this proved unsuccessful, as wages and prices continued to rise soon after the wages pause was lifted (Davis and Lansbury 1993, 112). This together with the advent of a deep recession with unemployment reaching 10% during 1982-83, signalled the failure of the attempt to use a resources boom (expanding the sales of minerals and resources) to 'trade out' of a recession (Sheehan et al. 1994, 77).

The Call for Reform in the 1980s and 1990s

For policy makers, the solution to Australia's trade problems was clear: Australia's economy needed to grow, foster efficient industries and become more export oriented. To achieve this end, a combination of macro and micro economic changes was necessary. The Industries Assistance Commission argued that microeconomic reform was about changing government policies, institutions and in the structure and performance of industry (IAC 1988, 1).

An influential report called *The Global Challenge* prepared for the Australian Manufacturing Council by Pappas et al. (1990) examined a range of factors. These included the impact of tariffs, financial export incentives, economic policies and workplace reform, all of which were considered necessary to create an export oriented work culture (1990, 2). The Report targeted poor manufacturing export performance, observing that Australia's participation in some major manufacturing industries that were now organised on a global scale, such as the automotive, information and telecommunications equipment industries, was marginal. Australia's adoption of new productive techniques and industrial culture had also been slow. These were disturbing results, given often repeated calls to adjust structurally, to add more value to raw materials, and to participate more in Asian markets (1990, 4). The Report went on to argue that Australia's trade balance would be transformed if we could achieve more of our potential to add value to our resource exports (1990, 10).

In relation to Australian manufacturing, the Report found that productivity remained relatively low and rated a mediocre sixth in productivity compared to its overseas competitors (1990, 25). The Report argued strongly against the notion of a 'level playing field' in favour of active government intervention in order to create a strong tradeable manufacturing sector to restore Australia's prosperity. It identified the kind of industries Australia could realistically develop in a resurgent manufacturing sector, given the country's resources, size and distance from significant markets. It advocated further industrial refinement of Australia's resource exports in order to generate added value and reduce shipping costs. It also suggested that Australia could remedy its inherent natural disadvantage in non-resource-based large-scale-intensive industries (such as the car, aerospace and information technology industries) by integrating local manufacture into the increasingly internationalised production process. It suggested that Australian companies should develop industrial complementarities with Asian manufacturing, to sustain knowledge-intensive industries.

In order to achieve improved workplace productivity, the report went on to argue that Australian industry needed to create a new vision based on a new workplace culture and world best practice. Industries would need to strive to achieve international productivity standards through improvements in labour relations and the introduction of training and new technology.

Reforms of the 1980s and 90s

It was not until 1983 with the incoming Federal Hawke Labor Government, that Australia began to implement far-reaching economic reforms. Many of these reforms were combined with changes in the Australian industrial relations system. During the next thirteen years the Hawke and then Keating Labor Governments, the following changes occurred:

- the deregulation of financial markets, the floating of the Australian dollar and the abolition of exchange controls in the mid 1980s
- reductions in business regulation, reforms in corporation law, moves towards common product standards across the states, improvements in government purchasing and customs procedures
- greater accountability of government business enterprises and reduction in staff levels
- selling off public assets, including the Commonwealth Bank, Qantas and Australian Airlines
- changes in the tax regime, including cuts in the company tax rate, removal of the additional tax on retained earnings of private companies, accelerated depreciation allowances, and the introduction of full dividend imputation (lower tax paid on share dividends by shareholders)
- greater effort to reduce overlaps between the three levels of government, Federal, State and local. The most important of these have been attempts to set up a national electricity grid and initiatives in standard gauge rail transport and telecommunications
- efforts to improve government department budgeting, staffing and purchasing procedures
- accelerated efforts by Australia to remove impediments to international trade in agricultural products, through the establishment of the Cairns Group of other rural exporters, and the set up of an Asia-Pacific Economic Co-Operation group

- reductions in tariff levels and other forms of industry assistance in order to force further manufacturing productivity
- introduction of targeted 'industry' plans, aimed at setting productivity targets through planned restructuring and reform. Examples are the car industry, which included rationalising domestic car production; phasing out of tariff quotas; introduction of greater model and component sharing; improvements in assembly technologies; increased volume of sales of smaller, more fuel efficient cars; introduction of export credits; and creating a more flexible workforce. A further example was the textile, clothing and footwear (TCF) industry plan associated with reduction in tariff quotas and financial assistance to TCF manufacturers to accrue import credits from export sales similar to the car industry plan (summarised from Clark (1995), 148-149).

Reports such as Pappas et al. (1990), and an emerging European literature, identified new long term trends in work organisation that emphasised more skilled workers and greater customisation of production (see Piore and Sabel 1984). Focusing attention on these ideas played an important part in resolving the future of Australian industrial relations. It helped to link industry, trade and economic policies by the common thread of labour market reform. According to Bray and Walsh (1993) these ideas can be clearly seen in the goals of the new Federal Labor Government and the ACTU in their advocacy of award restructuring and enterprise bargaining. The aim was to re-orient the Australian workplace towards more productive and cooperative industrial relations, a more highly skilled workforce, and better career prospects for workers based on higher incomes and more secure jobs. Accommodation between capital and labour would define the new employment relations in an open, competitive and global Australia.

THE INDUSTRIAL RELATIONS REFORM DEBATE: EMPLOYER APPROACHES

In the 1990s, economic debate has focussed on reducing government expenditure and controlling inflation. It has been widely accepted that to achieve this, greater labour market flexibility and reform is essential. At times the economic debate has been inseparable from the industrial relations reform debate. This became a trend amongst OECD countries during this period. Based on the assumptions of a rational free market, proponents of 'labour market flexibility' argued that organisations needed to become more adaptable in such areas as hours of work, the more efficient use of labour resources and, more flexible payment systems which linked pay levels to company productivity. The perceived rigidity and inertia of the Australian Industrial Relations system was seen as a major hindrance to improved workplace productivity.

The Business Council of Australia (BCA), for example, is the most articulate of those calling for greater labour market flexibility and influencing the reform agenda. The BCA commissioned a number of studies, in particular, *Avoiding Industrial Relations: A Better Way of Working* (1991), *The Invisible Barriers to Change in Australia's Industrial Relations* (1992), *Enterprise Based Bargaining Units; A Better Way of Working* (1989) and *Working Relations: A Fresh Start for Australian Enterprises* (1993). These reports focused on two separate, yet mutually reinforcing aspects of the Australian Industrial relations system: the continuing role of centralised wage fixation (discussed in this chapter) and the role of trade unions (discussed in Chapter 5). Essentially, these reports argued for a more decentralised system of industrial relations that was more responsive to workplaces' particular productivity requirements by reducing the role of third parties such as trade unions and the Commission. According to the BCA, Australian business urgently needed a fundamental reorientation of the industrial relations system, away from the existing system focused outside the enterprise and adversarial in nature, to one which was centred on the enterprise (BCA 1989, ix).

A major issue according to the BCA was the structural rigidity and influence of Australian trade unions. Australia had a strong union structure and a widespread multi-award system, set up largely on an occupational basis. The BCA argued that this complex structure of work classification and conditions has several undesirable results: it limited horizontal and vertical mobility within the enterprise; it impeded the adoption of flexible work practices; and it discouraged enterprise training and skill formation. The BCA argued that Australia needed to introduce a system where wages could be decided at workplace level. This in turn needed to be linked to an enterprise-based union structure. Consequently unions would be more likely to recognise that it was in their member's interests to cooperate with employers at the workplace level.

While the BCA promoted a reduction in the role of the arbitration system, this view was not supported by other employer associations such as the Metal Trades Industry Association (MTIA). The MTIA supported a strong centralised system. The federalist approach advocated by the MTIA was in keeping with its overall national approach. During 1990-1991, the MTIA effectively set itself apart from other employer groups with its preference for industry level wage settlements. Their two-tier approach was based upon the existing regulatory framework, or the first tier. A second tier would involve productivity-based agreements at workplace level. This process would be conducted under the scrutiny of the AIRC in a 'managed' decentralist environment, ensuring that the AIRC played the role of umpire (Evans 1989, 28).

The MTIA and its members operate in industries with a strongly organised union base through the Metal Trades Federation of Unions (MTFU). Employers that were party to the Federal Metal Industry Award for skilled trades workers were generally industrially weak in the face of an organised union campaign for wage increases during the 1960s and 1970s. As a consequence, the MTIA has traditionally opposed enterprise based wage outcomes because of fears that these would merely lead to flow-ons throughout the industry with scant regard to workplace productivity issues. The MTIA continues to support centralised dispute resolution and strong sanctions on unions taking industrial action.

The growth of the 'New Right' in Australia during the mid 1980s reflected some employers' disenchantment with employer associations and the so-called 'IR club'. They were seen as failing to address what the new right saw as the 'fundamental' problem of the centralised arbitration system namely, the presence of unions. The 'New Right' comprised a range of individuals opposed to state involvement in industrial relations in favour of individual contracts of employment.

The New Right called for a removal of the AIRC and the application of common law (the right to contract) to labour relations through a system of negotiated labour contracts, breach of which would entitle either party to sue for damages. According to the New Right, employers should circumvent the centralised arbitration system. This included the negotiation and signing of labour contracts, irrespective of awards, and recourse to common law to solve disputes. It also included the elimination of union closed shops and compulsory unionism. This was to be achieved through a variety of statutory and legal avenues, including sections 45D and 45E of the Trade Practices Act, (which allowed employers to sue unions for economic damages and loss caused by strikes or bans under certain circumstances), and the common law. The most celebrated of these cases were Mudginberri, Kitchen Maid and Dollar Sweets. In each of these cases, striking unions were prosecuted and common law courts awarded large damages. To finance these costly legal actions, employer groups such as the National Farmers Federation allegedly built up large employer indemnity or special contingency funds (reputedly up to $8 million). It is questionable what impact the New Right has had on mainstream industrial relations debate. Their radical views failed generally to galvanise mainstream employer groups. The New Right has had most influence on legislation introduced by Conservative State and Federal governments.

Despite the criticism of the perceived rigidity and inflexibility of the arbitration system, the system in fact has always displayed a reasonably high degree of adaptability and accommodation to change. The introduction of dispute settlement procedures and mediation processes ensured a relatively cheap and accessible dispute settlement process in a lay court setting, where legal representation was not necessary. The early wage formulas such as Higgins 'living' or 'basic' wage ensured not only equity and social justice, but guaranteed a level of income sufficient to foster growing consumerism at a time when Australian manufacturing was being developed. They also laid the foundation of high levels of consumption for goods and services based on early forms of consumer credit known as lay-by. This system of allowing consumers to purchase goods by paying them off by monthly instalments (free of interest, or with minor interest charges) coincided with a growing capacity of workers to spend their surplus household income on domestic goods.

CHANGING DIRECTIONS IN WAGES POLICY: POST 1983

Wages policy between 1983 and 1996 sought to balance issues of equity (distribution) and productivity (allocation), reflecting earlier concerns about the general level of wage growth and prices. For example, Davis and Lansbury (1993, 111), argue that during the 1970s the Commission sought to reduce the differences between award wages and relativities across different industries. This was done in order to limit the growth in leap-frogging (i.e. wage increases spreading across awards to maintain relativities between skilled and semi-skilled work) with its associated jump in aggregate wage costs across industries. The Commission also tried to limit over-award (e.g. playing above the award rate) bargaining and increases that contributed to further growth in real wage costs. But by 1973-74, the contribution of increases determined by National Wage Cases to total wage increases had declined to approximately 20 per cent, as unions bargained directly with employers for large over-award payments (Howard 1977). Collective bargaining between unions and employers had therefore become the dominant mechanism for wage increases. Such increases generally extended to the whole economy through application of the principle of comparative wage justice, by which similar work attracted similar pay irrespective of industry. This led to a view that unchecked wages growth was an outcome of the award system and a new system for fixing wages was necessary (Isaac 1977, 14).

Unions and the Accord: 1983 - 1996

The incoming Federal Labor Government in 1983 had as its centrepiece of economic policy, the Accord, which had a profound influence on wages policy. From 1983, economic outcomes were strongly influenced by the Accord, which was essentially an agreement on wages and prices, signed by the ALP and the ACTU just before Labor's win in the federal election of March 1983. Upon entering office in 1983, the Hawke Government was faced with low economic growth and continued high unemployment and inflation. Wages policy was based on the Accord and reflected a consensual approach to economic reform. The Accord covered such matters as movements in prices and incomes, price surveillance, social security, health, industry development, occupational health and safety, education, employment, and a return to centralised wage setting. The consensual approach to national bargaining underlying the Accord was a prerequisite to a less conflict-ridden approach to workplace relations and was seen by the government and the ACTU as essential for improving workplace efficiency and saving jobs (Macklin, et al. 1992, 27-28).

Wage setting during the life of the Hawke/Keating governments was dominated by the Accord agreement with the ACTU. The common approach of government policy, industry and trade unions, as well as the beginnings of structural reform of the Australian economy, can be traced to the 1983 National Economic Summit Conference. One of the decisions made by the Conference was that there should be a return to a centralised wage fixation as the most equitable means of pursuing the goals of wage justice, protecting jobs and reducing inflation.

A remarkable feature of the Accord was how it changed during the period of the Federal Labor Government from a one-off statement to a central plank of economic policy, to be renegotiated as economic circumstances changed. Each Accord was modified to reflect changes in economic priorities at the time. This is not to argue that the Accords were reducible to simple wages policy. Indeed, the original form of the Accord involved a very wide-ranging set of economic and social reforms. However, it is the wages policy element which came to dominate the Accords, as other elements of the original agreement were effectively subordinated to broader wages and economic policy (Stilwell 1993). The Accord also encouraged a disciplined trade union movement in a close (albeit at times strained) relationship with the Federal Government. The purpose of this relationship was to achieve flexibility and economic adjustment through consensus (Kyloh 1989). The Accord effectively made the ACTU the Labor government's 'wages policeman', ensuring a lid was kept on unacceptable wage increases by unions. This was achieved by unions giving commitments not to pursue wage claims above those agreed to under the Accord.

Since the introduction of centralised arbitration in 1904, wages policy formed a central plank (depending on the extent to which the government of the day sought to intervene in the labour market) in economic policy and has been closely aligned to control of wages. Since 1983, the Accord proved to be a flexible social contract that enabled the Federal Labor Government to pursue major structural reform aimed at improving Australia's international competitiveness.

Without the Accords (and trade union compliance), it is unlikely that any federal government could have embarked on such a broad agenda of change after 1983. Changes in wages policy during the Accord era went through a number of phases. The original Accord (Mark I) was a written agreement or social contract made between the ACTU and the ALP, then still in opposition. It focused on prices and price controls, and a return to centralised wage indexation, improvements in working conditions (e.g. a reduction in the working week from 40 to 38 hours), new forms of income (e.g. occupational superannuation and social security), taxation and government expenditure. The agreement was the product of a long period of negotiation, taking place in difficult economic circumstances. In the September 1983 National Wage Case proceedings, there was general agreement on the re-establishment of a centralised system, although there were differing views on the form it should take. The new Federal Labor Government put the case against decentralisation in these terms:

> ...with a piecemeal approach to wage settlements it is difficult to assess the cumulative economic effects of such settlements. The case-by-case approach simply does not enable a thorough investigation of national or international economic conditions and their ramifications for the overall capacity of the economy to afford wage increases. Consequently, there is no protection for the community as a whole, including the unemployed and those living on fixed incomes (National Wage Case, 23 September 1983, Print F2900, 14).

The first stage of the application of the Accord took shape in the September 1983 decision of the AIRC that recognised the role of the Accord and laid down a set of criteria holding unions and employers to a centralised system of wage determination based on wage indexation. The benefits of the new system in the form of automatic wage rises (based on cost of living increases) were denied to those unions which did not accept the ceiling imposed by the AIRC in the form of a commitment not to bargain outside the limits imposed by the AIRC. The Accord progressively evolved after 1983. The phases of the Accord are set out in Figure 8.1.

THE EMERGENCE OF DECENTRALISED PRODUCTIVITY BARGAINING: 1987-1998

A new phase in the evolution to a more decentralised wages system was the March 1987 decision of the Commission, which ended three years of semi-automatic wage indexation. During the case, the major employer associations and the ACTU in a joint statement advised the AIRC that:

> The parties also acknowledge that to achieve the necessary adjustments to take advantage of the situation requires the cooperation of the workforce and management. The question is not the need for change, but the process by which we achieve that change. The objective is to achieve change through cooperation and consultation, not confrontation, and to increase the prospect of meaningful and satisfying work and the fuller realisation of human potential (National Wage Case, 11 March 1987, Print G6800, 12).

The shift away from centralised wage fixation began in March 1987 with a two-tier system established by the AIRC and supported by the major employer associations and the ACTU. This experiment with productivity based wage setting was supported by Accord Mark III. The first tier involved provision for an across-the-board wage increase of $10.00 per week (based on traditional equity and cost of living considerations). A second tier offered the prospect of pay rises - up to a limit of 4 percent in exchange for productivity improvements, which met the AIRC's Restructuring and Efficiency Principle (REP). The REP emphasised (but did not confine itself to) changing restrictive work practices. The resultant cost savings or 'offsets' constituted the productivity gains basis for wage increases under the second tier (up to a ceiling of 4%). State tribunals adopted substantially the same system.

Figure 8.1 The Accords, 1983-1995

THE ACCORDS, 1983 - 1995
On assuming office in 1983, the Federal Government entered a policy accord with the Australian Council of Trade Unions (ACTU). The parties have progressively modified and updated the Accord to meet the changing circumstances of the economy. *Accord Mark I* aimed to tackling the problems of inflation and unemployment simultaneously, while working to restore profit share to business. It provided for the maintenance of real wages through full wage indexation for cost-of-living (price) inflation.
In 1985-86 a sharp depreciation of Australia's currency saw a change in the emphasis of the Accord in order to avoid higher import prices flowing through to wage settlements. Under *Accord Mark II*, implemented in September 1985, the parties negotiated to discount full wage indexation for a wage-tax-superannuation package designed to preserve real after-tax incomes and create a national occupational superannuation savings system. It stressed the importance of the government restraining prices through the Prices Surveillance Authority.
Accord Mark III, implemented in March 1987, supported the AIRC's two tier system for wages and abandoned full wage indexation. In addition to the first tier of generally available wage increases, workers could negotiate a second tier of additional wage increases as a trade-off for productivity enhancing measures at the workplace.
Accord Mark IV, implemented in August 1988, supported the AIRC's award restructuring process, which encouraged further measures to improve efficiency and provide workers with access to more varied, fulfilling and better-paid jobs. The award restructuring process aimed to encourage multi-skilling and minimise demarcation disputes.
Accord Mark V, implemented in August 1989, aimed to secure wage restraint at a time of overheating in the macro economy. It combined moderate wage increases with substantial cuts in personal income tax and improvements in the social wage, thereby raising real disposable income. It also included agreement on the need to continue the award restructuring process.
Support for award restructuring continued with *Accord Mark VI* (February 1990), which relied on a wage-tax-superannuation trade-off to maintain wage restraint. Building on the workplace changes made through award restructuring, the Accord supported enterprise bargaining to enable more flexible and productive ways of working at the enterprise level.
Accord Mark VII (March 1993), entitled *'Putting Jobs First'*, reflected concern with rising recession and worsening unemployment. The Accord aimed to create 500 000 new jobs during the years 1993 to 1996. It continued to support a movement to decentralised wage fixation. A major feature of this Accord was the commitment to an arbitrated safety net for lower paid workers who did not derive any gains from enterprise bargaining.
Accord Mark VIII (June 1995) re-affirmed the commitment to a decentralised wages system. It provided for a set of four safety net adjustments for low wage earners over the duration of the Accord (1995-1999). The ACTU committed itself to wage growth consistent with the previous ALP government's target of an underlying inflation rate around 2 to 3 per cent over the course of the business cycle. The government, in turn raised its target for employment growth to 600 000 over the next 3 years. A feature of the Accord's social wage was the government introducing a new means tested maternity allowance. The election of a Federal Coalition government in March 1997 saw the end of the Accord era.

To have such cost offsets ratified, employers and unions were required to submit agreed changes to the AIRC for alteration of the relevant award provisions (commonly as an enterprise specific annexe to the award). In a significant departure from the centralised tradition, most second tier agreements were settled at the enterprise level (McDonald and Rimmer 1988, 482). Nevertheless, the AIRC played an extensive oversight role in the two tier bargaining process by:

- providing a framework under which the parties bargained
- providing a conciliation and arbitration service to any parties that became deadlocked during the bargaining process

- imposing a penalty on any unions requiring arbitration by splitting the available increase into two phased instalments - to discourage the parties from relying on arbitral mechanisms (Romeyn 1994, 10).

The spread of second tier wage increases varied considerably across awards, with employees in small firms less able to negotiate increases because of their limited bargaining resources. This may have reflected the 'go-it-alone' approach individual unions took to the process, rather than coordinating their negotiations (McDonald and Rimmer 1988). Employers with few or no union members made little use of the REP (Romeyn 1994). Large, single union, single award enterprises, particularly in the public sector, were most successful in negotiating second tier rises.

The most frequent offsets achieved under the REP principle concerned greater flexibility in working hours, such as extending the span of hours during which employees could work at ordinary time rates and changing overtime arrangements (DIR 1990). Other offsets allowed for the removal of a variety of restrictive work practices, for example, permitting greater job sharing, reducing demarcation between unions, and greater flexibility in the employment of casual labour. But the extent of changes varied considerably across industries (Rimmer and Zappala 1988).

The REP principle also successfully introduced some flexibility to previously established wage differentials. It did this by discouraging the automatic flow-on of wage increases across industries from one award (usually a key award for setting rates of pay, such as the Metal Industry Award) to other secondary awards (McDonald and Rimmer 1988). However, while the two-tier system provided some improvement in workplace flexibility, the wages system remained firmly within the centralised and legalistic system of wage determination. A number of problems associated with the REP principle also emerged. Many offsets were once-off savings and therefore represented short term gains. In addition, the notion of 'cost offsets' or 'trade-offs' prevented the adoption of more far sighted productivity enhancing strategies and workplace changes (see Rimmer and Zappala 1988).

A problem of the 1987 National Wage Fixing Principle was a failure by Australian management to come to grips with the concept of productivity. This is not to overlook trade union resistance to removing unproductive and artificial manning levels (overtime restrictions such as one-in-all-in, demarcation and restrictions on multi-skilling). However, employer associations adopted primarily a cost minimisation strategy focused on award conditions. The emphasis was on generating 'cost offsets' in return for pay rises (Frenkle and Shaw 1989). This practice, according to the Economic Planning and Advisory Commission (EPAC), reinforced and popularised a view of productivity among management that was based on cost control measures and a production mentality. According to EPAC, the concentration on measuring competitiveness and productivity on inputs was understandable in the context of an accounting approach to productivity. This was especially true where firms operated in industries that produced substitutable products that competed largely on the basis of price. However, this kind of approach sat uncomfortably with the idea of competing on the basis of quality (Hilmer 1991, 9).

The 1987 wage principle was less than successful. The selective 'production mentality' or 'negative cost offsetting' approaches hampered genuine productivity bargaining under the 1987 REP Principle. Labour efficiency was understood in terms of cost inputs (number of hours worked, wage costs, award constraints on hours, penalty rates and so on) rather than focusing on productivity enhancement strategies such as work organisation, job redesign, training and skill formation (Frenkel and Shaw 1989). The Commission also expressed such sentiments. The AIRC concluded that while the March 1987 principles had been reasonably successful:

> The proper application of the restructuring and efficiency principle called for a positive approach by trade unions, their members and individual workers and by employer organisations, their members and individual employers. In the Commission's experience some were inadequate for the task. Many others made positive efforts: the best not only derived benefits which produced immediate efficiency and productivity improvements but also laid the foundation for future improvement (National Wage Case, 12 August 1988, Print H4000, 5).

THE IMPACT ON TRADE UNIONISM

The experience of the 1987-88 wage round also identified weaknesses in structure of trade unions in productivity bargaining and profoundly altered trade union strategy. Union strategy shifted from a concern with shop floor militancy to a more integrated and long term view of Australian unionism promoted by the ACTU. It was to be achieved by adopting union strategies that emphasised industry based awards and wages relativities based on skill and training structures. The purpose was to rebuild a strongly unionised industry base as suggested in the release of two key reports.

The publication of *Australian Reconstructed* (ACTU/TDC 1987) and *Future Strategies for the Trade Union Movement* (ACTU 1987) served to highlight the fragile state of Australian unionism. *Australia Reconstructed* (1987) was an ambitious and sophisticated political, social and economic blueprint for Australia and Australian Unions. The Report argued for the socio-economic policies it had studied overseas, and for their adaptation to Australian conditions. As the title suggests, the Report outlined proposals for a major reconstruction of national industry policy. The Report advocated collective capital formation, industry policy development, state intervention to promote industry rationalisation, adoption of new industrial technologies, and export facilitation measures. It also called for the introduction of labour market programs and the reform of work life (including radical changes to job classifications and union structures that broke with craft unionism). The Report on Future Strategies for the Trade Union Movement (1987) identified weaknesses in union workplace representation. The Report (prepared by the ACTU) identified weak union structures, poor membership representation and a multiplicity of union bargaining structures as barriers to effective industry unionism. It called for rationalisation and streamlining of unions into 20 broad industry groups through a process of amalgamation. The objective of the process was to create larger, better-resourced, more financially viable and more representative union structures.

Subsequent reports, such as the Metal Trades Federation of Unions/Metal Trades Industry Association (MTFU/MTIA) mission to Europe entitled *Towards a New Metal and Engineering Industry Award* (1988) and a similar report by the Australian Vehicle Manufacturing industry called *Award Restructuring* (1988), identified the need to reform current award structures to achieve increased productivity with equity if manufacturing was to survive in a global economy.

THE AWARD RESTRUCTURING PHASE: 1988-1990

A second phase of flexible, centralised collective bargaining began with the August 1988 National Wage Case decision (Print H4000). In its decision the AIRC stated that in order to build on the progress made under the REP the future focus of wages policy must address the more fundamental, institutionalised elements which reduce potential productivity and efficiency. To address these inadequacies the AIRC enunciated the Structural Efficiency Principle (SEP). The SEP Principle reflected concerns raised during previous National Wage cases, particularly the implementation of the March 1987 REP Principle.

The AIRC introduced the SEP, both to facilitate future improvements as well as to reflect post-second tier developments. To achieve this, the AIRC adopted the ALP/ACTU approach in the Accord Mark IV (tax cuts and pay rises linked to skill development) in order to encourage greater workplace reforms and move away from the perceived narrowness of the Accord Mark III. The 1988 wage principle sought to remove the obstacles to better productivity by freeing up award provisions. The new wages principle aimed at ensuring that work classifications were appropriate to each industry. The new wage principle often referred to as the 'award restructuring principle' sought to encourage the parties to examine their awards with a view to:

- establishing skill-related career paths which provide an incentive for workers to continue to participate in skill formation
- eliminating impediments to multi-skilling and broadening the range of tasks which a worker may be required to perform
- creating appropriate relativities between different categories at enterprise level
- ensuring that work patterns enhance flexibility and meet the competitive requirements of the industry.

The SEP made wage increases available to unions that committed themselves to a fundamental review of their industrial awards, described as award restructuring. The Federal Government supported the SEP because it addressed objectives of improving industry efficiency and providing workers with access to more varied, fulfilling and better paid jobs. For unions, the SEP Principle approved a vehicle to modernise wage rates by linking wages to skills, and establishing industry benchmarks for wages, relativities and skill.

The AIRC emphasised its central role in the reform process in these words:

> To sustain real improvement in productivity and efficiency, we must take steps to ensure that work classifications and functions and the basic work patterns and arrangements in an industry meet the competitive requirements of that industry. It is accepted, at least by some, that a more highly skilled and flexible labour force is required not only to assist in structural adjustments but also to provide workers with access to more varied, fulfilling and better paid jobs (National Wage Case, 12 August 1988, Print H4000, 5-6).

With the introduction of the SEP, the AIRC was attempting to ensure that the classification, functions, and basic patterns of work fulfilled the competitive requirements of industry. The intention of the SEP was that while the wage increases acted as a catalyst for trade union participation in award reviews, employers were also given the incentive and opportunity to maximise the potential benefits on offer by tailoring awards to the needs of each industry. This became the focus of the 1989 National Wage Case Decision.

In the August 1989 National Wage Case decision (Print H9100) the introduction of the new wage-fixing package continued the earlier award reform process under the 1988 SEP Principle and the Accord Mark V. The decision built upon the Commission's cautious, yet determined goal of creating decentralised, productivity-based, wage bargaining within a centralised framework. The August 1989 decision continued the emphasis upon efficiency and productivity originally introduced in the March 1987 decision. It clarified the acceptable forms of efficiency restructuring and exerted further pressure on employers and unions to engage in the process by linking pay increases to productivity enhancement. While industry level negotiations were conducted with respect to some awards, the focus for negotiating the structural efficiency principle shifted increasingly to workplace or enterprise level. Importantly, the August 1989 National Wage Case decision set the context within which work would be regulated by more modern industry awards as follows:

- introduction of broad banding and skill related career paths (NWC 1989, 8)
- review, and rationalisation of, conditions of employment (NWC 1989, 9-10)
- rationalising the number of awards and of award respondents (NWC 1989, 11)
- creation of new relativities between awards and within awards, and the introduction of new revamped comparative worth (NWC 1989, 12)
- introduction of minimum rates adjustment (NWC 1989, 11-14)
- establishment of new key classifications and relativities (NWC 1989, 12)
- phasing out of paid rates and rationalising the over-award system or supplementary payments (NWC 1989, 15)
- elimination of interstate wage differentials (NWC 1989, 17).

This process was to be accompanied by wages rises of $10.00, $12.50 and $15.00 (or 3%) for unskilled, semi-skilled and skilled workers, with payments in two stages phased over six months, provided under the Federal government/ACTU Accord Mark V agreement. In connection with this process, the Commission warned in February 1989 that 'any proposals for change must be carefully handled' (NWC 1989, May Review Print H8200, 4).

At the heart of the process was the changing nature of skill, which through broad banding of classifications and multi-skilling would render obsolete traditional craft boundaries and notions of job ownership. The structural efficiency process aimed to operate at two levels: at the level of industry and union structure, and at the enterprise level. For example, the trend of award restructuring was towards the realignment of wages and relativities within, and between awards towards a single parent-type industry award with an enterprise focus. Implicit in this process was the restructuring of unions from narrow occupational categories to larger and more comprehensive industry-based organisations.

A key element of the award restructuring process was the minimum rates adjustment. This aimed to provide a safety net of consistent minimum wage rates across awards. It involved modernising classifications and adjusting pay relativities within and between awards. The most common changes arising from award restructuring were:

- eductions in the number of job classifications
- establishment of new skills-related career paths
- multi-skilling.

The extent of award restructuring varied across industries, with the pacesetter industry being the metals industry, where the MTIA and Metal Unions implemented a number of important changes to work practices. This is set out in Figure 8.2

AWARD RESTRUCTURING IN ACTION: THE METAL INDUSTRY

Changes to the federal Metal Industry Award during the award restructuring process included:

- the collapse of over 300 job classifications and pay levels into a new 14 level, broad classification designed to increase the skills base of the industry, provide an opportunity to redesign jobs and establish career paths
- reduction in award wage relativities
- the establishment of enterprise-based consultative mechanisms and procedures
- enabled employers to direct employees to perform any work within their skill, competence and training provided it does not lead to de-skilling or compromise safety. This was an important tool in eliminating demarcation based on union membership and job function
- required a training program to be developed having regard to the current and future skill needs of the enterprise
- allowed for training to be undertaken on and off the job on the basis that any training undertaking during working hours shall be without loss of pay
- introduced an 'enterprise flexibility clause' to enable the parties at the enterprise to make an agreement on any measure designed to increase efficiency subject to meeting certain conditions
- enabled a more flexible application of key award provisions relating to hours of work, shift work, meal breaks, annual leave and annual close-downs
- included a provision for adult apprentices (previously banned by unions).

Figure 8.2 Award restructuring in action: the metal industry

To summarise, the introduction of the August 1989 National Wage decision (Print H9100) was the final part of three important wage decisions: The August 1988 decision (Print H4000) that introduced the SEP or award restructuring Principle; the February Review (May) 1989 (Print M8200) that defined its terms; and the August 1989 decision that set the framework for implementing the process of award reform and modernisation. The major thrust of the SEP Principle was to broaden classification structures, to encourage multi-skilling and the introduction of career, training and skill enhancement structures.

The SEP Principle also sought to create appropriate relativities between classifications, introduce greater flexibility in working patterns, eliminate discriminatory provisions in awards, and finally, to prevent the spread of over-award payments.

TRADE UNION STRATEGY UNDER AWARD RESTRUCTURING

The three National Wage cases from 1988 to 1989 were important for achieving the Federal Government's objective of modernising business by encouraging reform (e.g. tariff and taxation reform) and restructuring the arbitration system and work organisation. The major components of this strategy were: award restructuring, to broaden classifications and provide incentives to undertake training and skill formation; extension of information sharing and participatory working practices; legislative reforms to reduce the number of unions; and encouraging industry to provide increased training in order to raise the level of skill formation.

These decisions were also important for trade unions. Union strategy under the SEP process was outlined in the ACTU Report entitled A Draft ACTU Blueprint for Changing Awards and Agreements (December 1988) that saw the SEP process as a vehicle to achieve genuine workplace reform with 'full involvement of trade unions'. The Report was based on an earlier MFTU/MTIA document entitled Towards a New Metal and Engineering Industry Award (1988) in which the Metals Award was to be restructured to provide new classifications and career paths linked to training. This strategy was to be applied to the building, transport, warehousing, timber, hotel, retail, clerical, vehicle, textile clothes and footwear, furnishing, local government, steel and airlines industries and was based on three considerations:

1. higher wage rates for employees on minimum rates awards
2. the provision of eight or nine skill levels within each award
3. the linking of classifications to training and competency outcomes.

Union strategy sought to use award restructuring to achieve the following broader goals:
- maximise trade union solidarity by maximising understanding of relativities
- introduce new structures to provide opportunities for skill and career enhancement
- link the new structure of wages with education and training
- raise minimum rates of pay by the creation of national 'parent', or generic, awards with appropriate relativities
- introduce new organisational structures which broaden workers skills and responsibility and reduce middle management control
- reduce demarcation barriers through the increased broad skilling of workers
- promote the role of unions in training and in establishing appropriate wage structures
- introduce participatory and consultative structures in the workplace, (Timo 1989, 403).

The trade union movement's strategy for the future of Australian unions had been formulated within the protective umbrella of the Accord relationship. The Accord was seen as providing unions with the necessary gestation period in order to develop and grow more effective and efficient workplace union structures.

However, a lack of consensus over the direction of wages policy was reflected in the August 1989 National Wage Case decision, which established a program for tailoring awards to the needs of the enterprise. A number of agendas were at work here. On the one hand, the ACTU and Federal Government saw the SEP Principle as a vehicle for reforming the award structure in terms of better structures for wages, relativities and skills-based classifications. Individual unions saw these developments as necessary for improving the structure and membership base of unions. On the other hand, employers saw the process as yet another round of wage increases and questioned the extent to which the content of awards could be varied and modernised. In response, the AIRC redefined its wages policy by setting in train a series of award reviews. This review was intended to result in changes to the way in which work was performed under the relevant award, and thereby improve productivity and create greater efficiency at enterprises to which the award applied. That process would ordinarily result in variations to the award which might for example, extend the span of hours during which work might be performed at the ordinary rates of pay. A list, though not exhaustive, of measures that might be reviewed was set out in the August 1989 Decision and included:

- compensating overtime with time off
- flexibility in arrangements covering hours of work, including wider daily span of ordinary pay hours and job sharing
- rationalising the taking of annual leave to maximise production
- developing consultative procedures to deal with day to day matters of concern to employers and workers. (National Wage Case, 7 August 1989, Print H9100)

The AIRC stated that such changes should not be implemented in a 'negative cost cutting manner', but through agreement. To unions, however, it seemed an invitation to management to do the former. Nor was it clear what was intended. For example, consider the clause relating to part-time and casual employment. Was this an encouragement towards casual work, or was it indicating a desire to lighten the conditions under which casual employment took place? The 1989 decision gave rise to debates about the extent of award restructuring; what constituted 'no disadvantage' to employees; and the future role of awards. Larger organisations appeared to have greater success in bargaining under the SEP principle than smaller firms. To what extent was the SEP process a success? The outcome varied across industries, with some gaining much greater productivity and efficiency through more flexible and modern awards. One outcome was to pave the way for the move to enterprise bargaining. As Romeyn observes, this laid the groundwork for a greater workplace focus, by making awards more flexible and relevant, including the use of facilitative provisions, the introduction of enterprise flexibility clauses and encouraging the establishment of workplace consultative mechanisms (Romeyn 1994, 10-11).

THE ENTERPRISE BARGAINING PRINCIPLE: THE AIRC AND CONTROVERSY 1991-1992

The third phase of the gradual process of reform under the Accord occurred in 1990. During the period 1988 - 1990, trade unions became increasingly concerned about the failure of the Accord to safeguard real wage levels. In 1989, the ACTU had begun to argue that wage increases should be linked, not to past increases in cost of living, as under the original Accord, but to the predicted rates of inflation in the six months ahead. In 1990 the key issue had become whether the parties should be allowed to directly negotiate wages and conditions outside the centralised award system. In February 1990, the ACTU and the Federal Government reached agreement on the terms of the Accord Mark IV, which included provision for a modified 'no extra claims commitment' which allowed unions to negotiate at enterprise level for over-award payments based on productivity. Accord outcomes also included agreement to a wage rise of 1.5% during the December 1990 quarter, based on the expected September quarter CPI rise (reduced to 0.7% when the inflation figure came in lower than expected). There was also a flat $12 per week six months later. This was to be augmented by a tax cut from January 1991, averaging $7.85 per week. Enterprise bargaining, industry by industry, was agreed on the basis that additional over-award payments or profit sharing could be gained through demonstrable productivity increases by workers in individual enterprises (up to a ceiling of 7 per cent). Superannuation schemes were also to be improved by an amount equivalent to a further 3% of wages to be phased in over two years from May 1991.

In August 1990, the ACTU passed a resolution that unions could campaign for industry agreements 'in the field'. The building agreement was the first and it included a productivity bonus as set out in the Accord Mark IV to be negotiated site-by-site in the form of over award payments. Over the next two months, the ACTU secured agreements in over thirty large corporations and industry sectors (MTIA 1993).

The larger Employer Associations supported the move towards a greater degree of enterprise bargaining. The Confederation of Australian Industry (now the Australian Confederation of Commerce and Industry - ACCI) had argued on behalf of most employers for greater flexibility:

> ...the next wage system must continue to place emphasis on the need to reform industrial relations to improve productivity, efficiency and international competitiveness. The structural efficiency principle must continue to be the centrepiece of the wage system...The employment relationship takes place in the workplace, it does not take place at the award level. The worth or otherwise of any reforms made at other levels must ultimately be assessed by reference to their effect in the workplaces. The two award restructuring systems (1988 and 1989) focused on reforming industrial awards, an important and as yet uncompleted task, but did not focus sufficiently on workplace change (ACCI Submission to 1991 National Wage Case, 16 April, Print No. J7400, 23).

But not all employers agreed with the change. The MTIA strongly opposed the approach and argued that a move to a decentralised wage setting involving over award bargaining as set out in the Accord Mark IV system was premature. It predicted that the reintroduction of the system of over award bargaining would lead to widespread industrial disputation, pressures for flow-ons and wage breakouts as in earlier episodes of decentralised wage fixing. It 'would cause a reversion to the wide scale pattern of direct action and leap-frogging wage levels existing prior to 1982' (NWC April 1991, 31). The MTIA argued that true enterprise bargaining required enterprise level unions, as opposed to the current structure of numerous but well organised craft unions. It maintained that such union structures create instability, engendering the development of unregulated over-award payments in single enterprises which subsequently flowed on as industry standards. The MTIA argued for the need to control wage pressures within a centralised framework, but one which provided a broader scope for direct bargaining between the parties under AIRC supervision.

On 16 April 1991, the AIRC gave its controversial decision in the December 1990 wage case (Print J7400). The AIRC rejected the Accord Mark IV and instead approved a 2.5% wage increase for 1991 (non-retrospective), on an award-by-award basis. In addition, each union claim for the increase had to give a new no-extra claim commitment. The claim for extra superannuation was adjourned. The AIRC decision in effect was a rejection of key elements of the Accord Mark IV. The AIRC concluded that enterprise bargaining raised a number of concerns:

- incompleteness of the award reform process and its application at the enterprise level
- inadequate development of the 'receptive environment' necessary for the success of enterprise bargaining beyond the present system
- fundamental disagreements between the parties and interveners about the nature of the proposed forms of enterprise bargaining and their failure to deal with significant issues
- potential for excessive wage outcomes
- lack of agreement on quantifying productivity outcomes
- lack of agreement as to how 'no cost offsetting' and 'no disadvantage' tests should apply
- persistence by employers to continue to side-step awards by attracting labour through paying above award wages (over awards) would continue labour market instability (National Wage Case, 16 April 1991, Print no. J7400, 29-53).

The rejection by the AIRC of North American-style collective bargaining had a number of consequences. The ACTU saw enterprise bargaining as a means of revitalising a union structure softened through years of centralised wage handouts. The ACTU strategy was to bargain over productivity and profitability. So instead of sharing national income through national wage cases, the distribution would reflect relative union power. Unions that were successful would attract members. Those that were unsuccessful would surrender membership to the more successful unions. For employers, the move towards enterprise bargaining was an attempt to weaken unions and reduce wages by linking increases to workplace productivity. The result of the April decision was therefore fourfold. First, the ACTU took its campaign into the field (waterfront, metals and public sector). Second, the AIRC decision kept microeconomic reform firmly within the award system and under the auspices of the AIRC. Third, it introduced long lags in the pay system, as most unions would take some time to meet the structural efficiency criteria laid down by the AIRC for accessing the 2.5% increase. Finally, at a political level, it signalled the need for Federal Government legislation (supported by the ACTU) for increasing the spread of enterprise bargaining and for dealing with a reluctant AIRC.

At a Special Unions Conference in May 1991, the ACTU formally rejected the April National Wage Case decision and resolved to secure productivity agreements at industry and enterprise levels. Shortly afterwards, the Federal Government and the ACTU jointly released their own guidelines for workplace bargaining. The guidelines provided for the payment of a uniform wage increase of $12.00 per week, provided unions gave a continued commitment to award restructuring. Additional wage increases were to be available based on achieved productivity or profitability at their enterprise/workplace level.

In September 1991, the AIRC reluctantly commenced a review of wage fixation principles and requested that the employers and unions address the question of whether the Commission should continue to establish principles of wage fixation in National Wage Cases (Review of National Wage

Case, 13 August 1991, Print J8943). Employers and unions advocated a move towards enterprise bargaining, with the Commission simply setting down general guidelines and approving consent arrangements involving wage and conditions agreed to at the enterprise level. Although the Commission had earlier expressed reservations about the maturity and ability of the parties to engage effectively in enterprise bargaining, it reluctantly agreed to introduce a formal enterprise bargaining principle in the National Wage Case Review decision of October 1991 as follows:

> In all the circumstances confronting us, we are prepared on balance to determine an enterprise bargaining principle. In deciding the best way to proceed, we have taken account of views of the parties and interveners and the need to limit the risks inherent in the approach chosen (National Wage Case, 30 October 1991, Print K0300 1991, 3).

The AIRC's October 1991 decision opened the way to further the process of decentralising industrial arrangements, particularly wage determination. The AIRC amended its wage fixing principles to allow for enterprise bargaining in the federal system. These agreements had to satisfy the AIRC's new Enterprise Bargaining Principle (EBP) that required employers and unions to bargain according to the following criteria:

- enterprise agreements to be based on a broad agenda
- wage increases to be based on the actual implementation of efficiency measures designed to effect real gains in productivity
- a 'single bargaining unit' to negotiate agreements at the enterprise level
- a commitment to no further pay increases, other than through any subsequent national wage case decisions
- retention of basic award standards in relation to hours of work, annual leave etc.
- agreements would be for a fixed term and not be subject to re-negotiation while still active.

Of particular importance was a requirement that bargaining took place through 'single bargaining units', comprising representation drawn from unions and employees at the workplace. In the case of a section of an enterprise, the parties were required to show that the bargaining unit was discrete and would not restrict the implementation of the SEP or the EBP in that enterprise or other sections of the enterprise. The AIRC indicated that its primary role in enterprise bargaining would be to provide conciliation and to ratify agreements, and not to arbitrate outcomes. The AIRC indicated that it was returning to its traditional role by concentrating on setting minimum rates of pay and leaving the determination of total rates to the parties directly involved.

LEGISLATION FOR ENTERPRISE BARGAINING: 1992-1996

However, the EBP Principle under the 1991 NWC decision could only be accessed where trade unions had updated all of their awards with the $10.00 REP increase, plus both first and second SEP increases. This amounted to an effective wage pause for workers due to the time lag involved in modernising awards. Earlier in March 1989, the Federal ALP government had varied the Industrial Relations Act 1988 to provide for more effective enterprise bargaining through the introduction of certified involving both single or multiple employers which allowed employers and unions to access the EBP principle agreements. (See also Chapter 7 and 9, for discussions of Certified Agreements and a sample CA.) Under these arrangements however, both the certified agreement and the AIRC's enterprise bargaining (EBP) principle streams focused on awards and required the involvement of unions. Non-union enterprises were effectively excluded from the federal enterprise bargaining process.

The Federal Government was concerned with the slow uptake of enterprise agreements both under the Industrial Relations Act's certification process and the AIRC's new enterprise bargaining principle. With the cooperation of the ACTU, it amended the Industrial Relations Act in 1992. The July 1992 amendments created a new enterprise bargaining division in order to further facilitate enterprise agreements. The amendments removed the requirement of the Commission to consider the public interest when approving agreements covering a single business and replaced it with a 'no disadvantage' test. This effectively compelled the Commission to approve these agreements as long as the technical requirements of the Act were followed. The amendments also added a number of other statutory tests relating to consultation, dispute settling provisions and the use of single bargaining units. The AIRC, when certifying an agreement, could not scrutinise the agreement's productivity measures or wage increases. The amendments introduced greater flexibility in the determination of agreements at the workplace, placed responsibility on employers and unions for bargaining; and limited the scope of the AIRC to intervene in the bargaining process. The intent of the new legislation was to ensure that certified agreements were available as a real alternative to the mainstream award system and not reserved for exceptional circumstances.

The 1992 amendments, while devolving responsibility to the bargaining parties, continued to rely on awards (as the benchmark for the no disadvantage test) and union participation in the bargaining process. While the amendments limited the AIRC's scope to intervene, the AIRC continued to play an important role in deciding whether enterprise agreements put up for certification satisfied the statutory tests, including the no disadvantage test. Hence, like the 1988 arrangements, non-union firms were effectively excluded from the AIRC enterprise agreement process. The number of enterprise agreements approved by the AIRC increased once the July 1992 amendments became effective. Most parties to these agreements chose the amended certified agreements route, rather than the AIRC's enterprise bargaining principle (BIE 1996, 62-63).

In October 1993, the AIRC replaced its enterprise bargaining principle with the enterprise awards principle. This new principle allowed parties to make enterprise agreements as consent (e.g. by agreement) awards. It also provided scope for the AIRC to assist in the making of these agreements by arbitrating as a last resort. However, despite this more flexible approach, the role of the AIRC was rapidly changing to that of a defender of minimum award standards and one of 'lighthouse keeper', to keep the enterprise bargaining stream working while protecting the industrially weak.

The shift towards the Commission having a less overt role in the bargaining process reflected deliberate government policy. The wage decision of the AIRC must always be seen in the context of the legislative bind on the Commission's ability to influence workplace bargaining outcomes. For example, following the re-election of the Labor Government in March 1993, the government amended the Industrial Relations Act 1988 even further to encourage workplace agreements. The Industrial Relations Reform Act 1993 came into force in March 1994. It introduced new objectives for the Act. These new objectives focused on:

- the facilitation of enterprise bargaining
- the protection of wages and conditions of workers through awards and by ensuring that labour standards meet Australia's international obligations
- the provision of a framework of rights and responsibilities consistent with the move towards a more decentralised system (Brereton 1993).

The amended legislation placed the onus for bargaining directly on employers and unions. The role of the AIRC was limited to conciliation while diminishing its role in arbitration. The 1993 Reform Act made provision for Certified Agreements (CA's) in unionised workplaces. In order to accelerate the spread of enterprise bargaining to workplaces with little or no union coverage, the amendments also included Enterprise Flexibility Agreements (EFA's). Enterprise Flexibility Agreements were available to constitutional corporations (that is, organisations that were incorporated and covered by the corporations power under the Australian Constitution) whose terms and conditions of employment were covered by a federal award and did not require union involvement or provide a union veto (except that unions with members had to be invited to become parties to the agreement). (See also Chapter 7, for a discussion of these agreements, later known as Australian Workplace Agreements.)

This was reflected in the AIRC's August 1994 National Wage Case Decision where the new focus was on the award safety net, which was to be:

> Reviewed and adjusted from time to time, consistent with the Commission's obligations to ensure that employees are protected by awards that set fair and enforceable wages and conditions of employment that are maintained at a relevant level. Generally, the detailed nature and timing of any adjustments (of $8.00 per week) will be determined in the context of specific applications and in the light of prevailing economic, social and industrial circumstances (National Wage Case, 16 August 1994, Print L4700, 15).

The September 1994 National Wage Case (Print L5300) and the October 1995 Safety net adjustment and Section 150A Review (Print M5600) have continued the notion of a 'safety net' role. However, the October 1995 Review has allowed access to the third $8.00 safety net adjustment only under limited conditions, where awards had been reformed and modernised, to provide for greater enterprise flexibility and prevent automatic flow-ons.

The Labor Government's legislative intervention to reduce the role of the Commission in the bargaining process saw its role change to that of maintaining an award 'safety net'. This policy was continued and accentuated by the Coalition Government's Workplace Relations Act (1996) and was reinforced by National Wage Case decision on the safety net review handed down in April 1997. This decision related to two ACTU claims. The first sought to increase award rates in order to establish a minimum hourly rate of $12.00 for all hourly workers or a minimum weekly wage of $456.00 for weekly workers. The second claim sought a further $20.00 per week pay increase for those employees who had not received increases under enterprise bargaining. Both claims sought to re-structure award wages in order to upgrade the award safety net. The claim was subject to both government and employer opposition with the new Governor of the Reserve Bank supporting the Coalition argument that the AIRC should reject much of the ACTU claim on the basis that it might lead to inflation.

Following a lengthy hearing, the AIRC (in a majority decision, with Vice President Ross arguing that a greater wage increase than that awarded by the Full Bench should have been directed at lower paid employees) rejected the quanta contained in the ACTU claims deciding instead to:

- grant an arbitrated safety net increase of $10.00 per week
- to determine a new adult weekly wage of $359.40 to be called the 'federal minimum' wage
- the new weekly wage to absorbable against over award payments
- to fast track the payment of any outstanding $8.00 per week safety net adjustments.

The AIRC decision while rejecting the quantum of the ACTU claim, has given greater emphasis to the Commission's 'lighthouse keeper' role, keeping the Commission involved in wages policy while the government continues to implement an enterprise-based wages system (Stegman 1997, 152). The Commission regretted that it could not go higher. It argued, however, that the future transition from an inflationary to a non-inflationary environment might lower the level of wage settlements. This would, it suggested, 'leave space for a more generous treatment of workers substantially dependent on award rates' and who are unlikely to access increases under enterprise bargaining (April 1997 Safety Net Review, Print 1997, 70).

AN ASSESSMENT OF THE ACCORD 1983-1995

The years of the Accord remain unprecedented in terms of coordinated union policy. Organised labour adopted a long term outlook and agreed to endure real wage erosion, abandon long held union protections, such as union demarcation, and reduce the number of unions. The Accord was a centrepiece of Australian economic and wages policy from its inception. The use of the Accords to frame National Wage Case Principles created fundamental changes in the workplace. For example, although the 1987 decision and the 1988/89 Structural Efficiency Principle decisions did not necessarily required negotiations at a workplace level, many industry-wide restructuring agreements involved the implementation of change at a workplace level through joint employer-union consultation committees.

The features distinguishing this system of decentralisation from those associated with the later Industrial Relations Reform Act 1993 and the Workplace Relations Act 1996 were: the maintenance of an administration role for tribunals referred to earlier as 'managed decentralism'; the preservation of awards as the primary instrument of employment regulation; and the maintenance of trade unions as the sole bargaining representatives of employees.

The reluctance of the AIRC to embrace wholesale workplace bargaining as envisaged by the ACTU and Federal Labor Government during 1990-1993, laid the foundations for legislative intervention by both the Keating Labor and later Howard Coalition governments. The strategy adopted by the Labor Federal Government and the labour movement was to maintain and reform the centralised system of award regulation, by providing the opportunity for unions and employers to negotiate a prescribed range of changes at industry and workplace level. In October 1991, the AIRC took a step in line with this view by establishing the Enterprise Bargaining Principle following earlier rejection of this approach. Despite this April 1991 decision, the ongoing role of the AIRC in coordinating decentralised bargaining came under increasing scrutiny. Legislative changes since 1992 had reduced this role to that of 'overseeing' the bargaining process and applying a 'no disadvantage' test. Under the Labor Federal Government, the monopoly of the centralised tribunal system over wages policy since 1904 was broken. The rebuke given to the AIRC by both the Labor Government and the ACTU when the AIRC refused to endorse the enterprise bargaining provisions of the Accord Mark VI saw the power of the AIRC legislated away. The actions of the ALP/ACTU during this period showed a willingness to curtail the powers of the 'independent umpire'. This position was exploited later by the Howard Coalition Government in justifying even further reductions in the role of the AIRC.

The Accord brought discipline to union wage claims and allowed the Labor Government to pursue broader economic objectives such as limiting wage increases and fighting inflation. For employers, the Accord era provided certainty and wages restraint, and combined with workplace restructuring, saw an increase in labour productivity. Table 8.1 points to selected economic indicators for the period 1989-1995. By the late 1980s, the Accord effectively slowed the growth of real wages while allowing company profits to grow. As these grew, so did executive salaries.

Table 8.1 Australian economic indicators - 1989 - 1995

COMPARISON OF GROWTH RATES (%)								
	1989	1990	1991	1992	1993	1994	1995	Cumulative Total
Executive pay	11.5	11.5	5.2	4.4	3.2	6.0	6.02	58.6
Av weekly earnings	7.5	6.7	7.5	3.8	-0.2	3.1	5.1	38.4
Av award rates	6.9	5.8	3.3	3.2	1.2	1.3	1.0	24.8
Labour productivity	2.5	-0.5	0.2	2.5	1.9	2.7	4.3	14.4
Corporate profits	12.7	11.4	0.1	-1.7	4.7	8.5	7.9	51.4
Profitability	4.4	-3.5	-28.7	-19.6	21.2	9.9	na	-23.1
Share prices	15.6	11.3	-18.8	19.7	-2.0	39.0	-15.0	44.8

Source: Prices Surveillance Authority, Price Probe 1995, 7

Was the Accord a success? During the period of the Accord there was a reduction in real unit labour costs and as well as substantially reduced industrial disputation. Inflation in Australia in the most recent decade averaged 5 per cent per year, compared with almost 9 per cent in the earlier period. According to Bernie Fraser, former Governor of the Reserve Bank of Australia, the Accord has served the Australian economy well. In fact, in terms of reduced wages growth, increased profits and a slow down in industrial disputes, the effect of the Accord was dramatic. According to Bernie Fraser, a former Governor of the Reserve Bank of Australia, the Accord slowed wage increases. The growth in average weekly earnings between 1976 to 1985 was 10.2% compared to only 4.7% from 1986 to 1995. For the same period, profit share (non farm GDP) grew from 13.4% to 15.6% and the level of industrial disputes fell from 482 days lost (per '000 employees) to only 176 (Fraser, 'Sustaining Growth and Living Standards', speech to Australian Business Economists, Sydney, 28th March 1996).

Looking to international comparisons, the picture is less dramatic but is still positive compared with other OECD countries. Growth rates in Australia were largely unchanged in the last two decades, but this has meant Australia did a little better than the OECD countries during the Accord period. The picture is less positive if we compare Australia to other regional economies. During the period 1976 to 1985, Australia's growth in GDP was 3% (or 1.75% per head) as compared to 3% (or 2% per head) for OECD countries and 6% (or 3.75% per head) for the South East Asian countries Indonesia, Malaysia, the Philippines, Singapore and Thailand. For the period 1986 to 1995, Australia recorded again a 3% (1.75% per head) increase in GDP as compared to 2.5% (1.5% per head) for OECD countries and 7% (4.75% per head) for South East Asian countries (Fraser, 'Sustaining Growth and Living Standards', speech to Australian Business Economists, Sydney, 28th March 1996). Consequently, whilst the Accord managed to reduce wages and labour costs, it was perhaps an inadequate tool for lifting investment.

In summary therefore, under the Accord, the Australian labour market achieved reasonable flexibility. Real wages rose less rapidly allowing a rise in company profits. The data above confirms the Accord as a significant device for controlling wages, inflation and industrial unrest while enabling industry to improve profitability. However, in relation to employment, the Accord was less successful in stemming the rise in unemployment.

WHAT IS THE FUTURE OF INDUSTRIAL RELATIONS REFORM?

The federal industrial relations system has experienced a number of significant changes over the last decade. The system, once highly centralised and based on industry wide, multi-employer awards, has progressively evolved to a system of workplace agreements. Enterprise agreements, underpinned by an award structure, are now the system's major focus. Microeconomic reform in the Australian labour market over the past decade has been extensive in scope and is continuing. It is best described as a system-wide program of regulatory review and reform, rather than deregulation. However, the reform debate continues. For example, during the early 1990s, the Business Council of Australia has argued for even further labour market reform in order to make labour more responsive to individual enterprise needs. The BCA has suggest that wages should be even further deregulated in order to link company performance and market competition and that wages should rise and fall in accordance with market changes (BCA 1994, 12).

Major employer associations have also continued to seek substantial changes to the industrial relations system. Employer proposals broadly call for:

- awards to contain only 'core' minimum conditions, so that enterprise bargaining is more flexible
- unions' role in negotiating wage deals to be reduced so that employees have the right to choose who represents them
- strengthened powers for the AIRC to order an end to strikes
- legislative restrictions on unions acting as spoilers in non-union wage deals
- greater focus on employer-employee individual agreements
- introduction of voluntary unionism
- reducing the role of the AIRC to set wages and conditions between employer and employee (BIE 1996, 66-67).

The Federal Coalition Government, elected in March 1996, embarked on a radical overview of the industrial relations system in Australia through the introduction of the Workplace Relations Act 1996. Key areas of change are:

- reducing the legal coverage of awards to 20 minimum core conditions
- simplifying awards to provide an enforceable safety net of minimum wages and conditions with matters beyond these being for determination by workplace parties
- removing paid-rates awards and removing restrictions on the use of particular types of labour and hours for regular part-time work
- ending monopoly rights and compulsory membership of trade unions, facilitating greater choice for workers in selecting their bargaining agent, and ending uninvited third party intervention in the making of workplace agreements
- facilitating agreement making between employers and employees without union involvement
- restricting the right of unions and workers to take strike action.

Under the Coalition model the role of the AIRC is reduced further to one of maintaining safety net wages and conditions, placing the onus of workplace bargaining in the hands of employers and employees, and reducing the role of trade unions to that of a bystander. A more detailed analysis of these changes is found in Chapter 9 dealing with Enterprise Bargaining.

CONCLUSION

This chapter has set out the developments in wage fixation since 1983. As outlined earlier in this chapter, the election in 1983 of a Federal Labor Government ushered in a range of changes under a centrally designed wages system. The chapter illustrates how managed change varied from careful tinkering with the edges of centralisation to more bold initiatives towards enterprise-based bargaining.

The Accord was a main feature of government and Union cooperation during the period 1983 to 1996. But was the Accord worth it? A range of commentators has questioned the importance of the Accord and considerable debate has emerged over how the changes brought forth under the Accord should be evaluated. Essentially, the Accords were the product of the failure of the Whitlam government in the 1970s to control wages, industrial disputation and outdated workplace skill formation systems. The Accords, introduced against the backdrop of high wage inflation and high unemployment, enabled Australia to achieve a ceiling on wage increases and engender far-reaching workplace reforms. The Accord process and subsequent changes in work practices required by National Wage Cases since 1987, have modernised workplace award structures (through greater award flexibility) and encouraged the reform of trade union structures.

For trade unions, the Accords provided a means to achieve long term strategies of economic restructuring at national, industry and workplace levels. The union movement's agenda widened beyond distributional questions to include the processes by which income was produced. Its approach to economic restructuring became more positive, coordinated and strategic. The novelty and numerous achievements of this new strategy, however, cannot hide a range of failures, such as the continuing decline in trade union membership and high levels of unemployment. The election in March 1996 of a conservative federal government and the formal 'death' of the Accord process has left Australia without a central wages and incomes policy. Those who argue for a market driven wages system see the demise of the Accords as a necessary prelude to shifting wage outcomes to workplace level and diminishing the power of trade unions to bargain and influence wages. For unions, the new workplace is much more competitive and restricted by new laws that have removed unions as the exclusive bargaining agents of employees. For some employees, the Accord has laid the foundations for increased wages, more skill and better careers. For others, this period of wage fixation has led to greater job insecurity, intensification of work, and longer working hours, as employers have adjusted to more competitive labour-use practices. The era of planned and consensual wages policy appears now at be at an end. However, if Labor returns to power in Canberra, it is possible that a another era of Accords may commence.

REVIEW QUESTIONS

1. What role should the government have in setting a framework for wage setting?
2. What part did tariffs play in Australia's earliest centralised wage fixing system?
3. Briefly set out the main historical markers in the development of the centralised wage fixing system between 1970 and 1983.
4. Why did Awards arise and why did they proliferate?
5. What are the key criticisms of the Award system of wage fixation?
6. How did tariffs affect Australia's preparedness to embrace global competition between 1950 and 1981?
7. Why was economic reform tied to industrial relations reform in the 1980s?
8. What were the main economic reforms of the 1983-1996 Labor Governments?
9. What were the main steps during Accord period that altered the centralised wage fixing system to one focused on workplace enterprise bargaining?
10. In what ways was the Accord a success? A failure?
11. In a wages system, what balance should there be between equity (distributing wages across the economy) and allocation (distributing wages based on productivity)?
12. 'The best outcomes for firms are where employers and employees assess their own interests and engage in negotiations that produce a balanced outcome based on these interests'. Discuss.

FURTHER READING

Bramble, T. (1989) 'Award Restructuring and the Australian Trade Union Movement: A Critique', *Labour and Industry*, Vol. 2, No. 3, 372-398.

Buchanan, J. and Callus, R. (1993) 'Efficiency and Equity at Work: The Need for Labour Market Regulation in Australia', *ACIRRT Working Paper* No. 26, University of Sydney.

Gardner, M. (1992) 'The Consequences of Decentralised Wages Systems', *National Wages Policy and Workplace Wage Determination - The Critical Issues*, Proceedings of the Conference, ACIRRT Monograph No. 7, University of Sydney, 104-121.

Hall, R. and Harley, B. (1995) 'The Australian Response to Globalisation: Domestic Labour Market Policy and the Case of Enterprise Bargaining', in *Globalisation and its Impact on the World of Work*, ACIRRT Working Paper no. 38, Sydney, 71-96.

Lansbury, R. and Niland, J. (1994) 'Trends in Industrial Relations and Human Resource Policies and Practices: Australian Experiences,' *International Journal of Human Resource Management*, 5(3), 581-608.

Timo, N. (1989) 'Industrial change and Structural Efficiency: A Trade Union View' *Labour and Industry*, 2 (3), 399-412.

CHAPTER 9

Enterprise Bargaining and Workplace Change in Australia since 1996

'To change and to change for the better are two different things.'

German Proverb

LEARNING OBJECTIVES

The objectives of this chapter are to:
- Identify approaches to enterprise bargaining
- Gain an understanding of the legislative framework of enterprise bargaining
- Understand the processes of workplace bargaining
- Understand the trends in workplace bargaining.

INTRODUCTION

The workplace is dynamic. It is a place of activity, conflict and change, affected by managerial strategies, government policies, trade union activities and employee involvement etc. It is also a political place. In 1998, the Minister for Workplace Relations and Small Business outlined his approach to enterprise bargaining in a speech by reminding his business audience that they should never forget the history of politics and which side his conservative Coalition Federal Government was on. They were, he was reported as saying, on the side of making profits and of the owners of private capital (Peter Reith, speech to a Business Lunch, 9th July 1998, Perth, W.A.). Unions also approach enterprise bargaining from entrenched political positions. They often use it as a vehicle for recruiting new membership and for pursuing political as well as industrial goals, such as in the 1999-2000 Victorian building industry dispute over reduced working hours. Yet, despite the clear political context of enterprise bargaining, reaching consensus on workplace issues through negotiation between employers and employees has been around for a long time. Employers and employees have always bargained directly on issues such as work customs and practices, work methods, wages and working time. However, it was only in the early 1990s that enterprise level negotiations were elevated to the status of government policy in Australia (Callus 1997). It has only been since the mid 1990s, that Australia has moved towards setting wages at the workplace level. Whilst Australia's centralised system of arbitration and award making still exists, the role of enterprise bargaining has increasingly become the primary focus of public policy. The role of the Australian Industrial Relations Commission (AIRC) is being increasingly marginalised to one of maintaining minimum wages and conditions as a safety net for workers unable to reach enterprise bargaining agreements.

This chapter focuses on these developments in enterprise bargaining in Australia. First, there is an overview of what enterprise bargaining is and the issues it creates. Second, we outline the historical context of Australia's move to enterprise bargaining. Third, the legislative process of enterprise bargaining under the Commonwealth Workplace Relations Act 1996 (hereafter referred to as WRA) will be outlined. For illustrative purposes reference will also be made to the former Industrial Relations Act 1988 (as amended) where appropriate. Finally, the trends in enterprise bargaining and the impact at workplace level will be summarised.

WHAT IS ENTERPRISE BARGAINING?

Enterprise bargaining can be defined as a consensual process of negotiation that leads to agreed workplace changes in return for some form of reward (such as wage increases, improved productivity, greater working time flexibility etc.). It may involve direct employer and employee negotiations, or it may be conducted between an employer or employers and a union or unions. At its core, enterprise bargaining involves a shift away from a centralised and compulsory system for determining wages and conditions, to a consensual process of bargaining at workplace level. Enterprise bargaining is a complex process, often occurring at many different levels and influenced by a range of factors such as the prevailing legal, political and economic environment, government policy, market pressures and managerial and union strategies. The core of enterprise bargaining is that the rules and customs governing the workplace can be rearranged to suit the needs of one party or another or both. It is a process involving a freeing up of the rules that govern workplace regulation to achieve a satisfactory outcome for all parties. These rules generally involve:

Substantive rules that establish the content of the employment relationship such as wages and conditions of employment. In Australia these rules are illustrated predominantly in the making of awards and agreements under the auspices of the AIRC and state industrial tribunals.

Procedural rules that establish the processes whereby the rights and obligations between employers, employees and trade unions are determined, usually through the AIRC, but also, to a lesser extent, through common law courts. Such rules include matters relating to how awards are created, who are the parties, wage determination, national wage cases, tribunal policies on matters such as redundancies, hours of work etc. and the mechanics of how the tribunal system works.

Different Types of Agreements

In order to understand how enterprise bargaining works, however, it is important to understand some of the mechanics of the bargaining process. The terms 'enterprise bargaining agreements' or 'workplace agreements' are often used interchangeably. There are several different types of bargains made at the workplace. There are informal agreements (either in writing or verbal, though these should not be used because they are difficult to enforce) that form part of the custom and practice (the accepted way that things are done at the workplace). There are collective agreements negotiated at the workplace between a single employer and his/her employees, and there are those negotiated between a union or unions and multi employer(s). In the Australian context, collective agreements are generally approved (or registered) by industrial tribunals such as the AIRC, though it is common for some industries (such as the Queensland sugar industry) to negotiate non-registered industry agreements. In contrast to collective agreements, there are individual agreements often referred to as individual contracts made directly between employers and individual employees. These are enforceable at common law. Examples of individual agreements approved by a quasi-industrial tribunal are Australian Workplace Agreements (AWAs). These are individual contracts that are approved by the Office of the Employment Advocate, a separate body to the AIRC. The CRA case study at the end of this chapter illustrates how in some instances, individual agreements can be a set of common conditions and 'individualised' within a company. For convenience, AWAs are referred to as 'workplace contracts' to distinguish them from collective agreements. The parties to an agreement are those who are covered by the terms of the agreement. In summary, in Australia today, there are many different ways to make an enterprise or workplace agreement.

Enterprise bargaining suggests bargaining at a workplace. However, a 'workplace' is not always easy to define and may include multiple geographically separate workplaces under one employer. 'Bargaining structure' generally refers to the way that bargaining relationships, between employers, employees and unions, are formed and structured. A key issue here is whether the bargaining process involves a single workplace (or part of a workplace) and a single employer. 'Multiple bargaining' or 'employer – union bargaining' may involve an industry approach to bargaining, similar to collective bargaining, that affects a number of employers, unions and employees in the industry concerned. This may involve 'pattern bargaining' whereby a common or collective approach is taken to enterprise bargaining across an industry or industries in order to achieve a desired outcome for all. A 'single bargaining unit' generally refers to the way in which a small number of unions (usually the largest unions at a workplace or in an industry) agree to negotiate on behalf of all unions and employees in a workplace or industry with employers. This is usually in the form of a committee. A single bargaining unit may also involve a select number of employers involved in the bargaining process. Bargaining often occurs through the establishment of a bargaining unit where union and employers agree to set up a single representative body (often referred to as a 'joint consultative committee') to represent the interests of all of those (employers and employees) affected by the outcomes of the bargaining process.

A feature of enterprise bargaining legislation under both the Labor and Coalition Federal Governments has been the emphasis on enterprise bargaining directly at a single workplace. This has been achieved by discouraging the making of multiple employer and union agreements. Only a Full Bench of the AIRC, according to strict criteria, can approve multiple employer agreements.

While pattern bargaining has not been outlawed (at the time of writing), the legislative requirements for approving agreements has tended to dissuade employers and unions from making common multiple employer agreements except under special circumstances. The focus of enterprise bargaining, therefore, has tended towards the making of agreements negotiated directly at a single geographically identifiable workplace (for a review of enterprise bargaining arrangements and terms in the early 1990s, see Macklin et al. 1992).

ENTERPRISE BARGAINING OR COLLECTIVE BARGAINING?

Theoretically, wages and conditions that result from enterprise bargaining should not extend outside the firm. However, in practice, because of the award safety net and bargaining strategies of both parties, a set of common terms often tends to be included in agreements. Nevertheless, under enterprise bargaining, employers and employees are expected to negotiate an agenda that focuses on workplace issues. The parties then tailor pay and conditions to suit each workplace or firm, rather than accept or have imposed on them, a collective outcome, based on a broad set of conditions for the industry as a whole. An industry approach, on the other hand, is termed pattern bargaining and is used in many industries such as engineering, metal, health and the public sector as a way of harmonising wages and conditions. Pattern bargaining is similar to collective bargaining, in that it usually involves negotiations between employers and unions at industry, regional or national level. As a result collective bargaining inevitably has a narrower agenda that enterprise bargaining (because it cannot include individual workplace issues). It is, however, important to recognise that Australia in the late 1990s has a mix of different bargaining structures, processes and outcomes. The differences depended upon industry, size, location, levels of unionisation and whether there was a history of previous negotiations (e.g. whether employers and unions were active bargainers rather than inactive).

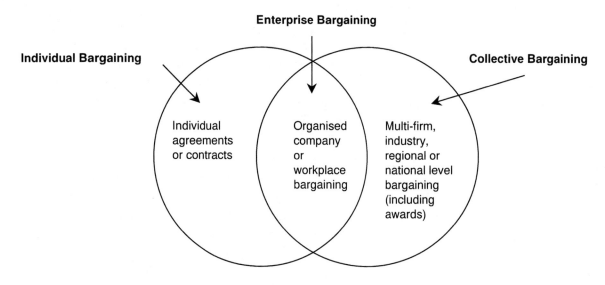

Figure 9.1 **Bargaining models**

A major issue is the extent to which unions are able to act collectively ('collective voice') on behalf of employees, thereby providing a counter to managerial power. Researchers studying enterprise bargaining not surprisingly demonstrated an a-symmetrical power relationship at the workplace that gives employers the upper hand when bargaining for a reduction in wages and conditions. (This issue is discussed later on in this chapter in relation to collectivist and individualist approaches to enterprise bargaining. See also the Chapter 5 on trade unions.) The distinctions between these forms of bargaining are illustrated in Figure 9.1.

ISSUES RAISED BY ENTERPRISE BARGAINING

Enterprise bargaining has both proponents and opponents. Those that oppose enterprise bargaining often have concerns for equity and the fair distribution of productivity increases. These concerns include:

- wage differences will widen so that better organised workers will achieve greater benefits, whereas those less organised or capable will fall behind
- working conditions will be reduced as employers try to negotiate trade-offs of employment conditions in return for wage increases
- employers will be reluctant to spend money on training (in case a competitor poaches employees)
- workplace change will lead to greater workforce insecurity as employers attempt to save costs by increasing work intensity or by using casual labour
- the enterprise bargaining process is complex and many employers and employees and their unions do not have sufficient skills in this area
- devolving wage negotiations to workplace level may simply increase unrest and industrial conflict as employers and employees attempt to gain the upper hand.

Proponents of enterprise bargaining argue that enterprise bargaining can deliver substantial benefits, such as:

- increases the firm's responsiveness to changing market conditions
- increase the commitment of the parties to each other and to the outcomes of bargaining
- increases the flexibility of labour
- focuses greater attention on efficiency and productivity at the workplace.

At a policy level, the shift towards enterprise bargaining raises a series of questions, including:

- What role should the AIRC play in the bargaining process?
- To what extent should minimum award standards be maintained and how?
- What role should unions have in the bargaining process?
- How do we obtain agreement on the bargaining agenda?
- How do we enforce workplace agreements?
- How do we bring the other party to the bargaining table?

ENTERPRISE BARGAINING AND PRODUCTIVITY

At the core of Australia's shift towards a system of enterprise bargaining is the simple belief that by devolving wage setting to the workplace, Australian firms would become more efficient and improve productivity. In reality of course, the shift towards enterprise bargaining has been driven by many different goals and motivations among the diverse groups involved. Yet even the simplest goal of 'productivity' has been fraught with difficulty, as there is no agreement on either a definition of productivity, or how it should be measured. (This issue is dealt with more fully later in this chapter.) As an example, over the past decade, Australia's gross domestic product (GDP) has improved. Yet according to the Australian Productivity and Competition Commission (ACCC, formerly known as the Productivity Commission) in the past 25 years, Australia has dropped from 10th to 20th position (excluding executive salaries that have risen some 250 per cent) in terms of per capita income. However, the ACCC also acknowledged that Australian workers are today far more productive than two and a half decades ago and that the levels of profitability of Australian Companies are at record levels (1996). At a policy level at least, enterprise bargaining has become a panacea for most of Australia's economic ills.

AUSTRALIA'S SHIFT TO ENTERPRISE BARGAINING: GLOBALISATION AND MICRO-ECONOMIC REFORM

The rise of enterprise bargaining should be seen in the context of a gradual shift in the industrial relations towards workplace agreements. Since the mid 1970s, successive Australian governments (both federal and state) have been moving Australia into the competitive global economy by gradually dismantling protective barriers and by micro-economic reforms based on less interventionist and more market-oriented policies. This has led to a reduction in the role of institutional regulatory agencies (Allan and Timo 1999). For example, from the mid 1970s, governments have reduced tariffs and allowed greater international competition across a range of industries such as telecommunications, finance, insurance, health, agriculture and education. In the mid 1980s, the finance sector was deregulated and exchange controls on the Australian dollar removed. Reform of the public sector has included privatisation and corporatisation of publicly owned organisations and assets, widespread contracting, the introduction of competitive tendering and a national competition policy (Quiggin 1996, 28).

While many of the above micro-economic reforms focused on capital and product markets, the labour market has also been gradually decentralised and deregulated (Harley 1995). These reforms have been occurring since the early 1980s and have shifted industrial relations and human resource issues to enterprise level (Lansbury and MacDonald 1995). Simultaneously, the relative strength of regulatory bodies such as the industrial tribunals and trade unions has been weakened as global markets and competition exert a greater influence on managerial decision making and labour utilisation strategies.

The shift to the enterprise focus has increased the freedom of management to alter the structure of employment relations by adjusting the substantive rules (wages and conditions) of work. This often occurs once governments have freed up the procedural rules in order to encourage workplace reform (Bennett 1999). Australia is not alone in this process. Many industrialised countries show trends towards declining trade union effectiveness and the devolution of labour regulation and rule making to the enterprise level. The result is greater flexibility in work and labour organisation, declining employment security and greater job mobility (Locke et al. 1995). However these effects driven by increased global competition on management strategy are mediated by a range of factors including the availability of new technology, the nature of management style, the competitiveness of particular markets, the effectiveness of the regulatory regime and the power of trade unions. These factors provide both opportunities and constraints that shape management choices and initiatives. By 1994, Australia was well down the path of deregulation through a mix of managed decentralisation and free market engineering. This was achieved by using industrial relations legislation and wages policy to promote labour market de-regulation while simultaneously encouraging efficiency and equity.

The shift towards greater workplace wage setting must be seen in context. Historically, Australian employers and unions have collectively bargained in relation to over award payments (payments above the legal minimum imposed by an award). However, the shift towards enterprise bargaining represents a fundamental shift away from centralisation to a greater degree of voluntarism (individual choice) (Short et al. 1993). Throughout the early 1990s, the Federal Labor Government sought to introduce legislation that promoted the use of workplace agreements. A contentious aspect this legislation was the 1993 amendments to the Industrial Relations Act 1988. This amendment made it easier for unions to obtain coverage under federal awards to circumvent, what was seen as anti-worker, anti-union state industrial legislation in conservative the states such as Victoria, South Australia and Western Australia. During the late 1980s, most States had introduced changes to industrial relations, ranging from the introduction of a system of non-union workplace agreements in New South Wales, South Australia and Tasmania to a more radical solution in Victoria, where the Kennett Government abolished awards altogether. Minimum conditions of employment (excluding annual leave loading and penalty rates) were set by statute, and employees were forced into individual contracts, unless the employer agreed to maintain their award.

In response to the 1993 Federal reforms, a number of Conservative State Governments challenged the constitutional validity of the amendments in the High Court. The challenge questioned the Commonwealth's powers (arising from Australia's international treaty obligations under the conventions of the International Labor Organisation (ILO)) to impose minimum conditions of employment including minimum wages, equal pay, termination of employment, discrimination in employment, family leave, collective bargaining and the right to strike.

In its decision, the High Court re-affirmed the ability of the Commonwealth to enter into and legislatively enforce international conventions, concluding that just because 'the obligations of the convention are expressed in broad general terms does not deny them the character of obligations enforceable by way of complaint pursuant to Article 26 of the Constitution' (Full Court of the High Court Australia, Victoria and Others v. The Commonwealth, September 1996, 66 Industrial Reports 392 at 411). The High Court also reaffirmed the right of the Commonwealth to make laws with respect to employment matters that affect employees employed by 'constitutional corporations' (66 Industrial Reports, 448). This finding was important because the Labor Government's 1993 enterprise bargaining amendments relied on the Commonwealth's corporations powers, rather than its more limited conciliation and arbitration powers (see Chapter 7). Consequently, future Federal Governments were free to use the corporate affairs power to make laws relating to enterprise bargaining so long as they either involved a corporation, or were the subject of a pre-existing industrial dispute.

IMPACT OF ENTERPRISE BARGAINING ON MANAGEMENT STRATEGIES

In order to understand the move to enterprise bargaining, we need to recognise that there were two important questions driving the reform process. First, how could the workplace be made more productive? Second, how could management and labour be made more productive? Over the past two decades, public policy endeavoured to provide answers to these questions by freeing up the procedural and substantive rules governing work. This was so companies could better pursue competitive strategies to become more productive, efficient and profitable. Theoretically, along the way, the living standards of employees and the community in general would also improve. This general pattern of change is not unique to Australia. NZ, the US and the UK over the past decade have also experienced a similar weakening of labour regulatory institutions during economic restructuring (Allan and Timo 1999).

The move to enterprise bargaining in the pursuit of competitiveness, profit and productivity has directly affected managerial strategies. Companies have increasingly interpreted competitive strategies into HRM strategies. In the pursuit of competitiveness, employers wished to connect pay and conditions more directly to the needs of the organisation and the market place (Boxal 1993). They increased union avoidance and increasingly adopted individualist approaches (direct employer and employee agreements) over the more traditional collectivist solutions (Bacon and Storey 1993 and 1996; Storey and Sisson 1993). This represents a significant shift to unitarist over pluralist approaches to labour relations. This process involves the demise of collectivism in favor of more individualist direct employer-employee employee relations and is part of a broader strategy to de-unionise the workplace (Peetz 1998; see also Chapter 1).

Theoretically individualism assumes common bonds between employer and employee, and favours organisational cultures built on cooperation and fairness. It values outcomes which foster 'high trust' in workplace relations (Fox 1966). However, the resultant HRM strategies vary between organisations, with the extreme variations being described as 'hard' and 'soft' (Legge 1989). Under the soft form, employees are considered assets with intellectual and creative skills which contribute to competitive advantage (human relations unitarism, see Chapter 1). Under the hard form, employees are viewed as another cost of production (scientific management unitarism, see Chapter 1)(Legge 1995). Research critical of the shift towards individualism tends to show that the hard form is more common (McCallum 1996). In the UK, some individualised (non-union) workplaces have seen significant growth in management power, OHS non-compliance, use of casual labour, absenteeism, dismissals, redundancies (Sisson 1993; Guest and Conway 1999). Individual contracts are often simply standardised contracts by-passing unions, rather than genuine results of individual bargaining (Evans and Hudson 1994; Timo 1997).

THE CHANGES UNDER THE *WORKPLACE RELATIONS ACT, 1996*
Background

During the 1996 federal election the Coalition promised fundamental changes in Australia's system of industrial relations by abandoning the award system in favour of a system of individual contracts. However these changes would be governed by the following commitments:

- a 'rock solid guarantee' that no worker would suffer a cut in take home pay
- employees would have a choice whether to stay in the award system or enter into a workplace agreement
- the maintenance of an award safety net

Behind the mask of 'freedom and equality', the Coalition model sought to strengthen managerial powers and reduce the protection afforded to employees under a pluralist conciliation and arbitration system. The policy was based on restructuring the current industrial relations system to provide for the following:

- ending union monopoly bargaining rights
- introducing collective and individual workplace agreements enforceable at common law
- reducing the scope of awards to core conditions
- outlawing 'closed shops' and preference clauses, and allowing employees to choose whether or not to join a union
- weakening the ability of unions to organise or take industrial action
- removing the jurisdiction of the AIRC to regulate the terms and conditions of employment of contractors
- limiting the rights of non-award employees to access unfair dismissal laws
- outlawing secondary boycotts and strikes under certain circumstances
- stripping back award conditions to a core of 20 minimum conditions
- freeing up the ability of employers to make agreements in either State or Federal jurisdictions
- removing limitations on the employment of part-time employees
- introduction of a non-arbitral body known as the Employment Advocate to assist employers and employees to make non-union agreements.

Following discussions with the Australian Democrats, a number of changes were made in the Coalition model. These included:

- reinforcing the role of awards as a minimum safety net
- greater employee protection in the making of workplace agreements
- allowing the AIRC to deal with a broader range of 'core' award matters
- strengthening the 'no disadvantage test'
- allowing workplace agreements (AWAs) to be vetted by the AIRC if referred by the employment advocate
- strengthening the unfair dismissal provisions
- strengthening the rights of unions to represent members (Agreement between the Commonwealth Government and the Australian Democrats on the Workplace Relations Bill, October 1996).

The Workplace Relations Act 1996 (WRA) became law in March 1997.

Objects of the WRA

WRA broadens the range of bargaining choices by reducing the role and involvement of unions in the bargaining process by:

- Ensuring that the primary responsibility for determining matters affecting the relationship between employers and employees rests with the employer and employees at the workplace or enterprise level
- Ensuring that wages and conditions of employment are determined as far as possible by the agreement of employers and employees at the workplace or enterprise level, upon a foundation of minimum standards
- Ensuring freedom of association, including the rights of employees and employers to join an organisation or association of their choice, or not to join an organisation or association ... (Section 3 - Objects of the Act).

The Role of Awards

Under WRA, awards continue to play an important role, albeit more in the form of providing a safety net to enterprise bargaining. However, WRA requires the AIRC to review and simplify awards, stripping them back to only 20 core or allowable matters (Section 89A). Briefly stated, these matters can be summarised as follows:

- Remuneration issues including: rates of pay generally, (including juniors, trainees or apprentices), piece rates, allowances, loadings for working overtime or for casual or shift work, penalty rates, redundancy pay, superannuation, pay and conditions of outworkers
- Conditions of employment including: ordinary hours of work, annual leave, long service leave, personal/carer's leave (including sick leave), parental leave, public holidays
- Procedural employment matters including: classification of employees, notice of termination, stand-down provisions, dispute settling procedures, jury service, type of employment (such as full-time, casual, regular part-time and shift work).

Employment issues outside of these 20 conditions cannot be included in an award. However, they can form part of a workplace agreement. These non-allowable matters if they are already in an award were meant to cease to have effect as from 30th June 1998. Other parts of the award simplification process involves removing discriminatory provisions and express award provisions in plain English.

Types of Workplace Agreements under WRA

In relation to agreement making, WRA provides five types of Certified Agreements (CAs) that can be approved by the AIRC. Employers that are Constitutional Corporations (except for agreements made in settlement of an industrial dispute) can only make CAs. The five types of CAs are as follows:

1. CAs made with one or more trade unions at a workplace (Section 170LJ)
2. Non-union CAs made with a 'valid majority' of employees at a workplace (similar to EFAs)(Section 170LK)

3. CAs made as greenfield agreements covering new work sites made with one or more trade unions which have the right to represent individuals who will become employees at a new business, before the new business engages employees (Section 170LL)
4. CAs made between an employer and a trade union in order to settle an 'industrial dispute' or to prevent an 'industrial situation' from giving rise to an 'industrial dispute' (Sections 170LO and 170 LP)
5. Multi-employer CAs made subject to a public interest test covering more than one employer, which are subject to special conditions being satisfied (Section 170LC).

Requirements for Approving Certified Agreements

All the CAs listed above require certain conditions to be satisfied before they are certified by the AIRC. These are as follows:

1. the CA must pass the 'no disadvantage' test (Section 170XA)
2. in the case of a CA reached between an employer and a trade union or trade unions:
   - employees must be provided with or have ready access to a copy of the proposed CA at least 14 days before the agreement is made
   - the terms of the agreement must be explained by the employer to all employees in ways appropriate to those particular employees (e.g. women, employees of a non-English speaking background and young persons)
   - a valid majority of employees must approve the agreement. A valid majority means a majority of employees covered by the agreement or if a vote is taken, a majority of employees who cast a vote approving the CA.
3. in the case of a CA made with employees directly:
   - the employer must ensure that every person to be covered by the agreement has at least 14 days written notice of intention to make the agreement and on or before that notice is given, has, or has ready access to, a copy of the proposed CA
   - the notice must advise that if a person is a member of a union with appropriate coverage, that person may request union representation
   - if an employee so requests, the union must be given reasonable opportunity to confer with the employer. That union can then intervene before the AIRC Commission when the application for certification is heard or request to become a party to the agreement
   - the employer must explain the proposed agreement to all employees to be covered by it
   - a valid majority of employees must approve the agreement.
4. in respect of all CAs:
   - the agreement must contain a dispute resolution clause
   - the agreement must have a nominal expiry date (up to a maximum of three years)
   - the application to certify the agreement must be made within 21 days after the agreement is approved by, or made with, employees.

The AIRC must refuse to certify the agreement under certain circumstances (Section 170LU) where:

- the agreement includes a provision which discriminates against an employee (excluding junior rates of pay) on the basis of sex, colour, age, race, religion (except in the case of a religious institution) etc.
- the agreement only applies to a part of an employer's business and that part is not a geographically distinct or distinct operational or organisational unit of the employer's business
- an employer has discriminated on the grounds of union membership or non-membership
- where the agreement fails to pass the no disadvantage test.

The 'no disadvantage test' (Section 170XA) applies on a global basis. This means that the contents of the agreement are compared 'globally' with the terms of the relevant award (or where there is no award, the AIRC can designate another award covering similar work in order to meet the 'no disadvantage test' (Section 170XE)). The award may be either a federal or state award (Section 170XA). An exception of where an agreement does meet the no disadvantage test but can still be approved is where the agreement seeks to award conditions that form part of a reasonable strategy to overcome a short-term business crisis (Section 170LT(4)).

The AIRC also has the option of accepting an undertaking from a party, or allowing the parties to amend the agreement, so as to make it certifiable. A CA will operate during the period for which it is expressed to operate (up to a maximum of 3 years) and thereafter it continues to operate even after it has passed its operative date. It only ceases to operate if:

- it is voluntarily terminated by the parties
- the AIRC terminates the agreement because it contains discriminatory provisions
- a party which gave an undertaking in relation to the operation of the agreement has breached that undertaking and the AIRC has ordered that the agreement terminate
- its nominal expiry date has passed and it is replaced by another CA. A CA can be extended for up to three years from the date on which the CA came into operation, if application is made to the AIRC before it expires and if a valid majority of employees approves the extension
- it contains conditions upon which it may be terminated after its nominal expiry date.

A CA can be varied by the Commission during its lifetime if the employer (and if bound, the union) and a valid majority of employees approve the variation (Section 170MC). The effect of a CA is that it prevails over any award or order of the AIRC. (See a sample CA in Appendix at end of this book.)

Persons Bound by Certified Agreements

CAs involving constitutional corporations are binding on the employer and all persons whose employment is subject to the agreement (Section 170M) as well as future employers and employees if the business is transmitted from one employer to the next (Section 170MB). CAs also bind unions that are parties to the agreement and their members (Section 170MA). Additionally, in the case of CAs made with a valid majority of employees, a union may apply to be made a party to the agreement. The AIRC can make that union bound by the CA provided that the union:

- has at least one member whose employment will be covered by the agreement
- has the right to represent the 'industrial interests' of that member
- was requested by the member to apply to the Commission to be bound by the agreement.

Bargaining Period and Negotiations for CAs and AWAs

The Act retains provisions dealing with the initiation of bargaining periods with the aim of concluding a CA. A bargaining period can be initiated by either an employer, a union, or by an employee acting on his/her own behalf or on behalf of other employees. The Act sets out detailed provisions concerning the notice requirements that initiates the bargaining period, which begins the day after the notice of bargaining was given (Section 170MK). An employer or employee may only take industrial action during the bargaining period known as 'protected action' (Section 170MI to 170ML). Industrial action cannot be taken before the nominal expiry date of an existing CA. If it is, then any action taken does not constitute 'protected action' and can be subject to claims for damages at common law.

The Acts sets out detailed requirements concerning the notice which must be given by the parties proposing to take industrial action (for instance, that the parties must have attempted to negotiate before taking industrial action). In addition, each party must inform the other by way of a written notice of at least 3 days setting out the nature of the action to be taken (Sections, 170MJ, 170MO and 170MP).

WRA allows the AIRC to suspend or terminate bargaining periods (170MW). Circumstances such as a party failing to negotiate before taking industrial action, or where industrial action endangers the life or personal safety or health or welfare of the population, or will cause significant damage to the Australian economy or a part of it, are grounds for the Commission to suspend or terminate a bargaining period. Once the Commission terminates a bargaining period, it must exercise its conciliation powers so as to facilitate the making of a CA or otherwise settle the matter or issues between the parties. In certain specified circumstances, if it is unable to facilitate the making of a CA, then it can exercise its arbitration powers to make an award dealing with the issues that were the subject of the negotiations. A Full Bench of the Commission, however, may only exercise these powers.

Australian Workplace Agreements (AWAs)

In addition to the types of CAs referred to above, WRA also enables employers (who are Constitutional Corporations) and employees to enter into Australian Workplace Agreement (AWAs). AWAs can be made either collectively with all employees (or a discreet section of the workplace) or with each employee individually. Unlike CAs, AWAs may be negotiated with employees on an individual or collective basis. Effectively, an AWA is an individual contract of employment that has the benefits of overriding a federal or state award or agreements (Sections 170VE and 170VF).

Making an AWA

The employer must explain the effect of the AWA to an employee between the time the employee first receives a copy of the AWA and the time the employee signs it. The employee must genuinely consent to making the AWA. In addition, either the employer or employee can appoint in writing a person to act as his or her bargaining agent and the other party must recognise that bargaining agent (170VK).

Approval of AWAs

Unlike CAs, AWAs are approved by a body separate from the AIRC known as the Office of the Employment Advocate (OEA). The OEA must approve an AWA provided the OEA is convinced that the AWA passes a 'no-disadvantage test' similar to CAs. Before the OEA approves an AWA, the OEA must ensure that the AWA meets a number of requirements. These are:

- the statutory requirements on discrimination, disclosure and dispute resolution
- the employees received a copy of the AWA the required number of days before signing it (i.e. five for a new employee and 14 of an existing employee)
- the employer explained the effect of the AWA to the employee between the employee first receiving and signing the AWA
- the employee genuinely consented
- an AWA in the same terms was offered to all 'comparable employees' (unless failure to do so was not unfair or unreasonable). A comparable employee is one carrying out similar kind of work.

If the OEA is not satisfied that the AWA meets the additional approval requirements, the OEA must refuse to approve the AWA. If the OEA has concerns about whether the AWA passes the no disadvantage test, but those concerns are resolved by a written undertaking by the employer accepted by the OEA, or other action by the parties, the OEA must approve the AWA. An AWA will fail the no disadvantage test only if it would result, on balance, in a reduction in the overall terms and conditions of employment under:

- the relevant award (i.e. a federal or state award which applies to the employment of employee)
- a designated award (i.e. a federal award when there is no relevant award)
- any other law that the OEA considers relevant.

The no disadvantage test is a global test rather than a line-by-line comparison with the award. However, a line-by-line consideration of reductions and increases in entitlements or protections may be required to form a judgement of whether, considered as a whole, there is no overall disadvantage. If the OEA has concerns, which are not resolved through undertakings, about whether the Awa passes the no disadvantage test, the OEA must refer the AWA to the AIRC. If an AWA is referred to the AIRC, either party may withdraw it. Where an AWA is referred to the AIRC, the AIRC must approve it, if satisfied it passes the no disadvantage test. If the commission has concerns about this, and written undertaking or other action resolves them, the AIRC must approve the AWA (Section 170VPG). If the AIRC considers it is not contrary to the public interest to do so, it must approve the AWA. An example is where the AWA is part of a reasonable strategy to deal with a short-term crisis in a business.

Effect of an Awa on Federal and State Awards, Agreements and Laws

An AWA prevails over a state law, award or agreement to the extent of any inconsistency (Section 170VR). An AWA operates to the exclusion of:

1. any federal award that would otherwise apply, except;
    - an award made by the AIRC following termination of a bargaining period
    - an exceptional matter included in an award or order, unless the AWA is inconsistent with that matter

2. any state award or agreement, except state award termination of employment provisions, which are able to operate concurrently with AWAs (Section 170VQ).

Employees with existing CAs will be able to pursue AWAs only after the nominal expiry date of the existing CA, because in some instances a CA will override an AWA.

Breach, Enforcement and Remedies

Neither party may breach an AWA nor engage in industrial action before the nominal expiry date of the AWA. The Court may grant an injunction in respect of a threatened or actual contravention. A party to an AWA may apply to the Court for imposition of a penalty for a breach of this part of the Act. Penalties are up to $10,000 for a body corporate and $2,000 for others. A party may also recover for loss or damage provided the action is brought within six years (Section 170VV). A new employee is entitled to be compensated for any shortfall in earnings under the AWA when compared with the appropriate award. A small claims procedure is available in such cases.

The 1999 Amendments to WRA: Workplace Relations Legislation Amendment Bill (More Jobs, Better Pay) Bill 1999

In 1999 the Government unsuccessfully sought to amend the terms of WRA by way of the Workplace Relations Legislation Amendment (More Jobs, Better Pay) Bill 1999. The importance of this failed proposal is that it provides a clear indication of the ongoing reform agenda of the Federal Coalition Government. The Bill had sought to amend WRA by linking the safety net role of awards and safety net adjustments to the low paid (awards had to be simplified before they had access to award safety net increases). It also sought to further reduce the right to strike by unions; to streamline the making of AWAs; to reduce the impact of award making by ensuring that unions are required to provide more information to employers when attempting to rope in employers under awards; to introduce a $500 conciliation fee per application to be charged by the AIRC; and introducing voluntary conciliation in relation to non-allowable matters; to reduce the right to strike during the bargaining period; to reduce employee access to unfair dismissal laws; and finally, to allow the AIRC to suspend the bargaining period in the case of pattern bargaining. The Government's proposed changes were highly technical and in some aspects sought to reintroduce changes that the Australian Democrats had previously rejected in 1996. The 1999 Bill was subsequently considered by the Senate Employment, Workplace Relations, Small Business and Education Legislative Committee and rejected by Labor and the Australian Democrats (Report on the Consideration of the Provisions of the Workplace Relations legislative Amendment (More Jobs, Better Pay) Bill, 1999, Australian Senate, Canberra, November 1999).

STATE LEGISLATIVE PROVISIONS

All Australian states have adopted some form of workplace agreement legislation. For example, under the Industrial Relations Act 1996 (N.S.W.) enterprise agreements may be made between:

- an employer or employers and their employees
- an employer or employers and one or more unions representing any of those employees.

A union may represent only employees who are, or are eligible to be, its members. In the case of agreements made directly between employers and employees, the enterprise agreement must be approved in a secret ballot by not less than 65 per cent of the employees who are to be covered at the time the ballot is conducted. Enterprise agreements may be made for any relevant group of employees, including employees of a single employer (whether all or a group or category of them), employees of two ore more associated employers (corporations and joint ventures) employees engaged in a project, and public sector employees.

Enterprise agreements are approved by the NSW Industrial Relations Commission (NSW IRC) provided they meet a number of relevant statutory requirements and criteria. Enterprise agreements prevail over awards. There is also provision for the making of enterprise awards (normally between a union and employer) to be approved by IRC.

Other states have similar legislation. Under the Industrial Relations Act 1999 (Queensland) certified agreements can be made covering:

- single employer or enterprise agreements
- multi-employer agreements
- project agreements
- new business agreements

Except in the case of new project agreements meant to cover 'greenfield sites', all agreements must be approved by a valid majority of employees. They are certified by the Queensland Industrial Relations Commission (QIRC) provided they do not disadvantage employees when compared to their conditions under the relevant award or the Act. In addition, the QIRC may also approve Queensland Workplace Agreements (QWAs) however, these forms of agreements can only be made with a person who is 18 years or older are no longer confidential (as under AWAs).

Under the Industrial and Employee Relations Act 1994 (S.A.) enterprise agreement may be made between:

- an employer or employers (who form a single business) and a group of employees
- an employer and a union
- an employer and the Employee Ombudsman and/or a union in order to cover a greenfields site or a group of employees who have not be previously employed by the employer in SA (this is called a provisional enterprise agreement).

An enterprise agreement cannot be approved if the agreement applies to part of a business and, unfairly, does not cover employees who should be covered. Enterprise agreements are approved by the Enterprise Agreements Division of the South Australian Industrial Relations Commission (S.A. IRC) and must contain a number of minimum conditions.

In Western Australia, there are three Acts that apply to making enterprise agreements, the Workplace Agreements Act 1993; Minimum Conditions of Employment Act 1993 and the Industrial Relations Act 1979. There are three types of workplace agreements that can be made Workplace Agreements Act 1993:

- Registered collective workplace agreements made between an employer and all or some of the employer's employees

- Registered collective workplace agreements made between an employer and all or some of the employer's employees who are covered by a federal award (Part 2A)
- Registered individual workplace agreements made between an employer and one of the employer's employees.

Unions have a limited role in workplace agreements. They must be authorised in writing to represent an employee. Workplace agreements override awards. The Commissioner for Workplace Agreements (CWA), who is independent of the W.A. Industrial Relations Commission (W.A. IRC) approves all workplace agreements. The W.A. IRC has no jurisdiction over workplace agreements. Collective workplace agreements are also registered with the CWA. The Industrial Relations Act 1979 also allows the making of Industrial Agreements made between employers or an organisation of employers and unions. Industrial Agreements are registered by the W.A. IRC.

Under the Industrial Relations Act 1984 and the as amended by Industrial Relations Amendment (Enterprise Agreements and Workplace Freedom) Act 1992 (Tasmania), an enterprise agreement may be made between any employer and any one of the following:

- one or more employee organisations representing persons employed in the enterprise
- each of at least 60 per cent of the individuals employed in one or more classes of employment in the enterprise
- an employee committee formed to represent persons employed in the enterprise
- any other person employed in the enterprise who is not already covered by an agreement, subject to the approval of the Enterprise Commissioner.

A registered enterprise agreement prevails over the provisions of any award, industrial agreement or order of the Tasmanian Industrial Commission (Tasmanian IC) that deal with the same matters. Enterprise agreements must be registered by the Enterprise Commissioner who is the deputy president of the Tasmanian IC. Industrial agreements can also be made under the Industrial Relations Act 1984. They are made between unions and employers. Industrial Agreements are registered with the Tasmania I.C.

The situation in Victoria is more complex. Under the Commonwealth Powers (Industrial Relations) Act 1996 Victoria referred certain matters within Victoria's jurisdiction to the Commonwealth on 1 January 1997. As a result, the Employee Relations Act 1992 (Victoria) was converted into the Long Service Leave Act 1992 and enterprise bargaining agreements are made under the Workplace Relations Act 1996 (WRA). WRA includes in Schedule 1A a safety net of minimum terms and conditions of employment maintaining those which existed under the (former) Victorian Act. The provisions of WRA apply in Victoria for making Certified Agreements and Australian Workplace Agreements (AWAs). The referral of industrial powers to the Commonwealth does not mean that federal awards apply to Victorian employers and employees. Collective and individual employment agreements made, under the (former) Victorian Act continue to operate. The minimum conditions of employment contained in Schedule 1A to WRA apply to those Victorian employees not covered by federal awards and agreements. The different forms of agreements that can apply in Victoria include:

1. Federal legislation (WRA):
   - Certified agreements (both union and non-union)
   - AWAs
   - Common law unregistered agreements (including Schedule 1A) for employees that are not covered by the minimum wage orders.

2. Existing agreements made under the Employee Relations Act 1992 (Victoria) covering:
   - Collective Employment Agreements
   - Individual Employment Agreements.

Both of these existing agreements continue to apply until superseded by an agreement made under WRA.

CASE LAW ON THE BARGAINING PROCESS
Case One

'A Right To Bargain?' The Asahi Case

In 1993 the Federal Labor Government amended the Industrial Relations Act, 1988 to give the AIRC the power (once a dispute was likely to occur) to order the parties to bargain in good faith (a concept derived from long standing US labour law). This meant the parties were required to agree to meet at reasonable times, comply with bargaining procedures, avoid capriciously adding or withdrawing items for negotiation, disclose relevant information etc. (Section 170QK(3). However, this right was removed in WRA 1996. Nevertheless, the AIRC under Section 170MX can use its arbitral powers to assess the bargaining agenda, merit, productivity issues and the extent to which the conduct of the parties was reasonable. However, these arbitral powers appear only to be able to be invoked where the parties have already begun the process of bargaining and have an established agenda. Australian unions, although they have the right to represent employees, apparently do not have the legal right to compel an employer to the bargaining table (a guaranteed formula for industrial conflict). This was the conclusion reached in the Asahi case.

Asahi Diamond Industrial Australia Pty Ltd ('Asahi') is a NSW based manufacturer of industrial diamonds and employed at the time 61 employees (of which 42 were covered by the Metal Industry Award 1984). In May 1994, the Automotive, Food Metals and Engineering Union ('AFMEU') served a demand on the Company that it negotiate an enterprise agreement with the union. When the Company refused, the AFMEU brought the matter before the AIRC seeking orders that the Company negotiate with the Union 'in good faith'. The AFMEU did not at that time have any members employed by the Company. The Company appealed the initial finding for the union. A key issue before the Full Bench (on appeal) was the question whether or not a union could compel a company to negotiate a workplace agreement where a company was not interested in making an enterprise bargaining agreement. A collateral issue was whether a union with no union members employed by the employer, could compel the employer to negotiate an enterprise agreement. In its decision, the Full Bench concluded that 'bargaining in good faith' applied only to a situation where the parties had commenced bargaining, but could not agree on bargaining outcomes. The Full Bench also made additional findings as follows:

- the Employer could not be forced to negotiate a workplace agreement where the Union had no members
- the Union had no members at Asahi and therefore had not been authorised to negotiate on behalf of the employees. This meant that the Union would not know whether the employees wished to enter into negotiations, or know what the employees claims were or how to respond to them
- the AIRC has the power to facilitate workplace bargaining process, but does not have the power to order an employer to negotiate or to make concessions
- the enterprise bargaining system facilitates and encourages direct bargaining where the parties wish to bargain. It is not a system of compulsory negotiation and concession making
- other factors relevant for determining whether the AIRC should become involved in assisting (but not compelling a party to bargain) include: the attitude of employees and employer, history of union involvement at the workplace, degree of unionisation, and the wishes of employer and employees
- 'bargaining in good faith' can only refer to a situation where two or more parties are 'negotiating' an agreement and suggests that the parties must have already entered negotiations with a view the concluding an agreement
- under enterprise bargaining, the responsibility for negotiating a workplace agreement rests solely on the parties' concerned involved in the bargaining process (Appeal, Full Bench of AIRC, Asahi Diamond Industrial Australia Pty Ltd v AFMEU 1995, 59 Industrial Reports, 385 at 419-21)

Case Two

'At The Bargaining Table: What Is Good Faith?' The ANF Case

Once at the bargaining table, what constitutes bargaining in 'good faith'? In 1996, the Australian Nursing Federation (ANF) commenced bargaining with a large number of employers in the health industry for a 10 per cent increase in wages across both public and private sector nursing awards. Despite the Union's vigorous pursuit of the claim, it had been met with limited success. The ANF applied to the AIRC to terminate the bargaining period and arbitrate. The ANF argued that arbitration was necessary in order to recognise fundamental changes in the nature of nursing work Australia-wide, and that despite its best efforts, the Union was having little success in reaching workplace agreements with employers. The ANF case centred on WA private hospitals and nursing homes, but was essentially a test case for all nursing awards. The ANF sought to promote its wages claim by serving demands on employers to begin bargaining. The ANF agreed to meet with employers but had insisted that employers enter into enterprise bargaining with the Union on the basis of:

- no loss of income of its members
- no erosion of national nursing standards or salary related conditions
- preservation of all national award standards and conditions of employment
- no changes to award hours of work arrangements or rostering provisions.

These demands underpinned the union's preparedness to commence bargaining. The matter went before a Full bench of the AIRC and following a lengthy hearing, found that the ANF had adopted a position that employers must agree in advance and not propose any trade-off, or they (ANF) would not negotiate. The AIRC went on to find that the ANF's position was in conflict with the Commission's previous decisions on structural efficiency and enterprise bargaining. They quoted the Full Bench from the October 1993 Review of Wage Fixing Principles decision [Print K9700]:

> In our view the essence of enterprise bargaining designed to achieve increased efficiency and productivity also requires the parties to demonstrate that they have considered a broad agenda in their enterprise negotiations. We do not intend that agenda be limited only to matters directly related to normal award prescriptions. It should cover the whole range of matters that ultimately determine an enterprise's efficiency, productivity and continuing competitiveness. ...Enterprise bargaining was not intended to apply in a negative cost-cutting manner ... [but] ... was intended to facilitate fundamental review to the overall advantage of both the employers and employees.

The AIRC concluded that the actions of the ANF did 'not constitute bargaining in good faith'. It found that the union's position of 'only being prepared to enter enterprise bargaining on their own terms is one which is in conflict with the broad thrust of [enterprise bargaining provisions of] the Act' (Full Bench of the AIRC, Australian Nursing Federation and Others, Print No. M9940, March 1996, 18-19).

Case Three

'Bargaining Over A Bargain: The No Disadvantage Test' Tweed Valley Fruit Processors Case

Once bargaining has commenced, what should we be bargaining about? The Tweed Valley Fruit Processing case in 1995 raises questions concerning the scope of the agenda of bargaining, the role of the award safety net, and a cost minimisation approach to enterprise bargaining (Woldring 1996). Tweed Valley Fruit Processing Company carries on business at Murwillumbah in Northern New South Wales, as a processor of fresh fruit and employed at the time about 29 employees. In late 1994 and early 1995 the General Manager of the Company set up an employee consultative committee with a view of making an Enterprise Flexibility Agreement (EFA). The Federal Labor Government amended the *Industrial Relations Act, 1988* in order to introduce EFAs in 1993 as a way of encouraging non-union agreements and these agreements had to pass a no disadvantage test similarly to Certified Agreements (CAs), and were approved by the AIRC. The idea was to use the EFA in order to replace the Food Preservers' (Interim) Award 1986. Employees in a secret ballot rejected the initial draft of the EFA. Subsequently, the EFA was amended and passed (this time by a show of hands) 26 votes in favour to 3 against.

> The agreement was opposed by the Automotive, Food Metals, Engineering, Printing and Kindred Industries Union (AFME/PKIU) which took advantage of the legislation that provided a union with hearing rights in the approval process of an EFA where the union is party to an award binding on the employer and affected by the making of the EFA. The agreement was

initially approved by a single Commissioner, but was appealed by the AFME/PKIU to a Full Bench of the AIRC. At the time the agreement was made, there was 29 employees covered by the agreement. The proposed EFA sought to reduce a number of conditions, such as reducing paid public holidays from 12 to 9, increasing the hours of work from 38 to 40 per week, pay out of sick leave, reduction in afternoon and night shift loadings from 15% and 30% to 10% and 20% respectively, reducing overtime rates of double time to time and a half, changing the age structure for junior rates from 75% of the adult rate for 18 and under to 19 years and under at 70%, eliminating the right of union entry, removing annual leave and casual loadings, and absorbing work related allowances on a one off basis into new aggregate hourly rate. According to the Company, these changes were offset by increases in the base rate of pay. The Company claimed that the EFA provided for a pay increase in two instalments of a total of 9% over the life of the EFA and that the reductions in award conditions amounted only to 9.7%. The unions on the other hand, claimed that day workers would loose 16.7%, casual day workers, 30.6% and night shift workers 38.3% as a percentage of weekly wages (Full Bench of AIRC, Automotive Food, Metals, Engineering, Printing and Kindred Industries Union v Tweed Valley Fruit Processors, 61 Industrial Reports, 212 at 218-221).

The Full Bench of the AIRC considered particular aspects of the EFA in terms of whether they breached 'accepted' community standards. In relation to sick leave, the Full bench said:

The question whether an entitlement to paid sick leave constitutes a community standard was raised in the proceedings before us. It was argued that if paid sick leave was a community standard then the Commissioner erred in not according the removal of this entitlement substantial weight in the determination of the no disadvantage test... In our view an entitlement to paid sick leave is a community standard (Full Bench of AIRC, Automotive Food, Metals, Engineering, Printing and Kindred Industries Union v Tweed Valley Fruit Processors, 61 Industrial Reports, 212 at 232)

The Full Bench went on to discuss the nature of the no disadvantage test and the extent to which an agreement can reduce award standards. Where the implementation of an agreement would result in a reduction in employee entitlements or protections the AIRC concluded that it must 'determine whether, in the context of the terms and conditions of the employees concerned, when considered as a whole, the reduction would be contrary to the public interest'. In practice this involves the AIRC considering 'the overall package of terms and conditions of employment to apply to the employees covered by the agreement. The reductions in employee entitlements and protections need to be balanced against the benefits provided in the agreement. Such benefits may include a wage increase or an improvement in conditions...' (61 Industrial Reports, 212 at 233). The AIRC went on to find that community standards were an important factor in deciding what constitutes the public interest. The decision was subsequently appealed to the Federal Industrial Court that up held the decision of the Full bench of the AIRC (Full Bench of the Industrial Relations Court of Australia, Tweed Valley Fruit Processors Pty Ltd v V.P. Ross and others, 65 Industrial Reports, 393 at 407). Whilst the decision was made under the previous Act (the now repealed *Industrial Relations Act, 1998*), it provides an interesting insight into how the AIRC and Federal Court have gradually begun to read into the enterprise bargaining process a charter of employee rights (see also the Case Study on the MUA Waterfront dispute).

Case Four

'Is All Fair In Love And War? The Right to Strike': Yallourn Energy Case

This last case illustrates the dynamic process of negotiation in reaching a bargaining agreement. Once we are bargaining, how do we advance our claims on the other party? Strikes are important in that they are an expression of the collective voice of employees as a lever in offsetting what would otherwise by an unequal power balance between employee rights and managerial power. In Australia, until very recently, there has never been a so-called 'right to strike' at law. Whilst strikes have occurred, sometimes with frequent regularity, by organising the strike weapon as a way of encouraging an employer to 'come across', unions have run the risk of common law damages under a tort of conspiracy (see Chapter 7). Two key concepts drawn from North American style bargaining and imported into the Australian enterprise bargaining framework are 'interest disputes' and 'rights disputes':

- 'interest disputes' are those disputes rising from the making of a new agreement and where it is allowable for employees, unions and employers to take strike action as part of the bargaining process in order to advance each sides interests
- 'rights disputes' are those disputes arising from the interpretation of the provisions of a workplace agreement that is in force and where strikes are outlawed whilst the agreement remains in force. It is expected that under such rights disputes, decisions about the interpretation of a provision of a workplace agreement rest with a common law or industrial court.

The key distinguishing factor between disputes concerning 'interests' and 'rights' is that strikes in relation to interest disputes are 'protected' from civil and common law damages claims by employers and the striking employees protected against dismissal (that is, are covered by unfair dismissal laws). Under the WRA (following similar provisions in the Industrial Relations Act 1988 as amended in 1993), unions and employers are able during an official bargaining period (that is, when either side initiates in writing a bargaining period) to take what is termed 'protective action'. This means the union can strike, or the employer may lock out employees, as a means for pressuring the other side to 'come across' on the terms of an enterprise bargaining agreement. Protected action enables unions to take industrial action without the fear of being prosecuted for damages under tort, and employees to take industrial action without fear of being dismissed by the employer. In the case of the employer, it can lock out employees without having to pay wages whilst then lock out is in progress (though the lock out does not break the employee's continuity of service). Once an agreement is reached and approved (either by the AIRC in the case of a certified agreement or the Employment Advocate in the case of an AWA), WRA outlaws strikes in relation to rights disputes whilst an agreement is in force. Whilst WRA maintains the concepts embodied in disputes of 'rights' and 'interests' as part of the bargaining process under both the making of Certified Agreements (Section 170ML) and Australian Workplace Agreements (Section 170WB), WRA places strict limits on the type of action (e.g. action may not injure innocent third parties or breach workplace health and safety obligations). Once industrial action has begun, the AIRC may terminate the bargaining period and arbitrate on any outstanding issues (Section 170MX). The AIRC may also order a secret ballot in relating to the proposed agreement or the taking of industrial action.

In order to understand the practical application of enterprise bargaining in the context of the right to strike it is useful to consider the decision by Justice Merkel in the Australian Workers' Union and ors v Yallourn Energy Pty Ltd (Australian Federal Court, V 23 of 2000, Case No. FCA 65, 8th February 2000). In this case, a number of unions were involved: the Australian Workers' Union (AWU), the Automotive Food Metals Engineering Printing and Kindred Industries Union of Australia (AMWU) and the Communications, Electrical, Energy, Information, Postal, Plumbing and Allied Services Union of Australia (ETU). These unions commenced proceedings against Yallourn Energy Pty Ltd seeking penalties and an injunction restraining Yallourn Energy from pursuing any action in tort against the unions, their officers or members. The proceedings related to the industrial action taken by the unions and their members in January 2000, at the mine and power plant site of Yallourn Energy. Yallourn Energy had already been involved in lengthy disputation with the unions and had at one time locked employees out. The unions and Yallourn Energy are parties to the Yallourn Energy Pty Ltd Enterprise Agreement 1997 that had expired in September 1999 and the disputation arose from a break down in negotiations over the making of new agreement. As discussed earlier in the chapter, provided that the appropriate notices were given by the union, industrial action taken during this period of bargaining are classified as interest disputes and are protected under WRA, meaning that the union is protected from common law conspiracy actions and other relevant laws.

In order to put heat on the union, on the 9th of November 1999 Yallourn Energy lodged an application with the AIRC under Section 170MH for terminating the Yallourn enterprise agreement. Under WRA enterprise agreements continue on in force even if they have expired until replaced by another agreement (Section 170LX). The AIRC may be asked by a party to an agreement to terminate it and the AIRC in deciding whether to terminate it or not must consider the public interest in doing so this includes whether by terminating the agreement, employees will loose the benefits under the agreement (Section 170MH). Unions retaliated by stepping up industrial action. In response, in a memorandum dated 18 January 2000, Yallourn Energy notified the unions that it would not accept part performance of duties by union members and that they would be locked out until they were prepared to perform all their duties. Although the employees were to be stood down and not paid, they were to continue to be employees of Yallourn Energy. As a consequence of the industrial action taken by both sides, Yallourn Energy's plant site was effectively closed down causing substantial financial loss and power shortages in Victoria.

On the 19th January 2000 Yallourn Energy applied to the AIRC for a certificate to enable the Company to take action in tort against the unions 'in relation to the bans, rolling stoppages and the failure or refusal of the members who were employees of Yallourn Energy to perform work as required by their contracts of employment' (FCA 65, 7). Section 166A of WRA grants unions and employers immunity under certain circumstances from prosecution under tort as long as the action is 'in contemplation of furthering industrial claims'. However, a party, usually an employer, may apply to the AIRC for a certificate that enables the party to commence tort proceedings against another. The AIRC may issue the certificate in certain circumstances, but if the industrial action complained of is not stopped by AIRC conciliation with 72 hours of the request for the certificate, the AIRC must issue the certificate. This Section essentially limits the powers of the AIRC to conciliate a dispute to 72 hours. At the hearing, Yallourn Energy sought and was granted a certificate in relation to the conduct of the unions (not the members) enabling Yallourn Energy to commence an action in tort in relation to the alleged tortious industrial action by the unions. However, Yallourn Energy also began action under tort against its employees who were involved outside the scope of the certificate (FCA 65, 16).

In response, unions applied to the Federal Court to seek penalties and an injunction on Yallourn Energy from proceeding with damages against the unions and their members. In their application, the unions contended that the proposed proceedings by Yallourn Energy contravened WRA in three areas. First, the unions claimed that their industrial action was 'protected action' and immune from tort proceedings (Section 170MT). Second, the unions argued that that by threatening to take action against the unions, the Company was in breach of Section 170MU(1). (This Section prohibits an employer from taking action likely prejudice employees who are union members because those employees are engaging in protected action.) Finally, the unions argued that the actions of the Company were tantamount to coercion and that 'a person must not ... threaten or threaten to take any industrial action or other action ... with the intent to coerce another person to agree, or not agree ... to making or varying an enterprise agreement' as set out in Section 170NC. The irony was that this Section was originally included in WRA as a method of limiting union recruitment and interference in non-union agreements. However, since the MUA decision the Federal Court has applied this power equally to the conduct of employers (see MUA Case Study).

In its decision, the Federal Court rejected the second proposition that by pursuing action against the unions (and not their members) that the Company had altered the position of employees to their prejudice. The Court reasoned that whilst the action might reduce the capacity of employees to gain assistance and advice from the union, this did not alter the position of employees (FCA 65, 16). However, the Court was more concerned about the Company's actions against its employees. It found the Company's actions made employees 'defendants in a case involving potentially costly litigation damages and liabilities' when on the evidence, employees were engaged in lawful conduct 'against their employer in order to advance claims in relation to an enterprise agreement' (FCA 65, 16). The Company claimed that it had suffered significant economic losses during the dispute. However, the Court found little evidence that Yallourn Energy was actually concerned about, or had sought information in relation to, the financial capacity of the unions or the employees to satisfy any judgment for damages that the Company might have incurred. The Court concluded that:

> ...each step and counter step by the parties in the current dispute appears to be intended to advance their respective bargaining positions in relation to the new enterprise agreement. ... Thus, whilst a reason for the proposed proceeding *might* be to recover loss, I would infer from the limited evidence before me that, on a prima facie basis, the proposed [tort] proceeding is another step to assist the position of Yallourn Energy in the bargaining process... [and the actions of the Company] is likely to have an intimidatory or coercive effect on the unions and the employees (FCA 65, 17).

The important principle underlying the Court's approach was its view that, if employers resorted to common law action against unions and employees, not to resolve some industrial wrong, but as part of a broader tactic to coerce unions and employees in the bargaining process, then that coercive step may be unlawful under WRA. On this point, the Court said:

> the stronger the case that the [union industrial] action is protected action, the more harmful and undermining [the Company's proposed] litigation is likely to be to the integrity intended to be given [by WRA] to the industrial bargaining process and the industrial action taken to support it (FCA 65, 19).

The Court did not issue the 'anti-litigation' injunction sought by the unions because Yallourn Energy agreed not to pursue their common law action. This decision is an important reminder that enterprise bargaining in Australia occurs on many levels and tactics vary according to opportunities and constraints set by the arbitral-legal system. It is also important to recognise that in the case of the Yallourn Energy Pty Ltd and in the Patrick/MUA dispute, specialist industrial law courts such as the Federal Court are increasingly prepared to intervene in the bargaining process, reading into WRA a charter of employee and union bargaining rights. In so doing, they are tilting the balance ever so slightly in favour of employees.

Case Five

'Pattern' Bargaining versus 'Individual' Bargaining: That Is The Question!

Ideally, under enterprise bargaining, each agreement made at workplace level should be unique to the needs of the firm and employees. 'Pattern bargaining' is a term used to describe a situation where a bargaining party attempts to seek an outcome consistent with one achieved in another workplace usually within the same industry or sector. Pattern bargaining usually involves a planned and coordinated approach to bargaining. For unions, it is about a set pattern of outcomes across industry. For employers, it usually takes the form of a common set of conditions within a company based on standardised HRM practices. According to the Australian Business Council (BCA):

> Rather than focusing on developing innovative agreements with employers on a workplace-by-workplace basis, it is unfortunate that some unions are still driven by out dated concerns with 'comparative wage justice' and how enterprise bargaining can be 'coordinated'.

> 'Pattern bargaining' continues to be a serious problem in the Australia labour relations system... The essential problem with pattern bargaining is that there is ... refusal of the union involved to actually bargain with the employer to meet the circumstances of the particular workplace ... A key rationale for enterprise bargaining is that of promoting discussions and agreement on the problems and promote prospects, and this key rationale is defeated by a pattern bargaining approach (Submission No. 375, BCA, Vol. 12, 2627, quoted in Senate Employment, Workplace Relations, Small Business and Education Legislative Committee Report on Consideration of the Provisions of the Workplace relations legislation Amendment (More Jobs, Better Pay) Bill, 1999, 117).

However, pattern bargaining is also a vehicle for maintaining key conditions of employment. According to the Health Services Union (HSUA), not every industry is suited to individualistic bargaining, particularly those dependant upon public funding:

> ...pattern bargaining in many sectors makes sense, particularly in the funded sectors, such as the aged care sector in various states and in the public hospital sector. The reality is that these sectors are totally dependent upon government funding. There is very little practical point in

seeking to negotiate and bargain individually with employers in these sectors; their hands are largely tied, and this is the message they deliver to unions... (Evidence from HSUA, 8th October, 1999, Melbourne, quoted in Senate Employment, Workplace Relations, Small Business and Education Legislative Committee Report on Consideration of the Provisions of the Workplace relations legislation Amendment (More Jobs, Better Pay) Bill, 1999, 118).

In practice, Australia has adopted a mixed approach to enterprise bargaining with some industries better at tailoring their needs in the enterprise bargaining process. However, employers and unions alike have adopted both pattern bargaining. For example, the metal unions have adopted a national approach to the next round of enterprise bargaining in the metal industry under the banner of 'Campaign 2000' that seeks a coordinated outcome in terms of wages and conditions across the industry including a wage increase to offset the impact of the goods and services tax (GST). Employers have equally been keen to adopt a coordinated approach. For example, Rio Tinto (formerly CRA), a significant member of the BCA, has used standard but individualised (by name of employee) contracts throughout the company as part of a broader de-unionisation strategy. A similar approach was adopted by BHP in its metalliferous mines in Western Australia. Employers in the health sector have also sought to standardise employment conditions. Clearly, employers and unions will use pattern bargaining in order to control the outcomes of enterprise bargaining.

IMPACT OF ENTERPRISE BARGAINING ON WORKING CONDITIONS
Sources of Data

Almost every academic industrial relations journal published since the early 1990s contains contributions purporting to 'discover' the effects of enterprise bargaining on particular industries, trade unions, equity or working conditions according to the political view of the writer. In practice, our knowledge of the effects of enterprise bargaining is limited to a handful of statistical sources, and some of these are possibly slanted towards a particular political view.

The largest survey of changes in the Australian workplace is found in the extensive surveys known as the Australian Workplace Industrial Relations Survey (or AWIRS) funded by the Federal Department of Industrial Relations (as it then was). Two AWIRS surveys have been conducted, one in 1990 (Callus et al. 1991) and another in 1995 (Morehead et al. 1997). The most recent, AWIRS 1995 represents a survey drawn from a population of 120,000 workplaces and nearly 4.4 million Australian workers involving both face to face interviews and questionnaires. AWIRS 1995 has been relied upon by researchers to highlight changes in the Australian workplace, although the data sets are now nearly five years old. Each State Department of Industrial Relations maintains a data base on state based workplace agreements. At a federal level, the former Department of Industrial Relations published two annual reports on enterprise bargaining, one covering trends in 1994 called *Annual Report 1994: Enterprise Bargaining in Australia*, (DIR 1995), the other covering trends in 1995. The latter report called *Annual Report 1995: Enterprise Bargaining in Australia*, (DIR 1996) covered trends and issues in enterprise bargaining both at federal and state levels for 1995. The annual report series were superseded in 1996 when the new Federal Coalition Government revamped the old Department of Industrial Relations renaming it as the Department of Employment, Workplace Relations and Small Business (or DEWRSB, but also referred to as the Department of Workplace Relations, Small Business or DWRSB). DEWRSB maintains a Workplace Agreements Database and issues a quarterly publication called Trends in Enterprise Bargaining (this publication provides interesting statistics on trends in enterprise bargaining and is available free of charge on the Internet at http://www.dwrsb.gov.au/publications/prodserv.htm).

An independent source of data on workplace agreements is produced by the Australian Centre for Industrial Relations Research and Training (ACIRRT) at the University of Sydney. The Centre maintains a workplace agreement database of over 6000 agreements known as the Agreements Database and Monitor (or ADAM). ACIRRT publishes (with CCH Australia) a regular report called the ADAM Report. This report provides an informative, topical and current review of selected features of enterprise agreements and is the most authoritative review of wages and enterprise bargaining trends. ACIRRT usually provides an overview of wages and enterprise bargaining tends in the March (annual review) issue of the *Journal of Industrial Relations*. Finally, the National Institute of Labour Studies at Flinders University (S.A.) under the title of *The Transformation of Australian Industrial Relations Project* has surveyed approximately 1500 workplaces. The project is sponsored by the Business Council of Australia and the Committee for Economic Development of Australia (CEDA) and many of the companies are drawn from the membership of these organisations. A book under the above title has recently been published drawing together the survey results (Wooden, 2000).

Extent of Agreement Making and Wage Increases under Agreements

Under a system of enterprise bargaining, one can expect the development of wage variations between industries and occupations due to differential bargaining power of those involved. Whilst the different data sources (above) give slightly different figures, the trends are fairly clear. In 1995-1996, under the last two years of the Federal Labor Government's Accord with the ACTU (see Chapter 8), real wages increased by about 0.9% and 0.3% respectively. This compares to increases of 4.2% and 2.5% during 1998-1999 under enterprise bargaining (Senate Report on the Consideration of the Provisions of the Workplace Relations Legislative Amendment (More Jobs, Better Pay) Bill, November, 1999, 390). The pace of agreement making is gradually increasing. Between October 1991 to the end of September 1999 almost 28,000 agreements were approved by the AIRC. It is estimated that there were 11,420 workplace agreements current as at 30 September 1999 covering 1.3 million workers. When one takes into account agreements approved by state industrial tribunals as well as AWAs, the number of agreements exceeds 130,000 (Trends in Enterprise Bargaining, September Quarter, DEWRSB, September, 1999).

The average duration of agreements approved by the Commission was between 14 and 20 months (DIR 1996, 128). It has been estimated by ACIRRT (ADAM Report No. 23, December, 1999, 4) that by September 1999, 75% of federal award employees were covered by enterprise bargaining agreements, 36% of employees in New South Wales, 47% of employees in Queensland, 65% of employees in South Australia, 73% in Western Australia and 64% of Tasmanian employees. Aggregate wage trends under enterprise agreements ranged from 4-6% between 1993-1996, a high of 5.7% for the period 1995-1996, 4.8% for the period 1996-1997 to just under 4% in the March quarter of 1998, giving an average aggregate wage increase of 3.5% per annum during the period 1991-1998 (DEWRSB, Trends in Enterprise Bargaining, September Quarter, 1999, 4. Chart 1).

Who are the Parties in the Bargaining Process?

Data from the DIR Survey (1996) suggests that unions remain important to the bargaining process, despite a decline in union membership (Campling and Gollan 1999). 63% of bargaining was found to occur with union members who were present in the workplace (DIR 1996, 253). Where union delegates were absent in the workplace, there was a much smaller chance that unions would be involved or act as bargaining agent (39%) (DIR 1996, 29, Table 2.5, federal award workplaces only). Despite the move towards workplace bargaining, the majority of agreements were negotiated at a higher level in the organisation and away from the workplace (62% for Federal agreements) (DIR 1996, 82, Table 3.1). Managers and full-time union officials tend to dominate the bargaining process. For example, of those involved in the bargaining process, 68% of managers in the workplace said that they were involved in the bargaining process. 60% of managers outside of the workplace said that they were involved in the bargaining process. 77% of full-time union officials were involved in bargaining. 49% of agreements involved consultative committees. Only 24% of employees acted collectively to initiate bargaining. Finally, only 24% of agreements involved employer associations (DIR 1996, 83, Table 3.2). In relation to formal (e.g. agreements approved by an industrial tribunal), 62% of federal and 77% of state registered agreements were negotiated with managers and union officials beyond the workplace. In comparison, 78% of unregistered or informal agreements were negotiated directly between management and employees at workplace level (DIR 1996, 273, Table S3.1).

Employment Size, Wages and Equity

Surveys by both the 1995 Report on Enterprise Bargaining in Australia (DIR 1996) and AWIRS 1995 (Morehead et al. 1997) suggested that workplace bargaining occurred formally (where the agreement is approved by an industrial tribunal), and informally (where agreement is reached between employer and employee). While bargaining was occurring across most industries, some workplaces were more likely to bargain than others. The 1995 DIR Report showed that some industries were much more likely to have bargaining workplaces than others. Industries with high proportions of bargaining workplaces (or active bargainers) included electricity, gas and water (85%) government administration (83%), communications (72%) and transport and storage (69%). Industries with low proportions of bargaining (or less active bargainers) included retail trade (21%), accommodation, café and hotels (29%) and property and business (29%). In these industries, workers tend to be less active in bargaining. The proportion of workers involved (as opposed to workplaces) in bargaining was only 26% of workers in retail trade workplaces, 45% of workers in accommodation, cafe and hotels industry, and 47% of workers in property and business (DIR 1976, 17). Workplace bargaining is also related to size. For example, only 48% of workplaces that employed less than 20 employees had an agreement. In workplaces that employed 20 employees or more, 63% of employees were covered by a workplace agreement (DIR 1996, 23). Clearly, the larger the workplace, the more likely workers are involved in enterprise bargaining.

The move towards a more deregulated industrial relations system has been accompanied by a growing pattern of differential wage outcomes between industries, types of agreements (formal versus informal agreements) and gender. Most industries show a range of wage increases, but the largest variations were found in mining/construction, metal manufacturing, financial services and community services. Buchanan et al. (1999a) show that wage outcomes vary considerably between industries. The highest average annual wage increases (AAWI) under agreements were in mining/construction and metal manufacturing (where 24.0% of agreements fell into the highest AAWI category), followed by financial services (22.5%) and community services (22.0%) followed by other manufacturing electricity, gas and water (15.0%), food beverage and tobacco manufacturing (10.4%). The lowest AAWI under agreements were in recreational services and public administration (0.3%), other manufacturing (0.6%) financial services and mining/construction (0.7%) (1999a, Table 3). What this suggests is that wage increases under enterprise bargaining do not flow evenly within or between industries. Agreements made with unions tend on average to have higher wage increases of between 1-2.5% above non-union agreements (ADAM Report No. 15, December 1997, 23).

However, does this suggest the emergence of a broader 'wages gap' under enterprise bargaining between active bargaining workplaces and less or non-active workplaces (including workplaces with no agreement or those relying solely on the award safety net)? Some researchers suggest that since 1992-93 there has been a growing disparity between weekly earnings and award rates of pay. As a consequence, the wages gap between workers under enterprise agreements and awards, is widening. This is particularly evident for workers under informal or individual agreements. Buchanan et al.(1997) suggest evidence of an emerging wages gap between workers covered by awards or enterprise agreements and those covered by informal or individual contracts. For example, using average wage movements for 1996, it was found that workers covered by both awards and registered enterprise agreements received an average wage increase of between 4% - 6%. On the other hand, workers solely covered by the award system, received an average wage increase of 1.3%, and workers solely covered by informal arrangements or individual contracts received an estimated average wage increase were between 0 (i.e. no wage increase) to a high of 8% (1997, 101, Table 2).

There are also implications for gender. There is evidence of a widening gap between male and female earnings. In 1998 (January-June), AAWI for women was 3.7% as compared to 3.9% for men (down from 4.1% and 4.7% respectively for 1997). Agreements where women make up less than 40% of the employees covered by an agreement, the AAWI was 3.8%. For agreements where women make up between 40% and 60%, the AAWI was 4.4%. Where women make up more than 60%, the AAWI drops back to 3.5%. In addition, the ratio of female to male hourly earnings for full-time adults recorded a low of 86.2% in May 1996, rose to 88.7% in November 1997, and dropped to 87.7% by June 1998. For part-timers, the AAWI in 1997 stood at 4.0% as compared to 4.5% for full-time employees. In 1998 (January-June) these figures were 3.6% and 3.8% respectively (DEWRSB 1998b, 8-10, and Table 4). What these figures show is that female workers are less likely to be able to achieve bargaining outcomes equal to that of males. This may be because women are found in industries where female employees lack bargaining power, or because they are employed as part-time or casual employees (the majority of whom are female) and either do not influence the bargaining process or are absent from it altogether (Pocock 1998, 594).

The Scope of the Bargaining Agenda and Outcomes

The extent to which workplace agreements totally replace awards is uncertain because of the 'no disadvantage test', which requires agreements to reflect core award conditions. Many agreements incorporate at least some award conditions and are therefore applied in conjunction with the award.

Table 9.1 Employee coverage and key provisions in federal enterprise agreements: public and private sectors, 1999 (January-June)

	Subject Matter	% of Agreements		% of Employees	
		Public	Private	Public	Private
Nature and scope of agreements	Section 170LK (Non-union, majority of workers CAs)	7.9	12.5	5.0	11.1
	Comprehensive	5.0	9.6	5.1	20.1
	Retains provisions removed through award simplification	34.6	44.2	37.9	15.7
	Provision for AWAs	9.7	1.5	41.6	2.6
	Exclusion of AWAs	3.2	13.5	1.5	18.1
Performance/ Productivity	Performance Indicators	10.6	9.2	26.1	9.5
	Multi-Skilling	22.6	49.5	29.9	41.4
	Benchmarking	13.2	24.6	7.1	10.9
Flexible work arrangements	Negotiable hours of work	12.6	8.4	20.3	11.2
	Job sharing	7.3	1.1	8.8	3.5
	Home based work	7.9	0.1	21.5	0.0
Flexible salary arrangements	Annualised salaries	9.1	4.4	5.6	4.9
	Salary packaging	51.3	7.0	34.5	16.6
Leave entitlements	Cashing out annual leave	2.3	2.6	0.4	3.4
	Cashing out long service leave	5.9	5.5	3.7	5.8
	Carers' leave (incl. sick leave)	24.6	22.6	31.1	50.9
	All purpose paid leave	9.7	50.9	18.8	10.7
	Paid maternity leave	39.6	4.4	27.9	10.3
	Training leave	32.3	36.2	46.4	38.1
	Purchase extra annual leave	8.2	0.6	41.3	8.5
	Sick leave insurance scheme	3.8	22.0	0.7	10.2
Employment opportunity and equity provisions	EEO provisions	16.1	10.8	51.6	23.1
	Child care provisions	3.5	0.3	14.9	0.5
	Family responsibilities	11.1	1.4	2.7	2.6
	Access and equity for people with disabilities	6.2	2.5	19.0	16.9
	Regular hours for part-timers	10.6	5.8	21.0	29.9
Redundancy provisions	TCR better than test case	17.9	20.4	25.9	40.0
	Redundancy scheme	3.8	48.4	1.6	12.6
	Employment security	20.8	7.7	56.2	29.0
Trace union matters	Union encouragement	1.5	19.1	0.6	29.9
	Deduction of dues	4.4	17.3	21.0	30.3

Source: DEWRSB, Trends in Enterprise Bargaining, June Quarter, 1999, 3, Table 3

The 1995 DIR Report estimated that only 13% of Federal and 22% of State agreements replaced all award conditions, 17% and 25%, respectively, replaced most award conditions and 70% and 53%, respectively, replaced some award conditions (DIR 1996, 311, Table S.4.9). The majority of workplace agreements appear to be 'add-ons' and are applied in addition to the conditions provided under the parent award. Pay rates, working hours and work practices contribute the majority of bargaining items. The range of employment provisions included under enterprise agreements in 1999 (January-June) is set out in Table 9.1.

Table 9.1 demonstrates that most agreements contain provisions which affect individual performance and productivity, flexible working and flexible leave entitlements. For example 22% of public agreements contained some form of multi-skilling, 12.6% contained flexible hours of work, and 24.6% contained provisions relating to family/carers' leave, (although this is usually included because it includes sick leave which is an award condition). However, the extent to which workers are happy with these arrangements remains uncertain. Enterprise agreements have been crucial to the transformation from a centralised system to a deregulated workplace-based system of wage negotiation, according to ACIRRT.

However, it is in the area of working time where agreements have had the most impact (ADAM Report No. 16, March, 1998, 41). According to ACIRRT (November 1998; 1999) workplace restructuring during the past decade has dramatically altered the way in which we work. Three trends are clear. First, up to a third of employees report a decline in job security (ACTU 1999, ACIRRT 1999). Job insecurity has traditionally been associated with changes in the labour market and business cycle. However, changes during the past decade suggest that job insecurity may be more closely linked to cost minimisation strategies and organisational restructuring. Between 1986 and 1998, over 3 million full-time workers were retrenched and by the mid 1990s, more than a quarter of Australian companies had undergone restructuring and downsizing (ACIRRT 1999; Dawkins et al. 1999). Second, as standard-time employment has declined, there has been an increase in atypical or non-standard forms of employment. These include higher levels of casual and temporary employment, and the growth of contract employment. Around a quarter of Australian workers are employed on a casual or part-time basis. In addition, the majority of new jobs are in service industries that are predominantly made up of casual, part-time and temporary forms of labour such as tourism, hospitality, cafe/restaurants, financial services, property services and personal services. Between 1984 and 1997 over 60% of the new jobs created were casual (Burgess and Campbell 1998, ACIRRT 1999). Women workers tend to dominate casual and part-time jobs (Pocock 1998).

Finally, the growth in atypical forms of employment places further pressure on standard-time work arrangements and job security. Currently, just over a third of the workforce works standard working hours (38 hours per week, Monday to Friday), whilst almost a third are working very long hours. 30% of full-time employees regularly work over 49 hours per week (up from below 20 % in the early 1980s). In addition, the intensity of work has increased leading to an unfair distribution of between those in jobs working longer and harder, and those unemployed or under employed seeking more work.

The intensification in working hours suggests that Australian workers are increasingly 'time poor'. The Australian Council of Trade Unions (ACTU) highlighted increased time poverty in a recent survey entitled, *Employment Security and Working Hours – A National Survey of Current Workplace Issues* (July 1999, Yann Campbell Hoare Wheeter). The survey involved 6,770 employees who took part in a self-completion survey between February and June 1999 covering approximately 100 industries. It also included additional surveys conducted by 3 separate unions covering a further 2,929 employees. In summary the survey found that with regard to hours of work, a total of 55% of respondents worked 40 or more hours per week on average, with 26% working 45 hours or more, and 12% working 50 hours or more on average. Almost half (45%) of the respondents do at least some unpaid overtime each week. This compared with only around a third (29%) being paid for working overtime.

Amongst those respondents who felt their working arrangements have contributed to health problems, 62% worked 40 or more hours per week. Similarly, amongst those who felt that their working arrangements have contributed to accidents or near misses, 63% work more than 40 hours. A total of 13% of respondents work 10 hours or more of unpaid overtime. Female workers were significantly more likely than males to report doing unpaid overtime. Around one third of males (35%) do up to 10 hours of paid overtime on average per week, while 11% of females reported the same. Respondents were asked whether they were happy working the number of hours that they did in their main job. Almost a third (31%) of respondents overall wanted to work fewer hours each week, with 34% of females indicating a preference for shorter hours compared with 28% of males. Amongst permanent workers, 32% overall would like to work fewer hours, although permanent full-time workers were significantly more likely (33%) to indicate a preference for fewer hours, than permanent part-time workers (19%). In comparison, only 13% of casual workers wanted to work fewer hours. Inversely, 22% of casual workers would like to work more hours per week, compared with 4% of permanent workers. It should be noted that casual workers made up only 5% of the survey population (n=317). Workers on fixed or limited term employment contracts were more likely to work unpaid overtime than permanent workers. They were also the least satisfied with their current hours of work compared to other groups, with only 52% happy with their hours and 37% preferring to work less hours (ACTU 1999).

Similarly, the Australian Bureau of Statistics (ABS) has found a dramatic shift away from the notion of a 'standard' working week. According to the ABS, in August 1998, of the 8.5 million people who were employed, 37% worked less than 35 hours per week and 17% worked for less than 16 hours per week. 36% of workers were found to be working between 35 and 44 hours a week while 27% worked more than 44 hours per week. 9% were found to work 60 or more hours per week (ABS, Australian Social Trends 1999, Cat No. 4102.0, 105-106). According to the ABS, the large disparities in hours worked among employed people mark a shift away from the norm of a full-time job of about 35-44 hours (and most commonly 40 hours) observed several decades ago. It also marks a reversal of the general trend in the 1980s towards shorter hours of full-time work. Moreover, these changes have continued throughout the last decade. Between 1988 and 1998, both the proportion of people working part-time hours and the proportion working at least 45 hours per week increased and as a result, the proportion working 35-44 hours fell from 42% to 36% (ABS, Australian Social Trends 1999, Cat No. 4102.0, 106).

According to the ABS, patterns of change have also differed for men and women in different age groups. The overall shift in proportions working long hours between 1988 and 1998 was about the same for both men and women (3.1%). However, those working longer hours were largely restricted aged between 25 and 64. The distribution shift was most pronounced for men aged 45-64 (among whom the proportion working 45 hours or more increased by 6.7%). According to the ABS, both young men and women (aged 15-24) were considerably more likely to work part-time than ten years earlier. Occupational groups displaying marked movements from standard working hours to long hour employment included skilled workers, professionals and supervisory occupations. Between 1988 and 1998, two service industries exhibited the most pronounced movement towards employing people for very short hours. These were cultural and recreational services (an increase of 4.9%) and retail trade (3.9%). These industries employ relatively high proportions of women and part-time workers. They are also industries experiencing strong growth in employment. In contrast, two production industries have experienced the largest proportional shift to very long hour employment: mining (an increase of 13.4%) and electricity, gas and water supply (7.5%).

These industries continue to be dominated by male full-time workers. They are also industries in which employment has been in decline. Employment in mining declined by 9% between 1988 and 1998 and in electricity, gas and water supply by 39%. The ABS also suggests that the growing diversity of working arrangements, described above, is also associated with an increase in work during 'unsocial hours' (in the evening or on weekends). For example, the proportion of people working between 6 p.m. and 6 a.m. increased from 35% to 37% including the proportion of people working on weekends (ABS, Australian Social Trends 1999, Cat No. 4102.0, 105-109). The importance of working time flexibility to cost minimisation is illustrated in Table 9.2.

Table 9.1 Employee coverage and key provisions in federal enterprise agreements: public and private sectors, 1999 (January-June)

HOURS OF WORK PROVISION	NON-UNION AGREEMENTS (%)	UNION AGREEMENTS (%)
Any flexible hours provision:	85	71
Working hours greater than 38 hours per week:	24	7
Ordinary hours Monday-Saturday:	7	10
Ordinary hours Monday-Sunday:	18	6
Averaging of hours of work (over any 7 days per week, or 52 weeks per year):	38	17
Overtime paid at single rate:	14	1
Time off in lieu of overtime at ordinary rate:	16	9

Source: DEWRSB, Trends in Enterprise Bargaining, June Quarter, 1999, 3, Table 3

According to Table 9.2, 85% of non-union agreements contain provisions for flexible hours as compared to 71% of union agreements. These differences are more stark when one considers that non-union agreements have a greater propensity to provide for longer working hours (24% as opposed to 7%); more likely to average hours over a week or year to absorb penalty rates and special payments for collective agreements in 1996-1997)working outside Monday to Friday (38% as opposed to 17%); and are more likely to pay overtime at single rates (14% as compared to 1%).

According to data from AWIRS 1995, workers are increasingly unhappy with the results of enterprise bargaining and the impact it is having on their working lives. The Table 9.3 summaries worker responses and shows just how prevalent work intensification has become in the mid-1990s.

The results in Table 9.3 suggest that workplace change has dramatically affected the attitude of employees towards change. A picture is emerging of an increase in the pace and intensity of work associated with increased job related stress. The relatively high proportion of respondents that indicated 'no change' suggests that the parties to enterprise bargaining are not skilled in developing consultation and outcomes that improve the working lives of employees. One reason may be that cost minimisation continues to dominate employer bargaining agendas. A gradual increase is evident in atypical forms of employment (irregular, casual and temporary jobs characterised by job insecurity), and in the absorption of both penalty rates and overtime payments. For example, 85% of non-union agreements and 71% of union agreements include provisions for flexible hours. 10% of non-union and union agreements make provisions for absorbing allowances and leave loadings (ADAM Report, No. 15, December, 1997, 22-23). Also, these changes appear interconnected. Allan et al. (1999) suggest a convergence in workplace change. They suggest that it is now possible to say that workers are experiencing a 'bundling' of simultaneous effects at the workplace level, including increases in the number of tasks performed, in the pace and intensity of work, and in the feeling of insecurity in their employment.

Table 9.3 Workers' views of the impact of workplace bargaining on selected employment conditions (AWIRS, 1995)

JOB CHARACTERISTIC	UP %	NO CHANGE %	DOWN %
Work Intensification/Effort require by the Job	59	37	4
The Pace of Work	46	50	4
Amount of Stress on the Job	50	42	7
Job Satisfaction	30	40	29
Impact on Working Hours	25	66	8
Job Related Training	18	70	11
Fair chance to have a say about Workplace Change	32	44	25
Better Balance between Job and Family Life	14	58	26
Overall Satisfaction with Workplace Agreement	31	42	24

Source: Data derived from AWIRS 1995, Employee Survey, Morehead et al. 1997, Appendix Tables.
Population: Persons in workplaces with more than 20 employees

Enterprise Bargaining and Occupational Health and Safety (OHS)

Occupational health and safety is a key element of workplace management. Most Australian States have, since the mid 1980s devolved the regulation of health and safety to workplace level by legislation that emphasises industry self-regulation and a duty of care. However, greater labour flexibility under enterprise bargaining has come at a cost. For example, according to ACIRRT, the problem of work intensification is not just one of perception. Stress also makes people sick. Between 1990 and 1994, stress claims under workers compensation doubled, even though stress is one of those illnesses where workers seldom make claims, preferring to use their sick leave or recreational leave to try to recover (ADAM Report, No. 6, September, 1995). In the AWIRS 1995 employee survey, nearly 5 per cent of respondents reported that stress had caused them to be ill - and 15 per cent of this group received workers compensation for their stress and 50 per cent took time off work (Morehead et al. 1997, 127-129).

Heiler (1996) has found that a managerial focus on cost minimisation concerned with labour costs, labour flexibility and individual performance has diverted attention from OHS issues under enterprise bargaining. Whilst 35% of agreements had provisions relating to OHS matters, these were mostly limited to statements of policy or provisions relating to working extended hours such as the introduction of 12-hour shifts, flexible rostering and rest breaks (Heiler 1994, 1996). Only 9% of agreements referred to safety training and only 6% of agreements made provisions for workplace health and safety committees. In addition, only 8% of agreements contained performance indicators that included workplace health and safety. According to ACIRRT, the expansion of shift working to include 12-hour shifts requires close attention, as there are a host of potential physical, social and emotional problems associated with such long working days. The lack of OHS procedures is illustrated by the fact that while 6.1% of agreements contain 12-hour shift provisions, only 1.9% referred to the ACTU code on working 12-hour shifts. (This code recommends that not more than 4 consecutive shifts should be worked without at least two days off, as well as covering rest breaks and the monitoring of fatigue levels.) In addition, OHS issues become even more difficult to monitor with the introduction of flexibility provisions, such as clauses that leave working hours to be organised 'by mutual arrangement' between employer and employee. Fear of recrimination and job insecurity may increase the willingness of employees to agree to work longer hours or reduce the number of day's off etc., thereby potentially increasing worker fatigue. The agenda for enterprise bargaining has been dominated by economic considerations. OHS issues remain a neglected item on the bargaining agenda (ADAM Reports, No, 5, March, 1995 and No. 6, September, 1995, 20-21).

ENTERPRISE BARGAINING AND THE PROBLEM OF MEASURING PRODUCTIVITY

A major reason for the deregulation of Australia's industrial relations system and the move towards workplace bargaining is that these changes will increase efficiency and productivity. So how effective has enterprise bargaining been in increasing industry productivity and efficiency? According to the DEWRSB Workplace Agreements Database, labour productivity has gradually risen since the early 1990s. Between June 1992 and February 1996, labour productivity had grown by approximately 3% (DEWRSB 1998b, 5-6, Chart 5). According to the ABS (measuring labour productivity as gross domestic product divided by the number of hours worked) there was a steady increase in labour productivity per hour worked. Productivity in the 'all industries' category increased by 2.4% per annum from June 1991 to September 1998, and at 3.1% per year to the September Quarter, 1998. The figure was 2.5% and 3.3% respectively for the same periods for the 'non-farming' category (ABS, *Labour Productivity, Australia, September 1998*, Cat. No. 5206.0).

However, linking labour productivity to enterprise bargaining outcomes is difficult. There are few reliable studies. To date, we have tended to rely on labour costs as a major indicator of productivity. However, this focus on wage outcomes has tended to place a greater emphasis on provisions under agreements such as individual performance appraisals, performance related pay, and productivity linked bonus schemes etc. as a means for determining expected productivity gains (Rimmer 1998, 614-615). In addition, identifying precisely which components of agreements increase productivity is difficult. While there are a variety of mathematical research methods used to measure productivity, the problem with productivity is that it is an imperfect term. It often does not take into account product market changes, government policy (e.g. minimum wages, taxation etc), managerial practices, skills and education, technology, and social measures such as standards of living, community expectations, unemployment rates, quality of production, morale of workers and so on. A simple example may serve to demonstrate the problem. If a hotel has 100 beds and employees 50 staff, and the hotel decides to retrench 25 staff whilst keeping the hotel trading with 100 beds, it is safe to assume that by increasing the intensity of work amongst the remaining 25 staff, staff productivity will increase by 100%! But at the same time, what are the costs in terms of moral, motivation, quality of service, turnover, absenteeism, and health and safety issues.

Thus, measuring the outcome of enterprise bargaining in terms of productivity is problematic. For some, it becomes a question of whether more deregulated industrial relations actually increase the productivity of firms (due to better working practices, introduction of new technology, better management or increased labour flexibility) or whether productivity increases are simply due firms doing more (or the same) but with fewer workers (ACIRRT 1999). For example, many banks justify restructuring to their shareholders by asserting productivity gains measured largely in terms of the number of jobs made redundant. A focus on labour costs may also increase the adoption of atypical and more precarious forms of employment (casual and less secure lower paid jobs) as management attempts to reduce costs by replacing full-time workers with casual and part-timers (ACIRRT 1996a).

An analysis of agreements by the Federal Department of Industrial Relations (now DEWRSB) in the 1996 Enterprise Bargaining Report (DIR 1996) found that most federal agreements contain provisions aimed at increasing productivity. These productivity gains are expected either through changes in work organisation, better use of technology and capital, or changes in employment conditions (such as greater numerical flexibility or working time flexibility, or function flexibility through training). Results of the survey are set out in Table 9.4.

Table 9.4 Management reporting on the effects of workplace agreements, 1994 - 1995

		Increased a lot %	Increased a little %	No change %	Decreased a little %	Decreased a lot %
Workplace Profitability:	(a)	9	38	42	9	2
	(b)	7	37	43	11	2
Skill Levels:	(a)	13	49	38	0	0
	(b)	11	59	28	2	0
Absenteeism:	(a)	9	41	50	0	0
	(b)	19	36	44	1	0
Labour Productivity:	(a)	9	36	52	3	0
	(b)	5	44	51	0	0
Product/Quality:	(a)	2	10	70	12	5
	(b)	0	13	65	18	4

Source: DIR 1996, 131-133, Tables 4.7, 4.8, 4.9, 4.10 and 4.11

(a) Federal Agreements
(b) All Agreements (Federal, state and informal or non-registered)

Table 9.4 suggests that management is generally satisfied with the outcomes of enterprise bargaining. 47% of managers under federal agreements reported profitability increased as a result of the agreement (44% under all agreements). Over half of managers stated that labour productivity had increased as a result of the agreement (DIR 1996). However, the proportion of agreements that link wage increases to productivity remains small. According to ACIRRT few industries are successful in linking wages to productivity, and in those that have, the proportion of agreements remain small (e.g. community services 15.6%, other manufacturing 11.7%, transport/storage 10.4%, metal manufacturing 9.1%, mining and construction 7.8%, electricity, gas and water 6.5%, and financial services 3.9%, recreational and personal services 0.0%). Interestingly, and reflecting a greater emphasis on outcomes, 15.6% of public service agreements contained wage increases linked to productivity but contained few means to measure productivity outcomes (ADAM Report No. 18, September 1998, 6). According to AWIRS 1995, whilst 84% of workplaces referred to key performance indicators in their agreements, only 14% used some form of productivity measure! In addition, whilst 79% of managers were involved in developing key performance indicators in the workplace, only 39% of employees said that they were involved in designing the measures (Morehead et al. 1997, 106-107, Tables 6.2 and 6.3).

Managers however were not entirely satisfied by outcomes. The *1996 MTIA Members' Survey on Enterprise Agreements* (ACIRRT 1996b) found that according to 33% of managers, the most significant failure of enterprise agreements was that they failed to reach set productivity targets and many productivity goals were not achieved during the life of the agreement. In addition, 18% of mangers complained that desired changes in work organisation were also not achieved. 23% of managers stated that they hoped to see provisions relating to productivity/performance included in their next agreement. The extent of management's satisfaction with their agreement was also a reflection of employee attitudes. 38% of managers conceded that employee resistance to change was a major factor to consider in future rounds of enterprise bargaining (ACIRRT 1996b, 4, Table 5).

In summary, Australian businesses have used the past decade under enterprise bargaining to undergo substantial restructuring and downsizing as the primary method of achieving increased efficiency. According to ACIRRT (1999), the focus on measuring productivity under enterprise bargaining overlooks the fact that many improvements in labour productivity have resulted from organisations doing more with fewer people as many organisations have restructured and downsized. ACIRRT concludes that organisational change has been largely responsible for contributing to productivity and efficiency through increasing the pace and intensity of work as well as through restructuring working-time by increasing the working hours of the remaining survivors of downsizing (ACIRRT 1999). The impact of this workplace restructuring is shown in Table 9.5.

Data on use of casual and agency workers, retrenchments, unpaid overtime and outsourcing based on workplaces with 20 or more employees. Data on proportion of employees at workplaces with more and less than 100 employees is based on estimates covering the whole sample).

Table 9.5 Key indicators of workplace restructuring in Australian workplaces, 1990-1995

FORM OF RESTRUCTURING	1990(%)	1995(%)
Workplaces using casual workers:	64	70
Workplaces using agency/contract workers:	14	21
Workplaces reporting retrenchments (all): • Workplaces with 200-499 employees: • Workplaces with 500+employees:	26 39 39	27 44 60
Employees whose working hours increased but whose pay did not:	na	23
Decreasing employment size: • Percentage of workplaces outsourcing since 1990: • Percentage of employees in 100+ workplaces:	 na 46	 35 41

Source: AWIRS 1995, Morehead et al. 1997, various Tables; also drawn from Buchanan et al. 1998, 113

IS THERE A DEMISE OF COLLECTIVIST EMPLOYMENT RELATIONS IN AUSTRALIA UNDER ENTERPRISE BARGAINING?

Has the move to enterprise bargaining led to an increase in managerial authority in the workplace? Has it led to a decline in union power? There are a number of trends in Australian employment relations suggesting that employers are choosing to by pass the collectivist system of industrial relations. Since the mid 1980s there has been a steady decline in the award coverage of employees with a rise in the use of informal workplace agreements or common law contracts in traditionally strong unionised areas such as mining (44%), construction (24%) and wholesale trade (29%) had some non-managerial employees on contract. In high growth areas such as cultural and recreational services (42%), personal services (25%), tourism (22% and finance and insurance (15%) had some employees on contract. In addition, up to a third of employees in these areas was found to be award free (Buchanan et al. 1997: 112, Table 4). AWIRS 1995 found that 26 per cent of workplaces had non-managerial employees on some form of individual contract (Morehead et al. 1997, 205-206). The number of AWAs approved by the Office of the Employment Advocate (OEA) has grown considerably from less than 5,000 in December 1997 to over 120,000 by May 2000 (Office of the Employment Advocate, personal communication).

There has also been a steady decline in Union membership. According to AWIRS 1995 the proportion of workplaces with at least one union member has declined from 80% in 1990 to 74% in 1995. This decline was most notable in smaller workplaces (20 to 49 employees) where the proportion of workplaces with at least one union member fell from 73% to 64%. AWIRS 1995 also found that 57% of workplaces with five or more employees were non-union (Morehead et al. 1997, 356). Most of the decline was in the private sector (Morehead et al. 1997, 139-140). AWIRS 1995 supports the picture of a steady decline in union density. Union membership has fallen significantly over the last decade: from 46 percent of the workforce in 1986 to 31 percent in 1996. In the private sector less than a quarter of the workforce remains unionised. This decline is attributable to structural changes in industry such as a decline in traditional manufacturing, the growth in services, and an increase in the use of various forms of precarious employment (such casual, temporary or seasonal and contract jobs) (see Chapter 5). This shift is compounded by the structural inability of union representation at workplace level to resist de-unionisation (Peetz 1998).

Legislative changes and the gradual deregulation of the labour market over the past decade has provided Australian employers with a wider range of options as to how they wish to manage employment relations. Increasingly management is opting to deal directly with employees rather than through collective processes involving trade unions. There has been a greater use of performance-based pay and individual appraisal systems and the wider utilisation of direct communication systems with the employees (Morehead et al. 1997, 243-245). There has also been a marked increase in the use of a range of employee monitoring devices. These include employee attitude surveys and customer/client feedback programs, and the monitoring of customer service and satisfaction linked to employee performance and productivity. This trend is often accompanied by a decline in joint decision-making or joint regulatory structures at workplace level (Morehead et al. 1997; Deery and Walsh 1998). This has been accompanied by an attitudinal change in Australian management. Early examples of enterprise bargaining during the 1990s overwhelmingly involved agreements made with trade unions with few opting for non-union agreements. However, once over the initial hurdle, management learnt the lessons of setting up consultative committees and the importance of employee communication. By the mid 1990s, managers were far more confident in dealing directly with their employees and union involvement became an optional extra. This suggested, as one Government report noted, that the 'potential benefits' of increased individual and direct working relationships, as advocated by human resource management adherents was being realised, putting in place the basis of ongoing improvements (LMC 1998, 45-46).

The decision by management to adopt individual agreements with employees rather than collective agreements with trade unions may be made for a number of reasons such as convenience, part of a competitive strategy etc. However, the decision to adopt it is increasingly being made as a matter of managerial industrial relations strategy. A survey by the BCA and Committee for the Economic Development of Australia (CEDA) found that 72% of managers preferred individual agreements as a matter of preference or strategy. Of this group 66% preferred them to obtain more favourable bargaining outcomes, 52% to improve employee relations, 35% because employees wanted them, 15% because the manager felt constrained by enterprise bargaining, and 12% because of increased competitive pressures (Wooden 1999a, 16, Figure 1). Whilst managers indicated that they were generally satisfied with the outcomes of bargaining (74% that said yes as opposed to 14% that said no), the level of satisfaction in most cases (81%) was higher for managers with informal (non registered) workplace agreements (DIR 1996, 134, Table 4.12). Clearly, Australian management is becoming bolder and adopting individual agreements as a matter of choice and strategy. Such findings are consistent with the view expressed by Deery and Walsh (1998) that preference for individualistic employment arrangements is a function of unitarist management styles. Individualism is also a vehicle for sidelining unions and collective labour.

DOES MANAGEMENT PREFERENCE FOR INDIVIDUALISTIC EMPLOYMENT RELATIONS MEAN BETTER EMPLOYEE RELATIONS?

Do individualist approaches to employee relations mean better employee relations and more employee involvement in the workplace? AWIRS 1995 found that the majority of managers rated their relationship with employees as good (49%) or very good (43%). Smaller workplaces rated their relationship as good (44%) and very good (51%) and was higher in the private sector (49% good, 45% very good) than the public sector (49% good, and 39% respectively) (Morehead et al. 1996, 131, Table 6.26). 58% of managers strongly preferred to deal directly with their employees and not through a union, with only 33% agreeing to deal with trade unions should any employees join one (Morehead et al. 1996, 133, Table 6.27, all workplaces). Does this mean that employees are more trusting of employers? Survey evidence suggests that nearly two thirds of workers do not trust management (with those in the public sector less likely to trust in their employer). According to AWIRS 1995, young people between 15-20 tend to be more trusting of management at 54%, but this trust tends to decline with work experience reaching a low of 31% for employees between 30-39 years of age. In addition, 56% of employees felt that they did not get a say in workplace changes, and that management made all the decisions (Morehead, et al 1997, 577-578, Tables A12.14b and A12.15a).

The AWIRS 1995 survey suggests that enterprise bargaining has facilitated the introduction of 'best practice' management and work organisation such as quality circles, autonomous work groups and joint consultative committees in order to improve productivity, efficiency, quality, employee communication and job satisfaction (Morehead et al. 1996, 190 - 192, Tables 9.9, 9.10, 9.11, 9.12, 9.13 and 9.14). However, the extent that these are applied at workplace level remains elusive. According to Campling and Gollan (1999) workplace data here is not encouraging. 84% of union agreements are likely to have grievance procedures as compared to 73% on non-union agreements. 41% of union agreements contains occupational health provisions as compared to 30% under non-union agreements. 55% of union agreements contain consultative provisions as opposed to 29% of non-union agreements. In addition, 58% of union agreements contain provisions related to training as compared to only 38% of non-union agreements (ACIRRT 1997, ADAM Report No. 15, December 1997, 24). In addition, regular newsletters, staff bulletins and structured regular and on-going consultative meetings (the hallmark of good employee relations) were more likely to be found in unionised workplaces. In addition, in unionised workplaces, employees are more likely to be consulted in relation to future staffing plans (84%) and company investment plans (56%) as compared to non-unionised workplaces (72% and 46% respectively) (Morehead et al. 1997, 505). In relation to new HRM management techniques, only 4% of non-union agreements contained gain/profit sharing schemes, 4% contained quality assurance schemes, 5% contained team work provisions, and only 5% contained bonus payments. For union agreements, the number of agreements containing these provisions were slightly higher, 6% (gain/profit sharing), 7% (quality assurance schemes), 10% (team work) and 7% (bonus payments) respectively. 7% of non-union agreements were found to use individual performance reviews as compared to only 4% of union agreements contained performance appraisals (ADAM Report, No, 15, December 1997, 22).

Is there evidence that Australian managers use the option for individual agreements (AWAs) to enhance HRM practices and employee relations? An analysis of non-union agreements by ACIRRT on the ADAM agreement database found a number of common characteristics of Australian Workplace Agreements (AWAs). For example, AWAs were largely concerned with increasing working time flexibility by extending the working day, or eliminating overtime etc. AWAs were also found to involve workplaces with large proportions of casual or temporary employees. Most AWAs surveyed had a life of between thirty months and three years (maximum allowed under WRA). Many did not provide for a wage increase during the life of the agreement, according to ACIRRT representing in effect 'fixed priced employment contracts' (Buchanan et al. 1998, 102). According to ACIRRT, the gap in wages between non-union agreements and union agreements was around 1%. ACIRRT also found that non-union agreements were concentrated in small to medium sized workplaces in infrastructure and services. Companies such as Rio Tinto were the exception to the rule (Buchanan et al. 1998 1999; ADAM Report No. 19, December 1998). A survey by the Department of Employment, Workplace Relations and Small Business (DEWRSB) of the introduction of AWAs in 1997-1998 revealed that only 19.8% of agreements (covering 15.8% of employers) were comprehensive and replaced the award. 28.1% (covering 45.5% of employers) made reference to including award provisions. According to the Report, the most common provisions found under these agreements related to occupational superannuation (77.5% of agreements covering 68.3% of employers), annual leave, sick leave and other leave provisions (70.5% covering 84.2% of employers) and long service leave (55.3% covering 57.9% of employers) (DEWRSB 1998a, 48-50). According to a review of the Report by ACIRRT, the most important finding related to the high level of pattern bargaining in AWAs, with 31.2% of AWAs (covering 24.3% of employers) found to be 'pattern agreements' (Buchanan et al. 1999b, 111).

In a similar survey of non-union Queensland Workplace Agreements (QWAs) for 1977-1998) found that the average wage increase was 2.6%, considerably lower than the 4.1% average wage increase provided for under collective agreements with unions during the same period. 58% of QWAs offered no pay increase and a significant number of these reduced award conditions such as reducing or removing overtime (43%), allowances (31%), and annual leave (18%). Other award conditions that were affected included the removal of weekend penalty rates (69%) and sick leave (19%). The report also found that that 39% of QWAs increased ordinary working hours at no extra pay, and 53% increased the span of hours that could be worked on any day without overtime. The report concluded that QWAs have focused on repackaging award provisions relating to hours of work and overtime to improve flexibility but did not introduce any significant reform measures or innovations to increase productivity in Queensland workplaces (DETIR 1998, ii). The conclusion seems to be that individual agreement making in Australia typically does not involve negotiations over wages and conditions with individual employees. Only a small proportion of non-union agreements focuses directly at the individual. In fact, in relation to non-union bargaining, most individual agreements are little more than standardised packages (Wooden 1999b, 442). They are more concerned with non-union collective bargaining than with developing unique agreements to suit the particular needs of individual employers and employees (Buchanan et al. 1999b, 111). The Australian experience appears to mirror some overseas studies, especially from the UK where the growth of individualist employee relations was not associated with the introduction of good HRM practices (Sission 1993; Guest and Conway 1999).

The use of individual agreements as part of a broader union avoidance strategy finds support when one considers that the main reasons management enter into bargaining. According to the 1995 DIR Enterprise Bargaining Report, 52% of managers sought to commence bargaining in order to improve productivity/efficiency; 31% to improve workplace and communication; 25% to improve quality; 18% as part of a corporate plan; 16% to reduce costs; 13%, to improve reliability and to reduce wastage; 9% to provide a wage increase (DIR 1996, 31, Table 2.7). Similarly, according to Wooden (using the NILS Survey) found that managers rated the drive for reducing costs (42%) and the need for greater labour flexibility (45%) as the top two significant drivers of change over the next five years. The NILS Survey also found that in relation to their business strategies, 60% of managers rated the use of individual agreements as important, 71% the use of part-time employment, 65% the use of casual employment and 69% the use of outsourcing and use of subcontractors (Wooden, 2000, 186, 194, Tables 8.1 and 8.4). Overall, from a managerial perspective, the overriding agenda for workplace bargaining is economic performance, cost cutting and labour flexibility, which are being pursued as part of a broader cost minimisation strategy (Helier 1996). Clearly, Australia managers have a long way to go if they are to embrace a broader innovative approach to workplace bargaining.

ARE WE HEADING TOWARDS BARGAINING FATIGUE?

A survey of enterprise bargaining suggests that Australia has adopted a 'mix or hybrid system' (Rimmer 1998, 609) with three broad streams. First, there are those employers that have adopted collective/individual agreements. Second, there are employers that have adopted a combination of both agreements and awards. Last, there are employers that have endeavoured to maintain informal or over award agreements. The extent to which public policy can continue to be the driver of change is questionable. As observed in the MTIA Survey discussed earlier (ACIRRT 1996b), maybe too much is expected from enterprise bargaining. There may only be so much that can be achieved from either side before employees start to rebel or management runs out of ideas. Enterprise bargaining should not be seen as the panacea for all economic ills. Agreements cannot improve workplace employee relations without positive action by management. How much more productivity can enterprise bargaining squeeze out of the workplace before 'bargaining fatigue' sets in? The ADAM *Reports* and AWIRS 1995 data suggest that we are perhaps nearing this point soon. Both employers and unions seem content pursuing pattern bargaining whether it is under collective or individual agreements. The idea of standardising bargaining outcomes whether under collective agreements or individual agreements may have deeper historical roots reflecting the persistence of a centralised ethos or approach in Australian industrial relations albeit under the guise of workplace bargaining.

Enterprise bargaining has important implications for unions. Writers such as the Webbs (1902) and Phelps Brown (1988) have argued that the basic reason for having unions is to provide mutual protection for workers from the unfeeling impact of market forces. This line of argument falls into the 'defensive' theories of the labour movement, where trade unionism is seen as representing the natural development of groups for advancing and protecting the collective interests of labour under industrialism. Acceptance of a role for unions in collective bargaining remains built upon notions of equity and equality in the work relationship manifested in group representation and responsibility (Frazer 1995, 54-5). Governments since the early 1990s have shifted the emphasis of the industrial relations system from being solely performing an arbitral function to overseeing a shift towards employer and employee workplace agreements. The introduction of WRA has accelerated a shift towards an individualist model of enterprise bargaining whilst reducing the rights of unions. The challenge for management is to manage the change process effectively to ensure that the productivity increases achieved are long term and gained with employee support. The challenge for unions, if they are to remain relevant, is to maintain representational structures in the face of a steady decline in union membership and a more hostile political and legislative environment.

CONCLUSION

This chapter has traced the development of workplace bargaining in Australia and has examined the steps and issues associated with the shift towards workplace wage outcomes. A number of significant debates and developments have also been detailed. The shift towards a system of workplace bargaining in Australia has essentially followed a 'managed decentralism' approach where legislation has been used by successive Federal Governments (both Labor and Coalition) to set the pace and direction of change. The provisions of WRA have also been detailed. The chapter has traced developments under enterprise bargaining concluding that the direction of change has placed a greater burden is carried by employees. We examined trends in enterprise bargaining suggesting that managers are more likely to adopt individualist approaches to employee relations. The implications for unions were also discussed.

SAMPLE CERTIFIED AGREEMENT

A genuine sample of a Certified Agreement can be found in the Appendix at the end of the book.

KEY POINTS TO REMEMBER

- consultation with all relevant persons is important
- provide training to all participants (e.g. interpersonal skills, literacy skills etc.) where necessary
- ensure all persons understand the bargaining process and have access to relevant information
- to ensure a valid majority of employees, a secret ballot is often the best option conducted by an 'independent' third party
- keep a written record of negotiations
- seek expert advice in case of difficulty
- keep it simple
- keep an open mind to options and alternatives
- build trust
- negotiating workplace agreements is not for everyone, nor can a workplace agreement solve all of a company's problems.

REVIEW QUESTIONS

1. Should markets dictate how we manage productivity?
2. What role should Government play in promoting enterprise bargaining?
3. What measures of productivity are there?
4. How should we measure productivity under enterprise bargaining?
5. What are the effects of enterprise bargaining on unions?
6. What are the effects of enterprise bargaining on equity?
7. There is only so much bargaining one can do, after that bargaining fatigue sets in! Discuss.
8. Occupational health and safety and enterprise bargaining do not mix! Discuss.
9. What items would you include in an enterprise bargaining agenda and why?
10. Your company is experiencing hard times, your costs are too high, you have good employees, the workplace is strongly unionised and militant. Your shareholders want a return on their money. Identify your options, and discuss the strengths and weaknesses of each.

NEGOTIATING AN ENTERPRISE AGREEMENT

Table 9.6 sets out a number of the important steps in negotiating an enterprise bargaining agreement.

Table 9.6 Steps in negotiating an Enterprise Agreement

Start the process
Involve everybody –managers, employees and his or her representatives.
Set the scene for cooperation.
Identify mutual benefits.
Establish Ground Rules
Establish ground rules.
Provide training for participants.
Consult with employees or bargaining agent, about what is happening through information sessions.
Consult
Establish consultative arrangements.
For collective Agreements, form a single bargaining unit that can represent everyone at the workplace.
Develop an agenda and timetable for negotiations.
Give Everyone a Say
Make sure everyone's interests and views are considered.
Help all individuals and groups to have their say in a way that meets their needs. Some groups, e.g. women, people of non-English backgrounds and younger people may have specials needs that should be considered.
Negotiate the Agreement
Set the goals for change.
Identify areas for discussion.
Listen to suggestions.
Reinforce mutual benefits.
Write the Agreement
Make sure the agreement follows all the requirements of the Industrial Relations Act, for example, that it contains dispute-settling procedures and is non-discriminatory.
Collect and identify material to support the agreement.
Inform employees and discuss/vote on the document.
For Certified Agreements, the employer, employees and/or unions must agree to the terms of the agreement.
For AWAs, a majority of employees must genuinely approve the agreements, or the individual must agree.
Finalise the Agreement
Lodge the agreement with the Australian Industrial Relations Commission for Certification or approval of Certified Agreement or the Office of the Employment Advocate in relations to AWAs.
Monitor the Agreement
Keep track of productivity changes through indicators.
Regularly discuss how the agreement is going.
Evaluate progress.
Renew the Agreement
Review the agreement before it expires. Identify subjects for discussion.
Start negotiations for renewal.

Modified from: *Making Workplace Agreements – It's Your Agreement*, Department of Industrial Relations, May 1994, Canberra.

FURTHER READING

Allan, C., O'Donnell, and Peetz, D. (1999) 'More Tasks, Less Secure, Working Harder: Three Dimensions of Labour Utilisation', *Journal of Industrial Relations*, Vol. 41, No. 4, 519-535.

Australian Center for Industrial Relations Research and Training (ACIRRT) (1999) *Australia at Work: Just Managing?* Prentice Hall, Sydney.

Buchanan, J., Callus, R. and Briggs, C. (1999) 'What Impact has the Howard Government had on Wages and Hours of Work?', *Journal of Australian Political Economy*, No.43, 1-21.

Callus, R. (1997) 'Enterprise Bargaining and the Transformation of Australian Industrial Relations', *Asia Pacific Journal of Human Resources*, Vol. 55, No. 2, 16-25.

Campling, J. and Gollan, P. (1999) *Bargained Out: Negotiating Without Unions in Australia*, Federation Press, Leichhardt, N.S.W.

Morehead, A. Steele, M. Alexander, M. Stephen, K. and Duffin, L. (1997) *Changes at Work: The 1995 Australian Workplace Industrial Relations Survey*, Melbourne, Addison Wesley Longman.

Peetz, D. (1998) *Unions in a Contrary World*, Cambridge University Press, Cambridge.

CASE STUDY

CRA (Rio Tinto)

Individual Contracts, Strategic HRM Practices and Trade Unions in Conflict in the Mining Industry

BACKGROUND

Historically, the emergence of the mining industry in Australia has had profound influences on industrial relations. Mining unions formed in the early 1870s and were the first examples of organised labour in colonial Australia. They, subsequently, played an important role in the establishment of a centralised conciliation and arbitration system. Historically, the mining industry has been divided into two groups:

1. black coal - dominated by the United Miners Federation (now the Construction, Forestry, Mining and Energy Union or CFMEU, following a series of amalgamations during the late 1980s)

2. metalliferous (metal ore) - dominated by The Australian Workers Union Union/Federation of Industrial, Manufacturing and Engineering Employees (AWU/FIMEE, referred to here as the AWU).

Maintenance work at mine sites has traditionally been covered by the Automobiles, Metals, Food and Engineering Union (AFMWU). Due to the importance of the coal industry, a specialist tribunal of the Australian Industrial Relations Commission (AIRC), the Coal Industry Tribunal, was responsible for arbitrating coal industry matters until the Tribunal was disbanded in 1996.

Since the mid 1970s, there has been a substantial expansion in Australian coal and metalliferous mining associated with the expansion in Asian demand for high quality coking coal and steel. This demand has been largely met by the expansion in open cut mining of metalliferous ore, coal and more recently bauxite. These mining methods are relatively inexpensive and provide Australia with a significant source of export income. There has been 'healthy competition' between unions for membership, especially in metalliferous mining. In this area, the AWU covered all operational workers and the Federated Engine and Firemen's Association (FEDFA, now amalgamated with the CFMEU), supported by the CFMEU, covered engine drivers, boiler attendants and earth moving plant/equipment operators. The tensions came to the surface during the later part of the 1970s when employment levels were affected by a decline in commodity prices and closure of mines. Competition between unions for the remaining employees intensified.

GLOBALISATION AND RESTRUCTURING OF WORK PRACTICES IN MINING

The story of Rio Tinto (previously RTZ and, for convenience, referred to here as CRA) has been told elsewhere (Hamberger 1995a and 1995b; Timo 1997). However, the dispute is significant because it involved not only a battle over the 'hearts and minds' of employees, but over ideas concerning the role of unions and how employment relations should be managed. During the mid 1980s, mining companies such as CRA moved away from a collectivist approach to industrial relations, preferring instead to adopt what they saw as a more individualist, employee relations approach. It was a change brought about in the context of globalisation, increasingly competitive commodity markets, and growing managerial militancy towards collectivist industrial relations. Mining companies are dominated by commodity prices. If global prices fall, the growth and even the viability of a company may be threatened. A recent survey of the threats perceived by mining companies, undertaken by Deloittes' South African and South Australian offices (*The Australian*, 4th June 1998), ranked the following in terms of importance:

- declining exploration
- increasing costs
- declining relative competitiveness
- declining commodity prices
- repatriation of profits.

Cost pressure and falling commodity prices have profoundly altered miners attitudes towards labour. Mining companies have responded by reshaping labour relations and HRM practices. This has involved the introduction of single union sites, bonus or performance pay, annual salaries and introduction of 12-hour continuous shifts. These changes also involve the introduction of a 'single stream workforce' on many mining sites.

The single stream workforce concept involves doing away with occupational classifications and dismantling the notion of a 'principal job' (important for determining union job rights). Under a single stream classification structure, employees are reclassified according to 'generic' job roles. A single stream structure provided for two categories or roles for employees:

1. production technician – who operated and maintained equipment
2. crew coordinator - a team leader managing about 10 employees in a production crew, within a production unit. The crew operated without demarcation was multi-skilled.

With the loss of specific job titles and duties, it was no longer clear to miners which union was the most relevant to their needs. The effect was to produce instability in the relationship between unions, who competed with each other for membership. No union was willing to forgo what they saw as lawful membership rights. According to CRA, unions and collectivist industrial relations had the effect of impeding effective workplace bargaining reducing CRA's international competitiveness.

CRA: THE COMPANY, PRODUCT MARKETS AND TRADE UNIONS

CRA is a major Australian mining and smelting company. It is 48.7 per cent owned by Rio Tinto Zinc (RTZ), a mining multinational company based in the United Kingdom. The company mines iron ore, bauxite, gold and coal. One of its main subsidiaries is Comalco, which operates smelters at Bell Bay in Tasmania and Boyne Island at Gladstone as well as a bauxite mine at Weipa in far north Queensland (bauxite is the raw mineral from which aluminium is refined). Other CRA operations are located in Papua New Guinea, Indonesia, New Zealand, United Kingdom, Holland, Taiwan and the United States (McIntosh Baring Report 1996). In 1997 the company became known collectively as Rio Tinto.

CRA had sales of $5.5 billion in 1994 and assets in excess of $5 billion. The company has been undergoing a period of restructuring, reflecting the turbulence in mining and commodity markets. CRA suffered a net loss of $17.4 million in 1996 down from a profit of $295 million in 1995 (Australian Mining and Oil Guide 1996). CRA's outputs are very price sensitive with small changes in the exchange rate having a large effect on the company's profitability. The events in this case study took place when the price of coal and metals had just declined by about 10 per cent. The response of CRA was to restructure its operations, introducing a significant change in management style and culture aimed at achieving a greater competitive advantage (IRM 1994, 4).

CRA is a large employer with approximately 15,000 employees directly employed and another 8,000 workers in associated companies such as Hamersley Iron and Comalco. The blue-collar workforce covering operational employees in Comalco was represented by the large amalgamated union, the AWU. Other unions included the CFMEU and the AMFEU. The restructuring of CRA across its various operations during the 1980s was the cause of considerable union tension, fuelled by a managerial approach that sought change at any cost. At Weipa, for example, CRA wanted changes in working conditions and manning levels. This included attempting to reduce the role of maintenance tradespeople by broadening the skill base of equipment operators. CRA also sought to train these operators (members of the AWU) to carry out bulk loading and crane operating functions, which were covered by members of FEDFA. The resultant demarcation dispute was eventually placed before the Australian Industrial Relations Commission (AIRC). The Commission used its demarcation powers to favour the AWU and excluded the FEDFA from coverage at Weipa.

This dispute substantially reduced intra-union cooperation, which in turn was further weakened when the FEDFA/CFMEU attempted to regain its membership at Weipa (reported in decision CRA [Comalco] Weipa, Demarcation Case, 42 Industrial Reports 336-351).

RESTRUCTURING AND THE DEMISE OF COLLECTIVE INDUSTRIAL RELATIONS AT CRA

In order to understand the attitude of CRA toward the unions, it is necessary to appreciate that changes in the company's attitude and strategy that had occurred. By the early 1980s, CRA management had begun to reappraise the value of the collectivist industrial relations system established by the Industrial Relations Act. In a memorandum in November 1981, the then Chairman of CRA, Sir Roderick Carnegie, told senior company managers that CRA's future competitiveness depended on organising and managing individual potential (rather than collective bargaining) (Ludeke 1996, 8). These comments, combined with the authoritarian attitude of most CRA mine managers (Gardner 1987, 106) sent clear signals to employees that collective (union) activities were incompatible with CRA's new workplace culture. This culture was based on breaking down the collectivist mindset underpinning unionism, and instilling a work ethic of individual performance and direct accountability to departmental mangers. The aim of this new strategy was to ensure that the interest of employees would be aligned to those of the company. CRA's new found managerial strength of purpose was based on adopting the ideas of the management writer Elliott Jaques. He argues that companies which restructure along the lines of his model of 'requisite organisation' are capable of achieving a 100 per cent increase in employee productivity and at the same time eliminate the disruptive effects of industrial unrest (Jaques 1989). The strategy advocated by Jaques was based on understanding the psychological needs of workers and the importance of individual accountability and responsibility to management. The vehicle used by CRA to achieve this was individualised contracts with employees. Contracts served the company's purpose of aligning the objectives of the business with the needs of the individual. Once signed, such contracts makes winning the 'hearts and minds' of employees unnecessary, as employees have cogent economic reasons to align their goals with those of the company. Unions were not parties to these contracts.

DE-CONSTRUCTING 'JOB RIGHTS' AT CRA AS A MANAGERIAL STRATEGY

The decision by CRA to adopt individual contracts was based on four key managerial assumptions about their business:

1. globalisation
2. cost minimisation
3. restructuring working time
4. labour control.

CRA argued that globalisation introduced a more competitive metals commodity market. Cheaper and more efficient production systems also enabled new players to enter the metals market, using new refining technology to mine and process ore deposits previously considered uneconomic. CRA, therefore, could not afford to carry excess costs. The company sought to reduce operating costs by:

- lowering labour costs - achieved by reducing the labour force and increasing work intensity amongst the remaining employees
- separating working time from payment systems - eliminating allowances, special rates and week end rates. It also included the capacity to intensify work effort without increasing the hourly rate through eliminating overtime payments. This involved extending the working day and restructuring working time on a just-in-time basis (when required only) by using fixed-term contracts or specific-task contracts.

The way to beat Australia's centralised wages and award system was to eliminate third-party intervention in the employment relationship. Contracting employees gave CRA management access to a more flexible labour force capable of working with the uncertainties of the product market. This process created a more effective match between labour supply, hours paid and hours worked.

THE INTRODUCTION OF INDIVIDUAL CONTRACTS

The introduction of staff contracts at CRA comprised two-stages. The first stage involved establishing a new company value system based on individualism (referred to as CRA's 'people system'). The second involved establishing the appropriate HRM systems and practices in order to reinforce individual accountability. These steps operated in tandem and were mutually reinforcing. CRA's new approach was first tested at its New Zealand smelter operations at Tiwai Point, operated by a CRA subsidiary, New Zealand Aluminium Smelters (NZAS).

The first stage of the process involved separating out collective bargaining and trade union involvement from the employment relationship. This was achieved by changing employee values and attitudes through the use of company-inspired 'myths'. The new narrative was kept simple, focusing on the negative role of the union in the company's efforts to protect jobs (NZAS Consultant Report 1992, 104-115). The aim was to soften up employee opposition to the introduction of individual contracts. These myths included common cliches such as: things would have to change if the company was to stay in business; the unions were forcing the company out of business; every individual's performance at work matters; and the company looks after the best interests of every employee (NZAS Consultant Report 1992,104). CRA's strategy also included separating and dividing employees, particularly those who were strong unionists. They were tagged as 'troublemakers' and 'poor performers'. Peer pressure was important in creating desired standards of behaviour. By dividing employee loyalty, the union workplace delegate structure gradually became ineffective and then redundant as union delegates became a priority target for retrenchments.

The same strategy for change was then systematically introduced to CRA's Australian sites. The unilateral nature of the changes introduced by CRA was criticised by the AIRC during proceedings concerning the legality of individual contracts. The AIRC concluded that the process of introducing these changes was conducted on the basis of 'a secretive and well organised campaign' where 'nothing was left to chance' and where 'senior management even extended the secrecy of the campaign to exclude supervisors from what was being proposed'. The campaign was kept secret so that even 'supervisors were deliberately deceived as to the real company purpose' and 'were only briefed as to the pro forma answers to be given to employees to encourage them to accept staff contracts' (AIRC decision, CRA, (Comalco) Bell Bay Case, Print no. L7449, reported in 56 Industrial Reports, 403, at 440).

The acceptance of contracts was made easier by the company insisting that no independent legal advice was necessary and that signing a staff contract represented an employee's trust in company management. Those who did not sign ran the risk of being tainted as troublemakers and disloyal. About 95 employees at Weipa and Bell Bay remained union members (CRA witnessing, (Comalco) Bell Bay Case, Print no. 7449, reported in 56 Industrial Reports 403 at 441, and CRA Employee witnesses, CRA (Comalco) Weipa Case, Print no. M8600, reported in 63 Industrial Reports 138 at 165-167). It would have been remarkable for the outcome to be any other than an acceptance of the offer (CRA [Comalco] Bell Bay Case, Print no. 7449, 56 Industrial Reports 403 at 440). Employees at CRA Comalco operations at Bell Bay and Weipa were being offered wage increases of 11 per cent to 15 per cent (an average of $7,000) under staff contracts, where they had not had a wage increase since 1991 due to the breakdown in collective negotiations. By the end of 1995, that vast majority of employees had agreed to sign staff contracts. Unions were not a party to these contracts. It was a case of the company offering a unilateral and non-negotiable offer and employees accepting the offer. Workers regarded this as the only real way to obtain a wage increase and possibly some form of secure employment in the short to medium term.

CRA, HRM AND INDIVIDUAL CONTRACTS

In order to replace collective employment relations with a work culture based on the individual, substantial changes to CRA's organisational structure, authority systems and HRM practices were necessary. First, leadership training for supervisors was a prerequisite for cultural change. In a paper prepared by the CRA Group Employment Systems Taskforce entitled, *Leadership: A New Direction*, strong emphasis was placed on gaining employee acceptance of managerial authority. It also proposed that for successful leadership, management needed to demonstrate to employees the values such as trust, honesty, fairness, dignity and love. These became the basis of CRA's 'people system' This was reinforced by employee value training sessions covering topics such as team-working, better communication, effective leadership and introduction of teams. A retrenchment system ensured that the unionised elements in the workforce (especially union delegates) had been gradually weeded out.

The success of teams at CRA was based on selecting the right people, an open and visible working environment, the sharing of group values and beliefs, peer control, peer evaluation, social bonding, and low profile management control. The unit manager, in order to maintain the social relations of the teams, could veto new appointments, determine who does what work, monitor and judge individual performance and initiate termination procedures (Johnson 1996, 8).

A further initiative under the contracts at CRA was to break the connection between payment systems and working hours. This involved a return to a 40-hour working week (up from 38), the introduction of 12 hour shifts, elimination of overtime payments and absorption (or buying out) of all allowances and special payments. To compensate employees for the different shift patterns or rosters, a role allowance was payable to certain employees. A geographical remoteness or area allowance of 25 per cent of the base salary was also part of the new salary package. The purpose was to augment the base salary by these allowances making it more attractive for employees to accept the contracts instead of award conditions.

Employee worth is assessed according to the 'CRA Work Performance Review' (PER). The PER review is conducted annually and managerial judgement is made of the employee's performance in three areas:

- technical abilities
- programming abilities
- people (teamworking) skills.

The employee is required, in the presence of the supervisor, to evaluate his or her own work standard as well as that of the supervisor. The supervisor is then required to assess the employee's performance under safety, team commitment, technical and work standard, and flexibility (reported in CRA (Comalco) Weipa Case, Print no M8600, 63 Industrial Reports 138 at 167, and Exhibit, PER Review Process, 42). Such assessment procedures are also linked to job tenure. A failure to meet company expectations could result in redundancy. Through a process of selected 'weeding out', up to a third of CRA's workforce was made redundant. CRA contracts provide for a company-based process of review. Where an employee who believes that he/she has been the subject of unfair treatment (including the salary determined by his/her supervisor), the employee has the right to appeal under a system known as the 'fair treatment process'. This involves the next management layer taking up the employee's complaint and either confirming or rejecting a decision of a lower ranked supervisor (Appendix to CRA Staff Contract, Source, AWU). The process is firmly in the hands of management and actionable by the employee only at common law. No third-party independent adjudication is provided for in this process.

UNION RESPONSE

Unions responded to the push for individual contracts by mounting a picket of company operations. They also made applications to the AIRC to use its arbitral powers to protect the role of the unions in collective bargaining. This involved trying to prevent CRA from using individual staff contracts or alternatively, in the face of widespread employee support for individual contracts, to have their terms brought formally into the collective bargaining system. This involved attempting to convert individual contracts into a 'paid rates' award (an award containing all wages and conditions paid under CRA's staff contracts).

The AIRC agreed with union claims that the company's individual contracts discriminated against those employees who sought to remain under the award. The AIRC concluded that the actions of the company were contrary to the objects of the Industrial Relations Act which 'provides for a legislated federal system of industrial relations based on the existence of registered organisations of employers and employees'. The AIRC found that the public interest would not be served by the 'effective elimination of [unions] in the employee/employer relationship and its replacement by a system of individual contracts' and decided to make an interim award as sought by the unions (CRA [Comalco] Bell Bay Case, Print no. L7449, 56 Industrial Reports 403 at 442). The AIRC decision was subsequently quashed on appeal by the Federal Industrial Court. The Court held on narrow technical grounds that the AIRC had the right to make the interim award but concluded that the AIRC erred in law in reaching the conclusions that it did (Decision, CRA [Comalco] Bell Bay Case, Appeal by CRA, 61 Industrial Reports 455).

Following the above Case, CRA began implementing staff contracts at its Weipa mine and refining operations. Unions began a new case in November 1995 before the AIRC, seeking to amend existing CRA awards at Weipa in order to insert annual salaries and related conditions based on those contained in CRA staff contracts. This approach relied on the AIRC's powers to apply equal pay for equal work as decided in the 1972 Equal Pay Case. The union case was given added publicity by being presented by former Australian Prime Minister R J Hawke (also a former President of the ACTU). The case centred on CRA's contention that a two party staff relationship is more productive than a collectively bargained (award) one (CRA Employer submission to AIRC, reported in CRA [Comalco] Weipa Case, 63 Industrial Reports 138, at 150-151).

After a lengthy hearing and a blockade of Weipa Port by the remaining award employees and a national stevedoring strike, the AIRC found that work practices at CRA's Comalco (Weipa) operations had improved as a 'direct consequence of the introduction of shift contracts'. However, the AIRC also found that the improvements in work practices at CRA could have been obtained 'through a system other than the staff contract system'. The AIRC rejected the union claim under the 1972 Equal Pay Case holding that the principle of equal pay only applied in cases of gender discrimination in pay. Gender was not an issue in contract pay (Decisions CRA [Comalco] Weipa Decision, 63 Industrial Reports 138, at 150, 190).

The AIRC agreed with unions that CRA had behaved in a discriminatory way to union members. The AIRC concluded that the policy of CRA was to 'discriminate against award employees solely on their choice to enter into collective bargaining through their respective union rather than negotiate [on a] one to one basis' (Decisions CRA [Comalco] Weipa Decision, 63 Industrial Reports 138, at 151). The AIRC found that it had a general obligation to resolve disputes between employers and registered organisations (unions) under the Industrial Relations Act. This also extended to furthering the bargaining rights of registered organisations in accordance with Australia's international treaty obligations with the International Labor Organisation (ILO).

At Weipa, the AIRC issued interim orders that CRA extend staff contract benefits to the remaining award employees (75 out of a workplace of about 650) on the basis that they were prepared to accept all the terms of the staff contracts. Despite the apparent union victory, problems remained in giving legal effect to the interim orders. Subsequently, the awards were varied to reflect the new conditions, but award employees also had to give commitments to work in accordance with the conditions contained in the staff contracts. Meanwhile, the vast majority of employees had already opted for contracts.

OUTCOMES

The move towards making individual employment contracts is often justified by arguments about the need to make labour relations as flexible as possible to better reflect and respond to unstable market conditions. The aim is to transfer risk from the market place into the employment relationship. This was certainly the case of CRA. Individual employment contracts resulted in a resurgence of managerial authority. Employee consent was manufactured by creating a new value system based on a company-controlled performance assessment and individual accountability system. This was underpinned by an internal system of justice and fairness without the recourse to third parties. It was designed to:

- ensure centralised financial control over wages and conditions
- link wages to market uncertainty
- protect the new system from disruption and uncertainty.

This process formed part of a broader competitive and cost minimisation strategy. Such a strategy was deemed necessary in order to win back employee relations (as opposed to industrial relations) and secure the company's long term competitive prospects. One irony of the CRA case is that it occurred not only in an industry with a strong collectivist history, but also under a Federal Labor Government. The experience of CRA shows how fragile union loyalties can be, given appropriate circumstances and inducements. It is also an example of a company adopting a strategic view of HRM, which was linked to broader business objectives that justified de-unionisation.

REVIEW QUESTIONS

1. Was CRA wrong in pursuing individual contracts?
2. To what extent was CRA's approach representative of a 'strategic' approach to HRM and IR?
3. Do unions need more sophisticated strategies to combat companies such as CRA?
4. What benefits and disadvantageous exist for both management and employees of the CRA approach?
5. Do individual contracts necessarily mean individual bargaining or merely a standardisation of HRM practice?

FURTHER READING

Ludeke, J. (1996) *The Line in the Sand: The Long Road to Staff Employment at Comalco*, Wilkinson Books, Melbourne.

Timo, N. (1997), 'The Management of Individualism in an Australian Mining Company', *Employee Relations*, 19(4), 337-351.

CHAPTER 10

Negotiation Skills

*'Here's the rule for bargains. "Do other men, for they would do you."
That's the true business precept.'*

Charles Dickens, 1812-70

LEARNING OBJECTIVES

After studying this chapter, you should be able to:

- understand main features of a bargaining relationship
- identify the sub-processes which occur in the negotiation process
- detail the main characteristics of the behavioural approach to bargaining and negotiation
- describe the negotiation processes commonly found in our selected five South East Asian countries and how they differ from those found in Australia.

INTRODUCTION

As we discussed in Chapter 2, managerial policy is one of the main causes of industrial disputes in Australia. This suggests that managers have not been particularly skilful when introducing change into the working lives of employees. This failure has in turn driven workers into the arms of their trade unions, which are seen as the only source of redress for workplace grievances. Arguably, one of the major reasons for this inadequacy is that managers have long been able to introduce a divisive policy or a change, and then leave it to their industrial relations specialists and industrial tribunals to sort out any problems that followed when workers took issue with the effect. The move towards decentralised bargaining and the desire on the part of a growing number of firms to implement human resource management programs suggest there is an increasing need for managers to think more seriously about their negotiation practices. The purpose of this chapter, therefore, is to focus on the use of negotiation skills in managing workers and handling industrial disputes in the workplace.

NEGOTIATION SKILLS

In this section we look at what it takes to be an effective negotiator. The personal characteristics of a negotiator can be vital to outcome of any bargaining process. It is generally accepted that two of the primary characteristics in this regard are honesty and integrity. The former Australian Prime Minister and former President of the ACTU (Australian Council of Trade Unions), Bob Hawke, believed it was these particular qualities which created a successful negotiator. Hawke maintained that one of the reasons behind his own success in negotiation was that other people accepted his honesty and integrity. They know, Hawke believed, that he had not told an untruth and that his word could be relied upon. Honesty was vital. Hawke felt that it was impossible to overstate the importance of telling the truth in negotiations (cited in McCarthy 1989, 6-7).

Another important quality is the ability to be detached. By this it is meant that a successful negotiator must be able to divorce the outcomes of negotiations from personal success or failure. Negotiators are representatives who should do their best for their constituency, but should not take an outcome personally (Holdsworth 1987, 64). Similarly, another quality is the ability to refrain from making personal attacks on those on the other side. There must be a willingness to recognise the interdependence that must occur between negotiating parties if a successful outcome is to be achieved. In this regard it is important to recognise that industrial relations is an ongoing process, and that it is very likely that the same representatives from each side will encounter one another again. It pays therefore to build a relationship of personal respect, whether one likes the people concerned or not.

Still other important qualities are the ability to be an effective communicator and the ability to be able to identify and effectively use different sources of influence over opponents. This, in turn, involves the ability to recognise and be able to cater for the needs of opponents, at least to some extent (Holdsworth 1987, 171-3). The ability to work in an atmosphere of ambiguity and uncertainty is also a substantial personal quality. This is because it is often the case that the true objectives of an opponent remain unknown, and are gradually ascertained by making and testing assumptions. Such a process involves a measure of risk-taking. A temperament that is capable of withstanding the tribulations of taking risks is thus an asset for a negotiator (Holdsworth 1987, 174-5). This of course may be stressful. One oil industry negotiator speculated that the unusually high number of industrial relations practitioners suffering heart attacks by their early fifties that he had witnessed, was the result of the stress involved in negotiation.

To these personal qualities of a negotiator, we can add the findings of research conducted by McCarthy (1989), who identified certain behavioural characteristics that appear to distinguish successful negotiators. These characteristics included:

- the propensity to ask many questions
- the inclination to test understanding of things, particularly when final decisions were close
- the predilection to 'flag' intentions to see the reaction from the other side before committing to a course of action
- the tendency to avoid giving away unnecessary information for fear providing the basis for counter-attacks by the other side (1989, 7).

The personal characteristics one brings to the art of negotiation are therefore important. However, such characteristics cannot be divorced from the negotiation process itself. Personal characteristics that allow a negotiator to be successful in legal or a diplomatic context may not be successful in an industrial context. For example, the adversarial nature of legal negotiations in a court room, where the combatants and their clients go their separate ways after the proceedings are concluded, lend themselves to a different bargaining style than is normally found in industrial relations. In industrial bargaining, the participants are often in an on-going relationship even after agreements have been reached. It is important therefore to look at the industrial negotiation process.

THEORIES OF NEGOTIATION PROCESSES

In this section we look at some of the main theories used to explain the nature and conduct of negotiation processes. According to Magenau and Pruitt (1979), there are essentially three approaches to studies in this area:

1. applied mathematics (or games theory), where theories are developed on the basis of how a 'rational' individual might be expected to behave during negotiation processes
2. empirical observation, where theories are developed on the basis watching how people actually behave in real world negotiation processes
3. experimental observation, where theories are made on the basis of how people behave in simulated negotiation settings (1979,181).

Theories developed by empirical observation have had the most influence in academic circles and among practitioners. Games theory and experimental observation have had a more limited impact. Games theory, because its assumptions of human rationality have been overly ambitious in describing behaviour where power and personalities play a major part in the dynamics. Experimental observation, because the findings gained from simulated settings have been difficult to transfer to uncontrolled settings of the real world. Consequently, we will confine further discussion to empirical observation theories. We will begin with a definition of negotiation processes, and then move on to examine some of the major theories developed from empirical observation.

Defining Negotiation Processes

As a way of defining the meaning of negotiation processes, Rubin and Brown (1975) have suggested that they normally involve:

1. at least two parties
2. a conflict of interest over one or more issues
3. a special kind of voluntary relationship between the parties
4. the exchange of resources
5. the resolution of intangible issues
6. the presentation and evaluation of demands or proposals, followed by concessions and counter-proposals (1975, 18).

In addition, industrial relations negotiations tend to differ from other types of negotiation, in that:

7. the relationship between management and trade unions is often on-going and can last for years
8. the parties do not usually, for legal and practical reasons, have the option of breaking off their relationship permanently
9. there are normally specific legal requirements governing the conduct of negotiations
10. negotiators need to understand the meaning and effect of labour contract clauses
11. labour contracts are relatively permanent and difficult to re-negotiate, and that attempts to renegotiate such issues tend to cause industrial problems (Loughran 1985, xxii-xxiii).

The Walton and McKersie Model

One of the most influential theories of negotiation processes in industrial relations is contained Walton and McKersie's (1965), *A Behavioral Theory of Labor Negotiations*. The theory put forward by these two authors provides many valuable insights into negotiation strategies and tactics, and has stood the test of time. Subsequent theories have either been derivatives or formulated as criticisms of Walton and McKersie's main arguments. The general theme of the theory argues that labour negotiations consist of four main systems of activity, each with its own function and internal logic for the interacting parties. These four activities are referred to as 'sub-processes'.

The first sub-process is called 'distributive bargaining', where the function is to resolve pure conflicts of interest. This refers to a situation where the basic goals of the parties are in conflict, either in respect of values or the allocation of resources. This type of bargaining or negotiation is referred to by the authors as a 'fixed sum situation' because the gains made by one party will be at the expense of the other. A typical issue falling within the rubric of this sort of bargaining is the allocation of company profits between shareholders and workers. Negotiations over a wage increase for workers, if successful, will invariably be at the expense of returns to shareholders.

The second sub-process is called 'integrative bargaining', where the function is to find common interests, and solve the problems confronting both parties. This type of bargaining refers to a situation where the goals of the parties are not in fundamental conflict, but can be integrated, at least to some degree. In this case, the nature of the problem allows solutions benefiting both parties. Such bargaining is referred to as a 'variable sum game'. Typical of issues with integrative potential are issues pertaining to health and safety, where both management and labour have a common interest in reducing accidents, injuries and diseases in the marketplace.

The third sub-process is called 'attitudinal structuring', where the function is to influence the attitudes of participants towards each other as a means of affecting their relationship. This particular process involves each party trying to influence the other to adopt a more favourable attitude towards it, using friendliness, offering trust, conferring respect and encouraging cooperation.

The final sub-process is call 'intra-organisational bargaining', where the purpose is to achieve consensus within each interacting group. This type of bargaining is essentially a socio-emotional processes. It is concerned with the reconciliation of attitudes and expectations within the constituencies represented (i.e. employers and workers), with outcomes seen as feasible and practical by the negotiators.

Each of these sub-processes has its own strategies and tactics, appropriate to the ends being sought. The strategy associated with the distributive model is to make a firm commitment to a position before the opponent is able to do so. Each party, it is suggested, should commence negotiations with a 'target' and a 'resistance' point. The former is the optimum outcome each side wishes to achieve at the end of the negotiations, the latter is the minimum outcome each side is prepared to accept. As each side commences negotiations in ignorance of the other's real target and resistance points, the early stages of negotiation are for eliciting information from the other side about its target and resistance points, while trying to reveal as little as possible about its own. Thus, the tactics of distributive bargaining may involve good amount of deception, bluff and threats. These, however, must be used with caution. For if wrongly used, or overdone, they may undermine the credibility of a party or cause the negotiations to break down altogether. Where threats are used, there must be the ability to carry out the threat (e.g. a trade union foreshadowing a strike), and the other side must be convinced that the threat will be carried out. Generally, subtle threats are more effective than blatant ones, and experienced negotiators know that those with strength need not make threats. The use of bluff or threats may be designed either to convey a misleading impression of one's own strength or to cause the other side to relax its resistance point, for example by a union manipulating management's aversion for industrial action (Walton and McKersie 1965, 58-72, 107-111).

At the conclusion of the initial phase of negotiations, the parties should have established a settlement range. This is the range within which an offer from the other side would be acceptable. At this point, the strategy of commitment comes into play. In essence, this involves assessing accurately the opponent's likely resistance point, and locking oneself in to a demand close to that resistance point. Walton and McKersie (1965) supply the following example. Suppose a company, in negotiations with a union, has a resistance point of a maximum pay increase of 15¢ an hour. The union negotiators accurately assess the resistance point, and succeed in conspicuously and irrevocably committing the union to a position of a pay demand of 14.5¢, although its own resistance point is a minimum of 9¢. Thereby, it is claiming virtually the whole of the settlement range, and management because of its own resistance point, will have to concede the demand (1965, 83). However, it is important for negotiators not to commit themselves too soon. Up to a certain point in time, flexibility is desirable, so as to be able to abandon untenable concessions, without loss of face. It is obviously important to have an accurate idea about the opponent's resistance point before acting to narrow the range. Part of the tactics may also involve preventing the opponent from becoming prematurely committed. This may be done by such devices as preventing the opponent from reducing his position to writing, breaking off communication temporarily or deliberately misunderstanding the opponent's position (Walton and McKersie 1965, 111-6).

The basic strategy of integrative bargaining is for both parties to hold-off making firm commitments, while discussing the causes of a problem, and possible alternative solutions. The aim is to ensure maximum exchange of information to fully identify mutual problems and the largest possible range of solutions. This is expected to ensure the maximum gain for each party. The tactics include first identifying the problem. This can be done with ongoing discussion without waiting for the commencement of formal negotiations for a new contract. Once formal negotiations are under way, problems that have integrative potential can be listed as agenda items to be discussed. Stating agenda items as problems rather than demands can also be helpful, as can setting them out in specific rather than broad terms. The general purpose of this tactic is to expose candidly differences between the two parties, as a first step towards an agreement.

Searching for alternative solutions is the second part of integrative bargaining. This involves giving advanced notice and allowing as much time as possible for the generation of possible options. It will also involve holding preliminary discussions, without the pressure of time or the threat of sanctions, to explore unfamiliar items jointly and informally. It also involves putting these types of items on the agenda first, where there is greater likelihood of success, and keeping any early resolutions tentative until everything is agreed. The third aspect of the tactic is selecting the best alternative. This involves discussing preferences for possible solutions accurately and avoiding the selective preferences of an opponent. It also involves making proposals divisible, so that parts of different proposals may be combined to give an integrative solution. The conditions necessary for integrative bargaining to succeed are genuine motivation on each side to settle, the full and free exchange of all relevant information, and the sufficient trust in each other's genuineness (Walton and McKersie 1965, 144-61).

The essence of 'attitudinal structuring' is changing the attitudes of the opponent towards your own side, and making them more positive. The tactics of attitudinal structuring are based on the interaction of two behavioural theories. These theories are 'balance theory' and 'cognitive dissonance'. Using this approach, the purpose is to create psychological stress in the opponent by encouraging the person to feel that, although he or she dislikes you, he or she has common preferences with your side. The theory suggests this tension will be resolved in terms of more favourable attitudes by the opponent. Ways of creating a perception of common preferences may involve references made to personal interests shared with an opponent, or the use of familiar arguments and reasoning. It may also involve introducing mutual problems or goals wherever possible. It may involve noting similar dislikes for outsiders, or emphasising the common fate of both parties, for example, in the event of a strike. It may involve emphasising common backgrounds in negotiation, or conferring status on an opponent, for example, by holding negotiations in a prestigious venue or allowing an opponent to use facilities such as telephones and photocopiers.

The strategy and tactics of intra-organisational bargaining are designed to achieve internal consensus and avoid unrealistic expectations among the negotiator's constituent body. Negotiators in this instance should seek to maintain flexibility by keeping preferences tentative. They can communicate information to their constituents about the feasibility of attaining any given objectives, and try to achieve a realistic agenda by limiting participation by aggressive and outspoken individuals. Tactics designed to revise unrealistic expectations by constituents include the use of expertise to argue rationally against exaggerated expectations, or the use of personal prestige and power to sway constituents. They can also involve efforts to revise expectations through personal experience (e.g. include a militant representative on the negotiating team, so that the person might acquire first-hand experience of the other side's position).

The Walton and McKersie (1965) theory has had a major influence on the way negotiators have engaged in industrial relations bargaining. Empirical research in the United States and New Zealand has been largely supportive of the theory. In their study of industrial relations negotiation in the United States, for example, Peterson and Tracy (1976) found in distributive bargaining, bargainers felt they were more successful when their own side's bargaining power was strong and work stoppages seemed unlikely. Integrative bargaining was seen as more successful when:

- the other side was cooperative and trustworthy
- the two sides had a long-standing bargaining relationship
- commitment was withheld by both sides until the causes and feelings about problems had been discussed
- information was freely available
- each party was free of constraints from their own constituents and from time pressure to reach agreement.

Attitudinal structuring was found to be positive when:
- the two sides experienced positive emotions about each other
- there were feelings of respect and recognition of each other's legitimacy
- praise was given by each side for the other's efforts
- both sides were far-sighted about their working relationship.

It was also found that success in integrative bargaining was significantly related to positive attitudinal structuring, which supported Walton and McKersie's (1965) views about the commonality of the tactics employed in these two sub-processes. In relation to intra-organisational bargaining, it was found that there was a greater likelihood of success when:
- negotiators could influence their constituents because the probability and costs of a work stoppage were high
- negotiators had power and authority within their own team
- negotiators were confident of approval from their constituents
- team mates were friendly
- there was freedom from constituent pressure (1976, 41-5).

Smith and Turkington's (1980) study of negotiation practices in New Zealand replicated Peterson and Tracy (1976) United States study. The results of were similarly supportive, except in relation to distributive bargaining. In this case it was found that management and unions in New Zealand felt that bargaining power had little bearing on the outcome of distributive bargaining. This finding was attributed to compulsory arbitration, which saw negotiated outcomes in trend-setting agreements reached between powerful trade unions and large employers 'flow on' to other agreements regardless of the bargaining power of the participants. As a consequence, those weaker, or less powerful parties felt they had relatively little control over the distributive bargaining process (Smith and Turkington 1980, 368). Smith and Turkington's (1976) findings had considerable relevance to Australia when compulsory arbitration was still a major force in collective agreements. But it is less relevant now that bargaining frameworks have been decentralised. Unfortunately, there are no equivalent broad Australian studies. A related study that is supportive of the Walton and McKersie's (1965) model was by Holdsworth (1987). As in Smith and Turkington's New Zealand study, Holdsworth found that the Australian system of compulsory arbitration imposed obstacles that influenced findings about negotiation processes. These obstacles included impediments to the free exchange of information; lack of commitment to achieving negotiated settlements; prevention of the development of mature relationships between the parties; suspicion on the part of trade unions and management of each other's motives; and denial by each side of the other's fundamental rights (1987, 170; see also, Fox et al. 1995, 574).

Studies criticising the theory have been thin on the ground, but two are worth noting. The first is by Morley (1979), who has suggested that the theory is too vague and should be refined and improved. It was argued that distributive bargaining and integrative bargaining should be viewed as major alternative processes, with attitudinal structuring and intra-organisational bargaining being treated as supporting sub-processes (1979, 214-7). The second critical study by Shea (1980) asserted that the theory has only reached the stage of classifying behaviour, rather than predicting when one kind of behaviour (e.g. distributive bargaining) should be adopted, rather than another (e.g. integrative bargaining) (1980, 715-6).

Other Theories

A number of other theories have adopted a similar approach to Walton and McKersie (1965) either refining, redefining or elaborating their description of negotiation processes. Cohen (1983), for example, has suggested that there are several ways in which negotiating parties can create the atmosphere of mutual trust and respect, both of which are needed if satisfactory settlements are to be reached. The practice arising from the theory in this case is that the parties should approach negotiations with the conviction that it is possible to achieve a 'win-win' outcome. They should also treat the process as more important than the outcome, and try to establish a long-term relationship with the other side. They should start the negotiations in a collaborative manner and on the basis that both sides are engaged in a mutual problem-solving exercise. In addition, they should start with congruent rather than divergent interests and try to establish a climate for success by initially agreeing on some matters. Quantifiable issues (e.g. wages) should be moved to the last item on the agenda, after other issues have been settled. They should also avoid making personal attacks on representatives of the other side, and allow plenty of time for negotiation because achieving results takes time. Finally, they should allow ample free round table discussion to enable the various attitudes and views of the parties to surface.

Fisher and Ury (1984) offer a win-win type theory that specifically deals with negotiating strategies for resolving industrial conflict. Referring to their approach as 'principled negotiation', the authors suggest that successful outcomes rest on four basic premises. First, 'people' engaged in negotiation must remain separate from the problem. Second, negotiators must focus on 'interests' and not positions. Third, negotiators must endeavour to generate a variety of 'options' before deciding on action. Fourth, the 'criteria' of assessment must be based on some objective standard. Fisher and Ury's (1981) concept of 'principled negotiation' is set out in Table 10.1.

The advantages of this approach to negotiation were summed up by the authors. They argued that unlike positional bargaining, principled negotiation focused on basic interests, mutually agreed options and fair standards, and as a result, a wise agreement normally produced. Principled negotiation allowed the parties to gradually and efficiently arrive at consensus, without the transaction costs digging into set positions, only to have to dig back out again. Separating people from the problem permitted each party to treat the other negotiator empathically as a human being. The result was amicable agreements (Fisher and Ury 1981, 14).

Table 10.1 Positional bargaining versus 'principled' or win-win negotiation

PRINCIPLED or WIN-WIN NEGOTIATION	POSITIONAL BARGAINING	
Negotiation is on the merits	Problem: which approach to take?	
	Soft Bargaining	Hard Bargaining
All parties are viewed as problem-solvers.	The other party is viewed as a friend	The other party is viewed as an adversary.
Negotiations aim to reach a wise agreement arrived at efficiently and amicably for mutual gain.	Negotiations aim to reach an agreement.	Negotiations aim to win.
The people and the problems are separated.	Concessions are made to build a relationship.	Concessions are demanded as the condition of a relationship.
Negotiators are treated softly, but problems dealt with firmly.	A soft approach is taken to both other party and to problems.	A hard approach is taken to both other party and to problems.
Negotiations are not concerned with issues of interpersonal trust.	The other party is trusted.	Other party is distrusted.
Attention is on interests, not positions.	Position is altered easily.	Position is held strongly.
Interests are examined.	Offers are made.	Threats are made.
'Resistance' points are avoided.	'Resistance' point is disclosed.	'Resistance' point is hidden.
New, mutually beneficial options are created.	Unequal concessions are granted to other party to obtain an agreement.	Unfair concessions are demanded of other party to reach agreement.
Numerous alternatives are generated and final choice between them is delayed.	A single solution agreeable to the other party is sought.	A single solution agreeable to own party is sought.
It is essential objective criteria are in agreement.	Agreement must be reached.	Position must be met.
Agreement is not concerned with issues of strength of will.	Contests of strength of will should be avoided.	Contests of strength of will should be won.
Reason and be open to reasons; yield to principle, not pressure.	Yield to pressure.	Apply pressure.

Source: Based on Fisher and Ury 1984, 13

In another theory, Kochan and Osterman (1995) have speculated on the success of negotiation processes in organisations termed 'mutual gains enterprises'. This term is used to describe enterprises that have developed in a way that allows Walton and McKersie's integrative bargaining strategies to be successfully employed. The study found that a number of interlocking factors at different levels of the organisation needed to develop if integrative bargaining practices were to be successful. Three levels of organisational activity were identified: (1) the workplace, (2) personnel policy-making, and (3) strategic decision-making.

The central argument of these authors is that policies need to reinforce one another at different levels in an organisation to produce the necessary support for a 'mutual gains enterprise'. This multi-level support is also necessary if the negotiation system is to achieve mutual benefits and yet maintain organisational competitiveness at our high standards of living (Kochan and Osterman 1995, 46-7). It is suggested that creating a mutual gains enterprise starts at the workplace level. Here the organisation must first hire employees with high levels of technical, analytical and behavioural skills, and positive attitudes towards work. Then there is a need for the firm to fully utilise the education and skills of workers on the job. Such utilisation must preclude a narrow approach to job design and instead must allow workers to move freely across task and function boundaries. Moreover, employees and their representatives must be allowed to engage in problem solving and decision-making in relation to their immediate work environment. Finally, there is a need to create a climate of trust between managers, workers and their representatives. Without such a climate, it is argued that it will not be possible to develop integrative forms of negotiation that span all the workplace issues necessary to produce and sustain mutual gains. Interestingly, Kochan and Osterman (1995) believe that establishing such a climate does not necessarily mean there will be no conflict. In fact, industrial relations specialists, trade union leaders and the like, are all held to be capable of improving a firm's competitive advantage because they act as agencies through which conflicts can be openly aired and quickly resolved (1995, 47-52).

At the personnel policy level, Kochan and Osterman (1995) suggest that the prospects of integrative bargaining are improved if firms follow three basic principles. First, it is recommended that organisations adopt staffing policies that, as far as possible, guarantee employment security. This is seen as promoting employee commitment, flexibility and loyalty. However, this does not mean that organisations must commit themselves to the principle of lifetime employment in the manner of large Japanese corporations. What it mean is that firms should instead be prepared to incur significant costs before resorting to lay-offs, and that this measure should only be used as a last resort. The second principle that firms should adopt is a strong commitment to training and development strategies. This is seen as particularly important because firms are not able to guarantee lifetime employment. The best they can do is to give their workers the skills that make them flexible, and allow them to transfer between functions and firms during course of their careers. In other words, it is recommended that both mangers and workers need to be encouraged to embrace a commitment to lifelong learning. The third principle concerns compensation. Organisations need to secure flexibility in the price of labour. Achieving this may be difficult, but the evidence provided in the study suggests that the best firms applying integrative bargaining techniques all utilise incentive schemes. Given that work is becoming increasingly group and team-based, in practice this means an increasing emphasis on group rather than individual incentive schemes. However, it is argued that these schemes should be carefully designed so that they do not lead individuals to maximise their own short-term compensation at the expense of long-term organisational goals (Kochan and Osterman 1995, 52-5).

At the strategic level, where integrative bargaining was working, firms tended to adopt policies and practices to create and sustain high employee commitment to the organisation. The central issue here was found to be the firm's competitive strategies. Companies that relied solely on lowering costs, and in particular lowering wage costs, were inclined to have a low-trust workplace and a competitive negotiation framework. Companies that relied on quality, innovation, flexibility, customer service and workforce training, had high-trust workplaces and integrative bargaining frameworks. In this connection the authors contrasted the strategies adopted by two United States airlines in the wake of the 1980s deregulation of the airline industry. The first, Continental, used a strategy of breaking labour contracts and lowering wages in order to cut airfares. The second, Delta Airlines, decided not to push for lower labour costs but to implement better quality control and provide more innovative times and routes. The end result was that Continental failed to generate employee commitment and for this and other reasons, eventually ended in bankruptcy. Delta, on the other hand, succeeded in maintaining profitability (though ultimately it too had to resort to lay-offs in 1993 when price wars broke out between the airlines) (Kochan and Osterman 1995, xxx).

Although Kochan and Osterman (1995) admit that the principles of their approach are idealised organisational practices, their survey suggests that the principles work in generating increased long-term productivity and quality, as well as greater worker satisfaction and more integrative negotiation processes. They also emphasise that there is no magic formula or single set of best practices for implementing the principles. Indeed, they cite evidence to suggest that, apart from green-field sites, there are no cases where all the principles have been implemented at once. At older work sites, for example, it was found that it was a matter of piecemeal and incremental change. At other work-sites it was the cumulative or combined effects of integrating their principles with other innovation in manufacturing and service delivery systems which was producing the best results.

In summary, a systemic approach through a number of levels of an organisation is needed to create the workplace climate conducive to improving integrative bargaining and thereby the foundations for a mutual gains enterprise (Kochan and Osterman 1995, 58-77). It needs to be recognised that the Australian negotiating environment is very different to the one in the United States. One obvious difference is the much higher level of unionisation in Australia. Also, as indicated earlier, there is little evidence that Australian companies are adopting the types of progressive human resource management policies which are required for fully fledged integrative bargaining systems. Having said this, the work Kochan and Osterman (1995) remains a valuable contribution to our understanding of what conditions need to be met for such systems to flourish.

Another theoretical approach to negotiation has been called 'phase models'. This approach both complements and addresses issues not covered by Walton and McKersie (1965). Fells (1985, 12), for example, has suggested that there are underlying but recognisable patterns in negotiations, which can be seen in the changing behaviour of those involved. Essentially, the idea is that negotiations pass through various stages. Typically, the first is an initial period of hard, competitive behaviour, in which the parties explore their differences. They then tend to move into a second, more cooperative, but still tentative phase, where they explore possible ways of resolving issues. Finally, they are said to revert to more competitive behaviour, in which they try to get the best possible deal for their respective sides (Fells 1995, 334). In another variation, Douglas (1957 1962) similarly suggests that negotiations pass through three phases. The first is said to be 'establishing the range', where the purpose is to establish the limits within which business can be done. The second is held to be 'reconnoitring the range', where the aim is to try to force the opponent into the least favourable part of the range. And the third is said to be 'precipitating the decision-making crisis', where the objective is to gain the feeling that each side has got the opponent to make its final best offer. Douglas (1962) argues that the two sides move from distributive behaviour in the first phase to integrative behaviour in the second, and to decision-making and action in the third stage.

WHEN NEGOTIATIONS STALL

Phase theories allow us to identify and tackle some important negotiating problems: first, how to ensure negotiating parties move from one stage of negotiation to the next at the same time, and second, how to overcome the deadlocks when they occur. Pruitt (1981), for example, has examined the problem of the 'concession dilemma', where one or both parties may wish to offer a concession to achieve a breakthrough in negotiations, yet hesitate to do so for fear of appearing weak. Such a phenomenon, it is suggested, can result in the continuation of distributive behaviour beyond an appropriate time, causing negotiations to collapse. Pruitt (1981) has suggested that, where trust is low, one party may test the other by indirect communication, involving disavowable conciliatory messages. The advantage of this, it is argued, is that it can be done simultaneously with the use of distributive tactics. One form of indirect communication can include sending signals by subtle nuances of wording to convey the possibility of a compromise. If a trade union, for instance, is prepared to lower its demands for a pay increase in return for a concession by management, a union negotiator might say: 'The proposal is unrealistic. Why, even 30¢ an hour would be too little.' This type of dialogue signals the possibility that a lower pay increase than initially demanded may be acceptable under certain circumstances. Another way of overcoming the concession dilemma is to organise private conferences between low-status members on the negotiating teams, or to use an (un)official intermediary to send a conciliation message to the other side.

However, deadlocks, according to Holdsworth (1987), should be viewed as an integral part of the bargaining process, rather than a sign that it has broken down, and may even be necessary as a tactical display of resolve or strength. When they do occur, it is not unusual for negotiators to express anger or frustration that their case has not been given a fair hearing. Holdsworth (1987) urges negotiators to resist these feeling, and to instead work through their feelings and allow their opponents to leave with a concrete proposal upon which to re-commence negotiations at some later stage. Moreover, it is suggested that when the parties do re-convene, they should try to avoid discussing why the negotiations broke down and confine themselves to the outstanding issues. This is to avoid the possibility of a repeat experience (1987, 101-2).

It is worth noting that useful distinctions have been made between different types of deadlocks. 'Process deadlocks', for example, are said to involve situations where the parties are not committed to the process of seeking a solution by negotiation. The symptoms include the failure of the real issues of the dispute to emerge, a lack of overlap in the parties' resistance points, and the use of pre-emptive, non-negotiation methods by one party. It is suggested that the only way out of a process deadlock is for the parties to re-negotiate their relationship and re-establish an agreed method for resolving their problems. They need to do so these things before they can address substantive issues.

'Issue deadlocks' are another form of deadlock. Normally these occur when one party's offer fails to match the other's demand. The parties in this instance may be aware of the direction in which they need to move to effect a settlement, but cannot transform their awareness into concrete and mutually acceptable solutions. This type of deadlock can often be resolved by a third party intervention, for example, by appointing a mediator. 'Image loss deadlocks' are yet another form, and these usually occur where the parties are aware of a mutually acceptable solution, but cannot commit themselves to it for fear of losing face. This may occur where one party is afraid to make a concession because this may present the appearance of weakness to the other side, or to the constituents they are representing. Concern about image loss is particularly strong in the presence of an audience, especially one which favours a hard line, or when a bargainer is accountable to constituents, or when future interaction with the same adversary is expected (Pruitt 1981, 23-5). Once again, third party intervention may be the only way to break a deadlock of this type (Pruitt 1981, 23-5; Fells 1985, 20-5). Overall, the most effective negotiators are those who are sufficiently prepared and imaginative to avoid or break deadlock situations (Fells 1995, 339).

Negotiation Skills

NEGOTIATION IN THE SELECTED FIVE SOUTH EAST ASIAN COUNTRIES

Each of the countries with which we have compared Australia in this book uses forms of collective bargaining to resolve disputes and to set wages and conditions. Malaysia and Singapore, in addition, use forms of compulsory arbitration similar to that applied in Australia. But the processes of negotiation which occur between trade unions and management in many South East Asian societies are very different from those which occur in Australia. This is partly because of the differences in economic, political and social contexts in which they are applied. It is also due to the differences in the cultural understandings and expectations of negotiations.

Looking more generally at the last of these differences, Hamzah-Sendut et al. (1990) have identified some interesting contrasts between the cultural contexts in which negotiations take place in western societies and Asian societies. In western societies, for example, it is suggested that the modes of interaction between managements and trade unions tend to be based on conflict and confrontation, with negotiations often taking on a 'win-lose' character. In Asian societies, however, there is held to be more of a tradition of harmony and cooperation, with negotiations taking on the character of working together toward a common corporate goal (1990, 14-5). Another significant difference that affects negotiations in Asian societies is the concept of 'face', a cultural trait that requires the giving of outward courtesy to others according to their social rank. This trait is closely tied to the high premium Asian cultures place on social harmony. To be made an object of public ridicule or criticism in front of others is a very painful experience in most Asian cultures. Consequently the on-going concern about preserving one's own face is matched only by giving of face to others. In this connection western cultures and Asian cultures have been contrasted, as respectively 'guilt' and 'shame' cultures. That is to say, in the west, behavioural controls are essentially internal, in the sense that people normally respond to the internal voice of their conscience. In Asia, however, the behavioural control mechanisms are external, in the sense that people normally respond to avoid losing face in front of others. To place this in the context of industrial relations, a negotiator that feels they have lost face may withdraw from negotiations altogether (1990, 21-3).

Another aspect of Asian cultures which differs from the west is the longer time-frame for decision making and the greater patience often demonstrated, a popular saying being 'patience brings peace' (Hamzah-Sendut et.al. 1990, 26). This can be a problem when east meets west in the context of business negotiations. Herb Cohen (1980), for example, relates the story of his first experience of negotiating with the Japanese over a business deal. His Japanese counterparts discovered his eagerness to conclude negotiations by a fixed deadline by innocently asking him about reserving a limousine to take him back to the airport for his return flight. After a week of entertainment, wining and dining and even enrolling him in a class to learn about Zen Buddhism, the actual negotiations only began on the eve of his departure, and were literally concluded as the limousine was approaching the airport. The result according to Cohen (1980), was the greatest Japanese victory since Pearl Harbor, with Cohen making all the concessions (1980, 93-5). A negotiator with more experience of the Japanese than Cohen, when asked about his deadline for finalising the deal, might have replied: 'As long as it takes' (Luthans 1992, 434).

Although there are some general cultural similarities between Asian societies, their experience of negotiation and collective bargaining is still very different. Details of the collective bargaining systems used in our South East Asian Five are discussed in Chapter 13. Here we highlight some issues relating to the negotiation process.

Japan

Observers of the Japanese industrial relations have remarked on the contrast between the public posturing of the Shunto, or spring offensive, in which trade unions engage in forms of ritual vilification of management, with the reality of negotiations between the parties at enterprise level. Shunto rituals may involve aggressive posturing; mass meetings and demonstrations; chanting of slogans; use of inflammatory placards; and the waving of special insignia, like arm and headbands. These rituals are to demonstrate solidarity in the face of the 'enemy'. However, these rituals are also little more than a show for external consumption (Ben Ari 1990, 106-7). As Shirai (1984) has noted, the processes of enterprise bargaining are marked by close cooperation between managers and trade unions. The mutual objectives and expectations of negotiations are seen as furthering the interests of the company. The permanent employees of large corporations expect to stay with their employers until retirement, and consequently bargaining is not viewed as a 'zero-sum' game, but rather as a mutual contribution to the success of a joint venture (1984, 314).

As such, it is not uncommon for trade union leaders to fraternise with management and to share information with them. During the actual bargaining process, there is a tendency to avoid public expression of differences and there is extensive collusion in behind-the-scenes negotiations as a means of reaching satisfactory settlements. As soon as wage problems are settled, strikes are normally called off and public demonstrations over noble causes are abruptly terminated (Ben Ari 1990, 107). Thus, the dominant emphasis in Japan is on integrative bargaining, to use Walton and McKersie's (1965) terminology. The culture of large Japanese organisations emphasises lifetime employment, the investment of substantial amounts of money in employee training and development, and their tradition of consultative decision-making. These factors all tend to generate employee loyalty and commitment, and no doubt bring Japanese enterprises close to Kochan and Osterman's ideal mutual gains type enterprise outlined above.

South Korea

The assumption that South Korea's industrial institutions are largely modelled on those of Japan is incorrect (a point we examine more fully in Chapter 13). The three 'sacred treasures' of Japanese management, namely, lifetime employment, seniority wages and enterprise unionism, have not developed as features of South Korean working life (Lee and Yoo 1987; Lie 1990). In South Korea, collective bargaining has not become legally institutionalised as in Japan. Unlike Japan, large-scale upheavals and open conflict have occurred from time to time, the most recent in 1998 and 1999 when changes were made in labour laws by the government of Kim Dae–Jung to make it easier for employers to sack workers.

The four dominant South Korean 'Chaebol' (large business conglomerates), unlike the Japanese 'Keiretsu' (large business corporations), have generally followed a policy of trying to crush or suppress independent trade unionism, and have done so ever since the end of the Korean War. They have been assisted in this task for most of the period by government policies. Devices such as the establishment of tame company unions, strikebreaking, using private armies of thugs (the so-called 'kusadae'), and calling in riot police to break up strikes and demonstrations have been commonplace in recent South Korean industrial history (Ogle 1990). Employers have only ever bargained when they have been forced to do so, such as when unions have been too strong to ignore. Even then, the approach by the companies has been little more than paternalistic gestures aimed at undermining worker support for the unions. Ogle (1990) reported that some managers even ordered lower management to use non-working hours to drink with workers to try to restore harmony in the workplace. The managers reported back that they were having a hard time digesting the copious intake of rice wine, but otherwise, little else had changed. (1990, 162).

Park (1993) agrees, noting that while changes in the laws introduced in 1987 have restricted the government from intervening on behalf of employers, it takes time before a new system of labour relations can emerge in the context of the rapid changes occurring in South Korean society (1993, 165). Under these circumstances, negotiation processes in South Korea have yet to take on the maturity of a developed industrial society. Consequently, Walton and McKersie's distributive bargaining, where outcomes are 'win-lose', remains the best description for the main form of negotiation in South Korea.

Singapore

The experience of Singapore presents a contrast to both Japan and South Korea. Since the mid-1960s, and following the succession of Singapore from the Malaysian federation, the trade union movement has almost become another arm of government. There has been a 'symbiotic relationship' between the ruling People's Action Party (PAP) and the National Trades Union Congress (NTUC) (Leggett 1993, 99). The dominant institution of Singaporean industrial relations has been the tripartite National Wage Council (NWC), set up in 1972, which consists of government, employer and trade union representatives. This has operated as a central or national wage fixing body that 'recommends' rates of annual wage increases. Considerable constraints are placed on collective bargaining by various legal controls, and attempts have been made to force the organised workforce into the NTUC, a body heavily influenced by the government. Singapore industrial relations institutions are also infused by a strong unitarist ideology, which emphasises the importance of national development and the subordination of sectional interests to this goal (Leggett 1993, 118).

Over the last 20 years, open conflict in the form of strikes has been rare, and labour-management relations have presented a peaceful appearance. Trade unions that have stepped out of line have been disbanded or re-structured in the name of maintaining the appearance of social harmony. In Singapore's circumstances, meaningful collective negotiations are confined to the national level, and even there, it is questionable how far the process is one of negotiation, given the nature of Singapore-style tripartism. Accordingly, it is difficult to make a precise judgement about what category of bargaining might best describe negotiations in Singapore. The tendency towards unitarist ideology and a dominant social culture of collectivism suggests Walton and Kersie's (1965) integrative bargaining. However, in a working world where managerial powers are beyond question and where workplace consultative mechanisms are all but non-existent, such a description is perhaps misleading, masking pluralist practices and bargaining processes which are better described as distributive bargaining.

Hong Kong

Hong Kong is an overwhelmingly Chinese society, even more than Singapore, but it presents many contrasts with Singapore. A largely British legal framework, based on principles of voluntarism, was established to regulate industrial relations in the colonial era. This framework was modified to accord with colonial circumstances and the government's policy of economic *laissez faire*. Over the past twenty years, Hong Kong's industrial relations have been relatively peaceful, at least in terms of industrial disputes. However, the statistics do not capture other forms of industrial action, which apparently have been more prevalent than in Singapore. Collective bargaining as a means of improving wages and conditions is still relatively undeveloped. A variety of reasons have been advanced to explain this situation. There is a lack of legislation compelling employers to recognise and bargain with trade unions. Trade unions are reluctant to make binding agreements for fear that they may hinder their freedom. Lastly, there is the lack of enthusiasm by trade union members to undertake industrial action to enforce their demands during negotiation (Levin and Ng 1993, 20-24, 41-8).

Survey evidence suggests that Hong Kong trade unionists generally prefer government legislation and formal joint consultation as methods for improving their terms and conditions of employment (Levin and Ng 1993, 42-3). Where formal procedures for joint consultation exist, they are often used by employees as *de facto* machinery for joint negotiations without trade union involvement. As in the case of Singapore, negotiations for job improvements tend to occur more at the individual than the collective level (Ng and Fung-Shuen 1989, 88-94). There is also a high level of labour turnover in most industries, so job dissatisfaction is often dealt with by labour mobility (Levin and Ng 1993, 43). Thus, in Hong Kong, as in Singapore, if for somewhat different reasons, models of negotiation based on the presumption of widespread collective bargaining have limited application. In terms of Walton and MeKersie's (1965) model, the same judgement applies, the dominant type of negotiation seems to be a weak form integrative bargaining.

Malaysia

The Malaysian system of industrial relations is based on a mixture of compulsory arbitration and collective bargaining. Tight government controls limit the right of workers to join unions and restrict trade union coverage of certain professions. The practice of collective bargaining is also severely constrained by various legal requirements. As a result, less than ten per cent of the workforce is currently covered by collective agreements. A major issue in Malaysia is the lack of recognition by employers of trade unions. If an employer refuses to recognise a trade union for collective bargaining purposes, the law stipulates that the matter can only be referred to the Director-General of Industrial Relations, a senior civil servant, and thence to the Minister of Human Resources. The latter has complete discretion, unfettered by any right of appeal to a court of law, to make the final decision. Employers have more often than not refused to recognise trade unions, and very few appeals to the Minister by trade unions have been successful.

Furthermore the legislative definition of collective bargaining effectively confines the process to the enterprise level, and to relations between single employers and single trade unions. There is also no obligation on the part of employers to bargain at all, even where recognition has been conceded to a trade union, or to bargain in good faith if the employer chooses not to negotiate. Finally, trade union rights to bargain in so-called 'pioneer enterprises' (i.e. those established with foreign capital) have been restricted to claims relating to minimum wages and conditions only (Ayudurai 1993, 84-5). In such an industrial relations climate, the scope for genuine negotiations between managers and workers is obviously very restricted. As such, the dominant type of negotiation, using Walton and McKersie's (1965) model, is distributive bargaining.

CONCLUSION

We have examined the personal attributes that distinguish successful negotiators and a range of theories relevant to the processes, strategies and tactics of negotiation. Such theories are useful tools for thinking and practicing the art of negotiation in industrial settings. But because of the complexity of negotiation processes, and the wide range of potential issues that can be the subject of bargaining, these theories should be used as broad guidelines only. The ability to compromise, make concessions, communicate effectively, and act with honesty, integrity and objectivity are as important as any theoretical understanding. As a general rule, organisations that have skilled negotiators, pro-active human resource practices, well understood avenues through which bargaining can take place, and an atmosphere trust between managers and workers, will find negotiations over wages and working conditions easier to conclude than organisations where these features are absent.

Our survey of our five selected South East Asian countries suggest that negotiation processes is different from those typically found in Australia because of the different cultural, economic, social and political contexts. Here again, as a general rule, it can be stated that the cultural values of these countries and their industrial relations systems are more unitarist than those found in Australia, a country with so-called 'western' values. A greater concern for outward harmony and a generally lower level of industrial disputes (South Korea being the exception) seem to suggest there is less need to be concerned about negotiation skills in the area of industrial relations. Having said this, however, there is much evidence of covert conflict in these South East Asian countries. This covert conflict is particularly evident in countries like Hong Kong and Singapore, where high levels of labour turnover are a natural part of working life. Consequently, there is a need in these countries to confront problems more openly and to develop more effective negotiation frameworks to deal with the hidden costs of covert conflict.

REVIEW QUESTIONS

1. How can improved negotiation skills on the part of management and unions contribute to a more harmonious and productive workplace?
2. What are the characteristics of a good negotiator?
3. Outline the main features of Walton and McKersie's (1965) behavioural theory of labour negotiations. How far is this model applicable to Australia?
4. What are the key features of a 'mutual gains enterprise'? How is such an enterprise related to Walton and McKersie's (1965) model?
5. Discuss the value of phase models to negotiation theory.
6. What general cultural differences are there between Asian and Western societies in terms of the negotiation process?
7. 'Models of negotiation developed in a western context are only applicable where collective bargaining is free and untrammelled by government regulation and control.' Discuss, in relation to the five selected South East Asian countries.

FURTHER READING

Deery, S. and Mitchell, R. (eds) (1993) *Labour Law and Industrial Relations in Asia,* Longman Cheshire, Melbourne.

Fisher, R. and Ury, Y. (1981) *Getting to Yes: Negotiating Agreement Without Giving In.* Houghton Miflin, Boston.

Holdsworth, W. (1987) *Advocacy and Negotiation in Industrial Relations*, 3rd Edn, Law Book Company.

Hudson, M. and Hawkins. L. (1995) *Negotiating Employee Relations,* Pitman, Melbourne.

McCarthy, (1989) *Developing Negotiating Sklls and Behaviour,* CCH, North Ryde, Sydney.

Stephenson, G. and Brotherton, C. (eds) (1979) *Industrial Relations: A Social-Psychological Approach,* John Wiley, Chichester.

Wertheim, E., Love, A., Peck, C. and Littlefield, L. (1998) *Skills for Resolving Conflict*, Eruditions Publishing, Melbourne.

CHAPTER 11

Equity in Industrial Relations

'We hold these truths to be self-evident: that all men and women are created equal'

Elizabeth Stanton, 1815-1902. (US Suffragette)

LEARNING OBJECTIVES

After reading this chapter you should be able to:

- define the concept of equity
- understand the significance of equity issues in industrial relations
- describe and evaluate the economic rationalist, civil libertarian and social justice approaches to equity
- explain the reasons for inequalities and continuing gender bias in the workplace in Australia
- describe and evaluate the position of women in the workforce in Japan, South Korea and Singapore.

INTRODUCTION

Few would disagree with the statement that there should be equity at work. However, this apparent consensus masks considerable disagreement about what constitutes 'equity'. For some equity simply means that talent should be rewarded irrespective of race or gender. Others regard large wage disparities, the growth of a class of working poor, a sizeable group of long term unemployed and high rates of injury and illness at work as inconsistent with fairness and equity. Clearly disagreements about equity involve disagreements about values. Currently, the dominant ideology of governments and policy-makers is one of economic rationalism. Economic rationalism is a philosophy that emphasises the primacy of the market in the organisation of society, where the overriding objective is to achieve an efficient and profitable economy. From this perspective, welfare benefits are seen as a privilege. They are reluctantly dispensed and must be earned, rather than granted as a right for those in need (McMahon,

Thomson and Williams, 2000, 20). Proponents of economic rationalism argue that individuals should be free to make choices without external controls. An alternative and opposing ideology is that of social justice. The social justice perspective holds that all citizens should be able to participate equally in economic, social and political life, and that it is the role of the state to try to reduce inequalities in respect of income, gender, race, age, location and disability. The state should also provide support for those who have suffered misfortunes such as unemployment, accidents, illness and marriage breakdown (Hawke and Howe 1991, 22). Advocates of social justice argue that human beings are entitled to some quality of life and that this encompasses such things as fair pay, safety in the work environment and decent medical care.

But these starkly different social values grow out of deeper underlying differences. Supporters of social justice and economic rationalists disagree about:

- what constitutes 'freedom'
- when an individual has a 'choice'
- what is 'fair'.

These disagreements are only partly about values. They are also partly about empirical questions such as 'what social conditions promote the ability of individuals to make choices for themselves?' and 'what economic/legal arrangements are most likely to produce fair wages?' Different approaches to the issue of equity involve assumptions about how the social world operates. In other words, each approach to equity makes assumptions about the world. If it can be shown that these assumptions are false then serious doubt will be cast on the approach and the social policies that are built upon it.

This is why so much debate over equity concerns itself with factual matters. Gender equity at work is a good example. Is the disparity in pay rates and working conditions between male and female workers the result of individual free choice or due to structural factors? The answer can be used to support the political, economic and legal arrangements advocated by the competing sides. If gender disparity is the result of free choice, as economic rationalists argue, then individual negotiations at the workplace are clearly the preferred form of industrial relations since this minimises external constraints on choice. If, on the other hand, the gender gap is due to structural factors, the argument for 'free choice' disappears and the social justice argument for social mechanisms such as unions, centralised wage-fixation and legislative action is strengthened.

A third strand of social philosophy competes with the economic rationalism and social justice for influence over contemporary public policy, especially in the area of industrial relations. This philosophy is civil libertarianism. Whilst we will examine this more fully below, briefly, it involves the acknowledgment that individuals have certain civil rights, or that they should be allocated those rights. In the context of industrial relations, a particularly important strand of civil libertarianism which has had considerable influence over public policy is the Equal Employment Opportunity (EEO) approach. This approach holds that it is necessary for the law to intervene to some extent in the employment relationship to ensure a level playing field so that discrimination does not occur in the hiring and treatment of workers on the basis of factors like gender and race. Unlike social justice, which tends to advocate broad spectrum economic policies like welfare programs, the EEO strand of civil libertarianism seeks to give individuals the right to legally enforce (or seek remedies for a breach of) specific legislated rights.

The debate between economic rationalists, advocates of social justice and civil libertarians has profound implications for social arrangements at work and beyond. Economic rationalists are currently dismantling many of the institutional mechanisms developed over the past 100 years by advocates of social justice. In the following section we will look briefly at economic rationalism, civil libertarianism and social justice. These approaches will then be put to a practical test. The final section of the chapter will explore how each approach deals with the issues of gender at work, inequality in the labour market and illness, injury and death at work.

ECONOMIC RATIONALISM

The 1990s in Australia has seen the cutting of public sector employment, the privatisation of government enterprises, a systematic move to out-sourcing in the public and private sectors, de-unionisation, the adoption of work for the dole schemes and the passage of legislation designed to deregulate the labour market. All these changes have significant implications for industrial relations and for equity at work and all are driven by economic rationalism.

Economic rationalism has a strongly individualist, free market orientation that reflects the cultural values of its country of origin, the United States. Economic rationalism combines a reliance on neoclassical economics with a particular form of political liberalism. From neoclassical economics it takes the idea that optimal efficiency and welfare are the result of perfect competition (Green 1995, 159-60). In the labour market this means that only unfettered competition can lead to full employment and the efficient allocation of workers to different jobs (Buchanan and Callus 1993, 521). From the American tradition of political liberalism, economic rationalism takes an emphasis on individualism, hostility to some state activities and a commitment to freedom of choice. Friedman, the 'father' of economic rationalism, tied his theory to the ideas embodied in the American Declaration of Independence. He interpreted this to mean that every person is entitled to pursue his own values (Friedman and Friedman 1980, 2). Economic rationalists see governments and trade unions as the major sources of power and threats to freedom. Protecting citizens against this potential tyranny requires perpetual vigilance.

Unlike many civil libertarians and social justice theorists, economic rationalists do not consider that power inequalities exist in a range of social contexts and give rise to a range of possible threats to the freedom of individuals. Rather, they take the view that power inequalities will effectively be minimised by limiting the role of government and institutionalising the free market. In order to maximise choice and promote competition, economic rationalists advocate the deregulation of the labour market. In other words they seek to restructure the labour market so that workers bargain in a one-on-one relationship with employers, unimpeded by statutory minimum conditions.

The libertarian social philosophy espoused by Friedman (1980) was brought to Australia over the last twenty years by economists who trained in the United States or at the London School of Economics and Political Science. Their views established the current thinking that the cure for all economic woes is deregulation and trust in market forces (Neville 1990, 74). The influence of such economists is also responsible for the continual support that has come from the federal Treasury and the Industry Commission for deregulation of the labour market (Buchanan and Callus 1993, 517).

Employer groups have also played an influential role in securing the implementation of economic rationalist ideas. A good example of this is The Business Council of Australia, which represents the largest corporations in Australia and is modelled on a similar body in the United States. The appeal to employer groups of economic rationalism, with its free market policies and libertarian social philosophy, is not surprising. In many respects economic rationalism is critical of the restraints imposed by governments and trade unions, which adversely affect profits and the efficient operation of business. But it fails to also recognise that employers exercise power over their employees in the workplace and exercise considerable power within the political process as a significant pressure group. Libertarianism assumes that workers need protection from unions but not from employers (Bennett 1994, 228).

CIVIL LIBERTARIANISM AND EQUAL EMPLOYMENT OPPORTUNITY

Civil libertarianism involves the acknowledgment or allocation of 'rights' to individuals. It has evolved into many forms, including the social libertarianism identified in the last section as one of the bastions of Friedman's economic rationalism. During the last two decades in Australia a somewhat different form of civil libertarianism (the EEO strand) has underlain many contemporary interventions in the workplace.

The starting point of the EEO strand of civil libertarianism has been in its rejection of some aspects of libertarian social philosophy particularly those concerned with equality of opportunity. Friedman's libertarian concept of equality of opportunity is that arbitrary obstacles should not prevent a person from achieving those positions that their abilities and values lead them to seek (Friedman and Friedman 1980, 132). At face value this appears fair and reasonable - that everyone in the same situation should be treated identically. Over time, however, some of those concerned with issues of racial and gender equality, came to regard this concept of equality of opportunity as too limited. (In fact, this definition in many respects captures the 'everyday' meaning of discrimination). They did not wholly reject libertarian philosophy but altered it in a number of important respects. Most importantly, they abandoned the assumption that equal opportunity meant treating individuals the same way irrespective of their sex, colour, political beliefs and so on. They came to the view that the 'same treatment' philosophy may, in fact, reinforce gender and racial inequalities. They argued that over time practices develop which effectively close off certain opportunities to those of a particular gender or race irrespective of the attitudes of those involved. Differences in the individual had to be taken into consideration. The playing field was not level.

Hunter (1992) argues that organisational procedures used to allocate positions and benefits in the workplace have normally been designed for Anglo-Australian, able-bodied, heterosexual males (the historically dominant group in public life). These patterns and attributes often differ markedly from those of women and minority groups. Women, almost exclusively, bear the responsibility for child rearing and home duties. This has a major impact on the pattern of their working lives.

Supporters of the new EEO strand of civil libertarianism argued that it is not simply a matter of asking whether attitudes are discriminatory, but also whether the processes that allocate individuals to positions in the society are discriminatory. In other words the EEO strand of civil libertarianism is intent on changing discriminatory structures as well as discriminatory behaviour and attitudes. Earlier versions of civil libertarianism accepted the social structure as it was, but those concerned with issues of gender and race argued that discrimination was historically a part of the social structure.

The EEO strand of civil libertarianism also breaks with classic political liberalism in its emphasis that power can be exercised in a number of different social contexts, not simply by governments. It acknowledges the exercise of economic power by employers, by landlords and by those who trade in goods and services as well as by trade unions and governments. However, key elements of political liberalism still remain. For both approaches the goal is to provide equality of opportunity for individual talent in a market economy, rather than benefits accruing on the basis of race or gender. The important points remain - freedom of choice, individualism, and equality of opportunity (Whitehouse 1992, 66). In addition the strategies for dealing with abuses of power remain the same and are highly individualised. Libertarianism, in both forms, seeks to curtail the abuse of power through the allocations of legal rights to individuals. It does not seek any substantial re-ordering of power relationships within society. Instead, individuals who can establish that their right to non-discrimination has been infringed may, at the discretion of a court or tribunal, be awarded compensation or, in theory, if the discrimination occurs at work be granted legal orders which compel their reinstatement or promotion.

EEO aims to minimise the impact of discriminatory social practices within a given social system but, unlike economic rationalism and social justice, it has a narrow focus. It does not deal with issues of how the economy should be structured or what should be the overall relationship between employers and workers. It is silent on the economic role of government. Questions of distribution are irrelevant. Many social issues relevant to the groups covered by anti-discrimination legislation are not addressed. For example, the rate of unemployment, although crucial to particular ethnic and indigenous groups, goes unaddressed by minimum employment protections.

In a sense it is precisely this social 'neutrality' which has allowed the passage of anti-discrimination legislation in countries that traditionally have taken very different approaches to issues of equity in the workplace. These include decentralised, relatively non-interventionist countries such as the United States, as well as countries with a strong tradition of social justice such as Australia. In Australia, the passage of such legislation was associated with the rise of women's and indigenous pressure groups. These groups did not seek support from local institutions and practices because the main elements of the Australian social justice system were both racist and sexist. Instead, they looked overseas and sought to introduce the legislative innovations of the United States, such as anti-discrimination legislation, into Australia. The idea that such legislation would open up the professions to women and encourage rewards on the basis of talent, rather than gender, was also particularly attractive to many of the middle class supporters of feminism.

SOCIAL JUSTICE

Historically the ideas of social justice have been influential in Australia, particularly in the field of industrial relations. The ideas of a living wage, of state support for trade unions and of controls over working hours, date back to the 19th Century and, until the last decade, were enshrined in both state and federal legislation.

Social justice promotes fairness, arguing that power inequalities have negative consequences (particularly in the workplace). It is argues that the operation of market forces can be oppressive and unjust and, at times, need to be tempered by institutions that promote more equitable relations at work. Unlike economic rationalism and civil libertarianism, social justice lacks a strong philosophical basis.

While the central ideas of economic rationalism, such as freedom of choice, can be traced back to the writings of philosophers (Sawer 1982, 20-37), the ideas of social justice were thrown up in the struggles between workers and capitalists in the 19th Century. Social justice is, unsurprisingly, marked by a concentration on 'everyday' problems. This pragmatic and institutional basis explains its tendency to focus on concrete problems rather than on theories of how society should operate. Although it too relies on theoretical concepts such as fairness, its treatment of equity tends to be more focused on issues such as in wage levels, work hours, the treatment of minority groups, industrial injury and sickness compensation, and social hierarchy.

Social justice tends to focus not on the particular position of a given individual but on the shared problems of groups of individuals. It tends to see problems as systemic, that is, in their historical and social context, rather than as aspects of a market-based economy. The methods for dealing with these problems also differs sharply from those advocated by economic rationalism and civil libertarianism. Social justice favours collective organisation within the economic sphere, by trade unions for example, and within the political sphere through political parties. Social justice believes the state cannot be neutral in areas such as industrial relations. Economic rationalism in comparison assumes that the state, particularly one where legal regulation is through the common law, is neutral. Those arguing from social justice would say that such a state effectively strengthens the employer's position. They would argue that historically employers have wielded significant influence within the political system and that the common law reinforces employer control over workers (see Chapter 7). In other words supporters of social justice claim that economic rationalism increases employer control over work and over workers.

Although less systematic and uniform than economic rationalism, social justice also addresses general issues of social structure, such as the nature of social welfare policy, and the correct approach to economic management (e.g. a significant reliance on incomes policies as opposed to monetary policy). Whereas economic rationalism assumes that the cumulative result of individual self-interested decisions is a society that functions rationally, this is not the case for social justice. Social justice assumes that the cumulative result of individual rational decisions may or may not be socially rational, and the appropriate result may require government intervention. For example, if some businesses can obtain a cost advantage by polluting the environment and paying workers subsistence wages they will do so, unless restrained by external controls. Once they have gained this 'advantage' it becomes irrational for their competitors not to follow suit. The cumulative results of such 'rational' behaviour - pollution and subsistence wages - are not socially desirable or rational, no matter how 'rational' the individual decisions may have been.

Social justice in Australia has a strong collectivist (control by the people/state) and institutionalist (control by organisations) history. It has long been associated with trade unions and the Labor Party. Underlying the activities of these organisations has been a belief that, given sufficient strength, they could secure a degree of influence in the state, which could then be used to bring about more equitable relations at work. So these organisations have played a key role in defining the social justice tradition in Australia. Social justice advocates have argued that the state must exercise power to counter inequities flowing from employers' superior economic power and the power given to employers by the common law. This belief that trade unions can influence the exercise of power by the state is one which has been held particularly strongly in countries such as Australia and reflects the trade unions' historical relationship with the Labor party and the arbitration system. In Britain and the United States unions have generally not been in a position to influence the exercise of state power and have sought to 'quarantine' (or keep strictly separate) industrial relations from active intervention by the state (Bennett 1994).

The ideas of social justice can currently be found in the policy documents of social welfare agencies, the mainstream churches and union journals. Within academia they are most likely to be found in industrial relations or labour history. In the 1970s and 1980s the rise of gender and race as issues saw the development of new criticisms of the Australian tradition of social justice. Critics looked overseas for new ideas. Forms of civil libertarianism and associated legislative strategies had a significant appeal to a number of feminists. In the 1980s and 1990s employers, business academics and economists also drew on developments in the United States. Many challenged the dominance of social justice approaches and sought to replace them with those based on economic rationalism.

EVALUATION

How can we evaluate the equity implications of economic rationalism, the EEO strand of civil libertarianism and social justice? One method is to look at these approaches in the context of a number of equity issues. This chapter will examine each approach on these issues:

- gender
- illness, injury and death at work
- labour market inequalities such as low wages.

A comprehensive treatment of these issues would take more than a chapter. Nevertheless certain key points can be made and the various approaches evaluated.

Gender

Although the interpretation and explanation of key aspects of women's participation in the workforce may be in dispute, the facts about that participation are not. Women are disproportionately located in low-paying jobs, they are heavily segregated into a relatively small number of industry and occupational areas and their career opportunities in the professions and management are more limited than those of men.

With the exception of agriculture, industries employing a high proportion of low paid employees in Australia are dominated by women workers. Such industries include clothing and footwear, personal services, retail trade, and private households employing staff (Buchanan and Watson 1997, 7, Table 3). Buchanan and Watson (1997) estimate on the basis of Bureau of Statistics data that, in 1993, 75,349 employees (who worked 16 hours a week or more) earned less than $9 an hour. A further 701,633 employees earned between $9.01-10.50 per hour. This represented 24.5 per cent of the male workforce, working a minimum of 16 hours per week and 33 per cent of the female workforce. Furthermore, not only are women workers disproportionately located within occupations which pay very low wages but within those occupations, they were more likely to be paid much lower than the men (1997, 5-7).

Whilst the pay and conditions for the majority of women is inferior to those enjoyed by men, the position of women at the top of the labour market has improved. There has been a marked increase in the number of women entering the professions and management. This represents a significant improvement in the position of some women but it is important to recognise that the gains made are less than might have been hoped for. One difficulty, unforseen by early feminism, was that women escaped from 'female' occupations into 'male' professions only to see the creation of new forms of gender segregation. In the legal profession, women have become concentrated in low paying, low prestige areas such as conveyancing and family law. In the medical profession, they are found disproportionately in general practice rather than in the high income, prestige specialisations. In management there is a tendency for women (middle) managers to leave large organisations to set up their own firms. This is frequently because movement of such women up the promotional ladder has been stopped by the existence of a 'glass ceiling'. These examples indicate that there is more to the elimination of gender segregation than the opening up of new areas for women. They do not support the idea that gender equality is 'just a matter of time' as women work their way into areas previously dominated by men. Rather they emphasise that there continues to be gender discrimination despite apparent commitment to equality of opportunity between the sexes.

So how can low pay, low prestige, poor conditions and the persistence of gender segregation be explained? Does it simply reflect the different choices made by men and women (economic rationalism)? Is it the result of prejudice and structural discrimination against women (EEO civil libertarianism)? Or is it to be explained by women's relative lack of choice due to their lack of bargaining power and the pursuit by employers and some trade unions of gender-biased policies (social justice)?

The economic rationalist approach to gender at work draws on neoclassical economics where differing 'returns' to workers is dependent on how much they invest in their career. According to this approach women choose to invest less in their career (human capital) since paid work is of less importance to them than their personal lives. In other words the different labour market experiences of women and men are a result of choice. This approach to women is exemplified by strategies that attempt to increase women's participation in management by increasing their motivation. They assume that the barriers to career progression are subjective rather than objective. Some companies have endeavoured to get more women into management positions by encouraging women to have higher aspirations, to increase their levels of commitment, to work harder and be prepared to accept more responsibility. These are attributes that have traditionally been associated with male career progression (Hunter 1992, 5). Evidence, however, does not support this.

First, studies have shown that even where men and women make identical investments in work and career, the returns on those investments differ. Comparative studies indicate that where men and women have equal qualifications, the returns on those qualifications will be less for women than for men. For example, there is a greater gap between the average earnings of men and women in Canada than in Sweden, despite the higher educational qualifications of Canadian women (Whitehouse 1990, 360-1).

Second, the presence or absence of particular qualifications is not necessarily a good measure of the time or difficulty inherent in doing a particular kind of work. In other words it is not necessarily a good measure of human capital. The dominance of men in educational and training institutions as well as the influence of male-dominated professional groups and trade unions can lead to men's work having credentials that women's does not. In other words, jobs may be more likely to require qualifications in male dominated occupations.

Third, and most problematically, economic rationalism functions with a very simple concept of 'choice'. A great deal of what occurs in the social world is omitted from the picture drawn by economic rationalism. In particular, it sees society presenting individuals with a particular range of choices. It does not query those choices, nor how they arose. Women, for instance, are presented as making a choice between family and career unlike male professionals or management. Economic rationalism does not go on to question a social structure which provides one gender with opportunities for a family and a career but requires the other to make a choice between them.

Civil libertarian approaches, on the other hand, stress the need to change social structures in a way that will enable both parents to participate in the workforce. Unlike economic rationalism, they address compensation for career time lost on maternity leave, they question promotion requirements, and explore ways of making management a more attractive for women including the need for appropriate child-care arrangements (Hunter 1992, 5-6).

Advocates of the EEO strand of civil libertarianism argue that equal participation requires the overhaul of organisational practices that may have negative effects on women. Promotion prerequisites, which include relocation or attendance at weekend courses, for instance, may count against women with domestic responsibilities. Equal participation by women requires supports such as quality childcare, maternity leave and carer's leave for sick children. They stress that economic rationalism simply overlooks the sexist aspects of some work cultures. In male dominated workplaces, lack of mentors for women, assumptions about their role and sexual harassment may combine to limit opportunities for women. In effect, channelling them into dead end and relatively poorly paid positions. In other workplaces, women's employment choices may be heavily constrained by social and religious attitudes. Recent immigrants, particularly from South East Asia and South America may find that language difficulties, the lack of an extended family for child care, and the high cost of long-day care, forces them to work from home while caring for their young children. They are effectively forced to become outworkers at below poverty line rates of pay.

The strength of EEO analysis lies in its ability to draw on gender studies to illustrate the mismatch between existing work structures and the career aspirations of some women. Such an analysis has less to say, however, about the position of the majority of women. For most women, the EEO analysis needs to supplemented by some discussion of how a lack of bargaining power creates poor wages and conditions. Social justice addresses this issue, linking women's pay and conditions to the occupations and industries where women disproportionately work and the impact of employer strategies.

The starting point of social justice analysis is the fact that women are concentrated in a limited range of industries and occupations, where they are often easily replaced. They, therefore, have little bargaining power and their wages and conditions are depressed. Women often work in the services sector and for small employers. These two groups often show hostility to any form of organisation that might improve pay or conditions. Effective organisation of employees is also made difficult by labour turnover and a high incidence of casual and part-time work. Union strategies, particularly the ACTU's insistence on global strategies such as amalgamations and enterprise bargaining, have also contributed. They have diverted attention and resources away from membership recruitment and organisation, concentrating instead on inter-union battles over coverage and workplace disputes with employers.

Despite these problems, a comparative study of gender inequality in OECD countries found that policies associated with social justice such as centralised wage-fixation and high levels of government employment had a positive effect on relative earnings. It concluded that the most successful efforts to reduce gender-based wage inequalities have been those driven by collective action. This study also pointed to the importance for women of active labour market policies designed to maintain full employment and facilitate structural adjustment. Such 'interventionist' policies have provided opportunities for women, which have served to lessen gender inequality in the labour market (Whitehouse 1992, 79).

The 1990s, however, saw a move away from a number of these social justice policies. The attempt by employers and governments to decentralise wage-fixation and improve flexibility impacted heavily on women. Conditions for many women workers deteriorated in the late 1980s and 1990s when employers sought to replace full-time permanent employees with a range of workers employed as contractors, casuals, outworkers, temps, and part-timers. Such changes swept through a range of industries where employment was predominantly male as well as through female dominated industries. The effects on women were more severe, however, since their conditions were poorer to begin with and their bargaining position was weaker.

Social justice policies have been attacked by proponents of economic rationalism, who see the gender gap as the result of choice and aim to increase the amount of choice by deregulating the labour market. The aim of economic rationalists is to ultimately dismantle all social justice programs and replace them with one-on-one face-to-face bargaining. The empirical evidence suggests that this will worsen the position of women workers. Victoria has moved most strongly in this direction and Pocock (1996) points out that in Victoria the gender gap has become widest. The Victorian ratio of female/male Average Weekly Ordinary Time Earnings (AWOTE) for full-time adults fell from 68.8 per cent in November 1991 to 65.3 per cent in August 1995. In contrast in Queensland, which operated a modified arbitration system at the time, the gender gap remained constant in this period at 65.2 per cent (1996, 57-8).

These findings are reinforced by the experience overseas. New Zealand provides a useful comparison since it has moved from a centralised awards-based system to a deregulated one, based on contract. Those supporting deregulation in Australia frequently point to New Zealand as a model. However, they tend not do so if they are looking at the gender effects of such industrial relations changes. A study of collective contracts in New Zealand by Hammond and Harbridge (1995) found that the employment contracts legislation had a significant effect on the gender gap. Their data showed that there has been a widening of the 'gender gap' between men's and women's wages from $7.75 per week in November 1992 to $17.10 per week in 1995. (These figures were calculated by comparing the lowest adult rate in each contract and weighting that rate by the number of men and women employees covered by the contract) (1995, 371).

Social justice approaches, which focus on structural changes in the labour market, point out some of the limitations of both EEO civil libertarianism and economic rationalism in areas such as gender. The EEO approach stresses that individuals must be free to compete for jobs and promotions, unhampered by considerations such as gender. However, the cumulative impact of fashionable managerial strategies and economic rationalism in the late 1980s and 1990s has been to drastically reduce the prospects for full-time employment particularly in areas that have normally entailed career opportunities. Massive retrenchments and the move to flatter management structures in the public and private sectors have drastically reduced opportunities to move upward. On one hand this has supported equity for women by altering career structures for management and eliminating some of the glass ceilings. On the other, it has made it even more difficult for women to compete because individuals, regardless of gender or race, now compete in a labour market where quality jobs are becoming scarcer and harder to hold.

Whitehouse (1992) argues that the strategies of economic rationalism and EEO civil libertarianism do not address the wider issues of social inequality, such as gender-biased evaluations of women's work or the concentration of women in certain occupations (1992, 66). In the 1990s such strategies can also be criticised for not addressing the impact of management strategies and government policies on women's working conditions. Allocating legal rights does nothing to touch the structural basis of gender inequality. Social justice institutions (e.g. unions and the ALP), despite their gender-biased history, have been much more effective in recent times. Success in reducing gender inequality in labour markets for the majority of women is attributable more to union-brokered wage fixing arrangements and labour market policies than to legislation. Arbitration has reduced inequalities for women (Whitehouse 1990, 368). Economic rationalism, however, appears likely to turn back the gains won by the majority of women workers and their professional and managerial counterparts.

Illness, Injury and Death at Work

The incidence of death, illness and injury due to road accidents, AIDS and conditions such as asthma have a relatively high public profile. The same cannot be said of the illnesses, injuries and deaths that occur at work or that are work related (e.g. the development of cancers due to exposure to carcinogenic substances). Yet this relative invisibility is not because the problem is insignificant. The former head of Worksafe, Joe Riordan pointed out that up to 2700 workplace related deaths occur annually. 500 occur as a result of traumatic accidents and up to 2200 are the consequence of workplace related disease. Around 650,000 persons suffer from non-fatal injuries each year and the total cost, as estimated by the Industry Commission, is as high as $20 billion a year (Riordan 1997, 27).

What is the appropriate response to such a problem? On this issue again economic rationalists and proponents of social justice have diametrically opposed views. Economic rationalists argue that employers and employees are in the best position to improve the situation for themselves, whilst social justice advocates argue for a variety of forms of intervention by unions and the state. Economic rationalists reason that occupational health and safety (OHS) is simply a matter of choice. If workers feel that the job is too risky they can refuse to take it. If employers have trouble recruiting they can offer additional money. Consequently, those workers, who are most in need of money or who are prepared to take greater risks, will take the most dangerous jobs while workers more concerned about safety issues will continue to avoid such work (Hopkins 1993, 179). It is thus a matter for the 'individuals' involved. In order to allow individuals to make such decisions about what is in their best interests economic rationalism argues that it is necessary to remove regulatory controls and collective bodies, such as unions. Only then will it be possible for workers and employers to freely choose, since free choice and competition are inextricably intertwined.

The critical assumption underlying the economic rationalist account is that workers are able to move between safe and unsafe jobs if they so choose. In other words that labour markets are like product markets and individuals can switch jobs in the way they can switch washing powders. Yet this is rarely the case. The opportunities open to workers, especially older ones, to move into new industries or occupations such as safer office and professional positions, are at best limited (Hopkins 1993, 179). This is particularly so in times when unemployment is high in specific skilled occupations. The economic vulnerability of such workers and their lack of effective choice in the labour market contradicts the economic rationalist assumption that the parties to the employment contract are equals and have equal bargaining power.

The empirical evidence also suggests that the policy of economic rationalism (i.e. intensified competition), can worsen outcomes for workers. In the area of occupational health and safety, the evidence is that intensified competition is associated with significantly increased incidence of occupational injury and death. Competitive practices such as outsourcing of labour have been shown to have potentially injurious consequences including both changes in the pattern and increases in the number of injuries. Self-employed workers are far more likely to be killed at work than are their employed colleagues (Mayhew and Quinlan 1997a, 2). Such empirical findings are consistent with social justice views of the inherent inequalities of the labour market. It is felt that competition may very well intensify inequalities of bargaining power, which will then produce a deterioration in wages and conditions, including a reduction in occupational health and safety.

Finally, economic rationalism can be faulted for its uncritical approach to the concept of choice. As was the case with gender inequality, economic rationalism focuses on the individual worker and his or her immediate (and superficial) situation. The extent to which the worker's individual choices are controlled by pre-existing and external factors is ignored, or more accurately, rendered invisible, by an analysis that concentrates on individual decision-making rather than on the processes which influence them. This can be seen more easily when the analysis moves down from the purely abstract to the concrete. In the building industry, for instance, the move by large firms to sub contract work intensifies competition. It often requires sub contractors to undercut one another by completing tasks in the shortest possible time. This often leads to subcontractors pushing themselves and their workers hard, working excessive hours and cutting corners in regard to safety (Mayhew, Quinlan and Ferris 1997, 3). These practices are linked to increased risk of injury. In the building industry 28 per cent of self-employed have chronic back pain. Instead of seeking medical attention, sub-contractors continue to work while they are injured. This occurs because they are economically insecure and have difficulty getting injury compensation (Mayhew and Quinlan 1997b, 198).

Hence, in a very unequal situation unacknowledged by economic rationalism, employers determine whether an industry will adopt contracting and this affects the pattern of risks which workers face. Workers, on the other hand, are not free to pick and choose between different types of work. They must either compete for sub-contracted work or leave the industry. This may not be recognised by the workers involved who regard the risks (and injuries) as just 'part of the job'. The macho behaviour of enduring injury and ill health, characteristic of many self-employed workers, often masks the intense economic pressures and few employment alternatives for those who are paid by their output (James 1993, 54).

The area of OHS also points to another problem with the concept of choice. That is, informed choice. The individual worker is generally not in a position to assess the risks involved in different areas of work. The carcinogenic (cancer causing) or tetrogenic (causing of abnormalities in the foetus) effects of chemicals is not something that the individual worker is in a position to research (even if aware of the possibility of such risks). Even when employers have such information they often do not pass it on. A recent strike in the building industry was caused by the employer's failure to inform workers that they were cutting material that was 60 per cent asbestos (the breathing of asbestos particles is known to cause fatal cancers in humans and there are no safe exposure levels) (Valiance 1997, 14). A dispute at the manufacturer Hoechst occurred when the employer failed to warn employees that they were handling DCBs which are known carcinogens in animals and suspected carcinogens in humans. This was despite the fact that the company's occupational hygienist had written a report two years earlier on the potential harm caused by the handling of DCBs (Berger 1993, 129). Even when workers are aware of the long-range risks, the more pressing needs of the moment, such as paying the rent, take precedence over their health (Hopkins 1993, 179).

A further key assumption, made by the economic rationalist account of OHS, is that allowing workers and employers to freely bargain does not impose substantial costs on others. This is not necessarily so. Costs can range from increased risk of injury and death to the general public to meeting the financial costs of the illnesses, injuries and deaths of workers. These include medical costs and social security costs for the workers themselves and their families. In the building industry a survey of 500 small builders found that only 9 per cent of 500 interviewees were aged over 55. The explanation for this is that by age 55 builders are worn out or chronically injured, many being on invalid pensions (Mahew and Quinlan 1997b, 198-9). Exposure of workers to asbestos in the building and mining industries will also impose massive costs on the medical system in the future. It has been estimated that it will take a further 20 years for the incidence of asbestos-related disease to peak in Australia. This is due to the long latency period between exposure to asbestos and diagnosis of its effects (which include the fatal lung cancer, mesothelioma). By 2010 there will be an additional 20,000 cases of diseases directly associated with exposure to asbestos plus 6,000 new cases of mesothelioma (Riordan 1997, 29).

The community generally meets these health costs through the medical and social security systems. Contractors tend not to take legal action against the businesses which employ them because they are economically vulnerable and because of the slowness and uncertainties of the law. Such businesses are then free to externalise the costs of injury and illness. Moreover because employers can externalise these costs they have less incentive to minimise illness and injury in the workplace by taking precautions. Consequently, the incidence and severity of injury and illness may be greater when businesses can pass the costs on to workers and third parties.

In certain areas increased risks of injury and illness may also extend beyond workers to the general public. This is the case in the transport industry with interstate and long-distance trucking and in certain areas of the building industry such as the highly dangerous and potentially lethal area of asbestos removal (Mayhew and Quinlan 1997a; Mayhew and Quinlan 1997b).

Important secondary effects on OHS also flow from economic rationalism, in particular its reliance on monetary policy. The building industry, for instance, is particularly susceptible to economic downturns and the use of monetary policy to contract the economy has significant effects on this industry and the health and safety of its workers. During downturns the competition is intense amongst subcontractors with the price of work dropping below basic wage levels. This results in increased workloads amongst subcontractors and their workers, as they try to complete more jobs to compensate for the lower returns. The OHS-related outcomes include fatigue, stress, burn-out and failure or delays in seeking treatment for work-related injuries (Mayhew and Quinlan 1997b, 193).

Economic rationalists generally accept that risks are associated with work. Social justice approaches, on the other hand, do not accept these risks. They use a series of measures to attempt to reduce the incidence of illness, injury and death due to work. Such measures seek to strengthen the labour market position of workers and to provide a regulatory system that encompasses a preventative approach. Economic rationalists argue that less intervention is needed, whereas social justice argues that more effective intervention is needed.

In Australia, the social justice policy of intervention in the workplace has been broadly adopted. This is achieved through legislation and government agencies, such as health and safety inspectors and Workcover. Such agencies can provide information on the nature of risks and develop practical measures for minimising them, for example, developing standards for safe work practices. They can prosecute employers who disregard such standards. They can also provide research on areas where the risks of various work processes are unclear. This can involve research on the risks associated with various forms of work organisation, the use of chemicals, exposure to noise and the impact of shifts. Such information can then be provided to employers, workers and unions.

Unions have also played a key role. As in the Hoechst and asbestos disputes discussed earlier, they can bring risks to the attention of workers and organise action designed to force a response from employers who are ignorant or indifferent to the health risks facing workers. Unions, unlike individual workers, have the resources to obtain information on the risks that arise in particular workplaces and also have the ability to lobby governments for effective enforcement and research.

Social justice criticisms also apply to the EEO strand of civil libertarianism. This approach does not provide mechanisms that reduce the incidence of injury and illness at work (other than by the threat of liability on employers). The EEO approach is basically reactive, responding to illness and injury at work, after it has occurred. Workers 'disabled' by injury or illness are given legal rights to ensure that they do not suffer discrimination in areas such as compensation, hiring, firing and promotion. But without a full range of retraining schemes and good employment prospects across all industries, such 'rights' achieve little. Such civil libertarian approaches have little to offer when it comes to analysing the broader social forces which impact on health and safety at work or when it comes to devising social and regulatory programs which will improve the health and safety of workers.

Inequality in the Labour Market

In recent years, the Australian labour market has been marked by increasing inequality. Well-paid permanent jobs have been (partially) replaced by poorly paid short-term and casual jobs. Full-time permanent employees have declined from approximately 66 per cent of the employed labour force in 1982 to 56.2 per cent in 1995 (Campbell 1996, 7). Many middle level jobs have disappeared. There is an increasing polarisation between a large number of poorly paid and a relatively small number of highly paid workers. A study that examined wage inequality from 1975 to 1989 found that for men low-wage employment increased from about 17 per cent in the mid-1970s to almost 25 per cent by

1989. For women, low-wage workers increased from 25 per cent to 33 per cent of working women, while the middle income group decreased from 70.83 per cent of all working women in 1975, to 57.64 per cent in 1989 (King, Rimmer and Rimmer 1991, 5).

Clearly, a substantial low-wage sector has developed. A study carried out for the Industrial Relations Commission's Living Wage Case 1996-7 found that the position of low paid workers relative to higher paid workers was deteriorating. They estimated that economy-wide one worker in ten is employed for less than $10 per hour and a further one in eight is probably earning less than $11.50 per hour (Buchanan and Watson 1997, 26-7). This low-waged sector includes a significant number of outworkers (often recent migrants and women) who work in conditions approximating those of third world countries. The Sydney Morning Herald reported a case mentioned by Jenny George (then president of the ACTU) of a Vietnamese woman who was contracted to make 240 wool blend coats for women at $14 per coat. Each coat took two and a half hours to make. The retailer imposed a 'lateness fine' and paid only $8.50 per coat so the outworker earned just over $3.50 an hour for working up to 16 hours a day. The coats later retailed at $200 each (SMH 1997a, 4).

This decline in wages and full-time employment can be explained by a number of factors. Structural changes and policy changes, such as tariff cuts, have reduced employment in areas which provide 'good' jobs such as manufacturing. Employment in areas which provide poor jobs, such as the services sector, has increased. The manufacturing sector's share of employment has shrunk from 21.6 per cent in 1975 to 13.9 per cent in 1995, while jobs in the services sector have expanded from 55.8 per cent to 67.8 per cent in the same period (Brosnan 1995, 16 Table 1). Linked to these changes are organisational policies that have focussed on downsizing, the replacement of full-time employees with contractors, casuals and temporary workers. Finally, employer strategies and government policies have driven down real wages. Cuts to public sector employment and the privatisation of government enterprises have contributed significantly, particularly in the 1990s. Public sector employment has traditionally provided quality jobs and many of these have been replaced by out-sourced labour, which is typically casual or contract based.

The development of wage polarisation is tied in with such trends. Casual workers, for instance, are more likely to be in low paid, unskilled occupations with little opportunity of developing a career path (Burgess and Campbell 1993, 193). Casual employment has expanded since the early 1980s. In August 1995, casuals represented 20.1 per cent of the employed labour force up from 10.8 per cent in August1982 (Campbell 1996, 7). This process has been particularly marked during recessions. In the 1990-1992 recession, for instance, 350,000 full-time jobs were lost while the number of part-time jobs increased by over 200,000 (Burgess and Campbell 1993, 193, 208).

In summary, privatisation, the cutting back of public sector employment, tariff cuts and the elimination of award protections are some of the reasons for the increasing labour market inequality. Not unexpectedly, these policies are all central to the economic rationalist idea of a 'small state' which does not 'interfere' in the operations of the market. Further movement in these directions will simply exacerbate labour market inequalities.

Economic rationalists frequently argue that wage flexibility (which in this context should be taken to mean the growth of a low-waged sector and precarious jobs) is necessary if unemployment is to be significantly reduced. They argue that interference in the market by unions for example, maintains wages at artificially high levels. High wages discourages additional employment, resulting in unemployment. Over the past decade, however, Australia has seen a significant growth in low-paid, precarious employment. However, this has been accompanied not by a decrease in unemployment but by an almost doubling in the rate of unemployment (from 5.4 per cent in 1975 to a peak of over 9 per cent in 1997-8, although it did begin to drop again in 1999-2000). Comparative work also undermines the 'link' between lowering wages and increasing employment. Highly centralised Nordic economies, for example, have performed well since the end of the long post-war boom in terms of employment and wage dispersal (Rowthorn 1992).

Economic rationalist policies also have effects on public redistribution programs that will intensify inequality between workers. The Federal Labor Government effectively subsidised low-wage jobs as part of the trade-off in the Accord period between 1983 and 1991 (see Chapter 8). Couples with children on very low income, recorded real increases in disposable income, only because of the introduction of the family allowance supplement (Harding and Landt 1992, 44-5). The economic rationalist rejection of a role for government in social welfare would impact heavily on such workers and their children. In metropolitan Sydney 13 per cent of children live in families which qualify for family income supplements because their families are working poor. A further 22 per cent of children are in families where the parents qualify because they are on some form of welfare (SMH 1997b, 1). Regional inequalities have increased with 56 per cent of children on the far North Coast of NSW living in families which qualify for income supplementation. In Sydney itself such children are heavily congregated in the poorer suburbs of the west (60 per cent in Auburn) (*SMH* 1997b, 1). Lower incomes for the working poor mean less money is spent on food, clothing and medical expenses (Buchanan and Watson 1997, Table 14, 24, 22).

The rejection by economic rationalism of incomes policies in favour of monetary policies (interest rates adjustments) means that from time to time it will be necessary to reduce economic activity, to prevent the economy overheating or to hasten a recession (Neville 1990, 77). When economic activity is depressed unemployment increases. Thus a heavy reliance on monetary policy effectively transfers some of the 'costs' of economic policy to those whose employment, or employment prospects, are precarious (e.g. school leavers and recent graduates).

Social justice approaches, on the other hand, combine a mixture of interventionist policies designed to stimulate the growth of 'quality' jobs with a range of measures aimed at improving wages and conditions at the bottom end of the labour market. This includes industry policies designed to stimulate the manufacturing sector (e.g. export incentives), fiscal policies designed to stimulate the growth of jobs (e.g. infrastructure spending to upgrade the transport system) and labour market policies to provide retraining particularly for the long-term unemployed. The low waged sector can be dealt with directly through improvements to award conditions, union campaigns and effective enforcement to deal with problems such as outworking. The aim of such policies is to improve the position of low paid workers and reduce the incidence of low paid work. In other words, social justice policies aim to reverse the labour market trends of the past two decades. Economic rationalism, on the other hand, would intensify these trends. EEO approaches simply ignores them, but insists that the small number of 'winners' be somehow balanced in terms of race, gender, sexuality, disability etc.

Loss of work, a decreasing living standard due to public sector cuts and the loss of well paid work have been associated in Europe and the United States with social instability. This has taken the form of right wing extremism and racist campaigns. The social consequences of economic rationalism need to be taken into account when the implications of the various approaches to equity are evaluated.

EQUITY ISSUES IN THE FIVE SELECTED SOUTH EAST ASIAN COUNTRIES

In Asian countries, as in the west, there is ample evidence of discrimination in the labour market. While many western countries have used equal opportunity legislation, however inadequate, to deal with race and sex discrimination in employment, this is not the case in most Asian countries.

Japan

In Japan an increasing number of women are now in the workforce. In 1975, 32 per cent of the workforce was composed of women. By 1997, this had risen to about 40 per cent. (*Economist* 1997). However, women mainly find themselves in dead-end jobs, often part-time, for which their pay is only half that of the average for their male counterparts (*Economist* 1988). By 1999, only 9.3 per cent of corporate executives in Japan were female, compared to 44.3 per cent in the United States, 30.6 per cent in Norway and 26.6 per cent in Germany (Amaha 1999, 34). Japanese women are among the most highly educated in the world, but their talents have remained largely unused because of social norms relegating them to second-class status. Even graduates of prestigious universities have been expected to work for only a few years until marrying and becoming full-time mothers (Amaha 1999, 35). Women are generally not given lifetime employment, and are part of the temporary and relatively disadvantaged part of the workforce. This is despite the fact that Japan is one of the few Asian countries which has ratified the United Nations Convention on the Elimination of All Forms of Discrimination Against Women, and passed the Equal Opportunity for Men and Women Act on 1 July 1985 (Bishop et al. 1992, 351-2).

Under this legislation, employers are required to give men and women equal opportunity in recruitment, training, fringe benefits, compulsory retirement age, resignation and dismissal. Female workers are to be assisted with vocational guidance, re-employment, health-care arrangements during pregnancy and child-care leave. Access to counselling and training centres is also required for women workers. The only enforcement mechanism under the Act, however, is an Equal Opportunity Mediation Commission, whose function is to mediate in disputes regarding employment conditions. The Commission's decisions have no binding legal force (Bishop et al. 1992, 354).

This legislation may contribute to the social recognition of female workers, however, it is doubtful whether the Act would be effective in achieving employment equality (The *Waseda Bulletin of Comparative Law*, vol.7, 50). An anonymous contributor to the *Economist* (1997) agreed with this assessment of the legislation, pointing out that its effect is to create two career tracks for women, one for those who aspired to enter management and another for those who did not. Women who entered management, however, found it difficult to continue down this path. Frequent transfers of their male spouses, long hours of work and lack of domestic help meant that women who wanted to bring up a family had little option but to stay at home. In 1996, 12 female bank employees successfully sued the Shiba Credit Association for discrimination against them, on the grounds of their sex, in denying them promotion. This was a landmark decision by Japanese standards.

In April and May 1999, the Japanese Diet passed new legislation to promote gender equality and a stronger and more effective equal opportunity law. For the first time in Japan, gender equity laws laid down the principle of equal and joint responsibility at home, at work and in society as a whole for men and women. The new equal opportunity law allows the government to intervene in labour disputes at the request of employees. It is also expected to make maternity leave more of a reality than under the old law, where employers theoretically allowed for 7 weeks leave, but in practice simply asked pregnant employees to resign. The new law also clamps down on sexual harassment, giving the Labour Ministry power to name publicly those companies which fail to deal effectively with harassment complaints. Public humiliation is abhorrent in 'face'-conscious Japan (see Chapter 13) and is, consequently, a very real deterrent. Gender–specific job advertisements are also banned under the new laws (Amaha 1999, 34-6).

While the new laws provide a foundation for more equal rights for women in Japan, it will take many years to break down established attitudes of prejudice in this male-dominated society.

South Korea

South Korea is another South East Asian country with a strong tradition of male domination in the workplace, as in the society as a whole. In 1995, the World Competitiveness Report, prepared by the International Institute for Management Development (IMD), a consulting and research body in Switzerland, compared South Korea's competitive standing with 48 countries around the world. In terms of career opportunities for women, South Korea was ranked last, despite the fact that women constituted 20 per cent of university graduates. Reasons for this ranking included society's expectations, traditional and cultural attitudes, business practices and the preferences of the women themselves. The Report found that South Korea's business sector, with the assistance of government and influenced by Confucianism, systematically worked to exclude women from employment. This was achieved through discriminatory practices in hiring and payment levels. In a newspaper report, an employment recruitment agency estimated that women made up only 8.1 per cent of college graduates hired by South Korea's top business groups. A government proposal which would have compelled state-invested corporations to recruit at least 20 per cent women to positions requiring undergraduate degrees was shelved because of opposition from government and business circles. It was argued that such a measure would involve discrimination against men (*Business Korea* 1995).

In South Korea, it has been common practice in the workplace for males to stare at female co-workers' bodies and to display nude posters in their offices. However, social attitudes are gradually changing, particularly as the country has faced a manpower shortage until the time of the Asian crisis. At the political level, President Kim Dae Jung has been the first major South Korean politician to champion women's rights. He created the Presidential Commission on Women's Affairs in 1997 and the National Assembly of South Korea recently legislated for equal opportunity in 1999. The new law makes it mandatory for all Korean companies with more than ten employees to provide yearly in-house training on the avoidance of sexual harassment. Companies are also required to discipline workers accused of sexual harassment. Disciplinary actions range from reprimand to firing. The Ministry of Labour oversees the enforcement of this law. While the definition of sexual harassment under the legislation is vague, some commentators have suggested that the new law could have a revolutionary impact on the male-dominated, Confucian office culture in South Korea. However, others have argued that while the law points in a new direction, it will still take generations to change the traditional South Korean mind-set (Song 1999, 35).

Singapore

In Singapore, there is no equal employment opportunity legislation. In relation to racial equality, the PAP Government has encouraged each major racial group to advance its economic status through voluntary, ethnically-based, community organisations, but it has refused to pass EEO legislation. In practice, the Chinese tend to occupy the top positions in business and the professions, while Malays and Indians form something of an economic underclass. However, in relation to gender equality, government policies have actively encouraged higher labour force participation rates by women, and their advancement into professional and managerial jobs. Labour force participation rates for women have been steadily increasing since 1970, in an economy, which, over most of the period, has been booming and experiencing full employment. In 1970, the female labour-force participation rate was 26.6 per cent. This increased to 35.5 per cent in 1982, 38 per cent in 1988, and had reached 39.7 per cent by 1991 (Le Poer 1989, 98, 140).

The Singapore Government's publicised positive attitudes to women in the workforce and its national policies of training programs for women, flexitime and child-care have led to increasing numbers of females in higher level administrative and managerial positions. This ranged from virtually none in 1965, to 18 per cent by 1983 (Bass 1990, 772). Within the civil service, by 1987, 70 per cent of female applicants for higher level positions in the first, second and third divisions were successful. Even in the traditionally exclusive male preserve of the armed services, women, who had previously been confined to clerical roles, have been allowed into professional and technical positions in support units since 1989, provided they possess the necessary formal qualifications (Le Poer 1989, 187, 241).

Notwithstanding the fact that women have made considerable strides in labour force participation in Singapore over the last 30 years, principally owing to the tight labour market, there is still evidence that they face the same obstacles to advancement as their counterparts in western countries. These obstacles include lack of suitable (especially female) role models, discrimination by male colleagues and supervisors, difficulty in obtaining promotions, maintaining a balance between family and career lives and exclusion from organisational decision-making processes (Petzall, et al. 1993, 94).

CONCLUSION

Economic rationalism, the EEO strand of civil libertarianism and social justice provide very different accounts of the social world and how equality can be achieved at work. Economic rationalism deals with the problems of distribution, fairness, equity, gender and race by leaving them to the impersonal workings of the free market. Its reliance on the market to solve problems has an appealing simplicity, but in fact there is no single, simple explanation that can exempt society and its institutions from extremely difficult individual choices (Lord Rolls 1992, 576). Much of the appeal of economic rationalism lies in its stress on 'freedom' and 'choice.' In practice, however, its uncritical approach to the social world means that it exaggerates the range of choices open to most of us within an unregulated market economy.

The examination of the choices faced by individuals in areas such as OHS, gender and low-waged work indicates that it is necessary to analyse not simply the situations in which individuals find themselves, but how those situations came to be. Groups with significant power are often in a position to determine the range of choices open to individuals. There is nothing in economic rationalism that is appropriate for dealing with such power inequalities and their consequences. In part, this is because economic rationalism focuses on political power to the exclusion of economic and social power. This blindness means that economic rationalism is more likely to exacerbate inequities than mitigate them, and the evidence tends to support this conclusion. Economic rationalism is not a neutral philosophy, its implementation increases power differentials to the disadvantage of the weak.

The economic approach adopted by economic rationalism is also problematic. Its assertions about improving the labour market are not supported by evidence, nor is its assertion that increased competition produces superior equity outcomes. Whether increased competition will produce overall increased social benefits cannot be determined easily. Sometimes it may produce these benefits and sometimes not, depending on a range of factors, not all of which fall within the subject matter of economics. Lastly, workplace economic rationalist theories do not prevent serious injuries or save lives, but potentially quite the opposite (Riordan 1997, 29).

The EEO strand of civil libertarianism focuses on the issues of gender and race (and also new areas such as sexuality and disability). In areas such as gender, the analysis is most helpful with respect to barriers to careers or career progression in the professions or management. The individualised rights-based strategies associated with EEO, however, offer little to the majority of women workers and the passage of EEO legislation has not been associated with significant improvements for them. The EEO approach has little, if anything, to offer in areas such as OHS and low-wage work.

Social justice approaches challenge the political and economic dominance of employer groups and seek to mitigate the harsher consequences of the unregulated market. They have traditionally been preoccupied with issues such as low-paid work and, to a lesser extent, OHS. They have sought to improve the position of low-paid workers through award-based protection and limitations on the extent of casual work.

In recent times business groups have made a concerted and partially successful attempts to replace the discourse of social justice in everyday life with that of economic rationalism. In many respects economic rationalism provides language which is the mirror image of that used by social justice. Where economic rationalism speaks of 'increased productivity', social justice talks of 'work intensification'. Where economic rationalism stresses the benefits of increased competition, social justice criticises increased economic insecurity. Implicit in the viewpoint of economic rationalism is the employer. Implicit in social justice is the worker, particularly those who fall outside the affluent, professional middle-class. The last two decades in Australia has seen the increasing success of economic rationalism, despite increasing workplace inequities (Galbraith 1992, 2).

Social justice institutions (particularly unions) have, however, omitted and at times worked against the interests of particular groups of workers. They have been heavily gender biased and often racist. Historically, for instance, women's work was valued less than men's and even today part-time work (dominated by women) is poorly paid and rarely attracts the conditions of full-time work. Another example is enterprise bargaining (originally opposed by the Industrial Relations Commission), which was supported by the ACTU and employer groups. Yet women workers with their lack of bargaining power inevitably do not do well under it.

Despite their gender-biased origins, the social justice institutions associated with arbitration and labour market programs have, since the late 1960s, played a key role in improving women's position and reducing the gender gap. This indicates that, where the gender-biased nature of social justice institutions is recognised and dealt with (if only partially), they have considerable power to improve the position of women. Social justice is also the only approach that currently offers any hope for softening the impact of decentralised enterprise bargaining on the wages and conditions (including OHS) of workers. Its ability to do so, however, is being undermined as economic rationalists consolidate the move to a society where equity is defined purely in terms of market outcomes.

In more economically developed South East Asian societies, women have been successful in increasing their participation rates in the labour force. In Japan and South Korea, despite having passed equal opportunity legislation (rare by Asian standards), the position of women in the workforce still remains greatly inferior to that of men, owing to the persistence of traditional values. In Singapore, on the other hand, a more progressive attitude on the part of government, together with a booming labour market, have greatly boosted the economic position of women over the last three decades. But even so, they still experience similar problems to their western counterparts in their quest for advancement to the higher ranks of business and the professions.

REVIEW QUESTIONS

1. What are the main elements of workplace equity?
2. What is the significance of equity issues in industrial relations?
3. How do economic rationalists, EEO civil libertarians and proponents of social justice view equity issues? How do each believe workplace equity can be secured?
4. Organisational rules and procedures used to decide the allocation of positions and benefits, have generally been designed, whether deliberately or thoughtlessly, around the behaviour and attitudes of the historically dominant social group (Anglo-Australian, able-bodied, heterosexual males). Discuss
5. What are the main reasons for the inequalities in Australian workplaces.
6. 'There should be positive discrimination in favour women in recruitment to firms and promotion to managerial positions' Discuss.
7. What position do women hold in Japanese, South Korean and Singaporean labour markets.

FURTHER READING

Bennett, L. (1994) *Making Labour Law in Australia: Industrial Relations, Politics and Law*, Law Book Company, Sydney.

Bennett, L. (1994) 'Women and Enterprise Bargaining: The Legal and Institutional Framework.' *Journal of Industrial Relations*, vol. 36, 191-212.

Bishop, E., Crawshaw, J.W., Shaw, Q.C. and Walton, M.J. (1992) 'Overcoming Sex Discrimination in Employment in the Asian and Pacific Region through Legislation' in Chen, E., Lansbury, R., Ng, S., and Stewart, S. (eds) *Labour-Management Relations in the Asia Pacific Region*, Centre of Asian Studies, University of Hong Kong.

Hunter, R. (1992) *Indirect Discrimination in the Workplace*, The Federation Press, Sydney.

Whitehouse, G. (1990) 'Unequal Pay: A Comparative Study of Australia, Canada, Sweden and the U.K.' *Labour and Industry*, vol. 3, nos. 2 and 3, 354-371.

CHAPTER 12

Multinational Corporations

'Beware of all enterprises that require new clothes.'

Henry Thoreau

LEARNING OBJECTIVES

After studying the material in this chapter, you should be able to:

- grasp the economic significance of multinational corporations in the economies of developed and developing countries
- understand their impact on industrial relations
- list organised labour's responses to the challenges and threats posed by multinational companies.

INTRODUCTION

The growth of multinational corporations (MNCs), or transnational enterprises (TNEs) as they are sometimes called, since the World War II has had a major impact on national economies and their industrial relations systems. This has been particularly true in Australia and the five South East Asian countries studied in this book, all of which have long histories foreign business investment. In each case, the establishment of MNCs has conferred a wide range of political, social and economic advantages and disadvantages. In this chapter we will review the advantages and disadvantages MNCs have had on national industrial relations systems, labour markets and trade unions. First, we will examine the global development and expansion of MNCs in recent years. Then we will move on to the effect MNCs have had on national employment and skill levels. We will also look at the problems they confront when dealing with industrial relations and the organisational approaches they use when dealing with them. We then examine the problems national governments and trade union movements confront when trying to limit the power of MNCs or regulate their activities. We conclude by discussing various international organisations that play a key role in trying to regulate the activities of MNCs.

THE GLOBAL SPAN OF MNCs

Multinational corporations (MNCs), have been the subject of controversy since their appearance as a major force in the global economy. According to a recent United Nations (UN) report, MNCs are estimated to account directly for a total of more than 73 million jobs worldwide, representing about three per cent of the world's total labour force. MNCs furthermore account for about 20 per cent of paid employment in non-agricultural activities, particularly in developed countries, but also increasingly in some developing countries. The indirect employment effects of MNC activities are also considerable. Estimates for developing countries suggest that for each worker employed by foreign affiliates, one to two additional jobs are created (UNCTAD 1994). In 1994, the UN estimated that $80 billion in Foreign Direct Investment (FDI) was flowing into developing countries, representing 39 per cent of total world FDI (UNCTAD 1995). Therefore, MNCs, which have already had a major presence in the advanced industrial countries, are also becoming increasingly significant in the economies of less developed countries. To give some sense of the global span of MNCs, Table 12.1 provides a ranking of the top 100 multinational corporations based on the foreign assets they hold.

The corporations listed in Table 12.1 represent only 0.3 per cent of all MNCs, they control most international production, and with the exception of financial and banking institutions they are all based in developed countries. The largest, with over $US100 billion of assets and around 106,000 employees is Royal Dutch Shell, the Anglo-Dutch oil refining and distribution conglomerate. Together, the 100 largest MNCs own about $US1.4 trillion of assets abroad, and account for approximately one third of global FDI. The highlights in the growth trends for these top 100 companies during the period 1990-94 were as follows. Collectively, their assets grew by six per cent and their sales went up by five per cent. In 1993, the sales of their foreign affiliates accounted for a quarter of their estimated $6 trillion worldwide sales. Total employment among companies was estimated in 1993 to be around 12 million, or 16 per cent of the estimated 73 million employed by all MNCs. The share of employment by MNCs did not change over the period, despite corporate re-structuring, but labour productivity nonetheless rose significantly by almost 30 per cent (UNCTAD 1996, 29).

The highlights for the regional and country trends among the top 100 MNCs spanning the period 1990-94 were as follows. The US was the country of origin of the largest number of MNCs, with 32 corporations making the list. These firms covered a wide range of industries, including oil and gas, pharmaceuticals, metals, electronics and electrical equipment, motor vehicles, food and beverages, and diversified services. There was particularly fast growth over the period in consumer goods. Furthermore, the fastest growing MNCs in the group were Japanese companies, which increased in number from 11 to 19. These figures suggest that Japanese MNCs were investing heavily abroad, even though the outflows of FDI from Japan during the period were relatively low. The most important new entrants among Japanese MNCs were in the field of electronics, through large acquisitions in the US and the construction of new plants in East and South East Asia. Japanese MNCs had the foreign sales of the largest value in the electronics industry, compared with the top MNCs domiciled in from other countries (UNCTAD 1996, 33). European MNCs on the list were particularly prominent in research and development industries, including chemicals and pharmaceuticals. In these industries, there was a wave of mergers and acquisitions over the period in question, which saw many corporations in the region experience the fastest growth of foreign assets. By country of origin, the largest group of European MNCs was those from the UK, followed by Germany and France (UNCTAD 1996, 33).

Table 12.1 The top 100 MNCs ranked by foreign assets, 1994

The Top 100 MNCs ranked by foreign assets, 1994 (billions of dollars and numbers of employees)									
Ranking by:									
Foreign Assets | Index[b]		Corporation	Country	Industry[a]	Foreign	Total	Foreign	Total	Foreign	Total	Index[b]
					assets		sales		employment	
1	27	Royal Dutch Shell[c]	UK/Nethrld	Petroleum	63.7	102.0	51.1	94.8	79000	106000	63.6
2	80	Ford	USA	Motor vehicles	60.6	219.4	38.1	128.4	96726	337778	28.6
3	26	Exxon	USA	Petroleum	56.2	87.9	72.3	113.9	55000	86000	63.8
4	85	General Motors	USA	Motor vehicles	..d	198.6	44.0	152.2	177730	692800	25.7
5	38	IBM	USA	Computers	43.9	81.1	39.9	64.1	115555	219839	56.4
6	30	Volkswagen	Germany	Motor vehicles	..d	52.4	29.0	49.3	96545	242318	60.4
7	97	General Electric	USA	Electronics	33.9	251.5	11.9	59.3	36169	216000	16.7
8	82	Toyota	Japan	Motor vehicles	.d	116.8	37.2	91.3	27567	172675	28.1
9	59	Daimler - Benz	Germany	Transprt/Commun	27.9	66.5	46.3	74.0	79297	330551	42.8
10	37	Elf Aquitaine	France	Petroleum	..d	48.9	26.2	38.9	43950	89500	56.7
11	32	Mobil	USA	Petroleum	26.2	41.5	44.1	66.8	27400	58500	58.7
12	74	Mitsubishi	Japan	Diversified	..d	109.3	67.0	175.8	11146	36000	31.0
13	8	Nesd6	Switzerland	Food	25.4	38.7	47.3	48.7	206125	212687	86.5
14	72	Nissan Motor	Japan	Motor vehicles	..d	80.8	27.3	65.6	34464	143310	32.2
15	6	ABB Asea Brown Boveri Ltd[e]	Switzerland	Electrical equipment	24.8	29.1	25.6	29.7	194557	207557	88.4
16	68	Matsushita Electric	Japan	Electronics	..d	92.2	39.2	78.1	112314	265397	39.8
17	4	Roche Holdings	Switzerland	Pharmaceutical	23.4	25.9	10.3	10.5	50869	61381	90.5
18	31	Alcatel Alsthom	France	Electronics	23.1	51.2	21.9	30.2	117000	197000	58.9
19	33	Sony	Japan	Electronics	..d	47.6	30.3	43.3	90000	156000	58.5
20	51	Fiat	Italy	Motor vehicles	22.5	59.1	26.3	40.6	95930	251333	47.0
21	14	Bayer	Germany	Chemicals	22.4	27.4	21.9	26.8	78300	146700	72.5
22	83	Hitachi	Japan	Electronics	..d	92.5	19.8	56.8	80000	331852	27.7
23	10	Unilever[f]	UK/Nethrld	Food	22.0	28.4	39.1	45.4	276000	307000	84.5
24	9	Philips Electronics	Netherlands	Electronics	..d	27.8	31.7	33.7	210000	253000	85.0
25	49	Siemens	Germany	Electronics	..d	50.6	30.1	52.1	158000	376000	47.3
26	55	Renault	France	Motor vehicles	..d	41.2	16.7	32.5	39982	138279	43.7
27	18	British Petroleum	UK	Petroleum	19.5	28.8	30.8	50.7	48650	66550	67.2
28	67	Philip Morris	USA	Food	10.0	52.6	24.2	65.1	85000	165000	41.0
29	28	Hanson	UK	Building mater'ls	18.0	34.0	10.3	17.7	58000	74000	63.3
30	78	Mitsui	Japan	Diversified	..d	82.5	64.5	171.5	23560	80000	29.5
31	62	Du Pont	USA	Chemicals	..d	36.9	18.6	39.3	35000	107000	42.0
32	79	Nissho Iwai	Japan	Trading	..d	55.5	34.3	118.4	2101	7245	29.0
33	20	B.A.T. Industries	UK	Tobacco	15.8	48.5	25.0	32.8	158205	173475	66.7
34	24	Hoechst	Germany	Chemicals .	15.7	26.2	23.9	30.6	92333	165671	64.6
35	29	Rh6ne - Poulenc	France	Chemical	15.6	22.9	9.4	15.5	46430	81582	61.8
36	25	Ciba - Geigy	Switzerland	Chemicals	15.5	31.8	15.4	22.0	63095	83980	64.6
37	81	ENI	Italy	Petroleum	..d	54.3	10.9	31.1	19527	91544	28.1
38	87	Sumitomo	Japan	Trading	..d	59.0	48.5	167.7	..g	22000	24.2
39	21	Volvo	Sweden	Motor vehicles	14.2	18.6	16.7	20.2	30664	75549	66.6
40	76	Chevron	USA	Petroleum	13.0	34.4	10.6	35.1	10636	45758	30.3
41	92	Toshiba	Japan	Electronics	..d	63.2	11.4	56.6	38000	190000	20.0
42	5	Sandoz	Switzerland	Pharmaceutical	..d	14.9	11.3	11.6	51258	60304	88.8
43	89	Itochu Corporation	Japan	Trading	..d	62.5	36.1	162.3	2706	10140	22.7
44	54	Texaco	USA	Petroleum	11.7	25.5	16.6	32.5	10640	29713	44.2
45	41	BASF	Germany	Chemicals	11.3	25.7	19.6	27.0	40297	106266	51.5
46	48	VIAG AG	Germany	Diversified	11.2	23.3	8.6	17.8	41288	86018	48.0
47	95	Marubeni	Japan	Trading	..d	78.8	37.3	153.8	1915	10006	19.1
48	52	Dow Chemical	USA	Chemicals	10.4	26.5	8.6	16.7	24165	53700	45.3
49	70	Xerox	USA	Scientfc/Photo Eq	10.2	38.6	7.9	16.8	32150	87600	36.7
50	3	RTZ	UK	Mining	..d	11.7	5.6	6.1	43112	44499	91.4
51	66	Honda	Japan	Motor vehicles	..d	28.3	25.0	37.5	19668	92800	41.0
52	7	Electrolux	Sweden	Electronics	..d	11.3	12.9	14.0	94469	114103	87.3
53	91	ITT	USA	Diversified Serv	..d	100.8	7.8	23.8	23366	110000	21:1
54	23	Saint - Gobain	France	Building material	..d	16.5	8.7	13.4	58364	80909	65.2
55	43	Procter & Gamble	USA	Soap/cosmetics	9.6	25.5	16.1	30.3	57500	96500	50.0
56	100	AT&T	USA	Electronics	9.4	79.3	7.3	75.1	32820	304500	10.8
57	94	NEC Corporation	Japan	Electronics	9.3	47.7	11.6	43.3	17569	151069	19.3
58	11	Glaxo Wellcomeb	UK	Pharmaceutical	9.1	12.1	7.7	8.5	35523	47378	80.2
59	65	Hewlett - Packard	USA	Computers	9.0	19.6	9.5	25.0	39435	98400	41.4
60	1	The Thomson Corp	Canada	Publishing/Print	9.0	9.4	5.9	6.4	43100	48600	92.3

Continued 2

Table 12.1 The top 100 MNCs ranked by foreign assets, 1994   (cont'd)

Ranking by: Foreign Assets	Index[b]	Corporation	Country	Industry[a]	Foreign assets	Total assets	Foreign sales	Total sales	Foreign employment	Total employment	Index[b]
61	13	Seagram	Canada	Beverages	9.0	11.7	6.5	6.8	..g	15805	78.6
62	19	News Corporation	Australia	Publishing/Print	9.0	19.4	7.3	8.4	..g	25844	66.8
63	86	Nippon Steel Corp	Japan	Metal	..d	51.3	8.8	34.0	15000	50438	24.4
64	88	Amoco	USA	Petroleum	8.5	29.3	7.1	30.3	7541	43205	23.3
65	50	Robert Bosch	Germany	Motor vehicles	..d	17.7	11.5	21.2	62343	153794	47.2
66	40	BMW AG	Germany	Motor vehicles	8.2	17.1	17.9	25.9	50474	109362	54.4
67	16	Michelin	France	Rubber/plastics	8.0	13.1	9.9	12.2	..g	117776	72.0
68	71	Canon Inc.	Japan	Computers	8.0	23.9	14.1	21.0	35101	72280	33.5
69	64	Sharp Corporation	Japan	Electronics	..d	109.9	7.3	14.6	29000	42853	41.6
70	90	Veba	Germany	Trading	7.7	38.6	12.4	43.7	23894	126875	22.4
71	2	Solvay	Belgium	Chemicals	7.7	8.3	7.4	7.8	35695	39874	92.2
72	77	Pepsico	USA	Food	7.6	24.8	8.2	28.5	140170	471000	29.8
73	17	Total	France	Petroleum	..d	10.3	19.1	25.6	29340	51803	68.0
74	42	McDonalds	USA	Restaurants	..d	13.6	4.2	8.3	..g	183000	50.5
75	98	Chrysler	USA	Motor Vehicles	..d	49.5	6.6	52.2	24000	121000	15.4
76	63	Grand Metropolitan	UK	Food	..d	15.5	4.7	11.8	27006	64300	42.0
77	75	BHP	Australia	Metals	6.6	20.5	4.3	12.6	12000	48000	30.3
78	47	Johnson & Johnsn	USA	Pharmaceutical	6.6	15.7	7.9	15.7	42374	81537	48.1
79	45	Minnesota Mining	USA	Mining	6.4	13.1	6.2	12.1	32581	69843	48.9
80	22	Cable & Wireless	UK	Telecommunctn	..d	11.1	4.8	7.1	31128	41348	65.9
81	36	Digital Equipment	USA	Computers	6.0	10.6	8.3	13.5	43598	82800	57.2
82	69	Mannesmann	Germany	Industrl/FarmEqmt	..d	13.3	6.4	18.7	40487	124914	37.3
83	99	GTE	USA	Telecommunctn	5.8	42.5	2.6	19.9	14793	111000	13.3
84	44	Carrefour	France	Trade	5.8	11.9	13.3	27.1	44200	90300	49.0
85	39	Thomson	France	Electronics	5.8	16.3	10.1	13.9	57148	98714	55.3
86	46	Sara Lee	USA	Food	5.8	11.7	5.8	15.5	84932	145874	48.3
87	15	Alcan Aluminium	Canada	Metal products	5.7	9.7	8.0	9.3	28000	39000	72.3
88	93	Atlantic Richfield	USA	Petroleum	5.6	24.6	2.6	15.0	4631	23200	20.0
89	56	Motorola Inc.	USA	Electronics	5.2	17.5	12.6	22.3	58900	132500	43.6
90	84	International Paper	USA	Paper	5.1	17.8	3.3	15.0	20500	70000	26.6
91	35	LVMH Moet-Hensy	France	Beverages	..d	12.0	3.4	5.0	11737	18779	57.4
92	53	Alcoa	USA	Metals	..d	12.4	4.3	9.9	31400	61700	44.9
93	12	Akzo	Netherlands	Chemicals	4.9	6.9	11.2	12.0	51700	70400	79.3
94	34	Pechiney	France	Metals	4.9	9.9	8.3	12.8	33800	58234	57.5
95	73	RJR Nabisco	USA	Food & Tobacco	4.9	31.4	4.9	15.4	33950	70600	31.9
96	58	Eastman Kodak	USA	Scientfc/Photo Eqmt	..d	15.0	7.2	13.6	42000	96300	43.0
97	96	Kobe Steel Ltd.	Japan	Metals	..d	38.3	2.5	14.8	5522	32485	17.0
98	61	UnitedTechnologies	USA	Aerospace	4.8	15.6	8.8	21.2	95600	171500	42.5
99	57	Norsl Hydro	Norway	Chemicals	4.7	13.8	4.5	9.8	16208	32416	43.5
100	60	Bridgestone	Japan	Rubber/Plastics	..d	20.1	9.0	18.8	52000	89711	42.7

Source: UNCTAD, World Investment Report, 1996, 30-2.

a   Industry classification for companies follows that in the "Fortune Global 500" list in Fortune, 25 July 1994, and the "Fortune Global Service 500" list in Fortune, 22 August 1994. Fortune classifies companies according to the industry or service that represents the greatest volume of their sales. Industry groups are based on categories established by the United States Office of Management and Budget. Several companies are, however, highly diversified. These companies include Asea Brown Boveri, General Electric, Grand Metropolitan, Hanson, Sandoz, Total and Veba.
b   The index of transnationality is calculated as the average of foreign assets to total assets, foreign sales to total sales and foreign employment to total employment.
c   Foreign sales are outside Europe whereas foreign employment figures are outside the United Kingdom and the Netherlands.
d   Data on foreign assets are either suppressed to avoid disclosure or they are not available. In the case of non-availability, they are estimated on the basis of the ratio of foreign to total employment, foreign to total sales and similar ratios for the trans nationality index.
e   The company's business includes electric power generation, transmission and distribution, and rail transportation. The company was formed by the merger of a Swedish and a Swiss firm. Data on foreign sales and assets are outside Switzerland.
f   Foreign sales, assets and employment figures are outside the United Kingdom and the Netherlands.
g   Data on foreign employment are suppressed to avoid disclosure.
h   Glaxo Wellcome was previously called Glaxo Holdings, but changed name after the acquisition of Wellcome, United Kingdom. The data provided is for Glaxo alone up to 30 June 1994.

Table 12.2 The top 50 MNCs based in developing countries, ranked by foreign assets, 1994

Top 50 MNCs based in Developing Countries, ranked by foreign assets, 1994 (millions of dollars and number of employees)

Ranking by: Foreign Assets	Index[a]	Corporation	Economy	Industry	Foreign assets	Total assets	Foreign sales	Total sales	Foreign employment	Total employment	Index[a]
1	11	Daewoo	Korea, Republ[b]	Electronics	..c	33000	16000	40000	100000	200000	33.0
2	10	HutchisnWhampoa	Hong Kong	Diversified	..c	52192	12500	30168	15086	26855	34.4
3	8	Cemex S.A.	Mexico	Cement	2847	7893	744	2101	8073	20997	36.6
4	5	Jardine Matheson	Hong Kong	Construction	2539	6350	6463	9559	50000	220000	43.4
5	..	China State Constr	China	Construction	2189	..e	1010	..e	..e	..e	..
6	..	China Chemicals	China	Trading	1915	..e	7914	..e	..e	..e	..
7	20	Samsung Co., Ltd.	Korea, Republ[b]	Electronics	..c	38000	21440	67000	42235	195429	19.5
8	17	LG Group	Korea, Republ[b]	Electronics	..c	25000	8600	43000	29061	59200	25.1
9	19	Grupo Televisa SA	Mexico	Media	1371	3260	286	1288	..f	21600	22.2
10	34	Hyundai	Korea, Republ[b]	Diversified	1293	9657	1610	13081	814	44835	9.2
11	15	Souza Cruz S.A.	Brazil	Tobacco	935	1246	316	3784	63	11387	28.0
12	23	Keppel Corporation	Singapore	Diversified	817	9118	248	1377	2847	12113	16.8
13	25	San Miguel Corp	Philippines	Food	806	2939	252	2599	2702	30965	15.3
14	14	Tatung Co. Ltd.	Taiwan	Electrical Eqmt	805	3983	1200	3621	9777	27769	29.5
15	7	Dong Ah Constr Ind	Korea, Republ[b]	Construction	734	3431	1134	2547	6828	12630	40.0
16	41	Petroleo Brasileiro	Brazil	Petroleum	715	30162	2316	26396	24	50295	3.7
17	..	China Metals/Minrls	China	Trading	710	..e	2270	..e	..e	..e	..
18	3	Acer	Taiwan	Electronics	665	2033	2079	3172	4164	9981	46.7
19	30	New World Devlt	Hong Kong	Diversified	624	6944	316	1721	2520	28000	12.1
20	2	Fraser & Neave Ltd	Singapore	Diversified	590	2728	839	1491	6547	8365	52.1
21	39	Singapore Telecom	Singapore	Telecommuns	577	4811	50	2490	411	11279	5.9
22	..	China Harbrs Eng	China	Construction	559	..e	409	..e	..e	..e	..
23	6	Sime Darby Berhad	Malaysia	Food	557	1189	1857	3159	7500	32000	43.0
24	21	Wing On Intl Ltd	Hong Kong	Diversified	491	1499	62	393	188	2792	18.4
25	..	China Shougang	China	Metals	446	..e	980	..e	..e	..e	..
26	..	China Cereals, Oil,	China	Trading	440	..e	6200	..e	..e	..e	..
27	18	CMPC Empresas	Chile	Paper	352	2612	380	891	1718	10465	24.2
28	42	Chinese Petroleum	Taiwan	Petroleum	349	14148	157	10748	19	21231	1.3
29	31	Formosa Plastic	Taiwan	Chemicals	327	1906	233	1491	60	3645	11.5
30	35	Empresas Ica Soc	Mexico	Construction	321	3264	95	1386	2136	25267	8.4
31	26	Sadia Concordia	Brazil	Food	313	1405	567	2784	57	32357	14.3
32	22	Desc SA de CV	Mexico	Diversified	313	1902	313	1633	3431	19288	17.8
33	..	China ForeignTrade	China	Transportatn	300	..e	300	..e	..e	..e	..
34	16	Hong Kong Hotels	Hong Kong	Hotel	292	2628	47	230	2756	5540	27.0
35	27	Grupo Indstrl Bimbo	Mexico	Food		1221	252	1252		42463	13.3
36	1	Creative Technol	Singapore	Electronics	224	445	638	658	883	2678	60.1
37	24	Amsteel Corp Ber	Malaysia	Diversified	209	1459	80	1066	7800	28200	16.5
38	..	China Iron/Steel	China	Metals	188	..e	257	..e	..e	..e	..
39	36	Co Cervejaria Brahma	Brazil	Food	187	1755	80	1249	476	9606	7.3
40	33	Sam Yang Co.	Korea,Republ[b]	Diversified	170	1964	115	1487	864	5795	10.4
41	37	China Steel Corp	Taiwan	Metal	170	5737	467	2492	6	9561	7.3
42	4	Hyosung Corp	Korea,Republ[b]	Trading	117	553	2206	2812	470	1460	43.9
43	38	Evergreen Marine	Taiwan	Transport	117	1678	80	1152	91	1298	7.0
44	9	Grupo Sidek	Mexico	Tourism	114	2831	25	575	10438	10774	35.1
45	40	TongYang Cement	Korea,Republ[b]	Cement	91	1733	39	736	116	2208	5.3
46	29	CharoenPokphand	Thailand	Food	82	642	109	857	1077	8440	12.8
47	12	Malaysn Intl Shipg	Malaysia	Transport	72	172	406	885	321	3004	32.8
48	28	Usimina -Siderurg	Brazil	Steel	63	3949	564	2280	1375	10448	13.2
49	32	Vitro Societad Ano	Mexico	Non-metallic	52	4338	800	2872	1000	36694	10.6
50	13	Aracruz Celulose	Brazil	Paper	..c	2593	482	529	..f	3378	31.1

Source: UNCTAD, *World Investment Report*, 1996, 34-5.

a The index of transnationality is calculated as the average of foreign assets to total assets, foreign sales to total sales, and foreign employment to total employment.
b The accounting standards of the Republic of Korea do not require the publication of consolidated financial statements including both domestic and foreign affiliates. The figures here are estimates as provided by the companies in response to a survey by UNCTAD. Depending on the availability of the data on foreign components, the data for business group totals are used.
c Data on foreign assets are either suppressed to avoid disclosure or they are not available. When non-availabile, they are estimated on the basis of the ratio of foreign to total employment, foreign to total sales and similar ratios for the trans nationality index.
d A subsidy of Jardine Matheson Holdings of Bermuda.
e Data are not available.
f Data on foreign employment are suppressed to avoid disclosure or are not available. In the case of non-availability of the data, they are estimated on the basis of other foreign components ratios for the transnationality index.

Table 12.2 sets out statistics relating to the top 50 MNCs based in developing countries. It shows that the 50 largest MNCs accounted for around ten per cent of the total of outward FDI coming from the countries in which they were domiciled. In 1994, more than half the MNCs in this group were based in Asia, the remainder being in Latin America. Of the countries discussed in this book, South Korea and Singapore were the most prominent countries represented (UNCTAD 1996, 33). The statistics also reveal that developing country FDI is usually directed to other developing countries, generally in the same region. For example, Daewoo is the largest foreign investor in Vietnam and Singapore's largest MNC, Keppel Corporation, a shipbuilding and repair company, derived about 18 per cent of its total earnings from projects in Vietnam. Furthermore, in recent years there has been the strong drive by corporations based in South Korea to shift from exports to outward investment, which has been driven by the government's desire to internationalise the country's national economy. Consequently, MNCs from South Korea have been motivated to invest abroad not only by lower costs, but also because they wish to access new markets and technology. A notable feature of this has been the way they have made large investments in developed countries (e.g. the United States and Europe). They have also targeted developing economies in central and Eastern Europe, including Hungary, Romania and Russia (UNCTAD 1996, 36).

MULTINATIONAL CORPORATIONS IN AUSTRALIA

Foreign ownership in Australia dates back to early colonial times. In the nineteenth century, for instance, the pastoral and mining industries, which became the backbone of the country's early economic growth, were largely developed using capital supplied by British investors. Twentieth century foreign ownership involved the arrival of MNCs from other countries, such as the United States and Japan, especially after Word War II. MNCs have therefore long occupied an extremely important position in the local economy. Information on the activities and their operations in Australia is sparse. But statistics taken during 1980s suggest that the Australian economy has one of the highest levels of foreign ownership of all the members of the OECD (Organisation for Economic Cooperation and Development). Foreign interests control around half of Australia's mining, and around one-third of the country's manufacturing and financial services (see, Renwick 1988, 3). There is little reason to believe these figures have declined over the course of the 1990s, and, if anything, have probably increased as a consequence of deregulatory policies introduced by various governments in the area of trade and investment.

This high degree of foreign ownership and control of Australian economic assets has made MNCs the subject of particularly close political scrutiny and controversy in this country. In the early 1970s, for example, the Whitlam Labor Government (1972-75) sought to implement a policy of economic nationalism. The aim of this policy was to 'buy back the farm' by replacing foreign ownership of Australian assets with local ownership (Crough and Wheelwright 1982, 5-6). The subsequent Liberal-National Coalition governments of Malcolm Fraser (1975-83) was similarly moved to imposed a number nominal regulations on the extent of foreign ownership and control, but these were never seriously enforced (Crough and Wheelwright 1982, 7-8). Since this time the political mood in the country has become more supportive of the activities of MNCs. Both the Hawke and Keating Labor Governments (1983-96), and the current Howard Coalition Government (1996-) have accepted the overall legitimacy and importance of multinational corporations in the development of the Australian national economy. Typical of arguments raised to support this approach have been the local benefits that flow from foreign investment. These, it is argued, include:

- the creation of jobs
- the transfer of technology
- the generation of greater competition
- the provision of cheaper goods and services.

The trade union movement and leftwing thinkers outside political circles, however, have been more sceptical of the benefits attributed to the local operations of MNCs, particularly in relation areas such employment, working conditions and national sovereignty. The general arguments from the unions range across a number of important areas including:

- the rapid development of technologies is making the location and direction of production less dependent on geography, with the result that goods in small volume and high value can be produced almost anywhere in the world. Whilst this in itself is not a bad thing, it allows firms to use the threat of relocation to bargain down the wages and conditions of workers. In other words, the ability to transfer or close production gives MNCs the capacity to 'play-off' one country's workers against the workers of another country
- the introduction of new technologies makes it possible to break down complex production processes into basic work units, and thereby fragment jobs and de-skill operations. Such is the sophistication of the new technology that production can be geared to a world-wide labour market, with widely different wage rates and skills
- because of the complex lines of organisational authority within MNCs, trade unions find it difficult to gain access to the key decision-makers, who may be located in the head office of a parent company located in another country
- for similar reasons, there are problems in obtaining appropriate access to information for negotiation purposes
- MNCs can exploit local labour markets because there is a lack of effective international laws to regulate labour practices.

The consequence is that the benefits of MNC operations must be offset against the damage they can cause to workers employment prospects and working conditions (McCarthy 1991, 228-9). On the issue of nation sovereignty, it is suggested that MNCs have the potential to suppress the political freedom of countries by threatening the stability of national economies. This line of argument holds that MNCs have the capacity to restrict their subsidiaries on exporting to third countries, which can be to the detriment of the economic interest of the host country. Indeed, such restrictions can result in resource under-utilisation, which in turn can negatively affect industry performance and the wages of workers. MNCs may also import from foreign suppliers to the detriment of local suppliers, with negative consequences for local business and employment. MNCs can use the threat of closure or relocation to put pressure on national political systems to secure their economic interests. MNCs may furthermore engage in 'transfer pricing' by manipulating important export prices to enhance global profits at the expense of tax revenue in the host country (McCarthy 1991, 228-9).

It must be said, however, that the extent to which such practices actually occur is open to question. As far as transfer pricing is concerned, for example, governments and researchers have found it extremely hard to gather evidence about the extent of this practice. One US House of Representatives study in 1990 claimed that about half of the nearly 40 foreign corporations surveyed had paid virtually no taxes for a ten year period. The loss of revenue through transfer pricing was estimated at $35 billion. A British study of 210 MNCs in 1995 also showed that 83 per cent had been involved in a transfer-pricing dispute. If it is difficult for Internal Revenue Services in advanced countries like the US and the UK to establish the extent of transfer pricing. It is even more difficult for developing countries to do so (Dicken 1998, 247).

THE IMPACT OF MNCs ON LOCAL LABOUR MARKETS

Much of the available evidence suggests that MNCs are a major force in generating employment in the world economy. One observer has cautioned against looking at the effects of MNCs on employment in aggregate terms because creation of new jobs in host countries by MNCs may result in displacement of jobs in local enterprises, which are unable to compete effectively against them. Thus, it is possible that net employment losses may occur in some cases (Dicken 1998, 257-8). On the other hand, there may also be positive effects, in terms of creating new opportunities for local businesses as suppliers, and stimulation of new enterprises through 'spin-off'. This latter term refers to managerial staff setting up their own businesses on the basis of skills and experience gained through working for foreign firms (Dicken 1998, 256-7).

However, there have been a number of concerns about the negative effects of MNCs on home country employment and quality of employment provided. Some see the establishment of enterprises overseas as being invariably accompanied by job losses in the home country. This has been a problem in the United States, where the implementation of the 'NAFTA' agreement (North American Free Trade Agreement) has seen many workers retrenched as companies relocate to Mexico to take advantage of that country's cheap labour (Enderwick 1994, 7). As for the quality of employment, the fear has been that MNCs have a detrimental impact on skill levels and employment security. This raises the question of what type of employment (skilled or unskilled) is generated by MNCs, and whether technological change results in the de-skilling of workforces and higher levels of job insecurity in host countries. The evidence is that MNCs are more heavily represented in capital and technology intensive industries. Conseqently, MNC subsidiaries in host countries have a greater need than local companies to train and retain the higher skilled workers needed to operate and service their more technologically sophisticated equipment (Enderwick 1994, 7-8).

As far as wages are concerned, the overall evidence suggest that MNCs pay above average wages compared with local firms in both developed and developing countries (UNCTAD 1994, 197-8). While this is obviously beneficial to workers employed by MNCs, it has often led to problems of income inequality when selective groups of local workers gain in comparison with other members of the labour force. The ability of MNCs to pay above average wages has nonetheless had the tendency to encourage 'credentialism' (i.e. the practice of making the selection for jobs dependent on the possession of formal qualifications). This has generally had a positive impact on the education levels of host country workforces, and particularly so in under-developed and developing countries (Lloyd 1982; Miller and

Zaidi 1982). However, a problem that has surfaced, particularly in Asian countries, in the mid-1990s, has been that MNCs have subcontracted work to local firms which have paid exceptionally low wages and whose working conditions have been very poor. In response, many MNCs have responded to this criticism by implementing codes of conduct to which their subcontractors must conform (Dicken 1998, 259).

The question of skill levels has already been touched upon in the previous passages. In the main, MNCs have had a positive impact on raising the skill levels of host country labour-forces. However, there is also much evidence to suggest that MNCs rarely improve the skill level of workers beyond the requirements necessary to run their plant and equipment. This is confirmed by the fact that most MNCs undertake a significant proportion of their research and development in the home country. In short, MNCs headquartered in industrialised countries are reluctant to employ or train skilled technicians and scientists in their overseas operations. On the more general issue of contribution to training and development, especially in less developed countries, the evidence is mixed. In general, it seems that MNCs provide as much training as their host country competitors. They also appear to play a significant role in developing management capacity and employee skills through the use of more advanced technology and by offering more sophisticated training opportunities than locally based competitors (UNCTAD 1994, 228-9).

One of the main problems posed by MNCs is their ability to transfer operations across borders, thus threatening the stability of employment in host countries. However, the evidence suggests that there is little difference in the level of employment security between local companies and MNCs. It has also been speculated that MNCs tend to react differently to local counterparts when confronted with national economic recessions. Both the Australian and Canadian governments have both expressed concerns over this issue. The concerns centred on the possible negative employment consequences if a profitable subsidiary of a MNC is downsized or closed because of economic difficulties faced by the parent company in its home country. It was nonetheless recognised there were no particular problems with employment stability among MNCs when compared with local companies (Franko 1994, 123-4).

The Australian car industry provides a good example of the MNC employment stability and organisational commitment issues within a host country. National government policy since the mid-1980s, for example, has been aimed at reducing the number of local manufacturers and the range of models they produce, and to increase the economic viability of the industry after some initial job-shedding. The aim was to stabilise employment at a lower level, while offering a range of product choices and quality to car buyers. As part of this policy, efforts have been made to reduce tariff protection, which was originally introduced to encourage overseas car manufacturers to set up in Australia. Some manufacturers, the most recent being Nissan, have withdrawn from manufacturing in Australia and have instead become importers. Other manufacturers, notably Ford and General Motors, have a long-term commitment to producing in Australia. These companies have been limited in the option of withdrawing because of the substantial Australian investments they have in plant and equipment (Renwick 1994, 93-4). The Japanese car manufacturers, Toyota, Nissan and Mitsubishi, have shown less commitment (Bamber and Shadur 1993, 45) because their combined investment has been lower and more recent (Renwick 1988, 94-8).

Nevertheless, the bargaining power of MNCs is not unlimited, and their ability to shift operations from one country to another is often constrained by factors such as existing levels of investment and profitability. In particular, firms in capital intensive industries are more difficult and costly to shift from one location to another. Of course, the bargaining power of MNCs may be greater in the case of under-developed and developing countries, where economies are more vulnerable and political processes are less stable. Certainly, the bargaining power of MNCs was increased by the economic downturn experienced by many South East Asian countries since 1997.

On the other hand, as Selvarajah (1991, 169) points out, there are other factors which can serve to diminish the power MNCs operating in under-developed and developing countries. In the context of a rapidly globalising economy, for example, the increased competition for market share has meant governments can play off one MNC against another. There has also been a tendency among many developing countries, for example, Singapore, Malaysia, South Korea and India, to develop their own MNCs. The Indian Oberoi chain of hotels, for example, is now a well-established MNC, which competes with international hotel chains around the world.

THE IMPACT OF MNCs ON LOCAL INDUSTRIAL RELATIONS SYSTEMS

There has been a significant degree of speculation on what impact MNCs have on industrial relations. Whilst there has been a growing literature on international human resource management and employee relations, surprisingly little is documented on how MNCs manage their human resources, particularly across national borders (Teo and Rodwell 1998, 2). Enderwick (1994) argues that there are several reasons for expecting differences between foreign-owned and locally owned firms. First, MNCs tend to be larger than their local counterparts, even in developed countries. This can influence a range of industrial relations practices, which in part appear to be a function of size. There may also be differences industrial relations are often a reflection of the culture of a society. Despite efforts made by the managers of foreign subsidiaries, the industrial relations practices of their organisations are invariably influenced by the traditions, customs and practices of the parent company and its the home country. It is not uncommon to find these periodically coming into conflict with the industrial relations traditions, customs and practices of the host country (Enderwick 1994, 15-6).

The combination of multi-nationality and authority structure of MNCs also have a bearing on their industrial relations practices. Where authority is highly centralised, it is often the case that local managers lack power to make decisions in collective bargaining forums, with decisions being made in distant corporate headquarters where there is little understanding, awareness or even interest in local circumstances (Dicken 1998, 260). From the trade union perspective, this is usually viewed as a deliberate attempt to frustrate or by-pass the bargaining process. A further problem exists in the way MNCs are able to make cross-national comparisons. Many efforts to introduce 'best practice' systems of people management on the basis of such comparisons have run into problems because they conflict with local industrial relations cultures.

Such problems, according to Enderwick, (1994), means that industrial relations is a major problem area for MNCs. In dealing with these problems some MNCs have been overtly anti-union and sought to avoid the unionisation of their workforces by setting up at 'green-field' sites in economically depressed areas. Others have sought to by-pass trade unions by negotiating individual contracts with employees. Many have sought to keep trade union coverage down to one union per site (Enderwick 1994, 17).

Other tactics used by MNCs have involved decentralising the function of dealing with industrial relations down to the local level. However, there is also contrary evidence to support the view that, while industrial relations is one of the most decentralised functions in MNCs, it is still subject to a higher degree of centralisation than in locally-based companies with multiple plants. In addition, the degree of centralisation also appears to be dependent on the nationality of the MNC. Japanese firms, for example, typically practise more centralised and more autocratic decision-making with regard to industrial relations issues than their British or American counterparts (see, Negandhi et al. 1985). The nature of the issues being collectively bargained and the performance of the subsidiary can also be factors affecting the degree of centralisation of decision-making (Enderwick 1994, 17).

The evidence about placing control over industrial relations in the hands of indigenous managers is mixed. Research has emphasised the diversity of MNCs in terms of their approach to management and staffing policies. Three types of strategy have been distinguished: (1) ethnocentricity, (2) polycentricity and (3) geocentricity. Ethnocentric enterprises are wholly owned and managed by managers in the host country, and are treated as direct extensions of the parent company. Polycentric enterprises are those where there are locally recruited managers and there may even be local participation in ownership. Geocentric enterprises have a management structure that transcends national differences and boundaries. The most qualified and effective managers from any country where the company operates may be promoted and sent to any other country of operation (Perlmutter 1969). Research indicates that American and European companies tend to apply polycentric staffing policies, whereas Japanese companies tend to apply ethnocentric staffing policies (see, Deresky 1994).

In a variation of this categorisation, Brunnecke et al. (1991) have classified MNCs on the basis of whether they play an 'adaptive' role or an 'ambassadorial' role when interacting with different industrial relation systems. Adapters, it is argued, accommodate themselves to the systems they find in place, whereas ambassadors attempt to bring about systematic change to the entire national systems of host countries. There is evidence that both American and Japanese MNCs are prone to play assertive ambassadorial roles in host countries. In this regard it has been noted that they are inclined to use their economic power to force changes, typically by blackmailing or bribing their workforces into accepting radical new working practices (Lucio and Weston 1994). This, quite naturally, has been a cause of some disquiet to many national trade union movements. This condition has not been helped by the fact that American and Japanese MNCs have tended to take a unitarist view of industrial relations. In contrast, the trade union movements of the host countries are normally wedded to a pluralist view, and expect that workers should enjoy the same rights to trade union membership and industrial action as their home country counterparts.

A further source of concern for trade union movements has been the information disclosure practices of MNCs. Issues which have arisen have included: the level at which information is compiled; the usefulness of the type of information disclosed; the timing of disclosure; and, the reliability of information provided. The practice of transfer pricing within MNCs may pose particular problems for unions in respect of information disclosure (Enderwick 1985, 114-5).

Trade unions from various countries have attempted to exert pressure on international organisations to obtain international regulatory codes of conduct. This pressure led to the ILO issuing a Tripartite Declaration of Principles concerning Multinational Enterprises and Social Policy in 1977, which includes information disclosure provisions (see below). However, for various reasons, these principles have had little practical impact. A code of conduct issued by the OECD has been more significant, but has still had very limited impact (Enderwick 1985, 134-8). The most comprehensive and influential provisions about information disclosure are those applying within the European Union, originating from the so-called Vredeling Directive (see below) (Blanpain 1983).

CULTURAL DIFFERENCES IN INDUSTRIAL RELATIONS PRACTICES

MNCs have traditionally pioneered introduction of new and innovative labour management practices. They have transferred successful practices from the home to the host countries, but in the context of often very different industrial relations systems in the host countries. In the early post-war era, most multinationals were American, and they introduced a range of new employment practices. These included merit and performance payment schemes, systematic job evaluation, longer term collective agreements, concession bargaining and no-strike agreements (Gennard 1972). More recently, the spotlight has been on Japanese MNCs whose numbers increased dramatically from the 1970s onwards. (See Table 12.1)

The hallmark of Japanese MNCs has been the search for labour flexibility. According to Rico (1987), new style work agreements by Japanese MNCs have a number of common features, including:

- preference for single union recognition or the rationalisation of multi-union structures
- uniform working conditions for different employee groups.

Equality in terms of working hours, holidays pensions and sickness pay is a means of promoting labour flexibility across functions. Japanese plants typically have workers at all levels dressed in the same uniforms, eating in the same canteens and with no special privileges for management, such as the executive washroom. No-strike clauses in agreements, often with provision for binding arbitration, are also frequently found in 'new style agreements'. There is also generally a strong emphasis on and investment in training, careful screening of new employees and a commitment of substantial resources to the personnel function (Enderwick 1994, 19).

As Enderwick (1994) comments, two features of transplanted Japanese-style management are noteworthy:

- The transplantation is almost invariably selective. The traditional features of management in Japan such as lifetime employment, seniority wages accompanied by company welfare schemes, and company unions, are rarely used in host countries. Research indicates that Japanese companies are in these respects very pragmatic and adapt their practices to conditions in the host countries

- Japanese management practices have generally been greeted with uncritical approval, because of their perceived superiority. As Enderwick (1994) argues, a problem with this is that Japanese practices may be introduced selectively without forming coherent packages. In many instances, these practices are introduced into an alien environment (where the attitudes of management and labour are typically more adversarial than in Japan) or are a response to a crisis situation. These circumstances are not conducive to success (1994, 19-20).

The experience of Japanese management, both in developed and underdeveloped countries, has brought to light a number of problems and criticisms. In the US, for example, there have been criticisms of Japanese production management methods, on the basis that they increase stress, and constitute safety hazards as assembly lines are speeded up and labour is used more intensively (Young 1992). Trade union opposition has also been aroused by the practice of creating 'tame' cooperative plant unions, with officials that act as team leaders and first line supervisors (Rehder 1990). In addition, Japanese employers have fallen foul of anti-discrimination laws in the US, with legal actions brought against them by women and members of minority groups (Negandhi et al. 1985; Johnson 1988; Woodward 1992).

As noted above, another criticism of Japanese management is its extremely centralised and autocratic nature when compared with other multinationals. While this has been somewhat tempered by market conditions and the existence of industrial democracy in advanced western countries, it is especially prevalent in less developed countries (Negandhi et al. 1985, 100). (This finding may appear contradictory to the picture of Japanese management presented in Chapter 3. Perhaps it is best explained by pointing out that Japan is a very homogeneous society and, within their own cultural context, Japanese relate to each other differently than when dealing with foreign nationals in host countries.)

There are a number of other problems that have been identified in the practice of Japanese management of MNCs, including the following:

- A low level of trust in local managers. Japanese companies will often restrict their trust to a few key local officials, who may suffer stress and conflict as a result of having to maintain a balance between two cultures
- Ethnocentric staffing policies at higher organisational levels. Japanese MNCs are the most ethnocentric of all the multinationals in terms of promotions to top management. There is typically a ceiling for locally employed managers, and Japanese managers enjoy superior employment privileges, compared with their local counterparts, as far as job security, training, fringe benefits and access to key information from head office are concerned.
- Problems with trade unions. The situation in the US has already been discussed. In less developed countries, such as Thailand, Malaysia, South Korea and the Phillipines, where labour has traditionally been in a weak position because of high unemployment and oppressive regimes (although this situation has recently changed in the Phillipines and South Korea) Japanese companies have been reported as engaging in overtly anti-union activities (Negandhi et al. 1985, 102-3). It is, however, true to say that US-based multinational corporations are hardly any better than their Japanese counterparts in their response to organised labour.
- Low wage policies. Japanese companies have become known for paying the lowest wages of all multinationals in South East Asia. Japanese firms have followed a systematic policy of moving labour intensive industries across borders into countries where labour costs are a fraction of those in Japan, in particular Thailand, Indonesia and South Korea. Often, low wages go with lack of technological sophistication. This tendency by Japanese companies is really an extension of the dual wages policy in Japan itself (Ozawa 1979, 201-6), where workers in large corporations enjoy much better pay and conditions than those working for small supplier companies. Once again, Japanese multinationals are not unique in seeking low labour costs, but they are at the extreme end of the spectrum.

More generally, recent literature suggests that MNCs are trying to balance employee relations issues by following host country norms for operational issues and adapting the style in which these practices are carried out to parent country norms (Teo and Rodwell 1998). Teo and Rodwell (1998) conclude that there are therefore few differences among MNCs, in respect to their practices directly associated with productivity and levels of cost. However, there are some differences in systems and structures which allow the expression of parent company style in host country operations. At the same time, pressures of global competition appear to be causing significant convergence of many MNC policies and practices.

A number of variables, both external and internal, influence MNCs human resource and employee relations practices. Industry factors, as well as each country's legal, social and political framework, can influence HR practices in different ways. For example, government economic development policies and intervention in the labour market have been very significant in shaping employee relations policies and practices in Malaysia and Singapore (Frenkel and Royal 1996). Where local laws require particular practices (e.g. EEO and affirmative action), or industrial relations practices are highly visible, involving considerable interaction with locals, there are strong pressures on MNCs to conform to local practices (Rosenzweig and Nohia 1993). On the other hand, where there are major internal inequities, or practices that require a high degree of interaction with the parent company, MNCs will be pressurised to conform to the practices of the parent company and country of origin. Internal factors which impact upon MNC practices include structure, size, degree of control exercised by the parent company, as well as the interactions between management, unions and government (Teo and Rodwell 1998, 5-6).

In some of the more recent literature, researchers have tried to group MNCs into three broad 'blocks', American, European and Asian, to try to highlight major policy trends in various countries. This body of research (Teo and Rodwell) has sought to describe the three approaches as follows:

- US MNCs are unitarist, with a high commitment of workers to employers and little need for trade unions
- Japanese MNC's are strong on team-working, flexibility, uniformity of status among workers, often accompanied by a single trade union, and extensive communication systems, including suggestion schemes and quality circles
- Europe (especially the UK) MNCs have anti-union systems with fewer constraints on management and an efficiency-driven approach to labour usage.

However, Ferner (1996) concludes that there is only a small body of literature on the 'country of origin' effect. Other researchers have disagreed on the issue of whether or not convergence is occurring in relation to ER practices within the same grouping of national cultures (Sparrow et al. 1994; Newman and Nollen 1996; Monk 1996). Thus, research concerning the influence of 'country of origin' on the choice of HRM practices by MNCs' has been inconclusive, including studies on the degree of head office control and the difference in national cultures between the host and parent countries (Teo and Rodwell 1998, 7).

LOCAL TRADE UNION RESPONSES TO THE MNCs

As a number of authors have argued, it is very difficult for organised labour to counter the challenges posed by the MNC and engage in effective multinational bargaining (see, Abbott 1998). In some countries, particularly underdeveloped countries, the labour movement is weak and disorganised. But even in more developed countries, there has been a general decline in trade union power during the 1980s and 1990s (Boswell and Stevis 1997, 2-3). In addition, even where there are stronger and better organised labour movements, they may be divided by ideological and religious differences, or their form of organisation may be fragmented, ill-suited to dealing with the challenges posed by the MNC. For example, in the USA, unions are organised on a plant basis ('locals'), with only very weak forms of federal organisation ('internationals'). Clearly, the UK, Australian and New Zealand emphasis on craft, industrial and general unions, provides a better basis for concerted action than the decentralised form of organisation in the USA (McCarthy 1991, 237).

But the biggest obstacle faced by organised labour is the fact that, at best, its organisation is national, and not equal to dealing with organisations which operate across national borders. Also, there can be conflicts of interest between the trade union movements of different countries. This can make it difficult for them to cooperate in dealing with MNCs. An alternative approach might be for unions to attempt to reduce the power of MNCs or increase the power of labour (Bergsten, et al. 1978).

Attempts to reduce the power of MNCs at national level have centred on host and source nation negotiation of Foreign Direct Investment (FDI) bilateral investment agreements. Trade unions in some home countries, such as the American Federation of Labor-Congress of Industrial Organisations (AFL-CIO), the equivalent of the ACTU in the US, did lobby governments to place restrictions on outward foreign investment to protect local jobs, but these attempts ultimately failed (Enderwick 1994, 303). Furthermore, while countries such as Canada and Australia systematically pursue anticipated benefits of foreign investment, these controls have been largely ineffective in view of global competition for scarce investment funds. Bilateral treaties providing for such matters as double taxation and insurance arrangements are also subject to shortcomings, such as the diversion of investment into non-participating economies (1994, 202-3).

TRADE UNIONS, INTERNATIONAL POLITICAL ORGANISATIONS AND MNCs

Trade unions have sought to work through established international agreements, or set up linkages through such agreements to deal with MNCs. Their efforts have centred on political lobbying, in some cases supported by local business interests, for negotiating international codes to regulate the behaviour of MNCs.

The international organisations through which unions have sought to channel their opposition to MNCs include the International Labour Organisation (ILO), the Organistin for Economic Cooperation and Development (OECD), the United Nations (UN) and its various specialised agencies, and the European Union (EU). The ILO is the last remnant of the now defunct League of Nations, dating back to 1919. International socialists originally hoped that the ILO would be a supranational body controlled by labour unions (Boswell and Stevis 1997). In the event, however, it was established as a tripartite organisation, consisting of representatives of governments, employers and trade unions. The ILO has the power to make conventions, setting labour standards for member countries, though these conventions have no binding force unless ratified by the legislatures of the member countries. As Boswell and Stevis (1997) put it, the adoption and implementation of ILO Conventions is in the hands of 'recalcitrant' states. Nevertheless, the ILO has had a major impact on the labour practices of both MNCs and local employers through the setting of minimum standards of compliance.

Between 1919 and 1968, the ILO introduced 128 binding conventions, and 132 recommendations. According to Enderwick (1994, 304) these international instruments have had a major impact. By 1968, there were more than 3,400 ratifications by 115 nations of 120 conventions. Moreover, the national legislation and practices of many countries has also been influenced by the non-mandatory recommendations adopted by the ILO Conferences. Some recent issues relating to minimum labour standards discussed by ILO Conferences have included matters relating to freedom of association, forced labour, discrimination and child labour. A particularly important ILO initiative was the ILO Tripartite Declaration on Multinational Enterprises and Social Policy (1977). This Declaration was the result of labour pressure and studies on the impact of MNCs. It contained a number of important procedural features:

- the recommended principles were non-mandatory
- the principles applied equally to all enterprises, regardless of ownership and multinationality
- the principles were very specific, covering only matters within the ILO authority, relating to employment and industrial relations
- the impact of the principles (on labour market practices of MNCs) was anticipated to be evolutionary
- provision was made for review and amendment over-time.

The ILO Declaration on MNCs addressed four major issues:

- its purpose was to act as a model for MNC employers in raising labour standards in developing countries. (In particular, there was much scope for MNCs to increase their training and development, as well as assisting in the development of union representation and collective bargaining.)
- it supplemented local custom and practice, because MNCs were viewed as increasingly likely to integrate into host nations' labour relations frameworks
- it sought to improve access of unions to corporate information for authentic bargaining purposes
- it supported bargaining at the national level as of prime importance. However, it did not rule out introduction of collective bargaining at industry or local level (Enderwick 1994, 306).

One of the most significant international labour codes currently in operation that relates to MNCs is from the Organisation of Economic Cooperation and Development (OECD), of which Australia is a member nation (Enderwick 1994). The OECD's code was formulated in 1976 and is important for two main reasons:

1. the OECD member countries are the main source of Foreign Direct Investment
2. the OECD has demonstrated flexibility by amending the guidelines to deal with changing circumstances brought to the attention of the Committee on International Investment and Multinational Enterprises (CIME) (Enderwick 1994, 307-8).

The OECD code has five key features:

1. it was developed consultatively with the the OECD's Trade Union Advisory Committee (TUAC) and the Business Advisory Committee (BIAC)

2. it embodies the principle of non-discrimination
3. it is voluntary
4. it complements national legislation
5. it provides for disclosure of information to union representatives for collective bargaining purposes.

The OECD Code has had a considerable impact on labour practices. However, there are a number of problems. The OECD's Trade Union Advisory Committee believes the provisions on information disclosure do not go far enough. They leave a number of loopholes that MNCs exploit by using inconsistencies in national accounting disclosure requirements. This can create large gaps in knowledge. In addition, while the Code has condemned cross-border transfers of strikebreaking labour as an unfair bargaining tactic, it has left untouched similar transfers from within the same nation. Many MNCs have more than one establishment in any particular country. There are also other difficulties, including:

- arriving at a satisfactory definition of a MNC
- providing a remedy for problems caused to labour by disinvestment (downsizing or closure) in the host country
- the settlement of disputes must be based on procedures in the host country
- the Committee on International Investment and Multinational Enterprises (CIME) is only entitled to discuss matters in dispute (Enderwick 1994, 309-10).

In the European Union information disclosure has also been a key issue. There has been pressure for supplementary provisions to enforce trade union access to information. This led to the drafting of the so-called Vredeling Directive. This Directive would have required extensive disclosure from MNCs about the organisational structure and economic performance, employment levels and trends, trends in production, sales and investments, as well as possible nationalisation and other matters which could impact on employee interests. But the Directive would have gone far beyond the requirements of most national legislation and intensive lobbying by US and Japanese business interests resulted in its being watered down (Enderwick 1994, 313-5). Following years of negotiation, the European Union finally adopted a modified form of the Directive, now known as the European Works Councils Directive. This Directive was to be implemented by September 22 1996 in member countries, either by way of legislation or agreements between management and trade unions. While a detailed examination of this Directive is beyond the scope of this chapter, some of the key issues addressed included:

- obligations on employers under certain circumstances to set up European Works Councils (EWCs), or information and consultation procedures
- obligations on management to initiate negotiations if requested by employees or their representatives
- establishment of Special Negotiating Bodies (SNBs) including the definition of their composition and tasks
- management's duties to include convening meetings and funding SNBs
- the scope of agreements which may be reached between management and SNBs
- management's rights to include withholding potentially damaging information, under certain circumstances

- an obligation on management and EWCs to work in a spirit of cooperation
- exemptions for firms which already had an agreement on transnational information and consultation by the Directive's implementation date.

The Directive also requires that a supplementary set of issues be addressed by member states relating to the operation of those multinationals covered by the Directive. There are a number of key areas here, such as the following:

- the definition of 'employees' representatives'
- methods for calculating workforce size thresholds under the Directive
- methods of appointment or election of SNBs
- confidentiality provisions relating to SNBs and EWCs procedures
- rights and protection for employee representatives carrying out their duties (e.g. paid time off)
- ensuring compliance with the Directive in all relevant cases, including provisions for enforcement
- methods for the election or appointment of employee representatives (*European Industrial Relations Review* [EIRR] 1995, 34-35).

Implementation of the EU Directive has been anticipated as one of the most difficult exercises ever attempted in EU legislation (*EIRR* 1995, 34) Apart from European multinationals, the major non-European multinationals affected by the Directive will be US and Japanese companies. The high level of foreign direct investment (FDI) by Japanese companies in Europe in recent years has made Japan the second biggest non-European investor, behind the USA. An estimated 27 large Japanese companies will be obliged to establish European Works Councils (*EIRR* 1995, 16).

In the view of many authorities on international business, the most effective long term response by organised labour to MNCs is some form of international trade union action. However, there are a number of major impediments to such action. Perhaps the most important has been that the structure of the international labour movement has not been conducive to united action. The international trade union movement has been dominated by three global organisations. The World Federation of Trade Unions, which drew its support mainly from the Communist bloc, claimed a membership of 11 Trade Union Internationals and 190 million members. However, the membership figure was probably grossly inflated for propaganda purposes and by counting unwilling conscripts. The International Confederation of Free Trade Unions (ICFTU), with 60 million members and 16 associated International Trade Secretariats (ITSs), is the main organisation covering national peak unions in the free world. There is also a third grouping, called the World Confederation of Labour (WCL), with an estimated five million members, and comprised of 12 industrial units, known as International Trade Federation (ITFs). Superimposed on these bodies have also been a variety of regional trade union organisations.

Since the collapse of Communism, in the early 1990s, the major ideological divide between the WFTU and the ICFTU has disappeared, but this has left a question mark over the future of WFTU. However, the ICFTU, which was established as the peak organisation for the free world's trade unions, has also had its problems. The organisation is confederate in nature, with very limited power over its constituent units. Its membership has included national unions with both socialist and non-socialist ideologies. Its current challenges are how to re-organise after the end of the Cold War and how to reconcile ideological differences between socialist and non-socialist members. One of the ICFTU's major problems has been the ambivalence of the American peak organisation, the AFL-CIO towards the organisation. During the 1950s and 1960s, the AFL-CIO participated in the ICFTU as a perceived bulwark against Communism. But from 1969-81, the AFL-CIO withdrew, because it disliked the pressure German unions were putting on the ICFTU for détente with Eastern Europe. Currently, however, the AFL-CIO is re-organising its stance on foreign policy and removing 'Cold Warriors' from positions of influence. Renewed interest and active participation by the AFL-CIO could help to revitalise the ICFTU, provided ideological differences between European trade unions, contained during the Cold War, can be resolved (Boswell and Stevis 1997, 292-4).

A second impediment to international trade union action towards MNCs is that union actions are always reactive, ad hoc and defensive. Unions have not been able to develop proactive strategies toward management (Enderwick 1994, 317-8). A third impediment lies in the differences in labour legislation and practices in different countries. This has made concerted action difficult. A fourth problem concerns multinational collective bargaining. While management has been strongly opposed to it, trade unions have also been unwilling or unprepared to engage in it. A fifth impediment is the deflection of trade union energy into protective national legislative campaigns, based on the mistaken belief that foreign direct investment is primarily concerned with lowering labour costs. Research, however, indicates that the motivation for FDI is more often a defensive strategy to retain market share. A sixth impediment occurs because the patterns of FDI have changed. There is now a focus on greater balance between investing countries (e.g. European firms penetrating the US market), with a less clear distinction between parent and host nations. There is also greater emphasis on indirect investment, which does not encourage multinational collective bargaining. For example, foreign companies may purchase large minority share-holdings in host country companies (Enderwick 1994, 320-2).

While there have been some well-documented cases of effective multinational collective bargaining, the obstacles mentioned above make widespread transnational collective bargaining unlikely (Enderwick 1994, 324). In practical terms, most coordinated international action between trade unions in the free world has occurred through the ICFTU and its 16 international ITSs. The affiliates of these ITSs are not peak union bodies, such as the ACTU, but individual trade unions. ITSs have provided forum for workers from different countries to meet and exchange information about MNCs operating in their countries. The most active ITSs in terms of size, diversification and ability to respond effectively to MNCs, have been the International Metal Workers Federation and the International Federation of Chemical, Engineering and General Workers Union (ICEF). These two organisations took the leadership in forming World Company Councils. These Councils were intended to bring together all the unions of a single multinational corporation to achieve multinational collective bargaining. Their success in this regard was modest, but they have provided a forum and a focus for international trade union action in a number of areas (McCarthy 1991, 240; Enderwick 1994, 319-20; Boswell and Stevis 1997, 295).

More recently, the ITSs have adopted a strategy of corporate campaigns for turning a particular MNC into the focal point for international action. In the view of two observers, such strategies have the potential to unite workers across national boundaries of countries at different stages of economic development. But to do so, they need to develop an agenda that can coordinate the different interests of national trade unions (Boswell and Stevis 1997, 295). In one case, an American union, the Automobile

Workers Union of America (UAW) was able to use an ITS effectively to provide evidence to the Australian Conciliation and Arbitration Commission in a case dealing with employees of GM Holden, a subsidiary of the US firm, General Motors (Enderwick 1994, 318-9).

While most commentators have concluded that the prospects for international collective bargaining are poor, it has been argued that less ambitious union strategies are more likely to enjoy success. Such strategies might include:

- strengthening of national union involvement in plant and company based bargaining
- research into the vulnerability of selected MNCs
- more effective international information exchange between national trade unions
- consolidation of company and industry-based international union movements (Enderwick 1994, 325).

Other scholars are somewhat more optimistic. They argue that forces of regional and global integration are bringing with them new incentives and opportunities for action. They particularly target the EU as the most promising arena within which unions can seek to organise themselves more effectively against MNCs. They also see the ICFTU as potentially capable of resolving union regional and sectional divisions, while dealing more effectively with national governments. However, they concede that to achieve this, the powers of the ICFTU and its secretariats will have to be strengthened, and their resources increased (Boswell and Stevis 1997, 299).

MNCs IN AUSTRALIAN INDUSTRIAL RELATIONS

It should now be clear that much of the debate about MNCs is ideological in nature. In order to discover the attitudes of both MNCs and trade unions in Australia on a range of issues, a limited survey was conducted of three major MNCs and four trade unions (Mc Carthy 1991). On the employer side, representatives were interviewed from ICI Australia Ltd, Monsanto Australia Ltd, and Ford Australia Ltd. On the union side, officials were interviewed from the Vehicle Builders Employees Federation (VBEF), the Federated Ironworkers Union (FIA) the Federated Clerks Union (FCU) and the Waterside Workers Federation (WWF). Each of these unions had substantial numbers of members employed by MNCs. The findings were as follows:

- the quality of industrial relations is not necessarily determined by the nationality of MNC ownership. It was felt by respondents that the attitudes to industrial relations of individual managers depended mainly on the nature of their functions, with different attitudes being displayed by managers involved in accounting, marketing and human resource management. Also, attitudes seemed to vary according to industries. In particular, it was suggested by one union that MNCs in manufacturing were less likely to be hostile to trade unions than those in the banking and retailing industries
- industrial relations had improved in the difficult economic circumstances of the 1980s and because some MNCs were recent entrants to Australia, they had avoided the confrontationist mentality of earlier times. The management styles of MNCs were seen as more consultative and less autocratic than previously

- all the companies surveyed claimed they enjoyed independence in industrial relations policies from their overseas parent companies
- the companies, however, noted that they still experienced difficulties in explaining cultural differences in Australian industrial relations practices to their parent companies e.g. in respect of multi-unionism in enterprises, the relationship between trade unions and government, trade unions' apparent freedom to break industrial agreements without sanctions and the working of the Conciliation and Arbitration system
- the MNCs surveyed were actually more highly unionised than many Australian companies, which perhaps was a function of their larger size
- the MNCs tended to provide pay and conditions superior to those of local companies. It was felt that this was because the MNCs were more capital-intensive and labour costs were less critical in their operation
- the MNCs all expressed a preference for collective bargaining, with their employees, as part of a strategy of closer identification between employees and their companies. Conciliation and Arbitration was seen as a last resort
- the MNCs were seen as practicing more modern management techniques than local companies and were more likely to employ skilled industrial relations staff
- at least one trade union official saw Research and Development (the lack of) as a more important issue than industrial relations in relation to MNCs
- MNCs were viewed as more pragmatic than indigenous companies and as adapting to the Australian multi-union environment even where they were anti-union. They were interested in avoiding stoppages, and were market-oriented. This made it easier for unions to establish precedents that could flow-on to the industry.

McCarthy (1991) concludes that generalisations about the quality of industrial relations in a particular MNC are fraught with danger. Some multi-national corporations in Australia have enjoyed better industrial relations than their large Australian counterparts. However, the quality of industrial relations can vary between different plants owned by the same company. For example, ICI's Botany plant in Sydney until recently had a poor strike record, while its plants in Victoria were peaceful. (From 1991, under difficult economic conditions, the company made a concerted effort to improve industrial relations at its Botany plant by introducing collaborative change, with encouraging results) (Mealor 1995, 130-45).

Overall, the pattern of industrial relations seems to depend on factors other than the nationality of company ownership (McCarthy 1991, 242-4). More recent evidence about human resource management and industrial relations practices of MNCs in Australia is provided by the 1990 Australian Workplace Industrial Relations Survey (AWIRS) (Callus, et al. 1990). The survey contained a substantial sample of foreign-owned companies (21 per cent) with headquarters outside Australia. Data from the survey has been used to examine similarities and differences in selected practices between Australian and foreign-owned companies (Teo and Rodwell 1998, 7-13). Companies were selected which were comparable in terms of industry type, and which operated within the same Australian legal, social and political environment. Also, the firms were conveniently grouped into US, Asian and European-owned companies. The statistical analysis of the data involved examining 8 variables. Significant differences were found in respect of three of those variables:

1. decentralisation of general managerial decision-making
2. use of performance appraisals
3. decentralisation of decision-making in relation to specific industrial relations practices, including: changing pay of non-managerial employees, dismissals, and the amount of time and resources allocated for in-house training.

Some of the other findings included: in respect to general decision-making, Australian firms allowed decisions about changes to be made at significantly lower levels i.e. lower to the shop floor than the European firms. However, Australian domestic firms centralised their decision-making significantly more than US firms. With regard to performance appraisals, the US firms used them to a significantly greater degree than their European counterparts. In respect to unionisation, there were significantly more unions in Asian firms than Australian firms. Otherwise, with regard to the degree of unionisation and the nature of employer-management relations, including use of contractors, casuals and the use of participatory practices such as quality circles, consultative committees and profit-sharing, there were no significant differences. The only other significant difference was that US firms were more likely to have a formal EEO policy compared to domestic firms.

The authors of the survey explained the apparent contradiction between the results for general decision-making and employment relations decision-making. They argued that Australian firms may be generally more decentralised and flexible than their European counterparts. However, the more unitary philosophy of the US firms involves overall direction at a high level, but devolution of responsibility for operational details. They also explained the surprisingly large number of unions in Asian companies, particularly compared with the stereotype of the Japanese corporation. They suggest that Asian firms may be particularly sensitive to their local environment and may have over-compensated in trying to adjust to perceived local norms. They argue too that the greater emphasis on EEO policies and performance appraisals in US companies reflects differences in parent company cultural norms. Thus, the general conclusion was that the nationality of the parent company did influence the subsidiaries in terms of structure and control, but had only a limited effect on human resource management and industrial relations practices (Teo and Rodwell 1998). This generally supports McCarthy's (1991) findings, and is also consistent with the majority of findings in other literature.

AUSTRALIAN COMPANIES AS MULTINATIONALS ABROAD

In the literature about MNCs, Australia is usually accorded the status of a 'client state'. As Helen Hughes (1969) noted, Australia has traditionally been a capital importing country. Its contribution to FDI is negligible, compared to the inflow of investment, and only a small proportion of its FDI goes to developing countries. Yet, it is often overlooked that a growing number of Australian companies are also multinationals, with overseas operations. It is a characteristic of Australian multinational companies that they are generally much smaller than their counterparts in countries such as the US. But the same developments have occurred in Australia as in other developed nations, with more and more companies of all sizes focusing on exporting or setting up their own operations overseas, especially in the areas of food products, manufactured goods and mining operations (Robbins, et al. 1997, 115).

BHP is the largest and most diversified Australian MNC, with operations in over 50 countries, including the US, Asia, Europe and the South Pacific. Its activities cover oil and gas, steel and a range of minerals, including copper, iron ore and coal. In 1997, the company was capitalised at $37,753,000 million, and employed 61,000 people (BHP 1997). Another well-known Australian company which has become a multinational company is Boral, a manufacturer of building and construction materials and a producer of natural gas, liquefied petroleum gas and electricity. The company operates in 23 countries in North and South America, Europe, Asia and the South Pacific. In 1997, shareholder equity exceeded $3 billion (Boral 1997). Another well known Australian company which has evolved into a MNCs is CSR, which originated as a sugar cane processing company in Queensland, but diversified into the building products area. Another was TNT, a road transport company that built a global network but nearly suffered economic collapse in the process, and was ultimately taken over by a Dutch firm.

Until recently, a frequently quoted example of an Australian success in internationalisation was Burns Philip, a food manufacturer and marketer, which in 1994 had operations in 33 countries and 10,000 employees (Robbins, et al. 1997, 115). Unfortunately the company was unable to manage its rapid global expansion and in 1997 was forced to sell its herbs and spices business in the US and Europe at a huge write-down. This resulted in a total loss of $875.5 million, which was announced just after a badly timed takeover by New Zealand investor, Graeme Hart (*Australian* 1997). In the field of services, there are also examples of Australian firms which have moved to internationalise, to take advantage of lucrative overseas markets. They include some large law firms, which have established offices in Asian financial centres, as well as in the US and Europe. In view of the trend towards Australian companies of all kinds becoming global corporations, it would be useful to examine their role in industrial relations, particularly in South East Asia. Unfortunately, the research in this area is both limited and out of date, not least because it was fuelled by an ideological view of MNCs that has now become unfashionable.

CONCLUSION

Although British companies had become established earlier, the growth and development of MNCs in the world economy since World War II has been spectacular. US companies spearheaded the post-war move to go international, later joined by companies from other nations, including Japan and Germany. The impact of MNCs on Australia has been considerable, given the high levels of foreign ownership and control in the Australian economy. Much of the writing about MNCs has been ideological in nature. In theory, MNCs can be the source of both economic advantages and disadvantages to a country. In practice, the benefits seem to outweigh the disadvantages, at least in more developed countries such as Australia, with most MNCs behaving overall as good corporate citizens.

From a labour perspective, MNCs also present a particular challenge. Partly because of the capital-intensive industries in which they usually operate, MNCs tend to pay above average wages and provide better working conditions. However, they have often been opposed to trade unions, and have sometimes had difficulty adapting their practices to the traditions and laws of the host countries. They have even sought to change national industrial relations systems by using their economic power. Trade unions have had problems in effectively countering the power of MNCs. This has been the result of the difficulty unions have in organising internationally to deal with MNCs operating across frontiers. Internal divisions, as well as conflicts of interest between union movements in different countries, have weakened union ability to put up a united front to MNCs.

However, organised labour has had some success in lobbying for codes of practice to regulate terms and conditions of employment offered by MNCs, though they have had little success in organising effective multinational collective bargaining. The only major exception appears to be the Works Council Directive in the European Union, and even here the effective the rights of labour may depend upon the respective power of management and trade unions in each of the EU states. Probably the best hope for organised labour to counter the power of MNCs in the short to medium run is to seek to bargain more effectively with them at a national and local level.

REVIEW QUESTIONS

1. Why do both the governments of host countries and national labour movements have concerns about the activities of multinational corporations?
2. In what ways do the industrial relations policies and practices of multinational corporations differ from those of national firms in host countries?
3. To what extent are cultural differences significant in the way multinational corporations deal with industrial relations in host countries? Comment specifically on Japanese companies in this regard.
4. How can organised labour respond to the power of multinational corporations on an international basis? Discuss attempts to lay down codes of conduct for multinational companies in industrial relations.
5. How do the industrial relations policies and practices of Australian companies abroad, particularly in the South East Asian region, compare with those originating from other countries?
6. 'Hostility to multinational corporations is essentially ideologically based. There is little evidence that multinational corporations are other than good corporate citizens.' Discuss.

FURTHER READING

Dicken, P. (1998) *Global Shift*, 3rd Edn, Guilford Press, London.

Enderwick, P. (ed) (1994) *Transnational Corporations and Human Resources*, Routledge, London.

Enderwick, P. (ed) (1985) *Multinational Business and Labour*, Croom Helm, London.

Selavarajah, C. and Cutbush-Sabine, K. (eds) (1991) *International Business*, Longman, Melbourne.

CHAPTER 13

Five Selected South East Asian Countries

'What do they know of England, who only England know?'

Rudyard Kipling

INTRODUCTION

In this chapter, we provide a brief overview of the history, economic development and industrial relations frameworks of Japan, South Korea, Malaysia, Singapore and Hong Kong. We seek to identify the key features of the industrial relations systems that have developed in these countries, and to supply reasons for the manner in which they have developed. Our survey suggests that systems of industrial relations vary from voluntarism in the case of Hong Kong prior to Chinese rule, to highly regulated and controlled systems in Singapore and Malaysia. The nature and extent of regulation depends on the role of government, as discussed in an earlier chapter, and on the particular priorities and problems of the five selected countries.

LEARNING OBJECTIVES

After reading this chapter, you should be able to:

- describe some of the main features of the history and economic development of five selected South East Asian countries
- outline the industrial relations regulatory frameworks in these countries
- explain the differences in the degree of independence of the labour movements in these countries
- discuss the different forms of industrial conflict occurring in these countries
- draw some comparisons between industrial relations in Australia and these five selected Asian nations.

JAPAN

Japan has a population of 122 million. It is one of the most socially homogeneous countries in the world, the only substantial ethnic minorities being 600,000 South Koreans and 500,000 Chinese (Matsuda 1993, 172).

History and Economic Development

Japan is one of the few countries in Asia never to have been colonised. After 200 years of closure to the West and the outside world, the country opened itself up in the second half of the nineteenth century. The Meiji Restoration in 1868 was the prelude to an era of modernisation and industrialisation. By the early twentieth century, Japan demonstrated that it had arrived as a world power by defeating Imperial Russia and destroying the Russian navy in the Russo-Japanese War of 1904-5. Industrialisation accelerated in the first two decades of the twentieth century, and by the 1930s, Japan turned to militarism and imperialism.

Following its defeat in World War II, the Allies under the command of General MacArthur occupied the country. The Occupation Forces imposed a democratic constitution on the defeated nation. In the following decades, Japan rapidly began to reconstruct its economy on the basis of the manufacture of consumer durables. This strategy was so successful that the country now ranks as a developed nation, the most economically advanced in Asia. In 1993, in terms of GDP per capita, Japan ranked third in the world, after the USA and Germany (*The Economist* 1994). The country enjoyed spectacular economic growth from 1955 to 1974. Real GNP increased at an average of 7.6% from 1955-9, and 11% from 1960-70. Growth slowed after the oil crisis of 1973, but by then Japan had already become an economically developed nation (Nimura 1994, 78-9 and 87). Since 1992, Japan has experienced a further severe recession. Growth slowed to less than 1% in 1994 and 1995 (Benson 1998, 208). Economic recovery was slow, but did pick up again in 1996, when growth approached 3% (Ito 1996, 16). In 1995 regular employment fell for the first time and at the end of that year unemployment reached a postwar high (Benson 1998, 208).

Successive Japanese governments have tried to 'kick-start' the economy by fiscal means. However, the banking sector experienced severe problems as the result of the collapse of the 'bubble economy' in the late 1980s, when the property market crashed. The rapid increase in the value of the yen against the $US was another factor contributing to the recession (Ito 1997, 16). While growth again faltered in 1998, the yen declined significantly in value against the $US, so Japanese exports began to rise again, particularly in key industries such as automobiles, ships and chemicals (Benson 1998, 219). While the seeds of economic recovery were thus evident at the end of the decade, in the view of some observers, the institutional roots of the earlier miracle economy may yet prove a source of weakness rather than strength in the future (Ito 1997, 16).

The Industrial Relations System

Background

Trade unions in Japan had their origins in craft guilds, with roots in the pre-Meiji feudal era. The first attempts at western-style unionism occurred at the end of the nineteenth century, among ironworkers, railway workers and typographers. The Government tried to suppress these early unions by legislation.

However, as industry developed after the Russo-Japanese War of 1904-5, the size of the factory workforce grew rapidly, and unions gained a permanent foothold among industrial workers. Yuaikai, the Friendly Society, was set up in 1912, and became the first union to achieve nationwide coverage. In 1921 it developed into Sodomei, the Japan Federation of Trade Unions (Matsuzaki 1994, 14-16).

During World War I, there was a greater concentration of capital, and the large conglomerates (Zaibatsu) established themselves as leaders in industry, commerce and finance. However, the 1920s were years of depression in Japan, which severely reduced labour mobility, even among the skilled industrial workforce. This was one reason for the beginning of the tradition of lifetime employment for sections of the workforce, as skilled workers kept their existing jobs. Another factor in the growth of lifetime employment was management strategy. Influenced by Taylorist ideas, the managers of large corporations sought to establish a trained and stable workforce to harness the new technologies that were then becoming available to industry. Companies sought to hire youths with good educational qualifications, who could be trained on the job to acquire the new skills. These recruits were encouraged to stay with the company for their whole careers. Seniority wages and company welfare benefits were also introduced to further encourage loyalty. Employers also sought to undermine independent unions and set up factory councils or committees, in effect a form of company unionism. Independent unions were thus mainly eliminated from large enterprises, and confined to medium and small firms.

After the invasion of Manchuria in 1931, there was pressure from the Government to further reduce industrial disputes and put Japanese industry on a war footing. Following the outbreak of war with China in 1937, the Sanpo (Industrial Service to the Nation) movement was set up by extreme right-wing elements in the labour movement, in combination with the Home Ministry's Police Bureau. The objectives of the Sanpo movement were to inculcate a spirit of national service to replace selfish personal interest and workplace confrontation. The movement became a tool for the repression of workers during World War II to maximise war production. Most trade union leaders, however, actively collaborated with the Sanpo (Matsumura 1994, 37-46).

Contemporary industrial relations

The postwar Constitution of 1946 was imposed on Japan by the Allied Occupation forces, with a view to instituting a form of western style democracy and safeguarding workers and trade union rights as a bulwark against the resurgence of militarism. Article 28 of the Constitution guarantees workers the right to organise and bargain collectively. The right to strike is also explicitly recognised by the Trade Union Law of 1945. Under the Trade Union Law, trade unions were allowed to acquire independent legal identity. They also acquired protection from criminal and civil law remedies, when in pursuit of their legitimate activities. Under this law, employers are obliged to bargain in good faith with unions. Collective agreements, properly concluded as formal contracts, are legally enforceable.

With encouragement from the occupying powers, in the immediate aftermath of World War II, trade unionism grew rapidly. By 1948, there were almost 7 million members, or more than 50% of the workforce. However, in the climate of anti-Communism of the early 1950s, management was able to re-assert its power and trade union growth slowed. At the turn of the 21st Century, trade union membership stands at around 12 million or 24% of the Japanese workforce, after peaking in 1993 at 12.7 million (Levine 1996, 222-223).

Legally, the resolution of disputes is divided in two based on the kind of dispute. An administrative tribunal, the Labour Relations Commission, has been set up in the private sector to deal with 'disputes of interest' (i.e. claims for improvements in wages and conditions, and adjudication of unfair labour practices, such as a refusal by employers to bargain in good faith). There is a Central Labour Relations Commission in Tokyo, which deals with cases of national importance. In each prefecture, there is also a local Labour Relations Commission to settle local disputes. The Central Commission, in addition to its original jurisdiction, acts as an appeals tribunal from the local bodies. The tribunals are tripartite in composition, including representatives of management, employees and the public. Similar arrangements exist in the public sector, where there is a separate dispute settling body, the Public Corporation and National Enterprise Labour Relations Commission. Despite the existence of these bodies, however, the parties (employers and unions) have preferred to use forms of voluntary conciliation for dispute resolution.

The second category of disputes, 'disputes of right', is the province of the ordinary civil courts. These disputes include such matters as established workers' rights under statute, collectively bargained agreements, and individual employment contracts. In practice, however, there is considerable overlap of jurisdiction between the civil courts and the Labour Relations Commission. This is particularly true in complaints of unfair labour practices, and because the courts exercise review powers over the tribunals (Matsuda 1993, 186-191).

The three pillars of Japanese industrial relations

Japan's industrial relations system has become known for three distinctive features: lifetime employment, seniority wages and enterprise trade unions. It should be noted, however, that these features apply only to a minority of the workforce, around 35%, who are permanent employees of large corporations and the Government (Petzall and Selvarajah 1991, 205). Those fortunate enough to be hired from school or university as permanent employees can look forward to lifetime employment with the corporation or government until the mandatory retirement age of 60. They enjoy steady advancement and increases in their wages, good retirement benefits and are the last to be laid off. However, as a substitute for layoffs, they can be transferred to subsidiary enterprises, a practice known as 'shukko' (Akita 1996, 244-5).

However, the majority of workers, even in large enterprises, are classified as temporary, and include almost all female employees. These temporary workers are non-unionised, receive few of the benefits of the permanent employees, and can be laid off in times of economic downturn (Petzall and Selvarajah 1991, 205). For example, in the recession following the collapse of the so-called 'bubble economy' of the 1980s, Toyota, a household name in the automobile industry, reduced its workforce by 15 per cent by 'releasing' workers on temporary contracts. The company thus reduced its labour costs, while avoiding the negative public relations effects of outright dismissals (Teramoto and Dirks 1996, 396).

Thus, Japan has a dual labour market. This has helped it to absorb the impact of economic shocks like the oil crisis of 1973, but at the expense of temporary workers. All permanent workers hired at a particular 'base grade' earn the same pay. Wage increases are largely determined by seniority, although since the 1970s, considerations of merit have been increasingly used in determining promotions (Nimura 1994, 86-7). The purpose of the seniority wage system, coupled with lifetime employment, is to bond permanent workers to their employers.

However, both lifetime employment and seniority wages came under increasing strain in the low growth and recessionary environment of the mid and late 1990s. The large motor manufacturer, Honda, for instance, in mid-1994 tied white-collar pay entirely to performance. Many firms have recently encouraged 'early retirement' (for women at ages as low as 30, without pensions), which constitutes a disguised abandonment of lifetime employment (*The Economist* 1994, 12). In 1993, 40 to 50 major firms openly announced redundancy plans for white-collar employees for the first time. (Robins 1994, 30). Observers however remain divided about the general trends in lifetime employment. In the view of Akita (1996, 244), despite increasing economic strain, most large Japanese companies have continued to meet what they see as their moral obligations to employ their regular workers until retirement, other than in exceptional financial circumstances. On the other hand, Benson (1998, 217) found that by 1995 larger firms were willing to adjust the numbers of permanent employees to meet variations in product demand. Perhaps these two views are reconcilable if larger firms use natural attrition rather than layoffs to achieve their objectives. Another strategy which large firms employ is to transfer or 'loan' permanent workers out to subsidiary companies, often on inferior terms and conditions of employment to those they previously enjoyed (Whittaker 1998, 289).

Enterprise unions

Over 90 per cent of Japan's 73,000 unions are enterprise-based unions. Membership is limited to the permanent employees of an individual large company. Consequently, union coverage in small companies is almost non-existent. A number of reasons have been advanced to explain how this form of unionism became dominant in Japan:

1. Destruction of the pre-war union movement left no convenient structure around which to organise unions. The Occupation forces encouraged the Japanese to form unions immediately after the war, and the most convenient way in which to do this was at the individual plant or enterprise level. The Occupation authorities also exercised production control through enterprise unions. In the 1950s, left-wing union leaders tried to raise class-consciousness among workers and to counter 'enterprise egoism' by wider attempts at union organisation and political participation, but their efforts were unsuccessful (Whittaker 1998, 281).

2. The practice of lifetime employment caused workers to identify strongly with their enterprises and to find common interests within the enterprise.

3. There was no western-style craft union tradition of regulating working conditions beyond the individual enterprise (Matsuda 1993, 95-6; Nimura 1994, 71).

Nevertheless, by the end of the 20th Century, many enterprise unions had been linked with union federations and, ultimately, Rengo, the Japanese Trade Union Confederation, the equivalent of the ACTU in Australia. After many years of disunity and fragmentation, Rengo was established as the dominant national peak organisation of the Japanese labour movement in 1989 (Levine 1996, 226).

Collective bargaining and joint consultation (including the Shunto or Spring Offensive)

In order to counter the relative weakness of enterprise unions compared with their employers, and to avoid damaging the competitive position of employers, the device of the Shunto or Spring Offensive was initiated in 1955. It has served as minimum wage fixing mechanism and a substitute for industry-wide bargaining. Certain strong unions in particular industries act as pacesetters for minimum wage increases throughout the industry. However, the size of increases awarded in individual enterprises varies according to the economic circumstances of each enterprise. On the surface, the Shunto has developed into a colourful ritual, emphasising working class solidarity and even being used to attack employers publicly. The reality, however, is a largely consensual, behind-the-scenes negotiation and settlement of disputes (Ben Ari 1991, 106-7). The tradition of consensus is of course assisted by the identification of individual workers with their enterprises, and the fact that almost 70 per cent of senior company executives have also been trade union officials earlier in their careers. (Matsuda 1993, 199).

Widespread forms of joint consultation have supplemented collective bargaining in Japan, using management-employee committees to resolve grievances and establish personnel policies. At the workplace level, more informal forms of consultation have also developed, including quality circles and zero defect groups. Such groups consist of workers who meet voluntarily after work hours to discuss ways of improving their enterprises. These practices are an outgrowth of the celebrated group methods of decision-making in Japanese enterprises, as well as the philosophy of Kaizen, or the search for continuous improvement (see, Petzall and Selvarajah 1991, 202). Such has been the pressure on workers to offer suggestions for improvements, that cases have been known of individuals who have committed suicide because they have had no suggestions to offer!

In summary, the pattern of Japanese industrial relations since the mid 1950s has been generally peaceful. In large enterprises, close ties of loyalty have been forged between employers and permanent employees. However, the traditional three pillars of Japanese industrial relations (lifetime employment, seniority wages and enterprise unions) were under increasing strain in the recessionary era of the 1990s.

Nevertheless, some observers who have studied individual industries in detail have challenged this somewhat idyllic broad picture of industrial relations. In particular, the automobile industry has been the subject of investigation. Kamata (1982) has painted a depressing picture of working life in a Toyota assembly plant. According to Kamata, workers are subjected to continuing assembly line speed-ups, high injury rates, poor safety precautions, bad working conditions and fatigue on the job. Privacy and individual freedom are also restricted. Other accounts of the pressures involved in working in Japanese automobile firms have lent support to this picture (Young 1992, 686-8). Even when moved to different cultural settings, there is evidence of the pressures which Japanese production methods impose on workers. Parker and Slaughter (1988) describe the operation of the production system at a joint venture between Toyota and General Motors in the US as 'management by stress'. Workers can never establish a comfortable work pace, because the philosophy of kaizen requires continuous pressure on the production line to expose areas of weakness, so that the process can be redesigned for greater efficiency. The result is that the line runs so fast that workers almost have to run to perform their tasks, and can barely keep up, let alone help others who may have fallen behind.

'Workaholism' is also a significant problem in Japanese industry. A workaholic has been defined as a person diagnosed with the personality disorder of obsessive-compulsive perfectionism (Kanai and Fling 1996, 223-4). Kanai and Fling (1996), in a study of male and female Japanese workers in industrial organisations found that workaholism was widespread, and had a significant impact on job stress and health complaints, especially for male workers. Further, it is well known that many workers take hardly any holidays because of the pressure of the Japanese work ethic. Workers have been reported to have literally died of exhaustion from overwork. In 1991, a widow made industrial history by successfully suing her late husband's employer for causing his death by overwork (*The Economist* 1994, 18). Following this, employers have begun to encourage or even require their workers to take more holidays, but most Japanese workers still work far longer hours than their Western counterparts.

It is clear, therefore, that great benefits have accrued to Japan from its economic miracle and its industrial relations system, which has contributed. However, there have also been considerable human costs involved in the process.

SINGAPORE

Singapore is an island state at the southern tip of the Malay Peninsula. In 1999, Singapore had a population of 3.7 million. The country is multi-racial with the majority (78%) being Chinese. Malays make up 14% and Indians 7% of the population. The remaining 1% consist of Arabs, Europeans and mixed races.

History and Economic Development

In 1819, Sir Stamford Raffles secured a trading concession for the British East India Company from Singapore's Malay ruler, the Sultan of Johore. The island had already been an important trading centre for at least 500 years, ideally located close to the Dutch East Indies and the strategically important sea routes to India and China. In 1824, Raffles negotiated the outright cession of Singapore to the British East India Company. At the same time, the British took over the Dutch settlement of Malacca on the Malay Peninsula, and supplanted the Dutch as the dominant power in Malaya. Singapore then became part of the Straits Settlements, governed from the capital of the island of Penang. Between 1826 and 1867, Singapore developed into a thriving tariff-free port, with a cosmopolitan population of 85,000. It attracted merchants and traders from many nations. Substantial immigration from China in the 1820's established the Chinese as the largest community by 1827. Smaller communities of Malays and Indians also made Singapore their home in the next half-century. The Straits Settlements was declared a Crown Colony on April 1, 1867.

Apart from its status as a free port, Singapore became a major British naval and military outpost, guarding the sea routes to India and other British possessions east of Suez. Despite its strong fortifications, however, it was occupied by the Japanese from 1942 to 1945. The British returned after the defeat of Japan in 1945, but self-government was conceded in 1959. Full independence came in 1963 when Singapore became part of the new Malaysian Federation. However, in 1965, Singapore withdrew to form a separate, independent state because of racial tension between the numerically dominant Malays on the Malay Peninsula, and the Chinese majority on the island of Singapore (Le Poer 1991, 1-57). Despite independence from Britain, English has been retained as the language of administration, and, in effect, the common language between the different cultural groups. Britain abandoned its naval base on the island to the Government of Singapore in 1967. This was subsequently developed into a thriving shipbuilding and repair facility.

Singapore's annual economic growth rate since the 1970s has exceeded 7%. Singapore's per capita GDP overtook Australia's in 1995 (*The Australian*, 8 May 1995). By 1996, Singapore's GDP per head had reached US$27,000, placing it fifth in the world after Luxemburg, the United States, Switzerland and Hong Kong (*The Economist*, May 8-15 1998). Another estimate, comparing purchasing power, places Singapore third in the world, behind Luxembourg and the United States, but ahead of Switzerland (Peebles 1999, 1061). The country has one of the highest savings rates in the world, with gross national savings at 46% of GNP (Bartol 1994, 657).

Singapore has a workforce of 1.9 million, mainly employed in manufacturing (29%), commerce (23%) and services (21%), reflecting a high level of industrialisation. The proportion of GNP accounted for by manufacturing grew from only 12 per cent in 1960 to 29 per cent by 1979, a figure which has remained constant to the end of the 20th Century (Begin 1995, 65). 55% of the workforce is now employed by multinational companies, the result of Government policies to attract foreign investment and encourage foreign companies to set up business on the island (Redding 1990, 24).

Singapore's industrial take-off dates to the mid-1960s. At that time, the Government initiated policies designed to encourage low value-added assembly operations, which would capitalise on Singapore's then low labour costs (Begin 1995, 65). In 1979, the Government announced a second phase of industrialisation, aimed at achieving high value-added production and product technologies. This was partly a response to increasing labour costs and shortages, and partly motivated by a desire to raise the standard of living (Begin 1995, 66).

Singapore's economy relies heavily on exports, more than any other developed or developing country, largely because of the small size of the country and its restricted internal market. In 1987, it exported 43.9 per cent of its GNP, compared with Japan (10.7%) and South Korea (39%) (Begin 1995, 85).

Industrial Relations System

Singapore's industrial relations system is best known for 'tripartism' or a close relationship between government, business and trade unions. Indeed, so close is the relationship now between the Peoples Action Party (PAP) Government and the National Trades Union Congress (NTUC), the Singapore equivalent of the ACTU, that it is commonly described as 'symbiotic' (Leggett 1993, 101; Sullivan 1991, 140).

In 1959, the democratic socialist PAP, led by Lee Kuan Yew, won a majority of seats in the Legislative Assembly, and retained power after independence from Britain and the split from the Malaysian Federation in 1965. Trade unions had played a leading role in the struggle for independence from Britain. There had been an uneasy cooperation to this end between unions associated with the PAP and the Communists. In 1961, the Singapore Trades Union Congress split, and the NTUC, closely associated with the ruling PAP, soon became the dominant federation. The rival Communist organisation was banned in 1963. The strong personal ties between the leaders of the PAP and the NTUC were formalised in 1980 when NTUC Secretary Ong Teng Cheong (subsequently Minister of Labour and later President of the Republic) was made a Minister without portfolio in the PAP Government. A NTUC-PAP Liaison Committee was established, comprising top leaders of both organisations. The NTUC Secretary

General has subsequently always been a senior minister in the Government (Sullivan 1991, 141). As Leggett has commented, the close relationship between the two organisations makes it hard to separate government from unions in Singapore's industrial relations (Leggett 1993, 101).

The PAP Government has dedicated its efforts to the economic development of Singapore. It has followed highly interventionist policies in regulating and controlling industrial relations, to create a favourable climate for foreign investment and multi-national companies. As Anantaraman has suggested, the authoritarian ideology of Singapore's political system (a kind of idealised corporatism) tends to operate under the creed that everything that conforms to the national interest is just and everything that is contrary to the national interest is unjust (Anantaraman 1990, viii). State intervention goes so far that Singapore is one of the few countries in the world to run a government matchmaking agency, the Social Development Unit, whose aim is to encourage graduates to marry and produce children with higher levels of intelligence.

Collective Bargaining

A key institution of industrial relations in Singapore is the tripartite National Wages Council (NWC), set up in 1972, with joint Government, employer and trade union representation. Technically, the NWC is a government advisory body, which recommends annual wage increases for the whole economy. It seeks to ensure orderly wage development to promote economic and social progress. It also assists in the development of incentive schemes to improve national productivity. The guidelines set by the NWC are not mandatory, but have been closely followed in the public sector and very influential in the private sector (Sullivan 1991, 143). Between 1979 and 1984, the NWC recommended large wage increases in support of the government policy to phase out labour-intensive, low-technology industries, in favour of more skilled, high-technology industries. This contributed to a serious recession in 1985-6, after which the NWC moved to a new more flexible wage policy. Under this policy, employers and unions were free to bargain over the amount of annual bonus, although this was limited by productivity growth in the economy, and a maximum cap, recommended by the NWC (Sullivan 1991, 7 and 144).

Apart from the influence of the NWC, collective bargaining in Singapore is carried on under the shadow of direct government regulation and control. The process is subject to restraints imposed by the Employment Act, the Industrial Relations Act and other legislation.

The Employment Act, first passed in 1968, lays down minimum employment conditions for a large part of the workforce. There is also a wage ceiling set by the Government from time to time ($1250 per month in 1984). However, the Employment Act also prohibits conditions more favourable than the minimum in new industrial undertakings. Thus, in effect these minimum conditions have actually become the maximum conditions for the bulk of Singapore's workforce and they cannot be exceeded in collective bargaining (Leggett 1993, 106). The Act does permit negotiation between the parties on NWC recommendations, but subject to the maximum prescribed annual bonuses. The parties are, however, free to enter into productivity agreements, consistent with the government's policy of encouraging increasing labour productivity.

The Industrial Relations Act (IRA) excludes from collective bargaining a number of key employer powers, including the rights of hiring and firing, of worker placement and of promotion (Leggett 1993, 107-9). In 1960 the IRA established an Industrial Arbitration Court (IAC), based on the West Australian model, to deal with disputes arising from collective bargaining by conciliation and arbitration (see below). But only unions registered under the Trade Union Act are able to bargain collectively with employers, and the overwhelming majority of such unions are NTUC affiliates.

Dispute Settlement

Where negotiations fail to produce an agreement, there is provision in Singapore for conciliation to be provided by the Ministry of Labour, which, under the IRA, may also call a compulsory conference of the parties. Unresolved industrial disputes must then be submitted to the IAC for resolution. This may be done by the parties, the Ministry of Labour, or the President of the Republic. Industrial action after submission of disputes to the IAC is illegal (Leggett 1993, 109-12). Sympathy strikes and strikes designed to coerce the Government are also illegal, under the Trades Disputes Act of 1966 (Leggett 1993, 117).

The IAC has power both to make binding awards and to certify industrial agreements reached by the parties. Despite a declining caseload in recent years, the Court continues to play an important role in the industrial relations system.

Trade Union Regulation

The Trade Union Act, originally dating back to colonial ordinances, provides for registration and control of unions. Under an amendment in 1982, unions could only be registered if their objectives include promotion of good industrial relations, improvement of workers' conditions and raising productivity. Registration gives unions immunity from civil and criminal action in pursuit of trade disputes, but also subjects them to controls over their internal affairs in respect of their rules, appointment of officers and use of funds. In effect, the Government has used registration as a tool to control unions, including union federations (Leggett 1993, 114).

In the last few decades the structure and role of the union movement in Singapore have been re-shaped. In the 1970s, the NTUC began establishing cooperatives to further the welfare of members. In the 1980s, general unions were re-structured on an industry basis, and further split into house unions, to improve union/management relations and promote company loyalty (Sullivan 1991, 142). Unions that have resisted government policies in terms of union re-structuring have been forcibly broken up (Leggett 1993, 121-2).

The Industrial Relations Record

These policies of government control and regulation have had the intended effect, to reduce overt industrial conflict. From 1978 to 1984, there were no recorded work stoppages and only two, which were quickly dealt with, during the remainder of the 1980s (Leggett, 121). However, there has been a cost in terms of declining trade union membership. Since 1976, when trade union membership stood at 25.5% of the workforce, it has declined to 16.2% in 1989 (Leggett 1993, 122). Other symptoms of a malaise in industrial relations include widespread lack of loyalty by workers towards their employers, unwillingness to undertake overtime, strict adherence to job specifications and more frequent job-hopping (Chew 1983, 79).

In 1988, The National Productivity Board established a Task Force on Job Hopping, which made a comprehensive analysis of the causes of labour turnover. It found that the problem was related to various features of the industrial relations system. In particular:

- salaries were low
- there was little concern for employee welfare
- there were limited opportunities for job advancement
- jobs were poorly designed, narrow and unchallenging
- supervisor-workers and peer relationships were poor
- there were deficiencies in the physical work environment
- shift work created problems
- job security was poor.

The Task Force made various recommendations, designed to increase worker commitment, including measures to ensure greater worker participation and job security (Begin 1995, 78). The Singapore Government subsequently (in 1995) announced an ambitious plan for upgrading the country to a 'high tech' stage of development, part of which involved an undertaking to remedy some of the deficiencies revealed by the 1988 Task Force on Job Hopping. However, to date there is not much evidence of progress, particularly in the area of worker participation. The recession in 1997, caused by the Asian currency crisis, temporarily improved the problem of labour turnover by tilting the labour market in favour of employers.

Thus, Singapore's regime of government regulation has been associated with high rates of economic growth and low incidences of industrial stoppages. There is evidence, however, that these achievements have come at a price, including worker apathy towards the official trade union movement, lack of worker identify with their enterprises, and considerable labour turnover. (HRM practitioners might also query whether quality of performance and production was also suffering in these circumstances.)

One observer has raised the question of whether Singapore's current industrial relations system is consistent with the desire of the Government to move to a second phase of industrialisation. It had been argued that sweeping changes and a loosening up of the controls may be necessary if the transition is to be successful (Begin 1995).

MALAYSIA

Malaysia consists of 13 states and two federal territories, has a population of 19 million and covers an area of 329,758 square kilometres. The country comprises 3 main ethnic groups: Malays (61%), Chinese (30%) and Indians (9%). It is centrally located in the heart of South East Asia and has a strong emphasis on capital intensive and value-added manufacturing, especially electrical and electronic products. In 1998 manufactured goods accounted for 80.3% of Malaysia's total exports. As in Singapore, the export sector is heavily dominated by multinational companies (*Malaysia Industrial Digest* 1995, 2; Bhopal 1997, 572-3; Malaysian Industrial Development Authority (MIDA) 1998). For Australia, Malaysia is the largest ASEAN education market.

History and Economic Development

Malaysia has a long history of economic significance, primarily due to its strategic positioning between Thailand and Singapore on the Malay Peninsula. This area was part of the trade route used by the European nations in previous centuries to gain access to the East Indies. The sultanate of Malacca played an important role in this trade. Malacca was an important trade centre in Asia and hence was of immense interest to the Portuguese, Dutch and eventually the British. Other regions such as Singapore and the northern areas of Borneo, Sarawak and Sabah, together with the isle of Labuan, were all added to the growing colonial assets of the British crown. The Pangkor Treaty of 1874 ensured that Britain held power on the Malay Peninsula until the Japanese invasion of 1941. After World War II, Britain granted independence to her Malay states in 1957, while Sarawak, Sabah and Singapore joined in 1963. In 1965, Singapore gained independence, leaving Malaysia with its present national structure (*Asia Yearbook* 1995, 165).

Before independence from Britain, Malaysia's economy depended largely on exports of primary commodities. Tin and rubber production accounted for 85 per cent of export earnings and 48 per cent of GDP. Large industries, including agriculture, mining, banking and external trade, were under the control of foreign interests (mainly the British), while ethnic Chinese and Indians owned small-scale industry. Ethnic Malays were largely concentrated in the rural and agricultural sectors. While Malays were 50 per cent of the population, they owned less than 10 per cent of registered businesses, and less than 1.5 per cent of the share capital of listed companies (Kuruvilla 1995, 41). During the period 1957-70, government economic policy focused on industrialisation through import substitution. The state's role was confined to the development of infrastructure and the rural sector, while industrialisation was left to the private sector. The Government sought to create a climate favourable to foreign investment in import-substitution industries.

These policies had mixed results. On the one hand, by 1969, Malaysia had recorded economic growth averaging 5 per cent per annum, and manufacturing growth of over 10 per cent. Private investment was up by over 7 per cent annually. On the other hand, the economic dominance of the Chinese and Indians relative to the Malays had increased, leading to communal riots in 1969. This induced a change of policy by the Malay-dominated UMNO coalition government. The state now assumed a more dominant role in import-substitution investment with a view to improving the position of Malays. Thus was born the so-called bhumiputra (sons of the soil) policy, designed to increase the Malays' share of their country's wealth (see chapter 6) (Kuruvilla 1995, 42-4).

However, these policies led to significant economic problems, as the Government was forced to borrow heavily abroad to buy stakes in companies on behalf of the Malays, driving up interest rates and foreign debt. In 1977, a new policy commenced, to encourage private and foreign investment. Emphasis was placed on developing infrastructure with numerous tax, labour and other incentives. Part of the new policy was to restrict the power of trade unions, and to create union-free development zones to attract foreign capital. After a second 'resources crunch', the Malaysian Government was forced to move away from import-substitution towards export-oriented policies. These policies were successful in attracting capital, particularly from the US and Japan, and manufacturing by 1995 accounted for 32 per cent of employment, 42 per cent of GDP and 40 per cent of export earnings (Kuruvilla 1995, 44-47). Thus Malaysia has been a centre of trade from early in its history. Its resources of tin, rubber, crude petroleum, gas and other minerals have helped ensure ongoing economic growth. From 1985-1995, Malaysia was the eighth-fastest growing economy in the world, averaging a rate of 8% per annum.

In 1997, as a result of the financial crisis which hit Malaysia and other countries in the region, growth slowed, and even became negative for five quarters in 1998-9. Some of Malaysia's more grandiose development projects were curtailed. Since July 1997, the Malaysian ringgit has fallen by over 33% against the US dollar and the stock market declined by over 60%. Currency controls were announced in September 1998, with the ringgit fixed at 3.6 to the US dollar. With the easing of the Asian financial crisis, these controls were relaxed the following year. By mid-1999, it was announced that the country had returned to positive growth. Malaysia enjoyed an average income per head of US$4,840 in 1997, placing it far behind its prosperous island neighbour, Singapore (Edwards 2000, 607).

Nevertheless, the country's achievements over the previous 40 years of independence, together with a stable form of government have made Malaysia a relatively attractive for investment from organisations seeking a foothold in the Asian region. In turn the Malaysian government has responded to this interest by providing tax incentives and guidelines for the protection of foreign investment. These initiatives complement Malaysia's Vision 2020, in which the country aims to be a fully developed nation by the year 2020. The success of this plan depends, to large measure, on the development of an efficient labour force and the continued attraction of foreign investment. By 1992, foreign ownership of corporate equity had risen to 32.4%.

The Industrial Relations History

The first piece of industrial relations legislation was introduced in 1940, however the Trade Union Act was delayed due to the Japanese invasion and was not enforced until 1946. This legislation required unions to be registered and by the following year there were 298 unions with a membership of just under 200,000. The period from 1948 to 1969 was marked by the achievement of independence, strikes, riots and confrontation with Indonesia. During the same period the Malayan Communist party lost its influence over the trade union movement.

Malaysia's industrial relations policies had been tailored to fit the needs of its industrialisation and social redistribution strategies. Thus, during the import-substitution period, from the late 1950s until about 1977, the emphasis was on a form of 'restricted pluralism'. Legislation, described below, did give the Government considerable power over trade unions, including control over registration of unions, collective bargaining, and compulsory conciliation and arbitration of disputes. Strikes were permitted, subject to various restrictions. However, despite having these considerable legislative powers, the state's actual administrative intervention was minimal during this period (Kuruvilla 1995, 47-48.)

From 1980 onwards, the state took a more interventionist role in industrial relations, as part of its new economic policies of encouraging foreign investment (see above). In that year, amendments were passed to the Trade Union Act and the Industrial Relations Act. The Government also assumed more control over unions and their activities in practice. These changes increased Government influence over trade union, while the union movement's power decreased. Industrial relations policy during this period of export-oriented industrialisation was characterised by a shift towards a more unitary ideology and greater repression of unions by both Government and employers.

The Industrial Relations System

There are three basic laws in Malaysia that deal directly with industrial relations and all three are administered by the Ministry of Human Resources through the Department of Industrial Relations and the Department of Labour Peninsular Malaysia (Ayadurai 1992, 4). These three acts, the Industrial Relations Act 1967, the Employment Act 1955 and the Trade Unions Act 1959 are all Federal laws and are enforced through the Industrial Court. Appeals against decisions made by this court are referred to the High Court, which can vary the decision of the Industrial Court. There is also a Labour Court or Tribunal that is empowered under the Employment Act to resolve disputes concerning wages and cash payments between employers and employees. This dual system stems from the different emphasis of the two principal pieces of legislation. The Industrial Relations Act is primarily concerned with unions and dispute resolution via the principles of arbitration and conciliation while the Employment Act is directed toward the terms and conditions of employment.

In 1990, there were 446 Trade Unions in Malaysia with a total membership of almost 660,000 out of a labour force of just over 7 million people. Thus just under 10% of the workforce was unionised. In the plantation sector, where Government intervention had been minimal, however, the level of union density is much higher, at about 46% (Kuruvilla 1995, 57). However as Ayadurai (1992, 53) points out, the definition of a trade union in Malaysia has helped fragment the union movement and caused a multiplicity of unions to occur. Under the Trade Union Act, a trade union in Malaya, Sabah or Sarawak, may only include employees (or employers), from a particular establishment, trade, occupation or industry, or from similar trades, occupations or industries in the opinion of the Director General for Trade Unions. In effect this definition often led to the establishment of several related small unions rather than large national unions. Nevertheless, a few large national unions do exist in Malaysia today.

The Collective Bargaining Process

The Industrial Relations Act allows employees, after being recognised as a union, to enter into negotiations with an appropriate employer, to produce a Collective Agreement. The offer by the union to negotiate can be refused by the employer and if this happens then a Trade Dispute arises. These agreements are primarily concerned with the terms and conditions of employment. Issues considered to be within the realm of management powers, such as transfers and promotions, are necessarily excluded from such agreements.

The Employment Act and the Wages Council Act both set out the minimum acceptable terms and conditions for all employees. So collective agreements must use these as their guide, and the terms and conditions agreed to by both employers and unions must either meet these standards or exceed them. Once the agreement is concluded and supported by both parties, it must be forwarded to the Industrial Court for approval and this court has the power to amend any parts which it considers has not complied with the legislation. Once this process is concluded, the agreement becomes an award of the Industrial Court.

The Employment Act provides the following minimum benefits: a contract of service; wages paid within seven days of the pay period; ten paid and gazetted holidays; the prohibition of women working between 10.00pm and 5.00am; 14-22 days sick leave depending on length of service; working hours of up to 8 hours a day or 48 hours a week; paid maternity leave for up to 60 days at the ordinary rate of pay; overtime at the rate of one and a half times the ordinary rate for work done on ordinary days; double time on rest days and triple time on public holidays. Annual leave is determined by length of service, such as 8 days leave for those with less than 2 years service, 12 days for those with service between 2 to 5 years and 16 days for staff with service greater than 5 years (MIDA).

The Employees Provident Fund Act 1951 provides for employers and employees to contribute 10% to 12% of an employee's monthly wages to the fund, with the money being fully paid to the employee at the age of 55.

The Industrial Relations Act (1967) is also extremely specific in what it requires from employers and unions. The Act establishes the right of employers, employees and their union as well as the protection of each. The Act excludes union members from holding any management, executive, confidential or security role. It also sets out the procedures for submitting claims as well as the scope of union representation and collective bargaining. The Act specifically excludes many items, such as transfers, recruitment, dismissal, promotion, retrenchment, reinstatement and the allocation of duties, from the process of collective bargaining and from being the cause of strike action. The Act allows for intervention by the Minister of Human Resources in trade disputes. It also excludes strike action when trade disputes have been referred to the Industrial Court and when a matter is already covered by collective agreement or by an award of the court. There is also protection for pioneer industries from unreasonable demands of trade unions, on the basis that collective agreements must be based on the minimum standards outlined in the Employment Act 1955.

In non-unionised workplaces, the practice is for an aggrieved employee to seek redress from the immediate supervisor or from management. If this proves to be unsatisfactory then the employee has the right to lodge a complaint with the Ministry of Human Resources which is then required to undertake an investigation of the dispute.

The Industrial Relations Record

Malaysia has set out to become a fully industrialised nation by the year 2020. It has been trying to attract foreign investors to develop the economy and increase the trade and education levels of its people. Consequently, it has been seen as essential that potential investors see the industrial relations situation in Malaysia as stable, and government policies and legislation have focused on achieving this goal. According to the Labour and Manpower Report of 1987/8 (Ayadurai 1992, 127) there were 1235 trade disputes pending settlement in 1986, 1282 in 1987 and 1234 in 1988. 796 of the 1986 cases were resolved through conciliation, 158 through arbitration and 281 were left to be settled the following year. Figures for 1987 and 1988 are similar, showing that 920 and 861 cases respectively settled by conciliation, which is 64-70% of disputes settled by this method. Figures supplied by the Ministry of Human Resources in 1990 (Ayadurai,1993, 87), show that between 1980 and 1989, there were 203 strikes involving 39,167 workers and resulting in 146,899 days lost. The number of strikes decreased from 24 in 1981 to 7 in 1989. However, the number of disputes increased from 498 in 1981 to 989 in 1988 (Kuruvilla 1995, 58). This shows that the system has been far from conflict-free, but the institutional controls are such that workers have had to rely on conciliation for settlements.

Thus it would appear that on balance, the Malaysian Government's policy of allowing controlled unionism was extremely successful, in terms of economic growth, at least until the crisis of 1997 hit the country. Malaysia's economy grew strongly until that time, and foreign investment increased in terms of both projects and capital investment, with Japan significantly increasing its investments (MIDA). But there was a cost associated with this in terms of workers' rights. Union-busting and union-substitution strategies have been widespread in Malaysian industry. Indigenous companies were the worst offenders, but foreign companies tended to follow union avoidance strategies. In the key electronics industry, despite workers' theoretical rights to belong to unions, tactics of intimidation have been widespread, and in any case only enterprise unions were permitted. By 1993, only one enterprise union in the electronics industry had ever been registered (Kuruvilla 1995, 59).

In 1990, according to the Department of Trade Unions, Ministry of Human Resources (Ayadurai 1992, 58), there were 180 unions in the services sector and 103 in the manufacturing sector. The next highest number of unions was 82 in the transportation, communications and storage sector, and there were 33 unions each in the agriculture and commerce sectors. However, as might be expected, the greatest increase in the number of unions was in manufacturing, where the tally increased from 92 in 1989 to 103 in 1990.

Another significant feature of the trade union movement in Malaysia is the increasing proportion of enterprise unions. In 1985-6, for example, of 28 new unions registered, 27 were enterprise unions. The Trade Union Ordinance of 1959 provided for the registration of such unions, but their numbers only increased after the Government of Dr. Mahatir introduced its 'Look East' policy of trying to emulate Japan in 1980. While there is an argument in favour of this form of unionism, in that it may promote closer loyalty between workers and their enterprises, another consideration in Government thinking was undoubtedly that enterprise unions are small and weak. It is also noteworthy that the 1959 legislation allows enterprise unions to affiliate with national unions, but does not allow the latter to represent them for trade union purposes (Kuruvilla 1995, 54-5). Further, in 1982, a new section 18 was inserted into the Industrial Relations Act, allowing the Minister of Labour and Manpower to exercise his absolute discretion to suspend any trade union for a period of up to six months where, in his opinion, it was being used for purposes prejudicial to the interests of the security or public order of the country (Win Min Aun 1982, 39).

It is clear that Malaysia has been determined for quite some time to work seriously toward the ideal of being a leading nation in the Asian region. This is embedded in the Vision 2020 program, which revolves around a successful high technology manufacturing industry and the continued attraction of foreign companies. The Government has therefore viewed the achievement of an efficient industrial relations system as critical to the future success of Malaysia. To this end, however, the power of unions has been carefully limited, and the trade union movement has been deliberately kept weak and fragmented. In Kuruvilla's view, rapid changes in technology call for changes in labour utilisation, particularly in the crucial electronics industry. Kuruvilla argues that Malaysia needs to develop a more highly skilled workforce. Failure to do this will cause rising labour costs, which will cause foreign investors to shift their enterprises elsewhere, as has already occurred in neighbouring Singapore. However, the development of a more skilled labour force will require less repressive and more collaborative state and employer labour policies. Although there are some early signs of this occurring (Kuruvilla 1995, 61-2), in due course some liberalisation of the controls on unions and freeing up of the collective bargaining process will be essential if Malaysia is to successfully continue its march towards its Vision 2020.

HONG KONG

In 1998 Hong Kong had a population of 6.6 million with a land area of 1097 square kilometres. It is situated off the south east coast of the People's Republic of China and consists of the Kowloon Peninsula and some 235 adjacent islands, as well as Hong Kong Island itself. For over 150 years, Hong Kong was a British colony. On 1 July 1997, following the expiry of a 99-year treaty, control over Hong Kong reverted back to China. At that date, Hong Kong became a Special Administrative Region of China, pursuant to an agreement between Britain and China. Under the so-called 'Basic Law', negotiated in 1984, Hong Kong was guaranteed continuation of its capitalist system of private enterprise, its own currency, and certain freedoms carried over from the colonial era for 50 years (the so-called 'one country, two systems' policy). However, the partially democratic Legislative Council, established under British rule, was abolished, and replaced by an appointed Provisional Legislature set up under rules laid down by Beijing. Elections were held for a new Legislative Council in May 1998, but under a very restricted franchise.

The future of Hong Kong under Chinese rule remains uncertain. However, the Chinese national government has shown great restraint, integrating Hong Kong's capitalist system as a separate economic zone. If significant changes to the laws, industrial practices and economy of Hong Kong are to occur under Chinese rule, it appears that they will be achieved incrementally over many years.

History and Economic Development

The early history of Hong Kong is a product of the dealings between China and Britain. The trade relationship between the two countries was at best uncomfortable and at the worst, volatile. The trade in opium caused much concern to the Chinese and led to the Opium wars between the two nations. The first of these wars resulted in Britain acquiring the island of Hong Kong in 1842 and in 1860 further hostilities saw Britain take the Kowloon Peninsula. Finally, in 1898 following the war between China and Japan, Britain was awarded a 99-year lease on the New Territories area adjacent to Kowloon and the 235 neighbouring islands. The harbours of Hong Kong offered many economic opportunities, and so, under British rule, many new industries grew in order to support the blossoming trade between China and the West.

From 1998, Hong Kong continued to expand economically as its people, largely of Chinese heritage, became accustomed to British rule. However, Japanese forces overran Hong Kong in 1941 and their occupation continued till 1945. During this period the population and resources were greatly diminished. But, following the end of World War II and the return of British rule, ongoing turmoil in China saw a steady exodus of people fleeing permanently to Hong Kong. The post war period allowed Britain to redevelop Hong Kong as a free port. Although ultimate authority remained vested in a Governor appointed by Westminster, indigenous people assumed much greater responsibility and involvement during the late stages of colonial rule. Growth was steady and Hong Kong achieved the status of a newly industrialised East Asian economy.

The economy of Hong Kong was originally built on manufacturing cheap goods for export. However, the manufacturing sector has declined from 23.7% of GDP in 1980 to 6.5% in 1997. The service sector, on the other hand, has grown from 68% in 1980 to 85% in 1997. Particularly important in this sector are trading activities, banking, insurance, shipping and tourism. However, these figures are somewhat misleading because thousands of companies have shifted their factories to mainland China, and although their activities are still manufacturing, they have been re-classified as traders (Lewis, 2000, 302).

The Industrial Relations History

Hong Kong has traditionally been seen as a cheap Asian manufacturing base that can provide access to China. The transition through which Hong Kong has moved, from a predominantly agricultural and fishing settlement to an industrial enclave, has been relatively smooth. To a large extent, the indigenous Chinese population of Hong Kong, have found economic opportunities under British rule and economic growth occurred with western and Japanese investment. As Dobbs-Higginson points out (1993, 122-123), during the colonial era, the people of the territory enjoyed low taxes, experienced little violence and crime, enjoyed a high per capita GDP, and were separated from the sometimes chaotic and always authoritarian rule of China. It is largely for these reasons that Hong Kong has experienced a reasonably stable history in its industrial relations. However, the country faces other problems, such as a lack of unskilled labour, which China will no doubt continue to supply. There was also an alarming exodus of middle and senior managers, prior to the return to Chinese rule. The integration of China's workforce with Hong Kong's capital and the reliance on tourism, manufacturing and exporting will, no doubt, pose challenges to existing and emerging organisations well into the future.

Hong Kong unions only commenced to develop in 1948, after World War II. Over the following decade there was a slow but steady increase in trade union membership. Yet the amount of industrial activity was minimal and many believed that Hong Kong's Chinese heritage set the pattern of an accommodating workforce and a low level of industrial disputes.

The British colonial administration adopted a laissez faire attitude towards industrial relations, and it was only in the late 1960s and early 1970s that there was some increase in Government intervention, to establish a regulatory framework beyond the minimalism of the earlier colonial era. In 1966-7, there was a wave of civil unrest, which alerted the Government to the social grievances and deprivations of an increasingly affluent population, lacking channels to give expression to its desires and aspirations. Another factor explaining the Government's increased preparedness to intervene in the private sector was to help erase Hong Kong's image as a sweatshop and thereby strengthen its hand in trade negotiations aimed to achieve access for Hong Kong textile exporters to the European Economic Community. Against this background, the Government embarked on a program of labour reforms, introducing a framework for greater legal regulation of industrial relations. Nevertheless, most of the measures introduced were ad hoc and stopgap in nature, only marginally addressing the problems of workers and employees (Ng 1996, 291-2).

The Industrial Relations System

At the end of 1992, there were 511 registered trade unions, of which 409 were classified as unions of employees. They claimed a total strength of 525,538 members, comprising 362,916 men and 162,622 women (Nish, Redding, Ng et al. 1996, 284). Levin and Ng (1993, 39) also note an increase in the number and membership of smaller unions and a corresponding decrease in the number and membership of larger unions (i.e. those with 5001 or more members). Thus, the density of union membership is low and therefore so too is the strength of the union movement. The fragmentation of the trade union movement in Hong Kong has been attributed partly to the association between unionism and Chinese politics, and partly to the refugee mentality of the older generation of immigrants, who have viewed union membership as irrelevant or marginal (Nish, Redding, Ng et al. 1996, 282).

As with most countries that have been under British rule at some stage in their history, during the colonial era, Hong Kong had a social and political system that was typically British in style. Hence, there were various pieces of legislation applying to industrial relations issues modelled on the British system, mostly administered by the Labour Department. This legislation continues, subject to the possibility of changes under Chinese rule. The key legislation that provides the legal framework for the industrial relations system in Hong Kong includes: the Employment Ordinance of 1968; the Trade Union Ordinance of 1971; the Labour Tribunal Ordinance of 1973; the Labour Relations Ordinance of 1975; and the Occupational Safety and Health Council Ordinance of 1988. There are also other supplemental enactments.

According to the Hong Kong Trade Development Council, there were 119 enactments of industrial legislation over the decade 1983-92. This helped Hong Kong achieve its goal of ensuring that policies covering the health, safety and welfare of employees were comparable to those provided by other countries in the region at a similar stage of development. In 1993, another 11 pieces of labour legislation were enacted to support this objective, mainly through amendments to existing legislation.

Collective bargaining by employers is completely voluntary and agreements reached between employers and employees are not legally binding unless they are contained in a contract of employment. Thus when disputes or 'claims' between an employer and an employee arise over rights and benefits, as outlined in the Employment Ordinance of 1968, these are referred to the Labour Tribunal for hearing. Either the employer or the employee may refer an individual claim to the Labour Relations Service of the Labour Department or directly, in some instances, to the Labour Tribunal. If the Labour Relations Department cannot settle the dispute then the matter is referred to the Labour Tribunal for consideration. However, appeals against decisions made by the Tribunal can be made to the High Court if the decisions are considered inappropriate or inconsistent with the relevant legislation. But disputes that are resolved by these means are usually claims made by individual employers or employees concerning the interpretation of contracts of employment.

Wider disputes that involve several employees or that result in strikes as a means of achieving desired benefits for employees are termed Trade Disputes and are resolved through another mechanism. These disputes are handled in a more legalistic manner, which involves government participation and a potentially lengthy method of settlement. The process does not necessarily involve an independent arbiter or conciliator, but instead is centred on the Labour Department and the Commissioner. Thus, when a dispute arises, the Commissioner for Labour is notified of the circumstances leading to the dispute. The Commissioner in turn appoints a conciliation officer from the Labour Relations Service. This form of conciliation is not compulsory and may be refused by either or both parties. However, should this form of settlement be unsuccessful, then formal conciliation under the Labour Relations Ordinance becomes compulsory. Should the dispute still not be settled, then the Commissioner for Labour can report the dispute to the Governor in Council who in turn can take further action at his discretion. This action can involve referring the matter for arbitration with the consent of both parties, or to a Board of Inquiry or any other action deemed necessary under the circumstances. However as Levin and Ng note (1993, 36), virtually all disputes have been resolved by the initial means of conciliation and have not progressed beyond this point.

It is interesting to note the Commissioner for Labour actually headed up the Labour Department, rather than having a separate and independent body that deals with major disputes. It is not surprising therefore that so much legislation was enacted over a relatively short period in time with the government, and in particular Labour Department, playing such a major role in the country's industrial relations system. Effectively the colonial government was the major influence on industrial disputation and subsequent resolution. However, it is interesting to note that the key method of dispute resolution was in fact conciliation rather than arbitration, or other formal means of settling disputes. Also a point of interest, the Hong Kong public service has always had its own separate method of dispute resolution, which has only been used infrequently.

The rather piecemeal nature of the regulatory framework was, however, called into question in 1993 in a much-publicised 17 day strike by 3,000 airline hostesses against the airline Cathay Pacific. In particular, this dispute raised questions such as: whether the law should make it obligatory for employees and unions to give employers notice of anticipated strikes; whether the government should intervene more actively in the private sector, with a view to settling prolonged work stoppages more quickly; and whether the legal rights of both parties involved in strikes should be clarified (Ng 1996, 293).

The Industrial Relations Record

According to figures supplied by the Hong Kong Trade Development Council, during 1993 there were 8,041 prosecutions by the Labour Department for breaches of the Ordinances and regulations which resulted in fines of HK$22,793,100. The Council material also shows that in 1993 there were 157 trade disputes that involved 21 or more workers and resulted in 10 work stoppages and a loss of some 16,204 working days. The Labour Relations Division also dealt with 17,856 separate claims regarding wages and other payments. These figures indicate the influence of the Employment Ordinance as amended. They also highlight the involvement of the colonial government and the view that Hong Kong wished to maintain an equal basis of employment conditions within the region, while sustaining an attractive image to foreign investors and those wishing to use the re-exporting and tourism facilities.

The Council material also shows that the Labour Tribunal heard 4,029 cases initiated by employees and another 375 cases that were initiated by employers. 86% of these cases were referred by the Labour Relations Division after they had been unsuccessful in their attempts to conciliate. Amounts totalling HK$54 million were awarded to the parties by the relevant officers in these cases. This, too, could be seen as evidence of the effectiveness of Hong Kong's industrial relations system under colonial rule.

Other figures provided by the Commissioner for Labour, Annual Department Reports and cited in Levin and Ng (1993, 47) show that the number of strikes and lockouts in recent years has been low. For the decade 1981-90, the average annual loss of working days for the territory was only 5,684. In 1991, there were only five work stoppages classified as strikes or lockouts (Nish, Redding, Ng et al. 1996, 271). These figures compare favourably with those for 1956-57, when there were 12 strikes and lock-outs, which resulted in 78,852 working days lost (Levin and Ng 1993, 47).

These statistics reflect an increase in industrial stability and a decline in major industrial conflict. The increasingly close relations between Hong Kong and China have no doubt influenced this result to some extent, as Hong Kong businesses relocated many factories to the mainland (as discussed earlier). Many of those living in Hong Kong had been crossing the border to China to work, long before the return to Chinese rule. This has made economic sense, as China can provide a huge number of unskilled and semi-skilled workers, thus markedly reducing labour costs. However, the supervisory, professional and technical skills to manage the labour force still needed to come from Hong Kong. It is likely that, as this situation continues to evolve further, it will have a lasting effect on the industrial relations policies and programs of both Hong Kong and China.

During the period leading up to the return to Chinese rule, there was much uncertainty, leading to an increase in job insecurity, and hence a reduction in the already low level of industrial disputes. Observers have outlined various explanations as to why industrial conflict was relatively low in Hong Kong, even during the colonial era.

These include the following:

- Chinese culture is averse to open conflict, and workers have traditionally shunned collective forms of organisation, such as trade unions
- workers have negatively associated unions with the politics of the communist China
- the labour shortage has led to job-hopping and a lesser need for unions
- the government successfully provided effective means to resolve conflict quickly and amicably through institutional channels, including legislation, a labour tribunal and an industrial conciliation service
- the Government set up a body in the 1980s to advance wages to workers where employers became bankrupt or defaulted on payment of wages for financial reasons. This undoubtedly provided a safety valve for workers who may otherwise have resorted to industrial action to recover their entitlements at a time when numerous insolvencies occurred (Kirkbride, Tang and Westwood 1991; Levin and Ng 1993, 48; Nish, Redding and Ng, et al. 1996, 272).

Whatever the reasons, Hong Kong has enjoyed a stable industrial relations environment to date. Legislation dating back to the colonial era is still in place to ensure that conflict can be settled mainly by conciliation. However, the need for a more thorough regulatory framework, particularly when it comes to strikes, has been raised above.

Despite the impact of a major recession which saw property prices plummet by up to 40% and unemployment rise to record levels, the return of Hong Kong to Chinese sovereignty has not led to the destruction of democratic rights and freedoms, which some observers feared. Mainland China has largely observed the conditions laid down in the 'one country, two systems' policy in the agreement for the return of Hong Kong to Chinese sovereignty.

SOUTH KOREA

Population and Basic Demographics

The Republic of Korea, more commonly known as South Korea, is located on the southern half of the Korean peninsula bordering the Sea of Japan and the Yellow Sea. The capital is Seoul and the total land area of the country is 98,190 square kilometres. The estimated population in 1999 was 46.9 million. The labour force is 20 million, represented by, mining and manufacturing 27%, agriculture, fishing, and forestry 21%, services and others 52% (Chung, 2000, 606). The country is 78% urbanised, which is less than Singapore and Hong Kong, but much greater than Taiwan at 58% (Leggett 1997, 64). The population is ethnically homogeneous, except for about 20,000 Chinese. Although about 49% of South Koreans are Christians and 47.5% are Buddhists, Confucianism has been the dominant philosophy behind the South Korean culture and moral codes since it was introduced to Korea from China. Confucian traditions have strongly influenced modern South Korean management practices (Lee and Yoo 1987). (See also Chapter 4.)

From an Australian perspective, South Korea is one of Australia's largest and fastest growing export markets for commodities (Lansbury and Zappala 1990).

History and Economic Development

Korea was annexed by the Japanese in 1910 and this occupation continued until the end of World War II when the United States Occupation forces, as well as occupying Japan, began their influence in South Korea. There was a conditional arrangement between the United States and Russia, for the Russia to assume responsibility for North Korea, because Russia was considered an ally at the time. This arrangement became strained with the onset of the Cold War and culminated in war between North and South Korea from 1950-53. The United States intervention in support of South Korea continued after the Korean War, with considerable influence exerted on the government and its policies. Much of this influence related directly to the strategic location of South Korea, as well as to the Cold War and the arms race between the United States and the USSR from the mid-1950s until the early 1990s.

After World War II, Korea was one of the world's poorest countries, heavily dependent on agriculture and financially dependent upon the U.S. foreign aid. The Korean War further devastated the already fragile economic system of Korea. After the installation of President Park in 1961, however, South Korea registered meteoric rates of economic growth in the period 1962-1986. This was a period during which it successfully planned and implemented a growth strategy based on producing low-cost, labour-intensive, manufactured goods targeted for export markets. The reasons for this economic success include: the state's control over market mechanisms and its willingness to intervene in markets; the rise of South Korea's large, diversified business groups called *chaebol*; and a state corporatist regime that held South Korea's relatively low wages-long hours pattern in place to ensure international competitiveness.

In this 25 year period, as part of the economic development strategy, there were significant controls exerted on industrial relations. The state dominated the affairs of South Korea's national union federation, the Federation of Korean Trade Unions, and its industry-wide affiliated unions. To varying degrees, business dominated the affairs of local unions (for example, bankrolling union conventions, bribing union delegates, or providing cash payments and other benefits to union leaders) (Bognanno, Budd and Lee 1994).

Following the assassination of President Park in 1979, his authoritarianism survived under the regime of his equally repressive successor, General Chun Doo Hwan. An example of this repression was a South Korean version of China's Tiananmen Square massacre in which the military crushed a 1980 pro-democracy demonstration in the city of Kwangju, killing at least 200 civilians (*The Economist* 1995). However, the early to mid-1980s saw a more tolerant approach by the government. When industrial workers and students took to the street demanding democracy in 1987, President Chun Doo Hwan finally conceded. Since 1988, South Korea has been ruled by presidents who have been properly elected to office, rather than seizing power like Presidents Park and Chun.

Although South Korea is a newcomer in the competitive world of industrialised and rapidly developing countries, the government's relationship with business has been a very important aspect of South Korean management. Many South Korean enterprises owe their success to government support. As well as this close relationship, the government's control of the banking system from the early 1960s has made it possible to steer investment into the industries that the government wanted to develop (Lee and Yoo 1987, 73).

Despite the intervention of government, South Korea's external debt in 1980 amounted to 49% of GNP - a heavier burden than famously indebted Brazil (31%) or Mexico (31%). In 1980 the current-account deficit soared to nearly 9% of GNP. The Oil Crisis in 1980 saw a 2.2% shrinkage of South Korea's GDP while inflation hit 29%. The currency (the won) was devalued. An International Monetary Fund austerity package was implemented together with a cut in the subsidies to heavy industry. However, despite these measures, two key features of the Park regime continued: the habit of state intervention and the damaging concentration of South Korean industry in the hands of the *chaebol* (*The Economist* 1995).

Since 1987, South Korea has been trying to undo Park Chung Hee's political model. Yet for all Park's faults and dangerous legacies, South Korea has developed strongly economically in the same period. The economy experienced average real growth between 1987-94 of over 8%, partly because of an extraordinary piece of good luck. Following the Plaza Accord of 1985, the yen appreciated dramatically, allowing South Korean exporters to capture a large share of markets previously dominated by Japan (*The Economist* 1995, 21).

The driving force behind the economy's dynamic growth has been the planned development of an export-oriented economy in a vigorously entrepreneurial society. Real GDP increased more than 10% annually between 1986 and 1991. This growth ultimately led to an overheated situation with a tight labour market, strong inflationary pressures, and a rapidly rising current account deficit. As a result, in 1992, economic policy focused on slowing the growth rate of inflation and reducing the deficit. Annual growth slowed to 5%, still above the rate of most other countries in the world, but returned to 8.7% in 1995. From being the 11th largest economy in the world in 1996, South Korea slipped to 17th place in 1998, as a result of the Asian financial crisis. The country also recorded a period of negative economic growth in 1998. However, as a result of reforms initiated by the South Korean Government, the economy was back on a recovery path by 1999, with an 8.8% growth rate, though some doubts have been expressed about the sustainability of such rates of growth in the future (Chung 2000, 607).

Comparisons with Japan

The inaccurate assumption that South Korean management is basically just like Japanese management has become widely accepted. This assumption comes partly from claims that Japan and South Korea share a similar cultural heritage, especially their inheritance of Chinese culture, and the value systems of Confucius and the Buddha. It is also partly due to the Japanese colonisation of South Korea for 36 years and its assiduous attempts to 'Japanise' the South Korean population. Commentators have assumed the former colonial power had provided an enduring model for South Koreans in government and business. However, there are numerous and significant differences between South Korea and Japan (Lie 1990).

First, there is the tradition until recently of massive Government repression, which unlike Japanese tradition, has not been conducive to cooperative labour-management relations at the enterprise level (Chang Hee-Lee 1998 369). Second, the structure of industry is also different (Petzall 1993), the chaebol, unlike their Japanese counterparts, are family-dominated conglomerates. Third, South Korean management styles are quite distinct from those practiced in Japan (see Chapters 3 and 4). Fourth, employment policies are substantially different between the two countries. In Japan, the policy of permanent employment assures job security, fosters employee loyalty, and leads to worker immobility (these have been referred to in the section on Japan as *'three pillars of Japanese industrial relations'*). Whatever the actual extent of permanent employment is in Japan, it is not widely practiced in South Korea, certainly it is not usual for the South Korean enterprises to guarantee lifetime employment to its employees. There is considerably more employee mobility among firms in South Korea than is customary in Japan and executive recruitment occurs primarily from outside, rather than inside, the corporate hierarchy (Lie 1990).

Lie (1990, 116) has commented that the lack of internal promotion and lifetime employment results in a de-valuation of 'seniority' in wage fixing. High worker mobility implies that things other than the length of time spent in the firm are affecting wage rates. Indeed, credentialism or formal education is very significant in South Korea. Hence, promotion is much less dependent on seniority in South Korea than in Japan. For example, there are few upper-level managers in their 40s in Japan, while in South Korea there are many.

The most striking contrast between Japan and South Korea is the low level of unionisation in South Korea and the tendency towards unions which are industry-based, rather than enterprise-based as is the case in Japan. In South Korea, all unions are grouped by industry under a single umbrella organisation, the Federation of Korean Trade Unions.

Industrial Relations History

South Korea has a volatile political and industrial relations environment with strikes and demonstrations that are often violent (Lansbury and Zappala 1990, 1). South Korea was a feudal state for 500 years until its economy was forcibly opened in 1876 by the Kaghwa Treaty with Japan. By the late 19th century, a capitalist society was beginning to form. An organised labour movement based on occupations such as miners, stevedores and textile workers can be traced to the early twentieth century. As early as 1898 a violent strike against Japanese employers was recorded (Leggett 1997, 65). Although forms of unionism existed prior to the Japanese annexation in 1910, these were either single issue or short-lived types of union organisation. Japanese colonialisation, however, brought the labour movement together in national political struggles against foreign rule. Japanese colonialists had a monopoly on capital and they exploited the low cost South Korean labour. South Korean workers were not permitted to organise in trade unions (Lansbury and Zappala 1990, 22; Park and Lee 1995, 28-9).

Industrialisation accelerated during World War I, and in the period leading up to World War II. A trade union structure of local, regional and industry-wide unions emerged in the 1920s, as well as the first attempt at national organisation. However, the early unions were divided by ideology, a division exploited by Japanese colonial labour management policies. Japanese policies became more repressive with the approach of World War II. Overt labour protests declined, with some activists joining the underground resistance (Leggett 1997, 65-6).

The end of World War II saw both the cessation of Japanese rule and the start of political faction fighting between left and right wing elements of the labour movement. The communist-led unions were defeated, while the victorious Federation of Korean Trade Unions collaborated with management and the new post-colonial government. Labour unrest still occurred, however, leading to the enactment of the first labour laws in 1953. These laws, subsequently amended several times, required that unions not involve themselves in political activity and pursue the goal of collective bargaining. Yet despite these labour policies and corrupt union leaders, and despite the unions' political dependence on, and collaboration with, the ruling power, havoc and political unrest still raged within the labour movement. Ultimately these events resulted in the fall of the Rhee government in 1960 (Lansbury and Zappala 1990, 23; Park and Lee 1995, 30-31).

The 1960s witnessed renewed political repression of labour unions by legislation that restricted the ability to strike and undertake political activity. This coincided with the introduction of an outward looking growth strategy. In the 1970s unions were restructured on an enterprise basis in order to weaken collective action by workers. Even as late as 1979 union autonomy in South Korea was illusory. Government controls were oppressive and many 'official' unions affiliated with the Federation of Korean Trade Unions (FKTU) did not enjoy the support of rank and file members. Many workers turned to underground and radical unions led by intellectuals (Lansbury and Zappala 1990, 23; Park and Lee 1995, 31-2).

South Korean industrial relations reached a climax in 1987. The democracy movement resulted in a reassessment of government industrial relations policies. With the democratic reforms of 1987, a 'free' industrial relations system was born. Autonomous unions began replacing corrupted unions. Professional industrial relations and human resources departments began replacing corporate control schemes of bribery and intimidation. The state assumed a more neutral, regulatory role over labour relations. In addition the principles of independent labour unions, meaningful collective bargaining, and the right to strike were all advanced. The new 1987 regime had ushered in a new industrial relations system. In fact, in 1987 the number of recognised local unions increased by 170 percent. The sharp rise in the number of disputes following the relaxation of restrictions on strike activity is quite apparent, with 3,749 labour disputes in 1987 compared to 276 in the previous year. Many of these strikes did not occur as a result of labour and management impasses over wages, hours or working conditions. Some were spontaneous demonstrations against the political regime or corrupt business leaders, while others were over recognition disputes or individual grievances. (Bognanno, Budd and Lee 1994, 358-9).

Even with the 1987 changes, the lack of local union democracy in South Korea remained a problem. The close correlation between higher echelon centralised union intervention and subsequent enterprise strike activity would seem to recommend relaxing the prohibition on dual unionism (the law allowed only one national union federation, one national union per industry, and one union per enterprise). Indeed, legislating in this area may not now be necessary following a decision of the South Korean Supreme Court on 23 December 1992, 'lifting the prohibition' at all levels of the labour movement.

In 1996, the Government of Kim Young-Sam set up the multi-representative Industrial Relations Reform Commission (IRRC). It was intended to allow the independent trade union movement (Daehan Nochong) to enter the official framework of trade unionism. (Daehan Nochong was the organisation set up, originally on the initiative of radical students and intellectuals, in the early 1980s as the independent rival of the Government-sponsored FKTU.) There was an immediate effect in terms of a revival of growth in the trade union movement, in decline since the 1980s. However, the Government's action was subsequently shown to be merely token and the chaebol continued to resist dealing with independent unions.

At the end of 1996, the Government further amended the trade union laws, but in a manner which still effectively prohibited trade unions from becoming involved in politics, and denied official recognition to Daehon Nochong until the 2000, and denying multi-unionism in enterprises until the year 2003. Public servants (including teachers) also continued to be prohibited from joining trade unions. The change that caused the biggest outcry, however, was an increase in authority to lay off workers, which had previously been tightly controlled. Employers had sought more flexibility in this regard to contain rising costs in the face of economic recession (Leggett 1997, 72).

Despite the election of a more pro-labour government, headed by Kim Dae-Jung in 1998 (*TheEconomist,* February 28-March 6 1998, 31), labour unrest flared again in 1998 and 1999. The new government was forced by the pressure of the International Monetary Fund to confirm the labour flexibility provisions introduced by its predecessor, as well as allowing for hiring of more temporary workers (although 30 days notice is now required for layoffs of permanent workers). This led to several national strikes.

However, the new South Korean Government also opened its economy more fully to foreign companies, allowing participation by foreign investors in all but 13 of 1,100 industry sectors previously closed to them. The new provisions allowed for special tax incentives for firms employing over 1,000 workers, which over time should help restore employment lost during the recession (Anonymous 1999). Also, despite employers' new found freedom to lay off workers, the chaebol have generally shown themselves unwilling to sack workers on a large scale. As one commentator has put it, South Korea continues to suffer from a Confucian' labour market, in which paternalistic managers bully and protect workers in equal measure. (*The Economist,* July 10-16 1999, 7) Thus, companies like Samsung and Hyundai have resorted to asking workers to take unpaid leave in preference to sacking them. (In the case of Samsung, both men and women have been asked to take unpaid 'paternity' leave!).

Bognanno, Budd and Lee (1994) have hypothesised that South Korea's labour relations will stabilise as the labour-management relationships mature (Bognanno, Budd and Lee 1994, 367). Leggett (1997, 73) and Lee (1997, 369) tend to agree with this view, pointing to changes in the key human resource management policies of chaebol (such as Hyundai). The new strategy of the chaebol, in response to the state no longer repressing labour, has been to counter the emergence of independent trade unionism with policies such as by the provision of welfare facilities and the automation of previously labour-intensive production systems (Kwon and O'Donnell 1999, 289).

On the other hand, Lansbury and Zappala (1990) have suggested that it is fallacious to interpret South Korean union behaviour in terms of a strict dichotomy between political and business unionism. South Korean unions should be acknowledged as having both political and economic roles. Such an acknowledgement can, they argue, lead to better industrial relations outcomes in actual disputes. Unions may be political at a macro level, by membership of tripartite councils, activity in party politics and so forth, without necessarily jeopardising their more traditional economic role at the micro level. It is important, within the South Korean context, that the labour movement's goals for mass political change are not necessarily interpreted as exclusively 'political unionism'. Union members are also citizens of the broader society. It may well be, however, that political reform at the macro level will automatically channel union energy to the micro level in the longer run. Hence, it can be seen in terms of a self-correcting mechanism (Lansbury and Zappala 1990, 30).

A key element in improving the industrial relations situation, as identified by a number of South Korean analysts, would be changing the role of the government. It is currently regarded as being too restrictive, especially in regard to bargaining over the distribution of economic gains in recent years. Another important area for state change would be the restrictive laws governing the rights of workers and their unions (Lansbury and Zappala 1990, 17).

One of the more significant debates in South Korean industrial relations relates to the appropriate role for trade unions in the labour market. The debate is cast in terms of business/economic unionism versus political unionism. Most commentators feel that unions should be concentrating more on their economic function at the workplace level, the so-called 'bread and butter' issues. Implicit in this line of argument is the view that unions can be seen in terms of a 'rational maximiser' of their members' wages. This view grows directly out of the traditional labour monopoly model of union behaviour (Lansbury and Zappala 1990, 29).

Types of Unions

Streeck (cited in Lansbury and Zappala 1990, 12; see also Chapter 1) proposed a three part model for considering industrial relations - the 'neo-liberal model'; the 'dualistic model'; and the 'quasi-corporatist model'. Lansbury and Zappala (1990, 12) suggest that South Korea appears to provide a fourth model, in that the unions are taking a highly political role (since 1987) while the labour market structures remain weak. They have labelled this a 'marginalist model' because the union movement as a whole is still not regarded as a clear and legitimate role (especially those unions which take an anti-government stance). The South Korean unions, employers and government therefore face an important choice, whether they will continue with a system in which industrial relations are 'marginalised', or whether they will move towards one of the other alternative models. Such alternatives might include a 'dualistic model' as in Japan; a 'quasi-corporatist model' as in Sweden and Australia; or a 'neo-liberal model' as in the United States (Lansbury and Zappala 1990, 12).

On the basis of recent reports it seems evident that the different actors in the South Korean industrial relations system wish move forward in different directions. The Federation of Korean Trade Unions has indicated its preference for the 'quasi-corporatist' model. The Government prefers the 'dualist model and many employers regard the neo-liberal model as the way forward. Given the many contradictory tendencies in South Korean society, such as the strong enterprise basis of South Korean trade unions, the political uncertainty and the civil unrest, the path that will be chosen is by no means clear (Lansbury and Zappala 1990, 12-13).

The Law and Unions

A number of South Korean labour laws have been critical in state control of labour. The core of the current labour law was enacted in 1953 in the form of the Labour Standards Law, The Trade Union Law, and the Labour Dispute Adjustment Law. A series of changes were made to the Trade Union Law and the Labour Dispute Adjustment Law in December 1980.

It is interesting to see how the law was used to weaken the labour movement and collective bargaining. First, the focus of organising and bargaining was shifted from the Federation of Korean Trade Unions and its industry union affiliates to the enterprise-level unions, where resources and expertise were lacking. In effect, this amendment designated higher echelon labour leaders 'third parties', making it a crime for them to participate in enterprise-level organising and bargaining (Trade Union Law 1980, article 12). The Federation of Korean Trade Unions and industry unions were also prohibited from participating in strikes (Labour Dispute Adjustment Law 1980, article 13). Second, it was made more difficult for local unions to obtain certification by a requirement of a minimum level of 'showing of interest', and the intimidating requirement that organising members supply their names and addresses (Trade Union Law 1980, article 13). Third, anyone with a criminal record was barred from holding union office (Trade Union Law 1980, article 23). Thus, to remove uncooperative union leaders from office, the state simply needed to convict and imprison them on any criminal charge. Moreover, the state had power to dissolve unions or require them to re-elect their officers where any violations of laws or regulations occurred. (Trade Union Law 1980, article 32). Finally, these changes left in place the established legal prohibition on dual-unionism, allowing only one national union federation, one national union per industry, and one union per enterprise.

The effect of these amendments was virtually to outlaw strikes (Labour Dispute Adjustment Law 1980, articles 12, 16, and 30). However, these provisions were ineffectual in preventing strikes, but they were often used to imprison union leaders and render them ineligible for office. Between 1981 and 1986, union and union membership growth were stagnant, union density declined and strike activity was rare (Bognanno, Budd and Lee 1994, 356-7).

In December 1986 and November 1987, as part of the democratisation process, the Trade Union Law and Labour Adjustment Law were again amended, but this time to remove many of the restrictions on labour. The minimum 'showing of interest' provision was repealed (Trade Union Law 1987, article 13). The 'prison record' and related tests for eligibility to hold union office were removed (Trade Union Law 1987, article 23). The provision allowing the state to dissolve a labour union and force union officials to be re-elected was dropped from the statute (Trade Union Law 1987, article 32). Trade unions were also given greater freedom to strike. Cooling-off periods were shortened (Labour Dispute Adjustment Law 1987, article 16). Laws authorising the state to mandate mediation and compulsory arbitration were severely restricted (Labour Dispute Adjustment Law 1986, article 30). On the other hand, the prohibition on dual unionism was retained, with the FKTU and its affiliates remaining the only officially recognised union organisations (Bognanno, Budd and Lee 1994, 357-8). As pointed out above, the law was only finally changed in 1996. From the year 2000 onwards, the independent Daehon Nochong may act as a rival trade union centre to the FKTU, but is still subject to the restriction that public sector workers may not join affiliated unions.

Union membership has grown steadily from 224,000 in 1963 to 1,615,000 in 1995. In 1995, the level of union density was 12.7 per cent of permanent employees (Park and Leggett 1998, 279). The pattern of growth has reflected South Korea's rapid industrialisation since the mid 1960s, although political factors have caused temporary fluctuations (Park and Lee 1995, 32-41). The recent slight decline in the level of unionism from its peak in 1990 has been explained by structural changes in the economy, with the level of unionisation in manufacturing declining. However, unionism remains strong in large companies, with an average membership of about 250 (Park and Leggett 1998, 281).

Collective Bargaining

Laws regulating collective bargaining in South Korea date back to the end of the Korean Conflict in 1953. These statutes parallel the provisions of the Taft-Hartley Act in the United States, but until recently the lack of enforcement reduced them to empty pronouncements. In 1980, new legislation made it even easier for the state and businesses to avoid collective bargaining (Kearney 1991). This changed in 1987 when South Korea took an important step toward free collective bargaining (Bognanno 1988; Rogers 1990). Decades of state corporatism - where government and business elites permitted unionisation and collective bargaining, but only within the limits they set - gave way to a new industrial relations system granting workers *genuine* rights to unionise, collectively bargain and strike (Rogers 1990). The number of local labour unions, union members, and strikes increased dramatically (Bognanno, Budd and Lee 1994, 353.)

Labour Relations

South Korea's labour policies were especially unpleasant. The country was built by men who worked appalling hours, led by obsessive bosses who, along with their workers, slept on the docks and construction sites. Kim Woo Chong, who founded the Daewoo industrial group in 1967, never took a day off until his son was killed in a car crash in 1990. His employees were expected to work six days a week, 12 hours a day, until the mid-1980s. Anybody who protested got fired, or jailed. Under Park Chung Hee and his successor soldier-president, Chun Doo Hwan, labour disputes were generally resolved by troops, tear gas and truncheons (*The Economist* 1995, 5).

A small but significant proportion of South Korea's post-1986 strikes have been expressive, being primarily over political issues such as freedom of speech, or recognition issues, such as management's refusal to recognise workers' legally certified bargaining agents. However, a majority of the post-1986 strikes were tactical, economic force was used to secure employer concessions regarding wages, hours and employment conditions (Bognanno, Budd and Lee 1994, 355).

In South Korea, employers have not adopted a rational labour relations management system as in the United States nor a permanent employment system like Japan. In sum, they wish to adopt terms advantageous to themselves. In addition to employers' attitudes, there have been political problems.

That is, labour unions have been kept on a tight leash that forbids outsiders from intervening in a dispute between an employer and his workers. This law makes it virtually impossible for a union to help workers bargain with their employers, and regulations on arbitration effectively outlaw strikes. Comparatively low labour costs and weak power of labour unions give an incredible combined advantage in international competition to South Korean enterprises. Nevertheless, relatively low wages and weak labour unions have resulted in some real problems. Since the early 1960s, low wages, a high employee turnover rate, worker pirating, distrust in entrepreneurs, poor social security, and poor working conditions have resulted in both social and managerial problems (Lee and Yoo 1987, 74).

South Korea faces important strategic decisions about the future direction of industrial relations. Among the issues to be considered are:

- the degree to which government will continue to be directly involved in industrial relations
- the recognition to be granted by government and employers to the trade union movement as a whole
- the roles which the trade unions will pursue at both the national, macro-level of the economy and the micro or enterprise-level.

The South Korean government at the moment appears uncertain whether to follow a United States style 'neo-liberal' approach or a more 'dualistic' pattern similar to Japan. The 'quasi-corporatist' model, as exemplified by recent Australian experience, may also be relevant to South Korea's needs (Lansbury and Zappala 1990, 36).

One of the major challenges facing the South Korean government is to develop an appropriate institutional framework for resolving industrial conflict. For such a system to operate effectively, however, it will be necessary for both employers and government to recognise the legitimacy of trade unions that have the genuine support of workers. Conversely, trade unions will need to operate within a legal framework that confers both rights and obligations on their members (Lansbury and Zappala 1990, 37).

CONCLUSION

In this chapter we have briefly examined the industrial relations systems of five selected South East Asian countries. This examination has shown that each of these countries has evolved its own unique system for dealing with industrial relations. In each case, history, culture, economics, politics and geographic location has played a role in shaping the institutions that have developed.

In Japan and South Korea, independent labour movements have developed, and trade unions play both an important and legitimate role in the industrial relations dynamics of the society. In both Japan and South Korea, collective bargaining is the chief method for fixing wages and settling industrial disputes, although Japanese industrial relations have been markedly more peaceful and stable than those in South Korea since the mid 1950s.

In Hong Kong, the attitude of the Colonial Government was generally laissez faire, but not actively hostile to trade unions. However, for other reasons, unions did not develop with the strength and independence as in Japan and South Korea. Collective bargaining is also practiced, but it is underdeveloped compared with Japan and South Korea. It remains to be seen what the long-term impact the 1997 return to Chinese rule will have on Hong Kong's industrial relations.

In Malaysia and Singapore, on the other hand, the Governments have actively sought to regulate, control and shape the labour movement to their own ends, and to subordinate them to the needs of national economic development. Collective bargaining in these countries is overshadowed by mechanisms of conciliation and arbitration, and direct government intervention.

Despite these different approaches, all of these Asian societies has experienced rapid economic growth in the last two decades. Japan, Singapore and Hong Kong have each overtaken Australia in terms of GDP per capita. While the financial crisis beginning in 1997 put a check on economic growth, it seems likely that the effects on the economies of the countries discussed in this chapter will only be temporary, and that reforms have been initiated which will return them to a long-term growth path.

REVIEW QUESTIONS

1. Discuss the role of history in the evolution of the different industrial relations systems and institutions of the five selected South East Asian countries.

2. To what extent do cultural differences explain the different systems developed in the five countries?

3. Why have Japan and South Korea developed independent labour movements, whereas in Hong Kong, Malaysia and Singapore, the respective labour movements are either weak or subject to government control?

4. Australia, Malaysia and Singapore all use variants of compulsory arbitration in the prevention and settlement of industrial disputes. Compare and contrast the experience of these countries in respect of their record of industrial disputes.

5. 'For forms of government, let fools contest,

    Whate'er is best administered is best.'

    (Alexander Pope).

    Discuss Pope's words in relation to the industrial relations systems of Australia and the five selected South East Asian nations.

FURTHER READING

Anantaraman, V. (1991) *Singapore Industrial Relations System*, McGraw Hill, Singapore.

Ayadurai, D. (1992) *Industrial Relations in Malaysia, Law and Practice*, Butterworths, Singapore.

Bamber, G. and Lansbury, R. (eds) (1998) *International and Comparative Employment Relations*, 3rd Edn, Allen and Unwin, Sydney.

Deery, S. and Mitchell, R. (eds) (1993) *Labour Law and Industrial Relations in Asia*, Longman, Melbourne.

Nish, I., Redding, G. and Ng, S. (eds) (1996) *Work and Society. Labour and Human Resources in East Asia,* Hong Kong University Press, Hong Kong.

Verma, A., Kochan, T. and Lansbury, R. (eds) (1995) *Employment Relations in the Growing Asian Economies*, Routledge, London and New York.

APPENDIX

QUEENSLAND INDUSTRIAL RELATIONS COMMISSION

Workplace Relations Act 1997, s 25

CLUB FREEFALL

AND

Australian Workers' Union

(No. CA ..6 of 1998)

CLUB FREEFALL

- CERTIFIED AGREEMENT 1998

COMMISSIONER R...Y

4 September 1998

APPLICATION FOR CERTIFICATION OF AGREEMENT

THIS AGREEMENT, is made in pursuance of the Workplace Relations Act 1997, this eighteenth day of August 1998 (being the date on which the first party signed this Agreement), between the CLUB FREEFALL and the Australian Workers Union of Employees, Queensland, witnesseth that it is hereby mutually agreed as follows:

ARRANGEMENT OF AGREEMENT

Subject Matter	Clause No:
PART 1: PRELIMINARY	
Title	1.1
Agreement Coverage	1.2
Date of Operation	1.3
Wage Increases	1.4
Club's Commitment to Staff	1.5
Club's Incorporated's Expectation of Staff	1.6
Posting of Agreement	1.7
Representation	1.8
PART 2: TERMS & CONDITIONS OF EMPLOYMENT	
Contract of Employment	2.1
Introduction of Changes, Termination of Employment	2.2
Time and Wages Records	2.3
Grievance Procedures	2.4
Counselling and Warning Procedures	2.5
Anti-discrimination	2.6
Structural Efficiency	2.7
Multi-hiring	2.8
Training and Education	2.9
Multi-skilling and Job Rotation	2.10
PART 3: DEFINITIONS, WAGES, SUPERANNUATION	
Definitions	3.1
Wages Permanents, Casuals, Juniors, and Trainees	3.2
Superannuation	3.3

PART 4:	HOURS OF WORK AND OVERTIME	
Hours of Work Full-time employees and Part-time employees		4.1
Rosters		4.2
Breaks		4.3
Overtime		4.4

PART 5:	LEAVE	
Annual Leave		5.1
Sick Leave		5.2
Bereavement Leave		5.3
Club Long Service Leave		5.4
Family Leave		5.5
Statutory Holidays		5.6

PART 6:	MISCELLANEOUS	
Uniforms and Protective Clothing		6.1
Destruction of Property		6.2
Consultative Mechanisms		6.3
Workplace Health and Safety		6.4

PART 1 PRELIMINARY

1.1 Title

This Agreement shall be titled the CLUB FREEFALL - Certified Agreement.

1.2 Agreement Coverage

1.2.1 This Agreement shall apply to
- (a) CLUB FREEFALL
- (b) All employees of the Club for which classifications and classes of work are contained in this Agreement where ever employed in the State of Queensland
- (c) The Australian Workers Union of Employees, Queensland.

1.2.2 Employees classified under this Agreement who are appointed in writing under this clause and paid in excess of $28,000.00 per annum shall be excluded from the operation of the following clauses of the agreement: 3.1, 3.2, 4.1, 4.2, 4.3 and 4.4.

1.2.3 This Agreement replaces all terms and conditions of the Club Employees Award - State (Excluding South East Queensland) and the Liquor and Accommodation Industry- Licensed Clubs - Managers and Secetaries Award 1996 or any other relevant safety net Award.

1.3 Date of Operation

1.3.1 This Agreement shall take effect and have the force of law as from the first pay period on or after the date of approval. It shall remain in force for a period of three years until September 3 2001. The Agreement shall be subject to review based on the operational needs of the Club after 18 months operation, or other period as determined by mutual agreement of the parties to this Agreement.

1.3.2 Each party reserves its right to raise matters of substantial concern during the life of the Agreement.

1.4 Wage Increases

The rates in this agreement shall increase by 3% from 1 July 1999 and a further 3% from 1 July 2000.

1.5 The Club's Commitment to Staff

The Club is committed to:
- (a) providing staff with ongoing permanent employment, where possible, which provides opportunities for personal and professional development and advancement
- (b) providing employees with a work environment which is satisfying, safe and challenging
- (c) encouraging a strong team ethic whilst providing individual opportunities and rewards.

1.6 The Club's Expectation of Staff

As well as being committed to all Club employees, the Club also has expectations of its Staff, these include:
- (a) striving to excel in the level of service provided to our member's and guests
- (b) seeking to enhance your individual skills through available training and development opportunities offered by the Club

(c) a desire to succeed both as part of the Club team and as an individual
(d) recognising that income earning capacity is based on personal performance as well as overall performance of the Club.

1.7 Posting of Agreement

A true copy of this Agreement shall be exhibited in a conspicuous place on the principal premises of the employer so as to be easily read by employees.

1.8 Representation

The Australian Workers Union is the representative of the employees of the Club in this Agreement. The Australian Workers Union will continue to encourage employees to remain or become members of the Australian Workers Union. The employer will encourage employees to be a member of the Union, and will arrange for Union dues to be deducted from the payroll and forwarded to the Union.

The Australian Workers Union with the employees are entitled to hold 2 paid meetings of 1 hr duration each 12 mth period, outside normal work hours, only employees attending meetings will be granted 1hr pay.

PART 2 TERMS AND CONDITIONS OF EMPLOYMENT

2.1 Contract of Employment

2.1.1 An employee shall on or prior to commencing employment, be provided by the employer with a written statement containing the following information:
   (a) Type of engagement, which shall be either full-time, part-time, casual, fixed term or specified period
   (b) Classification level
   (c) Rostered Hours of Duty
   (d) Rate of Pay
   (e) Date of Appointment
   (f) Probationary Period
   (g) any other specific conditions of employment.

2.1.2 Except in circumstances where the provisions of Clause B (Introduction of Changes) and Clause C (Redundancy) of the Statement of Policy of the Queensland Industrial Relations Commission apply, the following notice of termination of employment shall apply to all permanent employees:

Continuous Service	Notice Period
Not more than 1 year	1 week
More than 1 year but less than 3 years	2 weeks
More than 3 years but less than 5 years	3 weeks
More than 5 years	4 weeks.

2.1.3 The above periods of notice are increased by 1 week if the employee concerned is over 45 years of age and has served with the Club for more than 2 years.

2.1.4 If an employee does not give the prescribed notice to the Club, then the Club may deduct from the employee's termination monies an amount equal to the required period of notice.

2.1.5 If the Club terminates the employee they may elect to pay out the period of notice required to be given to the employee in lieu of the prescribed notice period at the employee's ordinary rate of pay. Alternatively the parties may mutually agree to have the employee work out part of the notice period and receive payment for the other part of the required period of notice.

2.1.6 The employee may be terminated without notice in any of the following instances:
   (a) drunkenness or being under the influence of drugs whilst rostered on duty
   (b) theft or unauthorised use of Club property, and fraud on the Club
   (c) refusal to obey a reasonable direction of the Club Manager or his/her's representative whilst rostered on duty
   (d) wilful neglect of duty
   (e) fighting, assaulting, or any form of violence to another employee, club member, or guest
   (f) issuing of members credit points to a person not entitled or authorised to receive such member's credit points
   (g) sexual harassment and discrimination of other employees, club members or guests
   (h) any other instances of misconduct a defined under the Workplace Relations Act 1997.

In all such cases, the employee is to be paid their wages and any other entitlements in accordance with this Agreement at the time of termination. Provided that if the employee is terminated outside usual office hours, payment shall be made no later than the next normal pay day.

2.1.7 All employees engaged under the terms and conditions of this Agreement are subject to a probationary period of 480 hours. The purpose of the probationary period is for both the employee and employer to assess their respective suitability for the position occupied within the Club. This assessment of suitability shall be determined by discussion between the employers representative or supervisor and the employee at regular intervals as determined by the Club.

2.1.8 No notice of termination shall apply to casual employees, probationary employees, trainees, apprentices, or fixed term employees.

2.2 Introduction of Changes, Termination of Employment in Cases of Redundancy.

Except as provided in clause 2.1, the employer and employees to whom this agreement applies will observe the terms and conditions of the Statement of Policy of Termination of Employment, Introduction of Changes and Redundancy of the Queensland Industrial Relations Commission as amended from time to time.

2.3 Time and Wages Records

2.3.1 The employer shall keep and have available a complete record of all employees subject to this agreement who are or were employed by the employer in accordance with the requirements of Chapter 9 of the Workplace Relations Act 1997.

2.3.2 Time sheets, time books and rosters will be provided by the employer, wherein the employee will enter their daily commencing and ceasing times of work including breaks taken during the shift. Rosters will be displayed in convenient places accessible to employees.

2.3.3 The employer may also store such information on an electronic timekeeping device.

2.4 Grievance Procedures

2.4.1 It is agreed that every effort will be made to amicably resolve any dispute or grievance that may arise by direct negotiations and consultation between the parties to this agreement.

2.4.2 The intention of this procedure is to facilitate the resolution of grievances at the workplace level within each section of the Club.

2.4.3 The matters to be dealt with in this procedure will include any grievance or dispute between an employee and the employer. The procedure may apply to a single employee or any number of employees.

2.4.4 The procedures in the event of a grievance or dispute shall be:
  (a) any grievance or dispute shall be raised as soon as possible with the employee's immediate supervisor.
  (b) if the matter cannot be resolved at this level, then the employee will discuss the issue of concern with the Manager as appropriate. If requested, a representative of the Union may be present at this interview.
  (c) if the matter continues to remain unresolved at this stage the issue may at the discretion of the parties be referred to representatives of the employer and employee for further advice and if necessary assistance to resolve the matter.
  (d) Should the discussions under the terms of this provision still fail to resolve the matter, the dispute may be referred to an Industrial Magistrate or to the Queensland Industrial Relations Commission, whichever is appropriate.
  (e) While this procedure is being followed, the status quo will prevail and work will continue normally, if safe, until settlement is reached. No party will be prejudiced as to the final settlement by the continuance of work in accordance with this provision.

2.5 Counselling and Warning Procedures

2.5.1. If an employee is performing work unsatisfactorily, then the employee will be formally counselled or warned. The employee shall be given an opportunity to respond to the allegations of unsatisfactory work performance before any warning is given to the employee by the Club.

2.5.2 If the employee's unsatisfactory work performance continues, a further written warning will issued or alternatively, if the circumstances warrant it, a final warning in writing will be given to the employee. A Union Representative or other witness may be present if a final warning is given. The employee an opportunity to respond to the allegations of unsatisfactory work performance before a further written warning or final warning is given to the employee by the Club.

2.5.3 If the employee's performance continues to be unsatisfactory and the employee has been given an opportunity to respond to all the allegations of unsatisfactory work performance that person may be terminated by the Club. Within 2 weeks of termination the Club will provide the employee concerned with a written notice of termination specifying the reasons for termination.

2.5.4 For the purposes of this clause, matters that directly affect customer or guest service, or failure to follow Club procedures will be considered as serious matters for the purposes of assessing employee performance.

2.5.5 Provided that for the purposes of this provision, nothing shall prevent the Club summarily dismissing or other lesser action as the Club deems appropriate should the circumstances warrant such action being taken, provided further that such actions are in accordance with the Workplace Relations Act 1997.

2.6 Anti-Discrimination

2.6.1 The Club has a policy of equal employment opportunity. This policy requires decisions to be made on employment matters on the basis of equality of opportunity without discrimination in recruitment and selection, alteration of employment or on termination of employment.

2.6.2 Merit will be the basis of all such decisions at all times.

2.7 Structural Efficiency

2.7.1 The parties are committed to on-going modernisation and review of the terms of this agreement so that it provides flexible working arrangements compatible with the operational needs of the enterprise. Also factors such as improved working conditions, increased job satisfaction and commitment, improved communications and increased skill levels are essential factors.

2.7.2 The parties recognise that business performance, growth and success can only be achieved with a partnership approach.

2.8 Multi-Hiring

2.8.1 Permanent employees may be separately engaged as casual employees for duties in a separate section of the Club. The employee will be paid the appropriate rate of pay for a casual employee engaged in that section of the Club.

2.8.2 For the purposes of this clause, 'a separate section of the Club' shall mean a discrete work location other than the employee's usual work location. Alternatively, shall mean a discrete set of duties other than the employee's usual duties, provided such duties are not wholly or substantially performed in the employee's usual work location, and shall not apply to work where overtime would ordinarily be performed.

2.9 Training and Education

2.9.1 The parties will cooperate in ensuring that appropriate training and cross skilling is available and that such training if required by the employer will be provided at the expense of the employer. The employer also agrees to cooperate in encouraging employees to avail themselves of the benefits of such training.

Accordingly, the parties commit themselves to:
- developing a more highly skilled and flexible workforce
- providing employees with career opportunities through appropriate training to acquire additional skills
- removing barriers to the utilisation of skills acquired.

2.9.2 The parties shall develop appropriate training programs to facilitate skill enhancement based on the following procedures:
   (a) training shall comply with the criteria and guidelines established by the employer
   (b) all employees shall have access to training and no barriers shall be placed on employees accessing such training provided that the training is relevant to the employees position or career path as determined by the employer
   (c) the employee shall not suffer any loss of ordinary pay if training undertaken on the job, provided it is during ordinary hours of work of the employee
   (d) where off the job training is required by the employer, an employee attending such training programs shall be entitled to paid at their ordinary rate of pay but such time shall not be regarded at time worked for the purposes of annual leave, sick leave or long service leave accruals.

2.10 Multi-skilling and Job Rotation

In recognition of the operational and efficiency requirements of the employer, and to create more varied and interesting work, it is a condition of employment that staff perform duties and functions for which they have the skills and training to perform. As the training of employees increases, additional tasks and functions may be required to be performed subject to the operational needs of the enterprise at all times.

Where a employee is appointed to a position of work of higher level duties, for a fixed period, all work performed at the higher level shall be paid at the higher level of pay.

PART 3: DEFINITIONS, WAGES, SUPERANNUATION, AND THE CLUB BONUS

3.1 Definitions of the Classes of Work

Your will be appointed to the following classification and it determine the pay rate applicable to the work you perform. If an employee is appointed work of a higher grade then they shall be paid at the higher rate for the hours worked at the higher grade.

The grades are as follows:

3.1.1 Introductory Club Employee

This level applies to new entry level employees where the employee has not been trained in or has no knowledge of the establishments systems or procedures nor the work performed in the complex and/or the Industry generally.

Work at this level for entry level employees requires direct supervision, direction and training. Training may be either on or off the job or a combination of both on and structured off the job training, depending on the position. A permanent employee when newly employed at the establishment commences a mandatory probationary period of 480 hrs. This period can be extended with the mutual agreement of both the employer and employee.

3.1.2 Club Employee Level 1

Positions at this level require no formal training but occupants can demonstrate skills to undertake tasks to the minimum level of proficiency to perform to the establishment's standards. Positions at this level are typically performed under direct supervision and have no decision making responsibility.

Indicative functions at this level include general cleaning, cleaning functions in kitchens, basic kitchen duties, basis f&b duties, cleaning and clearing tables, handling, storing and distributing goods, washing.

3.1.3 Club Employee Level 2

Positions at this level have some formal training (which is usually on the job training) where the occupants can demonstrate skills to undertake functions to a standard of proficiency requiring a lesser degree of supervision than level 1 positions and consistently meet the defined standards for the position. The level of knowledge of occupants in positions at this level, of the establishments systems and procedures is at a level, where they can give guidance and assistance to employees at a lower level. Positions at this level have authority to make limited decisions within defined parameters.

Indicative functions at this level in addition to level 1 duties include: food and beverage service, retail sales, operation point of sale systems, operation of gaming devices such as ClubTAB, Keno, or Poker machines, assisting in audit duties and clerical duties, basic food preparation, driving motor vehicles including parking, servicing general areas, assisting in the cellar, periodic use of a fork-lift and supervisory duties of employees at lower grades.

3.1.4 Club Employee Level 3

Work at this level requires employees to have gained significant experience in the industry. Occupants can demonstrate skills to undertake tasks at a medium level of proficiency to perform to establishment standards.

Positions at this level are typically performed at a relatively autonomous level, with a limited amount of decision making responsibility. Supervision and training of staff may be involved at this level and lower level duties. Attending to the operation and maintenance of gaming devices such as ClubTab, Keno, or Gaming machines, Audit functions and clerical duties, cellar duties, cooking meals and preparing food by persons without trade qualifications, but reasonable skill of grills, light meals, counter lunch and the like. Driving a Club Courtesy or Tour Coach of 25 passengers or less. Routine maintenance, that is non-trade nature of the buildings, grounds and surrounds. Security and lock up duties as and required

3.1.5 Club Employee Level 4

Employees at this level will have achieved formal training in their field (or with relevant trade qualifications). Tasks must be undertaken with a high level of proficiency and occupants must have a detailed understanding of the establishment and industry.

Occupants at this level will be responsible for supervising and training other staff, and trade duties. Level 4 employees' responsibilities will extend to decision making within the relevant department.

3.1.6 'Special Events Casual' shall mean a casual employee engaged for the purposes of a special event at or for the Club for which the employee will work the special event on a one off basis. Such class of employee shall be paid rates of pay as prescribed. The minimum engagement for such class of employee shall be two hours or two hours pay in lieu thereof.

3.2 Wages

3.2.1 It is the intention of the Club to operate its premises on 7 days per week on each available trading day. In view of this the parties agree that wage rates will apply regardless of the day of the week or time of the day worked. Employees will be rostered on an equitable basis to ensure that no worker will be disadvantaged.

3.2.2 Queensland Minimum Wage

The rates of wages prescribed by this Agreement in respect of adult employees are deemed to include and to be expressed by reference to the Guaranteed Minimum Wage declared from time to time pursuant to the provisions of the Workplace Relations Act 1997, and unless otherwise ordered such wages are to adjusted to accord with any variations to the Guaranteed Minimum Wage as follows:

Adults..$373.40

3.2.2 Subject to clause (2), the minimum wages to be paid to the following classes of employees shall be as follows:

	3.9.1998 to 1999		1.6.1999 to 2000		1.6.2000 to 2001	
CLASSIFICATION	Permanent	Casual	Permanent	Casual	Permanent	Casual
Club Employee Intro Level	$10.64	$12.13	$10.96	$12.50	$11.28	$12.87
Club Employee Level 1	$11.65	$13.29	$12.00	$13.68	$12.36	$14.10
Club Employee Level 2	$13.01	$14.83	$13.40	$15.28	$13.80	$15.74
Club Employee Level 3	$13.69	$15.61	$14.10	$16.08	$14.53	$16.56
Club Employee Level 4	$14.76	$16.84	$15.21	$17.34	$15.66	$17.86
Special Events Casual	$13.80		$14.21		$14.64	

* Annualised rates include an additional loading of 14% on base rates identified in schedule 1 to this Agreement. This schedule identifies anticipated work requirements for the Club. This loading compensates employees for work on public holidays, weekends and late work.

3.2.4 Junior Employees

The minimum rate of wages for junior employees shall be the undermentioned percentages of the rates prescribed for the appropriate adult classification for the work performed by the junior employee

Age	**Percentage**
17 years and under	70%
18 years	80%
19 years	90%
20 years and over	Full adult rate.

Junior rates shall be calculated to the nearest 10 cents. To determine the correct rate of pay, the employer may request proof of age from the employee. Should the Club deem a junior employee competent then they shall be paid the adult rate of pay.

3.2.5 Casual Employees

(a) Casual employees shall be paid for the time actually worked with a minimum engagement of 2 hours per shift.

(b) Casual rates of pay with the exception of the 'Special Events Casual', shall be calculated using the following formula:

Weekly base rate contained in Clause 3.2.3 of this Agreement divided by 40 plus 30% for ordinary hours Monday to Sunday inclusive.

(c) For work on any one day in excess of 10 consecutive hours, exclusive of breaks, the loading shall increase to 50% for the first three hours so worked on any one day then 100% thereafter.

(d) If a casual employee works on a public holiday then they shall be paid a loading of 150% additional on the appropriate base rate.

3.2.6 Payment of Wages

(a) All wages shall be paid on actual hours of work including any overtime worked during that period. Wages will be paid weekly or fortnightly on the nominated pay day into a bank account or account of some other financial institution preferred by the Club.

(b) Should the nominated pay day fall on a Public Holiday then the employee's wages shall be paid on the day following that day.

3.3 Superannuation

3.3.1 The superannuation provisions for all employees covered by this Agreement shall be in accordance with the Superannuation Guarantee (Administration) Act 1992.

3.3.2 The Club will contribute an amount, as prescribed in that Act, of the employee's wage into Queensland Super (the prescribed superannuation fund), on a monthly basis.

PART 4: HOURS OF WORK AND OVERTIME

4.1 Hours of Work - Full-time and Part-time Employees

4.1.1 Full-time Employees

The arrangements of hours of work for Full-time employees may be implemented within the combinations of one of the following:

(a) 160 hours over a 4 week cycle

(b) All ordinary hours are to be worked within a minimum of 3 hours per day and a maximum of 10 hours per day, provided that a maximum of 12 hours per day may be worked by mutual agreement between the employer and employee in writing

(c) All ordinary time shall be worked within a span of 14 hours on any one day from start to finish.

(d) Employees are entitled to 8 full days off duty each 4 week cycle.

(e) A maximum of 10 consecutive days may be worked in any 4 week cycle.

(f) Broken shifts may be worked within a maximum span of 14 hours on any one day or shift as appropriate.

4.1.2 Part-time Employees

The arrangements for Part-time employees shall be implemented as follows:

(a) Part-time employees shall be paid the ordinary hourly rate as prescribed for full-time employees.

(b) Part-time employees may work broken shifts, provided that the span of hours for the broken shifts does not extend 16 hours in any one (1) day, otherwise clause 4.4 will apply.

(c) Part-time employees who are employed at the date of introduction of this agreement shall work a minimum of 15 hours per week.

(d) The minimum engagement for part-time employees shall be 10 hrs per week or 3 hrs per day. Part-time employees may work up to 160 hrs over a 4 week cycle.

4.2 Rosters

4.2.1 Where practicable, rosters will be drawn up in consultation with employees and provide adequate rest pauses and rostered days off. It is Club policy that where possible rostered days off duty be constant. In addition, it is Club policy that rosters be drawn up with full consideration being given to health and safety considerations in accordance with the Health and Safety Policy of the Club.

4.2.2 Subject to the approval of the employer, it shall be acceptable for employees to mutually agree to temporarily change or swap rosters. Rosters so changed will be paid for at the rates applicable to the originally rostered time.

4.2.3 Rosters may be changed by the employer giving of not less than 2 days notice or in the case of an emergency 24 hours notice. If the employer and employee mutually agree, a change of roster may occur at an agreed lesser period than that specified in the clause.

4.3 Breaks

4.3.1 Meal Breaks

Every employee shall be entitled to a meal break of not less than 30 minutes nor more than 1 hour during their rostered hours of work, before the end of 6 hours work or at such later time as mutually agreed between the employer and employee.

4.3.2 Rest Pauses

Employees shall receive a paid rest pause of 10 minutes' duration if they work 4 or more hours. Rest Pauses shall be taken at times so as not to interfere with the operational needs of the Club.

4.4 Overtime

All time worked in excess of 160 hours by permanent employees in a four week cycle, outside the span of hours, outside the employee's agreed rostered hours, or on the employee's rostered day, will be paid as overtime at the rates of 50% additional to the base rate for the first 3 hours and 100% additional to the base rate thereafter.

PART 5 - LEAVE

5.1 Annual Leave

5.1.1 Full-time employees covered by this agreement will at the end of each year of continuous service be entitled to 4 weeks annual leave on full pay. Part-time employees at the end of each year are entitled to 4 weeks annual leave payable at the rate of their average ordinary weekly earnings for the year. Part-time employees may take their annual leave in equivalent full-time hours i.e. 2 weeks at 40 hours per week.

5.1.2 All permanent employees leave is exclusive of statutory holidays, which may fall during the period of such leave.

5.1.3 Leave accrues at the rate of 1.539 days per 28 days of continuous service.

5.1.4 Where the employee has accrued 6 weeks annual leave under this clause, the Club may request an employee to take any amount of the leave accrued, by giving 14 days notice.

5.1.5 Annual leave shall not accumulate during periods of sickness or accident of more than 520 hours.

5.1.6 ~~Full-Time or Part-Time employees who are terminated or resign before the completion of 12mths continuous~~ service will be paid annual leave accrued on the basis of 0.077 hrs per ordinary hour worked. Leave loading will not apply to this proportionate leave on termination.

5.1.7 All annual leave paid to an employee will have an additional 17.5% loading paid on the amount paid for the annual leave.

5.2 Sick Leave

5.2.1 Permanent employees are entitled to 8 days leave each year of service for personal illness or injury.

5.2.2 This entitlement for full-time employees accrues at the rate of 8 hours for each competed 6 weeks of service with the Club. Part-time employees will accrue such leave on a pro-rata basis.

5.2.3 If the employee is absent from work they must notify at the Club Manager or their immediate supervisor, at least 2 hours before the commencement of their shift, so that alternative arrangements can be made to cover the absence. Failure to do so without a reasonable excuse may result in disciplinary action against the employee concerned.

5.2.5 If the employee is absent from work for 2 or more consecutive days, they are required to provide a medical certificate to the Club Manager stating the reason for the absence and the likely duration of the absence, otherwise the employee concerned shall not be paid for the absence and may be disciplined by the Club.

5.2.6 Unused leave shall accumulate from year to year to a maximum amount of 13 weeks.

5.2.7 No sick leave shall be paid during any period in which an employee receives workers compensation.

5.3 Bereavement Leave

5.3.1 A permanent employee on the death of a wife, husband, father, mother, brother, sister, child or step child, parents in law, and grand parents, is entitled to, on notice, leave up to and including the day of the funeral of such relative. Such leave shall be without loss of pay for the period not exceeding 2 days. Proof of the death is to be furnished to the employer as a condition of approval and payment of the leave. Bereavement outside the state or considerable distance away within the state, employees are entitled to use portion of their accrued sick leave entitlements.

5.3.2 For the purposes of this clause the words 'wife' and 'husband' shall include a person who lives with the employee as a de facto wife or husband.

5.4 Club Long Service Leave

All employees shall be paid long service in accordance with the provisions of the Chapter 4 Part 4 of the Workplace Relations Act 1997.

5.5 Family Leave

The conditions of this type of leave are detailed in the Family Leave Award - State, as published in 139 QGIG 179-184 and amended in 150 QGIG 82-83.

5.6 Statutory Holidays

For the purposes of this Agreement, the following days are recognised as public holidays: Good Friday, Easter Saturday, Easter Monday, Labour day, Christmas day, Boxing day, ANZAC Day, Australia Day, Sovereigns Birthday, New Years day, Show Holiday or any other day appointed under the Holidays Act 1983.

PART 6 - MISCELLANEOUS PROVISIONS

6.1 Uniforms and Protective Clothing

6.1.1 Where uniforms and protective clothing are required to be worn, they will be provided by the employer free of charge to the employee.

6.1.2 A security deposit may be required by the employer for uniforms provided to employees. This deposit is refundable upon return of the uniforms in good condition, fair wear and tear excepted. Uniforms remain the property of the employer.

6.1.3 Black and white apparel and shoes and socks are not considered uniforms for the purposes of this provision.

6.2 Destruction of Property

The employer will not charge or deduct any sum from the wage of any staff in respect of accidental breakages except in the case of wilful destruction of property.

6.3 Consultative Mechanisms - Focus Group

6.3.1 The parties to this Agreement are committed to maximising the effectiveness of the business by ensuring that flexibility is maximised for the benefit of all. Specific measures to ensure that this occurs include:
   (a) Open communication to assist in the identification of obstacles to superior service and operation
   (b) Measures to monitor the effectiveness of the agreement and its operation within the opening of the Club.

6.3.2 A Club Focus Group will be established and comprised of a minimum and where possible equal number of representatives as follows:
- Elected employee representative
- General Manager of the Club
- Other representatives as required by the elected representatives.

6.3.3 Communications to staff of all Club activities in addition to those of the Focus Group will be via the following mediums:
- Staff Handbook
- Employee Newsletter
- Staff Notice Boards
- Departmental meetings.

6.3.4 The parties to this award agree that adequate consultation and communication, facilitates efficient and flexible operations, and productive employee and management practices.

6.4 Workplace Health and Safety

6.4.1 The parties to this Agreement are committed to providing a safe and healthy workplace and work practices. The parties recognise that illness or injury at the workplace is costly to the employer and the employee and also disruptive to the respective parties.

6.4.2 To facilitate healthy and safe work practices, the parties to the agreement are committed to discussing health and safety issues as they apply to the operations of the Club as part of the consultative measures under this Agreement.

6.4.3 The employer and employees under this Agreement may refer to their respective Industrial Representatives for appropriate advice or expertise in enhancing performance with due regard to health and safety initiatives.

The parties also recognise the importance of conducting regular audits of the Clubs operations, policies and procedures, including the employee's skills, knowledge, qualifications and application of healthy and safe work practices.

Signed for and on behalf of the CLUB FREEFALL   )

In the presence of   )

Signed for and on behalf of the   )

Australian Workers Union of Employees   )

In the presence of   )

SCHEDULE 1

1. Permanent rates used for the purposes of the calculation of the wages in clause 3.2.3 includes employees working on 56 public holidays hours per calender year, 224 Saturday hours 224 Sunday hours calender year, and 200 late work hours, based on the following rates:

Club Introductory Probation	373.40
Club Services Grade 1	408.80
Club Services Grade 2	456.40
Club Services Grade 3	480.40
Club Services Grade 4	518.00

   The casual rates are 1/40 plus 30% on the on the above rates.

2. Implicit in the working of traditional penalty times under this Agreement is the requirement for all employees so rostered to work rotating rosters are formulated equitably so as to share all such shifts across the Club workforce in the respective areas of the clubs operation.

3. The employee may after 12 months continuous service request an audit of their financial circumstances if they have good reason. 'Good reason' means that an employee has worked over the prescribed number of hours in paragraph 1. If the audit reveals a disadvantage then the employer will make up any shortfall.

   Should an employee for any personal reason request to work rosters that result in a disadvantage then the employer shall not be required to make up any shortfall.

This agreement is certified under the Workplace Relations Act 1997, chapter 2 part 1.

R...Y, Commissioner

Filed on this twenty-first day of August 1998, certified by the commission and given Register No. CA ..6 of 1998, in the Certified Agreements Register.

Dated this fourth day of September 1998

E...L

Registrar

Operative Date: 4 September 1998

REFERENCES

Abbott, K. (1993), 'Labour Flexibility, Industrial Relations and Productivity: A 'Conceptual Bias' Explanation', *Labour Economics and Productivity*, vol.5, no.2, September.

Abbott, K. (1999), 'Lessons for the Australian Trade Union Movement from the Industrial Relations Policy Experiences of Britain and New Zealand', *Policy, Organisation and Society*, no.18, winter, 39-58

ACIRRT (1995), *It Enterprise Bargaining Good for Your Health? The Occupational Health and Safety Implications of the Shift to Enterprise Bargaining in Australia*, Report Prepared for Worksafe Australia.

ACIRRT, (1996), *Agreements Database and Monitor*, no.11, University of Sydney.

Ahlstrand, B. (1990), *The Quest for Productivity: A Case Study of Frawley After Flanders*, Cambridge University Press, Cambridge.

Akita, J. (1996) 'Japanese Industrial Practices and the Employment Contract', in Nish, I, Redding, G. and Ng, S. (eds) (1996) *Work and Society. Labour and Human Resources in East Asia*. Hong Kong University Press, 241-252.

Allan, C., O'Donnell, and Peetz, D. (1999) 'More Tasks, Less Secure, Working Harder: Three Dimensions of Labour Utilisation', *Journal of Industrial Relations*, Vol. 41, No. 4, 519-535.

Allan, C. and Timo, N. (1999) 'Globalization and the Organization of Work: Case Studies of Three Service Industries', in *Employment Relations Perspectives: Globalization and Regionalisation in the Asia Pacific*, forthcoming.

Alexander, Robyn and John Lewer. *Understanding Australian Industrial Relations*. 5th ed. Sydney, Harcourt Brace, 1998.

Amaha, E. (1999), 'Blazing a Trail', *Far Eastern Economic Review*, July 1, 34-6.

Anantaraman, V., (1991), *Singapore Industrial Relations System*, McGraw Hill, Singapore.

Anonymous (1999) 'South Korean Labor in Flux', *World Trade*, July, 1999, 20-22.

Argy, V. (1992) *Australian Macroeconiomc Policy in a Changing World Environment*, Allen and Unwin, Sydney.

Ariff, M. (1993) 'Singapore' in Rothman, M, Briscoe, D., and Nacamulli, R. (eds) *Industrial Relations Around the World*. de Gruyter, Berlin, 345-365.

Ashenfelter, O. and Johnston, G. (1969), 'Bargaining Theory, Trade Unions and Industrial Strike Activity', *American Economic Review*, vol.59, no.1, 35-49.

Asia 1999 Yearbook. Far Eastern Economic Review.

Aun, Wu Min. (1982) The Industrial Relations Law of Malaysia, Singapore, Heinemann.

Australia. Bureau of Industry Economics (BIE) (1996) 'Setting the Scene: Micro-Economic Reform - Impacts on Firms', *Report 96/1*, AGPS, Canberra.

Australia. Bureau of Industry Economics (BIE) (1995) 'International Benchmarking – Waterfront 1995, *Research Report 95-16*, Australian Government Publishing Service, Canberra.

Australia. Bureau of Transport and Communications Economics (BTCE) (1990) 'Costs of Waterfront Unreliability', *Occasional Paper* no. 101, Australian Government Printing Service, Canberra.

Australia. Bureau of Transport and Communications Economics (BTCE) (1995) Review of the Waterfront Industry Reform Program, *Research Report* no. 91, Australian Government Printing Service, Canberra.

Australia. Bureau of Transport Economics (BTE) (1999) *Waterline,* BTE, Canberra.

Australia. Cabinet Briefing Paper (1997) *'Waterfront Strategy'*, Unpublished Paper, July, Canberra.

Australia. Department of Employment, Workplace Relations and Small Business (DEWRSB) (1998) *Trends in Enterprise Bargaining*, September Quarter, 1998, DEWRSB, Canberra.

Australia. Department of Employment, Workplace Relations and Small Business (DEWRSB) (1998a) *1997 Report: Agreement-Making under the Workplace Relations Act*, Prepared by the National Institute of Labour Studies at Flinders University, AGPS, Canberra

Australia. Department of Employment, Workplace Relations and Small Business (DEWRSB) (1998b) *1998 Update: Collective Agreement-Making under the Workplace Relations Act*, January to June 1998, DEWRSB, October, Canberra.

Australia. Department of Employment, Workplace Relations and Small Business (DEWRSB) (1999) *Trends in Enterprise Bargaining*, March Quarter, 1999, DEWRSB, Canberra.

Australia. Department of Employment, Workplace Relations and Small Business (DEWRSB) (1999) *Trends in Enterprise Bargaining*, June Quarter, 1999, DEWRSB, Canberra.

Australia. Department of Employment, Workplace Relations and Small Business (DEWRSB) (1999) *Trends in Enterprise Bargaining*, September Quarter, 1999, DEWRSB, Canberra.

Australia. Department of Industrial Relations (DIR) (1990) *Report on the Operation of the Restructuring and Efficiency Principle*, AGPS, Canberra.

Australia. Department of Industry Relations (DIR) (1992) *Workplace Bargaining: The First 100 Agreements*, Report of the Wages Policy Branch, DIR, AGPS, Canberra.

Australia. Department of Industrial Relations (DIR) (1994) *Making Workplace Agreements – It's Your Agreement*, DIR booklet, May, DIR, Canberra.

Australia. Department of Industrial Relations (DIR) (1995) *Annual Report 1994: Enterprise Bargaining in Australia*, DIR, AGPS, Canberra.

Australia. Department of Industrial Relations (DIR) (1996) *Annual Report 1995: Enterprise Bargaining in Australia*, DIR, AGPS, Canberra.

Australia. Department of Industrial Relations/Australian Manufacturing Council (DIR/AMC) (1992) *International Best Practice: Report of the Overseas Study Mission*, DIR/AMC, Canberra.

Australia. Industries Assistance Commission (AIC) (1988) *Annual Report*, 1987-1988, AGPS, Canberra.

Australia (1988) *Industrial Relations Act 1988*, Australian Government Printer, Canberra.

Australia. (1993) *Industrial Relations Reform Act 1993 (Cth)*, Australian Government Printer, Canberra.

Australia. Inter-State Commission (1989) *Waterfront Investigation,* (Volumes 1-5), Summary Report, Australian Government Publishing Service, Canberra.

Australia. Labour Ministers Council (LMC) (1998) *Individual Contracting - Australian and New Zealand Experiences*, Labour Market Research Program, Research Paper, DEWRSB, Canberra.

Australia. Minister for Workplace Relations and Small Business Peter Reith (1998) *Waterfront Reform: Seven Benchmark Objectives*, unpublished paper, 8th April, Canberra.

Australia. Prices Surveillance Authority (PSA) (1995) *Price Probe Report*, No. 23, PSA, Melbourne.

Australia. Productivity Commission (1998a) 'International Benchmarking of the Australian Waterfront', *Research Report,* AusInfo, Canberra.

References

Australia. Productivity Commission (1998b) 'Work Arrangements in Container Stevedoring', *Research Report*, AusInfo, Canberra.

Australia. Productivity Commission (1996) *Stocktake of Progress in Microeconomic Reform*, Productivity Commission, June, AGPS, Canberra.

Australia. Senate (1999) *Report on Consideration of the Provisions of the Workplace Relations Legislation Amendment (More Jobs, better Pay) Bill*, November, Senate Printing Unit, Parliament House, Canberra.

Australia. (1974) *Trade Practices Act 1974 (Cth)*, Australian Government Printer, Canberra.

Australia. (1996) (WRA) *Workplace Relations Act 1996 (Cth)*, Australian Government Printer, Canberra.

Australian Bureau of Statistics (ABS) (1996), *Trade Union Statistics*, June 1996, Cat. No. 6323.0, Canberra.

Australian Bureau of Statistics (ABS) (1998) *Labour Productivity, September, Australia*, Cat. No. 5206.0, ABS, Canberra.

Australian Bureau of Statistics (ABS) (1999) *Australian Social Trends 1999*, Cat No. 4102.0, ABS, Canberra.

Australian Bureau of Statistics (ABS) (1999) *Employee Earnings, Benefits and Trade Union Membership, Australia*, August 1999, Cat No. 6310.0, Canberra.

Australian Bureau of Statistics (ABS), *Industrial Disputes, Australia*, Cat. Nos. 6321.0 and 6322.0, AGPS, Canberra.

Australian Center for Industrial Relations Research and Training (ACIRRT) (1999) *ADAM Report*, No. 6, September, 1995.

Australian Center for Industrial Relations Research and Training (ACIRRT) (1999) *ADAM Report*, No. 15, December, 1997.

Australian Center for Industrial Relations Research and Training (ACIRRT) (1999) *ADAM Report*, No. 16, March, 1998.

Australian Center for Industrial Relations Research and Training (ACIRRT) (1999) *ADAM Report*, No. 18, September, 1998.

Australian Center for Industrial Relations Research and Training (ACIRRT) (1999) *ADAM Report*, No. 19, December, 1998.

Australian Center for Industrial Relations Research and Training (ACIRRT) (1999) *ADAM Report*, No. 23, December, 1999.

Australian Center for Industrial Relations Research and Training (ACIRRT) (1999) *Australia at Work: Just Managing?* Prentice Hall, Sydney.

Australian Center for Industrial Relations Research and Training (ACIRRT) (1996a) *Casual Workers, Employment Security and Economic Competitiveness in the Australian Hospitality Industry: Recent Developments and Implications for Policy*, ACIRRT, Sydney, University of Sydney.

Australian Center for Industrial Relations Research and Training (ACIRRT) (1996b) *1996 MTIA Members' Survey on Enterprise Agreements*, ACIRRT, July, University of Sydney, Sydney.

Australian Center for Industrial Relations Research and Training (ACIRRT) (1998) *Working/Time/Life: Reclaiming the Working Time Agenda: An Issues Paper for the Australian Trade Union Movement*, ACIRRT, University of Sydney, Sydney, November.

Australian Conciliation and Arbitration Commission (ACAC) (1983) *National Wage Case*, 23 September, Print F2900, Melbourne.

Australian Conciliation and Arbitration Commission (ACAC) (1987) *National Wage Case*, 11 March, Print G6800, Melbourne.

Australian Conciliation and Arbitration Commission (ACAC) (1988) *National Wage Case, 5* February 1988, Print H0900, Melbourne.

Australian Conciliation and Arbitration Commission (ACAC) (1988) *National Wage Case*, 12 August, Print H4000, Melbourne

Australian Conciliation and Arbitration Commission (ACAC) (1989) *National Wage Case*, February Review, 25 May, Print H8200, Melbourne

Australian Conciliation and Arbitration Commission (ACAC) (1989) *National Wage Case*, 7 August, Print H9100, Melbourne.

Australian Council of Trade Unions (ACTU) (1987), *Future Strategies for the Trade Union Movement*, September, Melbourne.

Australian Council of Trade Unions (ACTU) (1988) *Discussion Paper: A Draft ACTU Blue Print for Changing Awards and Agreements*, Melbourne.

Australian Council of Trade Unions (ACTU) (1995a) *The Future of Unions in Australia*, Background Paper, A.C.T.U. 1995 Congress, Melbourne.

Australian Council of Trade Unions (ACTU) (1995b) *Organising Works*, Pamphlet No. 2, Melbourne.

Australian Council of Trade Unions (ACTU) (1995c*), Recruitment: The Priority for 1995*, Background Paper, A.C.T.U., Melbourne.

Australian Council of Trade Unions (ACTU) (1999) *Employment Security and Working Hours – A National Survey of Current Workplace Issues*, prepared by Yann Campbell Hoare Wheeter, July, ACTU, Melbourne.

Australian Council of Trade Unions (ACTU) (1999) *Unions @t Work: The Challenge for Unions in Creating a Just and Fair Society*, ACTU, Melbourne.

Australian Council of Trade Unions and Trade Development Commission (ACTU/TDC) (1987) *Australia Reconstructed: Report of the ACTU/TDC Mission to Western Europe*, AGPS, Canberra.

Australian Democrats (1996) *Agreement between the Commonwealth Government and the Australian Democrats on the Workplace Relations Bill*, October, Canberra.

Australian Development Assistance Bureau, (1983) *Industrial Relations in Malaysia and the Role and Growth of Trade Unions*, International Training Institute: Department of Foreign Affairs, Sydney.

Australian Financial Review (newspaper) 25th June, 1998, 14th February, 1998, 29th April, 1999, 8th October, 1999.

Australian Industrial Relations Commission (AIRC) (1991), *CRA [Comalco] Weipa Demarcation Case*, 42 Industrial Reports 336-351.

Australian Industrial Relations Commission (AIRC) (1991), *National Wage Case*, Review, 13 August, 1991, Print J8943, Melbourne.

Australian Industrial Relations Commission (AIRC) (1991), *National Wage Case*, 16 April, Print J7400, Melbourne.

Australian Industrial Relations Commission (AIRC) (1991) *National Wage Case*, 30 October, 1991, Print K0300, Melbourne.

Australian Industrial Relations Commission (AIRC) (1993) *Review of Wage Fixation Principles*, 25 October, 1993, Print K9700, Melbourne.

Australian Industrial Relations Commission (AIRC) (1994), *Aluminium Industry CRA [Comalco] Bell Bay Case*, Full Bench Decision, Print No. L7449, 56 Industrial Reports 403-446.

Australian Industrial Relations Commission (AIRC) (1994) *Review of Wage Fixing Principles*, 16 August, 1994, Print L4700, Melbourne.

Australian Industrial Relations Commission (AIRC) (1994) *Safety Net Adjustments and Review - September*, Print L5300, Melbourne.

Australian Industrial Relations Commission (AIRC) (1995), *Aluminium Industry CRA [Comalco] Bell Bay Case*, Appeal by CRA, Full Bench Decision of the Federal Industrial Court, 61 Industrial Reports 455-486.

Australian Industrial Relations Commission (AIRC) (1995) Appeal, Full Bench of AIRC, re Asahi Diamond Industrial Australia Pty Ltd v Automotive, Food Metals and Engineering Union (AFMEU) and ors, 59 *Industrial Reports,* 385.

Australian Industrial Relations Commission (AIRC) (1995) *Third Safety Net Adjustment and Section 150A Review*, 9 October, Print M5600, Melbourne.

Australian Industrial Relations Commission (AIRC) (1996), *Aluminium Industry CRA [Comalco] Weipa Case*, Full Bench Decision, Print No. M8600, 63 Industrial Reports 138-193.

Australian Industrial Relations Commission (AIRC) (1996) 'Decision of the Full Bench of the AIRC, re Australian Nursing Federation (ANF) and ors', Dec 249/96 S Print No. M9940, 13 March, Sydney.

Australian Industrial Relations Commission (AIRC) (1996) Full Bench of AIRC, re Automotive Food, Metals, Engineering (AFMEU), Printing and Kindred Industries Union (PKIU) and ors v Tweed Valley Fruit Processors, 61 *Industrial Reports*, 212.

Australian Industrial Relations Commission (AIRC) (1997) *Safety Net Review*, Print No. p1997, Melbourne.

Australian Industrial Relations Commission (AIRC) (1999) Decision by Vice President McIntyre, Application for Registration by SMQ Enterprise Union, 27th October, 1999, Dec 1269/99 S Print S0298.

Australian Industry Group web page. Available at:

Australian Manufacturing Council (AMC) (1990) *The Global Challenge: Australia Manufacturing in the 1990s* Pappas Report, Melbourne.

Australian Mining and Oil Guide, (1996), Sydney

Australian Vehicle Manufacturing Industry (AVMI) (1989) *Award Restructuring: Report of Tripartite Study Mission to Japan, the U.S., G.F.R. and Sweden*, FVIU, VBEFA and FCAI, DIR, Canberra.

Ayadurai, Dunston (1992) *Industrial Relations in Malaysia: Law and Practice*, Singapore, Butterworths Asia.

Ayadurai, Dunston.(1993) 'Malaysia' in Deery, S. and Mitchell R.(eds) *Labour Law and Industrial Relations in Asia*. Melbourne, Longman, 1993, 61-95.

Bacharach, S. and Lawler, E. (1980) *Power and Politics in Organisations*, Jossey-Bass Publications, San Francisco.

Bacon N. and Storey J. (1993) 'Individualisation of the Employment Relationship and Implications for Trade Unions', *Employees Relations*, Vol. 15, No. 1, 5-17.

Bacon, N and Storey, J. (1996) 'Individualism and collectivism and the changing role of trade unions' in Ackers, P., Smith, C. and Smith, P. (eds) *The New Workplace and Trade Unionism: Critical Perspectives on Work and Organisation*, Routledge, London, 41-76.

Bain, G. and Price R. (1983) 'The Determinants of Union Growth', in G.Bain (ed), *Industrial Relations in Britain*, Blackwell, 1983, 12-33.

Bamber, G. and Lansbury, R. (eds) (1998), *International and Comparative Employment Relations*, 3rd Edn, Allen and Unwin, Sydney.

Bamber, G. and Shadur, M. (1993), 'The International Transferability of Japanese Management Strategies: An Australian Perspective', in Czerkawski, C. (ed), *Japanese Management: Challenges and Applications for Business Executives*, Academic Press, Hong Kong, 1993, 35-58.

Barbash, J. and Barbash, K. (eds) (1989), *Theories and Concepts in Comparative Industrial Relations*, University of Carolina Press, Columbia, SC.

Barney, J. and Griffin, R. (1992), *The Management of Organisations: Strategy, Structure and Behaviour*, Houghton Mifflin, Boston.

Barry, Michael. 'Employer Associations: Assessing Plowman's Reactivity Thesis', *The Journal of Industrial Relations*. 37\4 (1995), 543-561.

Bartol, M., Martin, D.C., Tein, M. and Matthews, G. *Management: A Pacific Rim Focus*, McGraw Hill, 1995.

Bass, B.M. (1990), *Bass and Stogdill's Handbook of Leadership: Theory, Research and Managerial Applications*, 3rd Edn, Free Press, New York.

Bean, R. Comparative Industrial Relations. Routledge, London, 1985.

Beardwell, I. and Holden, L. (1994), *Human Resource Management: A Contemporary Perspective*, Pitman, London.

Beasley, M. (1996) *Wharfies: A History of the Waterside Workers Federation of Australia*, Halstead Press, Sydney.

Beggs, J., and Chapman, B. (1987), 'An Empirical Analysis of Australian Strike Activity', *Economic Record*, vol.63, 46-60.

Begin, J. (1995) 'Singapore's Industrial Relations system: Is it Congruent with its Second Phase of Industrialisation?' in Frenkel, S., and Harrod, J. *Industrialization and Labor Relations. Contemporary Research in Seven Countries*, Cornell University, 64-87.

Bell, S. (1994) Australian Business Associations: New Opportunities and Challenges. *Australian Journal of Management*, vol. 19, no. 2, Dec., 137-158.

Bell, S. and Head, B. (1994), 'Australia's Political Economy: Critical Themes and Issues', in S. Bell and B. Head (eds) *State, Economy and Public Policy in Australia*, Oxford University Press, Melbourne.

Ben-Ari, E. (1990), 'Ritual Strikes, Ceremonial Slow Downs: Some Thoughts on the Management of Conflict in Large Japanese Enterprises', in Eisenstadt, S. and Ben Ari, E. (eds) *Japanese Models of Conflict Resolution*, Kegan-Paul, London, 94-124.

Bennett, L. (1994), *Making Labour Law in Australia: Industrial Relations, Politics and Law*, Law Book Company, Sydney.

Bennett, L. (1994), 'Women and Enterprise Bargaining: The Legal and Institutional Framework', *Journal of Industrial Relations*, vol.36, 191-212.

Bennett, L. (1999) 'Swings and Shifts in Australian Industrial relations: Employer Dominance in the 1990s', *New Zealand Journal of Industrial Relations*, Vol. 24, No. 3 231-256.

Benson, J. (1991) Labour management during recession: Japanese manufacturing enterprises in the 1990's. *Industrial Relations Journal*, vol. 29, no. 3, 207-221.

Bentley, P. and Hughes, B. (1971), 'Australian Cyclical Strike Patterns', *Journal of Industrial Relations*, vol.13, no.4, 352-67.

Berger, Y. (1993), ' The Hoechst Dispute: A paradigm Shift in Occupational Health and Safety' in M. Quinlan (ed.), *Work and Health: the Origins, Management and Regulation of Occupational Illness*, Macmillan, Melbourne, 126-39.

Bernstein, M. (1955), *Regulating Business by Independent Commission*, Princeton University Press, Princeton, NJ.

Berry, P. and Kitchener, G. (1989), *Can Unions Survive?* Industrial Printing and Publicity, Melbourne.

BHP (1997) *Report to Shareholders.*

References

Bishop, E., Crawshaw, J.W., Shaw, Q.C. and Walton, M.J. (1992), 'Overcoming Sex Discrimination in Employment in the Asian and Pacific Region Through Legislation' in Chen, E., Lansbury, R., Ng, S. and Stewart, S. (eds), *Labour-Management Relation in the Asia Pacific Region*, Centre of Asian Studies, University of Hong Kong, 347-63.

Blandy, R. and Sloan, J. (1986), 'The Dynamic Benefits of Labour Market Deregulation', *ACC/Westpac Economic Discussion Papers*, Canberra.

Blandy, R., Sloan, J. and Wooden, M. (1989), 'Reforming the Trade Union Structure in Australia', in *Australian Bulletin of Labour*, Vol. 15, No. 5, 370-381.

Blanpain, R. (1983), *The OECD Guidelines for Multinational Enterprises and Labour Relations, 1979-82: Experience and Mid-Term Report*, Kluwer, Deventer.

Blyton, P. and Turnbull, P. (1992), 'HRM: Debates, Dilemmas and Contradictions', in P. Blyton and P. Turnbull (eds), *Reassessing Human Resource Management*, Sage, London.

Bognanno, M.F., Budd, J.W. and Lee, Y-M, (1994), 'Institutional Turmoil and Strike Activity in Korea' *The Journal of Industrial Relations*, September 1994, 353-69.

Bongarzoni and Compton, R. (1986), 'The Impact of the Macro-Industrial Relations System on Relations at the Enterprise Level', in Blandy, R. and Niland, J. (eds) *Alternatives to Arbitration*, Allen and Unwin, Sydney, 128-143.

Boral (1997), *Annual Report for 1997*.

Bosanquet, B. [1899](1958), *The Philosophical Theory of the State*, Macmillan, London.

Boswell, T. and Stevis, D. (1997), *Work and Occupations*, vol.24, no.3, 288-308.

Bottomore, T. (1966), *Elites and Society*, Penguin, Harmondsworth.

Bowie, A. (1994), 'The Dynamics of Business Government Relations in Industrialising Malaysia', in A. Macintyre (ed) *Business and Government in Industrialising Asia*, Allen and Unwin, Sydney, 167-94.

Boxall, P. (1993) 'Strategic Human Resource Management: Beginnings of a New Orthodoxy?', *Human Resource Management Journal*, Vol. 2, No. 3, 66-79.

Bramble, T. (1989) 'Award Restructuring and the Australian Trade Union Movement: A Critique', *Labour and Industry*, Vol. 2, No. 3, 372-398.

Bramel, D. and Friend, R. (1981), 'Hawthorne, the Myth of the Docile Worker, and Class Bias in Psychology', *American Psychologist*, vol.36, no.8, 867-78.

Braverman, H. (1971), *Labour and Monopoly Capitalism*, Monthly Review Press, London.

Bray, M. and Walsh, P. (1993) 'Unions and Economic Restructuring in Australia and New Zealand', in Bray, M. and Haworth, N. (ed) *Economic Restructuring and Industrial Relations in Australia and New Zealand: A Comparative Analysis*, ACIRRT Monograph no. 8, 122-153.

Bray, M. and Walsh, P. (1995) 'Accord and Discord: The Differing Fates of Corporatism under Labo(u)r Governments in Australia and New Zealand', *Labour and Industry*, Vol. 6, No. 8, 1-26.

Brereton, L. (1993) News Release, Ministerial Document Service, no. 151 93-94, 25th March, Canberra.

Briggs, C. (1999) 'The Transformation and Decline of the ACTU During the 1990's: From a 'Governing Institution' to a 'Servicing' Organisation', *New Zealand Journal of Industrial Relations*, Vol. 24, No. 3, 257-289.

Brooks, B. (1988) *Why Unions?* 2nd Edn, CCH Australia Ltd, Sydney.

Brooks, A. (1993), 'The Contract of Employment and Workplace Agreements', in Ronfeldt, P. and McCallum, P. (eds) *A New Province for Legalism: Legal Issues and the Deregulation of Industrial Relations*, ACCIRRT Monograph, no.9, University of Sydney, 14-22.

Brosnan, P. (1995), *Labour Markets and Social Deprivation,* Inaugural Professorial Lecture Series, Griffith University, Brisbane.

Brunnecke, K., Faust, M., Jaunch, P. and Deutschmann, C. (1991), *Operative Decentralisation - the Influence of Different National Systems: Are Companies Adaptors or Ambassadors Overseas?* Paper to Workshop on Centralisation and Decentralisation in the Euro-Company, University of Warwick.

Buchanan, J. (1992) 'Industrial Relations and the Coalition's Fightback Package: An Assessment' *The Economic and Labour Relations Review,* Vol. 3, No. 1, 80-93.

Buchanan, J. (1995) 'Managing Labour in the 1990's', in Rees, S. and Rodley, G. (eds) *The Human Costs of Managerialism,* Pluto Press, Sydney, 55-67.

Buchanan, J. (1996) 'Industrial Relations, Enterprise Bargaining and the Continuing Relevance of Socialist Principles', unpublished paper, 10th AIRAANZ Conference, Department of Organisational and Labour Studies, University of Western Australia.

Buchanan, J. and Callus, R. (1993) 'Efficiency and Equity at Work: The Need for Labour Market Regulation in Australia', *Journal of Industrial Relations,* vol.35, no.4, 515-37.

Buchanan, J., Callus, R. and Briggs, C. (1999) 'What Impact has the Howard Government had on Wages and Hours of Work?', *Journal of Australian Political Economy,* No.43, 1-21.

Buchanan, J., O'Keeffe, S., and Bretherton, T. (1999) 'Wages and Wage Developments in 1998', *Journal of Industrial Relations,* Vol. 41, No. 1, 102-126.

Buchanan, J. and Watson, I. (1997), 'A Profile of Low Wage Employees', *ACIRRT Working Paper 47,* University of Sydney.

Buchanan, J., Woodman, M., O'Keeffe, and Arsovska, B. (1998) 'Wages Policy and Wage Determination in 1997', *Journal of Industrial Relations,* Vol. 40, No. 1, 88-118.

Buchanan, J., Van Barneveld, K., O'Laughlin, T., and Pragnell, B. (1997) 'Wages Policy and Wage Determination in 1996', *Journal of Industrial Relations,* Vol. 39, No. 1, 96-119.

Burgess, J. and Campbell, I. (1993), 'Moving Towards a Deregulated Labour Market: Part-Time Work and the Recession in Australia', *International Journal of Economic Studies,* vol.1, no.2, 192-211.

Burgess, J. and Campbell, I. (1998) 'Casual Employment in Australia: Growth, Characteristics, A Bridge or a Trap?' *The Economic and Labour Relations Review,* Vol. 9, No. 1, 31-54.

Business Council of Australia (BCA) (1989) *Enterprise-Based Bargaining Units: A Better Way of Working,* Report to the BCA by the Industrial Relations Study Commission and National Institute for Labour Studies, Flinders University, BCA, Melbourne.

Business Council of Australia (BCA) (1990) 'The Main Game: Rationalising Union Coverage', National Institute of Labour Studies Survey, *Business Council Bulletin,* May, 4-5.

Business Council of Australia (BCA) (1991) *Avoiding Industrial Action: A Better Way of Working.* Report to the BCA by the Industrial Relations Study Commission, BCA, Melbourne.

Business Council of Australia (BCA) (1992) 'The Invisible Barriers to Change in Australia's Industrial Relations', *Business Council Bulletin,* October, 15-20.

Business Council of Australia (BCA) (1992) 'Waterfront and Port Reform', *Business Council Bulletin,* No 91, 8-12.

Business Council of Australia (BCA) (1993) *Working Relations: A First Start for Australian Enterprises,* Report to the Employee Relations Study Commission by Hilmer, F., Angwin, M., Layt, J., Dudley, G., Barrat, P. and McLaughlin, P. Information Australia, Melbourne.

Business Council of Australia (BCA). (1994) *Annual Report 1993-4.* Melbourne, BCA.

References

Business Council of Australia (BCA) (1994) *Investing in Australia's Future: Achieving Australia 2010 Scorecard*, paper to 1994 National Business Summit, Sydney Conventions Centre, 9-10th March, Sydney.

Business Council of Australia (BCA) (1999) *Submission to Senate Employment, Workplace Relations, Small Business and Education Legislative Committee, Inquiry into the Consideration of the Provisions of the Workplace Relations Amendment (More Jobs, better pay) Bill*, Submission No. 375, BCA, Vol. 12, 2627.

Business Korea, Seoul, October 1995, 'Korea's Manpower Shortage'.

Byrt, W. (1985) *The Framework of Consensus*, Fan Book Company Ltd, Sydney.

Callus, R., Morehead, A., Cully, M. and Buchanan, J. (1991), *Industrial Relations at Work: The Australian Workplace*, Industrial Relations Survey, Australian Government Printing Service, Canberra.

Callus, R. (1997) 'Enterprise Bargaining and the Transformation of Australian Industrial Relations', *Asia Pacific Journal of Human Resources*, Vol. 55, No. 2, 16-25.

Campbell, I. (1996), *Casual Employment, Labour Regulation and Australian Trade Unions*, National Key Centre in Industrial Relations, Melbourne.

Campling, J. and Gollan, P. (1999) *Bargained Out: Negotiating Without Unions in Australia*, Federation Press, Leichhardt, N.S.W.

Carlye, T. (1911), *Past and Present*, Ward Lock, London.

Carney, Shaun. (1988) *Australia in Accord*. Sun Books, Melbourne.

Cawson, A. (1978), 'Pluralism, Corporatism and the Role of the State', *Government and Opposition*, vol.13, no.2.

Chang, Hee-Lee. (1998), 'New Unionism and the Transformation of the Korean Industrial Relations System.' *Economic and Industrial Democracy*, vol. 19, no. 2, 1998, 347-373.

Chen, M. (1995), *Asian Management Systems*, Routledge, London.

Chew, S. (1983), 'The Singapore Worker', *Singapore Management Review*, vol. 5, no. 1, 79-81.

Chew, S. (1988), *The Small Firm* Oxford University Press, Singapore.

Chew, S.B. and Chew, R. (1995) 'The development of industrial relations strategy in Singapore', in Verma, A, Kochan, T. and Lansbury, R. (eds) *Employment Relations in the Growing Asian Economies*. Routledge, London and New York, 62-87.

Child, J. (1969), *British Management Thought: A Critical Analysis*, George Allen and Unwin, London.

Child, J., Loveridge, R. and Warner, M. (1973) 'Towards an Organisational Study of Trade Unions', *Sociology* Vol. 1, No. 7, 1-22.

Chung-In M. (1994), 'Changing Patterns of Business-Government Relations in South Korea', in A. MacIntyre, (ed) *Business and Government Relations in Industrialising Asia*, Allen and Unwin, Sydney, 142-66.

Chung, J. (2000) *Korea. Economy. The Far East and Australasia 2000*, Europa, Surrey.

Clark, D. (1995) 'Microeconimc Reform' in Kriesler, P. (ed) *The Australian Economy: The Essential Guide*, Allen and Unwin, Sydney, 142-169.

Clark, G. (1983), 'Village Mentality Holds the Key to Japanese Success', *The Mirror*, November 15.

Clarke, T. and Clements, L. (eds) (1977), *Trade Unions Under Capitalism*, Fontana, Glasgow.

Clegg, H. (1975), 'Pluralism in Industrial Relations', *British Journal of Industrial Relations*, vol.13, no. 3, 309-316.

Clegg, H. (1976), *Trade Unionism Under Collective Bargaining: A Theory Based on Comparisons of Six Countries*, Blackwell, Oxford.

Clegg, H. (1979), *The Changing System of Industrial Relations in Great Britain*, Blackwell, Oxford.

Cohen, H. (1983), 'You Can Negotiate Anything: Bargaining a Way Out of Industrial Warfare' *Rydges*, vol. 61, no.9, 69-72.

Colingnon, R., Chikako, U. and Irwin, M. (1997), 'The Permeability of the Japanese Political Economy: Amakudari, in Association with Japanese Business Studies, *Making Global Partnerships Work, Best Paper Proceedings*, 10th Annual Meeting, Washington, 171-84.

Commons, J.R. (1909) ' American shoemakers, 1648-1895.' *Quarterly Journal of Economics*, 24. Also in, (1913), *Labor and Administration*, Macmillan, New York, 163-93.

Coppell, Bill. (1994) *Australia in Facts and Figures*. Penquin, Melbourne.

Confederation of Australian Industry (CAI) and Australian Council of Trade Unions (ACTU) (1988) *Joint Statement on Participative Practices*. CAI and ACTU, Melbourne.

Costa, M. and Duffy, M. (1991) *Labour, Prosperity and the Nineties*, Federation Press, Sydney.

Costello, P. (1989), 'Sue the Workers, Call in the Military: How the Labor Government Handled the Pilot's Dispute' *IPA Review*, vol.43, no.2, 15.

Costello, M. (1996), *Sanctions and Safety Nets: Criminal Prosecutions in Victoria, Australia, to Enforce Individual Employee Entitlements Under the Industrial Relations Act 1979 (Vic) and the Employee Relations Act 1992 (Vic)*, Thesis submitted in partial fulfilment of the requirements for the degree of Masters of Laws, Monash University.

Creigh, S. and Makeham, D. (1982), 'Strike Incidence in Industrial Countries: An Analysis', *Australian Bulletin of Labour*, vol.8, no.3, 139-49.

Creighton, B. (1982) 'Law and the Control of Industrial Conflict' in K. Cole (ed) *Power, Conflict and Control in Australian Trade Unions*, Ringwood, Vic. Penguin, 121-156.

Creighton, B. (1995), 'The Internationalisation of Labour Law' in Mitchell, R. (ed), *Redefining Labour Law: New Perspectives on the Future of Teaching and Research*, Centre for Employment and Labour Relations Law, Occasional Monograph Series, no.3, University of Melbourne, 90-120.

Creighton, B. and Stewart, A. (2000), *Labour Law: An Introduction*, 3rd Edn, Federation Press, Sydney.

Crosby, M. and Easson, M. (1992) *What Should Unions Do?* Pluto Press, Sydney.

Crouch, C. (1982) *The Politics of Industrial Relations*, 2nd Edn, Fontana, London

Crough, G. and Wheelwright, T. (1982), *Australia: a Client State*, Penguin, Sydney.

Cully, M. (2000) 'Unions @ a loss: Members and Earnings', *Australian Bulletin of Labour*, Vol. 26, No. 1, 11-17.

Dabschek, B. (1981), 'Theories of Regulation and Australian Industrial Relations', *Journal of Industrial Relations*, vol.23, 430-46.

Dabscheck, B. (1983), 'Of Mountains and Routes Over Them: A Survey of Industrial Relations', *Journal of Industrial Relations*, vol.25, no.4, 485-506.

Dabscheck, B. (1989), 'A Survey of Industrial Relations Theories', in J. Barbash and K. Barbash (eds), *Theories and Concepts in Comparative Industrial Relations*, University of South Carolina Press, Columbia.

Dabscheck, B. (1992), 'A Decade of Striking Figures' in B. Dabscheck, G. Griffin and J. Teicher (eds) *Contemporary Australian Industrial Relations*. Longman Cheshire, Melbourne.

Dabscheck, B. (1992), 'Industrial Tribunals and Theories of Regulation', in B. Dabscheck, G. Griffin and J. Teicher (eds.), *Contemporary Australian Industrial Regulations: Readings*, Longman Cheshire, Melbourne, 340-59.

Dabschek, B. (1993), 'Industrial Relations and Theories of Interest Group Regulation', in R. Adams and N. Meltz (eds), *Industrial Relations Theory: Its Nature, Scope and Pedagogy*, Scarecrow Press, Dabscheck, Braham. (1995) *The Struggle for Australian Industrial Relations*. Oxford University Press, Melbourne.

Dabscheck, B. (1994), 'A General Theory of (Australian) Industrial Relations', *Journal of Industrial Relations*, vol.36, no.1, 3-17.

Dabscheck, B. (1995) *The Struggle for Australian Industrial Relations*, Oxford University Press, Melbourne.

Dabscheck, B. and Niland, J. (1981), *Industrial Relations in Australia*, Allen and Unwin, Sydney.

Dahl, R. (1961), *Who Governs?*, Yale University Press, New Haven.

Dahrendorf, R. (1959), *Class and Conflict in Industrial Society*, Stanford University Press, Stanford.

Davis, E. (1996) 'The 1995 A.C.T.U. Congress: Recruitment and Retention', *Economic and Labour Relations Review*, Vol. 7, No. 1, 165-181.

Davis, E. and Lansbury, R. (1993) 'Industrial Relations in Australia', in Bamber, G. and Lansbury, R. (eds) *International and Comparative Industrial Relations*, 2nd Edn, Allen and Unwin, Sydney, 100-125.

Davis, R. (1979), 'Economic Activity, Incomes Policy and Strikes - A Quantitative Analysis', *British Journal of Industrial Relations*, vol.17, no.2, 205-23.

Dawkins, P., Littler, C., Valenzuela, M. and Jemsen, B. (1999) *The Contours of Restructuring and Downsizing in Australia*, Melbourne Institute of Applied Economic and Social Research, University of Melbourne, Melbourne.

Deery, S. (1983) 'Trade Union Amalgamations and Government Policy in Australia', *Australian Bulletin of Labour*, Vol. 9, No. 3, 190-205.

Deery, S. (1989) 'Union Aims and Methods' in Ford, G. and Plowman, D. (eds), *Australian Unions: An Industrial Relations Perspective*, 2nd Edn, Macmillan, Melbourne, 74-103.

Deery, S. and De Cieri, H. (1991) 'Determinants of Trade Union Membership in Australia', *British Journal of Industrial Relations*, Vol. 29, No. 1, 59-74.

Deery, Stephen and Mitchell, Richard J. (eds) (1993) *Labour Law and Industrial Relations in Asia*. Longman, Melbourne.

Deery, S. and Plowman, D. (1991), *Australian Industrial Relations*, 3rd Edn, McGraw-Hill, Sydney.

Deery, S., Plowman D. and Welsh, J. (1997), *Industrial Relation: A Contemporary Analysis*, McGraw-Hill, Sydney.

Deery, S., and Walsh, J. (1998) 'The Character of Individualised Employment Arrangements in Australia: Unitarism, Unilateralism and Utilitarianism', *Department of Management Working Paper in Human Resource Management and Industrial Relations*, No. 10, University of Melbourne, Melbourne.

D'Entreves, A. (1967), *The Notion of the State*, Clarendon Press, Oxford.

Deresky, H. (1994), *International Management*, Harper Collins, New York.

Dicken, P. (1998) *Global Shift*, 3rd Edn, Guilford Press, London.

Dobbs-Higginson, M.S (1993) *Asia Pacific: Its Role in the New World Disorder*, William Heinemann, Melbourne.

Dollinger, M. (1988), 'Confucian Ethics and Japanese Management Practices', *Journal of Business Ethics*, vol.7, 575-84.

Donovan, The Rt Hon Lord, Chairman. Royal Commission on Trade Unions and Employers' Associations 1965-1968. *Report*. (1971) Her Majesty's Stationery Office, London.

Dore, R. (1973) *British Factory, Japanese Factory*, Allen and Unwin, London.

Douglas, A. (1957), 'The Peaceful Settlement of Industrial and Intergroup Disputes', *Journal of Conflict Resolution*, vol.1, no.1, 69-81.

Douglas, A. (1962), *Industrial Peacemaking*, Columbia University Press, New York.

Douglas, K. (1993) 'Organising Workers: The Effects of the Act on the Council of Trade Unions and its membership,' in Harbridge, R. (ed) *Employment Contracts: New Zealand Experiences*, Victoria University Press, Wellington, 197-209.

Dowling, P. and Deery, S., (1985), 'The Australian Personnel and Industrial Relations Practitioners: a 1984 Profile', *Human Resource Management: Australia*, vol.23.

Drago, R., Wooden, M. and Sloan, J. (1992) *Productive Relations? Australian Workplace Relations and Workplace Performance*, National Institute of Labour Studies, Allen and Unwin, Sydney.

Drewry Shipping Consultants (Drewry Report) (1998) *World Container Terminals: Global Growth and Private Profit*, London, summary provided by The Australia Institute *'Productivity in Australian Container Terminals: New Evidence from an International Study'*, 25th April, Canberra.

Druckman, D. (ed) (1977), *Negotiations: Social-Psychological Perspectives*, Sage, London.

Dubin, R. (1954), 'Constructive Aspects of Industrial Conflict', in A. Kornhauser, R. Dubin and A. Ross (eds), *Industrial Conflict*, McGraw-Hill, New York.

Dubois, P. (1979), *Sabotage in Industry*, Penguin, Harmondsworth.

Dufty, Norman. F. (1972) *Industrial Relations in the Metal Industries*. West Publishing, Sydney.

Dufty, N.F and R.E Fells. (1989) *Dynamics of Industrial Relations in Australia*. Prentice-Hall, Sydney.

Dunlop, John T. (1958), *Industrial Relations Systems*, Holt and Co, New York. Republished (1977) Southern Illinios University Press, New York.

Dyson, K. (1980), *The State Tradition in Western Europe*, Martin Robertson, Oxford.

Eaton, M. and Stilwell, F. (1993) 'Economic Notes: Ten Years of Hard Labour', *Journal of Australian Political Economy*, No. 31, 89-105.

Edwards, C. (2000) Malaysia. The Far East and Australasia. *Economy*, Europa, London, 670-6.

Edwards, P. (1986), *Conflict at Work: A Materialist Analysis of Workplace Relations*, Blackwell, Oxford.

Edwards, R. (1979), *Contested Terrain: The Transformation of the Workplace in the Twentieth Century*, Basic Books, New York.

Edwards, P., Collinson, D., and Della Rocca, G. (1995), 'Workplace Resistance in Western Europe: A Preliminary Overview and a Research Agenda', *European Journal of Industrial Relations*, vol.1, no.3, 283-316.

EIRR (1995) 'European Works Councils Update - Trends and Issues', *European Industrial Relations Review*, no. 256, 14-36.

Eisenstadt, S. and Ben Ari, E. (1990), *Japanese models of Conflict Resolution*, Kegan-Paul, London.

Ely, R. (1890) *Ground Under Our Feet*, Macmillan, New York.

Enderwick, P. (ed) (1994) *Transnational Corporations and Human Resources*, Routledge, London.

Enderwick, P. (1985) *Multinational Business and Labour*, Croom-Helm, London..

Evans, A. (1989) *Managed Decentralism in Australian Industrial Relations*, MTIA Booklet, Sydney.

Evans R. (1985) 'Justice Higgins: Architect and Builder on an Australian Folly' in Hyde J. and Nurick, J. (eds) *Wages Wasteland: A Radical Examination of the Australian Wage Fixing System*, Hale and Iremonger, Sydney, 29-40.

Evans, S. and Hudson, M. (1994) 'From Collective Bargaining to 'Personal' Contracts: Case Studies in Port Transport and Electricity Supply', *Industrial Relations Journal*, Vol. 25, No. 4, 305-313.

Evatt Foundation (1995) *Unions 2001: A Blueprint for Trade Union Activism*, Evatt Foundation, Sydney.

References

Far Eastern Economic Review. Asia Year Book 1995, 'A Review of the Events of 1994.' Hong Kong.

Federal Court of Australia, (1978) Ascot Cartage Contractors Pty. Ltd. v Transport Workers' Union of Australia (1978) 32 *Federal Law Reports*, 148.

Federal Court of Australia (1998) Maritime Union of Australia and ors v Patrick Stevedores No 1 Pty Ltd, and ors, 79 *Industrial Reports* 281.

Federal Court of Australia (1998) Appeal to Full Bench Patrick Stevedores Operations No 2 Pty Ltd and ors v Maritime Union of Australia and ors, 79 *Industrial Reports* 305.

Federal Court of Australia (2000) 'Australian Workers' Union and ors v Yallourn Energy Pty Ltd', V 23 of 2000, Case No. FCA 65, 8th February, Melbourne.

Fells, R. (1985), *The Industrial Relations Negotiation Process*, Discussion Paper in Industrial Relations, University of Western Australia, Perth.

Fells, R. (1995), 'Negotiating Workplace Change', in Mortimer, D. Leece, P. and Morriss, R. (eds) *Workplace Reform and Enterprise Bargaining*, Harcourt Brace, 327-46.

Ferner, A. (1996), 'Country of Origin Effects and HRM in Multinational Companies, *Human Resource Management Journal*, nol.7, no.1, 19-37.

Fidler, J. (1981), *The British Business Elite: Its Attitudes to Class, Status and Power*, Routledge and Kegan Paul, London.

Fisher, R. and Ury, Y. (1981), *Getting to Yes: Negotiating Agreement Without Giving In*, Houghton Miflin, Boston.

Flanders, A. (1965), *What is Wrong with the System? An Essay on its Theory and Future*, Faber and Faber, London.

Ford, G. and Hearn, J. (1987), 'Conflict and Industrial Relations', in G. Ford, J. Hearn, and R. Lansbury (eds) *Australian Labour Relations: Readings*, 4th Edn, Macmillan, Melbourne, 2-19

Ford, W. (1994), 'The Constitution and the Reform of Australian Industrial Relations', *Australian Journal of Labour Law*, vol.7, no.2, 105-31.

Fox, A. (1966) 'Managerial Ideology and Labour Relations', *British Journal of Industrial Relations*, Vol. 4, No. 2, 366-378.

Fox, A. (1966), *Industrial Sociology and Industrial Relations*, Research Paper no.3, Royal Commission on Trade Unions and Employers Associations, Her Majesty's Stationery Office, London. Also reproduced in A. Flanders (ed), (1971) *Collective Bargaining*, Penguin, London.

Fox, A. (1971), *A Sociology of Work in Industry*, Collier-Macmillan, London.

Fox, A (1974), *Beyond Contract: Work, Power and Trust Relations*, Faber and Faber, London.

Fox, Carol B., Howard William A., and Pittard, Marilyn J., (1995) *Industrial Relations in Australia: Development, Law and Operation*, Longmans, Melbourne.

Franko, L. et al. (1994), 'MNE's and the Structure of Employment', in Enderwick, P. (ed) *Transnational Corporations and Human Resources*, 118-129.

Frazer, A. (1995) 'Trade Unions under Compulsory Arbitration and Enterprise Bargaining: A Historical Perspective', in Ronfeldt, P. and McCallum, R. (eds) *Enterprise Bargaining, Trade Unions and the Law*, Sydney, Federation Press, 52-81.

Fraser, B. (1996) 'Sustaining Growth and Living Standards', Speech to Australian Business Economists, Sydney, 28th March.

Freeman, R. and Medoff, J. (1984), *What do Unions Do?* Basic Books, New York.

French, R. and Raven, B, 'The Basis of Sociological Power', in D. Cartwright (ed), *Studies in Sociological Power*, Arbor, Michigan, 1959, 150-167.

Frenkel, S. (1977), *Industrial Relations Theory: A Critical Discussion*, University of New South Wales [unpublished research paper].

Frenkel, S. and Coolican, A. (1984) 'Unions Against Capitalism: A Sociological Comparison of the Australian Building and Metal Workers' Union, *Australian Studies in Industrial Relations*, George Allen and Unwin, Sydney.

Frenkel, S. and Royal, C. (1996), 'Globalisation and Employment Relations', *CCC Paper no. 063*, Kensington, Centre for Corporate Change, University of New South Wales.

Frenkel S. and Shaw, M. (1989) 'No Tears for the Second Tier: Productivity Bargaining in the Australian Metal Industry', *Australian Bulletin of Labour*, Vol. 15, No. 2, 90-114.

Friedman, M. and Friedman, R. (1963), *Capitalism and Freedom*, University of Chicago Press, Chicago.

Friedman, M.and Friedman, R. (1980), *Free to Choose: A Personal Statement*, Macmillan, Melbourne.

Fukuda, J. (1988), *Japanese Style Management Transferred*, Routledge, London.

Gahan, P. (1996) 'Did Arbitration Make for Dependent Unionism? Evidence From Historical Studies', *Journal of Industrial Relations*, Vol. 38, No. 4, 648-698.

Galbraith, J. (1963), *American Capitalism: The Concept of Countervailing Power*, Pelican, London.

Galbraith, J. (1992), *The Culture of Contentment*, Houghton Mifflin, Boston.

Galenson, W. (1954), 'Soviet Russia', in A. Kornhauser, R. Dubin and A. Ross (eds), *Industrial Conflict*, McGraw-Hill, New York.

Gardner, M. (1987) 'Australian Trade Unionism in 1986', *Journal of Industrial Relations*, 29(1), 102-110.

Gardner, M. (1989), 'Union Strategy: A Gap in Union Theory' in Ford, B. and Plowman, D. (eds.) *Australian Unions: An Industrial Relations Perspective*, 2nd Edn, Macmillan, Melbourne, 49-73.

Gardner, M. (1992) 'The Consequences of Decentralised Wages Systems', *National Wages Policy and Workplace Wage Determination - The Critical Issues*, Proceedings of the Conference, ACIRRT Monograph No. 7, University of Sydney, 104-121.

Gardner, M. and Palmer G., (1997), *Employment Relations: Industrial Relations and Human Resource Management in Australia*, 2nd Edn, Macmillan Educational, South Melbourne.

Gennard, J. (1972), *Multinational Corporations and British Labour: A Review of Attitudes and Responses*, British North American Committee, London.

Gill, H. and Griffin, V. (1981) 'The Fetish of Order: Reform in Australian Union Structure', *Journal of Industrial Relations*, Vol. 23, No. 3, 362-382.

Gladstone, A. 'Employers Associations in comparative perspective: functions and Activities'. In J.P Windmuller and A.Gladstone (eds) (1984) *Employers Associations and Industrial Relations: A comparative Study*. Clarendon Press, Oxford.

Gospel, H. and Palmer, G. (1993), *British Industrial Relations*, 2nd Edn, Routledge, London.

Green, R. (1995), 'Industrial Relations Legislation: All dressed Up and Nowhere to Go?' in Hunt, C. and Provis, C. *The New Industrial Relations in Australia*, Federation Press, Sydney.

Gregory, R. (1992) 'An Overview of the Microeconomic Reform Debate', in Forsyth, P. (ed) *Microeconomic Reform in Australia*, Allen and Unwin, Sydney, 305-314.

Griffin, G. and Svenson, S. (1996) *The Decline of Union Density, A Review*, National Key Centre in Industrial Relations, Working Paper No. 42, National Key Center in Industrial Relations, Monash University, Melbourne.

Guest, D. and Conway, N. (1999) 'Peering into the Black Hole: the Downside of the New Employment Relations in the UK', *British Journal of Industrial Relations*, Vol. 37, No. 3, 367-390.

Guilie, H., Sappey, D. and Winter, W. (1989), Can Industrial Relations Survive without Unions?, in M. Bray and D. Kelly (eds), *Issues and trends in Australasian Industrial Relations*, Proceedings of the 4th Biannial AIRAANZ Conference, University of Wollongong, Wollongong.

Hagan, J. (1977) *The A.C.T.U.: A Short History*, Reed, Sydney.

Hagan, J. (1981), *The History of the ACTU*, Longman Cheshire, Melbourne.

Hagan, J. (1983) 'Unions: Context and Perspective, 1850-1980', in Ford, B. and Plowman, D. (eds) *Australian Unions: An Industrial Relations Perspective*, Macmillan, Melbourne, 30-59.

Hagan, J. and Wells, A. (eds) (1994) *Industrial Relations in Australia and Japan*, Allen and Unwin, Sydney.

Hall, R. and Harley, B. (1995) 'The Australian Response to Globalisation: Domestic Labour Market Policy and the Case of Enterprise Bargaining', in *Globalisation and its Impact on the World of Work*, ACIRRT Working Paper no. 38, Sydney, 71-96.

Hamberger, J. (1995a) *Individual Contracts: Beyond Enterprise Bargaining?* Australian Centre for Industrial Relations Research and Training (ACIRRT), Working Paper No. 39, Sydney, University of Sydney.

Hamberger, J. (1995b) *Individual Contracts: What do They Mean for Australia?*, The Economic and Labour Relations Review, 65(2), 288-299.

Hamilton, Reg. (1993) 'Employer Matters in 1992'. In *The Journal of Industrial Relations* 35\1, 84 - 96.

Hammond, S. and Harbridge, R. (1995), 'Women and Enterprise Bargaining: The New Zealand Experience of Labour Market deregulation', *Journal of Industrial Relations*, vol.37, no.3, 359-76

Hampson, I. (1996) 'Accord: A Post Mortem', *Labour and Industry*, Vol. 7, No. 2, 55-77.

Hamzah-Sendut, Malsen, J. and Thong, G. (1990), *Managing in a Plural Society*, Longman, Singapore.

Hansen, A. (1921), 'Cycles of Strikes', *American Economic Review*, vol.11, no.4, 616-21.

Harbridge, R. and Moulder, J. (1993) 'Collective Bargaining and New Zealand's Employment Contracts Act: One Year On', *Journal of Industrial Relations*, Vol. 35, No. 1, 62-83

Harding, A. and Landt, J. (1992), 'Policy and Poverty: Trends in Disposable Incomes', *Australian Quarterly*, vol.64, no.19.

Harley, B. (1995) 'Labour Flexibility and Workplace Industrial Relations: The Australian Evidence', *ACIRRT Monograph* No. 12, Australian Center for Industrial Relations Research and Teaching, University of Sydney.

Hawke, A. and Wooden, M. (1998) 'The Changing Face of Australian Industrial Relations: A Survey', *The Economic Record*, No. 74, March, 74-88.

Hawke, R.J. and Howe, B. (1991) *Towards a Fairer Australia,* Australian Government Publishing Service, Canberra.

Hayek, F. (1960), *The Constitution of Liberty*, Routledge, London.

Health Services Union of Australia (1999) Evidence to Senate Employment, Workplace Relations, Small Business and Education Legislative Committee, *Inquiry into the Consideration of the Provisions of the Workplace Relations Amendment (More Jobs, Better Pay) Bill*, quoted in Report, Senate Printing Unit, Parliament House, Canberra, 118.

Helier, K. (1994) 'Enterprise Bargaining: Implications for Occupational Health and Safety', *ACIRRT Working Paper* No. 34, December, University of Sydney, Sydney.

Heiler K. (1996) 'Working Time Arrangements in Australia: A Policy Free Zone?' in Bryce M. (ed.) 'Industrial Relations Policy Under the Microscope', *ACIRRT Working Paper* No. 40, Australian Center for Industrial Relations Research and Training, University of Sydney.

Herbert, R.N. (1999) *About the AI Group*, 1-3.

Herzberg, F. (1966), *Work and the Nature of Man*, World Publishing, Cleveland.

Hibbs, D. (1976), 'Industrial Conflict in Advanced Societies', *American Political Science Review*, vol.70, no.4, 1033-58.

Higgins, H. (1922) *A New Province for Law and Order*, Sydney Workers' Educational Association of NSW, Sydney.

High Court of Australia (1996) State of Victoria and ors v The Commonwealth, September 1996, 66 *Industrial Reports* 392.

High Court of Australia (1998) Appeal to Full Bench, Patrick Stevedores Operations No 2 Pty Ltd and ors v Maritime Union of Australia and ors, 79 *Industrial Reports* 339.

Hilderbrand, G. (1988), 'Comment: Review Symposium on the Transformation of American Industrial Relations', *Industrial and Labor Relations Review*, vol.41, no.3, 1988.

Hilmer, F. (1990) 'Enterprise Bargaining – The Approach of the Business Council of Australia: Reply To Jamieson', *Australian Journal of Labour Law*, Vol. 3, No. 3, 304-309.

Hilmer, F. (1991) *Coming to Grips with Competitiveness and Productivity*, EPAC Discussion Paper 91/01.

Hilmer, F. (1995), *Competition Policy: Underlying Ideas and Issues*, Centre for Economic Policy Research, Canberra.

Hobson, S. (1920) *National Guilds and the State*, Bell, London.

Holdsworth, W. (1987), *Advocacy and Negotiation in Industrial Relations*, 3rd Edn, Law Book Company, Sydney.

Howard, W. (1977) 'Australian Trade Unions in the Context of Union Theory', *Journal of Industrial Relations*, Vol. 19, No. 3, 255-273.

Huczynski (1993), *Management Gurus, What Makes them and How to Become One*, Routledge, London.

Hudson, M. and Hawkins, L. (1995), *Negotiating Employee Relations*, Pitman, Melbourne.

Hunter, R. (1992), *Indirect Discrimination in the Workplace*, Federation Press, Sydney.

Hyman, R. and Fryer (1977), Trade Unions: Sociology and Political Economy, in T. Clarke and L. Clements, *Trade Unions Under Capitalism*, Fontana, Glasgow.

Hyman, R. (1971), *Marxism and the Sociology of Trade Unionism*, Pluto, London.

Hyman, R. (1975), *Industrial Relations: A Marxist Introduction*, Macmillan, London.

Hyman, R. (1978), 'Pluralism, Procedural Consensus and Collective Bargaining', *British Journal of Industrial Relations*, vol.16, no.1, 16-40.

Hyman, R. (1980), 'Theory in Industrial Relations:Toward a Materialist Analysis', in P. Boreham and G. Dow (eds), *Work and Inequality: Ideology and Control in the Capitalist Labour Process*, vol.2, Macmillan, South Melbourne, 38-59.

Hyman, R. (1989), *Strikes*, 4th Edn, Fontana, London.

Hyman, R. (ed) (1989), *The Political Economy of Industrial Relations: Theory and Practice in a Cold Climate*, Macmillan, London.

Ingham, G. (1974), *Strikes and Industrial Conflict*, Macmillan, London.

Industrial Relations Court of Australia (1996) Full Bench of the Industrial Relations Court of Australia, Tweed Valley Fruit Processors Pty Ltd v V.P. Ross and others, 65 *Industrial Reports*, 393.

Industrial Relations and Management Letter (1994) 'CRA's Bold: Some Believe Foolish Experiment in Industrial Relations', 11(1), 1-15.

International Labour Office (1993), *Sources and Methods: Labour Statistics*, vol.7, International Labour Office, Geneva

International Labour Organisation (various), *Year Book of Labour Statistics*, International Labour Office, Geneva.

Ippolito, D. and Walker, T. (1980), *Political Parties, Interest Groups, and Public Policy*, Prentice Hall, Englewood Cliffs, N.J.

Issac, J. (1977) 'Wage Determination and Economic Policy' *The Giblin Memorial Lecture*, Melbourne, University of Melbourne.

Ito, T. 'Japan's Economy Needs Structural Change.' *Finance and Development*, Washington, vol. 34, no. 2, June 1997, 16-19.

Jackson, M. (1982) Trade Unions, Longman, London.

Jackson, M. (1987), *Strikes: Industrial Conflict in Britain, U.S.A. and Australia,* Wheatsheaf Books, Brighton.

Jaques, E. (1989) *Requisite Organisation: The CEO's Guide to Creative Structure and Leadership*, Cason Hall and Co., New York.

Jamieson, S. (1990) 'Enterprise Bargaining – The Approach of the Business Council of Australia', *Australian Journal of Labour Law*, Vol. 3, No. 1, 77-82.

Jaynes, S., (1996), 'The Perpetuation of Managerial Ideology: A Critical Perspective', *Quarterly Journal of Ideology*, vol.19, no.1, June.

Jessop, B. (1982), *The Capitalist State, Marxist Theories and Methods,* Martin Robertson, London.

Johnson, C. (1988), 'Japanese-Style Management in America', *California Management Review*, vol.30, 34-45.

Johnson, I. (1996) *Speech on CRA Employee Relations Philosophy,* presented at the Australian Human Resources Institute Conference, Sydney.

Joskow, P. (1974), 'Inflation and Environmental Concern: Structural Change in the Process of Public Utility Price Regulation', *Journal of Law and Economics*, vol.17, no.2, 291-327.

Kallmargen, S. and Naughton, R. (1991) 'Change from within: Reforming Trade Union Coverage and Structure', *Journal of Industrial Relations*, Vol 33, No. 3, 369-394.

Kamata, S. (1982) *Japan In The Passing Lane*, Pentheon Press, New York.

Kanai, A and Fling, S.(1996) 'Workaholism among Japanese Employees: Male and Female Differences', in *Best Paper Proceedings, Association of Japanese Business Studies, 9th Annual Meeting*, Nagoya, Japan, 10-12 June, 1996, 223-236.

Kaufman, B. (1989), 'Models of Man in Industrial Relations Research', *Industrial and Labor Relations Review*, vol.43, no.1, 72-88.

Kaufman, B. (1993), *The Origins and Evolution of the Field of Industrial Relation in the United States*, IRL Press, New York.

Kaufman, B. (1999), 'Expanding the Behavioural Foundations of Labor Economics', *Industrial and Labor Relations Review*, vol.52, 361-92.

Kaufman, B. and Hotchkiss, J. (1999), *The Economics of Labor Markets*, 5th Edn, Dryden Press, New York.

Keenoy, T. and Kelly, D. (1998), *The Employment Relationship in Australia*, 2nd Edn, Harcourt Brace, Sydney.

Kelly, J. (1994), 'Does the Field of Industrial Relations Have a Future?' Annual Conference of the British Universities' Industrial Relations Association, Oxford.

Kelty, W. (1989), 'Speech' reprinted in *Business Review Weekly*, September, 92-97.

Kenyon, P. and Lewis, P. (1996) *The Decline in Trade Union Membership: What role did the Accord play?* Discussion Paper No. 96/8, Center for Labour Market Research, Curtin University of Technology.

Kerr, A. (1992) 'Why Public Sector Workers Join Unions: An Attitude Survey of Workers in the Health Service and Local Government', *Employee Relations*, Vol. 14, No. 2, 39-54.

Kerr, C. and Siegel, A. (1954), 'The Interindustry Propensity to Strike: An International Comparison', in

Kerr, C., Dunlop, J., Harbison, F. and Myers, C. (1962), *Industrialism and Industrial Man*, Heinemman, London.

Keys, J. and Miller, T. (1984), 'The Japanese Management Theory Jungle', *Academy of Management Review*, vol.9 , no.2, 342-53.

Kim, H.J. (1993) 'The Korean union movement in transition' in Frenkel, S. (ed.) *Organised Labour in the Asia Pacific: A Comparative Study of Trade Unionism in Nine Countries*. Ithaca, NY, International Labour Relations Press, 133-61.

King, J., Rimmer, S. and Rimmer, R. (1991), 'The Law of the Shrinking Middle: Inequality of Earnings in Australia 1975-1989', *Discussion Paper 17/91*, Department of Economics and Commerce, La Trobe University.

Kirkbride, P., Tang, S. and Westwood, R. (1991), 'Chinese Conflict Preferences and Negotiating Behaviour: Cultural and Psychological Influences, *Organisation Studies*, vol.12, 365-86.

Knights, D., Wilmot, H. and Collinson, D. (eds), (1985), *Job Redesign:Critical Perspectives on the Labour Process*, Gower, London.

Kochan, T. (1980), *Collective Bargaining and Industrial Relations*, Irwin, Homewood.

Kochan, T. and Barocci, T. (1985), *Human Resource Management and Industrial Relations*, Scott Foresman, Glenview, Ill.

Kochan, T., Katz, H. and McKersie, R. (1986), *The Transformation of American Industrial Relations*, Basic Books, New York.

Kochan, T. and Osterman, P. (1995), *The Mutual Gains Enterprise*, Harvard Business School Press, Boston.

Kochan, T. and Tamir, B. (1989) 'Collective Bargaining and New Technology: Some Preliminary Propositions', in Bamber, G. and Lansbury, R. (eds) *New Technology: International Perspectives on Human Resources and Industrial Relations*, Unwin Hyman, London, 60-74.

Koike, K. (1988), *Understanding Industrial Relations in Modern Japan*, Macmillan, London.

Kollmorgen, S. and Riekert, J. (1995), 'Social Policy and Judicial Decision-Making in Australian Employment Law', in Mitchell, R. (ed) *Redefining Labour Law: New Perspectives on the Future of Teaching and Research*, Centre for Employment and Labour Relations Law, Occasional Monograph Series, no.3, University of Melbourne, 167-198.

Komatsu, R. (1994), 'The Labour Movement and the Government in Japan', in Hagan, J.and Wells, A. (eds) *Industrial Relations in Australia and Japan*, Allen and Unwin, Sydney, 116-22.

Korea, South www.odci.gov/cia/publications/95fact/ks.html,.

Kornhauser, A., Dubin, R. and Ross, A. (eds) (1954), *Industrial Conflict*, McGraw-Hill, New York.

Korpi, W. and Shalev, M. (1979), 'Strikes, Industrial Relations and Class Conflicts in Capitalist Societies', *British Journal of Sociology*, vol.30, no.2, 164-87.

Kramer, R., McGraw, P. and Schuler, R. (1997), *Human Resource Management*, 3rd Edn, Longman, South Melbourne.

Kuhn, J. (1961), *Bargaining in Grievance Settlement: The Power of Industrial Work Groups*, Columbia University Press.

Kuruvilla, S. and Arudsothy, P. (1993) 'Economic Development Strategy and Government Labour Policy and Firm-level Industrial Relations Practices in Malaysia', in Verma, A., Kochan, T. and Lansbury, R. (eds) *Employment Relations in the Growing Asian Economies*. Routledge, London and New York, 1993, 158-193.

Kururilla, S. and Venkalaratram, C. (1996), 'Economic Development and Industrial Relations: The Case of South and South East Asia', *Industrial Relations Journal*, vol.27, no.1, 9-23.

Kuwahara, Y. (1996), 'The Impact of Globalisation on Industrial Relations: Corporate Governnance and Industrial Relations in Japan', *Democratisation, Globalisation and the Transformation of Industrial Relations in Asian Countries*, International Industrial Relations Association, Third Asian Regional Congress, Taipei, Taiwan, ROC.

Kuwahara, Y. (1998) 'Employment Relations in Japan' in Bamber, G. and Lansbury, R. (eds) *International and Comparative Employment Relations*, 3rd Edn, Allen and Unwin, Sydney, 249-274.

Kyloh, R. (1989) 'Flexibility and Structural Adjustment Through Consensus', *Industrial Labour Review*, Vol. 128, No. 1, 193-123.

Labour Council of New South Wales (1995) *Attitudes to Work and Unions: Focus Group Research Study*, Riley Research Pty Ltd, Sydney.

Laffer, K. (1974), 'Is Industrial Relations an Academic Discipline?', *Journal of Industrial Relations*, vol.16, no.1, 62-73.

Lall, S. (1995), 'Employment and Foreign Investment: Policy Options for Developing Countries' *International Labour Review*, vol.134, no.4-5, 521-40.

Lan, Z. (1997), 'A Conflict Resolution Approach to Public Administration', *Public Administration Review*, vol.57, no.1, 27-35.

Lang Corporation (1997) *Annual Report*, Sydney.

Lansbury R. and McDonald D. (1995) 'Public Policy and Industrial Relations: The Case of Australia', in Gollan, P. (ed) *Globalisation and its Impact on the World of Work*, Australian Centre for Industrial Relations Research and Teaching, ACIRRT Working Paper No. 38, University of Sydney, 40-57.

Lansbury, R. and Niland, J. (1994) 'Trends in Industrial Relations and Human Resource Policies and Practices: Australian Experiences,' *International Journal of Human Resource Management*, 5(3): 581-608.

Lansbury, R. and Zappala, J., (1990), *Korean Industrial Relations in Transition: The Relevance of Australian Experience*, Working Papers in Industrial Relations, Department of Industrial Relations, University of Sydney, No. 13.

Laughlin, P. (1989) 'Bargaining Structures: The Number One Labour Market Reform Priority', *Growth*, No. 37, 51-72.

Lee, S. and Yoo, S. (1987), 'The K-type Management: A Driving Force of Korean Prosperity', *Management International Review*, vol.27, no.4, 68-77.

Legge, K. (1989), 'Human Resource Management: A Critical Analysis', in Storey, J. (ed) *New Perspectives on Human Resource Management*, Routledge, London, 19-40.

Legge, K. (1995) 'HRM: Rhetoric, Reality and Hidden Agendas', in Storey, J. (ed) *Human Resource Management: A Critical Text*, Routledge, London, 33-59.

Legge, K. (1995), *HRM: Rhetoric and Realities*, Macmillan, Basingstoke.

Leggett, C. (1993) 'Singapore', in Deery, S. and Mitchell, R. (eds) *Labour Law and Industrial Relations in Asia*, Longman Cheshire, Melbourne, 96-136.

Leggett, C. (1997), 'Korea's Divergent Industrial Relations', *New Zealand Journal of Industrial Relations*, vol.22, no.1, 64-76

Lehmbruch, G. (1977), 'Liberal Corporatism and Party Government', *Comparative Political Studies*, vol.10, no.3.

Lenin, V. (1928), *What is to be Done?* International Publishers, New York (originally published 1902).

Le Poer, B. (ed) (1991), *Singapore: A Country Study*, 3rd Edn, Federal Research Division, Library of Congress, Washington DC.

Le Poer, B. (1991) 'Historical Setting' in Le Poer, B. (ed), *Singapore: A Country Study*, 3rd Edn, Federal Research Division, Library of Congress, Washington DC, 1-63.

Levin, D. and Chiu, S. (1995) 'Dependent Capitalism, a Colonial State and Marginal Unions: The Case of Hong Kong', in Frenkel, S. (ed) *Organised Labor in the Asia-Pacific Region. A Comparative Study of Trade Unionism in Nine Countries*, ILR Press, Ithaca, New York.

Levin, David and Ng Sek Hong. (1993) ' Hong Kong' in Deery, S. and Mitchell, R. (eds) *Labour Law and Industrial Relations in Asia*. Longman, Melbourne, 20-60.

Lewin, D. (1987), 'Industrial Relations as a Strategic Variable in Human Resources and the Performance of the Firm', in M. Kleiner, R. Block, M. Roomkin and S. Salsburg (eds), *Industrial Relations Research Association Series*, University of Wisconsin, Madison, 1987, 1-42.

Lewis, P. (2000) 'Hong Kong: Economy,' *The Far East and Australasia 2000*, 31st Edn, Europa, Surrey, UK, 301-6.

Lewis, P. and Spiers, D. (1990), 'Six Years of the Accord: An Assessment', *Journal of Industrial Relations*, vol. 32, no.1, 53-68.

Lie, J. (1990), 'Is Korean Management Just Like Japanese Management?', *Management International Review*, vol.30, no.2, 1990, 113-18.

Lindblom, C. (1977), *Politics and Markets*, Basic Books, New York.

Littler, C. and Salaman, G. (1984), *Class at Work*, Batsford Academic and Educational, London.

Lloyd P. (1982) *A Third World Proletariat?* Allen and Unwin, London.

Locke, R., Kochan, T. and Piore, M. (1995), 'Reconceptualising comparative industrial relations: lessons from international research', *International Labour Review*, 134(2) 139-161.

Longbottom, G. (1984), 'The Japanese Connection: Japanese Methodology in Australian Industry', *Human Resource Management in Australia*, vol.22, no.3, 30-5.

Loughran, C.(1985), *Negotiating a Labor Contract - A Management Handbook*, Washington D.C.

Low, L. (1990), 'Privitization Options and Issues in Singapore', in Gayle, D. and Goorich, J. (eds) *Privitization and Deregulation in Global Perspective*, Pinter, London, 291-311.

Lucio, M. and Weston, S. (1994), 'New Management Practices in a Multinational Corporation: The Restructuring of Worker Representation and Rights?', *Industrial Relations Journal*, vol.25, no.2, 110-21.

Ludeke, J. (1996) *The Line in the Sand: The Long Road to Staff Employment at Comalco*, Wilkinson Books, Melbourne.

Luthans, F. (1992), *Organizational Behaviour*, 6th Edn, McGraw-Hill, New York.

Mabey, C. Salaman, G. and Storey, J. (1998), *Human Resource Management: A Strategic Introduction*, 2nd Edn, Blackwell, Oxford.

McCallum, R. (1996) 'The New Millennium and The Higgins Heritage: Industrial Relations in the 21st Century', *Journal of Industrial Relations*, Vol. 38, No. 2, 294-312.

MaCarthy, P. (1970), 'The Living Wage in Australia - The Role of Government', *Labour History*, vol.18, 3-18.

McCarthy, P. (1989), *Developing Negotiating Skills and Behaviour*, CCH North Ryde, Sydney.

McCarthy, T. (1991), 'Free Trade Unions and International Business' in Selvarajah, C. and Cutbush-Sabine, K (eds) *International Business*, Longman Cheshire, Melbourne, 227-48.

McDonald, T. and Rimmer, M. (1989) 'Award Restructuring and Wages Policy', *Growth*, No. 37, 111-134.

McEvoy, K. and Owens, R. (1990), 'The Flight of Icarus: Legal Aspects of the Pilots' Dispute', *Australian Journal of Labour Law*, vol.3, no.2, 87-129.

McGregor, D. (1966), *Leadership and Motivation*, MIT Press, Cambridge, Mass.

McGregor [1957], 'The Human Side of Enterprise' in J. Ott (ed), (1989) *Classic Reading in Organisational Behaviour*, Brooks and Cole, Pacific Grove, 66-73.

McIntosh Baring Report, (1996) *Australian Research: Report on CRA Limited*, Melbourne.

MacIntosh, M.L. 'Australian Industrial Relations in 1992: Another Turning Point?'

Asia Pacific Journal of Human Resources. 31\2 Winter 1993, 52-64.

McIntyre, S. (1998) *The Maritime Dispute Then and Now* Unpublished Paper, Evatt Victoria Center, Melbourne.

McMahon, A., Thomson, J. and Williams, C. (2000) *Understanding the Australian Welfare State*, Tertiary Press, Melbourne.

Macken, J. (1997) *Australia's Unions: A Death or a Difficult Birth?* Federation Press, Sydney.

Macken, J., O'Grady, P. and Sappideen, C. (1997), *Macken, McCarry and Sappideen's The Law of Employment*, 4th Edn, LBC Information Services, Sydney.

Macklin, R., Goodwin, M. and Docherty, J. (1992) 'Workplace Bargaining Structures and Processes in Australia,' In Peetz, D., Preston, D. and Docherty, J. (eds) *Workplace Bargaining in the International Context*, , Industrial Relations Research Monongraph No. 2, DIR, Canberra, 3-70.

Magenau, J. and Pruitt, D. (1979), 'The Social-Psychology of Bargaining: A Theoretical Synthesis', in Stephenson, G. and Brotherton, C. (eds) *Industrial Relations: A Social-Psychological Approach*, John Wiley, Chichester.

Malaysian Industrial Development Authority (1998) *Growth of the Manufacturing Sector in Malaysia*. Department of Statistics, Malaysia, Jan-October, 1998.

Martin, R. (1980) *Trade Unions in Australia*. Penguin, Ringwood, Melbourne.

Martin, R. (1989) *Trade Unionism: Purposes and Forms*, Clarenden Press, Oxford.

Marx [1848] (1950), 'The Communist Manifesto' *Marx and Engles: Selected Works*, Moscow.

Marx, K. [1857] (1967) *Capital*, vol.1, International Publishers, New York.

Marx, K. [1891] (1978), 'Wages, Labour and Capital', in R. Tucker (ed), *The Marx-Engles Reader*, Lorton, New York, 167-90.

Maslow, A. (1954), *Motivation and Personality*, Harper and Row, New York.

Maslow, A. (1943), 'A Theory of Human Motivation', *psychological Review*, vol.50, 370-96.

Matsuda, Y. (1993), 'Japan', in Deery, S. and Mitchell, R. (eds) *Labour Law and Industrial Relations in Asia*, Longman Cheshire, Melbourne, 172-208.

Matsumura, T. (1994) 'Labour Relations in Japan between the wars', in Hagan, J. and Wells, A. (eds) (1994) *Industrial Relations in Australia and Japan*, Allen and Unwin, Sydney, 37-46.

Matsuzaki, H. (1994) 'Employers and employed in Meiji Japan', in Hagan, J. and Wells, A. (eds) (1994) *Industrial Relations in Australia and Japan*, Allen and Unwin, Sydney, 6-17.

Mayhew, C. and Quinlan, M. (1997a), 'The Management of health and Safety where Subcontractors are Employed', *Journal of Occupational Health and Safety - Australia and New Zealand*, vol.13, no.2.

Mayhew, R. and Quinlan, M. (1997b), 'Subcontracting and Occupational Health and Safety in the Residential Building Industry', *Industrial Relations Journal*, vol.28, no.3, 192-205.

Mayhew, C., Quinlan, M. and Ferris, R. (1997), 'The Effects of Subcontracting? Outsourcing on Occupational Health and Safety: Survey Evidence from Four Australian Industries' *Safety Science*.

Mayo, E. (1933), *The Human Problems of Industrial Civilisation*, Macmillan, New York.

Mayo [1933](1960), *The Human Problems of an Industrial Civilisation*, Harvard University Press, Cambridge.

Mealor, T. (1995), 'From Confrontation to Collaboration at ICI Botany' in Davis, E. and Lasnbury, R. (eds) *Managing Together*, Longman, Melbourne.

Metal Trades Industry Association (1990) *Review of the Operation of the Structural Efficiency Principle and the Minimum Rates Adjustment Exercise: MTIA Position*, MTIA, Canberra.

Metal Trades Industry Association (1993) *The Shift to Enterprise Bargaining*, MTIA Booklet, Sydney.

Metal Trades Industry Association (MTIA) (1995), *MTIA Annual Report 95*. MTIA, Canberra.

Metal Trades Industry Association/Metal Trades Federation of Unions (1988) *Towards a new Metal and Engineering Industry Award: Report of the DIR, MTIA and MTFU Mission to the UK, Sweden and West Germany*, Sydney, Breakout Press.

Meyrick and Associates and Tasman Pacific (1998) *Measures to Promote Effective and Efficient Container Port Practices*, Final report prepared for the Marine and Ports Group of the Australian Transport Council, October, Sydney.

Michels, R. (1959) *Political Parties*, Dover, New York.

Milgrom, P. and Roberts, J. (1990), *Economics, Organisation and Management*, Prentice Hall, Englewood Cliffs, NJ.

Miliband, R. (1969), *The State in Capitalist Society*, Weidenfeld and Nicolson, London.

Miller, P. and Mulvey, C. (1992) *What Do Unions Do?*, Discussion Paper, No. 92/8, The Western Australian Labour Market Research Centre, Perth.

Miller, R. and Zaidi, M. (1982), 'Human Capital and Multinationals: Evidence from Brazil and Mexico' *Monthly Labour Review*, no.105, 45-7.

Monks, K. (1996), 'Global or Local? HRM in the Multinational Company: The Irish Experience', *International Journal of Human Resource Management*, vol.7, no.3, 721-35.

Morehead, A (ed.), (1996), *Australian Workplace Industrial Relations Survey 1995*, Australian Government Printing Service, Canberra.

Morehead, A., Steele, M., Alexander, M., Stephen, K. and Duffin, L. (1997) *Changes at Work: The 1995 Australian Workplace Industrial Relations Survey*, Addison Wesley Longman, Melbourne.

Morley, I. (1979), 'Behavioural Studies of Industrial Bargaining', in Stephenson, G. and Brotherton, C. (eds) *Industrial Relations: A Social-Psychological Approach*, John Wiley, Chichester.

Morley, I. and Stephenson, G. (1977), *The Social Psychology of Bargaining*, George Allen and Unwin, London.

Mortimer, D and Leonie Still. (1999) 'The Role of Employer Associations in a Decentralised System: Evidence of a Proactive Response' in Morris, R. , Mortimer, D., Leece, P. (eds) *Workplace Reform and Enterprise Bargaining: Issues, Trends and Cases*, 2nd Edn, Harcourt Brace, Sydney, 276-288.

Mosca, G. [1896] (1939), *The Ruling Class*, [translated and edited by] A. Livingston, McGraw-Hill, New York.

Naugton, R. (1994), *The Industrial Relations Reform Act 1993*, Centre for Employment and Labour Relations Law, University of Melbourne.

Negandhi, A., Eshghi, G. and Yuen, E. (1985), 'The Management Practices of Japanese Subsidiaries Overseas', *California Management Review*, vol.27, No.4, 93-105.

Nelson, L. (1997), 'Managers and Enterprise Bargaining: Some Preliminary Findings', *Asia Pacific Journal of Human Resources*, vol.35, no.1.

Neumann, F. (1968), *The Structure and Practice of National Socialism: 1933-1944*, Harper, New York

Neville, J. (1990), 'The Case for Deregulation: Economic Science or Ideology', *Economic and Labour Relations Review*, vol.1, no.2, 71-80.

Newman, K. and Nollen, S. (1996), 'Culture and Congruence: The Fit Between Management Practices and National Culture, *Journal of International Business Studies*, vol.27, no.4, 753-79.

New Zealand Aluminium Smelters Consultant Report (1992) *The NZAS Experience and the Implications for CRA*, unpublished report prepared by G. Gunness and A. Lewis, CRA, NZAS.

Ng, S. (1996) 'The Development of Labour Relations in Hong Kong and Some Implications for the future', in Nish, I, Redding, G., and Ng, S. (eds) (1996) *Work and Society. Labour and Human Resources in East Asia,* 289-300.

Ng, S. and Fung-Shuen-Sit, V. (1989), *Labour Relations and Labour Conditions in Hong Kong*, Macmillan, Hong Kong.

Nicholson, N. (1978) 'Mythology, Theory and Research on Union Democracy', *Industrial Relations Journal*, Vol. 9, No. 4, 32-41.

Niland, J. (1978), *Collective Bargaining and Compulsory Arbitration in Australia*, University of New South Wales Press, Sydney.

Nimura, K. (1994) 'Post Second World War Labour Relations in Japan', in Hagan, J. and Wells, A. (eds) (1994) *Industrial Relations in Australia and Japan*, Allen and Unwin, Sydney, 64-91.

Nish, I., Redding, G. Ng, S., Labour Department of Hong Kong, Tam, Y., and Wong, Y. (1996) 'Industrial Harmony, the Trade Union Movement and Labour Administration in Hong Kong' in Nish, I., Redding, G. and Ng, S. (eds.) (1996) *Work and Society. Labour and Human Resources in East Asia*, Hong Kong University Press, 271-288.

Noon, M. (1992) 'HRM: A Map, Model or Theory? in P. Blyton and P. Turnbull (eds), *Reassessing Human Resource Management*, Sage, London.

Nordlinger, E. (1981), *On the Autonomy of the Democratic State*, Harvard University Press, Cambridge, Mass.

O'Brien. John. 'McKinsey, Hilmer and the BCA: The 'New Management' Model of Labour Market Reform'. *The Journal of Industrial Relations*. 36\4 (1994), 468-491.

O'Connor, J. (1973), *The Fiscal Crisis of the State*, St. Martins Press, New York.

Olsen, M. (1965), *The Logic of Collective Action*, Harvard University Press, Cambridge.

O'Neill, L. (1995), 'Linking Pay to Performance: Conflicting Views and Conflicting Evidence', *Asia Pacific Journal of Human Resources*, vol.33 no.2.

Osborne, J. (1992), 'Book Review', *Journal of Industrial Relations*, vol.34, no.1, 172.

Owen, B. and Braeutigan, R. (1978), *The Regulation Game: Strategic Use of the Administrative Process*, Ballinger, Cambridge, MA.

Oxnam, D. (1971), 'The Incidence of Strikes in Australia', in J. Isaac and G. Ford (eds), *Australian Labour Relations: Reading,* 2nd Edn, Sun Books, Melbourne.

Ozawa, T. (1979), *Multinationalism, Japanese style*, Princeton University Press, Princeton.

Paldam, M. and Pederson, P. (1982), 'The Macro-Economic Strike Model: A Study of Seventeen Countries 1948-1975', *Industrial and Labor Relations Review*, vol.35, no.4, 504-21.

Paldam, M. (1983), 'Industrial Conflicts and Economic Conditions', *European Economic Review*, vol.20, no.2, 231-56.

Pappas, Carter, Evans and Koop / Telesis (1990) *The Global Challenge: Australian Manufacturing in the 1990s*, Report to the AMC, Sydney.

Parato, V. [1916] (1935), *The Mind and Society*, Harcourt Brace, London.

Park, Young-Ki. (1993), 'South Korea', in Deery, S. and Mitchell, R. (eds) *Labour Law and Industrial Relations in Asia*, Longman Cheshire, Melbourne, 137-71.

Park, Y., and Lee, M. (1995) 'Economic Develoment, Globalization and Practices in Industrial Relations and Human Resource Management in Korea',. in Verma, A., Kochan, T., and Lansbury, R. (eds) (1995) *Employment Relations in the growing Asian Economies,* Routledge, London and New York, 27-61.

Park, Y. and Leggett, C. (1998), 'Employment Relations in Korea', in Bamber, G. and Lasnbury, R. (eds) *International and Comparative Employment Relations*, 3rd Edn, Allen and Unwin, Sydney, 275-93.

Parker, M. and Slaughter, J. (1988) 'Management by Stress', *Technology Review*, 91(7) 1988, 36-44.

Parsons, T. (1951), *The Social System*, Free Press, Chicago.

Peebles, G. 'Singapore: Economy.' *The Far East and Australasia 1999*, 30th Edn, Europa Publications, Surrey, UK.

Peetz, D. (1997a) *Why Join? Why Stay? Instrumentality, Beliefs, Satisfaction and Individual Decisions on Union Membership*, Discussion Paper, No. 356, Center for Economic Policy Research, Australian National University, Canberra.

Peetz, D. (1997b) *Why Bother? Union Membership and Apathy*, Discussion Paper No. 357, Centre for Economic Policy Research, Australian National University, Canberra.

Peetz, D. (1997c) *The Accord, Compulsory Unionism and the Paradigm Shift in Australian Union Membership*, Discussion Paper No. 358, Center for Economic Policy Research, Australian National University.

Peetz, D. (1998) *Unions in A Contrary World: The Future of the Australian Trade Union Movement*, Cambridge University Press, Melbourne.

Peetz, D. (1999) Submission no. 386, to Senate Employment, Workplace Relations, Small Business and Education Legislation Committee, Consideration of the Provisions of the Workplace Relations Legislation Amendment (More Jobs, Better Pay) Bill, 1999, Australian Senate, Parliament House, Canberra.

Perlman (1928), *A Theory of the Labor Movement*, Macmillan, New York. Republished (1949) Augustus Kelley, New York.

Perlmutter, H. (1969), 'The Tortuous Evolution of the Multinational Corporation', *Columbia Journal of World Business*, Jan-Feb, 9-18.

Perrow, C. (1986), *Complex Organisations*, Random House, New York.

Peterson, R. and Tracy, L. (1976), 'A Behavioural Model of Problem-Solving in Labor Negotiations', *British Journal of Industrial Relations*, vol.14, no.2, 159-73.

Peterson, R. and Tracy, L. (1977), 'Testing a Behavioural Theory Model of Labor Negotiations', *Industrial Relations*, vol.16, no.1, 35-50.

Petzall, S. (1993) 'Japanese Management: Can it be transferred to East and South-East Asia?' in Czerkawaski, C. (ed), (1993) *Japanese Management: Challenges and Applications for Business Executives*, Academic Press, Hong Kong, 1-37.

Petzall, S., Chan, S.K., Ong, S., and Sim, P. (1993), 'Women in Management: An Exploratory Singapore Study', *International Journal of Business Studies*, vol.1, no.1, 85-100.

Petzall, S. and Selvarajah, C. (1991), 'International Human Resource Management: Japanese Work Ethics', in Selvarajah, C. and Cutbush-Sabine, C. (eds) *International Business*, Longman Cheshire, Melbourne, 197-227.

Phelps Brown, H. (1990) 'The Counter-Revolution of Our Time', *Industrial Relations*, Vol. 29, No. 1, 1-14.

Pina, C. et al. (1994), 'Direct Employment Effects of MNE's in Developing Countries', in Enderwick, P. (ed) *Transnational Corporations and Human Resources*, Routledge, London, 130-59.

Piore, M. and Sabel, C. (1984) *The Second Industrial Divide*, Basic Books, New York.

Pittard, M. (1988), 'Trade Practices Law and the Mudginberri Dispute', *Australian Journal of Labour Law*, vol.1, 23-58.

Plowman, David. (1986) *Compulsory Arbitration and National Employer Coordination 1890-1980*, PhD Thesis, Flinders University of South Australia.

Plowman, D. (1989) 'Forced March: The Employers and Arbitration', in Macintyre, S. and Mitchell, R. (eds) *Foundations of Arbitration: The Origins and Effects of State Compulsory Arbitration 1890-1914*, Oxford University Press, Melbourne, 135-155.

Plowman, D. (1989), *Holding the Line: Compulsory Arbitration and National Employer Coordination in Australia*, Cambridge University Press, Cambridge.

Plowman, David. (1991) 'Models of national employer coordination, 1890 - 1980' in Savery, L. and Dufty, N. (eds) *Readings in Australian Industrial Relations*, Harcourt, Brace Jovanovich, Sydney, 146-175.

Plowman, David. (1992) 'Employer Associations and Industrial Reactivity.' In Dabscheck, B., Griffin, G. and Teicher, J. (eds) *Contemporary Australian Industrial Relations*, Longman Cheshire, Melbourne, 225-242.

Pocock, B. (1994) *Raising our Voices: Activism Amongst Women and Men in South Australian Unions*, Center for Labour Studies, University of Adelaide, Adelaide.

Pocock, B. (1995) 'Women in Unions: What Progress in South Australia', *Journal of Industrial Relations*, Vol. 37, No. 1, 3-23.

Pocock, B. (1996), 'Better the Devil You Know: Prospects for Women under Labor and Coalition Industrial Relations Policies' in Bryce, M. (ed), *Industrial Relations Under the Microscope ACIRRT Working Paper no.40*, University of Sydney.

Pocock, B. (1998) 'All Change, Still Gendered: The Australian Labour Market in the 1990s' *Journal of Industrial Relations*, Vol. 40, No. 4, 554-579.

Poggi, G. (1978), *The Development of the Modern State*, Hutchinson, London.

Poole, M. (1986), 'Management Strategies and 'Styles' in Industrial Relations: A Comparative Analysis', *Journal of General Management*, vol.12, no.1.

Poulantzas, N. (1973), *Political Power and Social Classes*, New Left Books, London.

Price, R. and G. Bain, (1983) 'Union Growth in Britain: Retrospect and Prospect', *British Journal of Industrial Relations*, Vol. 21, No. 1, 46-68.

Pross, P. (1992), *Group Politics and Public Policy*, Oxford University Press, Toronto.

Pruitt, D. (1981), *Negotiating Behavior*, Sage, New York.

Punch, P. (1989), *Law of Employment in Australia*, CCH. Sydney.

Purcell, P. (1987), Mapping Management Styles in Employee Relations', *Journal of Management Studies*, vol.24, no.5.

Purcell, P. and Ahlstrand B. (1989), 'Corporate Strategy and the Management of Employee Relations in the Multi-Divisional Company', *British Journal of Industrial Relations*, vol. 27, November.

Queensland. Department of Employment, Training and Industrial Relations (DETIR) (1998) *Report on the Effects of the Introduction of Queensland Workplace Agreements*, DETIR, Brisbane, August.

Quiggin, J. (1996) *Great Expectations: Microeconomic Reform and Australia*, Allen and Unwin, St Leonards, Sydney.

Quinlan, M. and Bohle, P. (1991), *Managing Occupational Health and Safety in Australia*, Macmillan, Melbourne.

Rawson, D. (1986) *Unions and Unionists in Australia*, 2nd Edn, Allen and Unwin, Sydney.

Redding, G. (1990), *The Spirit of Chinese Capitalism*, de Gruyter, Berlin.

Rehder, R. (1990), Japanese Transplants: After the Honeymoon', *Business Horizons*, vol.33, 87-98.

Renwick, N. (1988), *Australia and the Multinationals. A Study of Power and Bargaining in the 1980's* Department of International Relations, Australian National University, Canberra.

Ress, A. (1952), 'Industrial Conflict and Business Fluctuations', *Journal of Political Economy*, vol.60, no.5.

Richardson, J. and Jordan, A. (1979), *Governing Under Pressure*, Martin Robertson, Oxford.

Rico, L. (1987), 'The New Industrial Relations: British Electricians New Style Agreements', *Industrial and Labour Relations Review*, vol.11, 63-78.

Rimmer, M. (1981) 'Long-term Structural Change in Australian Trade Unionism', *Journal of Industrial Relations*, Vol. 23, No. 3, 323-344.

Rimmer, M. (1998) 'Enterprise Bargaining, Wage Norms and Productivity', *Journal of Industrial Relations*, Vol. 40, No. 4, 605-623.

Rimmer, M. and Zappala, J. (1988) 'Labour Market Flexibility and the Second Tier', *Australian Bulletin of Labour*, Vol. 14, No. 4, 564-591.

Riordan, J. (1997), 'A Window to the Worksafe Cuts', *Complete Safety Australia*, vol.4, 27-9.

Robins, F. (1994) 'A new Japanese management?' in Reitsperger, W. and Edelstein, B. (eds) (1994) *The Dynamics of Global Co-operation and Competition*, Proceedings of the International Symposium on Pacific Asian Business, Bangkok, Thailand, January, 1994.

Robbins, S. (1994), *Management,* 4th Edn, Prentice-Hall, New Jersey.

Robbins, S., Bergman, R. and Stagg, I. (1997), *Management*, Prentice Hall, Sydney.

Roethlishberger, F. (1965), *Management and Morale*, Harvard University Press, Cambridge.

Roll, E. (1992), *A History of Economic Thought*, 5th Edn, Faber and Faber, London.

Romeyn, J. (1994) 'The Law, Arbitration and Bargaining', *Industrial Relations Research Monograph*, No. 5, AGPS, Canberra.

Rosenzweig, P. and Nohria, P. (1993), 'Influences on Human Resource Management Practices in Multinational Corporations', *Journal of International Business Studies*, vol.23, no.2, 229-51.

Ross, A. and P. Hartman (1960) *Changing Patterns of Industrial Conflict*, Wiley, New York.

Rowthorn, R. (1992), 'Centralisation, Employment and Wage Dispersion', *Economic Journal*, vol.102, 506-23.

Royal Commission Report (1968) on Trade Unions and Employer Associations 1965-1968, *Report*, Cmnd 3623, HMSO, London.

Rubin, J. and Brown, B. (1975), *The Social Psychology of Bargaining and Negotiation*, Academic Press, New York.

Runciman, W. (1966), *Relative Deprivation and Social Justice*, Routledge and Kegan Paul, London.

Sakurai, K. (1985), 'Japanese Worker Attitudes: A Key factor in Productivity', *International Journal of Production Management*, vol.6, no.1, 42-53.

Sawer, M. (1982), 'Philosophical Underpinnings of Libertarianism in Australia' in Sawer, M. (ed) *Australia and the New Right*, George Allen and Unwin, Sydney, 20-37.

Schattsneider, E. *The Semi-Sovereign People*, Hold, Rinehart and Winston, New York.

Shea, G.P. (1980), 'The Study of Bargaining and Conflict Behaviour', *Journal of Conflict Resolution*, vol.24, no.4, 706-41.

Schienstock, G. (1981), 'Towards a Theory of Industrial Relations', *British Journal of Industrial Relations*, vol.19, no.2, 170-98.

Schmitter, P. (1974) 'Still the Century of Corporatism?', *Review of Politics*, vol.36.

Schmitter P. and Lehmbruch, G. (eds) (1979), *Trends Towards Corporatist Intermediation*, Sage, London.

Schulz, J. (1975), *Steel City Blues*, Penguin, Ringwood.

Scott, W., Mumford, E., McGivering, I. and Kirkby, J. (1963), *Coal and Conflict*, Liverpool University Press, Liverpool.

Selvarajah, C. (1991), Multinational Enterprises and Host Nation Responses', in Selvarajah, C. and Cutbush-Sabine, K. (eds) *International Business*, Longman Cheshire, Melbourne, 158-74.

Selvarajah, C. and Cutbush-Sabine, C. (eds) (1991) *International Business*, Longman Cheshire, Melbourne.

Shaw, J. (1986), 'Trade Practices Legislation and Industrial Relations: The Case for Reform', *The Australian Quarterly*, vol.58, no.2, 171-82.

Shaw, J., Walton, M. and Walton, C. (1990) 'A Decline in Union Membership: Some Ideas for Trade Unions in the 1990s', in *Labour Movement: Strategies for the 21st Century*, Evatt Foundation, Sydney, 93-104.

Sheehan, P. et al (1994) *The Rebirth of Australian Industry*, Centre for Strategic Economic Studies, Victoria University, Melbourne.

Sheldon, P. and Thornthwaite, L. (1993) 'Ex Parte Accord: The Business Council of Australia and Industrial Relations Change', *International Journal of Business Studies*, 1(1), 37-55.

Sheldon, P. and Thornthwaite, L. (1996) 'Re-evaluating the Impact of Employer Associations on the Accord: An Analysis of Changes to Bargaining Structures, 1983-1993', in Fells, R. and Todd, T. (eds), *Current Research in Industrial Relations*, AIRAANZ, Perth, 495-504.

Shenkar, O. (1988), 'Uncovering Some Paths in the Japanese Management Theory Jungle', *Human Systems Management*, vol.7, 221-30.

Sheridan, T. (1998) 'Regulating the Waterfront Industry 1950-1968', *Journal of Industrial Relations*, 40(3), 441-460.

Shirai, T. (1984), 'Recent Trends in Collective Bargaining in Japan', *International Labour Review*, vol.123, no.3, 307-18.

Short, M., Preston, A. and Peetz, D. (1993) *The Spread and Impact of Workplace Bargaining: Evidence from the Workplace Bargaining Research Project*, Workplace Bargaining Research Project, Department of Industrial Relations, AGPS, Canberra.

Shorter, E. and Tilly, C. (1974), *Strikes in France, 1830-1968*, Cambridge University Press, Cambridge.

Singapore Department of Statistics (1998) *Yearbook of Statistics*, Singapore.

Singh, R. (1976), 'Systems Theory in the Study of Industrial Relations: Time for a Reappraisal?', *Industrial Relations Journal*, vol.7, no.3, 59-71.

Sisson, K. (1993) 'In Search of HRM?', *British Journal of Industrial Relations*, Vol. 31, No. 2, 201-210

Slater, J. (1999) 'Labour Force', *Far Eastern Economic Review*, June 24, 56.

Sloan, J. (1995) 'Labour Market Reform: The Way Forward', *Business Council Bulletin*, No. 123, September, 10-15.

Sloan, J. (1998) 'An Economic Analysis of the 1988 Patrick Dispute', *The Economic and Labour Relations Review*, 9(2), 236-245.

Sloan, J. and Wooden, M. (1990) 'Trade Union Structure and Workplace Efficiency: An Agenda for Reform', *The Australian Quarterly*, Vol. 62, No. 3, 206-216.

Smith, C. et al. (1978), *Strikes in Britain*, Department of Employment, Manpower Paper 15, HMSO, London.

Smith, D. and Turkington, D. (1980), 'Testing a Behavioural Theory of Bargaining: An International Comparison', *British Journal of Industrial Relations*, vol.19, 361-9.

Smith, M. (1990), 'Pluralism, Reformed Pluralism and Neopluralism: The Role of Pressure Groups in Policy Making', *Political Science*, vol.38.

Snyder, D. (1975), 'Institutional Setting and Industrial Conflict', *American Sociological Review*, vol.40, no.3, 259-78.

Somers, G. (ed) (1969), *Essays in Industrial Relations Theory*, Iowa State University Press, Ames.

Song Jung A. (1999), 'Attitude Adjustment', *Far Eastern Economic Review*, July 1.

Sorrell, G. (1981), 'Equity in labour relations' in Troy, P. (ed) 'A Just Society?', *Essays on Equity in Australia*, George Allen and Unwin, Sydney, 154-61.

Sparrow, P., Schuler, R. and Jackson, S. (1994), 'Convergence or Divergence: Human Resources Practices and Policies for Comparative Advantage Worldwide', *International Journal of Human Resource Management*, vol.5, no.2, 267-99.

Stegman, T. (1997) 'Implications for Wages Policy in Australia of the Living Wage', *The Economic and Labour Relations Review*, Vol. 8, No. 1, 143-155.

Stigler, G. and Friedland, C. (1970), 'What Can Regulators Regulate: The Case of Electricity' in P. McAvoy, (ed), *The Crisis of Regulatory Commissions: An Introduction to a Current Issue of Public Policy*, Norton, New York.

Stilwell, F. (1993) 'Wages Policy and the Accord', in Mahony, G. (ed) *The Australian Economy under Labour*, Allen and Unwin, Sydney, 65-84.

Stone, R. (1998), *Human Resource Management*, 3rd Edn, John Wiley and Son, Brisbane.

Storey, J. (1992), *Developments in the Management of Human Resources*, Blackwell, Oxford.

Storey, J. (ed) (1994), *New Perspectives on Human Resource Management*, Routledge, London.

Storey J. and Sisson, K. (1993) *Managing Human Resources and Industrial Relations*, Open UP.

Strauss, G. (1988), 'Comment', *Industrial and Labor Relations Review*, vol.41, no.3.

Sullivan, M. (1991) 'The Economy', in Le Poer (ed) (1991) *Singapore: A Country Study*, 3rd Edn, Federal Research Division, Library of Congress, Washington DC, 123-174.

Supreme Court of Victoria - Practice Court (1998) Patrick Stevedores Operations Pty Ltd and ors v Maritime Union of Australia and ors, 79 *Industrial Reports*, 268.

Supreme Court of Victoria - Practice Court (1998) Patrick Stevedores Operations Pty Ltd and ors v Maritime Union of Australia and ors, 79 *Industrial Reports* 276.

Supreme Court of Victoria - Court of Appeal (1998) Maritime Union of Australia and ors v Patrick Stevedores Operations Pty Ltd and ors, 79 *Industrial Reports* 317.

Sydney Morning Herald (1 997a), "Shops of Shame' Targeted by Unions', May 31, 4.

Sydney Morning Herald (1 997b), 'Children in Welfare Net: the Toll Rises', May 31, 1.

Taira, K. (1993) 'Japan' in Rothman, M, Briscoe, D. and Nacamulli, R. (eds) *Industrial Relations Around the World*, De Gruyter, Berlin and New York, 217-233.

Tam, S. (1990), Centrigual vs. Cetripatal Growth Process: Contrasting Ideal Types for Conceptualising the Development Patterns of Chinese and Japanese Firms', in Clegg, S. and Redding, S. (eds) *Capitalism in Contrasting Cultures*, de Gruyter, Berlin, 153-63.

Tannenbaum, F. (1951), *A Philosophy of Labor*, Alfred A. Knopf, New York.

Tawney, R. (1961), *The Acquisitive Society*, Fontana, London.

Taylor, F. [1911] (1974), *Scientific Management*, Harper, New York.

Taylor, L. and Walton, P. (1971), 'Industrial Sabotage', in S. Cohen (ed), *Images of Deviance*, Harmondsworth, Penguin.

Teo, S. and Rodwell, J. (1998), 'MNC's in Australia: Striking the Right Balance in Employee Relations Practices' *Working Paper Series, No.14*, University of Technology, Sydney.

Teramoto, Y. and Dirks, D. (1996) 'Lessons from the Recession: Indications for a New Type of Japanese Management?' in *Best Paper Proceedings, The Association of Japanese Business Studies*, 9th Annual Meeting, Nagoya, Japan, June 10-12, 1996, 389-402.

The Age (1999), 27 February.

The Economist, 14 May 1988.

The Economist, July 9-15 1994, 'Survey of Japan', 1-18.

The Economist, June 3-9, 1995, 'The house that Park Built, A Survey of South Korea', 1-22.

The Economist, March 8 1997.

The Economist, April 12-18 1997, 25.

The Economist, February 28-March 6, 1998, 31.

Thomas, Shirley. Challenge. (1985) *The first 100 years of the VEF*. Victorian Employers Federation, Melbourne.

Thornthwaite, Louise and Peter Sheldon. ' The Metal Trades Industry Association, Bargaining Structures and the Accord.' *The Journal of Industrial Relations* 38\2 (1996), 171-195.

Tillett, A., Kempner, T., and Wills, G. (eds), *Management Thinkers* Penguin, Harmondworth.

Timo, N. (1997) The Management of Individualism in an Australian Mining Company, *Employee Relations*, Vol. 19, No. 4, 337-351.

Timo, N. (1989) 'Industrial change and Structural Efficiency: A Trade Union View' *Labour and Industry*, Vol. 2, No. 3, 399-412.

Timo, N. (1997), 'The Management of Individualism in an Australian Mining Company', *Employee Relations*, 19(4), 337-351.

Tolich, P. and Harcourt, M. (1999) 'Why Do People Join Unions? A Case Study of the New Zealand Engineering, Printing and Manufacturing Union', *New Zealand Journal of Industrial Relations*, Vol. 24, No. 1, 63-73.

Trinca, H. and Davies, A. (2000) *Waterfront: The Battle that Changed Australia*, Doubleday, Random House, Milsons Point, NSW.

Truman, D. (1951), *The Governmental Process*, Alfred A. Knopf, New York.

Tsui, T. (1979), 'The Bargaining Process in Hong Kong', in Casey, T. (ed), *Contemporary Labour Relations in the Asian Pacific Region*, Libra Press, Hong Kong, 20-8.

Tull, M. (1997) 'The Freemantle Port Authority: A Case Study in Micro Economic Reform', *Economic Papers*, 16 (4) 33-53.

Turner, I. (1976), *In Union is Strength*, Nelson, Melbourne.

Turner, H., Clack, G., and Roberts, G. (1967), *Labour Relations in the Motor Industry*, Allen and Unwin, London.

UNCTAD (1992), 'Transnational Corporations as Engines of Growth', *World Investment Report: 1992*, United Nations, New York.

UNCTAD (1993), 'Transnational Corporations and Integrated International Production' *World Investment Report: 1993*, United Nations, Geneva.

UNCTAD (1994), 'Transnational Corporations, Employment and the Workplace', *World Investment Report: 1994*, United Nations, Geneva.

UNCTAD (1995), *Recent Developments in International Investment and Transnational Corporations*, United Nations, Geneva.

UNCTAD (1996), 'Investment, Trade and International Policy Arrangements', *World Investment Report: 1996*, United Nations, Geneva.Valiance, D. (1997), 'Bleak Future for OHS Research', *Complete Safety Australia*, no.3, 14.

Verma, A. Kochan, T. and Lansbury R. (1995), *Employment Relations in the Growing Asian Economies*, Routledge, Londen.

Waddington, J. and Whitston, C. (1997) 'Why Do People Join Unions in a Period of Membership Decline', *British Journal of Industrial Relations*, Vol. 35, No. 4, 515-546.

Wallace-Bruce, N. (1998), *Employee Relations Law*, LBC Information Services, Sydney.

Wallace-Bruce, N. (1994), *Outline of Employment Law*, Butterworths, Sydney.

Walton, R. and McKersie, R. (1965), *A Behavioural Theory of Labor Negotiations*, McGraw-Hill, New York.

Wan Abdullah, Nik Mustapha and Abdul Manaf. In Abdul Rahman. (1983) *International Perspectives No 8*. Industrial Relations. Department of Foreign Affairs.

Waseda Bulletin of Comparative Law, vol. 7.

Waterfront Industry Reform Authority (WIRA) (1991) *Waterfront Reform - Port Status*, October, AGPS, Canberra.

Waters, M. (1982), *Strikes in Australia. A Sociological Analysis of Industrial Conflict*, Allen and Unwin, Sydney.

Webb, S. and Webb, B. (1896), *The History of Trade Unionism*, Longmans Green, London.

Webb, S. and Webb, B. (1902) *Industrial Democracy*, Longmans, Green and Co., London.

Weber, M. [1919](1948), 'Politics as a Vocation', in Gerth, H. and Wright Mills, C. (eds) *From Max Weber*, Routledge and Kegan Paul, London.

Wertheim, E., Love, A., Peck, C. and Littlefield, L. (1998) *Skills for Resolving Conflict*, Eruditions Publishing, Melbourne.

Whitehill, A. (1991), *Japanese Management: Tradition and Transition*, New York, Routledge.

Whitehouse, G. (1990) 'Unequal Pay: A Comparative Study of Australia, Canada, Sweden and the U.K', *Labour and Industry*, vol.3, nos.2 and 3, 354-71.

Whitehouse, G. (1992), 'Legislation and Labour Market Gender Inequality: An Analysis of OECD Countries', *Work, Employment and Society*, vol. 6, no.1, 65-86.

Whittaker, D.H. (1991) 'Labour Unions and Industrial Relations in Japan: Crumbling Pillar or Forging a 'Third Way'?' *Industrial Relations Journal*, vol. 29, no. 4, 280-294.

Williamson, O. (1985), *The Economic Institutions of Capitalism*, Free Press, New York.

Williamson, P. (1989), *Corporatism in Perspective: An Introductory Guide to Corporatist Theory*, Sage, London.

Windmuller, J. (1984) 'Employers Associations in Comparative Perspective: Organisation, Structure, Administration' in Windmuller, J.P. and Gladstone A. (eds) *Employers Associations and Industrial Relations: A Comparative Study*, Clarendon Press, Oxford.

Wiseman, J. (1998) 'Here to Stay? The 1997-1998 Australian Waterfront Dispute and its Implications', *Labour and Industry*, 9(1), 1-16.

Woldring, K. (1996) 'The Tweed Valley Fruit Processors Pty Ltd Enterprise Flexibility Agreement: A Regional test case with National Implications', in Dundas, K. and Woldring, K. (eds) *Towards Real Reforms in Employment Relations. Can the Adversarial Culture Be Replaced?* Proceedings of the Fourth Annual Conference of the International Employment Relations Association, Southern Cross University, 10-13 July, 523-534.

Wood, S. (1978), 'Ideology in Industrial Relations Theory', *Industrial Relations Journal*, vol.9, no.4, 42-56.

Wooden, M. (1995), 'Labour Absence in Australia: An Overview of the Dimensions, Causes and Remedial Strategies', *Australian Bulletin of Labour*, vol.21, no.4, 323-39.

Wooden, M. (1999a) 'Individual Agreement-Making', in *The Transformation of Australian Industrial Relations Project Executive Monograph Series*, No. 3, March, National Institute of Labour Studies, Flinders University, Adelaide.

Wooden, M. (1999b) 'Individual Agreement-Making in Australian Workplaces: Incidence, Trends and Features', *Journal of Industrial Relations*, Vol. 41, No. 3, 417-445.

Wooden, M. (2000) *The Transformation of Australian Industrial Relations*, Federation Press, Leichhardt, New South Wales.

Wooden, M. and Baker, M. (1994), 'Trade Unions and quits: Australian Evidence', *Journal of Labor Research*, vol.15, no.4, 403-18.

Wooden, M. and Hawke, A. (1999) 'The Changing Nature of Bargaining and the Consequences for Management and Trade Unions', *The Transformation of Australian Industrial relations Project*, Discussion Paper Series No. 7, National Institute of Labour Studies, Flinders University, Adelaide.

Woodward, D. (1992), Locational Determinants of Japanese Manufacturing Start-Ups in the United States', *Southern Economic Journal*, vol.58, 690-708.

Woodward, J. (1958), *Management and Technology*, HMSO, London.

Wren, D. (1987), *The Evolution of Management Thought*, Wiley and Son, New York.

Wright, Christopher. (1995) *The Management of Labour. A history of Australian Employers,* Oxford University Press, Melbourne.

Wright Mills, C. (1948), *New Men of Power: America's Labor Leaders*, Harcourt, New York.

Young, S. (1992), 'A Framework for Successful Adoption and Performance of Japanese Manufacturing Practices in the U.S.' *Academy of Management Review*, vol.17, no.4, 677-700.

Young-Ki, Parker. (1994) 'South Korea' in Deery, S. and Mitchell, R. (eds) *Labour Law and Industrial Relations in Asia*, Longman, Melbourne.

Zappala, J. (1988), *Workplace Industrial Relations in Australia: An annotated and Selected Bibliography 1970-87*, Business Council of Australia, Sydney.

INDEX TO REFERENCES BY AUTHOR

A

Abbott 1993 75
Abbott 1999 171
ACTU 1995a 1995b 1995c 149
ADAM 1997 270
ADAM 1998 267
Ahlstrand 1990 65
Akita 1996 360, 361
Alexander and Lewer 1998 88
Allan and Timo 1999 242, 244
Amaha 1999 327, 328
Anantaraman 1990 53, 365
Anantaraman 1991 154, 174
Argy 1992 210
Ariff 1993 154
Ashenfelter and Johnson 1969 48
Ayadurai 1992 370, 371, 372
Ayadurai 1993 155, 156, 177, 308, 371
Ayadurai 1994 103

B

Bacharach and Lawler 1980 68
Bacon and Storey 1993 244
Bacon and Storey 1996 244
Bain and Price 1983 136
Bamber and Lansbury 1998 17, 55
Bamber and Shadur 1993 341
Barbash and Barbash 1989 33
Barry 1995 88, 94, 102
Barry, Thornthwaite and Sheldon 107
Bartol 1994 364
Bass 1990 329
BCA 1989 214
BCA 1994 233
BCA Working Relations 1993 209
Bean 1985 100
Beardwell and Holden 1994 67
Beasley 1996 2
Beatrice and Sidney Webb *see* Webb and Webb
Beggs and Chapman 1987 56
Begin 1995 364, 367
Bell 1994 86
Bell and Head 1994 164
Ben Ari 1990 306
Ben Ari 1991 362
Bennett 1994 184, 194, 314, 317
Bennett 1999 242
Benson 1998 358

Bentley and Hughes 1971 52
Berger 1993 323
Bergsten, et al. 1978 347
Bernstein 1955 33
Berry and Kitchener 1989 148
Bhopal 1997 367
BIE 1996 208, 229, 233
Bishop et al. 1992 327
Blandy and Sloan 1986 171
Blandy et al. 1989 141
Blanpain 1983 344
Blyton and Turnbull 1992 69
Bognanno, Budd and Lee 1994
    379, 381, 382, 384
Bongarzoni and Compton 1986 209
Bosanquet [1899] 164
Boswell and Stevis 1997 347, 351, 352
Bottomore 1966 165, 166
Bowie 1994 177
Boxal 1993 244
Bramel and Friend 1981 26
Braverman 31, 32
Braverman 1971 67
Braverman 1974 67
Bray and Walsh 1993 213
Bray and Walsh 1995 148
Brereton 1993 230
Briggs 1999 142
Brookes 1988 124
Brooks 1993 183
Brosnan 1995 325
Brunnecke et al. 1991 343
Buchanan 1996 149
Buchanan and Callus 1993 313
Buchanan and Watson 1997 317, 325, 326
Buchanan et al. 1998 274, 277
Buchanan et al. 1999 277
Buchanan et al. 1999b 277
Burgess and Campbell 1993 325
Burgess and Campbell 1998 267
Byrt 1985 132

C

Callus 1997 238
Callus, et al. 1990 353
Campbell 1996 324, 325
Campling and Gollan 1999 276
Carlye 1911 19

Carney 1988 88, 91
Cawson 1978 167
Chang Hee-Lee 1998 380
Chen 1995 78, 79, 80, 81, 82
Chew 1983 366
Chew 1988 82
Child 1967 69
Child et al. 1973 125
Chung 2000 378, 379
Chung-in-Moon 1994 175
Clark 1983 77
Clark 1995 213
Clarke and Clements 1977 208
Clegg 1975 21
Clegg 1976 34, 46, 53
Clegg 1979 16
Cohen 1980 305
Cohen 1983 300
Colingnon et al. 1997 173
Commons 1909 89, 94
Commons 1913 34, 114
Coppell 1994 87
Costa and Duffy 1991 148
Costello 1989 171
Costello 1996 197
Creigh and Makeham 1982 49
Creigh and Markem 1982 52
Creighton 1982 125
Creighton and Stewart 1994 184, 185
Creighton and Stewart 2000 182
Crosby and Easson 1992 141
Crouch 1982 136
Crough and Wheelwright 1982 338
Cully 2000 140

D

Dabscheck 1983 24
Dabscheck 1992 62, 63, 168
Dabscheck 1993 33
Dabscheck 1994 31
Dabscheck and Niland 1981 24, 38
Dabscheck and Niland 1982 86
Dabschek 1989 22
Dabschek 1994 34
Dahl 1961 20, 165
Dahrendorf 1959 24
Davies 1996 148, 150
Davis 1979 48

Davis 1996 142
Davis and Lansbury 1993 211, 215
Deery 1989 128, 132
Deery and De Cieri 1991 136
Deery and Mitchell 1993 102
Deery and Walsh 1998 275
D'Entreves 1967 164
Deresky 1994 343
Dicken 1998 340, 341, 342
Dobbs-Higginson 1993 374
Dollinger 1988 78
Donovan 1971 88
Dore 1973 152
Douglas 1957 303
Douglas 1962 303
Douglas 1993 147
Drago et al. 1992 142, 206
Dubin 1954 45, 53
Dubin, R. 45
Dubois 1979 40
Dufty and Fells 1989 88
Dunlop, John 27, 31, 90, 91
Dunlop 1958 16
Dunlop 1977 90, 91
Dyson 1980 164

E

Edwards 1979 22, 67
Edwards 1986 22, 40
Edwards 2000 155, 156, 369
Edwards et al. 1995 39
Ely 1890 19
Enderwick 1985 343, 344
Enderwick 1994
    340, 342, 343, 344, 347, 348, 351, 352
Evans 1985 206
Evans 1989 214
Evans and Hudson 1994 244
Evatt Foundation 1995 171, 195

F

Fells 1985 303, 304
Fells 1995 303, 304
Ferner 1996 346
Fidler 1981 20
Fisher and Ury 1984 300, 301
Fisher and Ury's 1981 300

Flanders 1965 16
Ford and Hearn 1987 39, 40
Fox 1964 20
Fox 1966 19, 21, 244
Fox 1971 21, 71
Fox 1974 21
Fox et al. 1995 300
Franko 1994 341
Fraser 1996 233
Frazer 1995 279
Freeman and Medoff 1984 34, 134, 135, 170
French and Raven 1959 68
Frenkel 1977 23, 29
Frenkel and Coalican 1984 137
Frenkel and Royal 1996 346
Frenkel and Shaw 1989 219, 220
Friedman and Friedman 1963 34, 170
Friedman and Friedman 1980 313, 314
Fukuda 1988 81

G

Gahan 1996 118
Galbraith 1963 165
Galbraith 1992 330
Galenson 1954 39
Gardner 1987 286
Gardner 1989 130, 131
Gennard 1972 344
Gill and Griffin 1981 141
Gladstone 1984 99
Gospel and Palmer 1993 19
Gosper and Palmer 1992 164
Green 1995 313
Gregory 1992 210
Griffin and Svensen 1996 148, 149
Guest 1987 69
Guest and Conway 1999 244, 277
Guilie, Sappey and Winter 1989 20

H

Hagan 1977 142
Hagan 1981 195
Hagan 1983 120, 122, 123, 124
Hamberger 1995a 284
Hamberger 1995b 284
Hamilton 1993 97
Hammond and Harbridge 1995 320

Hampson 1996 148
Hamzah-Sendut et al. 1990 305
Hansen 1921 47
Harbridge and Moulder 1993 147, 148
Harding and Landt 1992 326
Harley 1995 242
Hartman, P 41–42
Hawke and Howe 1991 312
Hawke and Wooden 1998 148
Hayek 1960 19
Heiler 1994 271
Helier 1996 278
Herbert 1999 96
Herzberg 1966) 26
Herzerg 1968 51
Hibbs 1976 47, 49, 52
Hilderbrand 1988 76
Hilibrand 1988 31
Hilmer 1990 142
Hilmer 1991 219
Hilmer 1995 75
Hobson 1920 19
Holdsworth 1987 294, 299, 304
Hopkins 1993 321, 322, 323
Howard 1977 114, 117, 118, 131, 215
Huczynski, 1993 27
Hughes 1969 354
Hunter 1992 194, 314, 318, 319
Hyman 1971 22, 23
Hyman 1975 20, 21, 44, 114
Hyman 1989 16, 17, 38, 39, 40
Hyman and Fryer 1977 22
Hyman, R. 23, 44

I

IAC 1988 211
Ingham 1974 43, 54
Ippolito and Walker 1980 66
IRM 1994 285
Isaac 1977 215
Ito 1997 358

J

Jackson 1982 136
Jackson 1987 51, 55

Jackson and Sisson 90
James 1993 322
Jamieson 1990 142
Jaques 1989 286
Jaynes 1996 70
Jessop 1982 24
Johnson 1988 345
Johnson 1996 289
Joskow 1974 33
Justice Higgins 1922 205

K

Kallmargen and Naughton 1991 144
Kamata 1982 362
Kanai and Fling 1996 362
Karl Marx 22, 44, 166
Katz, H. 29
Kaufman 1989 34, 170
Kaufman 1993 16, 17
Kaufman and Hotchkiss 1999 34, 170
Kearney 1991 385
Keenoy and Kelly 1996 179
Keenoy and Kelly 1998 17, 38, 170
Kelly 1994 16, 17
Kenyon and Lewis 1996 148, 149
Kerr 1992 137
Kerr and Siegal 1954 50, 59
Kerr, Dunlop, Harbison and Myers 1964 90
Kerr et al. 1962 42, 53
Keys and Miller 1984 78
Kim 1993 160
King, Rimmer and Rimmer 1991 325
Kirkbride, Tang and Westwood 1991 377
Knights et al. 1985 32
Kochan 1980 19, 29, 34
Kochan and Barocci 1985 20
Kochan and Osterman 1995 301, 302, 303
Kochan and Tamir 1989 146
Kochan, Katz and McKersie 1986 29, 30, 65, 75, 146
Koike 1988 78, 152
Komatsu 1994 172
Kornhauser, A. 38
Kornhauser et al. 1954 38, 39
Korpi and Shalev 1979 46, 52, 53
Kramar, McGraw and Schuler 1997 18
Kuhn 1961 43

Kurunila and Venkalaratnam 1996 34
Kuruvilla 1995 368, 369, 370, 371, 372, 373
Kuruvilla and Arudsothy 1995 155, 156
Kuwahara 1996 34
Kuwahara 1998 152
Kwon and O'Donnell 1999 383
Kyloh 1989 216

L

Laffer 1974 16
Lan 1997 39
Lansbury and MacDonald 1995 242
Lansbury and Zappala 1990
    378, 380, 381, 383, 386
Laughlan 1989 141
Le Poer 1989 329
Le Poer 1991 363
Lee 1997 382
Lee and Yoo 1987 80, 81, 306, 379, 386
Legge 1989 17, 244
Legge 1995 17, 18, 244, 247
Leggett 1993 153, 307, 364, 365, 366
Leggett 1994 103
Leggett 1997 52, 378, 380, 381, 382
Lehmbruch 1977 167
Levin and Chiu 1995 157
Levin and Ng 1993
    156, 157, 308, 374, 376, 377
Levin and Ng Sek Kong 1994 104, 105
Levine 1996 359, 361
Lewin 1987 31
Lewin 1988 76
Lewis 2000 158, 374
Lewis and Spiers 1990 63
Lie 1990 81, 306, 380
Lindblom 1977 20, 165
Littler and Salaman 1984 32
Lloyd 1982 340
LMC 1998 275
Locke et al. 1995 243
Lord Rolls 1992 330
Loughran 1985 296
Low 1990 174
Lucio and Weston 1994 343
Ludeke 1996 286
Luthans 1992 305

M

Mabey, Salaman and Storey 1998 17, 18
MacIntosh 1993 97
Macken 1997 146
Macken et al. 1997 183, 185, 194
Macklin et al. 1992 216, 240
Magenau and Pruitt 1979 295
Marginson 1969 16
Martin 1980 121, 123
Martin 1989 110
Marx [1856] 166
Marx [1857][1891] 22
Maslow 1943 26
Maslow 1954 51, 69
Maslow, A. 26, 51
Matsuda 1993 53, 173, 358, 360, 361, 362
Matsumura 1994 359
Matsuzaki 1994 359
Mayhew and Quinlan 1997a 322, 323
Mayhew and Quinlan 1997b 322, 323, 324
Mayhew, Quinlan and Ferris 1997 322
Mayo 1933 26, 50, 54, 69
Mc Carthy 1991 352
McCaffree 89
McCallum 1996 244
McCarthy 1989 294
McCarthy 1991 339, 347, 351, 353, 354
McDonald and Rimmer 1988 218, 219
McEvoy and Owens 1990 184
McGregor 1957 26
McGregor's 1966 51
McIntosh Baring Report 1996 285
McIntyre 1998 2
McKersie, R. 29
McMahon, Thomson and Williams 2000 312
Mealor 1995 353
Meyrick and Associates and Tasman Asia Pacific
    1998 2
Michels 1959 125
Milgrom and Roberts, 1990 32
Miliband 1969 166
Miller and Mulvey 1992 135
Miller and Zaidi 1982 341
Monk 1996 346
Morehead et al. 1996 276
Morehead et al. 1997 133, 270, 274, 275

Morley 1979 300
Mortimer and Still 1999 97
Mosca [1896] 165
MTIA 1993 226

N

Naughton 1994 197
Negandhi et al. 1985 343, 345
Neumann 1968 39
Neville 1990 313, 326
Newman and Nollen 1996 346
Ng 1996 374, 376
Ng and Fung 1989 156, 157
Ng and Fung-Shuen 1989 178, 308
Nicholson 1978 126
Niland 1978 53
Niland, J. 24, 38
Nimura 1994 358, 360, 361
Nish, Redding, Ng et al. 1996 374, 375, 377
Noon 1992 17
Nordlinger 1981 165
NZAS Consultant Report 1992 287

O

O'Brien 1994 99
O'Connor 1973 166
Ogle 1990 306, 307
Olsen 1965 170
Olsen 1971 34
O'Neill, 1995 68
Osborne 1992 20
Owen and Braeutign 1978 33
Oxnam 1971 52
Ozawa 1979 345

P

Paldam 1983 48, 52
Paldam and Pederson 1982 48
Pappas et al. 1990 210, 211, 213
Pareto [1916] 165
Park 1993 175, 307
Park and Lee 1995 381, 385
Park and Leggett 1998 52, 159, 160, 385
Parker and Slaughter 1988 362
Parsons 1951 25
Peebles 1999 364
Peetz 1997a 1997b 1997c 137

Peetz 1998 137, 138, 146, 244, 275
Perlman 1928 34
Perlman 1949 24, 114, 115, 116
Perlmutter 1969 343
Perrow 1986 66
Peterson and Tracy 1976 298, 299
Petzal, et al. 1993 329
Petzall 1993 380
Petzall and Selvarajah 1991 173, 360, 362
Phelps Brown 1988 278
Phelps Brown 1990 137
Pittard 1988 194
Plowman 1982 86
Plowman 1986 90
Plowman 1989 71, 86, 117
Plowman 1991 98, 99
Plowman 1992 88, 93
Plowman, D. 93, 94, 107
Pocock 1994 138, 145
Pocock 1995 145, 146
Pocock 1996 320
Pocock 1998 265, 267
Poggi 1978 164
Poole 1986 73, 74, 83
Poulantzas 1973 166
Pross 1992 66
Pruitt 1981 303, 304
Purcell, P. 1987 65, 72, 73, 74, 83
Purcell and Ahlstrand 1989 76, 77

Q

Quiggin 1996 242
Quinlan and Bohle 1991 197

R

Rawson 1978 137
Rawson 1986 131, 137
Redding 1990 82, 364
Rehder 1990 345
Renwick 1988 341
Renwick 1994 341
Res 1952 48
Richardson and Jordan 1979 20, 165
Rico 1987 344
Rimmer 1981 141
Rimmer 1998 271, 278
Rimmer and Zappala 1988 210, 219
Riordan 1997 321, 323, 330

Robbins, et al. 1997 355
Robins 1994 361
Roethlishberger (1965) 26
Rogers 1990 385
Romeyn 1994 219, 226
Ross, A. 41–42
Ross and Hartman 1960 41, 42, 53
Rowthorn 1992 326
Rubin and Brown 1975 295
Runciman 1966 49

S

Sawer 1982 316
Schattsneider 1960 165
Schmitter 1974 167
Schmitter 1979 167
Schmitter and Lehmbruch 1979 33
Scott et al. 1963 39
Selvarajah 1991 342
Shaw et al. 1990 145
Shea 1980 300
Sheehan et al. 1994 210, 211
Sheehan, et al. 1995 210
Sheldon 1996 94
Sheldon and Thornthwaite 1993 142
Sheridan 1998 2
Shirai 1984 306
Short et al. 1993 243
Shorter and Tilly 1974 46, 52
Sission 1993 244, 277
Slater 1999 156, 158
Sloan 1995 209
Sloan 1998 3
Sloan and Wooden 1990 142
Sloan and Wooden 1991 141
SMH 1997a 325
SMH 1997b 326
Smith 1990 165
Smith and Turkington 1980 299
Smith, et al. 1978 50, 60
Snyder 1975 47, 52, 53
Somers 1969 16
Song 1999 328
Sparrow et al. 1994 346
Stegman 1997 231
Stigler and Friedland 1970 33
Stilwell 1993 216
Stone 1998 17, 18, 20, 69

Storey 1989 20
Storey and Sisson 1993 244
Strauss 1988 76
Streeck 91, 103
Sullivan 1991 173, 364, 365, 366

T

Taira 1993 152, 153
Tam 1990 82
Tannenbaum 1951 34, 94
Tawney 1961 19
Taylor 1911 69
Taylor and Walton 1971 40
Teo and Rodwell 1998 342, 346, 353, 354
Teramoto and Dirks 1996 360
Thomas 1985 87
Thornthwaite and Sheldon 1996 100
Tillett et al. 1970 26
Timo 1989 224
Timo 1997 244, 284
Tolich and Harcourt 1999 137
Trinca and Davies, 2000 1, 12, 13
Truman 1951 20
Tull 1997 5
Turner 1976 58, 59, 118, 119, 120, 121, 122
Turner et al. 1967 39

V

Valiance 1997 323
Verma et al. 1995 34

W

Waddington and Whitston 1997 137
Wallace-Bruce 1998 187, 189, 191, 193
Walton and Kersie's 1965 307
Walton and McKersie 1965 296, 297, 298, 299, 300, 303
Waters 1982 40, 53, 56
Webb and Webb 1894 34, 110, 111, 112, 113
Webbs 1902 278
Weber, [1919] 164
Whitehill 1991 80
Whitehouse 1990 318, 321
Whitehouse 1992 315, 320, 321
Whittaker 1998 361
Williamson 1985 32

Williamson 1989 167
Win Min Aun 1982 372
Windmuller 1984 92
Windmuller and Gladstone 1984 92
Woldring 1996 256
Wood 1978 28
Wooden 1995 40
Wooden 1999a 275
Wooden 1999b 277
Wooden 2000 263, 278
Wooden and Baker (1994 40
Wooden and Hawke 1999 138, 148
Woodward 1958 43, 60
Woodward 1992 345
Wren 1987 67
Wright 1995 87, 89
Wright Mills 1948 44, 53

Y

Young - Ki 1994 105
Young 1992 345, 362

INDEX

A

absenteeism 38, 40
absolute deprivation 49
Accords 63, 91, 170, 203
   1983-1995 218
   assessment 1983-1995 231
   ACTU 60
   Australian Labor Party (ALP) 60
   economic indicators 232
   failure to safeguard real wages 225
   managed decentralism 231
   response to Whitlam failure 234
   trade union decline 147
   unions and the Accords 216
ACTU 9, 60
   'Employment Security and Working Hours' 267
   formed in 1927 121
   MUA v Patrick Stevedores 9
   productivity bargaining 227
   structure 161
AIG
   range of services 96
air pilots' dispute 1989 185
AIRC 7, 101, 168, 187, 188–190, 207
   a safety net role 234
   CRA dispute 291
   curtailing the powers 232
   Enterprise Bargaining Principle (EBP) 228
   move to enterprise bargaining 228
   MUA waterfront disupute 7
   paper disputes 189
   rejects Accord Mark IV 227
   reluctance for workplace bargaining 231
   requirements for approving Certified Agreements 247
airline pilots' dispute 195
anti-discrimination legislation 193, 315
anti-union strategies 72
Australia
   recent strike statistics 59–62
Australian Chamber of Commerce and Industry (ACCI) 97
Australian Conciliation and Arbitration Commission
   equal pay decision 124

Australian Constitution 117
Australian Democrats 196
Australian Industry Group (AIG)
   formation MTIA and ACM 96
Australian Labor Party 194
Australian Waterfront Dispute, 1998 1–13
Australian Workplace Agreements 190, 192–193
Australian Workplace Agreements (AWAs) 249
Australian Workplace Industrial Relations Survey (AWIRS) 1 133
award restructuring
   metal industry 223
awards
   definition 206
AWAs. *See* enterprise bargaining

B

bargaining models 240
bargaining theory 33
benchmarking 4, 12
Bernie Fraser 232
BHP 132
Bracks Labor Victorian Government 101
Braverman, H. 31–32, 67
British trade unions 111
Business Council of Australia 3, 97, 98–99
   trade unions 141
   unitarism 142
business organisations 66–67
Button plan 93

C

Cabinet briefing paper 5, 8
   Waterfront Strategy 13
Canada
   strike statistics 57
capitalism 22, 51
capture theory 33
centralised arbitration system 117
Certified Agreement - Sample 389–400
Certified Agreements 190, 191–192
   dispute resolution clause 247

Certified Agreements cont'd
   no disadvantage 247
   persons bound 248
   valid majority 247
Chifley Labor Government 59, 122
China 114
Chinese management 82
   adversarial 83
   suspicious of workers 82
Chinese-run businesses 82
class struggle 23
collective bargaining 29, 46
   institutionalised 45
collectivism 20, 24, 73
Commonwealth Arbitration Court 120
communists
   in Australia 114
   in Japan 114
   in Singapore 114
company restructuring 7–9
Conciliation and Arbitration Act 1904 205
Confucian philosophy 78
Constitution 168
   High Court 186
   Section 51 186
   Section 52 186
containers (TEUs) 2
Corrigan, Chris 6
CRA
   AIRC suports union rights 291
   award employees get contract benefits 291
   commodity prices 284
   company details 285
   contracting employees 287
   equal pay for equal work 290
   globalisation 284
   individual contracts discriminated 290
   majority of employees signed Agreements 288
   New Zealand precursor 287
   Prime Minister R J Hawke 290
   restructuring work practices 284
   return to 40-hour week 289
   strategic view of HRM 291
   union response to contracts 289
   Work Performance Review 289
CRA (Rio Tinto) case study 283–292
Curtin, John 122

D

Dabscheck, B. 24, 38
de-unionising the docks 5
decentralised bargaining 171
decline in strikes in Australia
   Accords 63
   employee relations 63
   enterprise bargaining 63
   flexible labour markets 63
   trade union decline 63
   unemployment 63
definition
   awards 206
   employer associations 86
   enterprise bargaining 238
   equity 311
   human relations theory 26
   industrial conflict 38
   industrial relations 16–19
   labour process theory 31–32
   Marxism 22–24
   negotiation 295
   pluralism 20–22
   power 68
   scientific management 25
   strategic choice theory 29–31
   strikes 40
   systems theory 27–29
   the state 164
   trade union 110
   unitarism 19
   wage fixation 204
Dollar Sweets dispute 1988 101, 215
Dubai 6
Dubin, R. 45
Dunlop, John 91
   systems theory 27

E

economic rationalism 312, 313–314
   intensifying labour market inequalities 326
   worsens OHS 322
economic rationalism and OHS 321
economic reforms 1980s 212
   deregulation 212
   privatisation 212
   targeted industry plans 213
EEO strand of civil libertarianism
   equity 314–315

employer association theories
   Commons 89, 106
   defensive model 90
employer association theories cont'd
   Dunlop 91
   Hoxie 89, 106
   Jackson and Sisson 90, 107
   market model 91
   McCaffree 89, 106
   Plowman's reactivity theory 93, 107
   procedural model 90
   Streeck 91, 107
   Windmuller 92, 107
employer associations 85–107
   ACCI 97, 100, 107
   active role 101
   AIG 95, 95–97, 107
   alliance model 98
   Australian Chamber of Commerce and Industry (ACCI) 97
   Australian Chamber of Manufacturers (ACM) 86, 96
   Australian Industry Group (AIG) 86
   Australian Paint Manufacturers' Federation 95
   bargaining structures 99–101
   Business Council of Australia 3, 72, 88, 97, 98–99, 100, 107
   confederation model 98
   Confederation of Australian Industry (CAI) 88
   contact with government 100
   definition 86
   development of peak associations 88
   Employers' Federation of Hong Kong 104
   enterprise bargaining 100
   federation model 98
   fee for service 97
   history in Australia 86–87
   Hong Kong 104–105
   Housing Industry Association 95
   HR Nicholls Society 2, 72
   industry associations 87, 95–97
   Japan 102
   Malaysia 103–104
   Malaysian Employers' Federation (MEF) 103
   Metal Trades Industry Association (MTIA) 86
   MTIA 95–97, 100, 107
   mutual defence model 98
   National Farmers Federation 2
   Oil Industry Industrial Committee 95
   peak associations 97–99
   peak employer associations 87
   range of services 96
   Retailers Council of Australia 95
   secretariat model 98
   services 99
   Singapore 103
   Singapore Manufacturers Association 103
   Singapore National Employers Federation (SNEF) 103
   South East Asia 102–106
   South Korea 105–106
   structure 94
   theories 88–94
   umbrella associations 87
   Victorian Employers Federation (VEF) 87
   Workplace Relations Act 1996 101
Employment Advocate 193
employment relations 17
enterprise bargaining 72, 237–282
   a-symmetrical power relationship 241
   ACIRRT data 263
   AIRC approval of CAs 248
   alternative bargaining models 240
   approval of AWAs 250
   Australian Productivity and Competition Commission 242
   Australian Workplace Agreements (AWAs) 192–193, 239, 249
   Australian Workplace Industrial Relations Survey (AWIRS) 262
   Australia's mixed approach 262
   AWAs and no-disadvantage test 250
   AWAs cannot displace current CAs 251
   bargaining fatigue 278
   bargaining period 249
   bargaining structure 239
   breach, enforcement and remedies 251
   case law, Asahi case 254
   case law, ANF Case 255
   case law, Tweed Valley Fruit Case 256
   case law, Yallourn Energy Case 258
   Certified Agreements (CAs) 246
   collective agreements 239
   collective bargaining 240
   CRA case study 239
   definition 238
   demise of collectivism 274
   downsizing for efficiency 273
   effect of AWA on Awards 250
   effectively AWA is individual contract 249

enterprise bargaining cont'd
   Enterprise Flexibility Agreements (EFA) 190
   few links to productivity clauses 273
   globalisation 242
   greater efficiency and productivity 241
   greater job insecurity 241
   HRM strategies 244
   impact on working conditions 262–271
   implied charter of employee rights 257
   increased intensity of work 273
   increases flexibility of labour 241
   increases market responsiveness 241
   increasing job related stress 269
   individual agreements 239
   individual contracts, CRA 283
   Industrial Relations Reform Act 1993 229
   informal agreements 239
   issues 241
   joint consultative committee 239
   management strategies 244
   measuring productivity 271
   micro-economic reforms 242
   must bargain in good faith 256
   negotiating an Agreement 281
   no disadvantage test 247, 248, 257
   no right to compel employers to bargain 254
   NSW laws 252
   objects of the WRA 246
   Occupational Health and Safety 270–271
   Office of the Employment Advocate (OEA) 250
   OHS price of cost minimisation 271
   organisational restructuring 267, 274
   pattern bargaining 239, 240, 261
   persons bound by CAs 248
   procedural rules 238
   productivity 242
   Queensland laws 252
   record profitability 242
   requirements for approving CAs 247
   right to strike 259
   role of Awards 246
   slow uptake 229
   sources of data 262
   South Australia laws 252
   State legislation 251
   substantive rules 238
   Tasmanian laws 253
   time poverty 267
   transferring risk to employees, CRA 291
   types of agreements 239
   UK experience 244
   Victorian situation 253
   W.A. laws 253
   wage differences widen 241
   wages gap 265
   work conditions reduced 241
   workplace contracts 239
   Workplace Relations Act, 1996 244–251
   workplace wage setting 243
enterprise bargaining statistics
   Australian Workplace Agreements 277
   decline in union membership 274
   gender earnings gap grows 265
   growing atypical forms of employment 267
   management reasons for bargaining 278
   management view 272
   non-standard working week 268
   number of agreements 263
   number of AWAs 274
   public v. private sector agreements 269
   replacement of awards 266
   scope of bargaining agendas 266
   union v. non-union agreements 276
   wage increases attained 263
   which workplaces bargain 264
   who are the bargaining parties 264
   worker dissatisfaction 267
   worker view of impact 270
equity 311–332
   anti-discrimination legislation 315
   civil libertarianism 312
   death, illness and injury statistics 321
   definition 311
   economic rationalism and gender 318
   economic rationalism 311, 313–314
   economic rationalism and freedom of choice 313
   economic rationalism and individualism 313
   economic rationalism and inequality 322
   economic rationalism and labour market inequalities 325
   economic rationalism and OHS 321
   EEO grants legal rights to individuals 315
   EEO ignores labour market inequalities 326
   EEO narrow focus 315
   EEO re-active to OHS 324
   EEO strand of civil libertarianism 312, 314–315
   EEO strand of civil libertarianism and gender 319
   Equal Employment Opportunity (EEO) 312

equity cont'd
   fairness freedom and choice 312
   gender 317–321
   gender gap statistics 320
   gender statistics 317
   glass ceiling 318
   illness, injury and death at Work 321–324
   inequality in the labour market 324–327
   labour market inequality statistics 325
   New Zealand gender gap 320
   social inequality issues 321
   social justice 312, 315–317
   social justice and collectivism 316
   social justice and labour market inequalities 326
   social justice and OHS 324
   social justice and social welfare 317
   social justice focuses on groups 316
   social justice policies and gender 320
   South East Asia 327–329
exit 40

F

Fabian Socialists 111
Federal Court
   Justice North 10
   MUA v Patrick Stevedores 10
foot dragging 40
foreign ownership 355
France
   strikes 46, 57
Fraser Coalition Government 59, 123
French Revolution 118

G

glass ceiling 318
global competition 66
globalisation 2–4, 74, 209, 242, 284, 342
gold rush 119
Great Depression 58, 115, 121

H

Hartman, P 41–42
Hawke, R.J. 294
Hawthorne Studies 50
High Court 12, 243
   MUA waterfront dispute 12
Hilmer Report 75
   decentralising wage fixing 75
   restructuring unions 75

Hong Kong 373–377
   Cathay Pacific dispute 1993 376
   China one country, two systems 378
   Chinese cultural values 159
   collective bargaining 375
   Confederation of Trade Unions 157
   dispute statistics 377
   economic statistics 374
   employer associations 104–105
   Employers' Federation of Hong Kong 104
   Federation of Trade Unions 157
   Federation of Trade Unions (FTU) 105
   future state intervention uncertain 178
   hand-over to China 156, 178
   history and economy 373
   increasing industrial disputes 158
   industrial relations history 374
   industrial relations record 377
   industrial relations system 374
   integrative bargaining 308
   labour mobility 308
   low level government intervention 374
   management 81
   negotiation processes 307
   non-union joint consultation 308
   piecemeal regulatory framework 376
   return to China 377
   strike statistics 55, 57
   strikes 53
   the state 178
   trade union statistics 156, 374
   trade unions 113, 156–159
   unions docile and weak 157
Howard Coalition Government 5
HRM 16, 61
   definition of industrial relations 17
   employment relations 17
   internal conflict 69
   strategic HRM 17
   unifying culture 70
human relations theory 26–27
Hyman, R. 23, 44

I

ILO conventions 348
increasing competition 75
individualism 24, 83
industrial relations
   institutionalisation 44

industrial conflict 37–63. *See also* strikes
   capitalism 44
   covert 38, 39–41, 54
   definition 38
   deprivation 49
   economic expectations 47
   economic growth 48
   government policies 47
   human relations theories 54
   inflation 48
   inherent in business organisations 66–67
   institutionalised collective bargaining 45
   management strategies 69
   Marxism 23, 44
   measurement 54–56
   mining, CRA 283
   MUA v. Patrick Stevedores 1–13
   organisational communication 54
   organised 38
   overt 38, 39–41
   productivity losses 40
   recession 47
   role of state 47
   source of industrial conflict 23
   strikes 40
   theories applied 51–54
   theories of 41–51
   unemployment 49
   unequal distribution of power 41
   unorganised conflict 38
   wage relativities 48
   workplace morale 50
industrial conflict theories
   applied 51–54
industrial disputes. *See* strikes
industrial relations
   3 levels of activity 30
   corporate strategy 76
   defined 18
   definition 16–19
   managerial hierarchy 76
   theories of 24–34
   v. employment relations 17
industrial relations reform
   AIRC, a safety net role 234
   Award restructuring 221
   Business Council of Australia 214, 233
   Business Council of Australia (BCA) 213
   CRA case study 284

   enterprise-based union structure 214
   increased gender gap 320
   Industrial Relations Act 1988 challenged 243
   Industrial Relations Act ammended 1992 229
   Industrial Relations Reform Act 1993 229
   Kennett Victorian Government 243
   Metal Trades Industry Association (MTIA) 214
   micro-economic reforms 242
   move to enterprise bargaining 228
   National Economic Summit 1983 216
   National Wage cases 1988-89 224
   New Right 214
   restructuring and redundancies 267
   structural rigidity 214
   the future 233
   Workplace Relations Act 1996 234
   workplace wage setting 243
industrial relations theories
   human relations theory 26
   institutionalist theories 34
   labour market theories 33
   labour process theory 31–32
   regulation theories 33
   scientific management 25
   South East Asia 34
   strategic choice theory 29–31, 75
   systems theory 27–28
   transaction cost theory 32
industrial torts 184
inequality in the labour market 324–327
institutionalist theories 34
International Confederation of Free Trade Unions 350
International Labour Organisation (ILO) 169

J

Japan 358–363
   Amakudari 173
   centralised multinational corporations 343
   collective bargaining 361
   Confucian philosophy 78
   decline in unionism 151
   disputes of interest 360
   disputes of right 360
   dual labour market 360
   employee associations 152
   employer associations 102
   enterprise trade unions 116, 360
   enterprise unionism 80, 152
   enterprise unions 361

Japan cont'd
  equity 327–328
  gender equity laws 1999 327
  groupism 77
  history and economy 358
  Honda 361
  industrial conflict 52
  industrial relations system 358–363
  Japan Incorporated 172
  Japanese Federation of Employer Associations 102
  Japanese Trade Union Confederation ('Rengo') 102, 152
  joint consultation 362
  Labour Relations Commission 360
  lifetime employment 78, 360
  male-dominated society 328
  management 77–80
  management by stress 362
  MNCs have stress and other problems 345
  MNCs pay lowest wages 345
  MNCs seek labour flexibility 344
  mutual gains enterprises 306
  negotiation and public posturing 306
  negotiation processes 306
  no craft union tradition 361
  Occupation Forces 358
  philosophy of Kaizen 362
  post-war trade unionism 359
  residual feudal elements 51
  seniority wages 360
  Spring Offensive or 'Shunto' 102, 361
  state intervention 179
  state pervasive informally 173
  strike statistics 55
  strikes 53
  strikes statistics 57
  symbolic strikes 80
  temporary female employees 360
  the state 172–173
  Toyota 360, 362
  trade union statistics 151
  trade unions 80, 113, 151–153
  union and management fraternise 306
  women in dead end jobs 327
  workaholism 362
Japanese management
  bonuses 79
  collective responsibility 78
  decline in lifetime employment 80
  decline of enterprise unionism 80
  employee selection 78
  lifetime employment 78
  long-term planning 78
  more egalitarian remuneration 79
  promotion by seniority 79
Japanese managment
  unitarism 83
Japanese trade unions 80
job insecurity 39
Justice North 10
  MUA waterfront dispute 10

K

Karl Marx 22, 44, 166
Katz, H. 29
Kelty, Bill 141
Kennett Victorian Government 101
Kitchen Maid dispute 215
Kochan, T. 29
Kornhauser, A. 38

L

labour market theories 33
  perfect competition 33
labour power 31
labour process theory
  criticisms 32
  definition 31–32
Labour Supply Agreements (LSAs) 8
labour turnover 40
Lang Corporation 4, 8, 12
law 181–201
  AIRC 188–190
  AIRC and incidental matters 190
  AIRC, 20 allowable matters 189
  AIRC and no disadvantage test 196
  AIRC and Workplace Relations Act 1996 189
  AIRC national wage cases 189
  AIRC to encourage enterprise agreements 189
  anti-discrimination legislation 193
  Australian Federation of Air Pilots 185
  Australian Workplace Agreements 189, 190, 192–193
  AWA 200
  Awards 190
  Certified Agreements 191–192
  Coalition abstentionism 196
  conciliation and arbitration power 187

law cont'd
   Constitution s.51 186
   Constitution s.52 186
   corporations power 187
   courts and common law 182
   courts and contract of employment 182
   courts and interpretative power 185
   courts and tort of conspiracy 183
   doctrine of implied terms 183
   doctrine of precedent 182
   downgrading of the role of awards 201
   Enterprise Flexibility Agreements (EFA) 190
   external affairs power 187
   impact of industrial law 197
   Industrial Relations Legislation 187–188
   industrial torts 184
   International Labour Organisation (ILO) 187
   Mudginberri dispute 194
   non-industrial legislation 193
   occupational health and safety (OHS) 193
   Office of Employment Advocate 193
   paper disputes 189
   secondary boycotts 194
   social justice and equity 195
   sources 182
   The Australian Constitution 186
   trade and commerce power 187
   Trade Practices Act 1974 194
   weakening of the powers of the AIRC 201
   Workplace Relations Act 1996 187, 196
law of diminishing returns 34
Lenin, Vladamir 23, 113
Liberal-National Coalition 194
lifetime employment in Japan
   extensive socialisation 79
   promotion by seniority 79
   recruitment 78
Liverpool Dockers strike 1996 1
lockouts 39
London School of Economics and Political Science 313

M

Malaysia 367–373
   collective bargaining 370
   controlled unionism 372
   declining GNP 154
   distributive bargaining 308
   economic statistics 369
   employer associations 103–104
   enterprise level negotiation 308
   ethnic Chinese and Indians 368
   ethnic Malays 368
   fragmented unions 370
   history and economy 368–369
   independence from Britain 368
   Industrial Relations Act 371
   industrial relations record 371
   industrial relations system 370
   IR history 369
   Look East policy 177
   Malay-dominated government 176
   Malaysian Council of Employers' Organisations (MCE 104
   Malaysian Employers' Federation (MEF) 103
   Malaysian Trades Union Congress (MTUC) 104, 156
   management 81
   minimum benefits under Employment Act 370
   Minister of Human Resources 308
   ministerial powers 177
   negotiation processes 308
   New Economic Policy (NEP) 176
   Prime Minister Mahatir 177
   state intervention high 176
   strike statistics 55, 57
   strikes 53
   the state 176–177
   trade union statistics 154
   trade unions 113, 116, 154–156
   trade unions strictly controlled 155
   union statistics 372
   Vision 2020 104, 369, 372
management 65–66
   anti-union strategies 72
   behavioural theories 26
   Chinese nationals 81–83
   economic influences 74–75
   enterprise bargaining statistics 272
   forms of power 68
   Hong Kong 81
   ideology 20, 70–71
   individualism 244
   individualist approach 276
   IR responsibility at all levels 76
   Japan 77–80
   Japanese MNCs selective transfer of style 344
   Malaysia 81

management cont'd
- managerial hierarchy 76
- managerial style 72–74
- motivation 26
- neo-human relations 26
- new managerial values 29
- passive player 65
- pluralism 70
- power 21, 66
- power or prerogative 21
- pro-active labour strategies 66, 75
- reasons to enterprise bargain 278
- resolving organisational tensions 67–70
- resources of production 67
- scientific management 25
- Singapore 81
- sources of authority 20
- South East Asia 77–83
- South Korea 80–81
- strategic choice theory 30, 75–77
- strategic HRM practices, CRA 283
- unitarism 71
- women in management 318
- worker satisfaction 26

management ideology
- pluralism 70
- unitarism 71

management strategies
- chief executive officers 76
- for industrial conflict 69
- human resource management 244

management styles 72–74, 74
- employees as collectives 72
- employees as individuals 72
- pluralism 73
- Poole, M. 73
- Purcell, P. 73
- unitarism 73

management theories
- human relations 68, 69
- human resource management 68, 69
- scientific management 68, 69

manufacturing
- The Global Challenge 212

manufacturing in decline 1970s 210
Maritime Strike 1890 98
Maritime Union of Australia (MUA) 1, 110
Marxism
- bourgeoisie 22

Braverman 31
capitalism 22, 113
class conflict 113
criticisms 24
definition 22–24
false consciousness 22, 24, 114
labour process theory 31–32
Lenin 23, 113
proletariat 22
trade unions 113
v. pluralism 23

Maslow, A. 26
- self actualisation 26
- theory X and theory Y 51

Mayo 26, 50, 54
McKersie, R. 29
Metal Trades Industry Association (MTIA) 86
mining industry
- strike-prone 59
Minister for Workplace Relations and Small Busines 12
MUA
- Justice North 11
- members dismissed 9
- order of engagement 4
- over-manning 3
- redundancies 12
- victory over Patrick Stevedores 11
MUA v Patrick Stevedores 1–13
Mudginberri dispute 1985 101, 194, 215
multinational bargaining 346
multinational corporations 333–356
- 100 largest MNCs 334
- accounting disclosure 349
- adaptive role 343
- ambassadorial role 343
- Australian car industry 341
- Australian companies as MNCs 354
- Australian v. foreign companies 353
- AWIRS 1990 353
- best practice conflicts with local culture 342
- BHP 355
- centralisation depends on nationality 343
- cheap subcontracted work 341
- codes of conduct on IR 343
- cross-border transfers of strikebreaking labour 349
- CSR 355
- cultural differences in IR 344

multinational corporations cont'd
  developing countries own MNCs 342
  diverse management styles 343
  economic downturn increases power 342
  EEO 346
  ethnocentric staffing or no local managers 343
  EU European Works Councils Directive 349
  EU Vredeling Directive 349
  European style 346
  Ford Australia Ltd. 352
  geocentric staffing, or international staffing 343
  growth of 333
  home job losses 340
  HR practices 346
  ICI Australia Ltd 352
  ILO conventions 348
  impact on local industrial relations systems 342
  impact on local labour markets 340
  in Australia 338–340
  independent IR policies in Australia 353
  influenced locally by home culture 342
  instability of employment 341
  International Confederation of Free Trade Unions (ICFTU) 350
  International Labour Organisation (ILO) 347
  international trade union action 350
  Japanese approaches 346
  Japanese centralised autocratic 343
  Japanese ethnocentric 343
  legitimacy 339
  local benefits 339
  local trade unions 346
  loss of tax revenue 340
  MNCs in Australia 352–354
  Monsanto Australia Ltd 352
  multinational collective bargaining 351
  nationality irrelevant to IR practices 353
  OECD, UN, EU 347
  parent company style 346
  pay above average wages 340
  polycentric staffing, or some local managers 343
  poor information disclosure 343
  raise host country skill levels 341
  raising education levels 340
  reducing power 347
  research and development done at home 341
  spin-off 340
  statistics 334
  top 50 MNCs in developing countries 337
  trade unions 339
  transfer pricing 339
  transferring operations 341
  union inadequacy 347
  union obstacles 351
  US UK polycentric 343
  US unitarist 346
  Whitlam Labor Government 338
  World Federation of Trade Unions 350
multinational management
  management styles 344
multiple awards 93
mutual gains enterprise 301

N

National Farmers Federation 215
National Farmers Federation (NFF) 2, 7
National Institute of Labour Studies (NILS) 141
Nazi Germany 39, 172
negotiation
  negotiating an enterprise agreement 281
negotiation processes
  alternative solutions 298
  asian harmony and cooperation 305
  asian patience 305
  attitudinal structuring 296, 298
  definition 295
  distributive bargaining 296, 297
  giving and preserving face 305
  Hong Kong 307
  integrative bargaining 296, 297
  intra-organisational bargaining 296, 298
  Japan 306
  Kochan, T. 301
  Malaysia 308
  mutual gains and productivity 303
  mutual gains enterprise theory 301
  New Zealand 299
  Osterman, P. 301
  principled negotiation theory 300
  principled v positional negotiation 301
  Singapore 307
  South Korea 306–307
  Walton and McKersie Model 296
  Walton and McKersie model criticisms 300
  western v. asian 305
  win-win theory 300
negotiation skills 293–310
  concession dilemma 303

negotiation skills cont'd
   detachment 294
   disavowable conciliatory messages 304
   effective negotiator qualities 294
   empirical observation theories 295
   image loss deadlocks 304
   issue deadlocks 304
   process deadlocks 304
   risk-taking 294
   South East Asia 305–308
   telling the truth 294
   theories 295
   when negotiations stall 303–304
neo-human relations 26
New Zealand 147
New Zealand waterfront 1
Niland, J. 24, 38

O

occupational health and safety
   enerprise bargaining 270–271
occupational health and safety (OHS) 193
OECD international labour code 348
Organisation for Economic Cooperation and Development (OECD) 169
organisations
   business 66–67
   competing interests 67
   competing sources of authority 21
   motivation 26
   power and control 66
   restructuring 274
   restructuring and redundancies 267
   unequal distribution of power 41, 66, 70
   worker satisfaction 26, 69
organised conflict 38

P

P&O 4
Patrick Stevedores 1, 4–5
pattern bargaining 240
peak employer associations 100
perfect competition 33
Plowman, D. 93
Plowman's reactivity theory 88, 93–94
pluralism 24, 29, 34, 39, 165
   definition 20–22
power 68

   coercive power 68
   expert power 68
   legitimate power 68
   referent power 68
   reward power 68
Prices and Incomes Accords. *See* Accords
Prime Minister 8, 10
productivity 3, 12, 38, 209, 219
   declining 66
   enterprise bargaining 242, 271
   imperfect term 272
   mutual gains enterprise 303
   negative cost offsetting 219
   non-union workplaces 40
   waterfront 3
public sector conditions 63
Purcell, P. 72

R

rational economic maximisers 33
reduction of tariff protection 75
regulation theories 33
relative deprivation 49
Robe River dispute 1986 101
Ross, A. 41–42

S

scientific management
   management theory 25
self actualisation 26
shearing dispute 1984 2
Singapore 363–367
   collective bargaining 365–366
   dispute settlement 366
   distributive bargaining 307
   economic statistics 364
   employer associations 103
   Employment Act 365
   equity 329
   free trade and free markets 173
   high GNP 154
   highly interventionist policies 365
   history and economy 363–364
   independence from Britain 363
   Industrial Relations Act 365
   industrial relations record 366
   industrial relations system 364–365
   labour turnover 367
   Lee Kuan Yew 114, 364

Singapore cont'd
    Malaysian Federation 363
    management 81
    meteoric economic growth 174
    National Trade Union Congress (NTUC) 103, 116, 153, 174, 307, 364
    National Wages Council (NWC) 103, 174, 365
    negotiation processes 307
    Peoples Action Party (PAP) 364
    People's Action Party (PAP) 174, 307
    reduced overt conflict 366
    refused EEO legislation 329
    Singapore Manufacturers Association 103
    Singapore National Employers Federation (SNEF) 103
    Sir Stamford Raffles 363
    state houses 80% of people 173
    state housesing 173
    state is largest employer 173
    state owns 75% of land 173
    strikes 53, 154
    the state 173–174
    trade union regulation 366
    trade union statistics 153
    trade unions 113, 153–154
    tripartism 364
    union-government symbiosis 307
    unitarist ideology 307
    wage ceiling 365
    widespread covert conflict 366
    women face western-style obstacles 329
social justice 315–317
South East Asia 357–387
    covert industrial conflict 309
    equity 327–329
    giving and preserving face 305
    industrial conflict theories 51–54
    inferior position of women 331
    low level of strikes 52
    management 77–83
    Marxism 51
    multinational corporations 342
    negotiation and patience 305
    negotiation skills 305–308
    residual feudal elements 51
    the state 172–179
    theories of industrial relations 34
    trade unions 151–160

South Korea 378–386
    assassination of President Park in 1979 379
    chaebol 159, 174, 175, 306, 380
    collective bargaining 385
    comparisons with Japan 380
    Daewoo 385
    democracy movement 381
    democracy since 1988 379
    democratic movement 175
    demographics 378
    economic statistics 379
    employer associations 105–106
    equity 328
    Federation of Korean Industries (FKI) 105
    Federation of Korean Trade Unions (FKTU) 105, 159
    few unions 159
    government-dominated tripartite system 106
    high literacy rate 81
    history and economy 378–379
    Hyundai 175
    independent trade union movement (Daehan Nochong) 382
    industrial relations history 380–383
    industry-based unions 380
    Kim Dae-Jung 306
    Korean Chamber of Commerce and Industry (KCCI) 105
    Korean Confederation of Trade Unions (KCTU) 159
    Korean Federation of Employers' Associations (KFEA) 105
    Korean Federation of Trade Unions (KFTU) 175
    Korean Foreign Trade Association (KFTA) 105
    Korean War 1950-53 378
    labour relations 385
    Labour Relations Commission (LRC) 106
    Labour Union Law (LUL) 106
    law and unions 384
    long working hours and low pay 174
    low level of unionisation 380
    low trade union membership 81
    male-dominated workplaces 328
    negotiation processes 306–307
    new free industrial relations system 1987 381
    political repression of labour 381
    President Chun Doo Hwan 379
    President Kim Dae Jung 328
    state adopting less restrictive role 176

South Korea cont'd
   state and trade unions 175
   state highly interventionist 174
   strike statistics 55, 57
   strikes 52
   the state 174–176
   trade union statistics 159
   trade unions 113, 159–160
   uncertain future IR framework 386
   union membership 385
   unions and democratisation 160
   unions political and economic role 383
   win-lose negotiations 307
   women systematically excluded 328
South Korean management 80
   bureaucratic and paternalistic 80
   clan management 80
   Confucian and American 81
   pluralism 83
Soviet Union 114
state 163–180
   active government involvement 29
   as manager of discontent 179
   definition 164
   Hong Kong 178
   Japan 172–173
   Malaysia 176–177
   recent involvement 170–171
   Singapore 173–174
   South East Asia 172–179
   South Korea 174–176
   wage fixation 170
state influence
   Accords 170
   major employer 169
   political parties 169
   procedural and substantive rules 168
   signatory to international conventions 169
   social and economic environment 168
state intervention
   Australia 53, 179
   corporatist theories 167
   elite theories 165, 167
   Hong Kong 179
   Malaysia 53, 179
   Marxist theories 166, 167
   pluralist theories 165, 167
   Singapore 53, 179
   South East Asia 53

   South Korea 179
   theories of 164–167
stevedoring 2
strategic choice theory
   decline of trade unions 75
   definition 29–31
   human resource management 75
   updating systems theory 29
strike statistics 40
   Australia 55, 57, 58, 59–62
   Australian history 56
   causes in Australia 1984-98 61
   collection methods 55
   duration Australia 1984-98 62
   Hong Kong 55, 57
   international comparisons 56
   Japan 55, 57
   Malaysia 55, 57
   method of settling Australia 1984-98 62
   OECD countries 57
   Singapore 55, 57
   South East Asia 57
   South Korea 55, 57
   under-estimation of the number of strikes 56
strike-prone industries 50
strike-prone industry 59
strikes 39, 41–44. *See also* industrial conflict
   Accords 60
   Australian working days lost 60
   causes in Australia 1984-1998 61
   decline in Australia 63
   definition 40
   earning levels 49
   economic expectations 47
   economic factors 52
   economic growth 48
   establishment size 50
   France 46
   history in Australia 56
   human relations theories 50
   inflation 48
   labour intensity 49
   maritime workers 50
   Marxism 44
   miners 50
   product of business cycle 47–50
   product of industrialisation 41–44
   product of institutionalisation 44–45
   product of political factors 46–47

strikes cont'd
   product of social factors 50–51
   role of state 47
   statistical measures 55
   Sweden 46
   technological change 43
   unemployment 48
   unofficial and official 46
   wage relativities 48
   women workers 50
Sweden
   strikes 46
systems theory 30, 35
   actors 27
   binding Ideology 28
   body of rules 28
   critics 28
   definition 27–29
   environmental contexts 27
   John Dunlop 27

T

tariff protection 209
Taylor, Frederick 25
theory X and theory Y 51
tort of conspiracy 184
total value of cargo 2
trade union decline
   ACTU's 'Organising Works' Campaign 149
   dissatisfaction 146
   gender 145
   manufacturing 145
   role of management 146
   role of the State 146
   service sector 145
   the Accords 147
trade union democracy 126
   Workplace Relations Act 1996 126
trade union registration
   exclusive representation rights 125
   protection from tort of conspiracy 125
trade union statistics
   decline in membership 145, 148
   decline in public sector 139
   gender differences 139
   industry penetration 138
   occupational status differences 139
   part-time employees 139
   total membership 140

trade union theories
   relevance 117–118
Trade Unions
   MUA 1–13
trade unions 109–162
   8-hour day in 1856 119
   ACTU stemming the decline 142–144
   ACTU structure 161
   amalgamation 144
   amalgamations 195
   anti-Communist Movement 122
   Australia Reconstructed 143, 220
   Australian Constitution 117, 120
   Australian Council of Trade Unions (ACTU) 121
   Australian Labor Party (ALP) 110
   Australian Medical Association (AMA) 110
   award restructuring 224
   bargaining strategy 131
   BHP 132
   Business Council of Australia (BCA) 141
   business unionism 115
   centralised arbitration system 117
   class conflict 113
   closed shop 129, 137, 146, 208
   collective voice 135, 241
   common rule 111, 130
   Commons, John 114
   communist intellectuals 116
   Communist Party influence 122
   compulsory arbitration 117
   compulsory membership 137
   CRA dispute 283
   craft unions 128, 140
   debate over union structure 140–151
   decline in membership 135, 140, 144–149
   decline in union membership 29
   definition 110
   delegates 133
   democracy 124
   disamalgamation 127
   economic role 129
   enterprise unions 128
   equal pay for equal work 1969 124
   exclusive representation rights 125
   exclusive union coverage 144
   false consciousness 114
   Federal Coalition Government 150
   first recorded Australian strike 1829 119

trade unions cont'd
- formation of Australian Labor Party 120
- Future Strategies 143, 220
- gender and declining membership 145
- gender-biased history 321
- gold rush 119
- Great Depression 121
- great strikes 1890s 120
- Hilmer Report 75
- history in Australia 118–124
- Hong Kong 156–159
- Hyman, R. 114
- industry unions 128
- inefficient structure 142
- information disclosure by MNCs 343
- institutionalisation 44
- intellectuals 115
- internal vested interests 141
- international action against MNCs 350
- International Confederation of Free Trade Unions (ICFTU) 350
- involuntary conscripts 137
- job control and protection 129
- joining collective v. individual benefits 137
- joining for ideological reasons 136
- joining for industrial insurance 138
- joining for utilitarian reasons 136
- legislative control 124–127
- legitimacy 21, 46
- Lenin 23, 113
- loosing relevance 141
- Malaysia 154–156
- Maritime Union of Australia (MUA) 110
- Marxism 23, 113–114
- member dissatisfaction 146
- member services 138
- Michels 'iron' law of oligarchy 125
- monopoly and collective roles 134
- Mudginberri dispute 194
- multinational corporations 339, 346
- neutralising influence 73
- new organising model 150
- non-union contracts 132
- non-union workplace agreements 127
- occupational unions 128
- old servicing model 150
- one big union and AWU 121
- Organising Works 149
- paper disputes 189
- Perlman's theory 114–116
- political role 129
- protection of job rights 112
- purpose and goals 128–130
- reduced influence 72
- registration 125, 208
- rejuvenating trade unions 149
- restriction of numbers 111
- role of a union delegate 133
- scarcity consciousness 115
- scientific management 25
- secondary boycotts 194
- Singapore 153–154
- South East Asia 151–160
- South Korea 159–160
- South Korean state controlled 81
- statistics. *See* trade union statistics
- strategies of unions 130–132 143
- strikes 63
- super unions 144, 195
- theories of 111–117
- too many unions 141
- tort of conspiracy 125
- types of Australian unions 128
- union organisation 132
- union v. non-union workplace agreements 276
- Unions @t Work (1999) 150
- Webb labour theories 111
- why do workers join 135–138
- work rules 208
- Workplace Relations Act 1996 150
- workplace structures 133
- World Federation of Trade Unions 350

transaction cost theory 32

U

unemployment 39
unitarism 24, 26, 29
- definition 19–20

United Kingdom
- strike statistics 57

United States
- strike statistics 57

unorganised conflict 38

V

Victorian State Government 93
Vietnam War 59
voice 40

W

wage fixation 203–236
- Accord Mark I 216
- Accord Mark III 217

wage fixation cont'd
- Accord Mark IV 221
- Accord Mark V 222
- Accords 60
- ACTU rejects AIRC decision 227
- AIRC rejects Accord Mark IV 227
- assessing the Accords 231
- automatic cost-of-living adjustments 211
- award restructuring SEP 221
- award safety net minimum rates 222
- award wages linked to tariffs 206
- awards, quasi-legal status 208
- basic wage 206
- Business Council of Australia (BCA) 209
- centralised monopoly broken 232
- centralised system 204
- changing directions post 1983 215
- Constitution s.51 205
- critics of Award System 209
- decentralised 203
- decentralised productivity bargaining 217
- definition 204
- economic indicators 232
- Enterprise Bargaining Principle (EBP) 228
- Federal Metals Award 207
- Fraser Coalition Federal Government 211
- Harvester judgement of 1907 206
- Hawke Labor Government 60
- Hilmer Report 75
- Justice Higgins 1922 205
- Keating Labor Government 60
- Metal Trades Industry Association (MTIA) 214
- move to enterprise bargaining 228
- National Wage Case 1988 221
- National Wage Cases 215
- pacesetter awards 207
- productivity 219
- productivity bargaining 226
- reform, employer approaches 213
- Restructuring and Efficiency Principle (REP) 217
- second tier wage increases 219
- Structural Efficiency Principle (SEP) 221
- the Accords, 1983-1995 218
- the Award system 207–208
- The Global Challenge 211
- union registration 208
- unions and the Accords 216
- wage pause in early 80s 211
- wage rate 34, 204
- wages explosion 1970s 123
- Whitlam Federal Labor Government 211
- Workplace Relations Act 1996 234

wage indexation
- Accord Mark IV 226

waterfront duopoly 5
waterfront efficiency 1
Waterfront Industry Reform Authority (WIRA) 3
waterfront productivity 3
waterfront reform 3
Waterline quarterly survey 3
Webb and Webb 110
Webb Dock 7
whistle blowing 40
Whitlam Labor Government 59, 123

Windmuller
- five objectives 92

Women's Electoral Lobby 199
worker exploitation 44, 67, 113, 196

Workplace Relations Act 1996
91, 101, 150, 170, 190, 234
- 1999 Amendments defeated 251
- AIRC, a safety net 234
- approval of AWAs 250
- AWAs 192, 249
- balanced on social justice and equity 196
- bargaining period for CAs 249
- CAs 191
- Certified Agreements 192, 246
- disamalgamation of trade unions 127
- enterprise bargaining 244–251
- MUA waterfront dispute 7, 9
- no disadvantage test 199
- non-union workplace agreements 127
- objects of Act 102, 187, 246
- prohibited reason 9
- role of Awards 246
- trade union democracy 127
- union membership 13